HRW
ALGEBRA ONE
INTERACTIONS
COURSE 1

SOLUTION KEY

HOLT, RINEHART AND WINSTON
Harcourt Brace & Company

Austin • New York • Orlando • Atlanta • San Francisco • Boston • Dallas • Toronto • London

To the Teacher

HRW Algebra One Interactions Course 1 Solution Key contains the worked-out solutions for the exercises in the Practice & Apply, Look Back, Look Beyond, Chapter Review, Chapter Assessment, and Cumulative Assessment sections in *HRW Algebra One Interactions Course 1*. Answers for the Explorations and Communicate questions are found either with the question or in the Additional Answers section in *HRW Algebra One Interactions Course 1 Teacher's Answer Edition.*

ISBN 0-03-051284-0

1 2 3 4 5 6 7 066 01 00 99 98 97

TABLE OF CONTENTS

CHAPTER 1

DATA AND PATTERNS IN ALGEBRA

6. The table would show all possible pairs of teams A, B, C, and D.

Team	A	B	C	D	E
A		A vs. B	A vs. C	A vs. D	A vs. E
B			B vs. C	B vs. D	B vs. E
C				C vs. D	C vs. E
D					D vs. E

There are a total of 10 games.

7.

Teams	2	3	4	5	6	7	8	9	10	11
Number of games	1	3	6	10	15	21	28	36	45	55
Increase		+2	+3	+4	+5	+6	+7	+8	+9	+10

For 11 teams, there will be 55 games.

8. $15 + 11 = 66$

For 12 teams, there will be 66 games.

9. Find the total number of dots in the rectangular pattern: $5 \times 4 = 20$. Then divide by 2 to find the number of dots in the triangular pattern: $\frac{5 \times 4}{2} = 10$. The sum of the numbers being added is 10.

10. Find the total number of dots in the rectangular pattern: $9 \times 8 = 72$. Then divide by 2 to find the number of dots in triangular pattern: $\frac{9 \times 8}{2} = 36$. The sum of the numbers being added is 36.

11.
```
1 • • • • • • • 7      8×7
2 • • • • • • • 6     ─── = 28
3 • • • • • • • 5       2
4 • • • • • • • 4
5 • • • • • • • 3
6 • • • • • • • 2
7 • • • • • • • 1
   ←──── 8 ────→
```

12. $\frac{41 \times 40}{2} = 820$

13. In column A of a spreadsheet, enter the numbers from 1 to 50, one in each row. Enter the formula =SUM(A1...A50) in A51; the sum is 1275. Or form a rectangle of 50 dots by 51 dots. Find the total number of dots and divide by 2.
$\frac{(50 \times 51)}{2} = 1275$

14.
Sequence	4		9		14		19		24		[29]		[34]		[39]
Pattern		+5		+5		+5		+5		+5		+5		+5	

15.
Sequence	7		16		25		34		43		[52]		[61]		[70]
Pattern		+9		+9		+9		+9		+9		+9		+9	

16.
Sequence	9		19		29		39		49		[59]		[69]		[79]
Pattern		+10		+10		+10		+10		+10		+10		+10	

17.
Sequence	2		4		8		16		32		[64]		[128]		[256]
Pattern		×2		×2		×2		×2		×2		×2		×2	

18. Sequence 5   7   9   11   13   [15]   [17]   [19]
     Pattern   +2   +2   +2   +2   +2   +2   +2

19. Sequence 3   9   27   81   243   [729]   [2187]   [6561]
     Pattern   ×3   ×3   ×3   ×3   ×3   ×3   ×3

20. Sequence 8   10   12   14   16   [18]   [20]   [22]
     Pattern   +2   +2   +2   +2   +2   +2   +2

21. Sequence 16   8   4   2   1 $\left[\frac{1}{2}\right]$ $\left[\frac{1}{4}\right]$ $\left[\frac{1}{8}\right]$
     Pattern   ÷2   ÷2   ÷2   ÷2   ÷2   ÷2   ÷2

22. Sequence 5   12   19   26   23   [40]   [47]   [54]
     Pattern   +7   +7   +7   +7   +7   +7   +7

23.

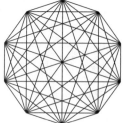

45 segments

24.

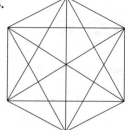

There are 9 diagonals. It is the same problem if the number of sides of the polygon are included.

25. 49 pairs

26. The numbers 50 and 100 would not be paired.

27. 49 · 100 + 50 + 100 = 5050

28. 10 × 10 = 100

29. 20 × 20 = 400

30.

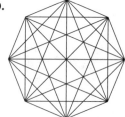

There are 28 phone lines.

31.

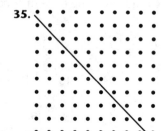

$$\frac{5 \cdot 10}{2} = \frac{50}{2} = 25$$

32. Triangular
numbers 1   3   6   10   15   21   28   36   45   [55]
     Pattern   +2   +3   +4   +5   +6   +7   +8   +9   +10
The 10th triangular number is 55.

33. Triangular
numbers 55   66   78   91   105   120   136   153   171   190   [210]
     Pattern   +11   +12   +13   +14   +15   +16   +17   +18   +19   +20
The 20th triangular number is 210.

34.

16 = 6 + 10

35.

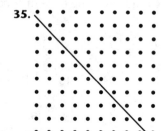

100 = 45 + 55

36. Number 1 3 5 7 9 1 13 15 17
Sum 1 4 9 16 25 36 49 64 81

37. Pattern 1^2 2^2 3^2 4^2 5^2 6^2 7^2 8^2 9^2
The sum of the first 100 odd numbers is 100^2, or 10,000.

38.

Number	1	2	3	4	5	6	7
Cube of the number	1	8	27	64	125	216	343
Sum of the cubes	1	9	36	100	225	441	784

39. Pattern 1^2 3^2 6^2 10^2 15^2 21^2 28^2; the sum of the first n cubes is $(1 + 2 + \cdots + n)^2$.
Continuing the pattern, the sum of the first 10 cubes is 55^2, or 3025.

PAGE 15, LOOK BACK

40. $\dfrac{196 \text{ cans}}{4 \text{ bags}} = 49$ cans per bag

41. $0.20 per pound; for 9 lb they will get $9 \times \$0.20$, or \$1.80.

42. $\dfrac{\$1.80}{4} = \$0.45$

Each person will get \$0.45.

43. Total collected $= 28 \times 2.75 = 77.00$
\$77.00 was collected.

44. Total number sold = number of student tickets + number of adult tickets
$= 6702 + 3749 = 10{,}451$
10,451 tickets were sold.

45. Area = length × width
$= 23 \times 23$
$= 529$
The square has an area of 529 cm².

46. $\dfrac{3}{5} = \dfrac{3 \times 2}{5 \times 2} = \dfrac{6}{10}$; $\dfrac{3}{5} = \dfrac{3 \times 3}{5 \times 3} = \dfrac{9}{15}$; $\dfrac{3}{5} = \dfrac{3 \times 4}{5 \times 4} = \dfrac{12}{20}$

47. $6(9 + 4) = 6(13)$
$= 78$

48. $\sqrt{225} = 15$

49. Amount left $= \$4.75 - \$3.12$
$= \$1.63$

PAGE 15, LOOK BEYOND

50.
Row 0   1
Row 1   1   1
Row 2   1   2   1
Row 3   1   3   3   1
Row 4   1   4   6   4   1
Row 5   1   5   10   10   5   1
Row 6   1   6   15   20   15   6   1
Row 7   1   7   21   35   35   21   7   1
Row 8 1   8   28   56   70   56   28   8   1

51.

Row	0	1	2	3	4	5	6	7	8
Sum	1	2	4	8	16	32	64	128	256

1.2 PAGES 21–23, PRACTICE & APPLY

7. Let p represent the number of persons. Then \$8 per person can be written as $8p$.

8. Let w represent the total wages and let h represent the number of hours. Then $w = 9h$.

9.

Number of medals m	Process: $25 = 0.30m$	Cost c
⋮	⋮	⋮
83	25 + 0.30(83)	\$49.90
84	25 + 0.30(84)	\$50.20
85	25 + 0.30(85)	\$50.50

Erin and Logan can purchase 85 small-sized medals.

10.

Reading r	Process	Temperature t
10°F	10 − 5	5°F
20°F	20 − 5	15°F
30°F	30 − 5	25°F
40°F	40 − 5	35°F
50°F	50 − 5	45°F
60°F	60 − 5	55°F
100°F	100 − 5	95°F

11. $r - 5$, where r represents the reading on the thermometer

12. Let t represent the temperature and let r represent the reading on the thermometer.
$t = r - 5$

13. Mary rides at a steady speed of 12.5 miles per hour, so $m = 12.5h$.

14. The base fee is $5 and the rate is $1.50 per hour, so $c = 1.5h + 5$.

15. Draw a diagram and count the number of sections of fence needed to create the required number of pens:

Number of pens	Number of sections
1	4
2	7
3	10
4	13
5	16
10	31

16.

Number of pens p	Process: $1 + 3p$	Number of sections $s = 1 + 3p$
1	$1 + 3(1)$	4
2	$1 + 3(2)$	7
3	$1 + 3(3)$	10
4	$1 + 3(4)$	13
5	$1 + 3(5)$	16
10	$1 + 3(10)$	31

17. $1 + 3p$, where p represents the number of pens

18. Let s represent the number of sections and let p represent the number of pens.
$s = 1 + 3p$

19. $0.50p$, where p represents the number of pounds

20. $85{,}000 - t$, where t represents the trade-in value

21. $12p$, where p represents the price per video

22. $24d$, where d represents the number of days

23. $1245 - a$, where a represents the amount of tax withheld

24. Let c represent the cost for parking and h represent the number of hours.
$c = 1.30h$

25. Let c represent the cost for parking and h represent the number of hours.
$c = 2 + 0.60h$

26. Airport Parking Lot Fees

Hours h	Cost c
0.5	$0.65
1.0	$1.30
1.5	$1.95
2.0	$2.60
2.5	$3.25
3.0	$3.90
3.5	$4.55
4.0	$5.20
4.5	$5.85
5.0	$6.50

27. Private Parking Lot Fees

Hours h	Cost c
0.5	$2.30
1.0	$2.60
1.5	$2.90
2.0	$3.20
2.5	$3.50
3.0	$3.80
3.5	$4.10
4.0	$4.40
4.5	$4.70
5.0	$5.00

28. The airport lot is cheaper until 2.5 hours. After that the private lot is cheaper.

29. $y = 2x$

x	y
1	2
2	4
3	6
4	8
5	10
10	20

30. $y = x - 1$

x	y
1	0
2	1
3	2
4	3
5	4
10	9

31. $y = x + 3$

x	y
1	4
2	5
3	6
4	7
5	8
10	13

32. $y = 2x - 2$

x	y
1	0
2	2
3	4
4	6
5	8
10	18

33. $y = 5x$

x	y
1	5
2	10
3	15
4	20
5	25
10	50

34. $y = x + 2$

x	y
1	3
2	4
3	5
4	6
5	7
10	12

35. $y = 3x - 3$

x	y
1	0
2	3
3	6
4	9
5	12
10	27

36. $y = 2x + 1$

x	y
1	3
2	5
3	7
4	9
5	11
10	21

37. $y = 4x$

x	y
1	4
2	8
3	12
4	16
5	20
10	40

38. $y = 2x - 1$

x	y
1	1
2	3
3	5
4	7
5	9
10	19

39. $y = 3x + 6$

x	y
1	9
2	12
3	15
4	18
5	21
10	36

40. $y = 4x - 2$

x	y
1	2
2	6
3	10
4	14
5	18
10	38

41. $y = 3x$

x	y
1	3
2	6
3	9
4	12
5	15
10	30

42. $y = 3x + 2$

x	y
1	5
2	8
3	11
4	14
5	17
10	32

43. $y = 4x + 3$

x	y
1	7
2	11
3	15
4	19
5	23
10	43

44. $y = -0.2x - 7$

x	y
1	−7.2
2	−7.4
3	−7.6
4	−7.8
5	−8.0
10	−9.0

PAGE 23, LOOK BACK

45. Sequence 1   3   5   7   9   [11]   [13]   [15]
  Pattern   +2   +2   +2   +2   +2   +2   +2

46. Sequence 1 1 2 3 5 8 13 [21] [34] [55]
  Pattern: Add the previous two terms together.

47. A 12-foot board divided into 2 foot pieces gives $12 \div 2$, or 6 pieces.

2 ft	2 ft	2 ft	2 ft	2 ft	2 ft

← ———————— 12 ft ———————— →

48. A liter contains 34 ounces, so 3 liters contains 34(3), or 102, ounces. Find the number of 12-oz cans to fill 3 liters: $102 \div 12 = 8.5$ cans. So it would take 8.5 cans of soda to fill the 3-liter bottle; however, 9 cans will need to be opened.

49. There are 60 students on each bus, so 4 buses would carry 60(4), or 240, students. This would leave 28 more students, so 5 buses would be needed.

50. There are 1000 meters in a kilometer, so there are 6(1000), or 6000, meters in a 6-kilometer track.
  $6000 \div 400 = 15$ You must run 15 laps to complete the race.

51.

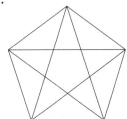

There are 10 games played.

52. $1 + 2 + 3 + 4 + 5 + 6 + 7 + 8 + 9 + 10 = \dfrac{10 \cdot 11}{2}$
$$= \dfrac{110}{2}$$
$$= 55$$

53.

Number n	Process: $n \cdot n$	Square number n^2
1	$1 \cdot 1$	$1^2 = 1$
2	$2 \cdot 2$	$2^2 = 4$
3	$3 \cdot 3$	$3^2 = 9$
4	$4 \cdot 4$	$4^2 = 16$
5	$5 \cdot 5$	$5^2 = 25$
10	$10 \cdot 10$	$10^2 = 100$

1.3 PAGES 28–29, PRACTICE & APPLY

6.

x	Process: $2.7x$	Outcome
10	2.7(10)	27
20	2.7(20)	54
30	2.7(30)	81
40	2.7(40)	108

7.

x	Process: $3x - 2$	Outcome
10	3(10) – 2	28
20	3(20) – 2	58
30	3(30) – 2	88
40	3(40) – 2	118

8.

h	Process: $4.25h + 10$	Outcome
10	4.25(10) + 10	52.50
20	4.25(20) + 10	95.00
30	4.25(30) + 10	137.50
40	4.25(40) + 10	180.00

9.

c	Process: $12c - 4$	Outcome
10	12(10) – 4	116
20	12(20) – 4	236
30	12(30) – 4	356
40	12(40) – 4	476

10. $d = 5$ when c is 31   **11.** $d = 12$ when c is 67.2

12. $d = 18$ when c is 88.8   **13.** $d = 100$ when c is 78

14.

Hours h	Formula: $5 + 2.25h$	Cost $c = 5 + 2.25h$
1	5 + 2.25(1)	$7.25
2	5 + 2.25(2)	$9.50
3	5 + 2.25(3)	$11.75
4	5 + 2.25(4)	$14.00
5	5 + 2.25(5)	$16.25

15. $14 = 5 + 2.25h$; solving for h gives 4, so you can rent the skates for 4 hours at a cost of $14.00.

16.

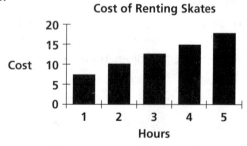

Cost of Renting Skates

17. 8 hours

18. Let A represent the amount of fencing around the region; then:

$$A = 2(40) + 2(40 + x)$$
$$A = 80 + 80 + 2x$$
$$A = 160 + 2x$$

19.

x	Process: $160 + 2x$	Amount of fencing $A = 160 + 2x$
0	$160 + 2(0)$	160 ft
5	$160 + 2(5)$	170 ft
10	$160 + 2(10)$	180 ft
15	$160 + 2(15)$	190 ft
20	$160 + 2(20)$	200 ft
25	$160 + 2(25)$	210 ft

20. Extend the table until you get $A = 240$ ft.

x	Process: $160 + 2x$	Amount of fencing $A = 160 + 2x$
⋮	⋮	⋮
30	$160 + 2(30)$	220
35	$160 + 2(35)$	230
40	$160 + 2(40)$	240

From the table, you can see that the amount of fencing is 240 ft when x is 40 ft. Thus, the dimensions are 40 ft by 80 ft.

21. Let A represent the amount of fencing:

$A = 2(50) + 2(50 + x)$
$A = 100 + 100 + 2x$
$A = 200 + 2x$

22.

Time (in hours) t	Distance (in miles) d
1	25
2	50
3	75
4	100
5	125
6	150
7	175
8	200

23. rate = distance · time

To find the rate in miles per hour, let the time in hours, t, be 1. When $t = 1$, $d = 25$ miles. Thus, the car is traveling at a constant rate of 25 miles per hour.

24. From the chart above, you can see that the car travels 75 miles in 3 hours.

25. Extend the table until you get $d = 250$ miles.

Time (in hours) t	Distance (in miles) d
⋮	⋮
9	225
10	250
11	275
12	300

From the table, you can see that if the car travels for 250 miles, it travels for 10 hours.

26. $25t$, where t represents the time in hours

27.

Hours h	Process: $24 + 12.5h$	Dollars a
1	$24 + 12.5(1)$	$36.50
2	$24 + 12.5(2)$	$49.00
3	$24 + 12.5(3)$	$61.50
4	$24 + 12.5(4)$	$74.00
5	$24 + 12.5(5)$	$86.50

28. Extend the table until you get $a = \$124.00$.

Hours h	Process: $24 + 12.5h$	Dollars a
⋮	⋮	⋮
6	$24 + 12.5(6)$	$99.00
7	$24 + 12.5(7)$	$111.50
8	$24 + 12.5(8)$	$124.00

Therefore, the mechanic will work 8 hours for $124.00.

29.

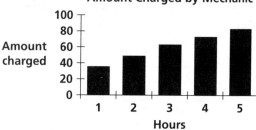

30. From the chart above, the mechanic will work for 6 hours.

PAGE 29, LOOK BACK

31.

15 games will be played.

32. $5p$, where p represents the number of people

33. $3 + 2r$, where r represents the number of rides

34. Let c represent the cost in dollars and p represent the number of pounds.
$$c = 4.5p$$

35. Let p represent the profit in dollars and x represent the number of people.
$$p = 5x$$

PAGE 29, LOOK BEYOND

36. $16 - 8 \cdot 2 = 16 - 16 = 0$

1.4 PAGES 34–35, PRACTICE & APPLY

6. $3x + 4 = 49$

Try $x = 10$.
$3x + 4 = 49$
$3(10) + 4 = 34$

10 is too small.
Try a larger number.

Try $x = 20$.
$3x + 4 = 49$
$3(20) + 4 = 64$

20 is too large.
Try a number
between 10 and 20.

Try $x = 15$.
$3x + 4 = 49$
$3(15) + 4 = 49$

15 is the correct
number; $x = 15$.

7. $4x + 3 = 51$

Try $x = 10$.
$4x + 3 = 51$
$4(10) + 3 = 43$

10 is too small.
Try a larger number.

Try $x = 15$.
$4x + 3 = 51$
$4(15) + 3 = 63$

15 is too large.
Try a smaller number.

Try $x = 12$.
$4x + 3 = 51$
$4(12) + 3 = 51$

12 is the correct
number; $x = 12$.

8. $14y$ is an expression.

For Exercises 9–12, let c equal the cost of each pencil.

9. Solve the expression $0c$. $0c = 0$
0 pencils cost $0.

10. Solve the expression $4c$. $4(0.20) = 0.80$
4 pencils cost $0.80.

11. Solve the expression $10c$. $10(0.20) = 2.00$
10 pencils cost $2.00.

12. Solve the expression $0.20p$. $cp = 0.20p$
p pencils cost $0.20p$.

13. Enter 6 and repeatedly add 2.

14. Enter 15 and repeatedly add 10.

15. Enter 100 and repeatedly subtract 10.

16. Enter 52 and repeatedly subtract 4.

17.

x	1	2	3	4	5
$4x$	4	8	12	16	20

18.

y	1	2	3	4	5
$5y$	5	10	15	20	25

19.

s	1	2	3	4	5
7s + 4	11	18	25	32	39

20.

n	1	2	3	4	5
3n	3	6	9	12	15

21. Beatrice tried choices for x until she found the value $x = 19$, which makes the equation true.

22. Substitute $x = 19$ and check whether the equation is true. $5(19) + 7 = 102$ True

23. Let t equal the number of tickets. Write the equation, $11t = 126$.

Try $t = 10$.
$11t = 126$
$11(10) = 110$
10 is too small.
Try a larger number for t.

Try $t = 11$.
$11t = 126$
$11(11) = 121$
11 is too small.
Try a larger number for t.

Try $t = 12$.
$11t = 126$
$11(12) = 132$
12 is too large.

The answer is between 11 and 12, but you cannot buy part of a ticket, so the answer is 11 tickets.

24. Let t equal the number of tickets. Write the equation, $9t = 135$.

Try $t = 10$.
$9t = 135$
$9(10) = 90$
10 is too small.
Try a larger number.

Try $t = 20$.
$9t = 135$
$9(20) = 180$
20 is too large.
Try a smaller number.

Try $t = 15$.
$9t = 135$
$9(15) = 135$

15 is the correct number.

You can buy 15 tickets.

25. Let a represent the number of apples. $30a = 99$

26. $30a = 99$

Try $a = 3\frac{3}{10}$.
$30a = 99$
$30\left(3\frac{3}{10}\right) \stackrel{?}{=} 99$
$30\left(\frac{33}{10}\right) \stackrel{?}{=} 99$
$99 = 99$ True

No; you cannot buy $\frac{3}{10}$ of an apple. With $0.99, you can buy 3 apples.

27. Let m represent the number of movie tickets.

Try $m = 6\frac{2}{5}$.
$5m = 32$
$5\left(6\frac{2}{5}\right) \stackrel{?}{=} 32$
$32 = 32$ True
$6\frac{2}{5}$ is the correct number.
You cannot buy $\frac{2}{5}$ of a movie ticket, so with $32 you can buy 6 movie tickets.

28. Let r represent the number of raffle tickets.

Try $r = 6$.
$5r = 32$
$5(6) = 30$
6 tickets would raise only $30.

Try $r = 7$.
$5r = 32$
$5(7) = 35$
7 tickets will raise $35.

To raise $32, you will have to sell 7 tickets.

29. Let s represent each person's share.
$s = \frac{32}{5}$
$s = \$6.40$
Each person's share is $6.40.

30. None, because you cannot have 3.18 people

31. A typical family would be 3 people.

PAGE 35, LOOK BACK

32. Three times the amount of each ingredient is needed.

3 Cups pecans or walnuts

$1\frac{1}{2}$ Cups dates

$2\frac{1}{4}$ Cups all-purpose flour

9 eggs

$4\frac{1}{2}$ Cups brown sugar

$2\frac{1}{4}$ Teaspoons baking powder, firmly packed

$\frac{3}{4}$ Teaspoon salt

33. In 2 cans there are 2(355) mL.

Each person will get $2\left(\frac{355}{5}\right)$, or 142 mL.

34. Number of pieces = 12(4)
= 48
In 4 pizzas there will be 48 pieces.

35. Students may draw dot patterns.
  Answers may vary. $4 = 1 + 3$
  $\qquad\qquad\quad 9 = 3 + 6$
  $\qquad\qquad\quad 16 = 6 + 10$
  $\qquad\qquad\quad 25 = 10 + 15$
  $\qquad\qquad\quad 36 = 20 + 16$

36. Yes; the number 1

37. $1 + 2 + 3 + 4 + 5 + 6 = 21$ and $\frac{6 \cdot 7}{2} = 21$
  $1 + 2 + 3 + 4 + 5 + 6 + 7 = 28$ and $\frac{7 \cdot 8}{2} = 28$
  The sum of the first n numbers will be $\frac{n(n+1)}{2}$.

38. $y = 4x + 1$

x	1	2	3	4	5
$4x + 1$	5	9	13	17	21

PAGE 35, LOOK BEYOND

39. $x^2 = 256$

Try $x = 12$.
$\quad x^2 = 256$
$\quad 12^2 = 144$

12 is too small.
Try a larger number.

Try $x = 18$.
$\quad x^2 = 256$
$\quad 18^2 = 324$

18 is too large.
Try a smaller number.

Try $x = 16$.
$\quad x^2 = 256$
$\quad 16^2 = 256$

16 is the correct
number; $x = 16$.

1.5 PAGES 41–42, PRACTICE & APPLY

7. $360 \div 1 = 360$ 1 and 360 are factors. $360 \div 8 = 45$ 8 and 45 are factors.
$360 \div 2 = 180$ 2 and 180 are factors. $360 \div 9 = 40$ 9 and 40 are factors.
$360 \div 3 = 120$ 3 and 120 are factors. $360 \div 10 = 36$ 10 and 36 are factors.
$360 \div 4 = 90$ 4 and 90 are factors. $360 \div 12 = 30$ 12 and 30 are factors.
$360 \div 5 = 72$ 5 and 72 are factors. $360 \div 15 = 24$ 15 and 24 are factors.
$360 \div 6 = 60$ 6 and 60 are factors. $360 \div 18 = 20$ 18 and 20 are factors.

We use 360 for the number of degrees in a circle because it has many factors and can be divided into different numbers of pieces.

8. Any even natural number greater than 2 would have at least 1, 2, and itself as factors. Therefore, it would have at least 3 factors.

9. Answers may vary. Some possible dimensions are listed.
$2500 \div 1 = 2500 \Rightarrow$ dimensions of 1 ft by 2500 ft
$2500 \div 2 = 1250 \Rightarrow$ dimensions of 2 ft by 1250 ft
$2500 \div 4 = 625 \Rightarrow$ dimensions of 4 ft by 625 ft
$2500 \div 5 = 500 \Rightarrow$ dimensions of 5 ft by 500 ft
$2500 \div 10 = 250 \Rightarrow$ dimensions of 10 ft by 250 ft
$2500 \div 20 = 125 \Rightarrow$ dimensions of 20 ft by 125 ft
$2500 \div 25 = 100 \Rightarrow$ dimensions of 25 ft by 100 ft
$2500 \div 50 = 50 \Rightarrow$ dimensions of 50 ft by 50 ft

10. $48 \div 1 = 48$
$48 \div 2 = 24$
$48 \div 3 = 16$
$48 \div 4 = 12$
$48 \div 6 = 8$
Factors of 48: 1, ②, ③, 4, 6, 8, 12, 16, 24, 48

11. $56 \div 1 = 56$
$56 \div 2 = 28$
$56 \div 4 = 14$
$56 \div 7 = 8$
Factors of 56: 1, ②, 4, ⑦, 8, 14, 28, 56

12. $72 \div 1 = 72$
$72 \div 2 = 36$
$72 \div 3 = 24$
$72 \div 4 = 18$
$72 \div 6 = 12$
$72 \div 8 = 9$
Factors of 72: 1, ②, ③, 4, 6, 8, 9, 12, 18, 24, 36, 72

13. $84 \div 1 = 84$
$84 \div 2 = 42$
$84 \div 3 = 28$
$84 \div 4 = 21$
$84 \div 6 = 14$
$84 \div 7 = 12$
Factors of 84: 1, ②, ③, 4, 6, ⑦, 12, 14, 21, 28, 42, 84

14. $51 \div 1 = 51$
$51 \div 3 = 17$
Factors of 51: 1, ③, ⑰, 51

15. 235 is not an even number, so it is not divisible by 2.
No, 235 is not divisible by 2, 5, and 10.

16. 522 is even, so it is divisible by 2.
522 does not end in a 5 or 0, so it is not divisible by 5.
No, 522 is not divisible by 2, 5, and 10.

17. 730 is even, so it is divisible by 2.
730 ends in a 0, so it is divisible by 5 and 10.
Yes, 730 is divisible by 2, 5, and 10.

18. 2895 is not even, so it is not divisible by 2.
No, 2895 is not divisible by 2, 5, and 10.

19. 6234 is even, so it is divisible by 2.
6234 does not end in a 5 or 0, so it is not divisible by 5.
No, 6234 is not divisible by 2, 5, and 10.

For Exercises 20–24, if a number is divisible by 2 and 3, then it is divisible by 6.

20. 1728 is even, so it is divisible by 2.
$1 + 7 + 2 + 8 = 18$, and 18 is divisible by 3.
Yes, 1728 is divisible by 2, 3, and 6.

21. 2500 is even, so it is divisible by 2.
$2 + 5 + 0 + 0 = 7$, and 7 is not divisible by 3.
No, 2500 is not divisible by 2, 3, and 6.

22. 7318 is even, so it is divisible by 2.
$7 + 3 + 8 + 1 = 19$, and 19 is not divisible by 3.
No, 7318 is not divisible by 2, 3, and 6.

23. 27,912 is even, so it is divisible by 2.
$2 + 7 + 9 + 1 + 2 = 21$, and 21 is divisible by 3.
Yes, 27,912 is divisible by 2, 3, and 6.

24. 60,992 is even, so it is divisible by 2.
$6 + 0 + 9 + 9 + 2 = 26$, and 26 is not divisible by 3.
No, 60,992 is not divisible by 2, 3, and 6.

For Exercises 25–29, if the sum of the digits in a number is divisible by 3, then the number is divisible by 3. If a number is divisible by both 2 and 3, then the number is divisible by 6. If the sum of the digits in a number is divisible by 9, then the number is divisible by 9.

25. $1 + 0 + 8 = 9$, and 9 is divisible by 3, so 108 is divisible by 3.
108 is even, so it is divisible by 2. Since it is divisible by 2 and 3, it is divisible by 6.
$1 + 0 + 8 = 9$, and 9 is divisible by 9, so 108 is divisible by 9.
Yes, 108 is divisible by 3, 6, and 9.

26. $3 + 5 + 0 + 7 = 15$, and 15 is divisible by 3, so 3507 is divisible by 3.
3507 is not divisible by 2 and 3, so 3507 is not divisible by 6.
No, 3507 is not divisible by 3, 6, and 9.

27. $5 + 1 + 7 + 2 + 6 = 21$, and 21 is divisible by 3, so 51,726 is divisible by 3.
51,726 is even, so it is divisible by 2. Since it is divisible by 2 and 3, it is divisible by 6.
$5 + 1 + 7 + 2 + 6 = 21$, and 21 is not divisible by 9, so 51,726 is not divisible by 9.
No, 51,726 is not divisible by 3, 6, and 9.

28. $3 + 3 + 4 + 5 = 15$, and 15 is divisible by 3, so 3345 is divisible by 3.
3345 is not divisible by 2 and 3, so 3345 is not divisible by 6.
No, 3345 is not divisible by 3, 6, and 9.

29. $4 + 2 + 6 + 6 = 18$, and 18 is divisible by 3, so 4266 is divisible by 3.
4266 is divisible by 2 and 3, so 4266 is divisible by 6.
$4 + 2 + 6 + 6 = 18$, and 18 is divisible by 9, so 4266 is divisible by 9.
Yes, 4266 is divisible by 2, 3, and 9.

For Exercises 30–34, if a number is divisible by 3 and 5, then it is divisible by 15.

30. $2 + 0 + 5 = 7$, and 7 is not divisible by 3.
No, 205 is not divisible by 3, 5, and 15.

31. $1 + 9 + 5 = 15$, and 15 is divisible by 3.
195 ends with a 5, so 195 is divisible by 5.
Yes, 195 is divisible by 3, 5, and 15.

32. $3 + 7 + 5 = 15$, and 15 is divisible by 3.
375 ends with a 5, so 375 is divisible by 5.
Yes, 375 is divisible by 3, 5, and 15.

33. $1 + 4 + 0 = 5$, and 5 is not divisible by 3.
No, 140 is not divisible by 3, 5, and 15.

34. $3 + 6 + 0 = 9$, and 9 is divisible by 3.
360 ends with a 0, so 360 is divisible by 5.
Yes, 360 is divisible by 3, 5, and 15.

35. $1 + 1 + 3 + 2 = 7$, and 7 is not divisible by 3.
Therefore, 3 people cannot share a $1132 prize evenly.

36. 61 is prime because it only has 1 and 61 as factors.

37. 57 is composite because it has factors of 1, 3, 19, and 57.

38. 185 is composite because it has factors of 1, 5, 37, and 85.

39. 1 is neither prime nor composite because 1 has only itself as a factor.

40. 372 is composite because it has more than 1 and 372 as factors.

41. 2 and 3 are primes, and their sum, $2 + 3 = 5$, is a prime.

42. 5 and 7, 11 and 13, 17 and 19

PAGE 42, LOOK BACK

43. Sequence 1   5   9   13   [17]   [21]   [25]   [29]
Pattern   +4   +4   +4   +4   +4   +4   +4
The next four terms in the sequence are 17, 21, 25, and 29.

44. $y = 2x + 1$

x	1	2	3	4	5	6	7	8	9	10
$2x + 1$	3	5	7	9	11	13	15	17	19	21

The y-values form a sequence of consecutive odd integers.

45. Multiply the speed, 60 mph, by 2.5 hours for a total of $60(2.5)$, or 150 miles.

Therefore, you can travel 150 miles in 2.5 hours.

PAGE 42, LOOK BEYOND

Answers may vary depending on the calculator.

46. Press $\boxed{\sqrt{}}$ followed by 2500.
Then press enter.
The answer is 50.
Therefore, the length of a side of the square with an area of 2500 square feet is 50 feet.

47. Answers may vary. Some possible perimeters are listed.

Dimensions	Perimeter
1 ft by 2500 ft	$1 + 1 + 2500 + 2500 = 5002$ ft
2 ft by 1250 ft	$2 + 2 + 1250 + 1250 = 2504$ ft
4 ft by 625 ft	$4 + 4 + 625 + 625 = 1258$ ft
5 ft by 500 ft	$5 + 5 + 500 + 500 = 1010$ ft
10 ft by 250 ft	$10 + 10 + 250 + 250 = 520$ ft
20 ft by 125 ft	$20 + 20 + 125 + 125 = 290$ ft
25 ft by 100 ft	$25 + 25 + 100 + 100 = 250$ ft
50 ft by 50 ft	$50 + 50 + 50 + 50 = 200$ ft

The square with 50-foot sides has the smallest perimeter.

1.6 PAGES 48–49, PRACTICE & APPLY

6. $5 \times 5 \times 5 \times 5 = 5^4$

7. $2 \cdot 2 \cdot 2 \cdot 2 \cdot 3 \cdot 3 \cdot 5 = 2^4 \cdot 3^2 \cdot 5$

8. $x \cdot x \cdot x \cdot y \cdot y = x^3 \cdot y^2$

9. $x \cdot x + 3 = x^2 + 3$

10. $2^4 = 2 \cdot 2 \cdot 2 \cdot 2 = 16$

11. $2^5 = 2 \cdot 2 \cdot 2 \cdot 2 \cdot 2 = 32$

12. $2^6 = 2 \cdot 2 \cdot 2 \cdot 2 \cdot 2 \cdot 2 = 64$

13. $10^3 = 10 \cdot 10 \cdot 10 = 1000$

14. $10^6 = 10 \cdot 10 \cdot 10 \cdot 10 \cdot 10 \cdot 10 = 1{,}000{,}000$

15. $8^4 = 8 \cdot 8 \cdot 8 \cdot 8 = 4096$

For Exercises 16–19, substitute the given measurement for e in the formula $V = e^3$:

16. $V = e^3$
$V = (6 \text{ in.})^3$
$V = 216 \text{ in.}^3$

17. $V = e^3$
$V = (4 \text{ cm})^3$
$V = 64 \text{ cm}^3$

18. $V = e^3$
$V = (3.2 \text{ m})^3$
$V = 32.768 \text{ m}^3$

19. $V = e^3$
$V = (1.8 \text{ yd})^3$
$V = 5.832 \text{ yd}^3$

20. $54 \div 2 = 27$
$27 \div 3 = 9$
$9 \div 3 = 3$
$54 = 2 \cdot 3^3$

21. $100 \div 2 = 50$
$27 \div 3 = 25$
$9 \div 3 = 5$
$100 = 2^2 \cdot 5^2$

22. $39 \div 3 = 13$
$39 = 3 \cdot 13$

23. $240 \div 2 = 120$
$120 \div 2 = 60$
$60 \div 2 = 30$
$30 \div 2 = 15$
$15 \div 3 = 5$
$240 = 2^4 \cdot 3 \cdot 5$

24. $399 \div 3 = 133$
$133 \div 7 = 19$
$399 = 3 \cdot 7 \cdot 19$

25. $63 \div 3 = 21$
$21 \div 3 = 7$
$63 = 3^2 \cdot 7$

26. $121 \div 11 = 11$
$121 = 11 \cdot 11 = 11^2$

27. $200 \div 2 = 100$
$100 \div 2 = 50$
$50 \div 2 = 25$
$25 \div 2 = 5$
$200 = 2^3 \cdot 5^2$

28. $91 \div 7 = 13$
$91 = 7 \cdot 13$

29. 101
 101 is a prime number.

30. $136 \div 2 = 68$
$68 \div 2 = 34$
$34 \div 2 = 17$
$136 = 2^3 \cdot 17$

31. $82 \div 2 = 41$
$82 = 2 \cdot 41$

32. $237{,}087 \div 3 = 79{,}029$
$79{,}029 \div 3 = 26{,}343$
$26{,}343 \div 3 = 8781$
$8781 \div 3 = 2927$
$237{,}087 = 3^4 \cdot 2927$

For Exercises 33–36, substitute the given values, and then multiply.

33. abc
$= (2)(3)(5)$
$= (6)(5)$
$= 30$

34. a^2bc
$= (2^2)(3)(5)$
$= (4)(3)(5)$
$= (12)(5)$
$= 60$

35. a^2b^3c
$= (2^2)(3^3)(5)$
$= (4)(27)(5)$
$= (108)(5)$
$= 540$

36. ab^3c^2
$= (2)(3^3)(5^2)$
$= (2)(27)(25)$
$= (54)(25)$
$= 1350$

37. $32{,}292 \div 2 = 16{,}146$
$16{,}146 \div 2 = 8073$
$8073 \div 3 = 2691$
$2691 \div 3 = 897$
$897 \div 3 = 299$
$299 \div 13 = 23$
$32{,}292 = 2^2 \cdot 3^3 \cdot 13 \cdot 23$

38. $45{,}220 \div 2 = 22{,}610$
$22{,}610 \div 2 = 11{,}305$
$11{,}305 \div 5 = 2261$
$2261 \div 7 = 323$
$323 \div 17 = 19$
$45{,}220 = 2^2 \cdot 5 \cdot 7 \cdot 17 \cdot 19$

39. $83{,}571 \div 3 = 27{,}857$
$27{,}857 \div 89 = 313$
$83{,}571 = 3 \cdot 89 \cdot 313$

40. $48{,}364 \div 2 = 24{,}182$
$24{,}182 \div 2 = 12{,}091$
$12{,}091 \div 107 = 113$
$48{,}364 = 2^2 \cdot 107 \cdot 113$

41. $4{,}500{,}000{,}000 \div 2 = 2{,}250{,}000{,}000$
$2{,}250{,}000{,}000 \div 2 = 1{,}125{,}000{,}000$
$1{,}125{,}000{,}000 \div 2 = 562{,}500{,}000$
$562{,}500{,}000 \div 2 = 281{,}250{,}000$
$281{,}250{,}000 \div 2 = 140{,}625{,}000$
$140{,}625{,}000 \div 2 = 70{,}312{,}500$
$70{,}312{,}500 \div 2 = 35{,}156{,}250$
$35{,}156{,}250 \div 2 = 17{,}578{,}125$
$17{,}578{,}125 \div 3 = 5{,}859{,}375$
$5{,}859{,}375 \div 3 = 1{,}953{,}125$
$1{,}953{,}125 \div 5 = 390{,}625$
$390{,}625 \div 5 = 78{,}125$
$78{,}125 \div 5 = 15{,}625$
$15{,}625 \div 5 = 3125$
$3125 \div 5 = 625$
$625 \div 5 = 125$
$125 \div 5 = 25$
$25 \div 5 = 5$
Prime Factorization
$5^9 \cdot 3^2 \cdot 2^8$

42. $150{,}000{,}000 \div 2 = 75{,}000{,}000$
$75{,}000{,}000 \div 2 = 37{,}500{,}000$
$37{,}500{,}000 \div 2 = 18{,}750{,}000$
$18{,}750{,}000 \div 2 = 9{,}375{,}000$
$9{,}375{,}000 \div 2 = 4{,}687{,}500$
$4{,}687{,}500 \div 2 = 2{,}343{,}750$
$2{,}343{,}750 \div 3 = 781{,}250$
$781{,}250 \div 5 = 156{,}250$
$156{,}250 \div 5 = 31{,}250$
$31{,}250 \div 5 = 6250$
$6250 \div 5 = 1250$
$1250 \div 5 = 250$
$250 \div 5 = 50$
$50 \div 5 = 10$
$10 \div 5 = 2$
Prime Factorization
$5^8 \cdot 3 \cdot 2^7$

43. $6000 \div 2 = 3000$
$3000 \div 2 = 1500$
$1500 \div 2 = 750$
$750 \div 3 = 250$
$250 \div 5 = 50$
$50 \div 5 = 10$
$10 \div 5 = 2$
Prime Factorization
$5^3 \cdot 3 \cdot 2^4$

44. Multiply the first 7 prime numbers.
$2 \cdot 3 \cdot 5 \cdot 7 \cdot 11 \cdot 13 \cdot 17 = 510{,}510$

45.

Sequence	2		5		4		7		6		9		8		[11]		[10]		[13]		[12]
First differences		+3		−1		+3		−1		+3		−1		+3		−1		+3		−1	

The first differences alternate between 3 and −1.
Therefore, the next four terms in the sequence are 11, 10, 13, and 12.

46.

x	1	2	3	4	5	10	100
y	2	7	12	17	22	47	497

47.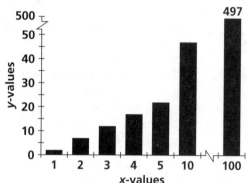

48. $67 + 53 = 53 + 67$ Yes
$6 \cdot 12 = 12 \cdot 6$ Yes

These expressions are equal because both addition and multiplication are commutative.

1.7 **PAGES 54–55, PRACTICE & APPLY**

7. $(28 - 2) \cdot 0 = 0$

8. $59 - 4 \cdot (6 - 4) = 51$

9. $57 \cdot 29 + 89 = 1742$

10. $72(98) + 12 = 7056 + 12$
$= 7068$

11. $89 + 57 \cdot 29 = 89 + 1653$
$= 1742$

12. $3(15) + 9 = 45 + 9$
$= 54$

13. $43 \cdot 32 + 91 \cdot 67 = 1376 + 6097$
$= 7473$

14. $45(75) + 9(24) = 3375 + 216$
$= 3591$

15. $\frac{28 + 59}{97 - 17} = 1.088$

16. $\frac{97 - 17}{72 + 7} = \frac{80}{79}$
≈ 1.013

17. $\frac{43 \cdot 91}{8 \cdot 25} = \frac{3913}{200}$
$= 19.565$

18. $157 - 29 + 23 \cdot 9 = 157 - 29 + 207$
$= 335$

19. $91 \div 7 + 6 = 13 + 6$
$= 19$

20. $187 - 34 \div 17 = 187 - 2$
$= 185$

21. Total area $= 15 \times 21 + 9 \times 12$
$= 315 + 108$
$= 423$
For house A, 423 sq ft of carpet are needed.

22. Total area $= 9 \times 14 + 12 \times 15 + 15 \times 15$
$= 126 + 180 + 225$
$= 531$
For house B, 531 sq ft of carpet are needed.

23. 423 sq ft $= \frac{423}{9}$ sq yds
$\frac{423}{9} \times \$12.99 = \$610.53$
For house A, the cost of carpeting is \$610.53.

24. 531 sq ft $= \frac{531}{9}$ sq yds
$\frac{531}{9} \times \$12.99 = \$766.41$
For house B, the cost of carpeting is \$766.41.

25. $2(5 + 4) \div 9 = 2(9) \div 9$
$= 18 \div 9$
$= 2$

26. $12 - 7 \cdot 3 + 9^2 = 12 - 7 \cdot 3 + 81$
$= 12 - 21 + 81$
$= -9 + 81$
$= 72$

27. $3 - 1 + 24 \div 6 = 3 - 1 + 4$
$= 2 + 4$
$= 6$

28. $7 + 6 \div 2 \cdot 10 = 7 + 3 \cdot 10$
$= 7 + 30$
$= 37$

29. $a + b - c = 5 + 3 - 4$
$= 8 - 4$
$= 4$

30. $a^2 + b^2 = 5^2 + 3^2$
$= 25 + 9$
$= 34$

31. $a^2 - b^2 = 5^2 - 3^2$
$= 25 - 9$
$= 16$

32. $(a + b) \cdot c = (5 + 3) \cdot 4$
$= (8) \cdot 4$
$= 32$

33. $a^2 - b - c = 5^2 - 3 - 4$
$= 25 - 7$
$= 18$

34. $a^2 - (b + c) = 5^2 - (3 + 4)$
$= 25 - 7$
$= 18$

35. 2100.3636
The calculator multiplies 32 by 38, then divides by 11, and then multiplies this answer by 19.

36. Class average $= \dfrac{4(100) + 12(90) + 7(80) + 1(60)}{24} = 87.5$

PAGE 55, LOOK BACK

37. $1 + 2 + 3 + 4 + 5 + 6 + 7 + 8 + 9 + 10 = \dfrac{10 \times 11}{2} = 55$

There will be 55 cans in the display.

38. Sequence   2   5   8   11   14   [17]   [20]
Pattern   +3   +3   +3   +3   +3   +3

The next two terms are 17 and 20.

39. Sequence   59   54   49   44   39   [34]   [29]
Pattern   −5   −5   −5   −5   −5   −5

The next two terms are 34 and 29.

40. Sequence   3   6   12   24   48   [96]   [192]

To get the next term, multiply the preceding term by 2.
The next two terms are 96 and 192.

PAGE 55, LOOK BEYOND

41. $2l + 2w = lw$

Try $l = 2$ and $w = 2$.   Try $l = 3$ and $w = 5$.   Try $l = 4$ and $w = 4$.
$2(2) + 2(2) \overset{?}{=} 2(2)$ $2(3) + 2(5) \overset{?}{=} 3(5)$ $2(4) + 2(4) \overset{?}{=} 4(4)$
$8 = 4$ False $16 = 15$ False $16 = 16$ True

If the length and width are both 4 units, then the area of the square is the same as its perimeter.

42. $(3 + 4)^2 = 3 + 4^2$
$7^2 \overset{?}{=} 3 + 16$
$49 = 19$ False
The equation is false.

43. $(3 + 4)^2 = (3 + 4)(3 + 4)$
$7^2 \overset{?}{=} (7)(7)$
$49 = 49$ True
The equation is true.

44. $(3 + 4)^2 = 3^2 + 2(3)(4) + 4^2$
$7^2 \overset{?}{=} 9 + 24 + 16$
$49 = 49$ True
The equation is true.

45. $(3 + 4)^2 = 3^2 + 4^2$
$7^2 \overset{?}{=} 9 + 16$
$49 = 25$ False
The equation is false.

1.8 PAGES 61–63, PRACTICE & APPLY

5. $(24 + 27) + 56 = (27 + 24) + 56$ Commutative Property
$= 27 + (24 + 56)$ Associative Property
$= 27 + 80$
$= 107$

6. $25 \cdot (27 \cdot 4) = 25 \cdot (4 \cdot 27)$ Commutative Property
$= (25 \cdot 4) \cdot 27$ Associative Property
$= 100 \cdot 27$
$= 2700$

7. $25(2 + 4) = 25 \cdot 2 + 25 \cdot 4$ Distributive Property

$= 50 + 100$

$= 150$

8. $(27 + 98) + 73 = (98 + 27) + 73$ Commutative Property

$= 98 + (27 + 73)$ Associative Property

$= 98 + 100$

$= 198$

9. $(45 \cdot 32) \cdot 0 = 45 \cdot (32 \cdot 0)$ Associative Property

$= 45 \cdot 0$

$= 0$

10. $(87 \cdot 5) \cdot 2 = 87 \cdot (5 \cdot 2)$ Associative Property

$= 87 \cdot 10$

$= 870$

11. $50 \cdot (118 \cdot 20) = 50 \cdot (20 \cdot 118)$ Commutative Property

$= (50 \cdot 20) \cdot 118$ Associative Property

$= 1000 \cdot 118$

$= 118,000$

12. $(688 + 915) + 312 = (915 + 688) + 312$ Commutative Property

$= 915 + (688 + 312)$ Associative Property

$= 915 + 1000$

$= 1915$

13. $(25 \cdot 78) \cdot 4 = (78 \cdot 25) \cdot 4$ Commutative Property

$= 78 \cdot (25 \cdot 4)$ Associative Property

$= 78 \cdot 100$

$= 7800$

14. $2 \cdot (129 \cdot 5) = 2 \cdot (5 \cdot 129)$ Commutative Property

$= (2 \cdot 5) \cdot 129$ Associative Property

$= 10 \cdot 129$

$= 1290$

15. $(133 + 52) + 67 = (52 + 133) + 67$ Commutative Property

$= 52 + (133 + 67)$ Associative Property

$= 52 + 200$

$= 252$

16. Commutative Property   **17.** Distributive Property   **18.** Distributive Property

19. Associative Property   **20.** Commutative Property   **21.** Distributive Property

22. Method 1

$9.50(7 + 8) = 9.50(15)$

$= \$142.50$

Method 2

$9.50(7) + 9.50(8) = 66.50 + 76.00$

$= \$142.50$

23. Method 1

$15(4 + 6) = 15(10)$

$= 150$

Method 2

$15(4) + 15(6) = 60 + 90$

$= 150$

Therefore, Marcia earned a total of $150.

24. $12(876) = 12(800 + 70 + 6)$

$= 12 \cdot 800 + 12 \cdot 70 + 12 \cdot 6$

$= 9600 + 840 + 72$

$= \$10,512$

25. 25 is less than 30, so the charge is $8.00 per person.

$25(8) = 25(4 + 4) = 25 \cdot 4 + 25 \cdot 4 = 100 + 100 = \$200$

$8(25) = 8(20 + 5) = 8 \cdot 20 + 8 \cdot 5 = 160 + 40 = \$200$

26. 49 is more than 30, so the charge is $6.00 per person.

$6(49) = 6(40 + 9) = 6 \cdot 40 + 6 \cdot 9 = 240 + 54 = \$294$

$6(49) = 6(50 - 1) = 6 \cdot 50 - 6 \cdot 1 = 300 - 6 = \$294$

27. $4 \cdot 28 = 4(20 + 8)$

$= 4 \cdot 20 + 4 \cdot 8$

$= 80 + 32$

$= 112$

28. $40 \cdot 28 = 40(20 + 8)$

$= 40 \cdot 20 + 40 \cdot 8$

$= 800 + 320$

$= 1120$

29. $9 \cdot 680 = 9(600 + 80)$

$= 9 \cdot 600 + 9 \cdot 80$

$= 5400 + 720$

$= 6120$

30. $90 \cdot 680 = 90(600 + 80)$
$= 90 \cdot 600 + 90 \cdot 80$
$= 54{,}000 + 7{,}200$
$= 61{,}200$

31. $95 \cdot 99 = 95(100 - 1)$
$= 95 \cdot 100 - 95 \cdot 1$
$= 9500 - 95$
$= 9405$

32. $68 \cdot 70 = (70 - 2) \cdot 70$
$= 70 \cdot 70 - 70 \cdot 2$
$= 4900 - 140$
$= 4760$

33. $12(5 + 4.5) = 12 \cdot 5 + 12 \cdot 4.5 = 60 + 54 = \$114$
Check: $12(5 + 4.5) = 12(9.5) = \$114$
Therefore, her total wages are \$114.

34. $(53 + 21 + 36) = (50 + 20 + 30) + (3 + 1 + 6)$
$= 100 + 10$
$= 110$

35. Answers may vary. A sample answer is given.
$2(3 - 2) = 2 \cdot 3 - 2 \cdot 2$
$= 6 - 4$
$= 2$

36. $xy + wy = (x + w)y$

37. $rs + rq = r(s + q)$

38. $9xy + 21xy = (3 + 7)3xy$

PAGE 63, LOOK BACK

39. $y = 3x$

x	3x	y
1	3(1)	3
2	3(2)	6
3	3(3)	9
4	3(4)	12
5	3(5)	15

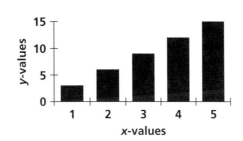

40. $y = 2x - 1$

x	2x – 1	y
1	2(1) – 1	1
2	2(2) – 1	3
3	2(3) – 1	5
4	2(4) – 1	7
5	2(5) – 1	9

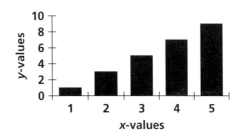

41. $c = 100 + 45h$

Hours h	Equation $100 + 45h$	Charge c
1	100 + 45(1)	\$145
2	100 + 45(2)	\$190
3	100 + 45(3)	\$235
4	100 + 45(4)	\$280
5	100 + 45(5)	\$325
6	100 + 45(6)	\$370
7	100 + 45(7)	\$415
8	100 + 45(8)	\$460

42. $360 = 2 \cdot 180$
$180 = 2 \cdot 90$
$90 = 2 \cdot 45$
$45 = 3 \cdot 15$
$15 = 3 \cdot 5$
$360 = 2 \cdot 2 \cdot 2 \cdot 3 \cdot 3 \cdot 5 = 2^3 \cdot 3^2 \cdot 5$

43. $V = (6)(6)(6) \text{ cm}^3$
$V = 216 \text{ cm}^3$

PAGE 63, LOOK BEYOND

44. $25 \cdot 76 = (20 + 5) + (70 + 6)$
$= 20 \cdot (70 + 6) + 5 \cdot (70 + 6)$
$= 20 \cdot 70 + 20 \cdot 6 + 5 \cdot 70 + 5 \cdot 6$
$= 1400 + 120 + 350 + 30$
$= 1900$

45. $26 \cdot 34 = (30 - 4) \cdot (30 + 4)$
$= (30 - 4) \cdot 30 + (30 - 4) \cdot 4$
$= 30 \cdot 30 - 4 \cdot 30 + 30 \cdot 4 - 4 \cdot 4$
$= 900 - 120 + 120 - 16$
$= 884$

1. Sequence 1   4   7   10   13   [16]   [19]   [22]
Pattern   +3   +3   +3   +3   +3   +3   +3

The next three terms are 16, 19, and 22.

2. Sequence 1   4   16   64   256   [1024]   [4096]   [16,384]

Each term is 4 times the previous term. The next three terms are 1024, 4096, and 16,384.

3. Sequence 27   9   3   1 $\frac{1}{3}$ $[\frac{1}{9}]$ $[\frac{1}{27}]$ $[\frac{1}{81}]$

Each term is one-third of the previous term. The next three terms are $\frac{1}{9}$, $\frac{1}{27}$, and $\frac{1}{81}$.

4. Equation $c = 8 + 2h$

Number of hours h	Process	Charge c
1	$8 + 2(1)$	$10
2	$8 + 2(2)$	$12
3	$8 + 2(3)$	$14
5	$8 + 2(5)$	$18
10	$8 + 2(10)$	$28

5. Include a row for $h = 6$ in your table.

Number of hours h	Process	Charge c
⋮	⋮	⋮
6	$8 + 2(6)$	$20

Therefore, the charge for 6 hours is $20.

6. Extend the table until you find the number of hours, h, that results in a charge, c, of $26.

Number of hours h	Process:	Charge c
⋮	⋮	⋮
7	$8 + 2(7)$	$22
8	$8 + 2(8)$	$24
9	$8 + 2(9)$	$26

You can rent a bike for 9 hours for $26.

7.

VCRs sold v	Process: $200 + 40v$	Wages w
1	$200 + 40(1)$	$240
2	$200 + 40(2)$	$280
3	$200 + 40(3)$	$320
4	$200 + 40(4)$	$360
5	$200 + 40(5)$	$400

8. Extend the table until you find the number of VCRs, v, which results in wages, w, of $520.

VCRs sold v	Process: $200 + 40v$	Wages w
⋮	⋮	⋮
6	$200 + 40(6)$	$440
7	$200 + 40(7)$	$480
8	$200 + 40(8)$	$520

Felix sold 8 VCRs.

9.

10. From the table you can see that Felix must sell at least 4 VCRs to earn at least $350.

11.

x	$8x - 2$
1	$8(1) - 2 = 6$
2	$8(2) - 2 = 14$
3	$8(3) - 2 = 22$
4	$8(4) - 2 = 30$
5	$8(5) - 2 = 38$

12. From the table in Exercise 11, $x = 2$.

13. $18 \div 1 = 18$
$18 \div 2 = 9$
$18 \div 3 = 6$
1, ②, ③, 6, 9, 18

14. $32 \div 1 = 32$
$32 \div 2 = 16$
$32 \div 4 = 8$
1, ②, 4, 8, 16, 32

15. $75 \div 1 = 75$
$75 \div 3 = 25$
$75 \div 5 = 15$
1, ③, ⑤, 15, 25, 75

16. $98 \div 1 = 98$
$98 \div 2 = 49$
$98 \div 7 = 14$
1, ②, ⑦, 14, 49, 98

17. $56 \div 2 = 28$
$28 \div 2 = 14$
$14 \div 2 = 7$
Prime factorization of $56 = 2^3 \cdot 7$

18. $102 \div 2 = 51$
$51 \div 3 = 17$
Prime factorization of $102 = 2 \cdot 3 \cdot 17$

19. 29 is a prime number.

20. $720 \div 2 = 360$
$360 \div 2 = 180$
$180 \div 2 = 90$
$90 \div 2 = 45$
$45 \div 3 = 15$
$15 \div 3 = 5$
Prime factorization of $720 = 2^4 \cdot 3^2 \cdot 5$

21. $18 - 4 \div 2 = 18 - 2$
$= 16$

22. $32 - 24 \div 6 - 4 = 32 - 4 - 4$
$= 28 - 4$
$= 24$

23. $3 \cdot 4^2 - [24 \div (6 - 4)] = 3 \cdot 4^2 - [24 \div 2]$
$= 3 \cdot 4^2 - 12$
$= 3 \cdot 16 - 12$
$= 48 - 12$
$= 36$

24. $(27 + 8) + 12 = 27 + (8 + 12)$ Associative Property
$= 27 + 20$
$= 47$

25. $(25 \cdot 87) \cdot 4 = (87 \cdot 25) \cdot 4$ Commutative Property
$= 87 \cdot (25 \cdot 4)$ Associative Property
$= 87 \cdot 100$
$= 8700$

26. $(6.2 + 7.1) + 3.8 = (7.1 + 6.2) + 3.8$ Commutative Property
$= 7.1 + (6.2 + 3.8)$ Associative Property
$= 7.1 + 10$
$= 17.1$

27. $(63 \cdot 20) \cdot 5 = 63 \cdot (20 \cdot 5)$ Associative Property
$= 63 \cdot 100$
$= 6300$

28. Let p represent the number of people.
$13p = 98$

Try $p = 7$.   Try $p = 8$.
$13p = 98$ $13p = 98$
$13(7) = 91$ $13(8) = 104$

7 is too small.   8 is too large, but since
Try a larger number.   it costs $104 for 8 tick-
ets, only 7 tickets can
be bought for $98.

29. Let t represent the number of tickets. The total cost of tickets is $22t$.
For 4 tickets, substitute 4 for t.
$22t = 22(4) = \$88$
For 8 tickets, substitute 8 for t.
$22t = 22(8) = \$176$

30. Let t represent the number of tickets and let c represent the total cost; then $c = 22t$.

PAGE 69   **CHAPTER 1 ASSESSMENT**

1. Sequence   4   8   16   32   64   [128]   [256]   [512]
Each term is two times the previous term. The next three terms are 128, 256, and 512.

2. Sequence   49   40   32   25   19   [14]   [10]   [7]
Pattern   −9   −8   −7   −6   −5   −4   −3
The next three terms are 14, 10, and 7.

For Exercises 3–5, let _n_ represent the number of notebooks. Then the cost of _n_ notebooks is 0.59_n_.

3. $0.59(2) = \$1.18$ **4.** $0.59(5) = \$2.95$ **5.** $0.59(12) = \$7.08$ **6.** $c = 0.59n$

7. To find the number of notebooks that cost $14.75, solve:

$$14.75 = 0.59n$$

Try $n = 20$.
   $0.59n = \$14.75$
   $0.59(20) = \$11.80$

20 is too small.
Try a larger number.

Try $n = 25$.
   $0.59n = \$14.75$
   $0.59(25) = \$14.75$

The total number of notebooks that cost $14.75 is 25.

8.

x	y = 250 + 20x
1	$250 + 20(1) = \$270$
2	$250 + 20(2) = \$290$
3	$250 + 20(3) = \$310$
4	$250 + 20(4) = \$330$
5	$250 + 20(5) = \$350$

9. Solve: $330 = 250 + 20x$

From the table in Exercise 8 you can see that to earn $330, Alice must sell 4 memberships.

10.

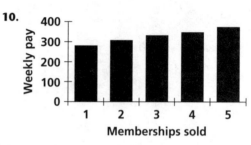

11. Selling 4 memberships results in earnings of only $330. To earn $340, Alice needs to sell at least 5 memberships.

12.

x	5x + 7
1	$5(1) + 7 = 12$
2	$5(2) + 7 = 17$
3	$5(3) + 7 = 22$
4	$5(4) + 7 = 27$
5	$5(5) + 7 = 32$

13. From the table in Exercise 12, you can see that $5x + 7 = 22$ when $x = 3$.

14. $20 \div 1 = 20$
$20 \div 2 = 10$
$20 \div 4 = 5$

1, ②, 4, ⑤, 10, 20

15. $42 \div 1 = 42$
$42 \div 2 = 21$
$42 \div 3 = 14$
$42 \div 6 = 7$

1, ②, ③, 6, ⑦, 14, 21, 42

16. $76 \div 1 = 76$
$76 \div 2 = 38$
$76 \div 4 = 19$

1, ②, 4, ⑲, 38, 76

17. Prime; the only factors of 19 are 19 and 1.

18. Composite; the factors of 30 include 1, 2, 3, 5, 6, 10, 15, and 30.

19. Prime; the only factors of 31 are 31 and 1.

20. $8 \div 2 = 4$
$4 \div 2 = 2$
$8 = 2^3$

21. $81 \div 3 = 27$
$27 \div 3 = 9$
$9 \div 3 = 3$
$81 = 3^4$

22. $105 \div 3 = 35$
$35 \div 5 = 7$
$105 = 3 \cdot 5 \cdot 7$

23. $252 \div 2 = 126$
$126 \div 2 = 63$
$63 \div 3 = 21$
$21 \div 3 = 7$
$252 = 2^2 \cdot 3^2 \cdot 7$

24. $3 + 27 \div 32 - (7 + 5) = 3 + 27 \div 32 - 12$
$= 3 + 27 \div 9 - 12$
$= 3 + 3 - 12$
$= 6 - 12$
$= -6$

25. $(9 + 37) + 11 = (37 + 9) + 11$ Commutative Property
$= 37 + (9 + 11)$ Associative Property
$= 37 + 20$
$= 57$

26. $20 \cdot (5 \cdot 19) = (20 \cdot 5) \cdot 19$ Associative Property
$= 100 \cdot 19$
$= 1900$

CHAPTER 2

PATTERNS WITH INTEGERS

6. integer

7. integer

8. integer

9. contains a decimal, not an integer

10. fraction, not an integer

11. integer

12. 20

13. −45

14. −500

15. 3

16. −9

17. 15

18. 2

19. −20

20. −6

21. −10

22. −17

23. 17

24. 0 is its own inverse.

25. 12

26. −6

27. $|-4| = 4$

28. $|0| = 0$

29. $|-3| = 3$

30. $|25| = 25$

31. $|-8| = 8$

32. $|14| = 14$

33. $|-2| = 2$

34. $|-30| = 30$

35. $|-25| = 25$

36. $|18| = 18$

37. −30

38. 20

39. 80

40. −50

41. 45

42. $711{,}407 - 678{,}974 = 32{,}433$

43. $427{,}799 - 448{,}159 = -20{,}360$

44. $990{,}957 - 904{,}078 = 86{,}879$

45. $441{,}154 - 403{,}213 = 37{,}941$

46. The temperature increased throughout the day: $30°F - (-20°F) = 50°F$

PAGE 77, LOOK BACK

47. $y = 2x + 1$

x	1	2	3	4	5	10
y	3	5	7	9	11	21

48. $y = 5x - 1$

x	1	2	3	4	5	10
y	4	9	14	19	24	49

49. $ab^2c = 3 \cdot 4^2 \cdot 2$
$= 3 \cdot 16 \cdot 2$
$= 48 \cdot 2$
$= 96$

50. $a^2bc = 3^2 \cdot 4 \cdot 2$
$= 9 \cdot 4 \cdot 2$
$= 36 \cdot 2$
$= 72$

51. $abc^2 = 3 \cdot 4 \cdot 2^2$
$= 3 \cdot 4 \cdot 4$
$= 12 \cdot 4$
$= 48$

52. $a^4 \cdot c^3 = 3^4 \cdot 2^3$
$= 81 \cdot 8$
$= 648$

53. $V = 7 \cdot 7 \cdot 7$
$V = 343 \text{ cm}^3$

54. $5 \cdot 13 \cdot 6 = (5)(10 + 3)(6)$
$= (50 + 15)(6)$ Distributive Property
$= 300 + 90$ Distributive Property
$= 390$

55. $78 + (23 + 22) = 78 + (22 + 23)$ Commutative Property
$= (78 + 22) + 23$ Associative Property
$= 100 + 23$
$= 123$

56. $8 \cdot 59 = (8)(50 + 9)$
$= 400 + 72$ Distributive Property
$= 472$

57. $y = |x|$

The graph of $y = |x|$ is an open ended V at the origin.

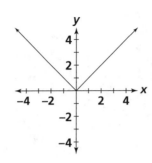

2.2 **PAGES 83–84, PRACTICE & APPLY**

5. Start with 5 negative tiles.
Add 2 negative tiles.
You are left with 7 negative tiles, so the sum is –7.

6. Start with 3 negative tiles.
Add 3 positive tiles
Remove all neutral pairs (the sum of a neutral pair is 0).
There is nothing left, so the sum is 0.

7. Start with 2 positive tiles.
Add 6 negative tiles.
Remove all neutral pairs.
There are 4 negative tiles remaining, so the sum is –4.

8. Start with 2 negative tiles.
Add 6 negative tiles.
Total up all of the negative tiles (there are 8).
The sum is –8.

9. Start with 8 positive tiles.
Add 3 negative tiles.
Remove all neutral pairs (this leaves you with 5 positive tiles).
The sum is 5.

10. Start with 4 negative tiles.
Add 5 negative tiles.
The sum is 9 negative tiles, so the sum is –9.

11. Start with 1 negative tile.
Add 5 positive tiles.
Remove the neutral pair.
The resulting sum is 4.

12. Start with 1 negative tile.
Add 2 negative tiles.
The sum is 3 negative tiles or –3.

13. $-28 + 50 = 22$

14. $17 + (-34) = -17$

15. $38 + (-72) = -34$

16. $54 + (-16) = 38$

17. $-13 + -18 = -31$

18. $31 + (-69) = -38$

19. $(-33) + (-5) = -38$

20. $43 + (-51) + 8 = -8 + 8$
$= 0$

21. $-61 + (-15) + 9 = -76 + 9$
$= -67$

22. $14 + (-29) + (-12) = -15 + (-12)$
$= -27$

23. $-43 + 82 + |-19| = 39 + |-19|$
$= 39 + 19$
$= 58$

24. $-308 + |-24| + (-29) = -308 + 24 + (-29)$
$= -284 + (-29)$
$= -313$

25. $(a + b) + c = (2 + (-3)) + 5$
$= -1 + 5$
$= 4$

26. $|a + b| + c = |2 + (-3)| + 5$
$= |-1| + 5$
$= 1 + 5$
$= 6$

27. $a + |b + c| = 2 + |-3 + 5|$
$= 2 + |2|$
$= 4$

28. $a + (b + c) = 2 + (-3 + 5)$
$= 2 + 2$
$= 4$

29. $a + (c + b) = 2 + (5 + (-3))$
$= 2 + 2$
$= 4$

30. $c + |a + b| = 5 + |2 + -3|$
$= 5 + |-1|$
$= 5 + 1$
$= 6$

31. Since protons have a charge of +1 and electrons have a charge of –1, we can use tiles to determine the total charge:

Start with 16 positive tiles.
Add 18 negative tiles.
Remove all neutral pairs.
The result is two negative tiles, so there is a total charge of –2.

32. Another way we can solve this problem is to first find the positive charge from the protons.

$$10(+1) = 10$$

Then we must find the negative charge from the electrons.

$$10(-1) = -10$$

The resulting sum is $10 + -10 = 0$, so there is 0 total charge.

33. To find the total loss or gain, we can sum up the gain or loss for each game separately:

Game 1
$$8 + (-4) + (-3) + 15 = 16$$

Game 2
$$-3 + (-5) + 4 + (-6) = -10$$

Now sum up the loss or gain for game 1 and game 2:

$$16 + (-10) = 6$$

Therefore, the total for both games is a gain of 6 yards.

34. Since losses are recorded in parentheses, we can rewrite the table as follows:

1st Quarter	2nd Quarter	3rd Quarter	4th Quarter
−389.75	−794.28	1796.50	−809.50

Adding from left to right:

```
    −389.75
 +  −794.28
  −1184.03
 +  1796.50
    612.47
 +  −809.50
   −197.03
```

Therefore, the business had a loss of $197.03 for the year.

35. The depth at 24 hours can be found by taking the original depth of −600 feet and adding the positive and negative changes over the 4 six-hour time intervals. You then get:

$$-600 + 128 + (-90) + 245 + (-116) + (-50) + 0 = ?$$

Working left to right, the sum is −483, so the depth at 24 hours is −483 feet.

PAGE 84, LOOK BACK

36. $1 + 2 + 3 + \cdots + 40 = \dfrac{40 \cdot 41}{2}$
$= \dfrac{1640}{2}$
$= 820$

37. Sequence   40   37   34   31   [28]   [25]
Pattern   3   3   3   3   3
The next two terms are 28 and 25.

38. Sequence   −5   −1   3   7   [11]   [15]
Pattern   4   4   4   4   4
The next two terms are 11 and 15.

39. Sequence   1   3   6   10   [15]   [21]
Pattern   2   3   4   5   6
The next two terms are 15 and 21.

40. $4(3.5) = 14$ cm
$= 19$

41. $15 - 21 + 3 + 4 = -6 + 3 + 4$
$= -3 + 4$
$= 1$

42. $[3(4 - 2)^2] + 7 = [3(2)^2] + 7$
$= (3 \cdot 4) + 7$
$= 12 + 7$

43. $12 + 3^2 + (9 - 6) = 12 + 9 + (9 - 6)$
$= 12 + 9 + 3$
$= 21 + 3$
$= 24$

44. $8 + 12 - 2 - 6 - 1 = 11$ yards
$12 - 6 + 8 - 2 - 1 = 11$ yards
$-2 - 6 - 1 + 8 + 12 = 11$ yards

45. integer

46. integer

47. decimal, not an integer

48. integer

PAGE 84, LOOK BEYOND

49. $(-2) + (-2) + (-2) + (-2) + (-2) + (-2) + (-2) = -14$

50. $-[7(-2)] = -[-14]$
$= 14$

5. $x + 5 = -1$
Try $x = -3$.
$x + 5 = -1$
$-3 + 5 = 2$

-3 is too large.
Try a smaller
number.

Try $x = -5$.
$x + 5 = -1$
$-5 + 5 = 0$

-5 is too large.
Try a smaller
number.

Try $x = -6$.
$x + 5 = -1$
$-6 + 5 = -1$

-6 is the correct
number; $x = -6$.

6. $-1 + x = -4$
Try $x = -2$.
$-1 + x = -4$
$-1 + -2 = -3$

-2 is too large.
Try a smaller
number.

Try $x = -4$.
$-1 + x = -4$
$-1 + -4 = -5$

-4 is too small.
Try a larger
number.

Try $x = -3$.
$-1 + x = -4$
$-1 + -3 = -4$

-3 is the correct
number; $x = -3$.

7. $4 + x = 2$
Try $x = -1$.
$4 + x = 2$
$4 + -1 = 3$

-1 is too large.
Try a smaller
number.

Try $x = -4$.
$4 + x = 2$
$4 + -4 = 0$

-4 is too small.
Try a larger
number.

Try $x = -2$.
$4 + x = 2$
$4 + -2 = 2$

-2 is the correct
number; $x = -2$.

8. $x + 1 = -1$
Try $x = 2$.
$x + 1 = -1$
$2 + 1 = 3$

2 is too large.
Try a smaller
number.

Try $x = 0$.
$x + 1 = -1$
$0 + 1 = 1$

0 is too large.
Try a smaller
number.

Try $x = -2$.
$x + 1 = -1$
$-2 + 1 = -1$

-2 is the correct
number; $x = -2$.

9. $-3 + x = -4$
Try $x = -2$.
$-3 + x = -4$
$-3 + -2 = -5$

-2 is too small.
Try a larger
number.

Try $x = 0$.
$-3 + x = -4$
$-3 + 0 = -3$

0 is too large.
Try a smaller
number.

Try $x = -1$.
$-3 + x = -4$
$-3 + -1 = -4$

-1 is the correct
number; $x = -1$.

10. $-7 + x = -2$
Try $x = 3$.
$-7 + x = -2$
$-7 + 3 = -4$

3 is too small.
Try a larger
number.

Try $x = 7$.
$-7 + x = -2$
$-7 + 7 = 0$

7 is too large.
Try a smaller
number.

Try $x = 5$.
$-7 + x = -2$
$-7 + 5 = -2$

5 is the correct
number; $x = 5$.

11. $x + (-4) = 0$
Try $x = 3$.
$x + (-4) = 0$
$3 + (-4) = -1$

3 is too small.
Try a larger
number.

Try $x = 5$.
$x + (-4) = 0$
$5 + (-4) = 1$

5 is too large.
Try a smaller
number.

Try $x = 4$.
$x + (-4) = 0$
$4 + (-4) = 0$

4 is the correct
number; $x = 4$.

12. $-4 + x = -4$
Try $x = -3$.
$-4 + x = -4$
$-4 + -3 = -7$

-3 is too small.
Try a larger
number.

Try $x = 2$.
$-4 + x = -4$
$-4 + 2 = -2$

2 is too large.
Try a smaller
number.

Try $x = 0$.
$-4 + x = -4$
$-4 + 0 = -4$

0 is the correct
number; $x = 0$.

13. $6 = 2 + x$
Try $x = 2$.
$6 = 2 + x$
$4 = 2 + 2$

2 is too small.
Try a larger
number.

Try $x = 5$.
$6 = 2 + x$
$7 = 2 + 5$

5 is too large.
Try a smaller
number.

Try $x = 4$.
$6 = 2 + x$
$6 = 2 + 4$

4 is the correct
number; $x = 4$.

14. $-6 = x + (-3)$
Try $x = -1$.
$-6 = x + (-3)$
$-4 = -1 + -3$

-3 is too large.
Try a smaller
number.

Try $x = -4$.
$-6 = x + (-3)$
$-7 = -4 + (-3)$

-4 is too small.
Try a larger
number.

Try $x = -3$.
$-6 = x + (-3)$
$-6 = -3 + -3$

-3 is the correct
number; $x = -3$.

15. $5 > -5$
$-5 < 5$

16. $-3 < -1$
$-1 > -3$

17. $0 > -2$
$-2 < 0$

18. $-3 > -7$
$-7 < -3$

19. $4 > -8$
$-8 < 4$

20. $-1 > -2$
$-2 < -1$

21. $-1 < 4$
$4 > -1$

22. $-4 < -2$
$-2 > -4$

23. $7 > -9$
$-9 < 7$

24. $10 > -8$
$-8 < 10$

25. $8 > -7$
$-7 < 8$

26. $15 > -15$
$-15 < 15$

27. $8 > -21$
$-21 < 8$

28. $-16 > -22$
$-22 < -16$

29. $14 > -7$
$-7 < 14$

30. $101 > -236$
$-236 < 101$

31. $16 > -17$
$-17 < 16$

32. $-9 > -18$
$-18 < -9$

33. $18 > 9$
$9 < 18$

34. $-1 > -200$
$-200 < -1$

35.
```
 -8 -7 -6 -5 -4 -3 -2 -1 0 1 2 3 4 5 6 7
```
Ascending order: $-5, -3, 1, 5$

36.
```
 -12 -11 -10 -9 -8 -7 -6 -5 -4 -3 -2 -1 0 1 2
```
Ascending order: $-10, -4, -2, -1, 0, 2$

37.
```
 -4 -3 -2 -1 0 1 2 3 4
```
Ascending order: $-3, -2, 0, 2, 3$

38.
```
 0 1 2 3 4 5 6 7 8
```
Ascending order: $2, 3, 4, 6$

39.
```
 -8 -7 -6 -5 -4 -3 -2 -1 0 1 2 3
```
Ascending order: $-6, -4, -3, -2, 1$

40.
```
 -8 -7 -6 -5 -4 -3 -2 -1 0 1 2 3 4 5 6 7 8
```
Ascending order: $-5, -4, 0, 5, 6$

41.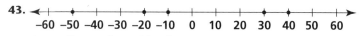

Ascending order: 10, 20, 30, 40

42.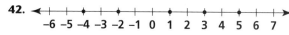

Ascending order: −4, −2, 1, 3, 5

43.

```
◄─┼──┼──●──┼──┼──●──┼──┼──┼──┼──●──┼──●──┼──►
  −60 −50 −40 −30 −20 −10  0  10  20  30  40  50  60
```

Ascending order: −50, −20, −10, 30, 40

44. $-5 + x = -2$

Try $x = 4$.	Try $x = 2$.	Try $x = 3$.
$-5 + x = -2$	$-5 + x = -2$	$-5 + x = -2$
$-5 + 4 = -1$	$-5 + 2 = -3$	$-5 + 3 = -2$
4 is too large. Try a smaller number.	2 is too small. Try a larger number.	3 is the correct number; $x = 3$.

Since $-5 + 3 = -2$ and 3 is a positive integer, the inequality $-5 < -2$ is true.

45. $-3 + x = -1$

Try $x = 0$.	Try $x = 1$.	Try $x = 2$.
$-3 + x = -1$	$-3 + x = -1$	$-3 + x = -1$
$-3 + 0 = -3$	$-3 + 1 = -2$	$-3 + 2 = -1$
0 is too small. Try a larger number.	1 is too small. Try a larger number.	2 is the correct number; $x = 2$.

Since $-3 + 2 = -1$ and 2 is a positive integer, the inequality $-3 < -1$ is true.

46. $-1 + x = 4$

Try $x = 3$.	Try $x = 6$.	Try $x = 5$.
$-1 + x = 4$	$-1 + x = 4$	$-1 + x = 4$
$-1 + 3 = 2$	$-1 + 6 = 5$	$-1 + 5 = 4$
3 is too small. Try a larger number.	6 is too large. Try a smaller number.	5 is the correct number; $x = 5$.

Since $-1 + 5 = 4$ and 5 is a positive integer, the inequality $-1 < 4$ is true.

47. $2 + x = 5$

Try $x = 2$.	Try $x = 4$.	Try $x = 3$.
$2 + x = 5$	$2 + x = 5$	$2 + x = 5$
$2 + 2 = 4$	$2 + 4 = 6$	$2 + 3 = 5$
2 is too small. Try a larger number.	4 is too large. Try a smaller number.	3 is the correct number; $x = 3$.

Since $2 + 3 = 5$ and 3 is a positive integer, the inequality $2 < 5$ is true.

48. $-8 + x = 7$

Try $x = 10$.	Try $x = 12$.	Try $x = 15$.
$-8 + x = 7$	$-8 + x = 7$	$-8 + x = 7$
$-8 + 10 = 2$	$-8 + 12 = 4$	$-8 + 15 = 7$
10 is too small. Try a larger number.	12 is too small. Try a larger number.	15 is the correct number; $x = 15$.

Since $-8 + 15 = 7$ and 15 is a positive integer, the inequality $-8 < 7$ is true.

49. $5 + x = 12$

Try $x = 5$.	Try $x = 8$.	Try $x = 7$.
$5 + x = 12$	$5 + x = 12$	$5 + x = 12$
$5 + 5 = 10$	$5 + 8 = 13$	$5 + 7 = 12$
5 is too small. Try a larger number.	8 is too large. Try a smaller number.	7 is the correct number; $x = 7$.

Since $5 + 7 = 12$ and 7 is a positive integer, the inequality $5 < 12$ is true.

50. $-3 + x = 4$

Try $x = 5$.	Try $x = 8$.	Try $x = 7$.
$-3 + x = 4$	$-3 + x = 4$	$-3 + x = 4$
$-3 + 5 = 2$	$-3 + 8 = 5$	$-3 + 7 = 4$
5 is too small. Try a larger number.	8 is too large. Try a smaller number.	7 is the correct number; $x = 7$.

Since $-3 + 7 = 4$ and 7 is a positive integer, the inequality $-3 < 4$ is true.

51. $-6 + x = -3$

Try $x = 2$.	Try $x = 5$.	Try $x = 3$.
$-6 + x = -3$	$-6 + x = -3$	$-6 + x = -3$
$-6 + 2 = -4$	$-6 + 5 = -1$	$-6 + 3 = -3$
2 is too small. Try a larger number.	5 is too large. Try a smaller number.	3 is the correct number; $x = 3$.

Since $-6 + 3 = -3$ and 3 is a positive integer, the inequality $-6 < -3$ is true.

52. −80°F, −50°F, −47°F, −40°F, −35°F, −17°F, −2°F, 12°F

53. Vermont, Iowa, and Alaska

54. Georgia, Florida, and Hawaii

55. $-80 < 12$

56. $-4 + x = -2$

Try $x = 3$.	Try $x = 1$.	Try $x = 2$.
$-4 + x = -2$	$-4 + x = -2$	$-4 + x = -2$
$-4 + 3 = -1$	$-4 + 1 = -3$	$-4 + 2 = -2$
3 is too large. Try a smaller number.	1 is too small. Try a larger number.	2 is the correct number; $x = 2$.

57. $y + 12 = 10$

Try $y = 1$.	Try $y = -1$.	Try $y = -2$.
$y + 12 = 10$	$y + 12 = 10$	$y + 12 = 10$
$1 + 12 = 13$	$-1 + 12 = 11$	$-2 + 12 = 10$
1 is too large. Try a smaller number.	−1 is too large. Try a smaller number.	−2 is the correct number; $y = -2$.

58. $5 + x = 2$

Try $x = -1$.
$5 + x = 2$
$5 + -1 = 4$
−1 is too large. Try a smaller number.

Try $x = -2$.
$5 + x = 2$
$5 + -2 = 3$
−2 is too large. Try a smaller number.

Try $x = -3$.
$5 + x = 2$
$5 + -3 = 2$
−3 is the correct number; $x = -3$.

59. $32 - x = -2$

Try $x = 30$.
$32 - x = -2$
$32 - 30 = 2$
30 is too small. Try a larger number.

Try $x = 35$.
$32 - x = -2$
$32 - 35 = -3$
35 is too large. Try a smaller number.

Try $x = 34$.
$32 - x = -2$
$32 - 34 = -2$
34 is the correct number; $x = 34$.

60. $32 + y = -21$

Try $y = -50$.
$32 + y = -21$
$32 + (-50) = -18$
−50 is too large. Try a smaller number.

Try $y = -55$.
$32 + y = -21$
$32 + (-55) = -23$
−55 is too small. Try a larger number.

Try $y = -53$.
$32 + y = -21$
$32 + (-53) = -21$
−53 is the correct number; $y = -53$.

61. $19 - x = -9$

Try $x = 25$.
$19 - x = -9$
$19 - 25 = -6$
25 is too small. Try a larger number.

Try $x = 30$.
$19 - x = -9$
$19 - 30 = -11$
30 is too large. Try a smaller number.

Try $x = 28$.
$19 - x = -9$
$19 - 28 = -9$
28 is the correct number; $x = 28$.

62. $2x = -8$

Try $x = -2$.
$2x = -8$
$2(-2) = -4$
−2 is too large. Try a smaller number.

Try $x = -6$.
$2x = -8$
$2(-6) = -12$
−6 is too small. Try a larger number.

Try $x = -4$.
$2x = -8$
$2(-4) = -8$
−4 is the correct number; $x = -4$.

63. $32 - y = -2$

Try $y = 30$.
$32 - y = -2$
$32 - 30 = 2$
30 is too small. Try a larger number.

Try $y = 32$.
$32 - y = -2$
$32 - 32 = 0$
32 is too small. Try a larger number.

Try $y = 34$.
$32 - y = -2$
$32 - 34 = -2$
34 is the correct number; $y = 34$.

64. $2z - 1 = -7$

Try $z = -1$.
$2z - 1 = -7$
$2(-1) - 1 = -3$
−1 is too large. Try a smaller number.

Try $z = -2$.
$2z - 1 = -7$
$2(-2) - 1 = -5$
−2 is too large. Try a smaller number.

Try $z = -3$.
$2z - 1 = -7$
$2(-3) - 1 = -7$
−3 is the correct number; $z = -3$.

65. $3x = -12$

Try $x = -2$.
$3x = -12$
$3(-2) = -6$
−2 is too large. Try a smaller number.

Try $x = -3$.
$3x = -12$
$3(-3) = -9$
−3 is too large. Try a smaller number.

Try $x = -4$.
$3x = -12$
$3(-4) = -12$
−4 is the correct number; $x = -4$.

66. $-12 + 2y = -6$

Try $y = 2$.
$-12 + 2y = -6$
$-12 + 2(2) = -8$
2 is too small. Try a larger number.

Try $y = 5$.
$-12 + 2y = -6$
$-12 + 2(5) = -2$
5 is too large. Try a smaller number.

Try $y = 3$.
$-12 + 2y = -6$
$-12 + 2(3) = -6$
3 is the correct number; $y = 3$.

67. $2z + 1 = -7$

Try $z = -5$.
$2z + 1 = -7$
$5(-5) + 1 = -9$
−5 is too small. Try a larger number.

Try $z = -3$.
$2z + 1 = -7$
$2(-3) + 1 = -5$
−3 is too large. Try a smaller number.

Try $z = -4$.
$2z + 1 = -7$
$2(-4) + 1 = -7$
−4 is the correct number; $z = -4$.

68. $-5 < -3$

69. $-5 + (-3) = -8$

70. $10 = -8 + x$

71. $a + a = b$
$2a = b$
$a = \dfrac{b}{2}$
$a < b$

72. $a + (2a) = b$
$3a = b$
$a = \dfrac{b}{3}$
$a < b$

73. $a + 0 = b$
$a = b$

74. $a - a = b$
$0 = b$
Since a is positive, $a > b$.

PAGE 92, LOOK BACK

75. $(23 + 48) + 77 = (48 + 23) + 77$
$= 48 + (23 + 77)$
$= 48 + 100$
$= 148$

76. $(4 \cdot 32) \cdot 25 = (32 \cdot 4) \cdot 25$
$= 32 \cdot (4 \cdot 25)$
$= 32 \cdot 100$
$= 3200$

77. $2 \cdot (95 \cdot 5) = 2 \cdot (5 \cdot 95)$
$= (2 \cdot 5) \cdot 95$
$= 10 \cdot 95$
$= 950$

78. $54 + (75 + 46) = 54 + (46 + 75)$
$= (54 + 46) + 75$
$= 100 + 75$
$= 175$

79. $24 \cdot 90 = (20 + 4) \cdot 90$
$= 1800 + 360$
$= 2160$

80. $26 \cdot 30 = (20 + 6) \cdot 30$
$= 600 + 180$
$= 780$

81. $40 \cdot 49 = 40 \cdot (40 + 9)$
$= 1600 + 360$
$= 1960$

82. $20 \cdot 99 = 20 \cdot (90 + 9)$
$= 1800 + 180$
$= 1980$

83. $|-4| = 4$ **84.** $|0| = 0$ **85.** $|-3| = 3$ **86.** $|25| = 25$ **87.** $|-8| = 8$ **88.** $|16| = 16$

PAGE 92, LOOK BEYOND

89. $2x = -6$

Try $x = -4$.	Try $x = -2$.	Try $x = -3$.
$2x = -6$	$2x = -6$	$2x = -6$
$2(-4) = -8$	$2(-2) = -4$	$2(-3) = -6$
-4 is too small. Try a larger number.	-2 is too large. Try a smaller number.	-3 is the correct number; $x = -3$.

90. $\frac{x}{2} = -14$

Try $x = -30$.	Try $x = -26$.	Try $x = -28$.
$\frac{x}{2} = -14$	$\frac{x}{2} = -14$	$\frac{x}{2} = -14$
$\frac{-30}{2} = -15$	$\frac{-26}{2} = -13$	$\frac{-28}{2} = -14$
-30 is too small. Try a larger number.	-26 is too large. Try a smaller number.	-28 is the correct number; $x = -28$.

91. $x^2 = 4$

Try $x = 3$.	Try $x = 2$.	Try $x = -2$.
$x^2 = 4$	$x^2 = 4$	$x^2 = 4$
$3^2 = 9$	$2^2 = 4$	$(-2)^2 = 4$
3 is too large. Try a smaller number.	2 is a correct number; $x = 2$.	-2 is a correct number; $x = -2$.

Notice that $x = 2$ and $x = -2$ are both solutions of $x^2 = 4$.

92. $2x = -4$

Try $x = -1$.	Try $x = -3$.	Try $x = -2$.
$2x = -4$	$2x = -4$	$2x = -4$
$2(-1) = -2$	$2(-3) = -6$	$2(-2) = -4$
-1 is too large. Try a smaller number.	-3 is too small. Try a larger number.	-2 is the correct number; $x = -2$.

2.4 PAGES 96–97, PRACTICE & APPLY

7. $67 - 3 = 64$

8. $42 - (-9) = 42 + 9$
$\qquad = 51$

9. $-10 - (-21) = -10 + 21$
$\qquad = 11$

10. $-35 - 17 = -52$

11. $33 - (-33) = 33 + 33$
$\qquad = 66$

12. $-78 + (-45) = -78 - 45$
$\qquad = -123$

13. $990 - (-155) = 990 + 155$
$\qquad = 1145$

14. $-97 - 88 = -185$

15. $-43 + 23 + (-43) = -43 + 23 - 43$
$\qquad = (-43 - 43) + 23$
$\qquad = -86 + 23$
$\qquad = -63$

16. $-77 - 77 + 5 = -154 + 5$
$\qquad = -149$

17. $108 + (-18) - 8 = 108 - 18 - 8$
$\qquad = 108 - 26$
$\qquad = 82$

18. $85 - (-12) - (-9) = 85 + 12 + 9$
$\qquad = 97 + 9$
$\qquad = 106$

19. $x - y = 5 - (-3)$
$\qquad = 5 + 3$
$\qquad = 8$

20. $x + y - z = 5 + (-3) - (-10)$
$\qquad = 5 - 3 + 10$
$\qquad = 15 - 3$
$\qquad = 12$

21. $(x - z) - y = [5 - (-10)] - (-3)$
$\qquad = [5 + 10] + 3$
$\qquad = 15 + 3$
$\qquad = 18$

22. $x - (z - y) = 5 - [-10 - (-3)]$
$\qquad = 5 - [-10 + 3]$
$\qquad = 5 - [-7]$
$\qquad = 5 + 7$
$\qquad = 12$

23. $y - x = -3 - 5 = -8$

24. $y - x + z = -3 - 5 + (-10)$
$\qquad = -3 - 5 - 10$
$\qquad = -8 - 10$
$\qquad = -18$

25. $(x + y) - (x - y) = [5 + (-3)] - [5 - (-3)]$
$\qquad = [5 - 3] - [5 + 3]$
$\qquad = 2 - 8$
$\qquad = -6$

26. $y - y - y - y = (-3) - (-3) - (-3) - (-3)$
$\qquad = -3 + 3 + 3 + 3$
$\qquad = -3 + 9$
$\qquad = 6$

27.

$9 - 4 = 5$ units

28.

$15 - (-6) = 15 + 6$
$\qquad = 21$ units

29.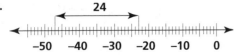

$$-23 - (-47) = -23 + 47$$
$$= 24 \text{ units}$$

30.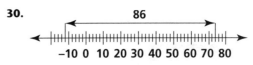

$$74 - (-12) = 74 + 12$$
$$= 86 \text{ units}$$

31. To determine the balance, subtract the withdrawal from the balance.

$$145 - 37 = 108$$

Mike has $108 left.

32. To determine the final temperature, subtract the first temperature from initial temperature, and then subtract the second temperature drop from the difference.

$$5 - 7 - 2 = 5 - 9$$
$$= -4$$

The final temperature should be −4°F.

33. To determine the wind-chill factor, locate 20°F in the air temperature column. Locate 20 mph under the wind-speed column. Find the intersection of the two columns.

The wind-chill factor is −10°F.

34. To determine the wind-chill factor, locate −10°F in the air temperature column. Locate 20 mph under the wind-speed column. Find the intersection of the two columns.

The wind-chill factor is −53; this means it feels like −53°F.

To find the difference in the feel of −10°F with no wind, subtract −10°F from the wind-chill factor.

$$-53 - (-10) = -53 + 10$$
$$= -43$$

It feels 43°F colder.

35. Determine the wind-chill factor for an air temperature of −10°F and a wind speed of 20 mph. The wind-chill factor is −34°F. Determine the wind-chill factor for an air temperature of −10°F and a wind speed of 30 mph. The wind-chill factor is −64°F. To determine the perceived change in temperature, subtract −34°F from −64°F.

$$-64 - (-34) = -64 + 34$$
$$= -30$$

The perceived drop in temperature is 30°F.

PAGE 97, LOOK BACK

37. $c = 40 + 0.25m$

38.

Miles m	Process: $40 + 0.25(m)$	Cost c
50	$40 + 0.25(50)$	$52.50
100	$40 + 0.25(100)$	$65.00
150	$40 + 0.25(150)$	$77.50
200	$40 + 0.25(200)$	$90.00

39. Substitute 72 for c:

$$72 = 40 + 0.25m$$
$$\underline{-40 \quad -40}$$
$$32 = 0.25m$$
$$\frac{32}{0.25} = m$$
$$m = 128$$

Therefore, you can travel 128 miles with $72.

40. no, not divisible by 6 or 9

41. no, not divisible by 6

42. no, not divisible by 9

43. yes

44.
$$36 - 12 \div 3 - 20 = 36 - 4 - 20$$
$$= 32 - 20$$
$$= 12$$

45.
$$3 \cdot 5 + 7 \div 2 = 15 + 7 \div 2$$
$$= 15 + 3.5$$
$$= 18.5$$

46.
$$28 \div 2 \cdot 7 + 4 = 14 \cdot 7 + 4$$
$$= 98 + 4$$
$$= 102$$

47. The opposite is 8; $|-8| = 8$.

48. The opposite is 0; $|0| = 0$.

49. The opposite is −6; $|6| = 6$.

50. The opposite is 25; $|-25| = 25$.

PAGE 97, LOOK BEYOND

51.

For a difference of 7 between x and 4, $x = 11$ or $x = -3$.

52.

For a difference of 10 between x and 4, $x = -6$ or $x = 14$.

6. $(-12)(-6) = 72$

7. $(-12) - (-6) = -12 + 6 = -6$

8. $(-8) - (-2) = -8 + 2 = -6$

9. $(-6.6) \div 3 = -2.2$

10. $(-0.8)(-2) = 1.6$

11. $(-8) \div (-2) = 4$

12. $(-8) + (-2) = -8 - 2 = -10$

13. $(-22) \div (-1) = 22$

14. $(-12) + (-6) = -12 - 6 = -18$

15. $(-1.2) \div (-6) = 0.2$

16. $(-5)[6 + (-6)] = -5(6 - 6)$
$= -5(0) = 0$

17. $(7)(4)(-6) = 28(-6)$
$= -168$

18. $(-9) - [8 + (-3)] = -9 - (8 - 3)$
$= -9 - (5)$
$= -9 - 5 = -14$

19. $(-54)(-115) = 6210$

20. $(-8)(-2)(-3) = 16(-3)$
$= -48$

21. $(-225) \div (-5) = 45$

22. $(-47)(23) = -1081$

23. $(-2108) \div (124) = -17$

24. $(-6942) \div (-78) = 89$

25. $(-90) \div (-15)(-3) = (6)(-3)$
$= -18$

26. $\dfrac{(7)(-1)}{-7} = \dfrac{-7}{-7} = 1$

27. $\dfrac{(-6)(-12)}{3} = \dfrac{72}{3} = 24$

28. $\dfrac{(-100)(-5)}{-25} = \dfrac{500}{-25} = -20$

29. $\dfrac{(-1)(10)(-80)}{-4} = \dfrac{(-10)(-80)}{-4}$
$= \dfrac{800}{-4} = -200$

30. True; the sum of two negatives is negative.

31. False; the difference of two negatives is not always a negative.

32. False; the product of two negatives is not negative; it is positive.

33. False; the quotient of two negatives is not negative; it is positive.

34. True; the average of a set of negative numbers is negative.

35. Let d represent the total deposit.
$d = 4(20) = 80$
Juan increased his account by $80 after his first deposit.

36. Let w represent the total amount of withdrawals made.
$w = 10 + 15 + 25 = 50$
Juan made a total withdrawal of $50.

37. Let b represent the current balance, d represent the deposits, and w represent the withdrawals.
$b = 20 + d - w$
$= 20 + 80 - 50$
$= 100 - 50 = 50$
Juan has a balance of $50.

38. Let y represent the total net yardage.
$y = -2 - 2 - 1 + 0 + 0 + 2 +$
$2 + 3 + 3 + 3 + 6 + 16$
$y = -5 + 35 = 30$
The net yardage was 30.

39. Order the set of data and find the middle number.
$-2, -2, -1, 0, 0, 2, 2, 3, 3, 3, 6, 16$
The middle number is 2. The median number of yards is 2.

40. To find the mode, locate the most frequently occurring number in the set of data.
$-2, -2, -1, 0, 0, 2, 2, 3, 3, 3, 6, 16$
The most frequently occurring number is 3. The mode is 3.

41. To find the mean, find the sum of the yardages and divide by the number of entries that were recorded in the data set.
$\text{mean} = \dfrac{(-2) + (-2) + (-1) + 0 + 0 + 2 + 2 + 3 + 3 + 3 + 6 + 16}{12}$
$= \dfrac{30}{12} = 2.5$
The average number of yards is 2.5.

42. According to the data, the longest run is 16 yds.

43. Answers may vary. Let the guess for the average be 100.

Errors	Differences from guess	Divide
95	$95 - 100 = -5$	$7 \div 7 = 1$
104	$104 - 100 = 4$	
87	$87 - 100 = -13$	
120	$120 - 100 = 20$	
102	$102 - 100 = 2$	
100	$100 - 100 = 0$	
99	$99 - 100 = \dfrac{-1}{7}$	

The average difference is 1. Add 1 to the guess of 100. The average score is 101. Check by adding all the scores and dividing by 7.

$$\text{Average} = \frac{(95 + 104 + 87 + 120 + 102 + 100 + 99)}{7}$$
$$= \frac{707}{7}$$
$$= 101$$

Since the average is 101, a guess of 100 is reasonable.

44. Answers may vary. Let the guess for the average be –20 (20 too few).

Errors	Differences from guess	Divide
–135	$-135 - (-20) = -115$	$50 \div 5 = 10$
–43	$-43 - (-20) = -23$	
–22	$-22 - (-20) = -2$	
38	$38 - (-20) = 58$	
111	$111 - (-20) = \dfrac{132}{50}$	

The average difference is 10. Add 10 to the guess of –20. The average number of beans is $-20 + 10 = -10$

Check by adding all the estimates and dividing by 5.

$$\text{Average} = \frac{-135 + (-43) + (-22) + 38 + 111}{5}$$
$$= \frac{-51}{5} = -10.2$$

Since the average error is –10.2, a guess of –20 is not reasonable.

PAGE 102, LOOK BACK

45. $-2 + (-7) = -2 - 7 = -9$ **46.** $-8 - (-3) = -8 + 3 = -5$ **47.** $|-7| = 7$ **48.** $|13| = 13$

49. $6 > -2$
$-2 < 6$

50. $-7 < 7$
$7 > -7$

51. $0 > -9$
$-9 < 0$

52. $1 > -3$
$-3 < 1$

53. $x + 2 = -2$

Try $x = -5$.	Try $x = -3$.	Try $x = -4$.
$x + 2 = -2$	$x + 2 = -2$	$x + 2 = -2$
$-5 + 2 = -3$	$-3 + 2 = -1$	$-4 + 2 = -2$
–5 is too small. Try a larger number.	–3 is too large. Try a smaller number.	–4 is the correct number; $x = -4$.

54. $-5 + x = -1$

Try $x = 3$.	Try $x = 5$.	Try $x = 4$.
$-5 + x = -1$	$-5 + x = -1$	$-5 + x = -1$
$-5 + 3 = -2$	$-5 + 5 = 0$	$-5 + 4 = -1$
3 is too small. Try a larger number.	5 is too large. Try a smaller number.	4 is the correct number; $x = 4$.

55. $x + (-7) = 0$
Try $x = 7$.   7 is the correct number; $x = 7$.
$x + (-7) = 0$
$7 + (-7) = 0$

PAGE 102, LOOK BEYOND

56. $\dfrac{6x + 12}{2} = \dfrac{2(3x + 6)}{2}$
$= 3x + 6$

57. $\dfrac{-5y - 25}{-5} = \dfrac{-5(y + 5)}{-5}$
$= y + 5$

58. $\dfrac{3w + 24}{-3} = \dfrac{-3(-w - 8)}{-3}$
$= -w - 8$

59. $\dfrac{5y - 45}{-5} = \dfrac{-5(-y + 9)}{-5}$
$= -y + 9$

2.6 PAGES 109–111, PRACTICE & APPLY

5. $y = 10 - x$

x	y	Ordered pair
–3	13	(–3,13)
–2	12	(–2,12)
–1	11	(–1,11)
0	10	(0,10)
1	9	(1,9)
2	8	(2,8)
3	7	(3,7)

6. $y = 10 + x - 2$

x	y	Ordered pair
–3	5	(–3,5)
–2	6	(–2,6)
–1	7	(–1,7)
0	8	(0,8)
1	9	(1,9)
2	10	(2,10)
3	11	(3,11)

7. $y = -1 - x$

x	y	Ordered pair
–3	2	(–3,2)
–2	1	(–2,1)
–1	0	(–1,0)
0	–1	(0,–1)
1	–2	(1,–2)
2	–3	(2,–3)
3	–4	(3,–4)

8. $y = 5 - x$

x	y	Ordered pair
−3	8	(−3,8)
−2	7	(−2,7)
−1	6	(−1,6)
0	5	(0,5)
1	4	(1,4)
2	3	(2,3)
3	2	(3,2)

9. $y = x - (-1)$

x	y	Ordered pair
−3	−2	(−3,−2)
−2	−1	(−2,−1)
−1	0	(−1,0)
0	1	(0,1)
1	2	(1,2)
2	3	(2,3)
3	4	(3,4)

10. $y = x - 4$

x	y	Ordered pair
−3	−7	(−3,−7)
−2	−6	(−2,−6)
−1	−5	(−1,−5)
0	−4	(0,−4)
1	−3	(1,−3)
2	−2	(2,−2)
3	−1	(3,−1)

11. $y = 2x - 12$

x	y	Ordered pair
−3	−18	(−3,−18)
−2	−16	(−2,−16)
−1	−14	(−1,−14)
0	−12	(0,−12)
1	−10	(1,−10)
2	−8	(2,−8)
3	−6	(3,−6)

12. $y = -3x + 12$

x	y	Ordered pair
−3	21	(−3,21)
−2	18	(−2,18)
−1	15	(−1,15)
0	12	(0,12)
1	9	(1,9)
2	6	(2,6)
3	3	(3,3)

13. $y = 5x - 30$

x	y	Ordered pair
−3	−45	(−3,−45)
−2	−40	(−2,−40)
−1	−35	(−1,−35)
0	−30	(0,−30)
1	−25	(1,−25)
2	−20	(2,−20)
3	−15	(3,−15)

14. $y = -12x$

x	y	Ordered pair
−3	36	(−3,36)
−2	24	(−2,24)
−1	12	(−1,12)
0	0	(0,0)
1	−12	(1,−12)
2	−24	(2,−24)
3	−36	(3,−36)

15. $y = x \div (-1)$

x	y	Ordered pair
−3	3	(−3,3)
−2	2	(−2,2)
−1	1	(−1,1)
0	0	(0,0)
1	−1	(1,−1)
2	−2	(2,−2)
3	−3	(3,−3)

16. $y = x \div (-2)$

x	y	Ordered pair
−3	$\frac{3}{2}$	$\left(-3,\frac{3}{2}\right)$
−2	1	(−2,1)
−1	$\frac{1}{2}$	$\left(-1,\frac{1}{2}\right)$
0	0	(0,0)
1	$-\frac{1}{2}$	$\left(1,-\frac{1}{2}\right)$
2	−1	(2,−1)
3	$-\frac{3}{2}$	$\left(3,-\frac{3}{2}\right)$

17. $y = 2x + 4$

x	y	Ordered pair
−3	−2	(−3,−2)
−2	0	(−2,0)
−1	2	(−1,2)
0	4	(0,4)
1	6	(1,6)
2	8	(2,8)
3	10	(3,10)

18. $y = -3x + 1$

x	y	Ordered pair
−3	10	(−3,10)
−2	7	(−2,7)
−1	4	(−1,4)
0	1	(0,1)
1	−2	(1,−2)
2	−5	(2,−5)
3	−8	(3,−8)

19. $y = 4x - 3$

x	y	Ordered pair
−3	−15	(−3,−15)
−2	−11	(−2,−11)
−1	−7	(−1,−7)
0	−3	(0,−3)
1	1	(1,1)
2	5	(2,5)
3	9	(3,9)

20. $y = 2x - (-5)$

x	y	Ordered pair
−3	−1	(−3,−1)
−2	1	(−2,1)
−1	3	(−1,3)
0	5	(0,5)
1	7	(1,7)
2	9	(2,9)
3	11	(3,11)

21. $A(-5, 2)$ **22.** $B(2, 3)$ **23.** $C(4, -4)$ **24.** $D(-3, -6)$

25. $y = x - 2$

x	y
−2	−4
−1	−3
0	−2
1	−1
2	0
3	1

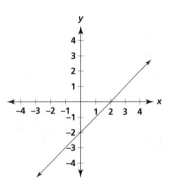

$y = -5$ when $x = -3$

26. $y = 4 - x$

x	y
−2	6
−1	5
0	4
1	3
2	2
3	1

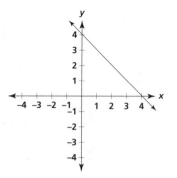

$y = 7$ when $x = -3$

27. $y = x + 2$

x	y
−2	0
−1	1
0	2
1	3
2	4
3	5

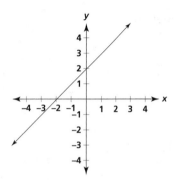

$y = -1$ when $x = -3$

28. $y = x - 5$

x	y
−2	−7
−1	−6
0	−5
1	−4
2	−3
3	−2

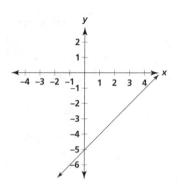

$y = -8$ when $x = -3$

29. $y = 2x - 3$

x	y
−2	−7
−1	−5
0	−3
1	−1
2	1
3	3

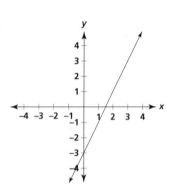

$y = -9$ when $x = 1 - 3$

30. $y = 1 - 2x$

x	y
−2	5
−1	3
0	1
1	−1
2	−3
3	−5

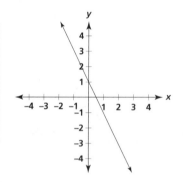

$y = 7$ when $x = -3$

31. $y = -2x - 1$

x	y
−2	3
−1	1
0	−1
1	−3
2	−5
3	−7

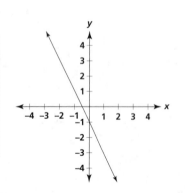

$y = 5$ when $x = -3$

32. $y = 2x - 8$

x	y
−2	−12
−1	−10
0	−8
1	−6
2	−4
3	−2

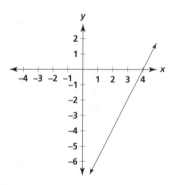

$y = -14$ when $x = -3$

33. Let x represent the time in hours, and let y represent the cost in dollars.

$y = 20 + 4x$

34. $y = 650 + 45x$

35. $y = 12 + 4x$

36. $y = 18x$

37. $y = 60x$

38. $y = 24x$

39.

x	−3	−2	−1	0	1	2	3
y	−2	−1	0	1	2	3	4

$y = x + 1$

40.

x	–3	–2	–1	0	1	2	3
y	9	6	3	0	–3	–6	–9

$y = -3x$

41.

x	–3	–2	–1	0	1	2	3
y	–5	–2	1	4	7	10	13

$y = 3x + 4$

PAGE 111, LOOK BACK

42.

Year	Number of CD sales	Number of tape sales
1991	333	360
1992	407	366
1993	495	339
1994	662	345

43. $360 - 333 = 27$

44. $662 - 345 = 317$

45. $49 = (7)(7)$
$\quad = 7^2$

46. $72 = (2)(36)$
$72 = (2)(6)(6)$
$72 = (2)(2)(3)(2)(3)$
$\quad = 2^3 \cdot 3^2$

47. $17 = (1)(17)$

48. 81
$81 = (9)(9)$
$81 = (3)(3)(3)(3)$
$\quad = 3^4$

49. $-2 > -5$
$-5 < -2$

50. $-3 < 1$
$1 > -3$

51. $0 > -3$
$-3 < 0$

52. $6 > -7$
$-7 < 6$

53. $-4 > -7$
$-7 < -4$

54. $4 > -1$
$-1 < 4$

55. $-2 > -3$
$-3 < -2$

56. $-5 < -2$
$-2 > -5$

PAGE 111, LOOK BEYOND

57. $y = -x + 1$

x	y	Ordered pair
–3	4	(–3,4)
–2	3	(–2,3)
–1	2	(–1,2)
0	1	(0,1)
1	0	(1,0)
2	–1	(2,–1)
3	–2	(3,–2)

$y = 2x - 8$

x	y	Ordered pair
–3	–14	(–3,–14)
–2	–12	(–2,–12)
–1	–10	(–1,–10)
0	–8	(0,–8)
1	–6	(1,–6)
2	–4	(2,–4)
3	–2	(3,–2)

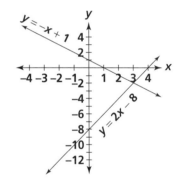

58. (3,–2) is the point of intersection.

2.7 PAGES 118–119, PRACTICE & APPLY

6.
Sequence 20 27 36 47 60
First differences 7 9 11 13
Second differences 2 2 2

7.
Sequence 18 32 46 60 74 [88] [102]
First differences 14 14 14 14 14 14

8.
Sequence 33 49 65 81 97 [113] [129]
First differences 16 16 16 16 16 16

9.
Sequence 20 21 26 35 48 [65] [86]
First differences 1 5 9 13 17 21
Second differences 4 4 4 4 4

10.
Sequence 30 31 35 42 52 [65] [81]
First differences 1 4 7 10 13 16
Second differences 3 3 3 3 3

11.   Sequence 100   94   88   82   76   [70]   [64]
First differences   −6   −6   −6   −6   −6   −6

12.   Sequence 44   41   38   35   32   [29]   [26]
First differences   −3   −3   −3   −3   −3   −3

13.   Sequence 12   12   18   31   53   87   [137]   [208]
First differences   0   6   13   22   34   50   71
Second differences   6   7   9   12   16   21
Third differences   1   2   3   4   5
Fourth differences   1   1   1   1

14.   Sequence 1   7   23   50   89   [141]   [207]
First differences   6   16   27   39   52   66
Second differences   10   11   12   13   14
Third differences   1   1   1   1

15.   Sequence 1   2   3   4   5
First differences   1   1   1   1
The first difference produces a constant, 1.

16.   Sequence 1 2^2 3^2 4^2 5^2
First differences   3   5   7   9
Second differences   2   2   2
The second difference produces a constant, 2.

17.   Sequence 1   8   27   64   125
First differences   7   19   37   61
Second differences   12   18   24
Third differences   6   6
The third difference produces a constant, 6.

18.   Sequence 1   16   81   256   625   1296
First differences   15   65   175   369   671
Second differences   50   110   194   302
Third differences   60   84   108
Fourth differences   24   24
The fourth difference produces a constant, 24.

19.   Sequence 7   11   16   [22]   [29]   [37]
First differences   4   5   6   7   8
Second differences   1   1   1   1
The next three terms would be 22, 29, and 37.

20.   Sequence 2   6   12   [20]   [30]   [42]
First differences   4   6   8   10   12
Second differences   2   2   2   2
The next three terms would be 20, 30, and 42.

21.   Sequence [5]   [9]   15   23   [33]
First differences   4   6   8   10
Second differences   2   2   2
The next five terms would be 5, 9, 15, 23, and 33.

22.   Sequence 2   [9]   [19]   [32]   [48]
First differences   7   10   13   16
Second differences   3   3   3

23. Maximum height = $\dfrac{\text{total flight time}}{2}$

$= \dfrac{20}{2} = 10$

The rocket reaches its maximum height after 10 seconds.

24. Maximum height times 2 is 24 × 2, or 48.
The rocket will hit the ground in 48 seconds.

25. C6 = B7 − B6   **26.** D5 = C6 − C5   **27.**

Side	1	2	3	4	5	6	7	8
Perimeter	4	8	12	16	[20]	[24]	[28]	[32]

28.

Sequence	4	8	12	16	[20]	[24]	[28]	[32]
First differences		4	4	4	4	4	4	4

Yes, the answers are the same as in the previous question.

29. From the table you can see that the boiling point of water drops 1 degree for every 1000-foot increase in altitude. Therefore, at 6170 feet in altitude, water would boil at approximately 94°C.

PAGE 119, LOOK BACK

30. $1 + 2 + 3 + 4 + \cdots + 18 = \frac{18 \cdot 19}{2} = \frac{342}{2} = 171$

31.

Sequence	43	49	55	61	67	[73]	[79]	[85]
First differences		6	6	6	6	6	6	6

The next three terms are 73, 79, and 85.

32. $c = 25 + 0.3m$

33.

m	Process: $25 + 0.3m$	c
25	$25 + 0.3(25)$	$32.50
50	$25 + 0.3(50)$	$40.00
75	$25 + 0.3(75)$	$47.50
100	$25 + 0.3(100)$	$55.00
125	$25 + 0.3(125)$	$62.50

34. In the formula in Exercise 32, substitute $58.00 for c and solve for m.

$58.00 = 25 + 0.3m$
$33.00 = 0.3m$
$110 = m$

You can drive the truck 110 miles for $58.

35. $(-11)(-6) = 66$ **36.** $(-12) \div (-4) = 3$ **37.** $369 \div (-3) = -123$ **38.** $(25)(-4) = -100$

PAGE 119, LOOK BEYOND

39.

Sequence	1	2	4	8	16	32	[64]	[128]	[256]

Each term is twice the previous term.

40.

Sequence	1	10	100	1000	10,000	[100,000]	[1,000,000]	[10,000,000]

Each term is 10 times the previous term.

PAGES 122–124 CHAPTER 2 REVIEW

1. $11 - 4 = 7$ **2.** $10 - 2 = 8$ **3.** $13 - 3 = 10$ **4.** $8 + (-9) = -1$

5. $-29 + (-37) = -66$ **6.** $-17 + 23 = 6$ **7.** $-41 + (-5) + 19 = -46 + 19$
$= -27$

8. $x + 3 = -3$

Try $x = -5$.	Try $x = -7$.	Try $x = -6$.
$x + 3 = -3$	$x + 3 = -3$	$x + 3 = -3$
$-5 + 3 = -2$	$-7 + 3 = -4$	$-6 + 3 = -3$
-5 is too large. Try a smaller number.	-7 is too small. Try a larger number.	-6 is the correct number; $x = -6$.

9. $-7 + x = 5$

Try $x = 10$.	Try $x = 15$.	Try $x = 12$.
$-7 + x = 5$	$-7 + x = 5$	$-7 + x = 5$
$-7 + 10 = 3$	$-7 + 15 = 8$	$-7 + 12 = 5$
10 is too small. Try a larger number.	15 is too large. Try a smaller number.	12 is the correct number; $x = 12$.

10. $9 + x = 2$

Try $x = -5$.	Try $x = -10$.	Try $x = -7$.
$9 + x = 2$	$9 + x = 2$	$9 + x = 2$
$9 + -5 = 4$	$9 + -10 = -1$	$9 + -7 = 2$
-5 is too large. Try a smaller number.	-10 is too small. Try a larger number.	-7 is the correct number; $x = -7$.

11. $x + (-2) = -5$

Try $x = -1$.	Try $x = -5$.	Try $x = -3$.
$x + -2 = -5$	$x + -2 = -5$	$x + -2 = -5$
$-1 + -2 = -3$	$-5 + -2 = -7$	$-3 + -2 = -5$
-1 is too large. Try a smaller number.	-5 is too small. Try a larger number.	-3 is the correct number; $x = -3$.

12.

Ascending order: $-6, -3, 0, 8$

13.

Ascending order: $-5, -4, 1, 4, 5$

14. $9 - (-15) = 9 + 15$
$= 24$

15. $48 - (-48) = 48 + 48$
$= 96$

16. $-13 - 28 = -41$

17. $39 - (-18) = 39 + 18$
$= 57$

18. $-67 - (-42) = -67 + 42$
$= -25$

19. $-23 - (-72) = -23 + 72$
$= 49$

20. $-43 - (-42) - 53 = -43 + 42 - 53$
$= -1 - 53$
$= -54$

21. $8 - 14 - 27 = -6 - 27$
$= -33$

22. $54 - (-42) = 54 + 42$
$= 96$

23. $-44 - 63 = -107$

24. $25 - 53 = -28$

25. $94 - (-33) = 94 + 33$
$= 127$

26. $(-12)(-5) = 60$

27. $54 \div (-9) = -6$

28. $(-6)(8) = -48$

29. $-64 \div (-4) = 16$

30. $(-121) \div (-11) = 11$

31. $(-6)(-3) \div (-9) = 18 \div (-9)$
$= -2$

32. $45[8 + (-8)] = 45(0)$
$= 0$

33. $(-5)(-5)(-1)(1) = (25)(-1)(1)$
$= (-25)(1)$
$= -25$

34. $(-45) \div [(-3)(-3)] = -45 \div 9$
$= -5$

35. $12(-2) \div [(-2)(3)] = 12(-2) \div -6$
$= -24 \div -6$
$= 4$

36. $-5[(-4) - 5] = -5(-9)$
$= 45$

37. $[(-4)(-7) \div (2)](-7) = (28 \div 2)(-7)$
$= (14)(-7)$
$= -98$

38. $y = x + 3$

x	-2	-1	0	1	2	3
y	1	2	3	4	5	6

39. $y = 3 - x$

x	-2	-1	0	1	2	3
y	5	4	3	2	1	0

40. $y = 2x - 4$

x	-2	-1	0	1	2	3
y	-8	-6	-4	-2	0	2

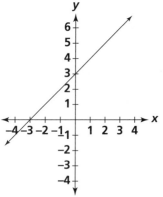

$y = 0$ when $x = -3$

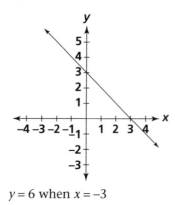

$y = 6$ when $x = -3$

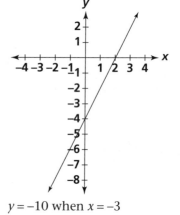

$y = -10$ when $x = -3$

41.

Time	0	1	2	3	4
Cost	9	16	23	30	37
Difference		7	7	7	7

Since there is a constant difference, the equation is linear.
$$c = 9 + 7t$$

42. $3 + (-7) + (-1) + 9 = 4$
There was a net gain of 4 yards.

43. $600 + 80 + 80 + 80 = 840$
Account balance: $840.00

44. $840 - 110 - 110 - 110 - 110 - 110 = 290$
Account balance: $290.00

PAGE 125 CHAPTER 2 ASSESSMENT

1. 8

2. -6

3. -5

4. $6 + (-5) = 1$

5. $-13 + (-7) = -20$

6. $-11 + 31 = 20$

7. $4 + (-11) + 6 = -1$

8. $-1 + (-7)1 + (-8) = -16$

9. $31 + (-56) + (-7) = -32$

10. $14 + |14| + (-6) = 22$

11. $-114 + |14| + |-15| = -85$

12. $x + 5 = -8$

Try $x = -10$.
$x + 5 = -8$
$-10 + 5 = -5$
−10 is too large. Try a smaller number.

Try $x = -15$.
$x + 5 = -8$
$-15 + 5 = -10$
−15 is too small. Try a larger number.

Try $x = -13$.
$x + 5 = -8$
$-13 + 5 = -8$
−13 is the correct number; $x = -13$.

13. $-4 + x = 12$

Try $x = 12$.
$-4 + x = 12$
$-4 + 12 = 8$
12 is too small. Try a larger number.

Try $x = 15$.
$-4 + x = 12$
$-4 + 15 = 11$
15 is too small. Try a larger number.

Try $x = 16$.
$-4 + x = 12$
$-4 + 16 = 12$
16 is the correct number; $x = 16$.

14. $x + (-41) = 42$

Try $x = 80$.
$x + (-41) = 42$
$80 + (-41) = 39$
80 is too small. Try a larger number.

Try $x = 85$.
$x + (-41) = 42$
$85 + (-41) = 44$
85 is too large. Try a smaller number.

Try $x = 83$.
$x + (-41) = 42$
$83 + (-41) = 42$
83 is the correct number; $x = 83$.

15. $3 + x = 1$

Try $x = -5$.
$3 + x = 1$
$3 + -5 = -2$
−5 is too small. Try a larger number.

Try $x = -3$.
$3 + x = 1$
$3 + -3 = 0$
−3 is too small. Try a larger number.

Try $x = -2$.
$3 + x = 1$
$3 + -2 = 1$
−2 is the correct number; $x = -2$.

16. $-13 + x = -6$

Try $x = 5$.
$-13 + x = -6$
$-13 + 5 = -8$
5 is too small. Try a larger number.

Try $x = 6$.
$-13 + x = -6$
$-13 + 6 = -7$
6 is too small. Try a larger number.

Try $x = 7$.
$-13 + x = -6$
$-13 + 7 = -6$
7 is the correct number; $x = 7$.

17. $18 + x = -18$

Try $x = -40$.
$18 + x = -18$
$18 + (-40) = -22$
−40 is too small. Try a larger number.

Try $x = -35$.
$18 + x = -18$
$18 + -35 = -17$
−35 is too large. Try a smaller number.

Try $x = -36$.
$18 + x = -18$
$18 + -36 = -18$
−36 is the correct number; $x = -36$.

18. $-47 = x + (-54)$

Try $x = 5$.
$-47 = x + (-54)$
$-49 = 5 + (-54)$
5 is too small. Try a larger number.

Try $x = 6$.
$-47 = x + (-54)$
$-48 = 6 + (-54)$
6 is too small. Try a larger number.

Try $x = 7$.
$-47 = x + (-54)$
$-47 = 7 + (-54)$
7 is the correct number; $x = 7$.

19. $6 + x = 17$

Try $x = 10$.
$6 + x = 17$
$6 + 10 = 16$
10 is too small. Try a larger number.

Try $x = 15$.
$6 + x = 17$
$6 + 15 = 21$
15 is too large. Try a smaller number.

Try $x = 11$.
$6 + x = 17$
$6 + 11 = 17$
11 is the correct number; $x = 11$.

20.

(number line from −10 to 10 with points at −8, −6, −4, 5, 7, 9)

Ascending order: −8, −6, −4, 5, 7, 9

21. $13 - (-13) = 26$

22. $17 - (-23) = 40$

23. $-51 - (-49) = -2$

24. $1 - 2 - 3 = -4$

25. $-9 - (-4) = -5$

26. $12 - 15 - (-2) = -1$

27. $45 - (-55) - 21 = 79$

28. $4 - (-4) = 8$

29. $11 - 3 = 8$

30. $10 - (-5) = 15$

31. $-97 - (-61) = 36$

32. $58 - (-34) = 92$

33. $12 - (-9) = 21$

34. $-35 - (-45) = 10$

35. $85 - (-61) = 146$

36. $43 - (-92) = 135$

37. $99(-2) = -198$

38. $-102 - 17 = -119$

39. $-20[-16 + (-14)] = -20(-30)$
$= 600$

40. $(-3)(-3)(-3) = 9(-3)$
$= -27$

41. $-7(27) \div (-9) = -189 \div -9$
$= 21$

42. $-80 \div [(-20)(-2)] = -80 \div 40$
$= -2$

43. $\dfrac{(-5)(-15)}{5} = \dfrac{75}{5} = 15$

44. $\dfrac{(-2)(12)(-28)}{21} = \dfrac{(-24)(-28)}{21}$
$= \dfrac{672}{21}$
$= 32$

45. $y = -2x + 5$

x	Process: $-2x + 5$	y
−3	$-2(-3) + 5$	11
−2	$-2(-2) + 5$	9
−1	$-2(-1) + 5$	7
0	$-2(0) + 5$	5
1	$-2(1) + 5$	3
2	$-2(2) + 5$	1
3	$-2(3) + 5$	−1

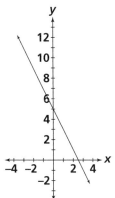

46.

Sequence	[2]		9		20		[35]		[54]
First differences		[7]		[11]		[15]		[19]	
Second differences			4		4		4		

The first five terms of the sequence are 2, 9, 20, 35, and 54.

47. The equation is linear because there is a common first difference.

Let t represent time and d represent distance; then:
$$d = 26(t)$$

1. eighth term in column A = 23
eighth term in column B = 18
column A > column B
∴ A is the correct response.

2. $-7 < 5$
column A < column B
∴ B is the correct response.

3. column A $2 + 8 \cdot 2 = 2 + 16 = 18$
column B $2 - 8 \cdot 2 = 2 - 16 = -14$
column A > column B
∴ A is the correct response.

4. column A: $9 \times 7 = 63$
column B: $7 \times 9 = 63$
∴ C is the correct response.

5. $150 - 80 + 170 - 195 = 45$
∴ c is the correct response.

6.

28 games are played.
∴ a is the correct response.

7. $-29 + |-24| + 3 = -29 + 24 + 3$
$$= -5 + 3$$
$$= -2$$
∴ b is the correct response.

8. $27 - (-61) = 88$
∴ d is the correct response.

9. $y = 3x - (-4)$
Substitute each ordered pair into the equation to find which ordered pair is *not* a solution.
d. $(-2,2)$ $2 \overset{?}{=} 3(-2) - (-4)$
$$2 \overset{?}{=} -6 + 4$$
$$2 \neq -2$$
∴ d is the correct response.

10.

Sequence	[3]		[9]		[17]		27		39
First difference		6		8		10		12	
Second difference			2		2		2		

The first three terms of the sequence are 3, 9, and 17.
∴ b is the correct response.

11. Sequence 729   243   81   [27]   [9]   [3]
Each term is $\frac{1}{3}$ of the previous term.

12.

x	Process: $3x - 2$	y
1	$3(1) - 2$	1
2	$3(2) - 2$	4
3	$3(3) - 2$	7
4	$3(4) - 2$	10
5	$3(5) - 2$	13

13. $w = 11.50h$

14. Substitute 80 for c, and solve for m.
$$80 = 20 + 0.30m$$
$$60 = 0.30m$$
$$200 = m$$
You can drive for 200 miles.

15. 533 is composite because $13 \cdot 41 = 533$. This means that 1, 13, 41, and 533 are factors of 533.

16. $7380 \div 2 = 3690$
$3690 \div 2 = 1845$
$1845 \div 3 = 615$
$615 \div 3 = 205$
$205 \div 5 = 41$
$7380 = 2^2 \cdot 3^2 \cdot 5 \cdot 41$

17. $-|-54| = -54$

18. $(68 + 26) + 32 = (26 + 68) + 32$ Commutative Property
$$= 26 + (68 + 32)$$ Associative Property
$$= 26 + 100$$
$$= 126$$

19.

Ascending order: −2, −1, 7, 9

20. $(-8)(7)(-36) + (-28) = (-56)(-36) + (-28)$
$= 2016 + (-28)$
$= 1988$

21. $341 = 11 \cdot 31$

The greatest prime factor of 341 is 31.

22. $x^3 y^z = 2^3 \cdot 4^3$
$= 8 \cdot 64$
$= 512$

23. $2(3 + 4) - 2 + 3^2(4) - 6 + 1 = 2(7) - 2 + 3^2(4) - 6 + 1$
$= 2(7) - 2 + 9(4) - 6 + 1$
$= 14 - 2 + 36 - 6 + 1$
$= 43$

24. $15(20) + 20 = 20(15 + 1)$
$= 20(16)$
$= 320$

25. $y = 3x - (-25)$
$y = 3(-4) - (-25)$
$y = -12 - (-25)$
$y = -12 + 25$
$y = 13$

CHAPTER 3

RATIONAL NUMBERS AND PROBABILITY

5.
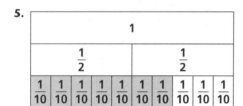

1									
$\frac{1}{2}$					$\frac{1}{2}$				
$\frac{1}{10}$	$\frac{1}{10}$	$\frac{1}{10}$	$\frac{1}{10}$	$\frac{1}{10}$	$\frac{1}{10}$	$\frac{1}{10}$	$\frac{1}{10}$	$\frac{1}{10}$	$\frac{1}{10}$

$\frac{7}{10}$ is closest to $\frac{1}{2}$.

6.

1		
$\frac{1}{2}$		$\frac{1}{2}$
$\frac{1}{3}$	$\frac{1}{3}$	$\frac{1}{3}$

$\frac{2}{3}$ is closest to $\frac{1}{2}$.

7.
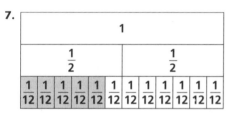

1											
$\frac{1}{2}$						$\frac{1}{2}$					
$\frac{1}{12}$	$\frac{1}{12}$	$\frac{1}{12}$	$\frac{1}{12}$	$\frac{1}{12}$	$\frac{1}{12}$	$\frac{1}{12}$	$\frac{1}{12}$	$\frac{1}{12}$	$\frac{1}{12}$	$\frac{1}{12}$	$\frac{1}{12}$

$\frac{5}{12}$ is closest to $\frac{1}{2}$.

8. $\frac{1}{2} = \frac{4}{8}$
$\frac{1}{2} \cdot \frac{4}{4} = \frac{4}{8}$

9. $\frac{2}{3} > \frac{6}{12}$
$\frac{2}{3} \cdot \frac{4}{4} = \frac{8}{12}$

10. $\frac{1}{3} > \frac{1}{6}$
$\frac{1}{3} \cdot \frac{2}{2} = \frac{2}{6}$

11. $\frac{4}{5} > \frac{30}{40}$
$\frac{4}{5} \cdot \frac{8}{8} = \frac{32}{40}$

12. $\frac{1}{2} < \frac{5}{6}$
$\frac{1}{2} \cdot \frac{3}{3} = \frac{3}{6}$

13. $\frac{2}{3} < \frac{5}{6}$
$\frac{2}{3} \cdot \frac{2}{2} = \frac{4}{6}$

14. $\frac{1}{3} > \frac{1}{21}$
$\frac{1}{3} \cdot \frac{7}{7} = \frac{7}{21}$

15. $\frac{3}{12} = \frac{1}{4}$
$\frac{1}{4} \cdot \frac{3}{3} = \frac{3}{12}$

16.
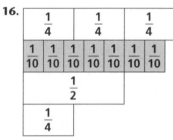

$\frac{7}{10}$ is closest to $\frac{3}{4}$.

17.

$\frac{2}{3}$ is closest to $\frac{3}{4}$.

18.

$\frac{2}{5}$ is closest to $\frac{1}{2}$.

19.

$\frac{7}{8}$ is closest to $\frac{3}{4}$.

20.

$\frac{6}{8}$ is equal to $\frac{3}{4}$.

21.
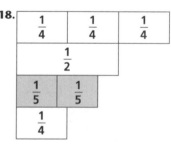

$\frac{7}{12}$ is closest to $\frac{1}{2}$.

22.

$\frac{1}{4}$	$\frac{1}{4}$	$\frac{1}{4}$
$\frac{1}{10}$ $\frac{1}{10}$ $\frac{1}{10}$ $\frac{1}{10}$ $\frac{1}{10}$		
$\frac{1}{2}$		
$\frac{1}{4}$		

$\frac{5}{10}$ is equal to $\frac{1}{2}$.

23.

$\frac{1}{4}$	$\frac{1}{4}$	$\frac{1}{4}$
$\frac{1}{12}$ $\frac{1}{12}$ $\frac{1}{12}$ $\frac{1}{12}$ $\frac{1}{12}$ $\frac{1}{12}$ $\frac{1}{12}$ $\frac{1}{12}$		
$\frac{1}{2}$		
$\frac{1}{4}$		

$\frac{8}{12}$ is closest to $\frac{3}{4}$.

24.

$\frac{1}{11}$ $\frac{1}{11}$ $\frac{1}{11}$ $\frac{1}{11}$ $\frac{1}{11}$ $\frac{1}{11}$ $\frac{1}{11}$ $\frac{1}{11}$ $\frac{1}{11}$ $\frac{1}{11}$		
$\frac{1}{4}$	$\frac{1}{4}$	$\frac{1}{4}$
$\frac{1}{2}$		
$\frac{1}{4}$		

$\frac{10}{11}$ is closest to $\frac{3}{4}$.

25.

$\frac{1}{10}$ $\frac{1}{10}$ $\frac{1}{10}$ $\frac{1}{10}$ $\frac{1}{10}$ $\frac{1}{10}$ $\frac{1}{10}$ $\frac{1}{10}$		
$\frac{1}{4}$	$\frac{1}{4}$	$\frac{1}{4}$
$\frac{1}{2}$		
$\frac{1}{4}$		

$\frac{8}{10}$ is closest to $\frac{3}{4}$.

26. $\frac{3}{10} < \frac{1}{2}$

$\frac{1}{2} \cdot \frac{5}{5} = \frac{5}{10}$

27. $\frac{2}{3} > \frac{1}{2}$

$\frac{2}{3} \cdot \frac{2}{2} = \frac{4}{6}$

$\frac{1}{2} \cdot \frac{3}{3} = \frac{3}{6}$

28. $\frac{3}{5} > \frac{1}{2}$

$\frac{3}{5} \cdot \frac{2}{2} = \frac{6}{10}$

$\frac{1}{2} \cdot \frac{5}{5} = \frac{5}{10}$

29. $\frac{5}{8} > \frac{1}{2}$

$\frac{5}{8} \cdot \frac{1}{1} = \frac{5}{8}$

$\frac{1}{2} \cdot \frac{4}{4} = \frac{4}{8}$

30. $\frac{3}{7} < \frac{1}{2}$

$\frac{3}{7} \cdot \frac{2}{2} = \frac{6}{14}$

$\frac{1}{2} \cdot \frac{7}{7} = \frac{7}{14}$

31. $\frac{9}{11} > \frac{1}{2}$

$\frac{9}{11} \cdot \frac{2}{2} = \frac{18}{22}$

$\frac{1}{2} \cdot \frac{11}{11} = \frac{11}{22}$

32. $\frac{7}{12} > \frac{1}{2}$

$\frac{1}{2} \cdot \frac{6}{6} = \frac{6}{12}$

33. $\frac{4}{12} < \frac{1}{2}$

$\frac{1}{2} \cdot \frac{6}{6} = \frac{6}{12}$

34. A-1 Video
Almundy Security
Cine Video

35. Software Today
Music Mart
CompuWare

36. A-1 Video
CompuWare
Almundy Security
Cine Video
Music Mart
Software Today
Edu-Corp
DNB Rentals

37. Answers may vary. Examples are given.

$\frac{2}{3} \cdot \frac{2}{2} = \frac{4}{6}$

$\frac{2}{3} \cdot \frac{3}{3} = \frac{6}{9}$

$\frac{2}{3} \cdot \frac{4}{4} = \frac{8}{12}$

$\frac{2}{3} \cdot \frac{5}{5} = \frac{10}{15}$

$\frac{2}{3} \cdot \frac{6}{6} = \frac{12}{18}$

PAGE 135, LOOK BACK

38. $-1 < 3$

39. $-3 > -5$

40. $-45 > -50$

41. $-100 < -98$

42. $x + 5 = -1$

Try $x = -4$.
$x + 5 = -1$
$-4 + 5 = 1$
-4 is too large. Try a smaller number.

Try $x = -5$.
$x + 5 = -1$
$-5 + 5 = 0$
-5 is too large. Try a smaller number.

Try $x = -6$.
$x + 5 = -1$
$-6 + 5 = -1$
-6 is the correct number; $x = -6$.

43. $3 - x = -2$

Try $x = 3$.
$3 - x = -2$
$3 - 3 = 0$
3 is too small. Try a larger number.

Try $x = 4$.
$3 - x = -2$
$3 - 4 = -1$
4 is too small. Try a larger number.

Try $x = 5$.
$3 - x = -2$
$3 - 5 = -2$
5 is the correct number; $x = 5$.

44. $2x = -6$

Try $x = -1$.
$2x = -6$
$2(-1) = -2$
-1 is too large. Try a smaller number.

Try $x = -2$.
$2x = -6$
$2(-2) = -4$
-2 is too large. Try a smaller number.

Try $x = -3$.
$2x = -6$
$2(-3) = -6$
-3 is the correct number; $x = -3$.

45. $2x + 1 = 5$

Try $x = 1$.
$2x + 1 = 5$
$2(1) + 1 = 3$
1 is too small. Try a larger number.

Try $x = 3$.
$2x + 1 = 5$
$2(3) + 1 = 7$
3 is too large. Try a smaller number.

Try $x = 2$.
$2x + 1 = 5$
$2(2) + 1 = 5$
2 is the correct number; $x = 2$.

46.

Sequence	5.00		7.50		10.00		12.50		15.00		17.50
First differences		2.50		2.50		2.50		2.50		2.50		

47. Let x represent the time (in hours), and y represent the cost (in dollars).

$$y = 5 + 2.50x$$

PAGE 135, LOOK BEYOND

48.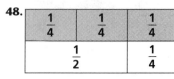

$$\frac{3}{4} = \frac{1}{2} + \frac{1}{4}$$

49.

$$\frac{5}{6} = \frac{1}{2} + \frac{1}{3}$$

50. $\frac{11}{24} = \frac{1}{4} + \frac{5}{24}$ **51.** $\frac{7}{9} = \frac{1}{3} + \frac{4}{9}$

3.2 PAGES 139–140, PRACTICE & APPLY

5. $\frac{8}{10} = \frac{8 \div 2}{10 \div 2} = \frac{4}{5}$

6. $\frac{12}{18} = \frac{12 \div 6}{18 \div 6} = \frac{2}{3}$

7. $\frac{5}{45} = \frac{5 \div 5}{45 \div 5} = \frac{1}{9}$

8. $\frac{108}{126} = \frac{108 \div 18}{126 \div 18} = \frac{6}{7}$

9. $\frac{17}{34} = \frac{17 \div 17}{34 \div 17} = \frac{1}{2}$

10. $\frac{13}{23}$ is in lowest terms because the GCF is 1.

11. $\frac{48}{64} = \frac{48 \div 16}{64 \div 16} = \frac{3}{4}$

12. $\frac{150}{600} = \frac{150 \div 150}{600 \div 150} = \frac{1}{4}$

13. $\frac{32}{88} = \frac{32 \div 8}{88 \div 8} = \frac{4}{11}$

14. $\frac{36}{45} = \frac{36 \div 9}{45 \div 9} = \frac{4}{5}$

15. $\frac{56}{72} = \frac{56 \div 8}{72 \div 8} = \frac{7}{9}$

16. $\frac{48}{72} = \frac{48 \div 24}{72 \div 24} = \frac{2}{3}$

17. $\frac{1}{2} < \frac{4}{5}$
$\frac{1}{2} \cdot \frac{5}{5} = \frac{5}{10}$
$\frac{4}{5} \cdot \frac{2}{2} = \frac{8}{10}$

18. $\frac{2}{3} < \frac{4}{5}$
$\frac{2}{3} \cdot \frac{5}{5} = \frac{10}{15}$
$\frac{4}{5} \cdot \frac{3}{3} = \frac{12}{15}$

19. $\frac{1}{3} > \frac{3}{16}$
$\frac{1}{3} \cdot \frac{16}{16} = \frac{16}{48}$
$\frac{3}{16} \cdot \frac{3}{3} = \frac{9}{48}$

20. $\frac{1}{2} > \frac{6}{14}$
$\frac{1}{2} \cdot \frac{7}{7} = \frac{7}{14}$

21. $\frac{2}{3} > \frac{4}{15}$
$\frac{2}{3} \cdot \frac{5}{5} = \frac{10}{15}$

22. $\frac{25}{32} > \frac{5}{8}$
$\frac{5}{8} \cdot \frac{4}{4} = \frac{20}{32}$

23. $\frac{2}{3} > \frac{5}{16}$
$\frac{2}{3} \cdot \frac{16}{16} = \frac{32}{48}$
$\frac{5}{16} \cdot \frac{3}{3} = \frac{15}{48}$

24. $\frac{7}{10} > \frac{2}{3}$
$\frac{7}{10} \cdot \frac{3}{3} = \frac{21}{30}$
$\frac{2}{3} \cdot \frac{10}{10} = \frac{20}{30}$

25. Express the fractions with common denominators and then compare them.

Bunny Run $\frac{1}{2} = \frac{5}{10}$ mi

Fox Chase $\frac{2}{5} = \frac{4}{10}$ mi

Moose Alley $\frac{6}{10} = \frac{6}{10}$ mi

Fox Chase is the shortest trail.

For Exercises 26–29, express the fractions with common denominators and then list them from least to greatest.

26. $\frac{3}{8} = \frac{9}{24}$
$\frac{2}{3} = \frac{16}{24}$
$\frac{1}{4} = \frac{6}{24}$
$\frac{1}{8} = \frac{3}{24}$
$\frac{1}{2} = \frac{12}{24}$
$\frac{1}{8}, \frac{1}{4}, \frac{3}{8}, \frac{1}{2}, \frac{2}{3}$

27. $-\frac{5}{8} = -\frac{15}{24}$
$-\frac{2}{3} = -\frac{16}{24}$
$\frac{1}{4} = \frac{6}{24}$
$-\frac{3}{4} = -\frac{18}{24}$
$\frac{1}{8} = \frac{3}{24}$
$-\frac{1}{2} = -\frac{12}{24}$
$-\frac{3}{4}, -\frac{2}{3}, -\frac{5}{8}, -\frac{1}{2}, \frac{1}{8}, \frac{1}{4}$

28. $\frac{1}{4} = \frac{4}{16}$
$\frac{5}{8} = \frac{10}{16}$
$\frac{1}{2} = \frac{8}{16}$
$\frac{5}{16} = \frac{5}{16}$
$\frac{3}{8} = \frac{6}{16}$
$\frac{7}{16} = \frac{7}{16}$
$\frac{1}{4}, \frac{5}{16}, \frac{3}{8}, \frac{7}{16}, \frac{1}{2}, \frac{5}{8}$

29.

$$\frac{1}{3} = \frac{10}{30}$$

$$\frac{2}{5} = \frac{12}{30}$$

$$\frac{4}{5} = \frac{24}{30}$$

$$\frac{1}{2} = \frac{15}{30}$$

$$\frac{7}{10} = \frac{21}{30}$$

$$\frac{2}{3} = \frac{20}{30}$$

$$\frac{1}{3}, \frac{2}{5}, \frac{1}{2}, \frac{2}{3}, \frac{7}{10}, \frac{4}{5}$$

30.

$$\frac{1}{8} = \frac{75}{600}$$

$$\frac{1}{3} = \frac{200}{600}$$

$$\frac{1}{4} = \frac{150}{600}$$

$$\frac{1}{5} = \frac{120}{600}$$

$$\frac{1}{6} = \frac{100}{600}$$

$$\frac{1}{2} = \frac{300}{600}$$

$$\frac{1}{100} = \frac{6}{600}$$

$$\frac{1}{100}, \frac{1}{8}, \frac{1}{6}, \frac{1}{5}, \frac{1}{4}, \frac{1}{3}, \frac{1}{2}$$

31. As the denominator increases, the fraction gets smaller.

32. Order the fractions by comparing the denominators. The larger the denominator, the smaller the fraction, so to order from least to greatest, list the the fractions with larger denominators first.

PAGE 140, LOOK BACK

33. Possible dimensions:

$546 \div 1 = 546$	546 ft by 1 ft
$546 \div 2 = 273$	273 ft by 2 ft
$546 \div 3 = 182$	182 ft by 3 ft
$546 \div 6 = 91$	91 ft by 6 ft
$546 \div 7 = 78$	78 ft by 7 ft
$546 \div 13 = 42$	42 ft by 13 ft
$546 \div 14 = 39$	39 ft by 14 ft
$546 \div 21 = 26$	26 ft by 21 ft

34. $82 \div 1 = 82$

$82 \div 2 = 41$

Possible dimensions are 82 cm by 1 cm and 41 cm by 2 cm.

35. $113 \div 1 = 113$

The only possible dimensions are 113 in. by 1 in.

36. $91 \div 1 = 91$

$91 \div 7 = 13$

Possible dimensions are 91 m by 1 m and 7 m by 13 m.

37. $|a + b| + c = |4 + (-2)| + (-3)$

$= |2| + (-3)$

$= 2 + (-3)$

$= -1$

38. $a + (c + b) = 4 + [(-3) + (-2)]$

$= 4 + (-5)$

$= -1$

39. $a + |b + c| = 4 + |(-2) + (-3)|$

$= 4 + |-5|$

$= 4 + 5$

$= 9$

40. $b + |b + c| + (-a) = -2 + |-2 + (-3)| + (-4)$

$= -2 + |-5| - 4$

$= -2 + 5 - 4$

$= 3 - 4$

$= -1$

41. $a + (-c) + (-b) = 4 + [-(-2)] + [-(-3)]$

$= 4 + 2 + 3$

$= 6 + 3$

$= 9$

42. $a + (-b) + (-a) = 4 + [-(-2)] + (-4)$

$= 4 + 2 + (-4)$

$= 6 - 4$

$= 2$

PAGE 140, LOOK BEYOND

43. $225.00 - 16.80 - 25.00 - 1.15 - 4.50 = 177.55$

Lorel's net pay is $177.55.

3.3 PAGES 146–148, PRACTICE & APPLY

6. $0.23 = \frac{23}{100}$

7. $0.8 = \frac{8}{10} = \frac{4}{5}$

8. $2.1 = 2\frac{1}{10}$

9. $5.7 = 5\frac{7}{10}$

10. $0.955 = \frac{955}{1000} = \frac{191}{200}$

11. $0.864 = \frac{864}{1000} = \frac{108}{125}$

12. $0.572 = \frac{572}{1000} = \frac{143}{250}$

13. $3.24 = 3\frac{24}{100} = 3\frac{6}{25}$

14. $5.08 = 5\frac{8}{100} = 5\frac{2}{25}$

15. $71.3 = 71\frac{3}{10}$

16. $125.4 = 125\frac{4}{10} = 125\frac{2}{5}$

17. $32.531 = 32\frac{531}{1000}$

18. $81\frac{44}{100} = 81\frac{11}{25}$

19. $894.32 = 894\frac{32}{100} = 894\frac{8}{25}$

20. $62.14 = 62\frac{14}{100} = 62\frac{7}{50}$

21. $0.005 = \frac{5}{1000} = \frac{1}{200}$

22. $4.015 = 4\frac{15}{1000} = 4\frac{3}{200}$

23. $45.45 = 45\frac{45}{100} = 45\frac{9}{20}$

24.
$$\begin{array}{r} 0.375 \\ 8\overline{)3.000} \\ -24 \\ \hline 60 \\ -56 \\ \hline 40 \\ 40 \\ \hline 0 \end{array}$$

25.
$$\begin{array}{r} 0.8 \\ 5\overline{)4.0} \\ -40 \\ \hline 0 \end{array}$$

26.
$$\begin{array}{r} -0.7 \\ 10\overline{)-7.0} \\ +70 \\ \hline 0 \end{array}$$

27.
$$\begin{array}{r} 0.41\overline{6} \\ 12\overline{)5.0000} \\ -48 \\ \hline 20 \\ -12 \\ \hline 80 \\ -72 \\ \hline 80 \\ -72 \\ \hline 8 \end{array}$$

28.
$$\begin{array}{r} -0.\overline{6} \\ 3\overline{)-2.00} \\ -(-18) \\ \hline -20 \end{array}$$

29.
$$\begin{array}{r} -0.\overline{11} \\ 9\overline{)-1.00} \\ -(-9) \\ \hline -10 \end{array}$$

30. $5\frac{3}{4} = \frac{23}{4}$
$$\begin{array}{r} 5.75 \\ 4\overline{)23.00} \\ -20 \\ \hline 30 \\ -28 \\ \hline 20 \\ 20 \\ \hline 0 \end{array}$$

31. $-7\frac{1}{2} = -\frac{15}{2}$
$$\begin{array}{r} -7.5 \\ 2\overline{)-15.0} \\ -(-14) \\ \hline -10 \\ 10 \\ \hline 0 \end{array}$$

32. $3\frac{2}{9} = \frac{29}{9}$
$$\begin{array}{r} 3.\overline{22} \\ 9\overline{)29.00} \\ -27 \\ \hline 20 \\ -18 \\ \hline 20 \\ -18 \\ \hline 2 \end{array}$$

33. $9\frac{7}{12} = \frac{115}{12}$
$$\begin{array}{r} 9.583\overline{3} \\ 12\overline{)115.0000} \\ -108 \\ \hline 70 \\ -60 \\ \hline 100 \\ -96 \\ \hline 40 \\ -36 \\ \hline 40 \end{array}$$

34. $-4\frac{1}{11} = -\frac{45}{11}$
$$\begin{array}{r} -4.\overline{09} \\ 11\overline{)-45.00} \\ -(-44) \\ \hline -100 \\ -(-99) \\ \hline -100 \end{array}$$

35.
$$\begin{array}{r} -0.\overline{142857} \\ -7\overline{)1.000000} \\ -7 \\ \hline 30 \\ -28 \\ \hline 20 \\ -14 \\ \hline 60 \\ -56 \\ \hline 40 \\ -35 \\ \hline 50 \\ -49 \\ \hline 10 \end{array}$$

For Exercises 36–41, rewrite the decimals using the same number of decimal places, and then reorder them.

36.
$0.4 = 0.400$
$0.38 = 0.380$
$0.49 = 0.490$
$0.472 = 0.472$
$0.425 = 0.425$

$0.38, 0.4, 0.425, 0.472, 0.49$

37.
$-0.035 = -0.035$
$-0.35 = -0.350$
$-0.5 = -0.500$
$-0.05 = -0.050$
$-0.53 = -0.530$

$-0.53, -0.5, -0.35, -0.05, -0.035$

38.
$5.32 = 5.320$
$5.2 = 5.200$
$4.97 = 4.970$
$5.037 = 5.037$
$5.3 = 5.300$

$4.97, 5.037, 5.2, 5.3, 5.32$

39. $6.091 = 6.091$

$6.01 = 6.010$

$6.009 = 6.009$

$6.9 = 6.900$

$6.19 = 6.190$

$6.009, 6.01, 6.091, 6.19, 6.9$

40. $-7.11 = -7.110$

$-7.011 = -7.011$

$-7.105 = -7.105$

$-7.01 = -7.010$

$-7.1 = -7.100$

$-7.11, -7.105, -7.1, -7.011, -7.01$

41. $-18.9 = -18.90$

$-19 = -19.00$

$-18.78 = -18.78$

$-19.25 = -19.25$

$-18.03 = -18.03$

$-19.25, -19, -18.9, -18.78, -18.03$

For Exercises 42–47, rewrite all numbers as either decimals or fractions then compare them.

42. $7.3 = 7.300$

$7\frac{3}{8} = 7.375$

$7.045 = 7.045$

$7\frac{5}{12} = 7.417$

$7\frac{1}{3} = 7.\overline{333}$

$7\frac{5}{12}, 7\frac{3}{8}, 7\frac{1}{3}, 7.3, 7.045$

43. $0.15 = 0.150$

$\frac{3}{8} = 0.375$

$-0.35 = -0.350$

$\frac{3}{4} = 0.750$

$\frac{679}{1000} = 0.679$

$\frac{3}{4}, \frac{679}{1000}, \frac{3}{8}, 0.15, -0.35$

44. $-5.6 = -5.600$

$-5\frac{5}{8} = -5.625$

$-5.55 = -5.550$

$-5\frac{2}{3} = -5.\overline{666}$

$-5\frac{2}{9} = -5.\overline{222}$

$-5\frac{2}{9}, -5.55, -5.6, -5\frac{5}{8}, -5\frac{2}{3}$

45. $-0.6 = -0.60$

$-\frac{2}{3} = -0.\overline{66}$

$-0.75 = -0.75$

$-\frac{3}{5} = -0.60$

$-0.5 = -0.50$

$-\frac{1}{3} = -0.\overline{33}$

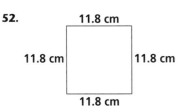 Equal

$-\frac{1}{3}, -0.5, -\frac{3}{5}, -0.6, -\frac{2}{3}, -0.75$

46. $8\frac{1}{9} = 8.\overline{11}$

$8.72 = 8.72$

$8\frac{6}{11} = 8.\overline{54}$

$8.56 = 8.56$

$8\frac{4}{9} = 8.\overline{44}$

$8.72, 8.56, 8\frac{6}{11}, 8\frac{4}{9}, 8\frac{1}{9}$

47. $\frac{14}{11} = 1.27\overline{27}$

$1.303 = 1.3030$

$1\frac{1}{3} = 1.333\overline{3}$

$0.133 = 0.1330$

$1\frac{1}{5} = 1.2000$

$1\frac{1}{3}, 1.303, \frac{14}{11}, 1\frac{1}{5}, 0.133$

48. First, round the cost of the fax modem to \$96.00. Next, round the cost of the memory chips to \$19.00.

$195 + 96 + 19 + 19 + 19 + 19 = \$367.00$

Since \$367.00 exceeds the \$350.00 that Ms. Jeffries has to spend, Ms. Jeffries does not have enough money to purchase the computer equipment.

49. Estimate: 6 boards can be cut from the available board.

Round 3.2 to 3.

Round 0.38 to $\frac{1}{2}$.

$3 \div \frac{1}{2} = 3 \cdot 2 = 6$

50. First, round \$2.95 to \$3.00.

$3 \times 5 = \$15.00$

$\$15.00 < \$17.00$

Yes, Amy has enough to purchase 5 notebooks.

51. Round \$10.95 to \$11.

$48 \div 11 = 4\frac{4}{11}$

Since Rico cannot purchase $\frac{4}{11}$ of a CD, he only has enough money to purchase 4 CDs.

52.

11.8 cm (top)

11.8 cm (left) 11.8 cm (right)

11.8 cm (bottom)

To estimate the perimeter of the square, first round 11.8 cm to 12.0 cm.

$P \approx 12.0 + 12.0 + 12.0 + 12.0$

$P \approx 4(12.0)$

$P \approx 48$ cm

53. To estimate Rachel's gas mileage, first round 425.8 miles to 425 miles and 25.3 gallons of gas to 25 gallons of gas.

$\text{gas mileage} = \frac{\text{number of miles traveled}}{\text{gallons of gas used}} \approx \frac{425}{25} = 17$

Rachel's gas mileage was approximately 17 mpg.

54. $3.2 = 3\frac{2}{10}$

$= 3\frac{1}{5}$

55. $47.032 = 47\frac{32}{1000}$

$= 47\frac{2}{125}$

56. $-8.48 = -8\frac{48}{100}$

$= -8\frac{12}{25}$

57. $-12.6 = -12\frac{6}{10}$

$= -12\frac{3}{5}$

58. $5.002 = 5\frac{2}{1000}$

$= 5\frac{1}{500}$

59. $-93.85 = -93\frac{85}{100}$

$= -93\frac{17}{20}$

60. $72.55 = 72\frac{55}{100}$

$= 72\frac{11}{20}$

61. $0.004 = \frac{4}{1000}$

$= \frac{1}{250}$

62. $0.56 = \frac{56}{100}$

$= \frac{14}{25}$

63. $-7.77 = -7\frac{77}{100}$

64. $66.66 = 66\frac{66}{100}$

$= 66\frac{33}{50}$

65. $6.59 = 6\frac{59}{100}$

66. $72.06 = 72\frac{6}{100}$

$= 72\frac{3}{50}$

67. $-0.001 = -\frac{1}{1000}$

68. $0.909 = \frac{909}{1000}$

69. $5.5 = 5\frac{5}{10}$

$= 5\frac{1}{2}$

70. Answers may vary. Sample answer: using the example 222.22, the value in the hundreds place, 200, is 10 times greater than the value in the tens place, 20, and so forth.

71. $72.26 = 72\frac{26}{100}$

$= 72\frac{13}{50}$

72. $505.025 = 505\frac{25}{1000}$

$= 505\frac{1}{40}$

73. $-0.00006 = -\frac{6}{100,000}$

$= -\frac{3}{50,000}$

74. $302.0075 = 302\frac{75}{10,000}$

$= 302\frac{3}{400}$

75. $16.1 = 16\frac{1}{10}$

76. $5.716 = 5\frac{716}{1000}$

$= 5\frac{179}{250}$

77. $22.2500 = 22\frac{2500}{10,000}$

$= 22\frac{1}{4}$

78. $0.667 = \frac{667}{1000}$

79. $0.333 = \frac{333}{1000}$

80. $1000.00001 = 1000\frac{1}{100,000}$

81. $\frac{\text{Hits}}{\text{At bats}} = \frac{45}{121} \approx 0.372$ batting average

82. $\frac{\text{Hits}}{\text{At bats}} = \frac{42}{127} \approx 0.331$ batting average

83. $\frac{\text{Hits}}{\text{At bats}} = \frac{43}{115} \approx 0.374$ batting average

84. Czarnecki (0.331), Rodriguez (0.372), Washington (0.374)

PAGE 148, LOOK BACK

85. $a^2 - b^2 = (-4)^2 - (2)^2$

$= 16 - 4$

$= 12$

86. False

$(3) - 7 \neq 4$

87. False

$(1) - 8 \neq 9$

88. True

$2(-1) + 6 = 4$

$-2 + 6 = 4$

89. False

$3(3) - 4 \neq 6$

$9 - 4 \neq 6$

90. True

$5(3) - 2(3) = 9$

$15 - 6 = 9$

91. False

$4(3) + 2(3) \neq 36$

$12 + 6 \neq 36$

92. $3x + 2 = 11$

Try $x = 2$.

$3x + 2 = 11$

$3(2) + 2 = 8$

2 is too small.
Try a larger number.

Try $x = 5$.

$3x + 2 = 11$

$3(5) + 2 = 17$

5 is too large.
Try a smaller number.

Try $x = 3$.

$3x + 2 = 11$

$3(3) + 2 = 11$

3 is the correct
number; $x = 3$.

93. First compare $3\frac{3}{8}$ with $3\frac{1}{3}$.

$3\frac{3}{8} = \frac{27}{8} = \frac{81}{24}$

$3\frac{1}{3} = \frac{10}{3} = \frac{80}{24}$

Since $3\frac{3}{8}$ is greater than $3\frac{1}{3}$, Helen cannot make the project with the amount of material she has on hand.

94. $\frac{1}{2} = \frac{n}{10}$

$\frac{1}{2} = \frac{1 \cdot 5}{2 \cdot 5} = \frac{5}{10}$

$n = 5$

95. $\frac{2}{9} = \frac{n}{18}$

$\frac{2}{9} = \frac{2 \cdot 2}{9 \cdot 2} = \frac{4}{18}$

$n = 4$

96. $\frac{n}{4} = \frac{3}{6}$

$6n = 4 \cdot 3$

$\frac{6n}{6} = \frac{12}{6}$

$n = 2$

97. $\frac{8}{12} = \frac{6}{n}$

$8n = 12 \cdot 6$

$\frac{8n}{8} = \frac{72}{8}$

$n = 9$

3.4 PAGES 152–153, PRACTICE & APPLY

6. Andrew's work hours

$5 + 6\frac{1}{4} + 8\frac{3}{4} + 4\frac{1}{2} + 3\frac{1}{4} = 5 + 6\frac{1}{4} + 8\frac{3}{4} + 4\frac{2}{4} + 3\frac{1}{4} = 27\frac{3}{4}$ hours

7. Bolla's work hours

$1\frac{1}{4} + 3\frac{1}{2} + 7\frac{1}{4} + 5\frac{3}{4} + 4\frac{1}{2} = 1\frac{1}{4} + 3\frac{2}{4} + 7\frac{1}{4} + 5\frac{3}{4} + 4\frac{2}{4} = 22\frac{1}{4}$ hours

8. Garza's work hours

$7\frac{1}{4} + 3\frac{3}{4} + 1\frac{1}{2} + 2\frac{1}{2} + 7\frac{3}{4} = 7\frac{1}{4} + 3\frac{3}{4} + 1\frac{2}{4} + 2\frac{2}{4} + 7\frac{3}{4} = 22\frac{3}{4}$ hours

9. Holland's work hours

$3\frac{1}{2} + 2\frac{1}{2} + 4\frac{1}{4} + 6 + 7 = 3\frac{2}{4} + 2\frac{2}{4} + 4\frac{1}{4} + 6 + 7 = 23\frac{1}{4}$ hours

10. Tate's work hours

$7\frac{1}{2} + 7\frac{1}{4} + 6\frac{1}{4} + 8\frac{3}{4} + 2\frac{1}{2} = 7\frac{2}{4} + 7\frac{1}{4} + 6\frac{1}{4} + 8\frac{3}{4} + 2\frac{2}{4} = 32\frac{1}{4}$ hours

11. Wuest's work hours

$6 + 4\frac{1}{2} + 6\frac{1}{2} + 3\frac{1}{4} + 0 = 6 + 4\frac{2}{4} + 6\frac{2}{4} + 3\frac{1}{4} + 0 = 20\frac{1}{4}$ hours

12. Work hours: $27\frac{3}{4} = 27.75$ hours

Wage: $7.25 per hour

Total wage: $7.25 \times 27.75 = \$201.19$

13. Work hours: $22\frac{1}{4} = 22.25$ hours

Wage: $6.75 per hour

Total wage: $6.75 \times 22.25 = \$150.19$

14. Work hours: $22\frac{3}{4} = 22.75$ hours

Wage: $7.75 per hour

Total wage: $7.75 \times 22.75 = \$176.31$

15. Work hours: $23\frac{1}{4} = 23.25$ hours

Wage: $7.58 per hour

Total wage: $7.58 \times 23.25 = \$176.24$

16. Work hours: $32\frac{1}{4} = 32.25$ hours

Wage: $7.95 per hour

Total wage: $7.95 \times 32.25 = \$256.39$

17. Work hours: $20\frac{1}{4} = 20.25$ hours

Wage: $6.65 per hour

Total wage: $6.65 \times 20.25 = \$134.66$

18. $5 + 1\frac{1}{4} + 7\frac{1}{4} + 3\frac{1}{2} + 7\frac{1}{2} + 6 = 5 + 1\frac{1}{4} + 7\frac{1}{4} + 3\frac{2}{4} + 7\frac{2}{4} + 6 = 30\frac{1}{2}$ hours

The total number of hours worked on Monday was $30\frac{1}{2}$ hours.

19. $6\frac{1}{4} + 3\frac{1}{2} + 3\frac{3}{4} + 2\frac{1}{2} + 7\frac{1}{4} + 4\frac{1}{2} = 6\frac{1}{4} + 3\frac{2}{4} + 3\frac{3}{4} + 2\frac{2}{4} + 7\frac{1}{4} + 4\frac{2}{4} = 27\frac{3}{4}$ hours

The total number of hours worked on Tuesday was $27\frac{3}{4}$ hours.

20. $8\frac{3}{4} + 7\frac{1}{4} + 1\frac{1}{2} + 4\frac{1}{4} + 6\frac{1}{4} + 6\frac{1}{2} = 8\frac{3}{4} + 7\frac{1}{4} + 1\frac{2}{4} + 4\frac{1}{4} + 6\frac{1}{4} + 6\frac{2}{4} = 34\frac{1}{2}$ hours

The total number of hours worked on Wednesday was $34\frac{1}{2}$ hours.

21. $4\frac{1}{2} + 5\frac{3}{4} + 2\frac{1}{2} + 6 + 8\frac{3}{4} + 3\frac{1}{4} = 4\frac{2}{4} + 5\frac{3}{4} + 2\frac{2}{4} + 6 + 8\frac{3}{4} + 3\frac{1}{4} = 30\frac{3}{4}$ hours

The total number of hours worked on Thursday was $30\frac{3}{4}$ hours.

22. $3\frac{1}{4} + 4\frac{1}{2} + 7\frac{3}{4} + 7 + 2\frac{1}{2} + 0 = 3\frac{1}{4} + 4\frac{2}{4} + 7\frac{3}{4} + 7 + 2\frac{2}{4} + 0 = 25$ hours

The total number of hours worked on Friday was 25 hours.

23.

	A	B	C	D	E	F	G
1				Payroll			
2							
3	Name	Mon. pay	Tue. pay	Wed. pay	Thur. pay	Fri. pay	Total pay
4							
5	Andrews	36.25	45.31	63.44	32.63	23.56	201.19
6	Bolla	8.44	23.63	48.94	38.81	30.38	150.19
7	Garza	56.19	29.06	11.63	19.38	60.06	176.31
8	Holland	26.53	18.95	32.22	45.48	53.06	176.24
9	Tate	59.63	57.64	49.69	69.56	19.88	256.39
10	Wuest	39.90	29.93	43.23	21.61	0.00	134.66

24. Round $15\frac{7}{16}$ to 16.

Round $12\frac{3}{8}$ to 12.

Estimated perimeter $\approx 16 + 16 + 12 + 12 = 56$

$$\begin{aligned}\text{Actual perimeter} &= 15\frac{7}{16} + 15\frac{7}{16} + 12\frac{3}{8} + 12\frac{3}{8} \\ &= 15\frac{7}{16} + 15\frac{7}{16} + 12\frac{6}{16} + 12\frac{6}{16} \\ &= 55\frac{10}{16} \\ &= 55\frac{5}{8}\end{aligned}$$

The estimated perimeter is 56, but the actual perimeter is $55\frac{5}{8}$.

25. Round $8\frac{3}{8}$ to 8.

Round $10\frac{5}{16}$ to 10.

Estimated perimeter $\approx 8 + 8 + 10 + 10 = 36$

$$\begin{aligned}\text{Actual perimeter} &= 8\frac{3}{8} + 8\frac{3}{8} + 10\frac{5}{16} + 10\frac{5}{16} \\ &= 8\frac{6}{16} + 8\frac{6}{16} + 10\frac{5}{16} + 10\frac{5}{16} \\ &= 37\frac{6}{16} \\ &= 37\frac{3}{8}\end{aligned}$$

The estimated perimeter is 36, but the actual perimeter is $37\frac{3}{8}$.

26. Round $5\frac{3}{16}$ to 5.

Round $7\frac{3}{4}$ to 8.

Estimated perimeter $\approx 5 + 5 + 8 + 8 = 26$

$$\begin{aligned}\text{Actual perimeter} &= 5\frac{3}{16} + 5\frac{3}{16} + 7\frac{3}{4} + 7\frac{3}{4} \\ &= 5\frac{3}{16} + 5\frac{3}{16} + 7\frac{12}{16} + 7\frac{12}{16} \\ &= 25\frac{14}{16} \\ &= 25\frac{7}{8}\end{aligned}$$

The estimated perimeter is 26, but the actual perimeter is $25\frac{7}{8}$.

27. Round $10\frac{5}{8}$ to 11.

Round $13\frac{1}{2}$ to 14.

Estimated perimeter $\approx 11 + 11 + 14 + 14 = 50$

$$\begin{aligned}\text{Actual perimeter} &= 10\frac{5}{8} + 10\frac{5}{8} + 13\frac{1}{2} + 13\frac{1}{2} \\ &= 10\frac{5}{8} + 10\frac{5}{8} + 13\frac{4}{8} + 13\frac{4}{8} \\ &= 48\frac{2}{8} \\ &= 48\frac{1}{4}\end{aligned}$$

The estimated perimeter is 50, but the actual perimeter is $48\frac{1}{4}$.

28. Round $60\frac{1}{2}$ to 61.

Round $36\frac{3}{4}$ to 37.

Estimated perimeter $\approx 61 + 61 + 37 + 37 = 196$

$$\begin{aligned}\text{Actual perimeter} &= 60\frac{1}{2} + 60\frac{1}{2} + 36\frac{3}{4} + 36\frac{3}{4} \\ &= 60\frac{2}{4} + 60\frac{2}{4} + 36\frac{3}{4} + 36\frac{3}{4} \\ &= 194\frac{2}{4} \\ &= 194\frac{1}{2}\end{aligned}$$

The estimated perimeter is 196, but the actual perimeter is $194\frac{1}{2}$.

For Exercises 29–34, answers may vary. Sample answers are given.

29. $4\frac{1}{3} = 2\frac{2}{3} + 1\frac{2}{3}$

30. $6\frac{3}{8} = 4\frac{7}{8} + 1\frac{1}{2}$

31. $-\frac{1}{2} = 2\frac{3}{4} + (-3\frac{1}{4})$

32. $11\frac{4}{7} = 9\frac{1}{7} + 2\frac{3}{7}$

33. $9\frac{7}{8} = 5\frac{1}{4} + 4\frac{5}{8}$

34. $-1\frac{1}{2} = 1\frac{1}{4} + (-2\frac{3}{4})$

For Exercises 35–40, answers may vary. Sample answers are given.

35. $4\frac{1}{3} = 6\frac{2}{3} - 2\frac{1}{3}$

36. $6\frac{3}{8} = 10\frac{7}{8} - 4\frac{1}{2}$

37. $-\frac{1}{2} = 4\frac{3}{4} - 5\frac{1}{4}$

38. $11\frac{4}{7} = 20\frac{6}{7} - 9\frac{2}{7}$

39. $9\frac{7}{8} = 15\frac{1}{2} - 5\frac{5}{8}$

40. $-1\frac{1}{2} = 3\frac{3}{4} - 5\frac{1}{4}$

41. $\dfrac{1}{2} + \dfrac{4}{5} = \dfrac{1 \cdot 5}{2 \cdot 5} + \dfrac{4 \cdot 2}{5 \cdot 2}$

$\phantom{\dfrac{1}{2} + \dfrac{4}{5}} = \dfrac{5}{10} + \dfrac{8}{10}$

$\phantom{\dfrac{1}{2} + \dfrac{4}{5}} = \dfrac{13}{10}$

$\phantom{\dfrac{1}{2} + \dfrac{4}{5}} = 1\dfrac{3}{10}$

42. $\dfrac{2}{3} - \dfrac{7}{12} = \dfrac{2 \cdot 4}{3 \cdot 4} - \dfrac{7}{12}$

$\phantom{\dfrac{2}{3} - \dfrac{7}{12}} = \dfrac{8}{12} - \dfrac{7}{12}$

$\phantom{\dfrac{2}{3} - \dfrac{7}{12}} = \dfrac{1}{12}$

43. $\dfrac{1}{3} + \dfrac{3}{16} = \dfrac{1 \cdot 16}{3 \cdot 16} + \dfrac{3 \cdot 3}{16 \cdot 3}$

$\phantom{\dfrac{1}{3} + \dfrac{3}{16}} = \dfrac{16}{48} + \dfrac{9}{48}$

$\phantom{\dfrac{1}{3} + \dfrac{3}{16}} = \dfrac{25}{48}$

44. $-\dfrac{1}{2} + \dfrac{2}{3} + 1\dfrac{2}{3} = -\dfrac{1}{2} + \dfrac{2}{3} + \dfrac{5}{3}$

$\phantom{-\dfrac{1}{2} + \dfrac{2}{3} + 1\dfrac{2}{3}} = \dfrac{-1 \cdot 3}{2 \cdot 3} + \dfrac{2 \cdot 2}{3 \cdot 2} + \dfrac{5 \cdot 2}{3 \cdot 2}$

$\phantom{-\dfrac{1}{2} + \dfrac{2}{3} + 1\dfrac{2}{3}} = \dfrac{-3}{6} + \dfrac{4}{6} + \dfrac{10}{6}$

$\phantom{-\dfrac{1}{2} + \dfrac{2}{3} + 1\dfrac{2}{3}} = \dfrac{1}{6} + \dfrac{10}{6}$

$\phantom{-\dfrac{1}{2} + \dfrac{2}{3} + 1\dfrac{2}{3}} = \dfrac{11}{6}$

$\phantom{-\dfrac{1}{2} + \dfrac{2}{3} + 1\dfrac{2}{3}} = 1\dfrac{5}{6}$

45. $\dfrac{3}{4} - \dfrac{1}{4} + 1\dfrac{3}{8} = \dfrac{3}{4} - \dfrac{1}{4} + \dfrac{11}{8}$

$\phantom{\dfrac{3}{4} - \dfrac{1}{4} + 1\dfrac{3}{8}} = \dfrac{3 \cdot 2}{4 \cdot 2} - \dfrac{1 \cdot 2}{4 \cdot 2} + \dfrac{11}{8}$

$\phantom{\dfrac{3}{4} - \dfrac{1}{4} + 1\dfrac{3}{8}} = \dfrac{6}{8} - \dfrac{2}{8} + \dfrac{11}{8}$

$\phantom{\dfrac{3}{4} - \dfrac{1}{4} + 1\dfrac{3}{8}} = \dfrac{4}{8} + \dfrac{11}{8}$

$\phantom{\dfrac{3}{4} - \dfrac{1}{4} + 1\dfrac{3}{8}} = \dfrac{15}{8}$

$\phantom{\dfrac{3}{4} - \dfrac{1}{4} + 1\dfrac{3}{8}} = 1\dfrac{7}{8}$

46. $3\dfrac{3}{4} + 2\dfrac{3}{16} = \dfrac{15}{4} + \dfrac{35}{16}$

$\phantom{3\dfrac{3}{4} + 2\dfrac{3}{16}} = \dfrac{15 \cdot 4}{4 \cdot 4} + \dfrac{35}{16}$

$\phantom{3\dfrac{3}{4} + 2\dfrac{3}{16}} = \dfrac{60}{16} + \dfrac{35}{16}$

$\phantom{3\dfrac{3}{4} + 2\dfrac{3}{16}} = \dfrac{95}{16}$

$\phantom{3\dfrac{3}{4} + 2\dfrac{3}{16}} = 5\dfrac{15}{16}$

47. $4\dfrac{1}{2} - 2\dfrac{3}{4} = \dfrac{9}{2} - \dfrac{11}{4}$

$\phantom{4\dfrac{1}{2} - 2\dfrac{3}{4}} = \dfrac{9 \cdot 2}{2 \cdot 2} - \dfrac{11}{4}$

$\phantom{4\dfrac{1}{2} - 2\dfrac{3}{4}} = \dfrac{18}{4} - \dfrac{11}{4}$

$\phantom{4\dfrac{1}{2} - 2\dfrac{3}{4}} = \dfrac{7}{4}$

$\phantom{4\dfrac{1}{2} - 2\dfrac{3}{4}} = 1\dfrac{3}{4}$

48. $8\dfrac{7}{10} - \dfrac{7}{8} = \dfrac{87}{10} - \dfrac{7}{8}$

$\phantom{8\dfrac{7}{10} - \dfrac{7}{8}} = \dfrac{87 \cdot 4}{10 \cdot 4} - \dfrac{7 \cdot 5}{8 \cdot 5}$

$\phantom{8\dfrac{7}{10} - \dfrac{7}{8}} = \dfrac{348}{40} - \dfrac{35}{40}$

$\phantom{8\dfrac{7}{10} - \dfrac{7}{8}} = \dfrac{313}{40}$

$\phantom{8\dfrac{7}{10} - \dfrac{7}{8}} = 7\dfrac{33}{40}$

49. $5 - \dfrac{3}{16} = \dfrac{80}{16} - \dfrac{3}{16}$

$\phantom{5 - \dfrac{3}{16}} = \dfrac{77}{16}$

$\phantom{5 - \dfrac{3}{16}} = 4\dfrac{13}{16}$

50. $-\dfrac{2}{3} - \dfrac{7}{12} = -\dfrac{2 \cdot 4}{3 \cdot 4} - \dfrac{7}{12}$

$\phantom{-\dfrac{2}{3} - \dfrac{7}{12}} = -\dfrac{8}{12} - \dfrac{7}{12}$

$\phantom{-\dfrac{2}{3} - \dfrac{7}{12}} = -\dfrac{15}{12}$

$\phantom{-\dfrac{2}{3} - \dfrac{7}{12}} = -1\dfrac{3}{12}$

$\phantom{-\dfrac{2}{3} - \dfrac{7}{12}} = -1\dfrac{1}{4}$

51. $-\dfrac{1}{3} + 1\dfrac{3}{4} = -\dfrac{1}{3} + \dfrac{7}{4}$

$\phantom{-\dfrac{1}{3} + 1\dfrac{3}{4}} = -\dfrac{1 \cdot 4}{3 \cdot 4} + \dfrac{7 \cdot 3}{4 \cdot 3}$

$\phantom{-\dfrac{1}{3} + 1\dfrac{3}{4}} = -\dfrac{4}{12} + \dfrac{21}{12}$

$\phantom{-\dfrac{1}{3} + 1\dfrac{3}{4}} = \dfrac{17}{12}$

$\phantom{-\dfrac{1}{3} + 1\dfrac{3}{4}} = 1\dfrac{5}{12}$

52. $-\dfrac{1}{2} + \left(-1\dfrac{7}{8}\right) + \left(-\dfrac{2}{3}\right) = -\dfrac{1}{2} + \left(-\dfrac{15}{8}\right) + \left(-\dfrac{2}{3}\right)$

$\phantom{-\dfrac{1}{2} + \left(-1\dfrac{7}{8}\right) + \left(-\dfrac{2}{3}\right)} = -\dfrac{1 \cdot 12}{2 \cdot 12} + \left(-\dfrac{15 \cdot 3}{8 \cdot 3}\right) + \left(-\dfrac{2 \cdot 8}{3 \cdot 8}\right)$

$\phantom{-\dfrac{1}{2} + \left(-1\dfrac{7}{8}\right) + \left(-\dfrac{2}{3}\right)} = -\dfrac{12}{24} + \left(-\dfrac{45}{24}\right) + \left(-\dfrac{16}{24}\right)$

$\phantom{-\dfrac{1}{2} + \left(-1\dfrac{7}{8}\right) + \left(-\dfrac{2}{3}\right)} = -\dfrac{57}{24} + \left(-\dfrac{16}{24}\right)$

$\phantom{-\dfrac{1}{2} + \left(-1\dfrac{7}{8}\right) + \left(-\dfrac{2}{3}\right)} = -\dfrac{73}{24}$

$\phantom{-\dfrac{1}{2} + \left(-1\dfrac{7}{8}\right) + \left(-\dfrac{2}{3}\right)} = -3\dfrac{1}{24}$

53. $9\dfrac{5}{6} - \dfrac{5}{6} = 9$

54. $6\dfrac{4}{5} - 9\dfrac{7}{8} = \dfrac{34}{5} - \dfrac{79}{8}$

$\phantom{6\dfrac{4}{5} - 9\dfrac{7}{8}} = \dfrac{34 \cdot 8}{5 \cdot 8} - \dfrac{79 \cdot 5}{8 \cdot 5}$

$\phantom{6\dfrac{4}{5} - 9\dfrac{7}{8}} = \dfrac{272}{40} - \dfrac{395}{40}$

$\phantom{6\dfrac{4}{5} - 9\dfrac{7}{8}} = -\dfrac{123}{40}$

$\phantom{6\dfrac{4}{5} - 9\dfrac{7}{8}} = -3\dfrac{3}{40}$

55. $-9\dfrac{5}{6} + 3\dfrac{11}{12} = -\dfrac{59}{6} + \dfrac{47}{12}$

$\phantom{-9\dfrac{5}{6} + 3\dfrac{11}{12}} = -\dfrac{59 \cdot 2}{6 \cdot 2} + \dfrac{47}{12}$

$\phantom{-9\dfrac{5}{6} + 3\dfrac{11}{12}} = -\dfrac{118}{12} + \dfrac{47}{12}$

$\phantom{-9\dfrac{5}{6} + 3\dfrac{11}{12}} = -\dfrac{71}{12}$

$\phantom{-9\dfrac{5}{6} + 3\dfrac{11}{12}} = -5\dfrac{11}{12}$

56. $-\dfrac{2}{3} + \left(1\dfrac{7}{8}\right) + \left(-8\dfrac{1}{2}\right) = -\dfrac{2}{3} + \dfrac{15}{8} + \left(-\dfrac{17}{2}\right)$

$\phantom{-\dfrac{2}{3} + \left(1\dfrac{7}{8}\right) + \left(-8\dfrac{1}{2}\right)} = -\dfrac{2 \cdot 8}{3 \cdot 8} + \dfrac{15 \cdot 3}{8 \cdot 3} + \left(\dfrac{-17 \cdot 12}{2 \cdot 12}\right)$

$\phantom{-\dfrac{2}{3} + \left(1\dfrac{7}{8}\right) + \left(-8\dfrac{1}{2}\right)} = -\dfrac{16}{24} + \dfrac{45}{24} + \left(-\dfrac{204}{24}\right)$

$\phantom{-\dfrac{2}{3} + \left(1\dfrac{7}{8}\right) + \left(-8\dfrac{1}{2}\right)} = \dfrac{29}{24} + \left(-\dfrac{204}{24}\right)$

$\phantom{-\dfrac{2}{3} + \left(1\dfrac{7}{8}\right) + \left(-8\dfrac{1}{2}\right)} = -\dfrac{175}{24}$

$\phantom{-\dfrac{2}{3} + \left(1\dfrac{7}{8}\right) + \left(-8\dfrac{1}{2}\right)} = -7\dfrac{7}{24}$

57. $82 \div 1 = 82$
$82 \div 2 = 41$ 1, ②, ㊶, 82

58. $54 \div 1 = 54$
$54 \div 2 = 27$
$54 \div 3 = 18$ 1, ②, ③, 6, 9, 18, 27, 54
$54 \div 6 = 9$

59. $75 \div 1 = 75$
$75 \div 3 = 25$ 1, ③, ⑤, 15, 25, 75
$75 \div 5 = 15$

60. $63 \div 1 = 63$
$63 \div 3 = 21$ 1, ③, ⑦, 9, 21, 63
$63 \div 7 = 9$

61. $-15 + (-12) = -27$

62. $-61 + (-8) + 7 = -69 + 7$
$\qquad\qquad\qquad = -62$

63. $24 + (-41) + (-9) = -17 + (-9)$
$\qquad\qquad\qquad\quad = -26$

64. $|-3| + (-7) = 3 + (-7)$
$\qquad\qquad\quad = -4$

65. $6 + (-12) + |7| = 6 + (-12) + 7$
$\qquad\qquad\qquad = -6 + 7$
$\qquad\qquad\qquad = 1$

66. $201 + (-32) + (-198) = 169 + (-198)$
$\qquad\qquad\qquad\qquad\quad = -29$

67. $x - \frac{1}{3} = 1\frac{2}{3}$

Try $x = 3$.
$x - \frac{1}{3} = 1\frac{2}{3}$
$3 - \frac{1}{3} = 2\frac{2}{3}$

3 is too large.
Try a smaller
number.

Try $x = 2$.
$x - \frac{1}{3} = 1\frac{2}{3}$
$2 - \frac{1}{3} = 1\frac{2}{3}$

2 is the correct
number; $x = 2$.

68. $x - \frac{3}{4} = 10\frac{1}{4}$

Try $x = 12$.
$x - \frac{3}{4} = 10\frac{1}{4}$
$12 - \frac{3}{4} = 11\frac{1}{4}$

12 is too large.
Try a smaller
number.

Try $x = 11\frac{1}{2}$.
$x - \frac{3}{4} = 10\frac{1}{4}$
$11\frac{1}{2} - \frac{3}{4} = 10\frac{3}{4}$

$11\frac{1}{2}$ is too large.
Try a smaller
number.

Try $x = 11$.
$x - \frac{3}{4} = 10\frac{1}{4}$
$11 - \frac{3}{4} = 10\frac{1}{4}$

11 is the correct
number; $x = 11$.

69. $\frac{x}{4} = 6\frac{1}{4}$

Try $x = 20$.
$\frac{x}{4} = 6\frac{1}{4}$
$\frac{20}{4} = 5$

20 is too small.
Try a larger
number.

Try $x = 23$.
$\frac{x}{4} = 6\frac{1}{4}$
$\frac{23}{4} = 5\frac{3}{4}$

23 it too small.
Try a larger
number.

Try $x = 25$.
$\frac{x}{4} = 6\frac{1}{4}$
$\frac{25}{4} = 6\frac{1}{4}$

25 is the correct
number; $x = 25$.

3.5 **PAGES 159–161, PRACTICE & APPLY**

5.
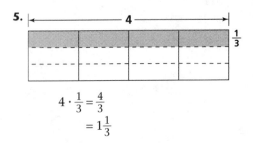

$4 \cdot \frac{1}{3} = \frac{4}{3}$
$\qquad = 1\frac{1}{3}$

6.
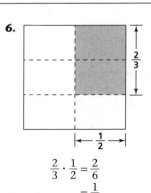

$\frac{2}{3} \cdot \frac{1}{2} = \frac{2}{6}$
$\qquad = \frac{1}{3}$

7.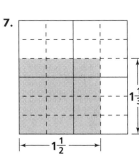

$$1\tfrac{1}{2} \cdot 1\tfrac{1}{3} = 12\left(\tfrac{1}{6}\right)$$
$$= 2$$

8.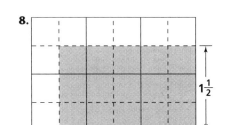

$$2\tfrac{1}{2} \cdot 1\tfrac{1}{2} = 15\left(\tfrac{1}{4}\right)$$
$$= \tfrac{15}{4}$$
$$= 3\tfrac{3}{4}$$

9. Round $2\tfrac{3}{4}$ to 3.

Round $5\tfrac{1}{3}$ to 5.

Estimated area $= 3 \cdot 5$
$$= 15 \text{ square inches}$$

Actual area $= 2\tfrac{3}{4} \cdot 5\tfrac{1}{3}$
$$= \tfrac{11}{4} \cdot \tfrac{16}{3}$$
$$= \tfrac{176}{12}$$
$$= 14\tfrac{2}{3} \text{ square inches}$$

10. Round $12\tfrac{5}{11}$ to 12.

Round $16\tfrac{1}{2}$ to 17.

Estimated area $= 12 \cdot 17$
$$= 204 \text{ square feet}$$

Actual area $= 12\tfrac{5}{11} \cdot 16\tfrac{1}{2}$
$$= \tfrac{137}{11} \cdot \tfrac{33}{2}$$
$$= \tfrac{137}{1} \cdot \tfrac{3}{2}$$
$$= \tfrac{411}{2}$$
$$= 205\tfrac{1}{2} \text{ square feet}$$

11. Round $\tfrac{1}{2}$ to 1.

Round $2\tfrac{3}{4}$ to 2.

Estimated area $= 1 \cdot 2$
$$= 2 \text{ square miles}$$

Actual area $= \tfrac{1}{2} \cdot 2\tfrac{3}{4}$
$$= \tfrac{1}{2} \cdot \tfrac{11}{4}$$
$$= \tfrac{11}{8}$$
$$= 1\tfrac{3}{8} \text{ square miles}$$

For Exercises 12–27, estimated answers may vary. Sample estimates are given.

12. Estimate $= 27$
$$9 \cdot 2\tfrac{2}{3} = 9 \cdot \tfrac{8}{3}$$
$$= \tfrac{72}{3}$$
Actual product $= 24$

13. Estimate $= 16$
$$2\tfrac{1}{4} \cdot 8 = \tfrac{9}{4} \cdot 8$$
$$= \tfrac{72}{4}$$
Actual product $= 18$

14. Estimate $= 36$
$$3\tfrac{1}{3} \cdot 12 = \tfrac{10}{3} \cdot 12$$
$$= \tfrac{120}{3}$$
Actual product $= 40$

15. Estimate $= 18$
$$10 \cdot 1\tfrac{3}{5} = 10 \cdot \tfrac{8}{5}$$
$$= \tfrac{80}{5}$$
Actual product $= 16$

16. Estimate $= 4$
$$1\tfrac{1}{2} \cdot 2\tfrac{1}{3} = \tfrac{3}{2} \cdot \tfrac{7}{3}$$
$$= \tfrac{21}{6}$$
$$= 3\tfrac{3}{6}$$
Actual product $= 3\tfrac{1}{2}$

17. Estimate $= 8$
$$3\tfrac{3}{4} \cdot 1\tfrac{2}{3} = \tfrac{15}{4} \cdot \tfrac{5}{3}$$
$$= \tfrac{75}{12}$$
$$= 6\tfrac{3}{12}$$
Actual product $= 6\tfrac{1}{4}$

18. Estimate $= 15$
$$4\tfrac{1}{2} \cdot 2\tfrac{2}{3} = \tfrac{9}{2} \cdot \tfrac{8}{3}$$
$$= \tfrac{72}{6}$$
Actual product $= 12$

19. Estimate $= 12$
$$6\tfrac{1}{4} \cdot 1\tfrac{3}{5} = \tfrac{25}{4} \cdot \tfrac{8}{5}$$
$$= \tfrac{200}{20}$$
Actual product $= 10$

20. Estimate $= 64$
$$8\tfrac{1}{5} \cdot 7\tfrac{1}{2} = \tfrac{41}{5} \cdot \tfrac{15}{2}$$
$$= \tfrac{615}{10}$$
Actual product $= 61\tfrac{1}{2}$

21. Estimate $= 8$
$$2\tfrac{2}{5} \cdot 4\tfrac{1}{6} = \tfrac{12}{5} \cdot \tfrac{25}{6}$$
$$= \tfrac{300}{30}$$
Actual product $= 10$

22. Estimate $= 15$
$$2\tfrac{5}{8} \cdot 5\tfrac{1}{4} = \tfrac{21}{8} \cdot \tfrac{21}{4}$$
$$= \tfrac{441}{32}$$
Actual product $= 13\tfrac{25}{32}$

23. Estimate $= 6$
$$1\tfrac{5}{6} \cdot 3\tfrac{1}{9} = \tfrac{11}{6} \cdot \tfrac{28}{9}$$
$$= \tfrac{308}{54}$$
$$= 5\tfrac{38}{54}$$
Actual product $= 5\tfrac{19}{27}$

24. Estimate = 128

$$8\frac{1}{4} \cdot 15\frac{3}{5} = \frac{33}{4} \cdot \frac{78}{5}$$
$$= \frac{2574}{20}$$

Actual product = $128\frac{7}{10}$

25. Estimate = 96

$$7\frac{2}{3} \cdot 12\frac{1}{8} = \frac{23}{3} \cdot \frac{97}{8}$$
$$= \frac{2231}{24}$$

Actual product = $92\frac{23}{24}$

26. Estimate = 22

$$2\frac{1}{6} \cdot 11\frac{1}{3} = \frac{13}{6} \cdot \frac{34}{3}$$
$$= \frac{442}{18}$$
$$= 24\frac{10}{18}$$

Actual product = $24\frac{5}{9}$

27. Estimate = 27

$$3\frac{1}{5} \cdot 8\frac{2}{3} = \frac{16}{5} \cdot \frac{26}{3}$$
$$= \frac{416}{15}$$

Actual product = $27\frac{11}{15}$

28. The reciprocal of $\frac{2}{3}$ is $\frac{3}{2}$.

$$\frac{2}{3} \cdot \frac{3}{2} = \frac{6}{6} = 1$$

29. $2\frac{1}{2} = \frac{5}{2}$

The reciprocal of $\frac{5}{2}$ is $\frac{2}{5}$.

$$\frac{5}{2} \cdot \frac{2}{5} = \frac{10}{10} = 1$$

30. $1\frac{2}{3} = \frac{5}{3}$

The reciprocal of $\frac{5}{3}$ is $\frac{3}{5}$.

$$\frac{5}{3} \cdot \frac{3}{5} = \frac{15}{15} = 1$$

31. $4\frac{4}{7} = \frac{32}{7}$

The reciprocal of $\frac{32}{7}$ is $\frac{7}{32}$.

$$\frac{32}{7} \cdot \frac{7}{32} = \frac{224}{224} = 1$$

32. $5\frac{2}{5} = \frac{27}{5}$

The reciprocal of $\frac{27}{5}$ is $\frac{5}{27}$.

$$\frac{27}{5} \cdot \frac{5}{27} = \frac{135}{135} = 1$$

33. $50 \div 2\frac{1}{2} = 50 \div \frac{5}{2}$
$$= 50 \cdot \frac{2}{5}$$
$$= \frac{100}{5}$$
$$= 20$$

There are 20 bags in one large sack.

34. $50 \div 3\frac{1}{3} = 50 \div \frac{10}{3}$
$$= 5 \cdot \frac{3}{10}$$
$$= \frac{150}{10}$$
$$= 15$$

There are 15 bags in one large sack.

35. $50 \div 1\frac{2}{3} = 50 \div \frac{5}{3}$
$$= 50 \cdot \frac{3}{5}$$
$$= \frac{150}{5}$$
$$= 30$$

There are 30 bags in one large sack.

36. $50 \div 1\frac{1}{2} = 50 \div \frac{3}{2}$
$$= 50 \cdot \frac{2}{3}$$
$$= \frac{100}{3}$$
$$= 33\frac{1}{3}$$

Since you cannot have $\frac{1}{3}$ of a bag, there are 33 $1\frac{1}{2}$-pound bags in the sack.

$33 \cdot 1\frac{1}{2} = 33 \cdot \frac{3}{2}$
$$= \frac{99}{2}$$
$$= 49\frac{1}{2}$$

There are $49\frac{1}{2}$ pounds of birdseed in the 33 bags. This leaves $\frac{1}{2}$ pound of birdseed left after all the bags are filled.

37. $17\frac{1}{2} \div 2\frac{1}{3} = \frac{35}{2} \div \frac{7}{3}$
$$= \frac{35}{2} \cdot \frac{3}{7}$$
$$= \frac{105}{14}$$
$$= 7\frac{1}{2}$$

Since you cannot make $\frac{1}{2}$ a loaf of bread, the baker can make 7 loaves of bread.

	MINUTES	FRACTION	UNITS PRODUCED
38.	10	$\frac{10}{60} = \frac{1}{6}$	$\frac{1}{6} \cdot 1200 = 200$
39.	15	$\frac{15}{60} = \frac{1}{4}$	$\frac{1}{4} \cdot 1200 = 300$
40.	20	$\frac{20}{60} = \frac{1}{3}$	$\frac{1}{3} \cdot 1200 = 400$
41.	25	$\frac{25}{60} = \frac{5}{12}$	$\frac{5}{12} \cdot 1200 = 500$
42.	30	$\frac{30}{60} = \frac{1}{2}$	$\frac{1}{2} \cdot 1200 = 600$
43.	35	$\frac{35}{60} = \frac{7}{12}$	$\frac{7}{12} \cdot 1200 = 700$
44.	40	$\frac{40}{60} = \frac{2}{3}$	$\frac{2}{3} \cdot 1200 = 800$
45.	45	$\frac{45}{60} = \frac{3}{4}$	$\frac{3}{4} \cdot 1200 = 900$
46.	50	$\frac{50}{60} = \frac{5}{6}$	$\frac{5}{6} \cdot 1200 = 1000$
47.	55	$\frac{55}{60} = \frac{11}{12}$	$\frac{11}{12} \cdot 1200 = 1100$
48.	60	$\frac{60}{60} = 1$	$1 \cdot 1200 = 1200$

49.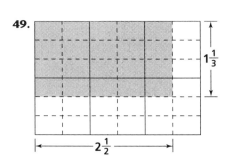

50.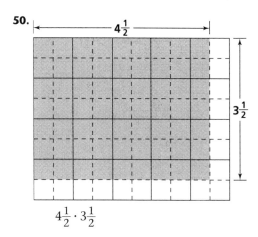

$$4\frac{1}{2} \cdot 3\frac{1}{2}$$

51.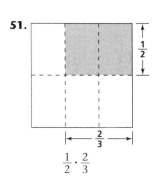

$$\frac{1}{2} \cdot \frac{2}{3}$$

52.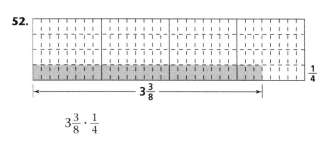

$$3\frac{3}{8} \cdot \frac{1}{4}$$

53.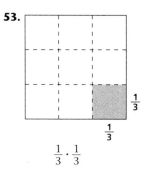

$$\frac{1}{3} \cdot \frac{1}{3}$$

54. $\frac{1}{2} \div \frac{2}{3} = \frac{1}{2} \cdot \frac{3}{2}$
$\qquad = \frac{3}{4}$

55. $7 \div 2\frac{1}{2} = \frac{7}{1} \div \frac{5}{2}$
$\qquad = \frac{7}{1} \cdot \frac{2}{5}$
$\qquad = \frac{14}{5}$
$\qquad = 2\frac{4}{5}$

56. $5 \div 1\frac{2}{3} = \frac{5}{1} \div \frac{5}{3}$
$\qquad = \frac{5}{1} \cdot \frac{3}{5}$
$\qquad = \frac{15}{5}$
$\qquad = 3$

57. $12 \div \frac{3}{4} = \frac{12}{1} \cdot \frac{4}{3}$
$\qquad = \frac{48}{3}$
$\qquad = 16$

58. $9 \div 2\frac{1}{4} = \frac{9}{1} \div \frac{9}{4}$
$\qquad = \frac{9}{1} \cdot \frac{4}{9}$
$\qquad = \frac{36}{9}$
$\qquad = 4$

59. $2\frac{2}{3} \div 8 = \frac{8}{3} \div \frac{8}{1}$
$\qquad = \frac{8}{3} \cdot \frac{1}{8}$
$\qquad = \frac{8}{24}$
$\qquad = \frac{1}{3}$

60. $3\frac{1}{3} \div 2 = \frac{10}{3} \div \frac{2}{1}$
$\qquad = \frac{10}{3} \cdot \frac{1}{2}$
$\qquad = \frac{10}{6}$
$\qquad = 1\frac{4}{6}$
$\qquad = 1\frac{2}{3}$

61. $10 \div 1\frac{2}{3} = \frac{10}{1} \div \frac{5}{3}$
$\qquad = \frac{10}{1} \cdot \frac{3}{5}$
$\qquad = \frac{30}{5}$
$\qquad = 6$

62. $4\frac{1}{2} \div 2\frac{1}{4} = \frac{9}{2} \div \frac{9}{4}$
$\qquad = \frac{9}{2} \cdot \frac{4}{9}$
$\qquad = \frac{36}{18}$
$\qquad = 2$

63. $3\frac{3}{4} \div 1\frac{2}{3} = \frac{15}{4} \div \frac{5}{3}$
$\qquad = \frac{15}{4} \cdot \frac{3}{5}$
$\qquad = \frac{45}{20}$
$\qquad = 2\frac{5}{20}$
$\qquad = 2\frac{1}{4}$

64. $1\frac{1}{2} \div 3 = \frac{3}{2} \div \frac{3}{1}$
$\qquad = \frac{3}{2} \cdot \frac{1}{3}$
$\qquad = \frac{3}{6}$
$\qquad = \frac{1}{2}$

65. $6\frac{1}{4} \div \frac{2}{3} = \frac{25}{4} \div \frac{2}{3}$
$\qquad = \frac{25}{4} \cdot \frac{3}{2}$
$\qquad = \frac{75}{8}$
$\qquad = 9\frac{3}{8}$

66. $3\frac{1}{5} \div \frac{4}{15} = \frac{16}{5} \div \frac{4}{15}$
$\qquad = \frac{16}{5} \cdot \frac{15}{4}$
$\qquad = \frac{4}{1} \cdot \frac{3}{1}$
$\qquad = 12$

67. $2\frac{1}{3} \div 1\frac{5}{6} = \frac{7}{3} \div \frac{11}{6}$
$\qquad = \frac{7}{3} \cdot \frac{6}{11}$
$\qquad = \frac{42}{33}$
$\qquad = 1\frac{9}{33}$
$\qquad = 1\frac{3}{11}$

68. $4\frac{1}{2} \div 2\frac{7}{10} = \frac{9}{2} \div \frac{27}{10}$
$\qquad = \frac{9}{2} \cdot \frac{10}{27}$
$\qquad = \frac{90}{54}$
$\qquad = 1\frac{36}{54}$
$\qquad = 1\frac{2}{3}$

69. $\frac{9}{10} \div 1\frac{1}{5} = \frac{9}{10} \div \frac{6}{5}$
$\qquad = \frac{9}{10} \cdot \frac{5}{6}$
$\qquad = \frac{45}{60}$
$\qquad = \frac{3}{4}$

70.

Sequence	4		9		16		25		[36]		[49]		[64]

First differences   5   7   9   11   13   15

Second differences   2   2   2   2   2

The next three terms in the sequence are 36, 49, and 64.

71. $76 \div 2 = 38$
$76 \div 4 = 19$
The greatest prime factor is 19.

72. $x + y \cdot z = -3 + 14 \cdot 2$
$= -3 + 28$
$= 25$

73. $y = 5x - 1$

x	1	2	3	4	5
y	4	9	14	19	24

74. $\left| -24 \right| = 24$

75. $(-4)(3)(-16) + (-8) = (-12)(-16) + (-8)$
$= 192 + (-8)$
$= 184$

76. $y = 2x - 1$

x	−3	−2	−1	0	1	2	3
y	−7	−5	−3	−1	1	3	5

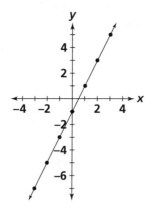

77. $y = 4 - x$

x	−3	−2	−1	0	1	2	3
y	7	6	5	4	3	2	1

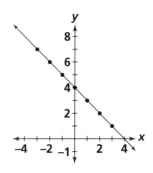

78. $y = 4x - 12$

x	−3	−2	−1	0	1	2	3
y	24	20	16	12	8	4	0

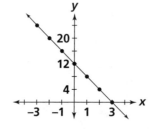

79. $\frac{1}{2} - \frac{4}{5} = \frac{1 \cdot 5}{2 \cdot 5} - \frac{4 \cdot 2}{5 \cdot 2}$
$= \frac{5}{10} - \frac{8}{10}$
$= -\frac{3}{10}$

80. $2\frac{2}{3} + 1\frac{7}{12} = \frac{8}{3} + \frac{19}{12}$
$= \frac{8 \cdot 4}{3 \cdot 4} + \frac{19}{12}$
$= \frac{32}{12} + \frac{19}{12}$
$= \frac{51}{12}$
$= 4\frac{3}{12}$
$= 4\frac{1}{4}$

81. $6 - \frac{3}{4} = \frac{24}{4} - \frac{3}{4}$
$= \frac{21}{4}$
$= 5\frac{1}{4}$

82. $Y = \frac{1}{X}$ can be used to make a list of reciprocals because for any X that is input, Y is its reciprocal, $\left(\frac{1}{X}\right)$.

For example:
$$X = 2 \Rightarrow Y = \frac{1}{2}$$
$$X = 3 \Rightarrow Y = \frac{1}{3}$$

83. There is an error message when X = 0 because $Y = \frac{1}{0}$ is undefined.

84. 0.5 can be rewritten as $\frac{1}{2}$. $\frac{1}{2}$ and 2 are reciprocals of each other.
$$X = \frac{1}{2} \Rightarrow Y = 2$$

3.6 PAGES 166–168, PRACTICE & APPLY

6. $\frac{3}{7} \cdot \frac{3}{3} = \frac{9}{21}$ **7.** $\frac{6}{8} = \frac{30}{40}$ **8.** $\frac{11}{12} = \frac{132}{144}$ **9.** $\frac{42}{54} = \frac{7}{9}$ **10.** $\frac{24}{27} = \frac{8}{9}$

11. $\frac{36}{42} = \frac{9}{10\frac{1}{2}}$ **12.** $\frac{48}{72} = \frac{6}{9}$ **13.** $\frac{49}{105} = \frac{7}{15}$ **14.** $\frac{3}{4} = \frac{30}{40}$ **15.** $\frac{49}{56} = \frac{7}{8}$

16. $\frac{63}{49} = \frac{9}{7}$ **17.** $\frac{20}{30} = \frac{2}{3}$ **18.** $\frac{72}{66} = \frac{12}{11}$ **19.** $\frac{3}{4} = \frac{123}{164}$ **20.** $\frac{75}{80} = \frac{15}{16}$

21. $\frac{65}{156} = \frac{5}{12}$

22. $\frac{3200}{55,600} = \frac{\text{number of households with at least two cars}}{\text{number of households surveyed}}$

$\frac{3200}{55,600} = \frac{32}{556} = \frac{16}{278} = \frac{8}{139}$ Reduced ratio

23. $\frac{1220}{55,600} = \frac{1220 \div 20}{55,600 \div 20} = \frac{61}{2780}$

24. $\frac{23,350}{55,600} = \frac{23,350 \div 50}{55,600 \div 50} = \frac{467}{1112}$

25. Let x represent the number of beef needed.
$$\frac{48}{2} = \frac{36}{x}$$
$$48x = 2 \cdot 36$$
$$\frac{48x}{48} = \frac{72}{48}$$
$$x = \frac{72}{48}$$
$$x = 1\frac{1}{2}$$
The width of the rectangle is 16 centimeters.

26. Let w represent the width of the rectangle.
$$\frac{3}{2} = \frac{24}{w}$$
$$3w = 2 \cdot 24$$
$$\frac{3w}{3} = \frac{48}{3}$$
$$w = 16$$
The width of the rectangle is 16 centimeters

27. Let h represent the number of expected hits.
$$\frac{3}{9} = \frac{h}{45}$$
$$9h = 45 \cdot 3$$
$$\frac{9h}{9} = \frac{135}{9}$$
$$h = 15$$
You would expect the baseball player to have 15 hits.

28. From the graph, the corresponding width is 6 feet.

29. From the graph, the corresponding width is 9 feet.

30. Let r represent the ratio of the length of the .
greenhouse to the width of the greenhouse.
$$r = \frac{\text{length}}{\text{width}} = \frac{12}{9} = \frac{4}{3}$$
The ratio of the length to the width is $\frac{4}{3}$.

31. The ratio of orange trees to grapefruit trees is $\frac{7}{4}$

32. Let x represent the number of grapefruit trees.
$$\frac{7}{4} = \frac{70}{x}$$
$$7x = 70 \cdot 4$$
$$\frac{7x}{7} = \frac{280}{7}$$
$$x = 40$$
The citrus grower should plant 40 grapefruit trees.

33. Let x represent the number of grapefruit trees.
$$\frac{7}{4} = \frac{98}{x}$$
$$7x = 98 \cdot 4$$
$$\frac{7x}{7} = \frac{392}{7}$$
$$x = 56$$
The citrus grower should plant 56 grapefruit trees.

34. Let x represent the number of orange trees.

$$\frac{7}{4} = \frac{x}{160}$$
$$4x = 160 \cdot 7$$
$$\frac{4x}{4} = \frac{1120}{4}$$
$$x = 280$$

The citrus grower should plant 280 orange trees.

35. Let $7x$ represent the number of orange trees, and let $4x$ represent the number of grapefruit trees.

$$7x + 4x = 264$$
$$11x = 264$$
$$\frac{11x}{11} = \frac{264}{11}$$
$$x = 24$$

Now substitute $x = 24$ into $7x$ and $4x$ to find the number of each kind of tree.

$$7x = 7(24) = 168$$
$$4x = 4(24) = 96$$

The citrus grower should plant 168 orange trees and 96 grapefruit trees.

36.

37. If the grower plants 28 orange trees, 16 grapefruit trees will be planted.

38. The ratio of missed serves to successful serves is $\frac{1}{4}$.

39. The ratio of successful serves to the total number of attempts is $\frac{4}{5}$.

40. Let x represent the number of successful serves.

$$\frac{4}{5} = \frac{x}{30}$$
$$5x = 4 \cdot 30$$
$$\frac{5x}{5} = \frac{120}{5}$$
$$x = 24$$

24 successful serves would be expected.

41.

42. 12 successful serves can be expected from 15 attempts.

43.

Length	Width	Ratio of dimensions
5	3	$\frac{5}{3} \approx 1.667$
8	5	$\frac{8}{5} = 1.6$
13	8	$\frac{13}{8} = 1.625$
21	13	$\frac{21}{13} \approx 1.615385$
34	21	$\frac{34}{21} \approx 1.619048$
55	34	$\frac{55}{34} \approx 1.617647$
89	55	$\frac{89}{55} \approx 1.618182$
144	89	$\frac{144}{89} \approx 1.617978$

44.

Sequence	32		44		56		68		80		92
First difference		12		12		12		12		12	

Let x represent the number of hours the plumber worked, and let y represent the plumber's fee.

$$y = 32 + 12(x - 1)$$
$$y = 32 + 12x - 12$$
$$y = 32 - 12 + 12x$$
$$y = 20 + 12x$$
$$y = 12x + 20$$

45. $-5 < 4; -5 + x = 4$
$$-5 + x = 4$$
$$5 + (-5) + x = 5 + 4$$
$$x = 9$$
Since x is positive, $-5 < 4$.

46. $-7 < -3; -7 + x = -3$
$$-7 + x = -3$$
$$7 + (-7) + x = 7 + (-3)$$
$$x = 4$$
Since x is positive, $-7 < -3$.

47. $y = 2x + 3$

x	−2	−1	0	1	2	3	4
y	−1	1	3	5	7	9	11

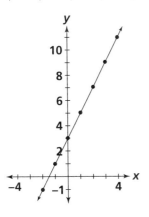

48. $y = 3x - 1$

x	−2	−1	0	1	2	3	4
y	−7	−4	−1	2	5	8	11

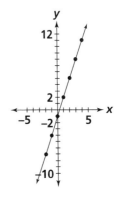

49. $13\frac{5}{8}$
$$13\frac{3}{4} = 13\frac{3 \cdot 2}{4 \cdot 2} = 13\frac{6}{8}$$
$$13\frac{3}{4} > 13\frac{5}{8}$$
The board that is $13\frac{3}{4}$ feet long is longer.

50. There is only one 5 on the 6-sided cube, so 5 can be expected 1 time.

51. There are 3 even numbers on the 6-sided cube, so an even number can be expected 3 times.

3.7 **PAGES 174–175, PRACTICE & APPLY**

6. $20\% = \frac{1}{5}$

0				1
$\frac{1}{5}$	$\frac{1}{5}$	$\frac{1}{5}$	$\frac{1}{5}$	$\frac{1}{5}$

7. $60\% = \frac{3}{5}$

0				1
$\frac{1}{5}$	$\frac{1}{5}$	$\frac{1}{5}$	$\frac{1}{5}$	$\frac{1}{5}$

8. $90\% = \frac{9}{10}$

9. $75\% = \frac{3}{4}$

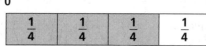

10. $125\% = 1\frac{1}{4}$

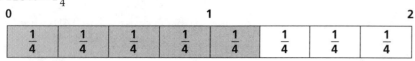

11. $140\% = 1\frac{2}{5}$

12. 80%

13. $\frac{2}{3} \approx 66.67\%$

14. 75%

15. $\frac{6}{9} \approx 66.67\%$

16. $0.8 \times 100 = 80\%$

17. $0.9 \times 100 = 90\%$

18. $0.82 \times 100 = 82\%$

19. $0.16 \times 100 = 16\%$

20. $3.5 \times 100 = 350\%$

21. $7.2 \times 100 = 720\%$

22. $0.815 \times 100 = 81.5\%$

23. $0.128 \times 100 = 12.8\%$

24. $0.359 \times 100 = 35.9\%$

25. $2.89 \times 100 = 289\%$

26. $8.14 \times 100 = 814\%$

27. $7.035 \times 100 = 703.5\%$

28. $1.133 \times 100 = 113.3\%$

29. $1.055 \times 100 = 105.5\%$

30. $0.1 \times 100 = 10\%$

31. $0.01 \times 100 = 1\%$

32. $0.546 \times 100 = 54.6\%$

33. $8.15 \times 100 = 815\%$

For Exercises 34–45, change the fraction to a decimal. Then multiply each decimal by 100, and add a percent sign.

34. $\frac{7}{8} = 0.875 \times 100 = 87.5\%$

35. $\frac{3}{4} = 0.75 \times 100 = 75\%$

36. $\frac{7}{12} = 0.583 \times 100 = 58.3\%$

37. $\frac{5}{6} = 0.833 \times 100 = 83.3\%$

38. $3\frac{9}{20} = \frac{69}{20}$

$\frac{69}{20} = 3.45 \times 100 = 345\%$

39. $2\frac{7}{10} = \frac{27}{10}$

$\frac{27}{10} = 2.7 \times 100 = 270\%$

40. $\frac{9}{12} = 0.75 \times 100 = 75\%$

41. $\frac{2}{3} = 0.667 \times 100 = 66.7\%$

42. $\frac{125}{150} = 0.5 \times 100 = 50\%$

43. $\frac{4}{5} = 0.8 \times 100 = 80\%$

44. $\frac{1}{8} = 0.125 \times 100 = 12.5\%$

45. $\frac{1}{5} = 0.2 \times 100 = 20\%$

46. Let x represent the number of students expected to pass the state exam.

$x = 79\% \cdot 1988$

$x = 0.79 \cdot 1988$

$x = 1570.52$

About 1570 students are expected to pass the state exam.

47. Let x represent the expected number of robberies or burglaries.

$x = 48\% \cdot 263$

$x = 0.48 \cdot 263$

$x = 126.24$

About 126 robberies or burglaries can be expected.

48. Let x represent the amount of salary increase.

$x = 9\% \cdot 1498.78$

New Salary

$1498.78 + 134.89 = \$1633.67$

$x = 0.09 \cdot 1498.78$

$x = 134.89$

The salary will increase by \$134.89. The employees new salary will be \$1633.67.

49. Let x represent the retail price increase.

$x = 35\% \cdot 239$

$x = 0.35 \cdot 239$

$x = 83.65$

The retail price will increase by \$83.65.

50. Let x represent the profit yield for the year.

$x = 9.8\% \cdot 4050$

$x = 0.098 \cdot 4050$

$x = 396.90$

The profit yield for the year will be \$396.90.

PAGE 175, LOOK BACK

51. $w = 9.50h$

52.

Sequence	1		5		12		22		35
First differences		4		7		10		13	
Second differences			3		3		3		

The second differences of the sequence are a constant 3.

53. Because the second differences of the sequence are constant, the function is quadratic.

PAGE 175, LOOK BEYOND

54. There are two sides to a coin, so you can expect heads to appear $\frac{1}{2}$ of the time. In 10 tosses you would expect the coin to land heads $\frac{1}{2}$ of the time, or $10\left(\frac{1}{2}\right) = 5$ times. This reasoning involves the use of the rational number $\frac{1}{2}$.

3.8 PAGES 183–184, PRACTICE & APPLY

7. Toss 4 coins, recording the result of each coin. One toss of all 4 coins represents 1 trial. Repeat for 10 trials. Count the number of trials where 4 heads or 4 tails show up. Divide the number by 10. The quotient represents the experimental probability.

8. Roll 2 number cubes. Record the results. This represents 1 trial. Repeat for 10 trials. Count the number of trials where at least 1 cube shows a 6. Divide the number by 10. The quotient represents the experimental probability.

9. Yes; both Fred and Ted will have the same results if all trials were successful or if all trials were unsuccessful. For example:
$\frac{15}{15} = \frac{16}{16}$ or $\frac{0}{15} = \frac{0}{16}$

For Exercises 10–13, let P represent the experimental probability, f the number of succussful events, and t the total number of trials. Then $P = \frac{f}{t}$, where $t = 20$.

10. Trials 2, 3, 5, 7, 14, 18, and 20 show results of 2 heads or 2 tails, so $f = 7$.
$$P = \frac{7}{20}$$
The probability of both coins showing heads or tails is $\frac{7}{20}$.

11. Trials 2, 3, 14, 18, and 20 show results of 2 heads. So $f = 5$.
$$P = \frac{5}{20}, \text{ or } \frac{1}{4}$$
The probability of both coins showing heads is $\frac{1}{4}$.

12. Trials 1, 2, 3, 4, 6, 8, 9, 10, 11, 12, 13, 14, 15, 16, 17, 18, 19 and 20 show results of at least 1 head, so $f = 18$.
$$P = \frac{18}{20}, \text{ or } \frac{9}{10}$$
The probability of at least 1 heads showing up is $\frac{9}{10}$.

13. Trials 5 and 7 show results of neither coin coming up heads, so $f = 2$.
$$P = \frac{2}{20}, \text{ or } \frac{1}{10}$$
The probability of obtaining no heads (or 2 tails) is $\frac{1}{10}$.

For Exercises 14 and 15, let $t = 10$.

14. Trials 3, 7, 8, and 9 show results where both numbers are less than 80, so $f = 4$.
$$P = \frac{4}{10}, \text{ or } \frac{2}{5}$$
The probability of both numbers being less than 80 is $\frac{2}{5}$.

15. Trials 1, 3, 4, 5, 8, and 10 show results where the first number is greater than the second, so $f = 6$.
$$P = \frac{6}{10}, \text{ or } \frac{3}{5}$$
The probability of the first number being greater than the second is $\frac{3}{5}$.

For questions 16–23, the number of trials chosen may vary. Answers may vary.

16. Toss a coin, and record the result. Repeat for 10 trials. Divide the number of trials in which tails show up by 10.

17. Toss a coin twice; record the result of each toss. Repeat for 10 trials. Divide the number of trials in which 2 tails show up by 10.

18. Roll a number cube; record the result. Repeat for 20 trials. Divide the number of trials in which a 3, 4, 5, or 6 shows up by 20.

19. Roll a number cube; record the result. Repeat for 20 trials. Divide the number of trials in which a 3 or 6 shows up by 20.

20. Roll 2 number cubes; record the result. Repeat for 40 trials. Divide the number of trials in which an odd sum shows up by 40.

21. Roll 2 number cubes; record the result. Repeat for 40 trials. Divide the number of trials in which the same number shows up on both cubes by 40.

22. Toss a coin 5 times; record the result after each toss. Repeat for 40 trials. Divide the number of trials in which at least 3 heads or at least 3 tails appear in a row by 40.

23. Toss a coin 5 times; record the result after each toss. Repeat for 40 trials. Divide the number of trials in which heads and tails alternate by 40.

24. RAND*2 output: numbers between 0 and 2, including 0, but not including 2

25. INT(RAND*2) output: integers 0 and 1

26. INT(RAND*2) + 1 output: integers 1 and 2

27. 100*(INT(RAND*2) + 1) output: integers 100 and 200

28. INT(RAND*5) + 10 output: 10, 11, 12, 13, and 14. Five different numbers are generated.

29. The smallest number of the five numbers is 10.

30. The greatest number of the five numbers is 14.

31. For an output of 0, 1, or 2, input INT(RAND*3).

32. For an output of 0, 1, 2, 3, 4, 5, 6, 7, 8, or 9, input INT(RAND*10).

33. For an output of 1, 2, 3, 4, 5, or 6, input INT(RAND*6) + 1.

34. For an output of 1, 2, 3, 4, 5, 6, 7, 8, 9, or 10, input INT(RAND*10) + 1.

PAGE 185, LOOK BACK

35. $y = 2x + 3$

x	0	1	2	3	4	5	6
y	3	5	7	9	11	13	15

36. Substitute 95 for c, and solve for m.
$$95 = 27 + 0.25m$$
$$95 - 27 = 27 - 27 + 0.25m$$
$$68 = 0.25m$$
$$\frac{68}{0.25} = \frac{0.25m}{0.25}$$
$$272 = m$$
You can drive 272 miles.

37. Answers may vary. The area of the playing field is approximately 130×70, or 9100 square yards.

38. $368 \div 2 = 184$
$184 \div 2 = 92$
$92 \div 2 = 46$ $\qquad 368 = 2^4 \cdot 23$
$46 \div 2 = 23$

39. $(19 + 21) + 22 = 40 + 22$
$= 62$

40.

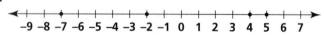

41. $-1 = 4 - x$

Try $x = 3$.
$-1 = 4 - x$
$1 = 4 - 3$

3 is too small. Try a larger number.

Try $x = 6$.
$-1 = 4 - x$
$-2 = 4 - 6$

6 is too large. Try a smaller number.

Try $x = 5$.
$-1 = 4 - x$
$-1 = 4 - 5$

5 is the correct number; $x = 5$.

42. $x + 5 = -2$

Try $x = -5$.
$x + 5 = -2$
$-5 + 5 = 0$

-5 is too large. Try a smaller number.

Try $x = -10$.
$x + 5 = -2$
$-10 + 5 = -5$

-10 is too small. Try a larger number.

Try $x = -7$.
$x + 5 = -2$
$-7 + 5 = -2$

-7 is the correct number; $x = -7$.

43. $2x + 1 = 1$

Try $x = 1$.
$2x + 1 = 1$
$2(1) + 1 = 3$

1 is too large.
Try a smaller number.

Try $x = -1$.
$2x + 1 = 1$
$2(-1) + 1 = -1$

−1 is too small.
Try a larger number.

Try $x = 0$.
$2x + 1 = 1$
$2(0) + 1 = 1$

0 is the correct number; $x = 0$.

44.

Sequence	1		5		14		30		55		[91]		[140]		[204]
First differences		4		9		16		25		[36]		[49]		[64]	
Second differences			5		7		9		[11]		[13]		[15]		
Third differences				2		2		[2]		[2]		[2]			

The next three terms in the sequence are 91, 140, and 204.

45.

Sequence	[−9]		[−3]		[5]		15		27
First differences		[6]		[8]		[10]		[12]	
Second differences			[2]		[2]		2		

The first three terms of the sequence are −9, −3 and 5.

46. $0.25 = \dfrac{1}{4} = \dfrac{2}{8}$

$\dfrac{2}{8} < \dfrac{3}{8}$

$0.25 < \dfrac{3}{8}$

47. $\dfrac{7}{100} = 0.07 \qquad \dfrac{3}{15} = 0.20$

$\dfrac{7}{100} < \dfrac{3}{15}$

48. $121.01 = 121.01$
$121.2 = 121.20$
$121.01 < 121.2$

49. $\dfrac{3}{4} + \left(-\dfrac{1}{8}\right) + \left(-\dfrac{3}{4}\right) + \left(-\dfrac{3}{8}\right) + \dfrac{1}{2} = \dfrac{6}{8} - \dfrac{1}{8} - \dfrac{6}{8} - \dfrac{3}{8} + \dfrac{4}{8} = 0$
The net change in the stock was 0.

50. The estimated number of students who voted for Sam was 60%.

$\dfrac{240}{400} = 0.6 \times 100 = 60\%$

PAGE 185, LOOK BEYOND

51. The red cube has 6 numbers. The green cube has 6 numbers. There are 36 possible pairs.

52. There are only 2 pairs that have a sum of 3: 1 and 2, and 2 and 1.

53. $1^2 - 0^2 = (1 - 0)(1 + 0) = (1)(1) = 1$

54. $2^2 - 1^2 = (2 - 1)(2 + 1) = (1)(3) = 3$

55. $3^2 - 2^2 = (3 - 2)(3 + 2) = (1)(5) = 5$

56. $4^2 - 3^2 = (4 - 3)(4 + 3) = (1)(7) = 7$

57. $5^2 - 4^2 = (5 - 4)(5 + 4) = (1)(9) = 9$

58. $6^2 - 5^2 = (6 - 5)(6 + 5) = (1)(11) = 11$

59. $100^2 - 99^2 = (100 - 99)(100 + 99)$
$= (1)(199) = 199$

60. $a^2 - (a - 1)^2 = [a - (a - 1)][a + (a - 1)]$
$= (a - a + 1)(a + a - 1)$
$= 1(2a - 1)$
$= 2a - 1$

3.9 PAGES 193–195, PRACTICE & APPLY

For Exercises 6–15 use the following chart to determine the theoretical probability of drawing one particular marble from the bag:

R	R	R	R	R	R	G	G	G	G	Y	Y

6. $P(G) = \dfrac{4}{12} = \dfrac{1}{3}$

R	R	R	R	R	R	G	G	G	G	Y	Y

7. $P(R) = \dfrac{6}{12} = \dfrac{1}{2}$

R	R	R	R	R	R	G	G	G	G	Y	Y

8. $P(Y) = \frac{2}{12} = \frac{1}{6}$

R	R	R	R	R	R	G	G	G	G	Y	Y

9. $P(not\ G) = \frac{8}{12} = \frac{2}{3}$

R	R	R	R	R	R	G	G	G	G	Y	Y

10. $P(not\ R) = \frac{6}{12} = \frac{1}{2}$

R	R	R	R	R	R	G	G	G	G	Y	Y

11. $P(not\ Y) = \frac{10}{12} = \frac{5}{6}$

R	R	R	R	R	R	G	G	G	G	Y	Y

12. $P(G\ or\ R) = \frac{10}{12} = \frac{5}{6}$

R	R	R	R	R	R	G	G	G	G	Y	Y

13. $P(G\ or\ Y) = \frac{6}{12} = \frac{1}{2}$

R	R	R	R	R	R	G	G	G	G	Y	Y

14. $P(R\ or\ Y) = \frac{8}{12} = \frac{2}{3}$

R	R	R	R	R	R	G	G	G	G	Y	Y

15. $P(G) + P(R) + P(Y) \overset{?}{=} 1$

$P(G) = \frac{1}{3} \qquad P(R) = \frac{1}{2} \qquad P(Y) = \frac{1}{6}$

$$\frac{1}{6} + \frac{1}{2} + \frac{1}{3} = \frac{1}{6} + \frac{3}{6} + \frac{2}{6}$$
$$= \frac{4}{6} + \frac{2}{6}$$
$$= \frac{6}{6}$$
$$= 1$$

16. Answers will vary but should be close to the respective theoretical probabilities.

17. Probability $= \frac{3}{6} = \frac{1}{2}$

1	2	3	4	5	6

18. Probability $= \frac{27}{36} = \frac{3}{4}$

	1	2	3	4	5	6
1	1,1	1,2	1,3	1,4	1,5	1,6
2	2,1	2,2	2,3	2,4	2,5	2,6
3	3,1	3,2	3,3	3,4	3,5	3,6
4	4,1	4,2	4,3	4,4	4,5	4,6
5	5,1	5,2	5,3	5,4	5,5	5,6
6	6,1	6,2	6,3	6,4	6,5	6,6

19. Probability $= \frac{18}{36} = \frac{1}{2}$

	1	2	3	4	5	6
1	1,1	1,2	1,3	1,4	1,5	1,6
2	2,1	2,2	2,3	2,4	2,5	2,6
3	3,1	3,2	3,3	3,4	3,5	3,6
4	4,1	4,2	4,3	4,4	4,5	4,6
5	5,1	5,2	5,3	5,4	5,5	5,6
6	6,1	6,2	6,3	6,4	6,5	6,6

20. Probability $= \frac{20}{36} = \frac{5}{9}$

	1	2	3	4	5	6
1	1,1	1,2	1,3	1,4	1,5	1,6
2	2,1	2,2	2,3	2,4	2,5	2,6
3	3,1	3,2	3,3	3,4	3,5	3,6
4	4,1	4,2	4,3	4,4	4,5	4,6
5	5,1	5,2	5,3	5,4	5,5	5,6
6	6,1	6,2	6,3	6,4	6,5	6,6

21. Probability $= \frac{1}{12}$

	1	2	3	4	5	6
H	H1	H2	H3	H4	H5	H6
T	T1	T2	T3	T4	T5	T6

22. Probability $= \frac{1}{12}$

	1	2	3	4	5	6
H	H1	H2	H3	H4	H5	H6
T	T1	T2	T3	T4	T5	T6

23. Probability $= 0$

Since it is impossible to roll a 7 on an ordinary number cube, the probability is 0.

24. $P(A) = \frac{1}{4}$

A	B	C	D

25. $P(B\ or\ C) = \frac{2}{4} = \frac{1}{2}$

A	B	C	D

26. $P(D\ and\ A) = \frac{2}{16} = \frac{1}{8}$

	A	B	C	D
A	AA	AB	AC	AD
B	BA	BB	BC	BD
C	CA	CB	CC	CD
D	DA	DB	DC	DD

27. $P(B\ or\ C) = \frac{12}{16} = \frac{3}{4}$

	A	B	C	D
A	AA	AB	AC	AD
B	BA	BB	BC	BD
C	CA	CB	CC	CD
D	DA	DB	DC	DD

28. Probability $= \frac{7}{16}$

	A	B	C	D
A	AA	AB	AC	AD
B	BA	BB	BC	BD
C	CA	CB	CC	CD
D	DA	DB	DC	DD

29. Probability $= \frac{1}{16}$

	A	B	C	D
A	AA	AB	AC	AD
B	BA	BB	BC	BD
C	CA	CB	CC	CD
D	DA	DB	DC	DD

30. independent events; $P(\text{R, then R}) = \dfrac{36}{144} = \dfrac{1}{4}$

2nd Draw

	R	R	R	R	R	R	G	G	G	G	Y	Y
R	R,R	R,R	R,R	R,R	R,R	R,R	R,G	R,G	R,G	R,G	R,Y	R,Y
R	R,R	R,R	R,R	R,R	R,R	R,R	R,G	R,G	R,G	R,G	R,Y	R,Y
R	R,R	R,R	R,R	R,R	R,R	R,R	R,G	R,G	R,G	R,G	R,Y	R,Y
R	R,R	R,R	R,R	R,R	R,R	R,R	R,G	R,G	R,G	R,G	R,Y	R,Y
R	R,R	R,R	R,R	R,R	R,R	R,R	R,G	R,G	R,G	R,G	R,Y	R,Y
R	R,R	R,R	R,R	R,R	R,R	R,R	R,G	R,G	R,G	R,G	R,Y	R,Y
G	G,R	G,R	G,R	G,R	G,R	G,R	G,G	G,G	G,G	G,G	G,Y	G,Y
G	G,R	G,R	G,R	G,R	G,R	G,R	G,G	G,G	G,G	G,G	G,Y	G,Y
G	G,R	G,R	G,R	G,R	G,R	G,R	G,G	G,G	G,G	G,G	G,Y	G,Y
G	G,R	G,R	G,R	G,R	G,R	G,R	G,G	G,G	G,G	G,G	G,Y	G,Y
Y	Y,R	Y,R	Y,R	Y,R	Y,R	Y,R	Y,G	Y,G	Y,G	Y,G	Y,Y	Y,Y
Y	Y,R	Y,R	Y,R	Y,R	Y,R	Y,R	Y,G	Y,G	Y,G	Y,G	Y,Y	Y,Y

1st Draw

dependent events; $P(\text{R, then R}) = \dfrac{30}{132} = \dfrac{5}{22}$

2nd Draw

	R	R	R	R	R	G	G	G	G	Y	Y
R	R,R	R,R	R,R	R,R	R,R	R,G	R,G	R,G	R,G	R,Y	R,Y
R	R,R	R,R	R,R	R,R	R,R	R,G	R,G	R,G	R,G	R,Y	R,Y
R	R,R	R,R	R,R	R,R	R,R	R,G	R,G	R,G	R,G	R,Y	R,Y
R	R,R	R,R	R,R	R,R	R,R	R,G	R,G	R,G	R,G	R,Y	R,Y
R	R,R	R,R	R,R	R,R	R,R	R,G	R,G	R,G	R,G	R,Y	R,Y
R	R,R	R,R	R,R	R,R	R,R	R,G	R,G	R,G	R,G	R,Y	R,Y
G	G,R	G,R	G,R	G,R	G,R	G,G	G,G	G,G	G,G	G,Y	G,Y
G	G,R	G,R	G,R	G,R	G,R	G,G	G,G	G,G	G,G	G,Y	G,Y
G	G,R	G,R	G,R	G,R	G,R	G,G	G,G	G,G	G,G	G,Y	G,Y
G	G,R	G,R	G,R	G,R	G,R	G,G	G,G	G,G	G,G	G,Y	G,Y
Y	Y,R	Y,R	Y,R	Y,R	Y,R	Y,G	Y,G	Y,G	Y,G	Y,Y	Y,Y
Y	Y,R	Y,R	Y,R	Y,R	Y,R	Y,G	Y,G	Y,G	Y,G	Y,Y	Y,Y

1st Draw

31. independent events; $P(\text{R, then G}) = \dfrac{24}{144} = \dfrac{1}{6}$

2nd Draw

	R	R	R	R	R	R	G	G	G	G	Y	Y
R	R,R	R,R	R,R	R,R	R,R	R,R	R,G	R,G	R,G	R,G	R,Y	R,Y
R	R,R	R,R	R,R	R,R	R,R	R,R	R,G	R,G	R,G	R,G	R,Y	R,Y
R	R,R	R,R	R,R	R,R	R,R	R,R	R,G	R,G	R,G	R,G	R,Y	R,Y
R	R,R	R,R	R,R	R,R	R,R	R,R	R,G	R,G	R,G	R,G	R,Y	R,Y
R	R,R	R,R	R,R	R,R	R,R	R,R	R,G	R,G	R,G	R,G	R,Y	R,Y
R	R,R	R,R	R,R	R,R	R,R	R,R	R,G	R,G	R,G	R,G	R,Y	R,Y
G	G,R	G,R	G,R	G,R	G,R	G,R	G,G	G,G	G,G	G,G	G,Y	G,Y
G	G,R	G,R	G,R	G,R	G,R	G,R	G,G	G,G	G,G	G,G	G,Y	G,Y
G	G,R	G,R	G,R	G,R	G,R	G,R	G,G	G,G	G,G	G,G	G,Y	G,Y
G	G,R	G,R	G,R	G,R	G,R	G,R	G,G	G,G	G,G	G,G	G,Y	G,Y
Y	Y,R	Y,R	Y,R	Y,R	Y,R	Y,R	Y,G	Y,G	Y,G	Y,G	Y,Y	Y,Y
Y	Y,R	Y,R	Y,R	Y,R	Y,R	Y,R	Y,G	Y,G	Y,G	Y,G	Y,Y	Y,Y

1st Draw

dependent events; $P(\text{R, then G}) = \dfrac{24}{132} = \dfrac{2}{11}$

2nd Draw

	R	R	R	R	R	G	G	G	G	Y	Y
R	R,R	R,R	R,R	R,R	R,R	R,G	R,G	R,G	R,G	R,Y	R,Y
R	R,R	R,R	R,R	R,R	R,R	R,G	R,G	R,G	R,G	R,Y	R,Y
R	R,R	R,R	R,R	R,R	R,R	R,G	R,G	R,G	R,G	R,Y	R,Y
R	R,R	R,R	R,R	R,R	R,R	R,G	R,G	R,G	R,G	R,Y	R,Y
R	R,R	R,R	R,R	R,R	R,R	R,G	R,G	R,G	R,G	R,Y	R,Y
R	R,R	R,R	R,R	R,R	R,R	R,G	R,G	R,G	R,G	R,Y	R,Y
G	G,R	G,R	G,R	G,R	G,R	G,G	G,G	G,G	G,G	G,Y	G,Y
G	G,R	G,R	G,R	G,R	G,R	G,G	G,G	G,G	G,G	G,Y	G,Y
G	G,R	G,R	G,R	G,R	G,R	G,G	G,G	G,G	G,G	G,Y	G,Y
G	G,R	G,R	G,R	G,R	G,R	G,G	G,G	G,G	G,G	G,Y	G,Y
Y	Y,R	Y,R	Y,R	Y,R	Y,R	Y,G	Y,G	Y,G	Y,G	Y,Y	Y,Y
Y	Y,R	Y,R	Y,R	Y,R	Y,R	Y,G	Y,G	Y,G	Y,G	Y,Y	Y,Y

1st Draw

32. independent events; $P(\text{R, then Y}) = \dfrac{12}{144} = \dfrac{1}{12}$

2nd Draw

	R	R	R	R	R	R	G	G	G	G	Y	Y
R	R,R	R,R	R,R	R,R	R,R	R,R	R,G	R,G	R,G	R,G	R,Y	R,Y
R	R,R	R,R	R,R	R,R	R,R	R,R	R,G	R,G	R,G	R,G	R,Y	R,Y
R	R,R	R,R	R,R	R,R	R,R	R,R	R,G	R,G	R,G	R,G	R,Y	R,Y
R	R,R	R,R	R,R	R,R	R,R	R,R	R,G	R,G	R,G	R,G	R,Y	R,Y
R	R,R	R,R	R,R	R,R	R,R	R,R	R,G	R,G	R,G	R,G	R,Y	R,Y
R	R,R	R,R	R,R	R,R	R,R	R,R	R,G	R,G	R,G	R,G	R,Y	R,Y
G	G,R	G,R	G,R	G,R	G,R	G,R	G,G	G,G	G,G	G,G	G,Y	G,Y
G	G,R	G,R	G,R	G,R	G,R	G,R	G,G	G,G	G,G	G,G	G,Y	G,Y
G	G,R	G,R	G,R	G,R	G,R	G,R	G,G	G,G	G,G	G,G	G,Y	G,Y
G	G,R	G,R	G,R	G,R	G,R	G,R	G,G	G,G	G,G	G,G	G,Y	G,Y
Y	Y,R	Y,R	Y,R	Y,R	Y,R	Y,R	Y,G	Y,G	Y,G	Y,G	Y,Y	Y,Y
Y	Y,R	Y,R	Y,R	Y,R	Y,R	Y,R	Y,G	Y,G	Y,G	Y,G	Y,Y	Y,Y

1st Draw

dependent events; $P(\text{R, then Y}) = \dfrac{12}{132} = \dfrac{1}{11}$

2nd Draw

	R	R	R	R	R	G	G	G	G	Y	Y
R	R,R	R,R	R,R	R,R	R,R	R,G	R,G	R,G	R,G	R,Y	R,Y
R	R,R	R,R	R,R	R,R	R,R	R,G	R,G	R,G	R,G	R,Y	R,Y
R	R,R	R,R	R,R	R,R	R,R	R,G	R,G	R,G	R,G	R,Y	R,Y
R	R,R	R,R	R,R	R,R	R,R	R,G	R,G	R,G	R,G	R,Y	R,Y
R	R,R	R,R	R,R	R,R	R,R	R,G	R,G	R,G	R,G	R,Y	R,Y
R	R,R	R,R	R,R	R,R	R,R	R,G	R,G	R,G	R,G	R,Y	R,Y
G	G,R	G,R	G,R	G,R	G,R	G,G	G,G	G,G	G,G	G,Y	G,Y
G	G,R	G,R	G,R	G,R	G,R	G,G	G,G	G,G	G,G	G,Y	G,Y
G	G,R	G,R	G,R	G,R	G,R	G,G	G,G	G,G	G,G	G,Y	G,Y
G	G,R	G,R	G,R	G,R	G,R	G,G	G,G	G,G	G,G	G,Y	G,Y
Y	Y,R	Y,R	Y,R	Y,R	Y,R	Y,G	Y,G	Y,G	Y,G	Y,Y	Y,Y
Y	Y,R	Y,R	Y,R	Y,R	Y,R	Y,G	Y,G	Y,G	Y,G	Y,Y	Y,Y

1st Draw

33. independent events; $P(G, \text{ then } R) = \dfrac{24}{144} = \dfrac{1}{6}$

2nd Draw

1st Draw	R	R	R	R	R	R	G	G	G	G	Y	Y
R	R,R	R,R	R,R	R,R	R,R	R,R	R,G	R,G	R,G	R,G	R,Y	R,Y
R	R,R	R,R	R,R	R,R	R,R	R,R	R,G	R,G	R,G	R,G	R,Y	R,Y
R	R,R	R,R	R,R	R,R	R,R	R,R	R,G	R,G	R,G	R,G	R,Y	R,Y
R	R,R	R,R	R,R	R,R	R,R	R,R	R,G	R,G	R,G	R,G	R,Y	R,Y
R	R,R	R,R	R,R	R,R	R,R	R,R	R,G	R,G	R,G	R,G	R,Y	R,Y
R	R,R	R,R	R,R	R,R	R,R	R,R	R,G	R,G	R,G	R,G	R,Y	R,Y
G	G,R	G,R	G,R	G,R	G,R	G,R	G,G	G,G	G,G	G,G	G,Y	G,Y
G	G,R	G,R	G,R	G,R	G,R	G,R	G,G	G,G	G,G	G,G	G,Y	G,Y
G	G,R	G,R	G,R	G,R	G,R	G,R	G,G	G,G	G,G	G,G	G,Y	G,Y
G	G,R	G,R	G,R	G,R	G,R	G,R	G,G	G,G	G,G	G,G	G,Y	G,Y
Y	Y,R	Y,R	Y,R	Y,R	Y,R	Y,R	Y,G	Y,G	Y,G	Y,G	Y,Y	Y,Y
Y	Y,R	Y,R	Y,R	Y,R	Y,R	Y,R	Y,G	Y,G	Y,G	Y,G	Y,Y	Y,Y

(The G,R cells are shaded.)

dependent events; $P(G, \text{ then } R) = \dfrac{24}{132} = \dfrac{2}{11}$

2nd Draw

1st Draw	R	R	R	R	R	R	G	G	G	G	Y	Y
R	R,R	R,R	R,R	R,R	R,R	R,G	R,G	R,G	R,G	R,Y	R,Y	
R	R,R	R,R	R,R	R,R	R,R	R,G	R,G	R,G	R,G	R,Y	R,Y	
R	R,R	R,R	R,R	R,R	R,R	R,G	R,G	R,G	R,G	R,Y	R,Y	
R	R,R	R,R	R,R	R,R	R,R	R,G	R,G	R,G	R,G	R,Y	R,Y	
R	R,R	R,R	R,R	R,R	R,R	R,G	R,G	R,G	R,G	R,Y	R,Y	
R	R,R	R,R	R,R	R,R	R,R	R,G	R,G	R,G	R,G	R,Y	R,Y	
G	G,R	G,R	G,R	G,R	G,R	G,R	G,G	G,G	G,G	G,Y	G,Y	
G	G,R	G,R	G,R	G,R	G,R	G,R	G,G	G,G	G,G	G,Y	G,Y	
G	G,R	G,R	G,R	G,R	G,R	G,R	G,G	G,G	G,G	G,Y	G,Y	
G	G,R	G,R	G,R	G,R	G,R	G,R	G,G	G,G	G,G	G,Y	G,Y	
Y	Y,R	Y,R	Y,R	Y,R	Y,R	Y,R	Y,G	Y,G	Y,G	Y,G	Y,Y	
Y	Y,R	Y,R	Y,R	Y,R	Y,R	Y,R	Y,G	Y,G	Y,G	Y,G	Y,Y	

(The G,R cells are shaded.)

34. independent events; $P(G, \text{ then } G) = \dfrac{16}{144} = \dfrac{1}{9}$

2nd Draw

1st Draw	R	R	R	R	R	R	G	G	G	G	Y	Y
R	R,R	R,R	R,R	R,R	R,R	R,R	R,G	R,G	R,G	R,G	R,Y	R,Y
R	R,R	R,R	R,R	R,R	R,R	R,R	R,G	R,G	R,G	R,G	R,Y	R,Y
R	R,R	R,R	R,R	R,R	R,R	R,R	R,G	R,G	R,G	R,G	R,Y	R,Y
R	R,R	R,R	R,R	R,R	R,R	R,R	R,G	R,G	R,G	R,G	R,Y	R,Y
R	R,R	R,R	R,R	R,R	R,R	R,R	R,G	R,G	R,G	R,G	R,Y	R,Y
R	R,R	R,R	R,R	R,R	R,R	R,R	R,G	R,G	R,G	R,G	R,Y	R,Y
G	G,R	G,R	G,R	G,R	G,R	G,R	G,G	G,G	G,G	G,G	G,Y	G,Y
G	G,R	G,R	G,R	G,R	G,R	G,R	G,G	G,G	G,G	G,G	G,Y	G,Y
G	G,R	G,R	G,R	G,R	G,R	G,R	G,G	G,G	G,G	G,G	G,Y	G,Y
G	G,R	G,R	G,R	G,R	G,R	G,R	G,G	G,G	G,G	G,G	G,Y	G,Y
Y	Y,R	Y,R	Y,R	Y,R	Y,R	Y,R	Y,G	Y,G	Y,G	Y,G	Y,Y	Y,Y
Y	Y,R	Y,R	Y,R	Y,R	Y,R	Y,R	Y,G	Y,G	Y,G	Y,G	Y,Y	Y,Y

(The G,G cells are shaded.)

dependent events; $P(G, \text{ then } G) = \dfrac{12}{132} = \dfrac{1}{11}$

2nd Draw

1st Draw	R	R	R	R	R	R	G	G	G	G	Y	Y
R	R,R	R,R	R,R	R,R	R,R	R,G	R,G	R,G	R,G	R,Y	R,Y	
R	R,R	R,R	R,R	R,R	R,R	R,G	R,G	R,G	R,G	R,Y	R,Y	
R	R,R	R,R	R,R	R,R	R,R	R,G	R,G	R,G	R,G	R,Y	R,Y	
R	R,R	R,R	R,R	R,R	R,R	R,G	R,G	R,G	R,G	R,Y	R,Y	
R	R,R	R,R	R,R	R,R	R,R	R,G	R,G	R,G	R,G	R,Y	R,Y	
R	R,R	R,R	R,R	R,R	R,R	R,G	R,G	R,G	R,G	R,Y	R,Y	
G	G,R	G,R	G,R	G,R	G,R	G,R	G,G	G,G	G,G	G,Y	G,Y	
G	G,R	G,R	G,R	G,R	G,R	G,R	G,G	G,G	G,G	G,Y	G,Y	
G	G,R	G,R	G,R	G,R	G,R	G,R	G,G	G,G	G,G	G,Y	G,Y	
G	G,R	G,R	G,R	G,R	G,R	G,R	G,G	G,G	G,G	G,Y	G,Y	
Y	Y,R	Y,R	Y,R	Y,R	Y,R	Y,R	Y,G	Y,G	Y,G	Y,G	Y,Y	
Y	Y,R	Y,R	Y,R	Y,R	Y,R	Y,R	Y,G	Y,G	Y,G	Y,G	Y,Y	

(The G,G cells are shaded.)

35. independent events; $P(G, \text{ then } Y) = \dfrac{8}{144} = \dfrac{1}{18}$

2nd Draw

1st Draw	R	R	R	R	R	R	G	G	G	G	Y	Y
R	R,R	R,R	R,R	R,R	R,R	R,R	R,G	R,G	R,G	R,G	R,Y	R,Y
R	R,R	R,R	R,R	R,R	R,R	R,R	R,G	R,G	R,G	R,G	R,Y	R,Y
R	R,R	R,R	R,R	R,R	R,R	R,R	R,G	R,G	R,G	R,G	R,Y	R,Y
R	R,R	R,R	R,R	R,R	R,R	R,R	R,G	R,G	R,G	R,G	R,Y	R,Y
R	R,R	R,R	R,R	R,R	R,R	R,R	R,G	R,G	R,G	R,G	R,Y	R,Y
R	R,R	R,R	R,R	R,R	R,R	R,R	R,G	R,G	R,G	R,G	R,Y	R,Y
G	G,R	G,R	G,R	G,R	G,R	G,R	G,G	G,G	G,G	G,G	G,Y	G,Y
G	G,R	G,R	G,R	G,R	G,R	G,R	G,G	G,G	G,G	G,G	G,Y	G,Y
G	G,R	G,R	G,R	G,R	G,R	G,R	G,G	G,G	G,G	G,G	G,Y	G,Y
G	G,R	G,R	G,R	G,R	G,R	G,R	G,G	G,G	G,G	G,G	G,Y	G,Y
Y	Y,R	Y,R	Y,R	Y,R	Y,R	Y,R	Y,G	Y,G	Y,G	Y,G	Y,Y	Y,Y
Y	Y,R	Y,R	Y,R	Y,R	Y,R	Y,R	Y,G	Y,G	Y,G	Y,G	Y,Y	Y,Y

(The G,Y cells are shaded.)

dependent events; $P(G, \text{ then } Y) = \dfrac{8}{132} = \dfrac{2}{33}$

2nd Draw

1st Draw	R	R	R	R	R	R	G	G	G	G	Y	Y
R	R,R	R,R	R,R	R,R	R,R	R,G	R,G	R,G	R,G	R,Y	R,Y	
R	R,R	R,R	R,R	R,R	R,R	R,G	R,G	R,G	R,G	R,Y	R,Y	
R	R,R	R,R	R,R	R,R	R,R	R,G	R,G	R,G	R,G	R,Y	R,Y	
R	R,R	R,R	R,R	R,R	R,R	R,G	R,G	R,G	R,G	R,Y	R,Y	
R	R,R	R,R	R,R	R,R	R,R	R,G	R,G	R,G	R,G	R,Y	R,Y	
R	R,R	R,R	R,R	R,R	R,R	R,G	R,G	R,G	R,G	R,Y	R,Y	
G	G,R	G,R	G,R	G,R	G,R	G,R	G,G	G,G	G,G	G,Y	G,Y	
G	G,R	G,R	G,R	G,R	G,R	G,R	G,G	G,G	G,G	G,Y	G,Y	
G	G,R	G,R	G,R	G,R	G,R	G,R	G,G	G,G	G,G	G,Y	G,Y	
G	G,R	G,R	G,R	G,R	G,R	G,R	G,G	G,G	G,G	G,Y	G,Y	
Y	Y,R	Y,R	Y,R	Y,R	Y,R	Y,R	Y,G	Y,G	Y,G	Y,G	Y,Y	
Y	Y,R	Y,R	Y,R	Y,R	Y,R	Y,R	Y,G	Y,G	Y,G	Y,G	Y,Y	

(The G,Y cells are shaded.)

36. independent events; $P(Y, \textit{then } R) = \dfrac{12}{144} = \dfrac{1}{12}$

2nd Draw

1st Draw	R	R	R	R	R	R	G	G	G	G	Y	Y
R	R,R	R,R	R,R	R,R	R,R	R,R	R,G	R,G	R,G	R,G	R,Y	R,Y
R	R,R	R,R	R,R	R,R	R,R	R,R	R,G	R,G	R,G	R,G	R,Y	R,Y
R	R,R	R,R	R,R	R,R	R,R	R,R	R,G	R,G	R,G	R,G	R,Y	R,Y
R	R,R	R,R	R,R	R,R	R,R	R,R	R,G	R,G	R,G	R,G	R,Y	R,Y
R	R,R	R,R	R,R	R,R	R,R	R,R	R,G	R,G	R,G	R,G	R,Y	R,Y
R	R,R	R,R	R,R	R,R	R,R	R,R	R,G	R,G	R,G	R,G	R,Y	R,Y
G	G,R	G,R	G,R	G,R	G,R	G,R	G,G	G,G	G,G	G,G	G,Y	G,Y
G	G,R	G,R	G,R	G,R	G,R	G,R	G,G	G,G	G,G	G,G	G,Y	G,Y
G	G,R	G,R	G,R	G,R	G,R	G,R	G,G	G,G	G,G	G,G	G,Y	G,Y
G	G,R	G,R	G,R	G,R	G,R	G,R	G,G	G,G	G,G	G,G	G,Y	G,Y
Y	**Y,R**	**Y,R**	**Y,R**	**Y,R**	**Y,R**	**Y,R**	Y,G	Y,G	Y,G	Y,G	Y,Y	Y,Y
Y	**Y,R**	**Y,R**	**Y,R**	**Y,R**	**Y,R**	**Y,R**	Y,G	Y,G	Y,G	Y,G	Y,Y	Y,Y

dependent events; $P(Y, \textit{then } R) = \dfrac{12}{132} = \dfrac{1}{11}$

2nd Draw

1st Draw	R	R	R	R	R	R	G	G	G	G	Y	Y
R	R,R	R,R	R,R	R,R	R,R	R,R	R,G	R,G	R,G	R,G	R,Y	R,Y
R	R,R	R,R	R,R	R,R	R,R	R,R	R,G	R,G	R,G	R,G	R,Y	R,Y
R	R,R	R,R	R,R	R,R	R,R	R,R	R,G	R,G	R,G	R,G	R,Y	R,Y
R	R,R	R,R	R,R	R,R	R,R	R,R	R,G	R,G	R,G	R,G	R,Y	R,Y
R	R,R	R,R	R,R	R,R	R,R	R,R	R,G	R,G	R,G	R,G	R,Y	R,Y
R	R,R	R,R	R,R	R,R	R,R	R,R	R,G	R,G	R,G	R,G	R,Y	R,Y
G	G,R	G,R	G,R	G,R	G,R	G,R	G,G	G,G	G,G	G,G	G,Y	G,Y
G	G,R	G,R	G,R	G,R	G,R	G,R	G,G	G,G	G,G	G,G	G,Y	G,Y
G	G,R	G,R	G,R	G,R	G,R	G,R	G,G	G,G	G,G	G,G	G,Y	G,Y
G	G,R	G,R	G,R	G,R	G,R	G,R	G,G	G,G	G,G	G,G	G,Y	G,Y
Y	**Y,R**	**Y,R**	**Y,R**	**Y,R**	**Y,R**	**Y,R**	Y,G	Y,G	Y,G	Y,G	Y,Y	Y,Y
Y	**Y,R**	**Y,R**	**Y,R**	**Y,R**	**Y,R**	**Y,R**	Y,G	Y,G	Y,G	Y,G	Y,Y	Y,Y

37. independent events; $P(Y, \textit{then } G) = \dfrac{8}{144} = \dfrac{1}{18}$

2nd Draw

1st Draw	R	R	R	R	R	R	G	G	G	G	Y	Y
R	R,R	R,R	R,R	R,R	R,R	R,R	R,G	R,G	R,G	R,G	R,Y	R,Y
R	R,R	R,R	R,R	R,R	R,R	R,R	R,G	R,G	R,G	R,G	R,Y	R,Y
R	R,R	R,R	R,R	R,R	R,R	R,R	R,G	R,G	R,G	R,G	R,Y	R,Y
R	R,R	R,R	R,R	R,R	R,R	R,R	R,G	R,G	R,G	R,G	R,Y	R,Y
R	R,R	R,R	R,R	R,R	R,R	R,R	R,G	R,G	R,G	R,G	R,Y	R,Y
R	R,R	R,R	R,R	R,R	R,R	R,R	R,G	R,G	R,G	R,G	R,Y	R,Y
G	G,R	G,R	G,R	G,R	G,R	G,R	G,G	G,G	G,G	G,G	G,Y	G,Y
G	G,R	G,R	G,R	G,R	G,R	G,R	G,G	G,G	G,G	G,G	G,Y	G,Y
G	G,R	G,R	G,R	G,R	G,R	G,R	G,G	G,G	G,G	G,G	G,Y	G,Y
G	G,R	G,R	G,R	G,R	G,R	G,R	G,G	G,G	G,G	G,G	G,Y	G,Y
Y	Y,R	Y,R	Y,R	Y,R	Y,R	Y,R	**Y,G**	**Y,G**	**Y,G**	**Y,G**	Y,Y	Y,Y
Y	Y,R	Y,R	Y,R	Y,R	Y,R	Y,R	**Y,G**	**Y,G**	**Y,G**	**Y,G**	Y,Y	Y,Y

dependent events; $P(Y, \textit{then } G) = \dfrac{8}{132} = \dfrac{2}{33}$

2nd Draw

1st Draw	R	R	R	R	R	R	G	G	G	G	Y
R	R,R	R,R	R,R	R,R	R,R	R,R	R,G	R,G	R,G	R,G	R,Y
R	R,R	R,R	R,R	R,R	R,R	R,R	R,G	R,G	R,G	R,G	R,Y
R	R,R	R,R	R,R	R,R	R,R	R,R	R,G	R,G	R,G	R,G	R,Y
R	R,R	R,R	R,R	R,R	R,R	R,R	R,G	R,G	R,G	R,G	R,Y
R	R,R	R,R	R,R	R,R	R,R	R,R	R,G	R,G	R,G	R,G	R,Y
R	R,R	R,R	R,R	R,R	R,R	R,R	R,G	R,G	R,G	R,G	R,Y
G	G,R	G,R	G,R	G,R	G,R	G,R	G,G	G,G	G,G	G,G	G,Y
G	G,R	G,R	G,R	G,R	G,R	G,R	G,G	G,G	G,G	G,G	G,Y
G	G,R	G,R	G,R	G,R	G,R	G,R	G,G	G,G	G,G	G,G	G,Y
G	G,R	G,R	G,R	G,R	G,R	G,R	G,G	G,G	G,G	G,G	G,Y
Y	Y,R	Y,R	Y,R	Y,R	Y,R	Y,R	**Y,G**	**Y,G**	**Y,G**	**Y,G**	Y,Y
Y	Y,R	Y,R	Y,R	Y,R	Y,R	Y,R	**Y,G**	**Y,G**	**Y,G**	**Y,G**	Y,Y

38. independent events; $P(Y, \textit{then } Y) = \dfrac{4}{144} = \dfrac{1}{36}$

2nd Draw

1st Draw	R	R	R	R	R	R	G	G	G	G	Y	Y
R	R,R	R,R	R,R	R,R	R,R	R,R	R,G	R,G	R,G	R,G	R,Y	R,Y
R	R,R	R,R	R,R	R,R	R,R	R,R	R,G	R,G	R,G	R,G	R,Y	R,Y
R	R,R	R,R	R,R	R,R	R,R	R,R	R,G	R,G	R,G	R,G	R,Y	R,Y
R	R,R	R,R	R,R	R,R	R,R	R,R	R,G	R,G	R,G	R,G	R,Y	R,Y
R	R,R	R,R	R,R	R,R	R,R	R,R	R,G	R,G	R,G	R,G	R,Y	R,Y
R	R,R	R,R	R,R	R,R	R,R	R,R	R,G	R,G	R,G	R,G	R,Y	R,Y
G	G,R	G,R	G,R	G,R	G,R	G,R	G,G	G,G	G,G	G,G	G,Y	G,Y
G	G,R	G,R	G,R	G,R	G,R	G,R	G,G	G,G	G,G	G,G	G,Y	G,Y
G	G,R	G,R	G,R	G,R	G,R	G,R	G,G	G,G	G,G	G,G	G,Y	G,Y
G	G,R	G,R	G,R	G,R	G,R	G,R	G,G	G,G	G,G	G,G	G,Y	G,Y
Y	Y,R	Y,R	Y,R	Y,R	Y,R	Y,R	Y,G	Y,G	Y,G	Y,G	**Y,Y**	**Y,Y**
Y	Y,R	Y,R	Y,R	Y,R	Y,R	Y,R	Y,G	Y,G	Y,G	Y,G	**Y,Y**	**Y,Y**

dependent events; $P(Y, \textit{then } Y) = \dfrac{2}{132} = \dfrac{1}{66}$

2nd Draw

1st Draw	R	R	R	R	R	R	G	G	G	G	Y
R	R,R	R,R	R,R	R,R	R,R	R,R	R,G	R,G	R,G	R,G	R,Y
R	R,R	R,R	R,R	R,R	R,R	R,R	R,G	R,G	R,G	R,G	R,Y
R	R,R	R,R	R,R	R,R	R,R	R,R	R,G	R,G	R,G	R,G	R,Y
R	R,R	R,R	R,R	R,R	R,R	R,R	R,G	R,G	R,G	R,G	R,Y
R	R,R	R,R	R,R	R,R	R,R	R,R	R,G	R,G	R,G	R,G	R,Y
R	R,R	R,R	R,R	R,R	R,R	R,R	R,G	R,G	R,G	R,G	R,Y
G	G,R	G,R	G,R	G,R	G,R	G,R	G,G	G,G	G,G	G,G	G,Y
G	G,R	G,R	G,R	G,R	G,R	G,R	G,G	G,G	G,G	G,G	G,Y
G	G,R	G,R	G,R	G,R	G,R	G,R	G,G	G,G	G,G	G,G	G,Y
G	G,R	G,R	G,R	G,R	G,R	G,R	G,G	G,G	G,G	G,G	G,Y
Y	Y,R	Y,R	Y,R	Y,R	Y,R	Y,R	Y,G	Y,G	Y,G	Y,G	**Y,Y**
Y	Y,R	Y,R	Y,R	Y,R	Y,R	Y,R	Y,G	Y,G	Y,G	Y,G	**Y,Y**

39. In each case, the sum of probabilities is 1.

P (independent events) $= \frac{1}{4} + \frac{1}{6} + \frac{1}{12} + \frac{1}{6} + \frac{1}{9} + \frac{1}{18} + \frac{1}{12} + \frac{2}{33} + \frac{1}{36} = 1$

P (dependent events) $= \frac{5}{22} + \frac{2}{11} + \frac{1}{11} + \frac{2}{11} + \frac{1}{11} + \frac{2}{33} + \frac{1}{11} + \frac{2}{33} + \frac{1}{66} = 1$

40. Probability $= \frac{1}{36}$

	1	2	3	4	5	6
1	1,1	1,2	1,3	1,4	1,5	1,6
2	2,1	2,2	2,3	2,4	2,5	2,6
3	3,1	3,2	3,3	3,4	3,5	3,6
4	4,1	4,2	4,3	4,4	4,5	4,6
5	5,1	5,2	5,3	5,4	5,5	5,6
6	6,1	6,2	6,3	6,4	6,5	6,6

41. Probability $= \frac{4}{12} = \frac{1}{3}$

	B	G	G
B	BB	BG	BG
B	BB	BG	BG
G	GB	GG	GG
G	GB	GG	GG

42. Probability $= \frac{2}{20} = \frac{1}{10}$

	B	G	G	G
B	BB	BG	BG	BG
B	BB	BG	BG	BG
G	GB	GG	GG	GG
G	GB	GG	GG	GG
G	GB	GG	GG	GG

43. Probability $= \frac{2}{20} = \frac{1}{10}$

	R	R	Y	Y
R	RR	RR	RY	RY
R	RR	RR	RY	RY
Y	YR	YR	YY	YY
Y	YR	YR	YY	YY
B	BR	BR	BY	BY

44. Probability $= \frac{4}{20} = \frac{1}{5}$

	R	Y	Y	B
R	RR	RY	RY	RB
R	RR	RY	RY	RB
Y	YR	YY	YY	YB
Y	YR	YY	YY	YB
B	BR	BY	BY	BB

45. Probability $= \frac{1}{36}$

	1	2	3	4	5	6
1	1,1	1,2	1,3	1,4	1,5	1,6
2	2,1	2,2	2,3	2,4	2,5	2,6
3	3,1	3,2	3,3	3,4	3,5	3,6
4	4,1	4,2	4,3	4,4	4,5	4,6
5	5,1	5,2	5,3	5,4	5,5	5,6
6	6,1	6,2	6,3	6,4	6,5	6,6

PAGE 195, LOOK BACK

46. Substitute 240 for m, and solve for c.

$c = 0.12m + 50$

$c = 0.12(240) + 50$

$c = 28.8 + 50$

$c = 78.8$

You would expect to pay $78.80.

47. $67 - (-92) + (-23) = 67 + 92 - 23$
$= 159 - 23$
$= 136$

48. $(-155) + 1245 - (-145) = (-155) + 1245 + 145$
$= 1090 + 145$
$= 1235$

49. Sequence $\quad \frac{1}{2} \quad \frac{1}{3} \quad \frac{1}{4} \quad \frac{1}{5} \quad \frac{1}{6} \quad \left[\frac{1}{7}\right] \quad \left[\frac{1}{8}\right] \quad \left[\frac{1}{9}\right] \quad \left[\frac{1}{10}\right] \quad \left[\frac{1}{11}\right] \quad \left[\frac{1}{12}\right]$

$\frac{1}{2} = 0.500$

$\frac{1}{3} = 0.\overline{333}$

$\frac{1}{4} = 0.250$

$\frac{1}{5} = 0.200$

$\frac{1}{6} = 0.167$

$\frac{1}{7} = 0.143$

$\frac{1}{8} = 0.125$

$\frac{1}{9} = 0.111$

$\frac{1}{10} = 0.100$

$\frac{1}{11} = 0.091$

$\frac{1}{12} = 0.083$

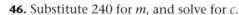

$\frac{1}{2}, \frac{1}{3}, \frac{1}{4}, \frac{1}{5}, \frac{1}{6}, \frac{1}{7}, \frac{1}{8}, \frac{1}{9}, \frac{1}{10}, \frac{1}{11}, \frac{1}{12}$

50. Sequence $\quad\dfrac{1}{2}\quad\dfrac{2}{3}\quad\dfrac{3}{5}\quad\dfrac{5}{8}\quad\dfrac{8}{13}\quad\left[\dfrac{13}{21}\right]\quad\left[\dfrac{21}{34}\right]\quad\left[\dfrac{34}{55}\right]\quad\left[\dfrac{55}{89}\right]\quad\left[\dfrac{89}{144}\right]\quad\left[\dfrac{144}{233}\right]$

$\dfrac{1}{2} = 0.500000$

$\dfrac{2}{3} = 0.666667$

$\dfrac{3}{5} = 0.600000$

$\dfrac{5}{8} = 0.625000$

$\dfrac{8}{13} = 0.615385$

$\dfrac{13}{21} = 0.619048$

$\dfrac{21}{34} = 0.617647$

$\dfrac{34}{55} = 0.618182$

$\dfrac{55}{89} = 0.617978$

$\dfrac{89}{144} = 0.618056$

$\dfrac{144}{233} = 0.618026$

$\dfrac{2}{3},\ \dfrac{5}{8},\ \dfrac{13}{21},\ \dfrac{34}{55},\ \dfrac{89}{144},\ \dfrac{144}{233},\ \dfrac{55}{89},\ \dfrac{21}{34},\ \dfrac{8}{13},\ \dfrac{3}{5},\ \dfrac{1}{2}$

51. The number of employed persons is 55,700 – 5600, or 50,100

$$\dfrac{55,700}{50,100} = \dfrac{55,700 \div 100}{50,100 \div 100} = \dfrac{557}{501}$$

The ratio of the total number of people to the number of people employed is $\dfrac{557}{501}$.

PAGE 195, LOOK BEYOND

52. Since the Earth is 30% land, it is 100 – 30, or 70% water.

$$70\% = \dfrac{70}{100} = \dfrac{7}{10}$$

The probability that the satellite would hit water is $\dfrac{7}{10}$.

53. Let $P(S_n)$ represent the probability of an object hitting water on the nth time.

$P(S_1) = \dfrac{7}{10}$

$P(S_2) = \dfrac{7}{10}$

$P(S_3) = \dfrac{7}{10}$

$\quad\vdots$

$P(S_{12}) = \dfrac{7}{10}$

$$\begin{aligned} P(S_1) \cdot P(S_2) \cdot P(S_3) \cdot \ldots \cdot P(S_{12}) &= \dfrac{7}{10} \cdot \dfrac{7}{10} \cdot \dfrac{7}{10} \cdot \ldots \cdot \dfrac{7}{10} \\ &= \left(\dfrac{7}{10}\right)^{12} \\ &= (0.7)^{12} \\ &\approx 0.014 \end{aligned}$$

The probability of 12 objects in a row hitting water would be approximately 0.014×100, or 1.4%.

PAGES 198–200 ## CHAPTER 3 REVIEW

1. $\dfrac{3}{8}$ is closest to $\dfrac{1}{3}$.

1

$\dfrac{1}{3}$	$\dfrac{1}{3}$

$\dfrac{1}{8}$	$\dfrac{1}{8}$	$\dfrac{1}{8}$

$\dfrac{1}{3}$

2. $\dfrac{1}{4}$ is closest to $\dfrac{1}{3}$.

1

$\dfrac{1}{3}$	$\dfrac{1}{3}$

$\dfrac{1}{3}$

$\dfrac{1}{4}$

3. $\frac{7}{10}$ is closest to $\frac{2}{3}$.

1

$\frac{1}{10}$	$\frac{1}{10}$	$\frac{1}{10}$	$\frac{1}{10}$	$\frac{1}{10}$	$\frac{1}{10}$	$\frac{1}{10}$

$\frac{1}{3}$	$\frac{1}{3}$

$\frac{1}{3}$

4. $\frac{5}{6}$ is exactly between $\frac{2}{3}$ and 1.

1

$\frac{1}{6}$	$\frac{1}{6}$	$\frac{1}{6}$	$\frac{1}{6}$	$\frac{1}{6}$

$\frac{1}{3}$	$\frac{1}{3}$

$\frac{1}{3}$

5. $\frac{9}{18} = \frac{9 \div 9}{18 \div 9} = \frac{1}{2}$

6. $\frac{21}{27} = \frac{21 \div 3}{27 \div 3} = \frac{7}{9}$

7. $\frac{26}{52} = \frac{26 \div 26}{52 \div 26} = \frac{1}{2}$

8. $\frac{42}{54} = \frac{42 \div 6}{54 \div 6} = \frac{7}{9}$

9. $\frac{1}{2} > \frac{2}{5}$

$\frac{1}{2} = \frac{1 \cdot 5}{2 \cdot 5} = \frac{5}{10}$

$\frac{2}{5} = \frac{2 \cdot 2}{5 \cdot 2} = \frac{4}{10}$

10. $\frac{2}{3} > \frac{5}{12}$

$\frac{2}{3} = \frac{2 \cdot 4}{3 \cdot 4} = \frac{8}{12}$

11. $\frac{3}{8} > \frac{1}{4}$

$\frac{1}{4} = \frac{1 \cdot 2}{4 \cdot 2} = \frac{2}{8}$

12. $\frac{4}{5} < \frac{9}{10}$

$\frac{4}{5} = \frac{4 \cdot 2}{5 \cdot 2} = \frac{8}{10}$

13. $0.49 = \frac{49}{100}$

14. $6.4 = 6\frac{4}{10} = 6\frac{2}{5}$

15. $2.94 = 2\frac{94}{100} = 2\frac{47}{50}$

16. $0.64 = \frac{64}{100} = \frac{16}{25}$

17. $\frac{7}{8} = 0.875$

$$
\begin{array}{r}
0.875 \\
8\overline{)7.0000} \\
-64 \\
\hline
60 \\
-56 \\
\hline
40 \\
-40 \\
\hline
0
\end{array}
$$

18. $\frac{1}{12} = 0.83\overline{3}$

$$
\begin{array}{r}
0.83\overline{3} \\
12\overline{)1.000} \\
-96 \\
\hline
40 \\
-36 \\
\hline
40 \\
-36 \\
\hline
4
\end{array}
$$

19. $-6\frac{1}{3} = -6.3\overline{3}$

$-6\frac{1}{3} = -\frac{19}{3}$

$$
\begin{array}{r}
-6.3\overline{3} \\
3\overline{)-19.00} \\
-18 \\
\hline
10 \\
-9 \\
\hline
10 \\
-9 \\
\hline
1
\end{array}
$$

20. $\frac{2}{7} = 0.\overline{285714}$

$$
\begin{array}{r}
0.285714 \\
7\overline{)2.000000} \\
-14 \\
\hline
60 \\
-56 \\
\hline
40 \\
-35 \\
\hline
50 \\
-49 \\
\hline
10 \\
-7 \\
\hline
30 \\
-28 \\
\hline
2
\end{array}
$$

21. $0.06 = 0.0600$
$0.008 = 0.0080$
$0.4 = 0.400$
$0.0203 = 0.0203$
$0.008, 0.0203, 0.06, 0.4$

22. $2.14 = 2.140000$
$2\frac{1}{7} = 2.142857$
$2.4 = 2.400000$
$2.1 = 2.100000$
$2.1, 2.14, 2\frac{1}{7}, 2.4$

23. $\frac{1}{4} + \frac{1}{2} = \frac{1}{4} + \frac{1 \cdot 2}{2 \cdot 2}$

$= \frac{1}{4} + \frac{2}{4}$

$= \frac{3}{4}$

24. $\frac{5}{6} - \frac{2}{3} = \frac{5}{6} - \frac{2 \cdot 2}{3 \cdot 2}$

$= \frac{5}{6} - \frac{4}{6}$

$= \frac{1}{6}$

25. $\frac{1}{5} + \frac{3}{8} = \frac{1 \cdot 8}{5 \cdot 8} + \frac{3 \cdot 5}{8 \cdot 5}$

$= \frac{8}{40} + \frac{15}{40}$

$= \frac{23}{40}$

26. $9\frac{1}{3} - \frac{7}{9} = \frac{28}{3} - \frac{7}{9}$

$= \frac{28 \cdot 3}{3 \cdot 3} - \frac{7}{9}$

$= \frac{84}{9} - \frac{7}{9}$

$= \frac{77}{9}$

$= 8\frac{5}{9}$

27. $5 \div 1\frac{1}{4} = 5 \div \frac{5}{4}$

$\qquad = 5 \cdot \frac{4}{5}$

$\qquad = \frac{20}{5}$

$\qquad = 4$

28. $4\frac{1}{3} \cdot 6 = \frac{13}{3} \cdot 6$

$\qquad = \frac{78}{3}$

$\qquad = 26$

29. $8\frac{1}{2} \div 9 = \frac{17}{2} \div 9$

$\qquad = \frac{17}{2} \cdot \frac{1}{9}$

$\qquad = \frac{17}{18}$

30. $2\frac{3}{4} \div 3\frac{5}{8} = \frac{11}{4} \div \frac{29}{8}$

$\qquad = \frac{11}{4} \cdot \frac{8}{29}$

$\qquad = \frac{88}{116}$

$\qquad = \frac{22}{29}$

31. $\frac{2}{5} = \frac{10}{?}$

$\frac{2}{5} \cdot \frac{5}{5} = \frac{10}{25}$

32. $\frac{5}{9} = \frac{?}{45}$

$\frac{5}{9} \cdot \frac{5}{5} = \frac{25}{45}$

33. $\frac{?}{82} = \frac{1}{2}$

$\frac{1}{2} \cdot \frac{41}{41} = \frac{41}{82}$

34. $\frac{54}{?} = \frac{6}{17}$

$\frac{6}{17} \cdot \frac{9}{9} = \frac{54}{153}$

35. $\frac{5}{8} = 62.5\%$

36. $\frac{3}{20} = 15\%$

37. $\frac{7}{10} = 70\%$

38. $5\frac{1}{3} = 533\%$

39. From the chart given on page 200, the probability that one of the coins is heads is $\frac{4}{5}$.

40. From the chart given on page 200, the probability that both coins are tails is $\frac{1}{5}$.

41. Probability $= \frac{9}{25}$

	B	B	G	G	G
B	BB	BB	BG	BG	BG
B	BB	BB	BG	BG	BG
G	GB	GB	GG	GG	GG
G	GB	GB	GG	GG	GG
G	GB	GB	GG	GG	GG

42. Probability $= \frac{6}{20} = \frac{3}{10}$

	B	B	G	G
B	BB	BB	BG	BG
B	BB	BB	BG	BG
G	GB	GB	GG	GG
G	GB	GB	GG	GG
G	GB	GB	GG	GG

PAGE 201 CHAPTER 3 ASSESSMENT

1. $\frac{9}{10}$ is closest to $\frac{7}{8}$.

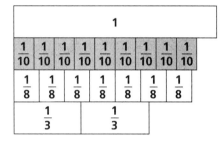

2. The LCD of $\frac{2}{3}$ and $\frac{5}{8}$ is 24.

$\frac{2}{3} \cdot \frac{8}{8} = \frac{16}{24}$

$\frac{5}{8} \cdot \frac{3}{3} = \frac{15}{24}$

$\frac{2}{3} > \frac{5}{8}$

3. $0.16 = 0.160$
$0.06 = 0.060$
$0.016 = 0.016$
$0.106 = 0.106$

$0.016, 0.06, 0.106, 0.16$

4. $1.8 = 1.800$
$1.08 = 1.080$
$1\frac{7}{8} = 1.875$
$1.78 = 1.780$

$1.08, 1.78, 1.8, 1\frac{7}{8}$

5. $\frac{7 \div 7}{14 \div 7} = \frac{1}{2}$

6. $\frac{35 \div 5}{40 \div 5} = \frac{7}{8}$

7. $\frac{29}{92}$ is in lowest terms.

8. $\frac{3}{7} = 0.\overline{428571}$

$$\begin{array}{r} 0.428571 \\ 7)\overline{3.000000} \\ -2\,8 \\ \hline 20 \\ -14 \\ \hline 60 \\ -56 \\ \hline 40 \\ -35 \\ \hline 50 \\ -49 \\ \hline 10 \\ -7 \\ \hline 3 \end{array}$$

9. $\frac{2}{3} + \frac{5}{6} = \frac{2 \cdot 2}{3 \cdot 2} + \frac{5}{6}$

$\qquad = \frac{4}{6} + \frac{5}{6}$

$\qquad = \frac{9}{6}$

$\qquad = 1\frac{3}{6}$

$\qquad = 1\frac{1}{2}$

10. $5\frac{5}{6} - 4\frac{1}{4} = \frac{35}{6} - \frac{17}{4}$

$\qquad = \frac{35 \cdot 2}{6 \cdot 2} - \frac{17 \cdot 3}{4 \cdot 3}$

$\qquad = \frac{70}{12} - \frac{51}{12}$

$\qquad = \frac{19}{12}$

$\qquad = 1\frac{7}{12}$

11. $\frac{1}{8} + \frac{1}{9} = \frac{1 \cdot 9}{8 \cdot 9} + \frac{1 \cdot 8}{9 \cdot 8}$

$\qquad = \frac{9}{72} + \frac{8}{72}$

$\qquad = \frac{17}{72}$

12. $\frac{1}{4} - \frac{1}{3} = \frac{1 \cdot 3}{4 \cdot 3} - \frac{1 \cdot 4}{3 \cdot 4}$
$= \frac{3}{12} - \frac{4}{12}$
$= -\frac{1}{12}$

13. $\frac{2}{3} + 2\frac{1}{6} = \frac{2}{3} + \frac{13}{6}$
$= \frac{2 \cdot 2}{3 \cdot 2} + \frac{13}{6}$
$= \frac{4}{6} + \frac{13}{6}$
$= \frac{17}{6}$
$= 2\frac{5}{6}$

14. $\frac{5}{7} + \frac{4}{8} = \frac{5 \cdot 8}{7 \cdot 8} + \frac{4 \cdot 7}{8 \cdot 7}$
$= \frac{40}{56} + \frac{28}{56}$
$= \frac{68}{56}$
$= 1\frac{12}{56}$
$= 1\frac{3}{14}$

15. $5 \cdot 4\frac{1}{3} = 5 \cdot \frac{13}{3}$
$= \frac{65}{3}$
$= 21\frac{2}{3}$

16. $8\frac{5}{8} \cdot 3 = \frac{69}{8} \cdot \frac{3}{1}$
$= \frac{207}{8}$
$= 25\frac{7}{8}$

17. $1\frac{3}{4} \cdot 2\frac{1}{5} = \frac{7}{4} \cdot \frac{11}{5}$
$= \frac{77}{20}$
$= 3\frac{17}{20}$

18. $-4\frac{1}{3} \cdot 6 = -\frac{13}{3} \cdot \frac{6}{1}$
$= -\frac{78}{3}$
$= -26$

19. $5\frac{1}{4} \cdot \left(-\frac{3}{5}\right) = \frac{21}{4} \cdot \left(-\frac{3}{5}\right)$
$= -\frac{63}{20}$
$= -3\frac{3}{20}$

20. $\frac{1}{2} \cdot \frac{1}{2} \cdot \frac{1}{3} = \frac{1}{4} \cdot \frac{1}{3}$
$= \frac{1}{12}$

21. $\frac{2}{7} = \frac{?}{21}$
$\frac{2}{7} \cdot \frac{3}{3} = \frac{6}{21}$

22. $\frac{5}{15} = \frac{?}{3}$
$\frac{5 \div 5}{15 \div 5} = \frac{1}{3}$

23. $\frac{3}{7} = \frac{12}{?}$
$\frac{3}{7} \cdot \frac{4}{4} = \frac{12}{28}$

24. $\frac{?}{8} = \frac{18}{24}$
$\frac{18 \div 3}{24 \div 3} = \frac{6}{8}$

25. $1.96 = 1\frac{96}{100}$
$= 1\frac{24}{25}$

26. $0.6 = \frac{6}{10}$
$= \frac{3}{5}$

27. $2.25 = 2\frac{25}{100}$
$= 2\frac{1}{4}$

28. $8.55 = 8\frac{55}{100}$
$= 8\frac{11}{20}$

29. $0.75 = \frac{75}{100}$
$= \frac{3}{4}$

30. $0.43 \times 100 = 43\%$

31. $2.03 \times 100 = 203\%$

32. $\frac{7}{20} \times 100 = \frac{700}{20}$
$= 35\%$

33. $1\frac{3}{8} = \frac{11}{8} \times 100$
$= \frac{1100}{8}$
$= 137.5\%$

34. Probability $= \frac{6}{36} = \frac{1}{6}$

	1	2	3	4	5	6
1	1,1	1,2	1,3	1,4	1,5	1,6
2	2,1	2,2	2,3	2,4	2,5	2,6
3	3,1	3,2	3,3	3,4	3,5	3,6
4	4,1	4,2	4,3	4,4	4,5	4,6
5	5,1	5,2	5,3	5,4	5,5	5,6
6	6,1	6,2	6,3	6,4	6,5	6,6

35. Probability $= \frac{6}{36} = \frac{1}{6}$

	1	2	3	4	5	6
1	1,1	1,2	1,3	1,4	1,5	1,6
2	2,1	2,2	2,3	2,4	2,5	2,6
3	3,1	3,2	3,3	3,4	3,5	3,6
4	4,1	4,2	4,3	4,4	4,5	4,6
5	5,1	5,2	5,3	5,4	5,5	5,6
6	6,1	6,2	6,3	6,4	6,5	6,6

36. Probability $= \frac{6}{20} = \frac{3}{10}$

	R	R	R	G
R	RR	RY	RR	RG
R	RR	RR	RR	RG
R	TR	RR	RR	RG
G	GR	GR	GR	GG
G	GR	GR	GR	GG

CHAPTER 4

GEOMETRY CONNECTIONS

For Exercises 6–14, measures are approximate. Allow a range of ±3.

6. 45°   **7.** 120°   **8.** 40°   **9.** 140°   **10.** 90°

11. 170°   **12.** 90°   **13.** 115°   **14.** 75°   **15.** parallel lines

16. a ray   **17.** a point   **18.** the line formed where the sky and the ocean meet

19. part of a plane   **20.** a line segment

21. plane *ABC*, plane *K*   **22.** ray *PD*, $\overrightarrow{PD}$; ray *PF*, $\overrightarrow{PF}$

23. line *n*, line *ML*, line *LM*, $\overleftrightarrow{ML}$, $\overleftrightarrow{LM}$ **24.** segment *CK*, $\overline{CK}$, segment *KC*, $\overline{KC}$

25. ∠2, ∠*WXY*, ∠*YXW*, ∠*X*   **26.** ∠1, ∠*TSR*, ∠*RST*, ∠*S*

27. *G*   **28.** no   **29.** Name of the plane may vary; *CBD*.

30. $\overleftrightarrow{KJ}$ or $\overleftrightarrow{JK}$ or line *m*   **31.** Name of the plane may vary; *CBD*.

32.
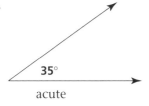
35°
acute

33.
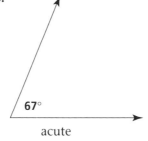
67°
acute

34.
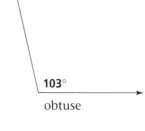
103°
obtuse

35.
170°
obtuse

36.
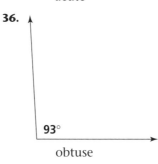
93°
obtuse

37.
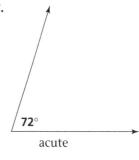
72°
acute

38.
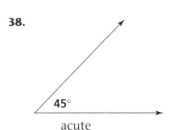
45°
acute

39.
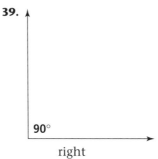
90°
right

40.
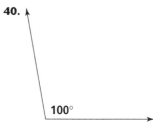
100°
obtuse

41.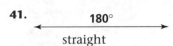
180°
straight

42.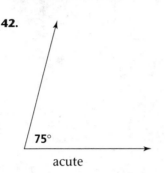
75°
acute

43.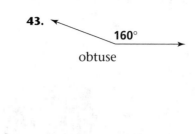
160°
obtuse

44. Roofs with an acute angle retain less snow than roofs which are flat. If a roof accumulates too much snow, the weight of the snow can cause the roof to collapse.

45. $\overrightarrow{WT}$ and $\overrightarrow{WV}$

46. Y

47. $\angle TWV$ or $\angle VWT$

48. protractor

49. Their measures are the same.

50. protractor

51. Answers may vary.
$\angle DGE$, $\angle AFE$, $\angle GFB$

52. $\angle FAB$

53. $\angle GFA$

54. $m\angle GFE = 180° - 130° = 50°$

55. $m\angle AFB = 180° - 130° = 50°$

56. No; in any triangle the sum of the measures of the angles equals 180°; $\angle ABF = 180° - 45° - 50° = 85°$. Since a right angle measures 90°, $\angle ABF$ is not a right angle.

PAGE 210, LOOK BACK

57. $\frac{2}{3} - 2.25 = \frac{2}{3} - 2\frac{1}{4}$
$= \frac{2}{3} - \frac{9}{4}$
$= \frac{8}{12} - \frac{27}{12}$
$= -\frac{19}{12}$, or $-1\frac{7}{12}$

58. $\frac{2}{3} \cdot 2.25 = \frac{2}{3} \cdot \frac{9}{4}$
$= \frac{3}{2}$, or $1\frac{1}{2}$

59. $\frac{2}{3} \div 2.25 = \frac{2}{3} \div \frac{9}{4}$
$= \frac{2}{3} \cdot \frac{4}{9}$
$= \frac{8}{27}$

60. $2{:}3 = \frac{2}{3}$
$= .66\overline{6}$
$= 66.\overline{6}\%$

61. $8{:}12 = \frac{8}{12}$
$= .66\overline{6}$
$= 66.\overline{6}\%$

62. $4{:}5 = \frac{4}{5}$
$= .8$
$= 80\%$

63. To find the percent of students who walk to school, convert $\frac{162}{645}$ to a percent. To estimate, first round the fraction to $\frac{160}{640}$, then reduce and convert to a percent. $\frac{160}{640} = \frac{16}{64} = \frac{1}{4} = 25\%$. Approximately 25% of the students at Northlake Middle School walk to school.

PAGE 210, LOOK BEYOND

64. Side and angle measure may vary for each triangle.
a. acute isosceles   b. acute right   c. right   d. obtuse isosceles

4.2 PAGES 214–215, PRACTICE & APPLY

7. $m\angle 2 + 15.5 = 90$
$m\angle 2 = 74.5°$

8. Vertical angles have equal measures; $m\angle 4 = 15.5°$

9. $m\angle 3 = m\angle 2 = 74.5°$

10. Answers may vary. $\angle 2$, $\angle 3$, and $\angle 4$ are all acute angles.

11. $\angle 1$

12. $\angle 2$ and $\angle 3$, or $\angle 4$ and the angle which measures 15.5°

13. $\angle 3$ and $\angle 4$; $\angle 2$ and the 15.5° angle; $\angle 2$ and $\angle 4$; or $\angle 3$ and the 15.5° angle

14. $m\angle BFC = 90 - 25$
$= 65°$

15. $m\angle BFD = m\angle BFC + m\angle CFD$
$= 65 + 90$
$= 155°$

16. m∠*DFE* = m∠*BFA* (vertical angles)
       = 25°

17. m∠*CFD* = 180 – m∠*CFA*
       = 180 – 90
       = 90°

18. m∠*BFE* = 180°

19. ∠*DFA* and ∠*EFB* are two straight angles.

20. Two right angles are ∠*DFC* and ∠*CFA*.

21. Two pairs of vertical angles are:
       ∠*DFE* and ∠*BFA*
       ∠*DFB* and ∠*EFA*.

22. Two pairs of complementary angles are:
       ∠*CFB* and ∠*BFA*
       ∠*DFE* and ∠*CFB*

23. Supplementary angle pairs include:
       ∠*EFD* and ∠*DFB*
       ∠*EFC* and ∠*CFB*
       ∠*DFC* and ∠*CFA*
       ∠*DFB* and ∠*BFA*
       ∠*EFA* and ∠*AFB*
       ∠*DFE* and ∠*EFA*

For Exercises 24–27, let *a* represent the angle, *c* represent the complement of the angle, and *s* represent the supplement of the angle.

24. $a + c = 90$
     $a + 15 = 90$
         $a = 75°$

25. $a + c = 90$
     $a + 82 = 90$
         $a = 8°$

26. $a + s = 180$
     $a + 35 = 180$
         $a = 145°$

27. $a + s = 180$
     $a + 125 = 180$
         $a = 55°$

28. Let *a* represent each congruent angle.
     $a + a = 90$
       $2a = 90$
         $a = 45°$
Each angle measures 45°.

29. $a + a = 180$
     $2a = 180$
       $a = 90°$
Each angle measures 90°.

30. $a + a + a = 180$
       $3a = 180$
         $a = 60°$
Each angle measures 60°.

31. Let *a* represent one of the angles and 2*a* represent the other.
     $a + 2a = 90$
        $3a = 90$
          $a = 30°$
The angles measure 30° and 60°.

32. The exterior angle measured by the goniometer is 60°, so the angle between the faces of the crystal is 120°.

33. The angle measured by the goniometer and the angle between the faces of the crystal will always create a straight angle, so their measures will always be supplementary.

34. Answers may vary. An example is provided:

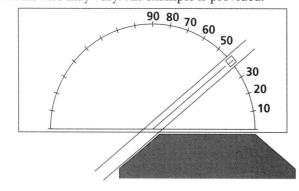

35. m∠7 = 90°

36. m∠2 = 90°

37. m∠3 = 90 – m∠4
       = 90 – 12.5
       = 77.5°

38. m∠4 = m∠1 = 12.5°

39. m∠5 = 90 – m∠1
       = 90 – 12.5
       = 77.5°

40. m∠6 = m∠1 + m∠2
       = 12.5 + 90
       = 102.5°

41. This is true in most cases; however, each angle could have a measure of 90°. Then neither would be obtuse, but they would still be supplementary.

42. $|10| = 10$ **43.** $|-7| = 7$ **44.** $|-0.8| = 0.8$ **45.** $\left|-\frac{2}{3}\right| = \frac{2}{3}$ **46.** $|0.01| = 0.01$

47. $\frac{2}{9} = 0.22\overline{2}$ **48.** $\frac{2}{5} = 0.4$ **49.** $\frac{1}{3} = 0.33\overline{3}$ **50.** $\frac{3}{8} = 0.375$ **51.** $\frac{5}{2} = 2.5$

52. $\frac{1}{8} = 12.5\%$ **53.** $\frac{3}{4} = 75\%$ **54.** $\frac{2}{5} = 40\%$ **55.** $\frac{9}{3} = 300\%$ **56.** $\frac{8}{9} = 88.\overline{8}\%$

57. $x + 2x = 90$
$3x = 90$
$x = 30$

58. $2x + 3x = 180$
$5x = 180$
$x = 36$

7. $m\angle 2 = 140°$ **8.** $m\angle 3 = 40°$ **9.** $m\angle 4 = 40°$ **10.** $m\angle 5 = 140°$

11. $m\angle 6 = 40°$ **12.** $m\angle 1 = 140°$ **13.** $m\angle 8 = 140°$

14. alternate interior angle pairs:
$\angle 2$ and $\angle 5$; $\angle 6$ and $\angle 3$

15. alternate exterior angle pairs:
$\angle 1$ and $\angle 8$; $\angle 4$ and $\angle 7$

16. corresponding angle pairs:
$\angle 7$ and $\angle 3$; $\angle 1$ and $\angle 5$; $\angle 2$ and $\angle 8$; $\angle 6$ and $\angle 4$

17. consecutive interior angle pairs:
$\angle 2$ and $\angle 3$; $\angle 5$ and $\angle 6$

18. Answers may vary. For example, $\angle 5$ and $\angle 3$ form a straight angle, so the sum of their measures is 180°, and they are supplementary angles. $\angle 3$ and $\angle 6$ are alternate interior angles, so their measures are the same. Therefore, $\angle 5$ and $\angle 6$ must also have measures that add up to 180° and that are supplementary.

19. Ten pairs of supplementary angles are:
$\angle 7$ and $\angle 2$; $\angle 2$ and $\angle 6$; $\angle 6$ and $\angle 1$; $\angle 1$ and $\angle 7$;
$\angle 3$ and $\angle 8$; $\angle 8$ and $\angle 4$; $\angle 4$ and $\angle 5$; $\angle 5$ and $\angle 3$;
$\angle 2$ and $\angle 3$; $\angle 5$ and $\angle 6$

20. right scalene triangle **21.** obtuse scalene triangle **22.** acute isosceles triangle

23. $x + 90 + 72 = 180$
$x = 18°$

24. $x + 30 + 130 = 180$
$x = 20°$

25. Since the triangle is isosceles,
$y = 70°$
$x + y + 70 = 180$
$x + 140 = 180$
$x = 40°$

26. No; in a right triangle, one angle has a measure of 90°. That leaves 90° to be divided between the other two angles. An obtuse angle is greater than 90°, which is not possible for any of the angles in a right triangle.

27. Yes; in a right triangle, the two angles that are not the 90° angle can be equal. Therefore, the triangle would have congruent base angles, and it would be isosceles.

28. No; if one angle in a triangle is 90°, the remaining 90° has to be distributed between the other two angles. Neither one could equal 90° because then the third would be 0° and there would be no triangle.

29. No; an obtuse triangle has one angle with a measure greater than 90°. An equilateral triangle has all angles equal to 60°.

30. Yes; the vertex angle of an isosceles triangle can be obtuse (greater than 90°), while the base angles are congruent.

31. Yes; an isosceles triangle is equilateral when the third side (or angle) equals the other two.

32. $m\angle C + 32 + 90 = 180$
$m\angle C = 58°$

33. $\angle A$ and $\angle C$ are complementary angles. In any right triangle, the sum of the measures of the two non-right angles must be 90°; therefore, they must be complementary.

34. Let *a* represent the measure of each congruent angle in a triangle.

$$a + a + a = 180$$
$$3a = 180$$
$$a = 60$$

Each angle measures 60°.

35. 1st Street, 2nd Street, and 3rd Street are all parallel. They all have corresponding angles which are congruent.

36. Eight other angles have the same measure as angle 11. Four of these angles are numbered: 10, 12, 13, 14.

37. Eight angles are supplementary to angle 10. Four of these angles are numbered: 11, 12, 13, 14.

38. Four angles have a measure of 120°. Three of these angles are numbered: 3, 5, 7.

39. Five angles are supplements of 120°. Five of these angles are numbered: 1, 2, 4, 6, 8.

For Exercises 40–45, use the following computation:

$$m\angle 2 + m\angle 4 = 180$$
$$x + 2x = 180$$
$$3x = 180$$
$$x = 60$$
$$2x = 120$$
$$m\angle 2 = 60° \text{ and } m\angle 4 = 120°$$

40. $m\angle 1 = 120°$

41. $m\angle 3 = 60°$

42. $m\angle 6 = 60°$

43. $m\angle 5 = 120°$

44. $m\angle 7 = 60°$

45. $m\angle 8 = 120°$

For Exercises 46–51, $\overline{DE} \parallel \overline{CB}$ and $m\angle ADE = m\angle AED$.

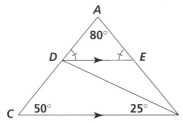 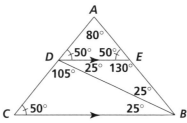

Since $\overline{DE} \parallel \overline{CB}$, $\angle ADE \cong \angle ACB$ and $\angle AED \cong \angle ABC$ (corresponding angles). $m\angle ACB$: $m\angle ADE = m\angle AED = m\angle ABC = 50°$. Other angles may be found using any of the following: the sum of measures of angles in a triangle equals 180°; the measure of a straight angle is 180°; alternate interior angles are congruent.

46. $m\angle ADE = 50°$

47. $m\angle AED = 50°$

48. $m\angle DEB = 130°$

49. $m\angle BDE = 25°$

50. $m\angle CDB = 105°$

51. $m\angle ABD = 25°$

52. corresponding

53. alternate interior

54. alternate exterior

55. none of these

56. corresponding

57. none of these

58. corresponding

59. none of these

60. alternate interior

61. none of these

62. corresponding

63. alternate interior

64. $m\angle 1 = 45°$, $m\angle 2 = 90°$, $m\angle 3 = 45°$, $m\angle 4 = 135°$; $m\angle 1 + m\angle 2 = m\angle 4$

65. $m\angle 4 + m\angle 1 + m\angle 5 = 180°$ because $\angle 4$, $\angle 1$, and $\angle 5$ create a straight angle. $\angle 3$ and $\angle 5$ are congruent alternate interior angles; $\angle 2$ and $\angle 4$ are congruent alternate interior angles. $\angle 3$ can be substituted into the equation for $\angle 5$, and $\angle 2$ can be substituted for $\angle 4$, so the equation becomes $m\angle 2 + m\angle 1 + m\angle 3 = 180°$.

66. Not necessarily; two angles can each equal 90°. They would then be supplementary to each other, but neither angle is obtuse.

67. In any triangle, the longest side is opposite the largest angle. If a triangle is a right triangle, the largest angle will be the 90° angle, so the side opposite it, the hypotenuse, will always be the longest side.
Examples:

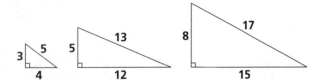

68. $n - 2$
  $n = 6$: $n - 2 = 6 - 2 = 4$
  $n = 8$: $n - 2 = 8 - 2 = 6$
  $n = 10$: $n - 2 = 10 - 2 = 8$

69. $(n - 2)\,180$
  $n = 6$: $(n - 2)180 = (6 - 2)180 = 4 \cdot 180 = 720$
  $n = 8$: $(n - 2)180 = (8 - 2)180 = 6 \cdot 180 = 1080$
  $n = 10$: $(n - 2)180 = (10 - 2)180 = 8 \cdot 180 = 1440$

70. $\dfrac{(n - 2)180}{n}$

  $n = 6$: $\dfrac{(n - 2)180}{n} = \dfrac{(6 - 2)180}{6} = \dfrac{720}{6} = 120$

  $n = 8$: $\dfrac{(n - 2)180}{n} = \dfrac{(8 - 2)180}{8} = \dfrac{1080}{8} = 135$

  $n = 10$: $\dfrac{(n - 2)180}{n} = \dfrac{(10 - 2)180}{10} = \dfrac{1440}{10} = 144$

71. $-2 < 5$

72. $3 > -3$

73. $-5 < 2$

74. $\dfrac{2}{3} = \dfrac{6}{n}$
  $18 = 2n$
  $9 = n$

75. $\dfrac{n}{8} = \dfrac{3}{12}$
  $24 = 12n$
  $2 = n$

76. $\dfrac{14}{x} = \dfrac{35}{45}$
  $\dfrac{14}{x} = \dfrac{7}{9}$
  $\dfrac{2}{x} = \dfrac{1}{9}$
  $x = 18$

77. $25\% = 0.25$

78. $5\% = 0.05$

79. $4.5\% = 0.045$

80. $112\% = 1.12$

81. $66.6\% = 0.666$

82. $2x + 6x + x = 180$
  $9x = 180$
  $x = 20$
  $2x = 40$
  $6x = 120$

83. $x + 3x + 2x = 180$
  $6x = 180$
  $x = 30$
  $2x = 60$
  $3x = 90$

5.

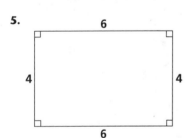

6.

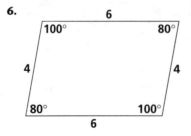

7.

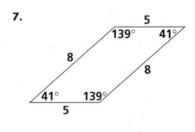

8.

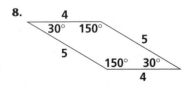

9. convex, hexagon **10.** convex, octagon **11.** convex, heptagon

12. concave, dodecagon **13.** concave, hexagon

For Exercises 14–20, figures may vary. Sample figures are given.

14. true

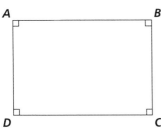

A rectangle has four angles. $\overline{AB}$ and $\overline{CD}$ are transversals across $\overline{AD}$ and $\overline{BC}$. m∠A + m∠B = 180 and m∠D + m∠C = 180, so $\overline{AD} \parallel \overline{BC}$ by supplementary consecutive interior angles. In the same manner, $\overline{AB} \parallel \overline{DC}$. Therefore, quadrilateral *ABCD* is a parallelogram.

15. true

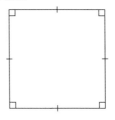

Every square has four right angles and all sides congruent.
Every rectangle has four right angles and opposite sides congruent, so every square is also a rectangle.

16. false

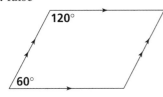

Parallelograms do not necessarily have 90° angles, which are necessary for a rectangle.

17. false

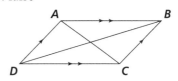

In ∆*ADC* and ∆*DAB*, let ∠*DAB* > ∠*ADC*. Since the sides of ∠*ADC* are congruent to the sides of ∠*DAB* and one angle is larger than the other, the sides opposite those angles have the same relationship, that is, one is longer than the other one.

18. true

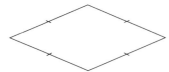

For a quadrilateral to be a parallelogram, both pairs of opposite sides must be congruent, which is true for this figure.

19. true

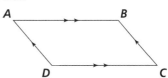

$\overline{AD}$ is a transversal across $\overline{AB}$ and $\overline{DC}$, which are parallel to each other. ∠A and ∠D are therefore supplementary adjacent interior angles. In the same manner, the other 3 pairs of adjacent interior angles of parallelogram *ABCD* are supplementary.

20. false

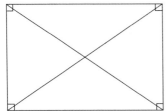

The only rectangle with perpendicular diagonals is a square, and not all rectangles are squares.

For Exercises 21–25, use the formula $m = (n - 2)$ 180, where n is the number of sides of a polygon and m is the sum of the interior angle measures of the polygon.

21. $n = 7$

$m = (n - 2)180$
$= (7 - 2)180$
$= 5 \cdot 180$
$= 900°$

22. $n = 5$

$m = (n - 2)180$
$= (5 - 2)180$
$= 3 \cdot 180$
$= 540°$

23. $n = 10$

$m = (n - 2)180$
$= (10 - 2)180$
$= 8 \cdot 180$
$= 1440°$

24. $n = 8$

$m = (n - 2)180$
$= (8 - 2)180$
$= 6 \cdot 180$
$= 1080°$

25. $n = 9$

$m = (n - 2)180$
$= (9 - 2)180$
$= 7 \cdot 180$
$= 1260°$

For Exercises 26–30, use the formula $a = \dfrac{(n-2)180}{n}$, where n is the number of sides of a regular polygon and a is the measure of one interior angle of the polygon.

26. $n = 3$

$a = \dfrac{(n-2)180}{n}$
$= \dfrac{(3-2)180}{3}$
$= \dfrac{180}{3}$
$= 60°$

27. $n = 6$

$a = \dfrac{(n-2)180}{n}$
$= \dfrac{(6-2)180}{6}$
$= 4 \cdot \dfrac{180}{6}$
$= 120°$

28. $n = 5$

$a = \dfrac{(n-2)180}{n}$
$= \dfrac{(5-2)180}{5}$
$= 3 \cdot \dfrac{180}{5}$
$= 108°$

29. $n = 8$

$a = \dfrac{(n-2)180}{n}$
$= \dfrac{(8-2)180}{8}$
$= 6 \cdot \dfrac{180}{8}$
$= 135°$

30. $n = 7$

$a = \dfrac{(n-2)180}{n}$
$= \dfrac{(7-2)180}{7}$
$= 5 \cdot \dfrac{180}{7}$
$= 128\frac{4}{7}°$

31. Let x represent the measure of each of the congruent angles of the pentagon. The sum of the interior angles of a pentagon is 540° (see Exercise 22).

$540 = 90(3) + 2x$
$540 = 270 + 2x$
$270 = 2x$
$135 = x$

Each angle measures 135°.

32.

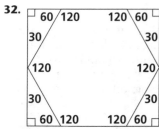

PAGE 231, LOOK BACK

Guess-and-check is used to solve Exercises 33–39. Answers may vary.

33.

x	Equation $x + 2 = -1$	Simplified expression	True?
2	$2 + 2 = -1$	$4 = -1$	no
0	$0 + 2 = -1$	$2 = -1$	no
-2	$-2 + 2 = -1$	$0 = -1$	no
-3	$-3 + 2 = -1$	$-1 = -1$	yes

The solution is $x = -3$.

34.

x	Equation $5 - x = -1$	Simplified expression	True?
2	$5 - 2 = -1$	$3 = -1$	no
0	$5 - 0 = -1$	$5 = -1$	no
4	$5 - 4 = -1$	$1 = -1$	no
6	$5 - 6 = -1$	$-1 = -1$	yes

The solution is $x = 6$.

35.

x	Equation $2x = -7$	Simplified expression	True?
-1	$2(-1) = -7$	$-2 = -7$	no
-3	$2(-3) = -7$	$-6 = -7$	no
-4	$2(-4) = -7$	$-8 = -7$	no
$-3\frac{1}{2}$	$2\left(-3\frac{1}{2}\right) = -7$	$-7 = -7$	yes

The solution is $x = -3\frac{1}{2}$.

36.

x	Equation $2x + 1 = 8$	Simplified expression	True?
2	$2(2) + 1 = 8$	$5 = 8$	no
3	$2(3) + 1 = 8$	$7 = 8$	no
4	$2(4) + 1 = 8$	$9 = 8$	no
$3\frac{1}{2}$	$2\left(3\frac{1}{2}\right) + 1 = 8$	$8 = 8$	yes

The solution is $x = 3\frac{1}{2}$.

For Exercises 37–39, $l = 2\frac{1}{2}$ and $w = 4$.

37. $l \cdot w = \left(2\frac{1}{2}\right)4$
$= \frac{5}{2} \cdot \frac{4}{1}$
$= 10$

38. $l + w + l + w = 2\frac{1}{2} + 4 + 2\frac{1}{2} + 4$
$= 2\left(2\frac{1}{2}\right) + 2(4)$
$= 5 + 8$
$= 13$

39. $2l + 2w = 2\left(2\frac{1}{2}\right) + 2(4)$
$= 5 + 8$
$= 13$

40. 25% of $400 = \frac{1}{4} \cdot 400$
$= \frac{400}{4}$
$= 100$

41. 10% of $50 = \frac{1}{10} \cdot 50$
$= \frac{50}{10}$
$= 5$

42. 75% of $60 = \frac{3}{4} \cdot 60$
$= 3\left(\frac{1}{4} \cdot 60\right)$
$= 3(15)$
$= 45$

PAGE 231, LOOK BEYOND

43. $y = x^2 + 1$

x	-3	-2	-1	0	1	2	3
y	10	5	2	1	2	5	10

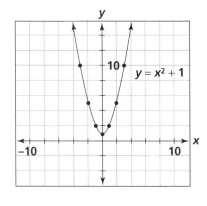

44. $y = x^2 - 2$

x	-3	-2	-1	0	1	2	3
y	7	2	-1	-2	-1	2	7

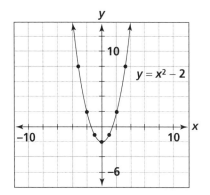

45. $y = x^2 + 2x + 1$

x	-3	-2	-1	0	1	2	3
y	4	1	0	1	4	9	16

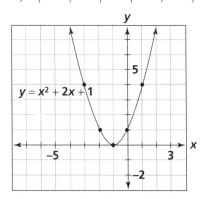

Use the grids to estimate the perimeter and area for each figure. Answers may vary.

8. $P \approx 26$ units, $A \approx 42$ square units

9. $P \approx 15$ units, $A \approx 10$ square units

10. $P \approx 20$ units, $A \approx 25$ square units

11. $P \approx 21$ units, $A \approx 28$ square units

12. $P \approx 16$ units, $A \approx 14$ square units

13. $P \approx 24$ units, $A \approx 20$ square units

14. $P = 2l + 2w$
$= 2(95) + 2(48)$
$= 190 + 96$
$= 286$ meters
$A = l \cdot w$
$= 95 \cdot 48$
$= 4560$ square meters

15. $P = 2l + 2w$
$= 2(2.5) + 2(5.75)$
$= 5 + 11.5$
$= 16.5$ yards
$A = l \cdot w$
$= (2.5)(5.75)$
$= 14.375$ square yards

16. $P = 2l + 2w$
$= 2\left(15\frac{3}{16}\right) + 2\left(15\frac{3}{16}\right)$
$= 4\left(15\frac{3}{16}\right)$
$= 4\left(\frac{243}{16}\right)$
$= \frac{243}{4}$
$= 60\frac{3}{4}$ inches
$A = l \cdot w$
$= \left(15\frac{3}{16}\right)\left(15\frac{3}{16}\right)$
$= (15.1875)^2$
≈ 230.66 square inches

17. $P = 2l + 2w$
$= 2(8.5) + 2(4.4)$
$= 17 + 8.8$
$= 25.8$ centimeters
$A = l \cdot w$
$= (8.5)(4.4)$
$= 37.4$ square centimeters

18. $P = 2l + 2w$
$= 2(2.5) + 2(5.75)$
$= 5 + 11.5$
$= 16.5$ meters
$A = l \cdot w$
$= (2.5)(5.75)$
$= 14.375$ square meters

19. $P = 2l + 2w$
$= 2(18) + 2\left(2\frac{1}{2}\right)$
$= 36 + 5$
$= 41$ inches
$A = l \cdot w$
$= 18\left(2\frac{1}{2}\right)$
$= 45$ square inches

20. $P = 2l + 2w$
$= 2(110) + 2(110)$
$= 4(110)$
$= 440$ feet
$A = l \cdot w$
$= (110)(110)$
$= 12,100$ square feet

21. $P = 2l + 2w$
$= 2(2.5) + 2(5.2)$
$= 5 + 10.4$
$= 15.4$ miles
$A = l \cdot w$
$= (2.5)(5.2)$
$= 13$ square miles

22. $P = 2l + 2w$
$= 2\left(5\frac{2}{3}\right) + 2\left(1\frac{1}{2}\right)$
$= 2\left(\frac{17}{3}\right) + 2\left(\frac{3}{2}\right)$
$= \frac{34}{3} + 3$
$= 11\frac{1}{3} + 3$
$= 14\frac{1}{3}$ yards
$A = l \cdot w$
$= \left(5\frac{2}{3}\right)\left(1\frac{1}{2}\right)$
$= \frac{17}{3} \cdot \frac{3}{2}$
$= \frac{17}{2}$
$= 8\frac{1}{2}$ square yards

23. $P = 2l + 2w$
$= 2\left(1\frac{3}{4}\right) + 2\left(\frac{7}{8}\right)$
$= 2\left(\frac{7}{4}\right) + \frac{7}{4}$
$= \frac{21}{4}$
$= 5.25$ inches
$A = l \cdot w$
$= \left(1\frac{3}{4}\right)\left(\frac{7}{8}\right)$
$= \frac{7}{4} \cdot \frac{7}{8}$
$= \frac{49}{32}$
$= 1\frac{17}{32}$ square inches

24. side $a = 80 - (15 + 15)$
$= 80 - 30$
$= 50$
side $b = 100 - (50 + 25)$
$= 100 - 75$
$= 25$
dimensions: 50 feet by 25 feet
perimeter $= 2l + 2w$
$= 2(50) + 2(25)$
$= 150$ feet
area $= l \cdot w$
$= 50 \cdot 25$
$= 1250$ square feet

25. side $a = 100 - 30 = 70$
side $b = 90 - 75 = 15$
dimensions: 70 feet by 15 feet
perimeter $= 2l + 2w$
$= 2(70) + 2(15)$
$= 140 + 30$
$= 170$ feet
area $= l \cdot w$
$= 70 \cdot 15$
$= 1050$ square feet

26. side $a = 100 - 30 = 70$

side $b = 500 - 75 = 425$

dimensions: 70 feet by 425 feet

perimeter $= 2l + 2w$

$\qquad = 2(70) + 2(425)$

$\qquad = 140 + 850$

$\qquad = 990$ feet

area $= l \cdot w$

$\qquad = 70 \cdot 425$

$\qquad = 29{,}750$ square feet

27. side $a = 100 - 30 = 70$

side $b = 120 - 75 = 45$

dimensions: 70 feet by 45 feet

perimeter $= 2l + 2w$

$\qquad = 2(70) + 2(45)$

$\qquad = 230$ feet

area $= l \cdot w$

$\qquad = 70 \cdot 45$

$\qquad = 3150$ square feet

For Exercises 28–33, solutions are indicated in bold print in the table. Individual computations for each rectangle are shown following the table.

	Length	Width	Perimeter	Area
28.	4	**5**	18	**20**
29.	4	**4**	**16**	16
30.	**1**	1.5	5	**1.5**
31.	**4**	2.5	**13**	10
32.	**2**	20	**44**	40
33.	16	**2.5**	37	**40**

28. $P = 2l + 2w$

$18 = 2(4) + 2w$

$18 = 8 + 2w$

$10 = 2w$

$5 = w$

$A = l \cdot w$

$\quad = 4 \cdot 5$

$\quad = 20$

29. $A = l \cdot w$

$16 = 4w$

$4 = w$

$P = 2l + 2w$

$\quad = 2(4) + 2(4)$

$\quad = 16$

30. $P = 2l + 2w$

$5 = 2l + 2(1.5)$

$5 = 2l + 3$

$2 = 2l$

$1 = l$

$A = l \cdot w$

$\quad = 1(1.5)$

$\quad = 1.5$

31. $A = l \cdot w$

$10 = l(2.5)$

$4 = l$

$P = 2l + 2w$

$\quad = 2(4) + 2(2.5)$

$\quad = 13$

32. $A = l \cdot w$

$40 = l \cdot 20$

$2 = l$

$P = 2l + 2w$

$\quad = 2(2) + 2(20)$

$\quad = 44$

33. $P = 2l + 2w$

$37 = 2(l6) + 2w$

$5 = 2w$

$\dfrac{5}{2} = w$ or $w = 2\dfrac{1}{2}$

$A = l \cdot w$

$\quad = 16\left(\dfrac{5}{2}\right)$

$\quad = 40$

	Fixed perimeter	Length	Width	Area
34.	250	20	**105**	**2100**
35.	250	40	**85**	**3400**
36.	250	60	**65**	**3900**
37.	250	80	**45**	**3600**
38.	250	100	**25**	**2500**
39.	250	120	**5**	**600**

40. The pen with dimensions 60 feet by 65 feet has an area of 3900 square feet.

41. The pen with dimensions 120 feet by 5 feet has the smallest area, 600 square feet.

42.

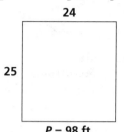

Answers may vary. One example is a pen with a width of 62.5 feet.

43. Answers may vary. Examples of rectangular plans are shown. As the rectangle gets closer to square in shape, the perimeter of the rectangle gets smaller.

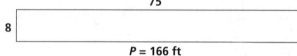

24
25
$P = 98$ ft

60
10
$P = 140$ ft

75
8
$P = 166$ ft

40
15
$P = 110$ ft

150
4
$P = 308$ ft

PAGE 238, LOOK BACK

44.

x	Equation $60 = \frac{600}{x}$	Simplified expression	True?
5	$60 = \frac{600}{5}$	$60 = 120$	no
6	$60 = \frac{600}{6}$	$60 = 100$	no
8	$60 = \frac{600}{8}$	$60 = 75$	no
10	$60 = \frac{600}{10}$	$60 = 60$	yes

The solution is $x = 10$.

45.

x	Equation $8 = \frac{x}{100}$	Simplified expression	True?
5	$8 = \frac{5}{100}$	$8 = \frac{1}{20}$	no
50	$8 = \frac{50}{100}$	$8 = \frac{1}{2}$	no
500	$8 = \frac{500}{100}$	$8 = 5$	no
800	$8 = \frac{800}{100}$	$8 = 8$	yes

The solution is $x = 800$.

46.

h	Equation $50 = 20 + 2h$	Simplified expression	True?
2	$50 = 20 + 2(2)$	$50 = 24$	no
5	$50 = 20 + 2(5)$	$50 = 30$	no
10	$50 = 20 + 2(10)$	$50 = 40$	no
15	$50 = 20 + 2(15)$	$50 = 50$	yes

The solution is $h = 15$.

47. For a pentagon, $n = 5$. Let a represent the measure of one angle in the regular pentagon.

$$a = \frac{(n-2)180}{n}$$
$$= \frac{(5-2)180}{5}$$
$$= \frac{3 \cdot 180}{5}$$
$$= 108$$

The measure of one angle in a regular pentagon is 108°.

PAGE 238, LOOK BEYOND

For Exercises 48–50, $b = 2\frac{1}{2}$ and $h = 4$.

48. $\frac{1}{2}(b \cdot h) = \frac{1}{2}\left(2\frac{1}{2}\right)(4)$

$= \frac{1}{2}\left(\frac{5}{2}\right)\left(\frac{4}{1}\right)$

$= 5$

49. $\frac{bh}{2} = \frac{\left(2\frac{1}{2}\right)(4)}{2}$

$= \frac{\left(\frac{5}{2} \cdot \frac{4}{1}\right)}{2}$

$= \frac{10}{2}$

$= 5$

50. $\frac{b}{h} = \frac{2\frac{1}{2}}{4}$

$= \frac{\frac{5}{2}}{4}$

$= \frac{5}{2} \cdot \frac{1}{4}$

$= \frac{5}{8}$

5. $A = \frac{1}{2}bh$
$= \frac{1}{2}(4)(5)$
$= 10$ square units
Perimeter ≈ 16 units

6. $A = \frac{1}{2}bh$
$= \frac{1}{2}(6)(5)$
$= 15$ square units
Perimeter ≈ 16 units

7. $A = bh$
$= 3 \cdot 6$
$= 18$ square units
Perimeter ≈ 18 units

8. $A = bh$
$= 3 \cdot 5$
$= 15$ square units
Perimeter ≈ 16 units

9. $A = \frac{(b_1 + b_2)h}{2}$
$= \frac{(4 + 7)4}{2}$
$= 22$ square units
Perimeter ≈ 19 units

10. $A = \frac{(b_1 + b_2)h}{2}$
$= \frac{(2 + 4)5}{2}$
$= 15$ square units
Perimeter ≈ 16 units

For Exercises 11–13, divide each figure into regions and find the area of each region. Regions may vary. Examples are shown below.

11.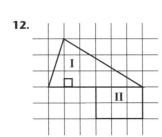

Region I: $A = \frac{(b_1 + b_2)h}{2}$
$= \frac{(1 + 4)5}{2}$
$= \frac{25}{2}$, or 12.5 square units

Region II: $A = \frac{1}{2}bh$
$= \frac{1}{2} \cdot 2 \cdot 4$
$= 4$

Total area $= 12.5 + 4 = 16.5$ square units
Perimeter ≈ 17 units

12.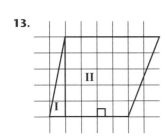

Region I: $A = \frac{1}{2}bh$
$= \frac{1}{2} \cdot 6 \cdot 3$
$= 9$

Region II: $A = l \cdot w$
$= 3 \cdot 2$
$= 6$

Total area $= 9 + 6 = 15$ square units
Perimeter ≈ 18 units

13.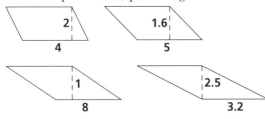

Region I: $A = \frac{1}{2}bh$
$= \frac{1}{2} \cdot 1 \cdot 5$
$= \frac{5}{2}$, or 2.5

Region II: $A = \frac{(b_1 + b2)h}{2}$
$= \frac{(4 + 6)5}{2}$
$= 25$

Total area $= 2.5 + 25 = 27.5$ square units
Perimeter ≈ 21 units

For Exercises 14–16, answers may vary. Examples are shown for each.

14. Area = 8 square units; parallelograms

15. Area = 8 square units; triangles

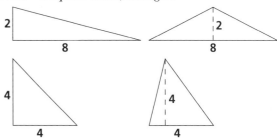

16. Area = 8 square units; trapezoids

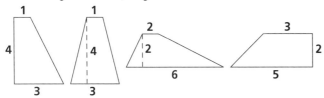

17. $A = \frac{1}{2}bh$

$\quad = \frac{1}{2}(9)(4.8)$

$\quad = 21.6$ square centimeters

18. $A = \frac{1}{2}bh$

$\quad = \frac{1}{2}(1.7)(5)$

$\quad = 4.25$ square millimeters

19. $A = \frac{1}{2}bh$

$\quad = \frac{1}{2}\left(5\frac{1}{2}\right)\left(5\frac{1}{2}\right)$

$\quad = \frac{1}{2}\left(\frac{11}{2}\right)\left(\frac{11}{2}\right)$

$\quad = \frac{121}{8}$, or $15\frac{1}{8}$ square inches

20. $A = \frac{1}{2}bh$

$\quad = \frac{1}{2}\left(8\frac{3}{4}\right)(5)$

$\quad = \frac{1}{2}\left(\frac{35}{4}\right)(5)$

$\quad = \frac{175}{8}$

$\quad = 21\frac{7}{8}$ square feet

21. $A = \frac{1}{2}bh$

$\quad = \frac{1}{2}(6)(4)$

$\quad = 12$ square inches

22. $A = \frac{1}{2}bh$

$\quad = \frac{1}{2}(2.5)(8)$

$\quad = 10$ square millimeters

23. $A = \frac{1}{2}bh$

$\quad = \frac{1}{2}\left(2\frac{2}{3}\right)\left(5\frac{1}{2}\right)$

$\quad = \frac{1}{2}\left(\frac{8}{3}\right)\left(\frac{11}{2}\right)$

$\quad = \frac{88}{12}$, or $\frac{22}{3}$

$\quad = 7\frac{1}{3}$ square inches

24. $A = \frac{1}{2}bh$

$\quad = \frac{1}{2}\left(7\frac{1}{4}\right)(5)$

$\quad = \frac{1}{2}\left(\frac{29}{4}\right)(5)$

$\quad = \frac{145}{8}$

$\quad = 18\frac{1}{8}$ square feet

25. $A = \frac{1}{2}bh$

$\quad = \frac{1}{2}(8)(11)$

$\quad = 44$ square centimeters

26. $A = \frac{1}{2}bh$

$\quad = \frac{1}{2}(8.4)(12.2)$

$\quad = 51.24$ square meters

27. $A = bh$

$\quad = (8)(14.4)$

$\quad = 115.2$ square centimeters

28. $A = bh$

$\quad = \left(12\frac{1}{4}\right)\left(5\frac{3}{4}\right)$

$\quad = \left(\frac{49}{4}\right)\left(\frac{23}{4}\right)$

$\quad = \frac{1127}{16}$, or $70\frac{7}{16}$ square feet

29. $A = bh$

$\quad = (13)(7.1)$

$\quad = 92.3$ square millimeters

30. $A = bh$

$\quad = (11)(4.25)$

$\quad = 46.75$ square centimeters

31. $A = bh$

$\quad = (18)(9.4)$

$\quad = 169.2$ square meters

32. $A = bh$

$\quad = (12.5)(5.75)$

$\quad = 71.875$ square feet

33. $A = bh$

$\quad = (18)\left(10\frac{1}{8}\right)$

$\quad = (18)\left(\frac{81}{8}\right)$

$\quad = \frac{1458}{8}$, or $\frac{729}{4}$

$\quad = 182\frac{1}{4}$ square inches

34. $A = bh$

$\quad = (4.9)(9.2)$

$\quad = 45.08$ square centimeters

35. $A = \frac{(b_1 + b_2)h}{2}$

$\quad = \frac{(4 + 2.5)11}{2}$

$\quad = \frac{(6.5)11}{2}$

$\quad = \frac{71.5}{2}$

$\quad = 35.75$ square feet

36. $A = \frac{(b_1 + b_2)h}{2}$

$\quad = \frac{(24 + 12)10}{2}$

$\quad = \frac{(36)10}{2}$

$\quad = \frac{360}{2}$

$\quad = 180$ square centimeters

37. $A = \frac{(b_1 + b_2)h}{2}$

$\quad = \frac{(12.7 + 11)18.3}{2}$

$\quad = \frac{(23.7)18.3}{2}$

$\quad = \frac{433.71}{2}$

$\quad = 216.855$ square centimeters

38. $A = \frac{(b_1 + b_2)h}{2}$

$\quad = \frac{\left(6 + 9\frac{3}{4}\right)15}{2}$

$\quad = \frac{\left(15\frac{3}{4}\right)15}{2}$

$\quad = \frac{\frac{63}{4} \cdot \frac{15}{1}}{2}$

$\quad = \frac{945}{4} \cdot \frac{1}{2}$

$\quad = \frac{945}{8}$, or $118\frac{1}{8}$ square feet

39. $A = \frac{(b_1 + b_2)h}{2}$

$\quad = \frac{(3.4 + 6.7)8.9}{2}$

$\quad = \frac{(10.1)8.9}{9}$

$\quad = \frac{89.89}{2}$

$\quad = 44.945$ square millimeters

40. $A = \frac{(b_1 + b_2)h}{2}$

$\quad = \frac{(18 + 12)5.2}{2}$

$\quad = \frac{(30)5.2}{2}$

$\quad = \frac{156}{2}$

$\quad = 78$ square meters.

For Exercises 41–43, divide the figure into polygons for which there are area formulas. Solutions may vary.

41.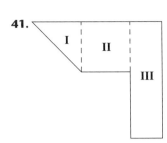

A = region I + region II + region III
$$= \tfrac{1}{2}bh + l \cdot w + l \cdot w$$
$$= \tfrac{1}{2}(3)(3) + (3)(3) + (2)(7)$$
$$= 4.5 + 9 + 14$$
$$= 27.5 \text{ or } 27\tfrac{1}{2} \text{ square units}$$

42.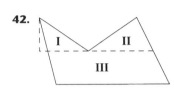

A = region I + region II + region III
$$= \tfrac{1}{2}bh + \tfrac{1}{2}bh + bh$$
$$= \tfrac{1}{2}(2)(2) + \tfrac{1}{2}(4)(2) + (6)(2)$$
$$= 2 + 4 + 12$$
$$= 18 \text{ square units}$$

43.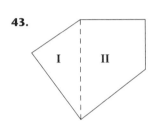

A = region I + region II
$$= \tfrac{1}{2}bh + \frac{(b_1 b_2)\, h}{2}$$
$$= \tfrac{1}{2}(6)(3) + \frac{(3+6)\, 4}{2}$$
$$= 9 + \frac{(9)\, 4}{2}$$
$$= 9 + \frac{36}{2}$$
$$= 9 + 18$$
$$= 27 \text{ square units}$$

	Base	**Height**	**Area**
44.	8	**3**	12
45.	**5**	10	25
46.	3	**4**	6
47.	**20**	1.5	15

	Base₁	**Base₂**	**Height**	**Area**
48.	10	5	**2**	15
49.	5	**3**	4	16
50.	**24**	12	2	36
51.	8	12	**5**	50

52.
$$A = \frac{(b_1 + b_2)h}{2}$$
$$= \frac{(40 + 150)90}{2}$$
$$= \frac{(190)(90)}{2}$$
$$= \frac{17{,}100}{2}$$
$$= 8550 \text{ square feet}$$

The area of one face of the pyramid is 8550 square feet.

53. Since all faces of the pyramid are congruent, the total area of all four sides is four times the area of one side.
$$A = 4\left(\frac{(b_1 + b_2)h}{2}\right)$$
$$= 2(b_1 + b_2)h$$

54. Since all faces of the pyramid are congruent, the base is a square with side lengths of 150 feet.
$$A = s^2$$
$$= (150)^2$$
$$= 22{,}500 \text{ square feet}$$

The area of the bottom of the pyramid is 22,500 square feet.

55. The top of the pyramid is a square with side lengths of 40 feet.
$$A = s^2$$
$$= (40)^2$$
$$= 1600 \text{ square feet}$$

The area of the top of the pyramid is 1600 square feet.

56.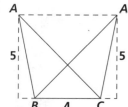

Let $\triangle ABC$ be the original triangle, where $b = 4$ and $h = 5$. Let $\triangle A'BC$ be the transformed triangle. The base, $\overline{BC}$, is 4 units and the height is 5 units.

$$A_{\triangle ABC} = \frac{1}{2}bh \qquad A_{\triangle A'BC} = \frac{1}{2}bh$$
$$= \frac{1}{2}(4)(5) \qquad\qquad = \frac{1}{2}(4)(5)$$
$$= 10 \text{ square units} \qquad = 10 \text{ square units}$$

PAGE 247, LOOK BACK

For Exercises 57–59, substitute the values given for a and b into $a^2 + b^2$ to evaluate.

57. $a^2 + b^2 = 3^2 + 4^2$
$= 9 + 16$
$= 25$

58. $a^2 + b^2 = 4.5^2 + 6^2$
$= 20.25 + 36$
$= 56.25$

59. $a^2 + b^2 = 3^2 + 3^2$
$= 9 + 9$
$= 18$

60.

x	Equation $x + (-3) = -5$	Simplified expression	True?
1	$1 + (-3) = -5$	$-2 = -5$	no
0	$0 + (-3) = -5$	$-3 = -5$	no
-1	$-1 + (-3) = -5$	$-4 = -5$	no
-2	$-2 + (-3) = -5$	$-5 = -5$	yes

The solution is $x = -2$.

61.

x	Equation $x - 4 = -1$	Simplified expression	True?
-1	$-1 - 4 = -1$	$-5 = -1$	no
5	$5 - 4 = -1$	$1 = -1$	no
4	$4 - 4 = -1$	$0 = -1$	no
3	$3 - 4 = -1$	$-1 = -1$	yes

The solution is $x = 3$.

62.

x	Equation $x + 3 = 5$	Simplified expression	True?
0	$0 + 3 = 5$	$3 = 5$	no
4	$4 + 3 = 5$	$7 = 5$	no
3	$3 + 3 = 5$	$6 = 5$	no
2	$2 + 3 = 5$	$5 = 5$	yes

The solution is $x = 2$.

63.
```
5      0     -3    -4    -3    [0]   [5]   [12]
   -5    -3    -1     1    [3]   [5]   [7]
      2     2     2   [2]   [2]   [2]
```

64.
```
17      7     1    -1     1    [7]   [17]  [31]
  -10    -6   -2     2   [6]   [10]  [14]
      4    4     4   [4]   [4]   [4]
```

65.
```
21     11     5     3     5   [11]  [21]  [35]
  -10    -6   -2     2   [6]   [10]  [14]
      4    4     4   [4]   [4]   [4]
```

66.
```
3     6    10    15    21   [28]  [36]  [45]
  3    4     5     6    [7]   [8]   [9]
    1    1     1   [1]   [1]   [1]
```

PAGE 247, LOOK BEYOND

67. When both the base and height of a triangle are doubled, the area increases by a factor of four. When the base and height are tripled, the area increases by a factor of nine. To demonstrate algebraically, let x represent the amount that the area increases.

$$A = \frac{1}{2}bh$$
$$x \cdot A = \frac{1}{2}(2b)(2h) \qquad x \cdot A = \frac{1}{2}(3b)(3h)$$
$$x \cdot A = 4\left(\frac{1}{2}bh\right) \qquad x \cdot A = 9\left(\frac{1}{2}bh\right)$$
$$x \cdot A = 4 \cdot A \qquad\qquad x \cdot A = 9 \cdot A$$
$$x = 4 \qquad\qquad\qquad x = 9$$

68. When the base and height of a parallelogram are both doubled, the area increases by a factor of four. When the base and height are tripled, the area increases by a factor of nine.

$$A = bh$$
$$x \cdot A = (2b)(2h) \qquad x \cdot A = (3b)(3h)$$
$$x \cdot A = 4(bh) \qquad\qquad x \cdot A = 9(bh)$$
$$x \cdot A = 4 \cdot A \qquad\qquad x \cdot A = 9 \cdot A$$
$$x = 4 \qquad\qquad\qquad x = 9$$

For Exercises 5–28, values may vary for the nearest tenth estimation.

	Lies between perfect squares	Estimating: nearest whole number	nearest tenth	Value to nearest hundredth
5.	$\sqrt{4} < \sqrt{5} < \sqrt{9}$	2	2.2	2.24
6.	$\sqrt{9} < \sqrt{10} < \sqrt{16}$	3	3.1	3.16
7.	$\sqrt{9} < \sqrt{12} < \sqrt{16}$	3	3.4	3.46
8.	$\sqrt{16} < \sqrt{20} < \sqrt{25}$	4	4.4	4.47
9.	$\sqrt{25} < \sqrt{27} < \sqrt{36}$	5	5.2	5.20
10.	$\sqrt{36} < \sqrt{39} < \sqrt{49}$	6	6.3	6.24
11.	$\sqrt{36} < \sqrt{42} < \sqrt{49}$	6	6.5	6.48
12.	$\sqrt{49} < \sqrt{50} < \sqrt{64}$	7	7.1	7.07
13.	$\sqrt{49} < \sqrt{60} < \sqrt{64}$	8	7.7	7.75
14.	$\sqrt{64} < \sqrt{72} < \sqrt{81}$	8	8.5	8.49
15.	$\sqrt{81} < \sqrt{95} < \sqrt{100}$	10	9.8	9.75
16.	$\sqrt{100} < \sqrt{110} < \sqrt{121}$	10	10.5	10.49
17.	$\sqrt{121} < \sqrt{143} < \sqrt{144}$	12	11.9	11.96
18.	$\sqrt{169} < \sqrt{170} < \sqrt{196}$	13	13.1	13.04
19.	$\sqrt{169} < \sqrt{180} < \sqrt{196}$	13	13.5	13.42
20.	$\sqrt{196} < \sqrt{200} < \sqrt{225}$	14	14.2	14.14
21.	$\sqrt{81} < \sqrt{84} < \sqrt{100}$	9	9.2	9.17
22.	$\sqrt{144} < \sqrt{149} < \sqrt{169}$	12	12.2	12.21
23.	$\sqrt{81} < \sqrt{99} < \sqrt{100}$	10	9.9	9.95
24.	$\sqrt{64} < \sqrt{74} < \sqrt{81}$	9	8.6	8.60
25.	$\sqrt{196} < \sqrt{212} < \sqrt{225}$	15	14.5	14.56
26.	$\sqrt{16} < \sqrt{23} < \sqrt{25}$	5	4.8	4.80
27.	$\sqrt{121} < \sqrt{130} < \sqrt{144}$	11	11.5	11.40
28.	$\sqrt{225} < \sqrt{255} < \sqrt{256}$	16	15.9	15.97

For Exercises 29–48, use $a^2 + b^2 = c^2$, where c corresponds to the longest side of each triangle and a and b correspond to the other two sides.

29. $a^2 + b^2 = c^2$
$1^2 + 1.5^2 = 2^2$
$1 + 2.25 = 4$
$3.25 \neq 4$
no; not a right triangle

30. $a^2 + b^2 = c^2$
$5^2 + 12^2 = 13^2$
$25 + 144 = 169$
$169 = 169$
yes; right triangle

31. $a^2 + b^2 = c^2$
$6^2 + 8^2 = 10^2$
$36 + 64 = 100$
$100 = 100$
yes; right triangle

32. $a^2 + b^2 = c^2$
$30^2 + 40^2 = 50^2$
$900 + 1600 = 2500$
$2500 = 2500$
yes; right triangle

33. $a^2 + b^2 = c^2$
$5^2 + 6^2 = 8^2$
$25 + 36 = 64$
$61 \neq 64$
no; not a right triangle

34. $a^2 + b^2 = c^2$
$10^2 + 24^2 = 26^2$
$100 + 576 = 676$
$676 = 676$
yes; right triangle

35. $a^2 + b^2 = c^2$
$12^2 + 16^2 = 20^2$
$144 + 256 = 200$
$400 = 400$
yes; right triangle

36. $a^2 + b^2 = c^2$
$7^2 + 8^2 = 10^2$
$49 + 64 = 100$
$113 \neq 100$
no; not a right triangle

37. $a^2 + b^2 = c^2$
$18^2 + 24^2 = 30^2$
$324 + 576 = 900$
$900 = 900$
yes; right triangle

38. $a^2 + b^2 = c^2$
$4^2 + 6^2 = 7^2$
$16 + 36 = 49$
$52 \neq 49$
no; not a right triangle

39. $a^2 + b^2 = c^2$
$27^2 + 36^2 = 45^2$
$729 + 1296 = 2025$
$2025 = 2025$
yes; right triangle

40. $a^2 + b^2 = c^2$
$7^2 + 7^2 = 9^2$
$49 + 49 = 81$
$98 \neq 81$
no; not a right triangle

41. $a^2 + b^2 = c^2$
$12^2 + 13^2 = 18^2$
$144 + 169 = 324$
$313 \neq 324$
no; not a right triangle

42. $a^2 + b^2 = c^2$
$40^2 + 96^2 = 104^2$
$1600 + 9216 = 10,816$
$10,816 = 10,816$
yes, right triangle

43. $a^2 + b^2 = c^2$
$1.5^2 + 2^2 = 2.5^2$
$2.25 + 4 = 6.25$
$6.25 = 6.25$
yes; right triangle

44. $a^2 + b^2 = c^2$
$15^2 + 20^2 = 25^2$
$225 + 400 = 625$
$625 = 625$
yes; right triangle

45. $a^2 + b^2 = c^2$
$8^2 + 10^2 = 13^2$
$64 + 100 = 169$
$164 \neq 169$
no; not a right triangle

46. $a^2 + b^2 = c^2$
$10^2 + 24^2 = 26$
$100 + 576 = 676$
$676 = 676$
yes; right triangle

47. $a^2 + b^2 = c^2$
$(0.3)^2 + (0.4)^2 = (0.5)^2$
$0.09 + 0.16 = 0.25$
$0.25 = 0.25$
yes; right triangle

48. $a^2 + b^2 = c^2$
$9^2 + 9^2 = 13^2$
$81 + 81 = 169$
$162 \neq 169$
no; not a right triangle

49. $a^2 + b^2 = c^2$
$9^2 + 12^2 = c^2$
$81 + 144 = c^2$
$225 = c^2$
$\sqrt{225} = c$
$15 = c$

50. $a^2 + b^2 = c^2$
$24^2 + b^2 = 30^2$
$576 + b^2 = 900$
$b^2 = 324$
$b = \sqrt{324}$
$b = 18$

51. $a^2 + b^2 = c^2$
$a^2 + 12^2 = 20^2$
$a^2 + 144 = 400$
$a^2 = 256$
$a = \sqrt{256}$
$a = 16$

52. $a^2 + b^2 = c^2$
$20^2 + 48^2 = c^2$
$400 + 2304 = c^2$
$2701 = c^2$
$\sqrt{2704} = c$
$52 = c$

53. $a^2 + b^2 = c^2$
$a^2 + 13^2 = 85^2$
$a^2 + 169 = 7225$
$a^2 = 7056$
$a = \sqrt{7056}$
$a = 84$

54. $a^2 + b^2 = c^2$
$12^2 + b^2 = 13^2$
$144 + b^2 = 169$
$b^2 = 25$
$b = \sqrt{25}$
$b = 5$

55. $a^2 + b^2 = c^2$
$8^2 + 12^2 = c^2$
$64 + 144 = c^2$
$208 = c^2$
$\sqrt{208} = c$
$14.4 \approx c$

56. $a^2 + b^2 = c^2$
$16^2 + b^2 = 26^2$
$256 + b^2 = 676$
$b^2 = 420$
$b = \sqrt{420}$
$b \approx 20.5$

57. $a^2 + b^2 = c^2$
$10^2 + 20^2 = c^2$
$100 + 400 = c^2$
$500 = c^2$
$\sqrt{500} = c$
$22.4 \approx c$

58. $a^2 + b^2 = c^2$
$15^2 + 30^2 = c^2$
$225 + 900 = c^2$
$1125 = c^2$
$\sqrt{1125} = c$
$33.5 \approx c$

59. $a^2 + b^2 = c^2$
$4^2 + 4^2 = c^2$
$16 + 16 = c^2$
$32 = c^2$
$\sqrt{32} = c$
$5.7 \approx c$

60. The ladder represents the hypotenuse of a right triangle, and the two measurements given represent the lengths of the legs. To solve for the length of the ladder, use the "Pythagorean" Right-Triangle Theorem.

$$a^2 + b^2 = c^2$$
$$10^2 + 30^2 = c^2$$
$$100 + 900 = c^2$$
$$1000 = c^2$$
$$\sqrt{1000} = c$$
$$31.6 \approx c$$

The ladder is approximately 31.6 feet long.

61.

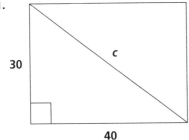

Let c represent the length of the diagonal of a rectangular pool.

$$a^2 + b^2 = c^2$$
$$30^2 + 40^2 = c^2$$
$$900 + 1600 = c^2$$
$$2500 = c^2$$
$$\sqrt{2500} = c^2$$
$$50 = c$$

The diagonal of a 30 feet by 40 feet pool is 50 feet.

62. Let c represent the distance traveled by the hiker.

$$a^2 + b^2 = c^2$$
$$4^2 + 4^2 = c^2$$
$$16 + 16 = c^2$$
$$32 = c^2$$
$$\sqrt{32} = c$$
$$5.7 \approx c$$

The hiker is approximately 5.7 miles from camp.

63. Let c represent the length of the diagonal between trees.

$$a^2 + b^2 = c^2$$
$$30^2 + 30^2 = c^2$$
$$900 + 900 = c^2$$
$$1800 = c^2$$
$$\sqrt{1800} = c$$
$$42.4 \approx c$$

For the trees to form a square, the diagonal should be approximately 42.4 feet long.

64. Let c represent the length of the diagonal between trees.

$$a^2 + b^2 = c^2$$
$$40^2 + 40^2 = c^2$$
$$1600 + 1600 = c^2$$
$$3200 = c^2$$
$$\sqrt{3200} = c$$
$$56.6 \approx c$$

The diagonal should be approximately 56.6 feet in order for the trees to form a square.

65. Let c represent the length of the cable.

$$a^2 + b^2 = c^2$$
$$105^2 + 60^2 = c^2$$
$$11{,}025 + 3600 = c^2$$
$$14{,}625 = c^2$$
$$14{,}625 = c$$
$$120.9 \approx c$$

The cable is approximately 120.9 feet long.

PAGE 255, LOOK BACK

66.

x	−2	−1	0	1	2	3	4
y	−5	−4	−3	−2	−1	0	1

The pattern is that the y-value is 3 less than the x-value, so the equation is $y = x - 3$.

67.

x	−2	−1	0	1	2	3	4
y	−3	−1	1	3	5	7	9

The pattern is that the y-value is 1 more than twice the x-value, so the equation is $y = 2x + 1$.

68. $A = \frac{1}{2}bh$

$$= \frac{1}{2}(3)(4)$$
$$= 6 \text{ square units}$$

69. $A = bh$

$$= (6)(4.5)$$
$$= 27 \text{ square units}$$

70. $A = \frac{(b_1 + b_2)\,h}{2}$

$$= \frac{(4 + 6)\,3}{2}$$
$$= \frac{30}{2}$$
$$= 15 \text{ square units}$$

PAGE 255, LOOK BEYOND

71. $(AB)^2 = 4^2 + 3^2$

$$= 16 + 9$$
$$= 25$$
$$AB = \sqrt{25}$$
$$= 5$$

72. $(AC)^2 = 4^2 + 4^2$

$$= 16 + 16$$
$$= 32$$
$$AC = \sqrt{32} \approx 5.6$$
$$AC \approx 5.66$$

73. $AD = 5$

D is 5 units from A horizontally; no right triangle is needed.

74. $(AE)^2 = 8^2 + 5^2$

$$= 64 + 25$$
$$= 89$$
$$AE = \sqrt{89} \approx 9.4$$
$$AE \approx 9.43$$

75. $(AF)^2 = 9^2 + 2^2$

$$= 81 + 4$$
$$= 85$$
$$AF = \sqrt{85} \approx 9.2$$
$$AF \approx 9.22$$

	Scale factor	Length	Width
	original	8 cm	10 cm
5.	2	16 cm	20 cm
6.	3	24 cm	30 cm
7.	4	32 cm	40 cm
8.	$\frac{1}{2}$	4 cm	5 cm
9.	0.8	6.4 cm	8 cm

	Scale factor	Length	Width
	original	12 cm	15 cm
10.	25%	3 cm	3.75 cm
11.	175%	21 cm	26.25 cm
12.	0.6	7.2 cm	9 cm
13.	$\frac{3}{4}$	9 cm	$11\frac{1}{4}$ cm
14.	2.5	30 cm	37.5 cm

15.

Length	Width	Perimeter
8 cm	10 cm	36 cm
16 cm	20 cm	72 cm
24 cm	30 cm	108 cm
32 cm	40 cm	144 cm
4 cm	5 cm	18 cm
6.4 cm	8 cm	28.8 cm

Length	Width	Perimeter
12 cm	15 cm	54 cm
3 cm	3.75 cm	13.5 cm
21 cm	26.25 cm	94.5 cm
7.2 cm	9 cm	32.4 cm
9 cm	$11\frac{1}{4}$ cm	$40\frac{1}{2}$ cm
30 cm	37.5 cm	135 cm

The ratio of the perimeter of the similar rectangle to the perimeter of the original rectangle is the same as the scale factor.

16.

Length	Width	Area
8 cm	10 cm	80 sq cm
16 cm	20 cm	320 sq cm
24 cm	30 cm	720 sq cm
32 cm	40 cm	1280 sq cm
4cm	5 cm	20 sq cm
6.4 cm	8 cm	51.2 sq cm

Length	Width	Area
12 cm	15 cm	180 sq cm
3 cm	3.75 cm	11.25 sq cm
21 cm	26.25 cm	551.25 sq cm
7.2 cm	9 cm	64.8 sq cm
9 cm	$11\frac{1}{4}$ cm	$101\frac{1}{4}$ sq cm
30 cm	37.5 cm	1125 sq cm

The ratio of the area of the similar rectangle to the area of the original rectangle is the square of the scale factor.

	Leg	Leg	Scale factor
	4 cm	8 cm	original
17.	40 cm	80 cm	10
18.	20 cm	40 cm	5
19.	4 cm	8 cm	1

	Leg	Leg	Scale factor
	3 cm	4 cm	original
20.	9 cm	12 cm	3
21.	27 cm	36 cm	9
22.	33 cm	44 cm	11

23.

Leg	Leg	Area
4 cm	8 cm	16 sq cm
40 cm	80 cm	1600 sq cm
20 cm	40 cm	400 sq cm
4 cm	8 cm	16 sq cm

Leg	Leg	Area
3 cm	4 cm	6 sq cm
9 cm	12 cm	54 sq cm
27 cm	36 cm	486 sq cm
33 cm	44 cm	726 sq cm

The ratio of the area of the similar triangle to the area of the original triangle is the square of the scale factor.

24.

Leg	Leg	Area
4 cm	8 cm	20.94 sq cm
40 cm	80 cm	209.44 sq cm
20 cm	40 cm	104.72 sq cm
4 cm	8 cm	20.94 sq cm

Leg	Leg	Area
3 cm	4 cm	12 sq cm
9 cm	12 cm	36 sq cm
27 cm	36 cm	108 sq cm
33 cm	44 cm	132 sq cm

The ratio of the perimeter of the similar triangle to the perimeter of each original triangle is the same value as the scale factor.

25. $\dfrac{\text{tree's height}}{\text{Katrina's height}} = \dfrac{13}{1.4} \approx 9.29$

Multiply the length of Katrina's shadow by the scale factor, 9.29, to find the length of the tree's shadow. $(1.1)(9.29) \approx 10.2$

The tree's shadow is approximately 10.2 meters long.

26. $\dfrac{\text{building's shadow}}{\text{Katrina's shadow}} = \dfrac{3.4}{1.1} \approx 3.09$

Multiply Katrina's height, 1.4 meters, by the scale factor, 3.09, to find the height of the building. $(1.4)(3.09) \approx 4.3$

The building is approximately 4.3 meters tall.

27. $\dfrac{\text{tree's height}}{\text{Katrina's height}} = \dfrac{13}{1.6} \approx 8.13$

Multiply the length of Katrina's shadow by the scale factor, 8.13, to find the length of the tree's shadow. $(1.1)(8.13) \approx 8.9$

The tree's shadow is approximately 8.9 meters long.

28. From Exercise 26, the scale factor is 3.09. Multiply Katrina's height by the scale factor to find the height of the building. $(1.5)(3.09) \approx 4.6$

The building is approximately 4.6 meters tall.

29. Scale factors may vary. Examples are shown.

Original triangle	Scale factor	New triangle
3-4-5	2	6-8-10
3-4-5	3	9-12-15
3-4-5	$\frac{1}{2}$	$\frac{3}{2}$-2-$\frac{5}{2}$
3-4-5	$\frac{1}{3}$	1-$\frac{4}{3}$-$\frac{5}{3}$

30. To find the scale factor, first convert the dimensions of the negative into the same units as the print: 24 mm × 36 mm = 2.4 cm × 3.6 cm.

Scale factor = $\dfrac{\text{length of print}}{\text{length of negative}} = \dfrac{12}{36} = 3.3\overline{3}$

or

Scale factor = $\dfrac{\text{width of print}}{\text{width of negative}} = \dfrac{8}{2.4} = 3.3\overline{3}$

The print was enlarged $3\frac{1}{3}$ times the size of the negative.

31. Scale factor = $\dfrac{9}{3.6} = 2.5$

Width of print = scale factor × width of negative
$= (2.5)(2.4)$
$= 6$ cm

The scale factor is 2.5. The width of the print is 6 centimeters.

32. Scale factor = $\dfrac{\text{new drawing height}}{\text{original drawing height}} = \dfrac{8.9}{24.8}$, or approximately $0.3589 \approx 36\%$

The scale factor is approximately 36%.

33. The approximate map distance between Harvard and MIT is 1.8 centimeters, so the scale factor is $\dfrac{1.8}{2.0}$, or 0.9. The approximate actual distance is $(0.9)(3)$, or 2.7 kilometers.

34. The approximate map distance between Franklin Park Zoo and Radcliff is 5.2 centimeters.

scale factor = $\dfrac{5.2}{2.0} = 2.6$

actual distance = $(2.6)(3) = 7.8$ kilometers

35. original rectangle: 8 centimeters long × 4 centimeters wide
scale factor = 150% = 1.5
new rectangle:

length = scale factor × original length
    = (1.5)(8)
    = 12

width = scale factor × original width
    = (1.5)(4)
    = 6

dimensions of new rectangle = 12 centimeters by 6 centimeters

$$P = 2l + 2w \qquad\qquad A = l \cdot w$$
$$= 2(12) + 2(6) \qquad\qquad = 12 \cdot 6$$
$$= 24 + 12 \qquad\qquad = 72 \text{ square centimeters}$$
$$= 36 \text{ centimeters}$$

dimensions of old rectangle = 8 centimeters by 4 centimeters

$$P = 2l + 2w \qquad\qquad A = l \cdot w$$
$$= 2(8) + 2(4) \qquad\qquad = 8 \cdot 4$$
$$= 16 + 8 \qquad\qquad = 32 \text{ square centimeters}$$
$$= 24 \text{ centimeters}$$

36. $\dfrac{\text{Perimeter of enlargement}}{\text{Perimeter of original graphic}} = \dfrac{36}{24} = 1.5 = \text{scale factor}$

$\dfrac{\text{Area of enlargement}}{\text{Area of original graphic}} = \dfrac{72}{32} = 2.25 = (\text{scale factor})^2$

When comparing perimeters or any other linear measure of two similar figures, the ratio of the new figure to the original figure will always be the same as the scale factor. When comparing areas of two similar figures, the ratio of the new figure to the original figure will always be the square of the scale factor. The perimeter is 150% larger and the area is 225% larger.

37.

Scale factor (%)	Scale factor (decimal)	Width	Length	Perimeter	Area
100%	1	4 cm	8 cm	24 cm	32 sq cm
150%	1.5	6 cm	12 cm	36 cm	72 sq cm
200%	2	8 cm	16 cm	48 cm	128 sq cm
300%	3	12 cm	24 cm	72 cm	288 sq cm
75%	0.75	3 cm	6 cm	18 cm	18 sq cm
50%	0.5	2 cm	4 cm	12 cm	8 sq cm

38. To find the perimeter of an enlarged or reduced figure, multiply the scale factor by the original perimeter. To find the area of an enlarged or reduced figure, multiply the square of the scale factor by the original area.

PAGE 263, LOOK BACK

39. 26% of $348 \approx \frac{1}{4} \cdot 348 \approx 87$
26% of $348 = (0.26)(348) = 90.48$

40. $\dfrac{458}{1020} \approx \dfrac{450}{1000} \approx \dfrac{45}{100} \approx 0.45 \approx 45\%$
$\dfrac{458}{1020} \approx 0.449 \approx 44.9\%$

41. 34 ft · 93 ft $\approx 35 \cdot 90 \approx 3150$ square feet
34 ft · 93 ft $= 3162$ square feet

42. $\dfrac{8.12}{96.03} \approx \dfrac{8}{96} \approx \dfrac{1}{12} \approx 0.08 \approx 8\%$
$\dfrac{8.12}{96.03} \approx .0846 \approx 8.5\%$

43. $7\frac{7}{16}$ in. $\cdot\, 9\frac{3}{8}$ in. $\approx 7\frac{1}{2} \cdot 9 \approx 63 + 4\frac{1}{2} \approx 67\frac{1}{2}$ sq in.
$7\frac{7}{16}$ in. $\cdot\, 9\frac{3}{8}$ in. $= 69\frac{93}{128}$ sq in. ≈ 69.7 sq in.

44. $\dfrac{\$8.48}{\$0.25} \approx \dfrac{\$8.50}{\$0.25} \approx 8\frac{1}{2} \cdot 4 \approx 32 + 2 \approx \$34$
$\dfrac{\$8.48}{\$0.25} = \$33.92$

92 CHAPTER 4

45. Let x represent the angle.

$$x + 18 = 90$$
$$x = 90 - 18$$
$$x = 72$$

The angle measures 72°.

46. Let x represent the angle.

$$x + 15 = 90$$
$$x = 90 - 15$$
$$x = 75$$

The angle measures 75°.

47. Let x represent the angle.

$$x + 45 = 180$$
$$x = 180 - 45$$
$$x = 135$$

The angle measures 135°.

48. Let x represent the first angle and $2x$ represent the second angle.

$$x + 2x = 180$$
$$3x = 180$$
$$\frac{3x}{3} = \frac{180}{3}$$
$$x = 60, 2x = 2(60) = 120$$

The angles measure 60° and 120°.

49. A decagon has 10 sides, so let $n = 10$.
sum of angles in polygon with n sides $= (n - 2)\ 180$

$$(n - 2)180 = (10 - 2)180$$
$$= 8 \cdot 180$$
$$= 1440$$

The sum of the angle measures in a decagon is 1440°.

PAGE 263, LOOK BEYOND

		A	B	C	$\overline{AB}$	$\overline{BC}$
	Original	(–2, 1)	(–2, –3)	(1, –3)	4	3

	Scale factor	A′	B′	C′	$\overline{A'B'}$	$\overline{B'C'}$
50.	2	(–4, 2)	(–4, –6)	(2, –6)	8	6
51.	3	(–6, 3)	(–6, –9)	(3, –9)	12	9
52.	4	(–8, 4)	(–8, –12)	(4, –12)	16	12

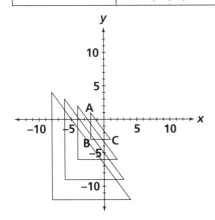

PAGES 266–268 CHAPTER 4 REVIEW

1.

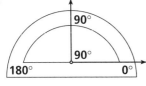

right angle

2.

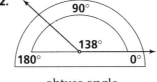

obtuse angle

3.

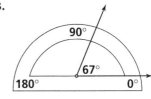

acute angle

For Exercises 4–6, let c represent the complement of the given angle, and let s represent its supplement.

4. $65 + c = 90$ $65 + s = 180$
    $c = 90 - 65$ $s = 180 - 65$
    $c = 25$ $s = 115$

The complement is 25°, and the supplement is 115°.

5. $89 + c = 90$ $89 + s = 180$
    $c = 90 - 89$ $s = 180 - 89$
    $c = 1$ $s = 91$

The complement is 1°, and the supplement is 91°.

6. $36.4 + c = 90$ $36.4 + s = 180$
    $c = 90 - 36.4$ $s = 180 - 36.4$
    $c = 53.6$ $s = 143.6$

The complement is 53.6°, and the supplement is 143.6°.

7. Let x represent the angle.
    $x + 135 = 180$
       $x = 180 - 135$
       $x = 45$

The angle measures 45°.

8. corresponding angles

9. alternate exterior angles

10. consecutive interior angles

11. alternate interior angles

12. (a) and (b) are true for all rectangles. (c) is true only when the rectangle is a square.

13. $P = 2w + 2l$
    $= 2(42) + 2(100)$
    $= 84 + 200$
    $= 284$ yards
$A = w \cdot l$
    $= 42 \cdot 100$
    $= 4200$ square yards

14. $P = 2w + 2l$
    $= 2(7.9) + 2(6.1)$
    $= 15.8 + 12.2$
    $= 28$ meters
$A = w \cdot l$
    $= (7.9)(6.1)$
    $= 48.19$ square meters

15. $P = 2w + 2l$
$$= 2\left(5\tfrac{1}{4}\right) + 2\left(3\tfrac{3}{8}\right)$$
$$= 2\left(\tfrac{21}{4}\right) + 2\left(\tfrac{27}{8}\right)$$
$$= \tfrac{42}{4} + \tfrac{27}{4}$$
$$= \tfrac{69}{4}$$
$$= 17\tfrac{1}{4} \text{ inches}$$
$A = w \cdot l$
$$= \left(5\tfrac{1}{4}\right)\left(3\tfrac{3}{8}\right)$$
$$= \tfrac{21}{4} \cdot \tfrac{27}{8}$$
$$= \tfrac{567}{32}$$
$$= 17\tfrac{23}{32} \text{ square inches}$$
or 17.71875 square inches

16. $A = \tfrac{1}{2} bh$
    $= \tfrac{1}{2}(10)(24)$
    $= 120$ square millimeters

17. $A = \tfrac{1}{2}(b_1 + b_2)h$
    $= \tfrac{1}{2}(7 + 9)\left(5\tfrac{1}{2}\right)$
    $= \tfrac{16}{2} \cdot \tfrac{11}{2}$
    $= \tfrac{176}{4}$
    $= 44$ square inches

18. $A = bh$
    $= (14.5)(6.3)$
    $= 91.35$ square yards

For Exercises 19–20, let a and b represent the lengths of the legs of the given right triangles, and let c represent the hypotenuse.

19. $a^2 + b^2 = c^2$
    $4^2 + 7.5^2 = c^2$
    $16 + 56.25 = c^2$
        $72.25 = c^2$
     $\sqrt{72.25} = c$
          $8.5 = c$

The hypotenuse of the triangle is 8.5.

20. $a^2 + b^2 = c^2$
    $12^2 + b^2 = 30^2$
    $144 + b^2 = 900$
         $b^2 = 900 - 144$
         $b^2 = 756$
          $b = \sqrt{756}$
          $b \approx 27.5$

The length of the other leg is 27.5.

21. Scale factor $= \dfrac{\text{length of leg on new triangle}}{\text{length of leg on original triangle}} = \dfrac{18}{6} = 3$
missing leg = scale factor × original $= 3 \cdot 9 = 27$

22. Scale factor $= \dfrac{\text{new triangle's leg}}{\text{original triangle's leg}} = \dfrac{18}{9} = 2$
missing leg = scale factor × original $= 2 \cdot 6 = 12$

23. Scale factor = $\dfrac{\text{new triangle's leg}}{\text{original triangle's leg}} = \dfrac{21}{6} = 3.5$

  missing leg = scale factor × original = (3.5)(9) = 31.5

24. Let x represent the length of the pipe.

$$52^2 + 52^2 = x^2$$
$$2704 + 2704 = x^2$$
$$5408 = x^2$$
$$\sqrt{5408} = x$$
$$73.5 \approx x$$

The pipe is approximately 73.5 ft long.

25. Scale factor = $\dfrac{\text{length of building's shadow}}{\text{length of Janice's shadow}} = \dfrac{36}{8} = 4.5$

  Height of building = scale factor × Janice's height
  = (4.5)(5)
  = 22.5

The building is 22.5 feet tall.

PAGE 269 # CHAPTER 4 ASSESSMENT

1.
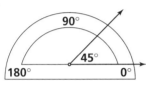
acute angle

2.
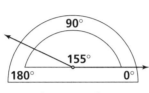
obtuse angle

3.
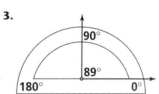
acute angle

4.
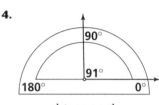
obtuse angle

For Exercises 5–7, let c represent the complement of the angle, and let s represent the supplement of the angle.

5. $23 + c = 90$
  $c = 90 - 23$
  $c = 67$

  The complement is 67°.

6. $23 + s = 180$
  $s = 180 - 23$
  $s = 157$

  The supplement is 157°.

7. $178 + s = 180$
  $s = 180 - 178$
  $s = 2$

  The supplement is 2°.

8. alternate interior angles:
  $\angle 6$ and $\angle 3$
  $\angle 8$ and $\angle 5$

9. alternate exterior angles:
  $\angle 4$ and $\angle 7$
  $\angle 1$ and $\angle 2$

10. corresponding angles:
  $\angle 1$ and $\angle 8$
  $\angle 4$ and $\angle 3$
  $\angle 6$ and $\angle 7$
  $\angle 5$ and $\angle 2$

11. consecutive interior angles:
  $\angle 6$ and $\angle 8$
  $\angle 5$ and $\angle 3$

For Exercises 12–17, answers may vary. Sample diagrams are shown below.

12.
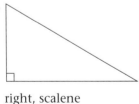
right, scalene

13.
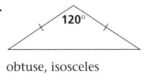
obtuse, isosceles

14.
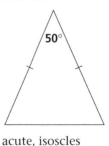
acute, isoscles

15.

convex, quadrilateral

16.

concave, hexagon

17.
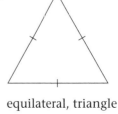
equilateral, triangle

18. $P = 2l + 2w$
$= 2(250) + 2(15)$
$= 500 + 30$
$= 530$ centimeters
$A = l \cdot w$
$= 250 \cdot 15$
$= 3750$ square centimeters

19. $P = 2l + 2w$
$= 2(14.5) + 2(6.8)$
$= 29 + 13.6$
$= 42.6$ feet
$A = l \cdot w$
$= (14.5)(6.8)$
$= 98.6$ square feet

20. $A = \frac{1}{2}bh$
$= \frac{1}{2}\left(4\frac{1}{8}\right)\left(3\frac{3}{4}\right)$
$= \frac{1}{2} \cdot \frac{33}{8} \cdot \frac{15}{4}$
$= \frac{495}{64}$
$= 7\frac{47}{64}$ square meters,
or 7.734375 square meters

21. $A = \frac{1}{2}(b_1 + b_2)(h)$
$= \frac{1}{2}(3 + 8)(5.5)$
$= \frac{11}{2} \cdot \frac{11}{2}$
$= \frac{121}{4}$
$= 30\frac{1}{4}$ square feet

22. $A = bh$
$= (5.7)(2.1)$
$= 11.97$ square centimeters

For Exercises 23–25, let a and b represent the legs of a right triangle, and let c represent its hypotenuse.

23. $a^2 + b^2 = c^2$
$3^2 + b^2 = 5^2$
$9 + b^2 = 25$
$b^2 = 25 - 9$
$b^2 = 16$
$b = \sqrt{16}$
$b = 4$ cm
The length of the third side is 4 centimeters.

24. $a^2 + b^2 = c^2$
$7.5^2 + 6^2 = c^2$
$56.25 + 36 = c^2$
$92.25 = c^2$
$\sqrt{92.25} = c$
9.6 ft $\approx c$
The length of the third side is approximately 9.6 feet.

25. $a^2 + b^2 = c^2$
$a^2 + 10^2 = 15^2$
$a^2 + 100 = 225$
$a^2 = 225 - 100$
$a^2 = 125$
$a = \sqrt{125}$
$a \approx 11.2$ in.
The length of the third side is approximately 11.2 inches.

26. scale factor $= \dfrac{\text{large triangle}}{\text{small triangle}} = \dfrac{12}{8} = \dfrac{3}{2}$ or 1.5
$a = \dfrac{10}{1.5} = 6\frac{2}{3}$
$b = 7 \cdot 1.5 = 10.5$

PAGES 270–271 # CHAPTERS 1–4 CUMULATIVE ASSESSMENT

1. C
$23 \cdot 43 + 23 \cdot 59 = 989 + 1357$
$= 2346$
$23 \cdot (43 + 59) = 23 \cdot (102)$
$= 2346$

2. A
$-17 - (-46) = -17 + 46$
$= 29$
$-17 - 46 = -63$

3. C
$(-144) \div 48 = -3$
$144 \div (-48) = -3$

4. B
$\frac{2}{3} = \frac{4}{6} < \frac{5}{6}$

5. b;
Charge c equals \$10 plus \$5 per hour, h
$c = 10 + 5 \times h$

6. b
4   19   44   79   124
15   25   35   45
10   10   10

7. d
a. $5\frac{1}{4} + 2\frac{7}{8} = 5\frac{2}{8} + 2\frac{7}{8}$
$= 7\frac{9}{8}$
$= 8\frac{1}{8}$

b. $12\frac{1}{8} - 3\frac{3}{8} = 11\frac{9}{8} - 3\frac{3}{8}$
$= 8\frac{6}{8}$

c. $6\frac{3}{4} + 1\frac{5}{6} = 6\frac{9}{12} + 1\frac{10}{12}$
$= 7\frac{19}{12}$
$= 8\frac{7}{12}$

8. b

$0.509 = 0.509 \cdot 100\%$
$= 50.9\%$

9. b
The marked angles are on opposite sides of the transversal and lie outside the two lines that the transversal cuts.

10. $\dfrac{301}{473} = \dfrac{43 \cdot 7}{43 \cdot 11}$
$= \dfrac{7}{11}$

11. From greatest to least, the numbers are as follows:

$4.4,\ 4\tfrac{1}{7},\ 4.14,\ 4.139,\ 4.014$

12. $56 \div 3\tfrac{1}{2} = 56 \div \tfrac{7}{2}$
$= 56 \cdot \tfrac{2}{7}$
$= \tfrac{112}{7}$
$= 16$

Walter can fill 16 bags.

13. $\dfrac{72 \text{ hamburgers}}{18 \text{ lb of beef}} = 4 \text{ hamburgers/lb}$
$\dfrac{120 \text{ hamburgers}}{4 \text{ hamburgers/lb}} = 30 \text{ lb of beef}$

14.

1	2	3
4	5	6

P (rolling a number > 2) $= \tfrac{4}{6}$, or $\tfrac{2}{3}$

15. Obtuse; the angle is larger than a right angle, but smaller than a straight angle.

16. Let x represent the angle.

$x + 45 = 90$
$x = 90 - 45$
$x = 45$

The angle measures $45°$.

17. A square; it has the right angles of a rectangle and the equilateral sides of a rhombus.

18. $P = 2l + 2w$ $A = l \cdot w$
$= 2(6.8) + 2(2.7)$ $= (6.8)(2.7)$
$= 13.6 + 5.4$ $= 18.36$ square feet
$= 19$ feet

19. $A = \tfrac{1}{2} bh$
$= \tfrac{1}{2}(5)(3)$
$= \tfrac{15}{2}$
$= 7\tfrac{1}{2}$ square units

20.

x	Equation $-8 + x = -3$	Simplified expression	True?
3	$-8 + 3 = -3$	$-5 = -3$	no
2	$-8 + 2 = -3$	$-6 = -3$	no
4	$-8 + 4 = -3$	$-4 = -3$	no
5	$-8 + 5 = -3$	$-3 = -3$	yes

The solution is $x = 5$.

21. $0.36 = \dfrac{36}{100}$
$= \dfrac{9}{25}$

22. let x represent the first angle. Then $2x$ represents the second angle.

$x + 2x = 180$
$3x = 180$
$\tfrac{1}{3} \cdot 3x = \tfrac{1}{3} \cdot 180$
$x = 60$
$2x = 2(60) = 120$

The larger angle measures $120°$.

23. Let a and b represent the lengths of the legs of the right triangle, and let c represent the length of the hypotenuse.

$a^2 + b^2 = c^2$
$7^2 + 24^2 = c^2$
$49 + 576 = c^2$
$625 = c^2$
$\sqrt{625} = c$
$25 = c$

The hypotenuse has a length of 25 centimeters.

24. Scale factor $= \dfrac{\text{short leg of new triangle}}{\text{short leg of original triangle}} = \dfrac{8}{4} = 2$

long leg of new triangle = scale factor × long leg of original triangle

$= 2 \times 15$
$= 30$

The long leg of the second triangle measures 30 feet.

CHAPTER 5

ADDITION AND SUBTRACTION IN ALGEBRA

5.1 **PAGES 277–279, PRACTICE & APPLY**

7. $(5a - 2) + (3a - 6) = (5a + 3a) + (-2 - 6)$
$= 8a + (-8)$
$= 8a - 8$

8. $(2x + 3) + (7 - x) = (2x - x) + (3 + 7)$
$= x + 10$

9. $(4x + 5) + (x + 9y) = (4x + x) + 9y + 5$
$= 5x + 9y + 5$

10. $(1.1a + 1.2b) + (2a - 0.8b)$
$= (1.1a + 2a) + (1.2b - 0.8b)$
$= 3.1a + 0.4b$

11. $\left(\frac{x}{2} + 1\right) + \left(\frac{x}{3} - 1\right) = \left(\frac{x}{2} + \frac{x}{3}\right) + (1 - 1)$
$= \left(\frac{3x}{6} + \frac{2x}{6}\right) + 0$
$= \frac{5}{6}x$

12. $\left(\frac{2m}{5} + \frac{1}{2}\right) + \left(\frac{m}{10} + \frac{5}{2}\right) = \left(\frac{2m}{5} + \frac{m}{10}\right) + \left(\frac{1}{2} + \frac{5}{2}\right)$
$= \left(\frac{4m}{10} + \frac{m}{10}\right) + \frac{6}{2}$
$= \frac{5m}{10} + 3$
$= \frac{1}{2}m + 3$

13. $(2a + 3b + 5c) + (7a - 3b + 5c) = (2a + 7a) + (3b - 3b) + (5c + 5c)$
$= 9a + 10c$

14. $(x + y + z) + (2w + 3y + 5) = 2w + x + (y + 3y) + z + 5$
$= 2w + x + 4y + z + 5$

15. Let x represent the number of x-tiles, and let the constants represent the number of 1-tiles.
$(6x + 3) + (2x + 1) = (6x + 2x) + (3 + 1)$
$= 8x + 4$

Use the following method for Exercises 16–18:
To determine the height of the framed picture, add the width of the frame above and below the picture to the height of the picture.

16. $12 + 3 + 3 = 15 + 3$
$= 18$
The height of the framed picture is 18 inches.

17. $20 + 3 + 3 = 23 + 3$
$= 26$
The height of the framed picture is 26 inches.

18. $h + 3 + 3 = h + 6$
The height of the picture is $(h + 6)$ inches.

Use the following method for Exercises 19–21:
To determine the total height of the box, add the lid thickness to the height of the box.

19. $10 + 1 = 11$
The height of the box is 11 inches.

20. $27.5 + 1 = 28.5$
The height of the box is 28.5 inches.

21. The height of the box is $(x + 1)$ inches.

22. Let b represent the number of boxes of tapes, and let the constants represent the number of single tapes.
$$(2b + 3) + (b + 7) = (2b + b) + (3 + 7)$$
$$= 3b + 10$$
John bought 3 boxes of tapes and 10 additional tapes.

23. Let b represent the number of cookies in a box.
Total cookies – friend's cookies = Don's cookies
$$7 \times 2 \times b - 14 = \text{Don's cookies}$$
$$14b - 14 = \text{Don's cookies}$$
Don has $14b - 14$ cookies for himself during the 7 months.

24. Let l represent the length of one of the 12 pieces of fabric. Then the length of the original piece of fabric is $12l + 3$.

25. If m represents an integer, then $m + 1$ and $m + 2$ represent the next two consecutive integers.

26. If n represents an odd integer, then $n + 2$ and $n + 4$ represent the next two odd integers.

27. Let a represent the number of apples, b the number of bananas, p the number of plums, and C the total cost. Then the total cost, in dollars, is $C = 0.30a + 0.25b + 0.20\,p$.

Use the following method for Exercises 28–30:
To determine the expression for the perimeter of each figure, add the expressions for the side lengths and simplify. Let P represent the perimeter of each figure.

28. $P = (3m + 2r) + (5r - m) + (4r + 2m) + (r - 5m)$
$$= (3m - m + 2m - 5m) + (2r + 5r + 4r + r)$$
$$= -m + 12r$$

29. $P = 2(4b - 2c) + 2(3a + b + c)$
$$= (8b - 4c) + (6a + 2b + 2c)$$
$$= 6a + (8b + 2b) + (-4c + 2c)$$
$$= 6a + 10b + (-2c)$$
$$= 6a + 10b - 2c$$

30. $P = (3s - 3t) + (5t - 4s + p) + (2p - 5s)$
$$= (3s - 4s - 5s) + (-3t + 5t) + (p + 2p)$$
$$= -6s + 2t + 3p$$
$$= 3p - 6s + 2t$$

31. Let A represent the area of the larger rectangle. Find the length times the width: $x(y + z)$. You can distribute the x over the addition of y and z: $x(y + z) = xy + xz$. Also, you can find the sum of each of the small rectangles: $A = xy + xz$. Use the distributive property to factor out the common x: $x(y + z)$.

32. $3(5 + 7) = 3(5) + 3(7) = 15 + 21$

33. $6(x - 3) = 6(x) - 6(3) = 6x - 18$

34. $(x + y)n = xn + yn$

35. $(4 \cdot 3 + 4 \cdot 5) = 4(3 + 5)$

36. $4x - 4 \cdot 7 = 4(x - 7)$

37. $az + bz = z(a + b)$ or $(a + b)z$

38. The product $25 \cdot 12$ can be found by expressing 12 as $10 + 2$. Then use the Distributive Property.
$$25 \cdot 12 = 25(10 + 2)$$
$$= 25 \cdot 10 + 25 \cdot 2$$
$$= 250 + 50$$
$$= 300$$

 PAGE 279, LOOK BACK

39. Sequence: 10, 20, 40, 80, 160, . . .
To find the next three terms, determine the rule. For this sequence, each term is the previous term multiplied by 2. The next three terms are 320, 640, and 1280.

40. Let $w = Y_1$, and enter the right-hand side of the equation as $5x + 12$.

Set up a table of values for the equation entered, where x has a minimum value of 35 and increases in increments of 1.

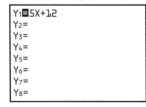

X	Y₁
35	187
36	192
37	197
38	202
39	207
40	212
41	217

X=38

The table shows that X is 38 when Y_1 is 202. So h is 38 when w is 202.

41. $12 + 3.5 = 12 + 15$
$\qquad\qquad\quad = 27$

42. $|-12| + |-3| = 12 + 3$
$\qquad\qquad\qquad\; = 15$

43. $(-10)(-2) \div (-5) = 20 \div (-5)$
$\qquad\qquad\qquad\qquad\; = -4$

44. $16 \div 5\frac{1}{3} = 16 \div \frac{16}{3}$
$\qquad\qquad\; = \frac{16}{1} \cdot \frac{3}{16}$
$\qquad\qquad\; = 3$

45. If a constant appears when determining the second differences, the function is quadratic.

46. $A = \frac{b_1 + b_2}{2} \cdot h$
$\quad = \frac{8 + 12}{2} \cdot 16$
$\quad = \frac{20}{2} \cdot 16$
$\quad = 10 \cdot 16$
$\quad = 160$ square inches

47. $a^2 + b^2 = c^2$
$\quad 7^2 + 9^2 = c^2$
$\quad 49 + 81 = c^2$
$\qquad\quad 130 = c^2$
$\qquad \sqrt{130} = c$
$\qquad\; 11.4 \approx c$

PAGE 279, LOOK BEYOND

---

48. $(3a + 2b + 4p) - (5a + 3p) = 3a + 2b + 4p - 5a - 3p$
$\qquad\qquad\qquad\qquad\qquad\quad = (3a - 5a) + 2b + (4p - 3p)$
$\qquad\qquad\qquad\qquad\qquad\quad = -2a + 2b + p$

49.

	x	$(x + y)$ y
x	x^2	xy
$(x + y)$ y	xy	y^2

50. One possible method of solving this problem is tracing the routes in an organized way. Let R represent a movement to the right, and let U represent a movement upward. The possible pathways from A to B are as follows:

1 change of direction = 2 pathways
4R   3U
3U   4R

2 changes of direction = 5 pathways
3R   3U   1R
2R   3U   2R
1R   3U   3R
2U   4R   1U
1U   4R   2U

3 changes of direction = 12 pathways
3R   2U   1R   1U
3R   1U   1R   2U
2R   2U   2R   1U
2R   1U   2R   2U
1R   2U   3R   1U
1R   1U   3R   2U
2U   3R   1U   1R
2U   1U   1U   3R
2U   2R   1U   2U
1U   3R   2U   1R
1U   1R   2U   3R
1U   2R   2U   2U

4 changes of direction = 9 pathways
2R   1U   1R   2U   1R
2R   2U   1R   1U   1R
1R   1U   2R   2U   1R
1R   2U   2R   1U   1R
1R   1U   1R   2U   2R
1R   2U   1R   1U   2R
1U   3R   1U   1R   1U
1U   1R   1U   3R   1U
1U   2R   1U   2R   1U

5 changes of direction = 6 pathways
2R   1U   1R   1U   1R   1U
1R   1U   2R   1U   1R   1U
1R   1U   1R   1U   2R   1U
1U   2R   1U   1R   1U   1R
1U   1R   1U   2R   1U   1R
1U   1R   1U   1R   1U   2R

6 changes of direction = 1 pathway
1R   1U   1R   1U   1R   1U   1R

There are 35 possible pathways.

5.2 PAGES 283–285, PRACTICE & APPLY

---

8. $-(17) = -17$

9. $-(-13) = 13$

10. $-(2x) = -2x$

11. $-(-6) = 6$

12. $-(9y + 2w) = -9y - 2w$

13. $-(5a + 3b) = -5a - 3b$

14. $-(2n - 3m) = -2n + 3m$

15. $-(9c - 5d) = -9c + 5d$

16. $-(-7x + 9) = 7x - 9$

17. $-(-7r + 4s) = 7r - 4s$

18. $-(-3p - q) = 3p + q$

19. $-(-j - k) = j + k$

20. $9x - 3x = 6x$

21. $8y - 2y = 6y$

22. $5c - (3 - 2c) = 5c - 3 + 2c$
$= (5c + 2c) - 3$
$= 7c - 3$

23. $7d - (1 - d) = 7d - 1 + d$
$= (7d + d) - 1$
$= 8d - 1$

24. $(7r + 2s) + (9r + 3s) = (7r + 9r) + (2s + 3s)$
$= 16r + 5s$

25. $(9k + 2k) + (11j - 2j) = 11k + 9j$

26. $(2a - 1) - (5a - 5) = 2a - 1 - 5a + 5$
$= (2a - 5a) + (-1 + 5)$
$= -3a + 4$

27. $(9v - 8w) - (8v - 9w) = 9v - 8w - 8v + 9w$
$= (9v - 8v) + (-8w + 9w)$
$= v + w$

28. $(2x + 3) - (4x - 5) + (6x - 7) = 2x + 3 - 4x + 5 + 6x - 7$
$= (2x - 4x + 6x) + (3 + 5 - 7)$
$= 4x + 1$

29. $(4y + 9) - (8y - 1) + (7 - y) = 4y + 9 - 8y + 1 + 7 - y$
$= (4y - 8y - y) + (9 + 1 + 7)$
$= -5y + 17$

30. $x - (y + z) = x - y - z$; therefore,
$x - (y + z) = x - y + z$ is a false statement.

31. $x - (y - z) = x - y + z$; therefore,
$x - (y - z) = x - y - z$ is a false statement.

32. $-x + (y - z) = -x + y - z$; therefore,
$-x + (y - z) = -x - y - z$ is a false statement.

33. Since the statement is false when x is negative, the statement is false.

34. According to the graph, there were approximately 75 million females in the United States in 1950.

35. According to the graph, there were approximately 75 million males in the United States in 1950.

36. According to the graph, there were approximately 150 million people in the United States in 1950.

37. According to the graph, there were approximately 110 million females in the United States in 1980.

38. According to the graph, there were approximately 110 million males in the United States in 1980.

39. According to the graph, there were approximately 220 million people in the United States in 1980.

40. True; the heights of the population bars are increasing over time.

41. True

42. False; the height of the gender population bars are approximately the same for any given year.

43. Let C represent the revenue in dollars from selling 89 deluxe and 234 regular fruitcakes.
$C = 89 \times 3 + 234 \times 2$
$= 267 + 468$
$= 735$
The total revenue is $735.

44. Let C represent the revenue in dollars from selling the cakes, d represent the number of deluxe fruitcakes, and r represent the number of regular fruitcakes. Then,
$C = 3d + 2r$.
The total revenue can be determined by the equation, $C = 3d + 2r$.

45. Let C represent the revenue in dollars from selling 89 deluxe and 234 regular fruitcakes, d represent the price of one deluxe fruitcake, and r represent the price of one regular fruitcake.
$C = 89d + 243r$
$= 89 \times 3.75 + 234 \times 2.50$
$= 333.75 + 585.00$
$= 918.75$
The total revenue is $918.75.

46. Let C represent the revenue in dollars from the sale of the fruitcakes, d represent the number of deluxe fruitcakes sold at a price of $3.75 each, and r represent the number of regular fruitcakes sold at a price of $2.50 each. Then, $C = 3.75d + 2.50r$.

The total revenue can be determined by the equation $C = 3.75d + 2.50r$.

47. Let C represent the total revenue from Joni's and Wang's sales in dollars, d represent the number deluxe fruitcakes sold, and r represent the number regular fruitcakes sold.

Total revenue = Joni's sales + Wang's sales

$$C = (3.75 \times 9 + 2.50 \times 23) + (3.75 \times 7 + 2.50 \times 27)$$
$$= (33.75 + 57.50) + (26.25 + 67.50)$$
$$= 91.25 + 93.75$$
$$= 185.00$$

The total revenue was $185.00.

48. To determine the difference in sales, subtract the smaller revenue (Joni's sales) from the greater revenue (Wang's sales). From Exercise 47, Wang's sales were $93.75 and Joni's sales were $91.25.

$93.75 - 91.25 = 2.50$

Wang earned $2.50 more than Joni.

49. Let c represent a case of juice, and let the constants represent single cans of juice. Let T be the total amount of juice distributed during lunch.

$$T = \text{beginning amount} - \text{ending amount}$$
$$= (11c + 3) - (6c)$$
$$= 11c - 6c + 3$$
$$= 5c + 3$$

Five cases and 3 single cans of juice were distributed during lunch.

50.

$11 + 5$

51.

$23 - 12$

PAGE 285, LOOK BACK

---

52. Let C represent the total charge, and let h represent number of hours.

$C = 16h$

53.
$$72 = 1 \times 72$$
$$= 2 \times 36$$
$$= 3 \times 24$$
$$= 4 \times 18$$
$$= 6 \times 12$$
$$= 8 \times 9$$

The factors of 72 are 1, 2, 3, 4, 6, 8, 9, 12, 18, 24, 36, and 72.

54.
$$150 = 15 \times 10$$
$$= (3 \times 5) \times (2 \times 5)$$
$$= 2 \times 3 \times 5^2$$

55. No parentheses are needed since $28 \div 2 - 4 \cdot 1 = 10$.

56. $16 \div (5 + 3) \div 2 = 1$

57. $40 \cdot (2 + 10 \cdot 4) = 1680$

58. Let r represent the current reading. To determine the current reading, add the recorded changes to 100.

$$r = 100 + (-4) + 51 + 0 + 7 + (-12) + (-78) + 2 + (-13) + (-1)$$
$$= 100 - 4 + 51 + 0 + 7 - 12 - 78 + 2 - 13 - 1$$
$$= (100 + 51 + 0 + 7 + 2) + (-4 - 12 - 78 - 13 - 1)$$
$$= 160 + (-108)$$
$$= 160 - 108$$
$$= 52$$

The current reading is +52.

59. Answers may vary. Substitute different values for x into the equation to see if a true statement results.

$x - 7 = -3$	$x - 7 = -3$	$x - 7 = -3$
Let $x = 5$.	Let $x = 2$.	Let $x = 4$.
$5 - 7 \overset{?}{=} -3$	$2 - 7 \overset{?}{=} -3$	$4 - 7 \overset{?}{=} -3$
$-2 \overset{?}{=} -3$	$-5 \overset{?}{=} -3$	$-3 = -3$
false, so $x \neq 5$	false, so $x \neq 2$	true, so $x = 4$

60.
$$A = \frac{1}{2}bh$$
$$= \frac{1}{2}(15)(21)$$
$$= 157.5$$

The area of the triangle is 157.5 square centimeters.

61. Let x represent the test score needed for an average of 85.

$$\frac{87 + 74 + 90 + x}{4} = 85$$

$$87 + 74 + 90 + x = 85(4)$$

$$251 + x = 340$$

$$x = 340 - 251$$

$$x = 89$$

Fred needs a score of 89 points on the next test.

62. To determine the time to travel around the lake one time, divide the distance around the lake by the speed of travel. Let t represent the travel time in minutes.

Find the time it takes Paul to travel around the lake one time.

Paul: $t = \frac{2}{12} = \frac{1}{6}$ hour

Find the time it takes Dan to travel around the lake one time.

Dan: $t = \frac{2}{10} = \frac{1}{5}$ hour

Convert the amount of hours to minutes.

Paul: $\frac{1}{6} \cdot 60 = 10$ minutes   Dan: $\frac{1}{5} \cdot 60 = 12$ minutes

Paul can sail around the lake in 10 minutes. Dan can sail around the lake in 12 minutes. Create a table to show the number of minutes each takes as they travel around the lake 1, 2, 3, 4, 5, and 6 times.

Number of times around the lake	1	2	3	4	5	6	
Paul	10	20	30	40	50	60	← minutes traveled around the lake
Dan	12	24	36	48	60	72	← minutes traveled around the lake

In 60 minutes, Paul and Dan will pass the starting point at the same time. The time will be 1:00 P.M.

5.3 **PAGES 289–291, PRACTICE & APPLY**

7. $x - 3 = 2$ **8.** $x + 3 = -5$ **9.** $-6 = 2 + x$

10. $2 + x = -3$

11. $x - 4 = -5$ **12.** $x + 2 = -3$

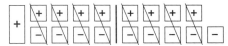

$$x - 4 = -5$$
$$x - 4 + 4 = -5 + 4$$
$$x = -1$$

$$x + 2 = -3$$
$$x + 2 - 2 = -3 - 2$$
$$x = -5$$

13. $3 = -4 + x$ **14.** $5 = x + 7$

$$3 = -4 + x$$
$$3 + 4 = -4 + 4 + x$$
$$7 = x$$

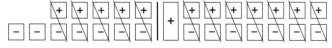

$$5 = x + 7$$
$$5 - 7 = x + 7 - 7$$
$$-2 = x$$

15. $4 + x = -4$ **16.** $-8 = 5 + x$

$$4 + x = -4$$
$$4 - 4 + x = -4 - 4$$
$$x = -8$$

$$-8 = 5 + x$$
$$-8 - 5 = 5 - 5 + x$$
$$-13 = x$$

17. $5 + x = -3$

$$5 + x = -3$$
$$5 - 5 + x = -3 - 5$$
$$x = -8$$

18. $x - 3 = -8$

$$x - 3 = -8$$
$$x - 3 + 3 = -8 + 3$$
$$x = -5$$

19.
$$x + 3 = 4$$
$$x + 3 - 3 = 4 - 3$$
$$x = 1$$

20.
$$t - 5 = -2$$
$$t - 5 + 5 = -2 + 5$$
$$t = 3$$

21.
$$x + 5 = -2$$
$$x + 5 - 5 = -2 - 5$$
$$x = -7$$

22.
$$3 = x + 2$$
$$3 - 2 = x + 2 - 2$$
$$1 = x$$

23.
$$-3 = y - 6$$
$$-3 + 6 = y - 6 + 6$$
$$3 = y$$

24.
$$-4 = x - 2$$
$$-4 + 2 = x - 2 + 2$$
$$-2 = x$$

25.
$$x - 3 = -3$$
$$x - 3 + 3 = -3 + 3$$
$$x = 0$$

26.
$$x - 2 = -2$$
$$x - 2 + 2 = -2 + 2$$
$$x = 0$$

27.
$$m + 6 = -1$$
$$m + 6 - 6 = -1 - 6$$
$$m = -7$$

28.
$$a + 4 = -3$$
$$a + 4 - 4 = -3 - 4$$
$$a = -7$$

29.
$$-5 = y + z$$
$$-5 - 2 = y + 2 - 2$$
$$-7 = y$$

30.
$$-3 = w + 3$$
$$-3 - 3 = w + 3 - 3$$
$$-6 = w$$

31.
$$x + 7 = 2$$
$$x + 7 - 7 = 2 - 7$$
$$x = -5$$

32.
$$-4 = n + 1$$
$$-4 - 1 = n + 1 - 1$$
$$-5 = n$$

33.
$$y - 8 = 10$$
$$y - 8 + 8 = 10 + 8$$
$$y = 18$$

34.
$$h - 65 = 65$$
$$h - 65 + 65 = 65 + 65$$
$$h = 130$$

35.
$$b + 10 = -6$$
$$b + 10 - 10 = -6 - 10$$
$$b = -16$$

36.
$$5 + t = -7$$
$$5 - 5 + t = -7 - 5$$
$$t = -12$$

37.
$$9 = v - 3$$
$$9 + 3 = v - 3 + 3$$
$$12 = v$$

38.
$$d - 5 = 11$$
$$d - 5 + 5 = 11 + 5$$
$$d = 16$$

39.
$$5 = -8 - x$$
$$5 + x = -8 - x + x$$
$$5 + x = -8$$
$$5 - 5 + x = -8 - 5$$
$$x = -13$$

40.
$$y - 4 = -5$$
$$y - 4 + 4 = -5 + 4$$
$$y = -1$$

41.
$$3 = p + (-2)$$
$$3 + 2 = p + (-2) + 2$$
$$5 = p$$

42.
$$(-5) + t = 9$$
$$(-5) + 5 + t = 9 + 5$$
$$t = 14$$

43. $p = 52$
$$p = 21 + w + 21 + w$$
$$52 = 21 + w + 21 + w$$
$$52 = 42 + 2w$$

44. $g = a - h$
$$g = 180 - 30$$
$$g = 150 \text{ mph}$$

45.
$$g = a - h$$
$$475.2 = a - 94.7$$
$$569.9 \text{ mph} = a$$

46.
$$g = a - h$$
$$525.5 = a - 72$$
$$597.5 \text{ mph} = a$$

PAGE 291, LOOK BACK

47. $12 < 18$
$18 > 12$

48. $16 > 10$
$10 < 16$

49. $9 > 0$
$0 < 9$

50. $-3 < 0$
$0 > -3$

51. $-8 > -12$
$-12 < -8$

52. $-17 < -8$
$-8 > -17$

53. $-15 < 7$
$7 > -15$

54. $18 > -4$
$-4 < 18$

55. $(-5)(3) + (-2)(-3) = -15 + 6$
$$= -9$$

56. $-24 \div -12 = 2$

57. $(-8)^2 + (-4)^2 = 64 + 16$
$$= 80$$

58. $[(-8) + (-4)]^2 = [-12]^2$
$$= 144$$

59. Let x be the missing length in the left triangle, and let y be the missing length in the right triangle. Since the triangles are similar, proportions can be set up as follows:

$$\frac{6}{y} = \frac{9}{36} = \frac{x}{20}$$

Solve individually:

$$\frac{6}{y} = \frac{9}{36} \qquad \frac{9}{36} = \frac{x}{20}$$

$$\frac{6}{y} = \frac{1}{4} \qquad \frac{1}{4} = \frac{x}{20}$$

$$24 = y \qquad 4x = 20$$

$$x = 5$$

The missing side lengths are 5 in the left triangle and 24 in the right triangle.

60. $(2x - 7) + (9x - 6) = (2x + 9x) + (-7 - 6)$
$\qquad\qquad\qquad\qquad\quad = 11x - 13$

61. $(4x - 3) - (5 - x) = (4x - 3) + (-5 + x)$
$\qquad\qquad\qquad\qquad\quad = (4x + x) + (-3 - 5)$
$\qquad\qquad\qquad\qquad\quad = 5x - 8$

PAGE 291, LOOK BEYOND

62. Answers may vary. One solution is the following:

$$4x - 2 = 3x + 1 \qquad \Rightarrow \qquad x - 2 = 1$$

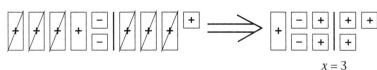

$$x = 3$$

 5.4 **PAGES 296–298 PRACTICE & APPLY**

6.

$$x + 9 = 6$$
$$x + 9 - 9 = 6 - 9$$
$$x = -3$$

7.

$$x - 7 = 3$$
$$x - 7 + 7 = 3 + 7$$
$$x = 10$$

8.

$$x - 10 = -4$$
$$x - 10 + 10 = -4 + 10$$
$$x = 6$$

9.

$$x + 6 = -4$$
$$x + 6 - 6 = -4 - 6$$
$$x = -10$$

10. Use the Addition Property of Equality.
$$a - 16 = 15$$
$$a - 16 + 16 = 15 + 16$$
$$a = 31$$

11. Use the Subtraction Property of Equality.
$$t + 29 = 11$$
$$t + 29 - 29 = 11 - 29$$
$$t = -18$$

12. Use the Subtraction Property of Equality.
$$m + 54 = 36$$
$$m + 54 - 54 = 36 - 54$$
$$m = -18$$

13. Use the Addition Property of Equality.
$$r - 10 = -80$$
$$r - 10 + 10 = -80 + 10$$
$$r = -70$$

14. Use the Addition Property of Equality.
$$l - 27 = 148$$
$$l - 27 + 27 = 148 + 27$$
$$l = 175$$

15. Use the Addition Property of Equality.
$$b - 109 = 58$$
$$b - 109 + 109 = 58 + 109$$
$$b = 167$$

16. Use the Subtraction Property of Equality.
$$y + 37 = -110$$
$$y + 37 - 37 = -110 - 37$$
$$y = -147$$

17. Use the Subtraction Property of Equality.
$$396 = z + 256$$
$$396 - 256 = z + 256 - 256$$
$$140 = z$$

18. Use the Subtraction Property of Equality.
$$x + \frac{3}{4} = \frac{5}{4}$$
$$x + \frac{3}{4} - \frac{3}{4} = \frac{5}{4} - \frac{3}{4}$$
$$x = \frac{2}{4}$$
$$x = \frac{1}{2}$$

19. Use the Subtraction Property of Equality.
$$7.4 + t = 5.2$$
$$t = 5.2 - 7.4$$
$$t = -2.2$$

20. Use the Subtraction Property of Equality.
$$r + 5.78 = 7$$
$$r + 5.78 - 5.78 = 7 - 5.78$$
$$r = 1.22$$

21. Use the Addition and Subtraction Properties of Equality.
$$\frac{3}{8} - x = \frac{3}{4}$$
$$\frac{3}{8} - x + x = \frac{3}{4} + x$$
$$\frac{3}{8} - \frac{3}{4} = x + \frac{3}{4} - \frac{3}{4}$$
$$\frac{3}{8} - \frac{6}{8} = x$$
$$-\frac{3}{8} = x$$

22.
$$a + b = c$$
$$a + b - b = c - b$$
$$a = -b + c$$

23.
$$a - b = c$$
$$a - b + b = c + b$$
$$a = b + c$$

24.
$$a + b = -c$$
$$a + b - b = -c - b$$
$$a = -b - c$$

25.
$$a - b = -c$$
$$a - b + b = -c + b$$
$$a = b - c$$

26.
$$a - \frac{2}{3} = 4$$
$$a - \frac{2}{3} + \frac{2}{3} = \frac{12}{3} + \frac{2}{3}$$
$$a = \frac{14}{3}$$
$$3a = 3\left(\frac{14}{3}\right)$$
$$= 14$$

27.
$$2.5 + s = 5.3$$
$$2.5 - 2.5 + s = 5.3 - 2.5$$
$$s = 2.8$$
$$2s - 3 = 2(2.8) - 3$$
$$= 5.6 - 3$$
$$= 2.6$$

28.
$$x + 35 = 96$$
$$x + 35 - 35 = 96 - 35$$
$$x = 61$$

29.
$$x - 35 = 96$$
$$x - 35 + 35 = 96 + 35$$
$$x = 131$$

30. Both require the use of an equality property; equation a requires the Subtraction Property of Equality, while equation b requires the Addition Property of Equality.

31. Let y represent the number of yards that the second-string running back ran.
$$89 + y = 94$$
$$(89 + y) - 89 = 94 - 89$$
$$y = 5$$

The second string running back gained 5 yards.

32. Let y represent the number of yards that the second-string running back ran.
$$94 + y = 89$$
$$(94 + y) - 94 = 89 - 94$$
$$y = -5$$

The second string running back lost 5 yards.

33. Let c represent the combined yardage of both running backs.
$$94 + 89 = c$$
$$183 = c$$

The total distance run is 183 yards.

34. Let d represent the number of days until Carl's birthday.
$$d + 288 = 355$$
$$d = 67$$

There are 67 days before Carl's birthday.

35. Let w represent the amount of water, in cups, to be added.

$$w + \frac{7}{8} = 1\frac{1}{2}$$
$$w + \frac{7}{8} - \frac{7}{8} = \frac{3}{2} - \frac{7}{8}$$
$$w = \frac{12}{8} - \frac{7}{8}$$
$$w = \frac{5}{8}$$

$\frac{5}{8}$ of a cup of water needs to be added.

36. Let m represent the odometer reading at the start of the trip in miles.

$$m + 149 = 23{,}580$$
$$m + 149 - 149 = 23{,}580 - 149$$
$$m = 23{,}431$$

The odometer reading was 23,431 miles.

37. Let m represent the odometer reading at the end of the trip in miles.

$$m - 149 = 23{,}580$$
$$m - 149 + 149 = 23{,}580 + 149$$
$$m = 23{,}729$$

The odometer reading was 23,729 miles.

38. Let t represent the tax amount in dollars and cents.

$$12.98 + 14.95 + t + 0.39 = 30.00$$
$$28.32 + t = 30.00$$
$$28.32 - 28.32 + t = 30.00 - 28.32$$
$$t = 1.68$$

The tax was $1.68.

39. Let L represent the lowest score.

$$28 = 47 - L$$
$$28 + L = 47 - L + L$$
$$28 + L = 47$$
$$28 - 28 + L = 47 - 28$$
$$L = 19$$

The lowest score is 19.

40. Let a represent the measure of the angle in degrees.

$$s + a = 180$$
$$92 + a = 180$$
$$92 - 92 + a = 180 - 92$$
$$a = 88$$

The measure of the angle is 88°.

41. Let a represent the measure of the third angle in degrees.

$$2(50) + a = 180$$
$$100 + a = 180$$
$$100 - 100 + a = 180 - 100$$
$$a = 80$$

The measure of the third angle is 80°.

42. Let x represent the measure of the angle SRT in degrees.

$$x + 30 = 70$$
$$x + 30 - 30 = 70 - 30$$
$$x = 40$$

The measure of angle SRT is 40°.

43. Let x represent the measure of angle SRT in degrees.

$$x + 18 = 70$$
$$x + 18 - 18 = 70 - 18$$
$$x = 52$$

The measure of angle SRT is 52°.

44. Let x represent the measure of angle TSP.

$$32 + x = 180$$
$$32 - 32 + x = 180 - 32$$
$$x = 148$$

The measure of angle TSP is 148°.

45. Let y represent the measure of angle UVZ.

$$y + 28 = 90$$
$$y = 28 - 28 = 90 - 28$$
$$y = 62$$

The measure of angle UVZ is 62°.

46. Enter the following command after the prompt:
solve (X + 12345.6789 = 55555555);

47. Enter the following command after the prompt:
solve (A + B = C + D,D);

48. Let s represent the weight of a squirrel, d represent the weight of a dog, and c represent the weight of a cat.

$$s + d = 2c$$
$$d = 2s + c$$

Substitute $2s + c$ for d in $s + d = 2c$ to solve for c in terms of s.

$$s + d = 2(3s)$$
$$s + d = 6s$$
$$s - s + d = 6s - s$$
$$d = 5s$$

Five squirrels will balance the dog.

49. Sequence 6   0   12   6   18   12   [24]   [18]   [30]
Difference   −6   +12   −6   +12   −6   +12   −6   +12

Subtract 6 from the first term to get the second. Add 12 to the second term to get the third. Subtract 6 from the third term to get the fourth, and so on.

First term: $12 + 12 = 24$
Second term: $24 − 6 = 18$
Third term: $18 + 12 = 30$

The next three terms are 24, 18, and 30.

50. Let n represent the number of poster boards that can be bought.

$n = 2.50 \div 0.39 \approx 6.4$

Shannon can purchase 6 poster boards.

51. To order rational numbers from least to greatest, convert each to equivalent fractions with the same denominator:

$\frac{5}{8}, \frac{1}{4} = \frac{2}{8}, \frac{1}{8}, \frac{3}{4} = \frac{6}{8}, \frac{1}{2} = \frac{4}{8}$

From least to greatest, the numbers are $\frac{1}{8}, \frac{1}{4}, \frac{1}{2}, \frac{5}{8},$ and $\frac{3}{4}$.

52. Let P represent the perimeter of the square, and let s represent the length of each side in inches.

$P = s + s + s + s$
$\quad = 4 \cdot s$
$\quad = 4 \cdot 2.5$
$\quad = 10.0$

The perimeter of the square is 10 inches.

53. $(3x − 7) − (x − 4) = 3x − 7 − x + 4$
$\qquad\qquad\qquad = 3x − x − 7 + 4$
$\qquad\qquad\qquad = 2x − 3$

54. $2(8 − 7y) + 5(2y) = 16 − 14y + 10y$
$\qquad\qquad\qquad = 16 − 4y$ or $− 4y + 16$

55. $−4(n − 2) − (−3n + 4) = −4n + 8 + 3n − 4$
$\qquad\qquad\qquad\qquad = −4n + 3n + 8 − 4$
$\qquad\qquad\qquad\qquad = −n + 4$

56. Model the left side of the equation with 1 x-tile and 3 negative 1-tiles and the right side with 8 positive 1-tiles. Add 3 positive 1-tiles to each side of the equation. Simplify the left side of the equation by removing 3 neutral pairs of 1-tiles. Eleven positive 1-tiles remain on the right side; therefore, $x = 11$.

57. Model the left side of the equation with 2 x-tiles and the right side with 12 positive 1-tiles. Separate the x-tiles on the left side into two groups, and separate the 12 positive 1-tiles on the right side into 2 groups, one group for each of the x-tiles on the left side. There are 6 positive 1-tiles in each group; therefore, $x = 6$.

58. Model the left side of the equation with 2 x-tiles and 5 positive 1-tiles and the right side with 11 positive 1-tiles. Take away 5 positive 1-tiles from each side. Separate the 6 positive 1-tiles on the right side into 2 groups, one for each of the x-tiles on the right side. There are 3 positive 1-tiles in each group; therefore, $x = 3$.

5. $\qquad 2x − 3x − 4 = −x − 4$
Check:

Let $x = 10$.
$2(10) − 3(10) − 4 \overset{?}{=} −10 − 4$
$\qquad\qquad\qquad −14 = −14$ True

Let $x = −10$.
$2(−10) − 3(−10) − 4 \overset{?}{=} −(−10) − 4$
$\qquad\qquad\qquad\qquad 6 = 6$ True

6. $\qquad 1 + 3x − 1 = 3x$
Check:

Let $x = 10$.
$1 + 3(10) − 1 \overset{?}{=} 3(10)$
$\qquad\qquad 30 = 30$ True

Let $x = −10$.
$1 + 3(−10) − 1 \overset{?}{=} 3(−10)$
$\qquad\qquad −30 = −30$ True

7. $\qquad 4x + 3 − 2x = 2x + 3$
Check:

Let $x = 10$.
$4(10) + 3 − 2(10) \overset{?}{=} 2(10) + 3$
$\qquad\qquad\qquad 23 = 23$ True

Let $x = −10$.
$4(−10) + 3 − 2(−10) \overset{?}{=} 2(−10) + 3$
$\qquad\qquad\qquad −17 = −17$ True

8. $2x^2 - 5 - x^2 = x^2 - 5$
Check:
Let $x = 4$.
$2(4)^2 - 5 - 4^2 \overset{?}{=} 4^2 - 5$
$11 = 11$ True
Let $x = -4$.
$2(-4)^2 - 5 - (-4)^2 \overset{?}{=} (-4)^2 - 5$
$11 = 11$ True

9. $-3b + b + 1 = -2b + 1$
Check:
Let $b = 10$.
$-3(10) + 10 + 1 \overset{?}{=} -2(10) + 1$
$-19 = -19$ True
Let $b = -10$.
$-3(-10) + (-10) + 1 \overset{?}{=} -2(-10) + 1$
$21 = 21$ True

10. $5a + 6 - 2a = 3a + 6$
Check:
Let $a = 10$.
$5(10) + 6 - 2(10) \overset{?}{=} 3(10) + 6$
$36 = 36$ True
Let $a = -10$.
$5(-10) + 6 - 2(-10) \overset{?}{=} 3(-10) + 6$
$-24 = -24$ True

11. $x^2 + 2x^2 - 3x = 3x^2 - 3x$
Check:
Let $x = 2$.
$2^2 + 2(2)^2 - 3(2) \overset{?}{=} 3(2)^2 - 3(2)$
$6 = 6$ True
Let $x = -2$.
$(-2)^2 + 2(-2)^2 - 3(-2) \overset{?}{=} 3(-2)^2 - 3(-2)$
$18 = 18$ True

12. $-x^2 - 3x^2 + 2x = -4x^2 + 2x$
Check:
Let $x = 2$.
$-2^2 - 3(2)^2 + 2(2) \overset{?}{=} -4(2)^2 + 2(2)$
$-12 = -12$ True
Let $x = -2$.
$-(-2)^2 - 3(-2)^2 + 2(-2) \overset{?}{=} -4(-2)^2 + 2(-2)$
$-20 = -20$ True

13. $2x^2 + 3x - x^2 = x^2 + 3x$
Check:
Let $x = 2$.
$2(2)^2 + 3(2) - 2^2 \overset{?}{=} 2^2 + 3(2)$
$10 = 10$ True
Let $x = -2$.
$2(-2)^2 + 3(-2) - (-2)^2 \overset{?}{=} (-2)^2 + 3(-2)$
$-2 = -2$ True

14. $2x^2 - x - 4x = 2x^2 - 5x$
Check:
Let $x = 2$.
$2(2)^2 - 2 - 4(2) \overset{?}{=} 2(2)^2 - 5(2)$
$-2 = -2$ True
Let $x = -2$.
$2(-2)^2 - (-2) - 4(-2) \overset{?}{=} 2(-2)^2 - 5(-2)$
$18 = 18$ True

15. $-4x + 3 + 2x^2 - x = 2x^2 - 5x + 3$
Check:
Let $x = 2$.
$-4(2) + 3 + 2(2)^2 - 2 \overset{?}{=} 2(2)^2 - 5(2) + 3$
$1 = 1$ True
Let $x = -2$.
$-4(-2) + 3 + 2(-2)^2 - (-2) \overset{?}{=} 2(-2)^2 - 5(-2) + 3$
$21 = 21$ True

16. $-3x^2 + 1 + 3x - 1 = -3x^2 + 3x$
Check:
Let $x = 10$.
$-3(10)^2 + 1 + 3(10) - 1 \overset{?}{=} -3(10)^2 + 3(10)$
$-270 = -270$ True
Let $x = -10$.
$-3(-10)^2 + 1 + 3(-10) - 1 \overset{?}{=} -3(-10)^2 + 3(-10)$
$-330 = -330$ True

17. $4x + 3 - 2x^2 - 5 = -2x^2 + 4x - 2$
Check:
Let $x = 2$.
$4(2) + 3 - 2(2)^2 - 5 \overset{?}{=} -2(2)^2 + 4(2) - 2$
$-2 = -2$ True
Let $x = -2$.
$4(-2) + 3 - 2(-2)^2 - 5 \overset{?}{=} -2(-2)^2 + 4(-2) - 2$
$-18 = -18$ True

18. $2x^2 - 5 - x^2 + 4 = x^2 - 1$
Check:
Let $x = 2$.
$2(2)^2 - 5 - 2^2 + 4 \overset{?}{=} 2^2 - 1$
$3 = 3$ True
Let $x = -2$.
$2(-2)^2 - 5 - (-2)^2 + 4 \overset{?}{=} (-2)^2 - 1$
$3 = 3$ True

19. $-3a + 8 - 2b$ Simplified

20. $5a^2 + 6 - 2a$ Simplified

21. $x^2 + 3x - 2x^2 + 4x = -x^2 + 7x$
Check:
Let $x = 2$.
$2^2 + 3(2) - 2(2)^2 + 4(2) \overset{?}{=} -2^2 + 7(2)$
$10 = 10$ True
Let $x = -2$.
$(-2)^2 + 3(-2) - 2(-2)^2 + 4(-2) \overset{?}{=} -(-2)^2 + 7(-2)$
$-18 = -18$ True

22. $2x^2 - (-4x + 3) = 2x^2 + 4x - 3$
Check:
Let $x = 2$.
$2(2)^2 - (-4(2) + 3) \overset{?}{=} 2(2)^2 + 4(2) - 3$
$13 = 13$ True
Let $x = -2$.
$2(-2)^2 - (-4(-2) + 3) \overset{?}{=} 2(-2)^2 + 4(-2) - 3$
$-3 = -3$ True

23. $2x^2 + (-x^2 - 2) = x^2 - 2$
Check:
Let $x = 2$.
$2(2)^2 + (-2^2 - 2) \stackrel{?}{=} 2^2 - 2$
$2 = 2$ True
Let $x = -2$.
$2(-2)^2 + (-(-2)^2 - 2) \stackrel{?}{=} (-2)^2 - 2$
$2 = 2$ True

24. $-x^2 - x - (-3x^2 - x) = 2x^2$
Check:
Let $x = 2$.
$-2^2 - 2 - (-3(2)^2 - 2) \stackrel{?}{=} 2(2)^2$
$8 = 8$ True
Let $x = -2$.
$-(-2)^2 - (-2) - (-3(-2)^2 - (-2)) \stackrel{?}{=} 2(-2)^2$
$8 = 8$ True

25. $(-2x - 3) + (2x + 2) = (-2x + 2x) + (-3 + 2)$
$= 0 + (-1)$
$= -1$

26. $(x^2 - 2) + (3x^2 + 1) = (x^2 + 3x^2) + (-2 + 1)$
$= 4x^2 - 1$

27. $(-x^2 + 1) + (x^2 - 1) = (-x^2 + x^2) + (1 - 1)$
$= 0$

28. $(x^2 + 2x) + (2x^2 + 3x) = (x^2 + 2x^2) + (2x + 3x)$
$= 3x^2 + 5x$

29. $(x^2 + x) + (-x^2 - 2x) = (x^2 - x^2) + (x - 2x)$
$= -x$

30. $(x^2 + 2x) + (-2x^2 - x) = (x^2 - 2x^2) + (2x - x)$
$= -x^2 + x$

31. $(-2x - 3) + (2x + 2) \stackrel{?}{=} -1$
$(-2(3) - 3) + (2(3) + 2) \stackrel{?}{=} -1$
$-9 + 8 \stackrel{?}{=} -1$
$-1 = -1$ True

32. $(x^2 - 2) + (3x^2 + 1) \stackrel{?}{=} 4x^2 - 1$
$((-3)^2 - 2) + (3(-3)^2 + 1) \stackrel{?}{=} 4(-3)^2 - 1$
$7 + 28 \stackrel{?}{=} 35$
$35 = 35$ True

33. $(-x^2 + 1) + (x^2 - 1) \stackrel{?}{=} 0$
$(-10^2 + 1) + (10^2 - 1) \stackrel{?}{=} 0$
$-99 + 99 \stackrel{?}{=} 0$
$0 = 0$ True

34. $(x^2 + 2x) + (2x^2 + 3x) \stackrel{?}{=} 3x^2 + 5x$
$((-5)^2 + 2(-5)) + (2(-5)^2 + 3(-5)) \stackrel{?}{=} 3(-5)^2 + 5(-5)$
$15 + 35 \stackrel{?}{=} 75 - 25$
$50 = 50$ True

35. $(x^2 + x) + (-x^2 - 2x) \stackrel{?}{=} -x$
$(5^2 + 5) + (-5^2 - 2(5)) \stackrel{?}{=} -5$
$30 + (-35) \stackrel{?}{=} -5$
$-5 = -5$ True

36. $(x^2 + 2x) + (-2x^2 - x) \stackrel{?}{=} -x^2 + x$
$(7^2 + 2(7)) + (-2(7)^2 - 7) \stackrel{?}{=} -7^2 + 7$
$63 + (-105) \stackrel{?}{=} -42$
$-42 = -42$ True

37. $(x^2 + x) + (-x^2 - 2x) = -x$

On a graphics calculator, enter left side of equation for Y_1 and right side of equation for Y_2.

```
Y₁▉(X²+X)+(-X²-2X)
Y₂▉-X
Y₃=
Y₄=
Y₅=
Y₆=
Y₇=
```

The Y_1 and Y_2 columns in the table should have the same corresponding values.

X	Y₁	Y₂
-3	3	3
-2	2	2
-1	1	1
0	0	0
1	-1	-1
2	-2	-2
3	-3	-3

X=-3

38. $(x^2 + 2x) + (-2x^2 - x) = -x^2 + x$

On a graphics calculator, enter the left side of the equation for Y_1 and the right side of the equation for Y_2.

```
Y₁▉(X²+2X)+(-2X²-X)
Y₂▉-X²+2
Y₃=
Y₄=
Y₅=
Y₆=
Y₇=
```

The Y_1 and Y_2 columns in the table should have the same corresponding values.

X	Y₁	Y₂
-3	-12	-12
-2	-6	-6
-1	-2	-2
0	0	0
1	0	0
2	-2	-2
3	-6	-6

X=-3

39. $(2x + 5) + (3x + 4) = (2x + 3x) + (5 + 4)$
$= 5x + 9$

40. $(-3x + 1) + (-3x + 1) = (-3x + (-3x)) + (1 + 1)$
$= -6x + 2$

41. $(4x + 3) + (2x - 5) = (4x + 2x) + (3 - 5)$
$= 6x - 2$

42. $(2x^2 - 5) + (x^2 + 4) = (2x^2 + x^2) + (-5 + 4)$
$= 3x^2 - 1$

43. $(-3b + 8) + (2b + 1) = (-3b + 2b) + (8 + 1)$
$= -b + 9$

44. $(5a + 6) + (-2a - 4) = (5a - 2a) + (6 - 4)$
$= 3a + 2$

45. $(x^2 + 3x) + (-2x^2 + 4x) = (x^2 - 2x^2) + (3x + 4x)$
$= -x^2 + 7x$

46. $(-x^2 - x) + (-3x^2 - 2x) = (-x^2 - 3x^2) + (-x - 2x)$
$= -4x^2 - 3x$

47. $(2x^2 + 3x) + (-x^2 - 2) = (2x^2 - x^2) + 3x - 2$
$= x^2 + 3x - 2$

48. $(2x^2 - x) + (-4x + 3) = 2x^2 + (-x - 4x) + 3$
$= 2x^2 - 5x + 3$

49. $(2x + 5) - (3x + 4) = 2x + 5 - 3x - 4$
$= (2x - 3x) + (5 - 4)$
$= -x + 1$

50. $(-3x + 1) - (-3x + 1) = -3x + 1 + 3x - 1$
$= (-3x + 3x) + (1 - 1)$
$= 0$

51. $(4x + 3) - (2x - 5) = 4x + 3 - 2x + 5$
$= (4x - 2x) + (3 + 5)$
$= 2x + 8$

52. $(2x^2 - 5) - (x^2 + 4) = 2x^2 - 5 - x^2 - 4$
$= (2x^2 - x^2) + (-5 - 4)$
$= x^2 - 9$

53. $(-3b + 8) - (2b + 1) = -3b + 8 - 2b - 1$
$= (-3b - 2b) + (8 - 1)$
$= -5b + 7$

54. $(5a + 6) - (-2a - 4) = 5a + 6 + 2a + 4$
$= (5a + 2a) + (6 + 4)$
$= 7a + 10$

55. $(x^2 + 3x) - (-2x^2 + 4x) = x^2 + 3x + 2x^2 - 4x$
$= (x^2 + 2x^2) + (3x - 4x)$
$= 3x^2 - x$

56. $(-x^2 - x) - (-3x^2 - 2x) = -x^2 - x + 3x^2 + 2x$
$= (-x^2 + 3x^2) + (-x + 2x)$
$= 2x^2 + x$

57. $(2x^2 + 3x) - (-x^2 - 2) = 2x^2 + 3x + x^2 + 2$
$= (2x^2 + x^2) + 3x + 2$
$= 3x^2 + 3x + 2$

58. $(2x^2 - x) - (-4x + 3) = 2x^2 - x + 4x - 3$
$= 2x^2 + (-x + 4x) - 3$
$= 2x^2 + 3x - 3$

59.

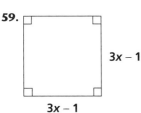

$P = (3x - 1) + (3x - 1) + (3x - 1) + (3x - 1)$
$= 12x - 4$
Substitute $x = 4$:
$P = 12(4) - 4$
$= 48 - 4$
$= 44$

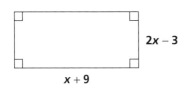

$P = (2x - 3) + (2x - 3) + (x + 9) + (x + 9)$
$= 6x + 12$
Substitute $x = 4$:
$P = 6(4) + 12$
$= 24 + 12$
$= 36$
The square has the larger perimeter.

60.

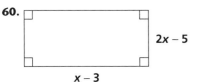

$P = (2x - 5) + (2x - 5) + (x - 3) + (x - 3)$
$= 6x - 16$

61.

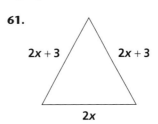

$P = (2x + 3) + (2x + 3) + 2x$
$= 6x + 6$

62.

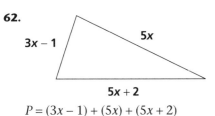

$P = (3x - 1) + (5x) + (5x + 2)$
$= 13x + 1$

63.

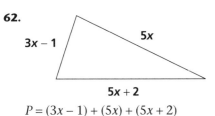

$P = (3x - 4) + (3x - 4) + (3x - 4) + (3x - 4)$
$= 12x - 16$

64. $450 = 45 \cdot 10$
$= (9 \cdot 5) \cdot (2 \cdot 5)$
$= (3 \cdot 3 \cdot 5) \cdot (2 \cdot 5)$
$= 2 \cdot 3^2 \cdot 5^2$

65. $484 = 4 \cdot 121$
$= (2 \cdot 2) \cdot (11 \cdot 11)$
$= 2^2 \cdot 11^2$

66. $318 = 3 \cdot 106$
$= 3 \cdot (2 \cdot 53)$
$= 2 \cdot 3 \cdot 53$

67. $18,900 = 189 \cdot 100$
$= (3 \cdot 63) \cdot (10 \cdot 10)$
$= (3 \cdot 3 \cdot 21) \cdot (2 \cdot 5 \cdot 2 \cdot 5)$
$= (3 \cdot 3 \cdot 3 \cdot 7) \cdot (2 \cdot 2 \cdot 5 \cdot 5)$
$= 2^2 \cdot 3^3 \cdot 5^2 \cdot 7$

68. From least to greatest, the fractions in order are $\frac{1}{2}, \frac{2}{3}, \frac{3}{4}, \frac{4}{5}, \frac{5}{6}, \frac{7}{8}$, and $\frac{99}{100}$.

69. For a fraction in which the numerator is one less than the denominator, as the denominator increases, the fraction's value gets larger and closer in value to one.

70. These types of fractions may be ordered by comparing denominators: the smaller the denominator, the smaller the fraction, and the larger the denominator, the larger the fraction.

71. The reciprocal of $\frac{1}{3}$ is $\frac{3}{1}$, or 3.
$\frac{1}{3} \cdot \frac{3}{1} = \frac{3}{3} = 1$

72. The reciprocal of $\frac{3}{4}$ is $\frac{4}{3}$.
$\frac{3}{4} \cdot \frac{4}{3} = \frac{1}{12} = 1$

73. To find the reciprocal of $2\frac{1}{2}$, convert the mixed number to an improper fraction, $\frac{5}{2}$. The reciprocal is $\frac{2}{5}$.
$\frac{5}{2} \cdot \frac{2}{5} = \frac{10}{10} = 1$

74. $(2x^2 - 3x + 5) + (-3x^2 + x - 4) = (2x^2 - 3x^2) + (-3x + x) + (5 - 4)$
$= -x^2 - 2x + 1$

Check: Let $x = 10$.
$(2(10)^2 - 3(10) + 5) + (-3(10)^2 + 10 - 4) \stackrel{?}{=} -(10)^2 - 2(10) + 1$
$(200 - 30 + 5) + (-300 + 10 - 4) \stackrel{?}{=} -100 - 20 + 1$
$175 + (-294) \stackrel{?}{=} -119$
$-119 = -119$ True

75. $(2x^2 - 3x + 5) - (-3x^2 + x - 4) = 2x^2 - 3x + 5 + 3x^2 - x + 4$
$= (2x^2 + 3x^2) + (-3x - x) + (5 + 4)$
$= 5x^2 - 4x + 9$

Check: Let $x = 10$.
$(2(10)^2 - 3(10) + 5) - (-3(10)^2 + 10 - 4) \stackrel{?}{=} 5(10)^2 - 4(10) + 9$
$(200 - 30 + 5) - (-300 + 10 - 4) \stackrel{?}{=} 500 - 40 + 9$
$175 - (-294) \stackrel{?}{=} 469$
$469 = 469$ True

76. On a graphics calculator, enter the left side of each equation for Y_1, and the right side of each equation for Y_2.

```
Y₁◗(2X²-3X+5)+(-3X²+X-4)
Y₂◗-X²-2X+1
Y₃=
Y₄=
Y₅=
Y₆=
Y₇=
```

```
Y₁◗(2X²-3X+5)-(-3X²+X-4)
Y₂◗5X²-4X+9
Y₃=
Y₄=
Y₅=
Y₆=
Y₇=
```

Equations from Exercise 74

Equations from Exercise 75

The Y_1 and Y_2 columns in each table should have the same corresponding values.

X	Y₁	Y₂
-3	-2	-2
-2	1	1
-1	2	2
0	1	1
1	-2	-2
2	-7	-7
3	-14	-14

X=-3

Table of values from Exercise 74

X	Y₁	Y₂
-3	66	66
-2	37	37
-1	18	18
0	9	9
1	10	10
2	21	21
3	42	42

X=-3

Table of values from Exercise 75

5.6 PAGES 311–312, PRACTICE & APPLY

6. $x < 3$

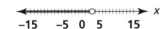

7. $x \leq -1$

8. $x > 4$

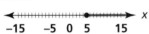

9. $x \geq 5$

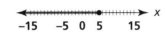

10. $x \leq 5$

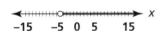

11. $x \geq -12$

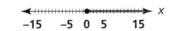

12. $x > -5$

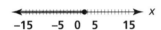

13. $x \geq 0$

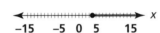

14. $x \geq -3$

15. $x \leq 2$

16. $4 \leq x$

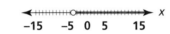

17. $-3 > x$

18. $x < -2$

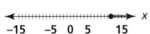

19. $-4 < x$

20. $3 < x$

21. $12 \leq x$

22. $6 > x$

23. $x > -11$

24. A represents the amount of money in a bank account.

$$A \geq 500$$

25. M represents the amount of money in an account.

$$M + 350 \leq 1240$$

26. Let x represent the amount of money Tamara had before lunch.

$$0 \leq x - 5.45 < 5.00$$

27.
$$0 \leq x - 5.45 < 5.00$$
$$0 + 5.45 \leq (x - 5.45) + 5.45 < 5.00 - 5.45$$
$$5.45 \leq x < 10.45$$

28. Let x represent the amount of money in Randy's bank account.

$$x + 50 \geq 180$$
$$(x + 50) - 50 \geq 180 - 50$$
$$x \geq 130$$

Randy had at least $130 in his bank account.

29. Let x represent the amount needed to purchase a VCR.

$$x \geq 280 - 90$$
$$x \geq 190$$

Rhonda still needs at least $190 to purchase a VCR.

30. Possible solution: 2
Check: substitute 2 for x in the inequality.

$$x + 3 > -1$$
$$2 + 3 > -1$$
$$5 > -1 \quad \text{True}$$

2 is a solution to the inequality.

31. Possible solution: 1
Check: substitute 1 for x in the inequality.

$$x - 4 \geq 2$$
$$1 - 4 \geq 2$$
$$-3 \geq 2 \quad \text{False}$$

1 is not a solution to the inequality.

32. Possible solution: 2

Check: substitute 2 for z in the inequality.

$z + 3 \leq 5$

$2 + 3 \leq 5$

$5 \leq 5$ True

2 is a solution to the inequality.

33. Possible solution: 14

Check: substitute 14 for x in the inequality.

$x + 5 \leq 9$

$14 + 5 \leq 9$

$19 \leq 9$ False

14 is not a solution to the inequality.

34. Possible solution: 5

Check: substitute 5 for y in the inequality.

$y - 2 \leq 3$

$5 - 2 \leq 3$

$3 \leq 3$ True

5 is a solution to the inequality.

35. Possible solution: −1

Check: substitute −1 for y in the inequality.

$y - 2 < -3$

$-1 - 2 < -3$

$-3 < -3$ False

−1 is not a solution to the inequality.

36. Possible solution: −1

Check: substitute −1 for w in the inequality.

$w + 5 \leq 2$

$-1 + 5 \leq 2$

$4 \leq 2$ False

−1 is not a solution to the inequality.

37. Possible solution: 12

Check: substitute 12 for w in the inequality.

$w - 5 \leq 9$

$12 - 5 \leq 9$

$7 \leq 9$ True

12 is a solution to the inequality.

38. Possible solution: −3

Check: substitute −3 for s in the inequality.

$s - 4 \geq -1$

$-3 - 4 \geq -1$

$-7 \geq -1$ False

−3 is not a solution to the inequality.

39. Possible solution: −2

Check: substitute −2 for m in the inequality.

$6 + m < 4$

$6 + (-2) < 4$

$4 < 4$ False

−2 is not a solution to the inequality.

40. Possible solution: 5

Check: substitute 5 for n in the inequality.

$n - 7 > -2$

$5 - 7 > -2$

$-2 > -2$ False

5 is not a solution to the inequality.

41. Possible solution: −5

Check: substitute −5 for z in the inequality.

$z + 4 < 6$

$-5 + 4 < 6$

$-1 < 6$ True

−5 is a solution to the inequality.

42.

$x - 3 < 7$

$x - 3 + 3 < 7 + 3$

$x < 10$

43.

$y - 4 > 9$

$y - 4 + 4 > 9 + 4$

$y > 13$

44.

$x - 3 < 4$

$x - 3 + 3 < 4 + 3$

$x < 7$

45.

$p - 4 < -4$

$p - 4 + 4 < -4 + 4$

$p < 0$

46.

$d - 1 \leq 5$

$d - 1 + 1 \leq 5 + 1$

$d \leq 6$

47.

$y + 6 \geq 3$

$y + 6 - 6 \geq 3 - 6$

$y \geq -3$

48.

$w + 3 \leq -7$

$w + 3 - 3 \leq -7 - 3$

$w \leq -10$

49.

$z + 5 < -12$

$z + 5 - 5 < -12 - 5$

$z < -17$

50.

$k + 2 < -2$

$k + 2 - 2 < -2 - 2$

$k < -4$

51.

$s - 0.5 \geq 5.5$

$s - 0.5 + 0.5 \geq 5.5 + 0.5$

$s \geq 6$

52.

$m - 4 < 2$

$m - 4 + 4 < 2 + 4$

$m < 6$

53.

$2 \geq x + 9$

$2 - 9 \geq x + 9 - 9$

$-7 \geq x$

54. $\left|-12\right|+\left|16\right|=12+16$
$= 28$

55. $\left|-12+16\right|=\left|4\right|$
$= 4$

56. $-16+(-9)+32=-25+32$
$= 7$

57. $-154-(-198)-127=-154+198-127$
$= 44-127$
$= -83$

58. $\dfrac{1}{2}+\dfrac{4}{5}=\dfrac{5}{10}+\dfrac{8}{10}$
$= \dfrac{13}{10},$ or $1\dfrac{3}{10}$

59. $\dfrac{3}{4}-1\dfrac{7}{8}=\dfrac{3}{4}-\dfrac{15}{8}$
$= \dfrac{6}{8}-\dfrac{15}{8}$
$= -\dfrac{9}{8},$ or $-1\dfrac{1}{8}$

60. $\dfrac{4}{7}\cdot 2\dfrac{1}{4}=\dfrac{4}{7}\cdot\dfrac{9}{4}$
$= \dfrac{9}{7},$ or $1\dfrac{2}{7}$

61. $\dfrac{2}{3}\div\dfrac{3}{8}=\dfrac{2}{3}\cdot\dfrac{8}{3}$
$= \dfrac{16}{9},$ or $1\dfrac{7}{9}$

62. $(7w-3)+(8w-7)=(7w+8w)+(-3+(-7))$
$= 15w-10$

63. $3y-7y=-4y$

64. $(12x-3)-(8x-12)=12x-3-8x+12$
$= (12x-8x)+(-3+12)$
$= 4x+9$

65. $-8<-1$

Multiply each side by 2:
$-8\cdot 2<-1\cdot 2$
$-16<-2$ True

Multiply each side by –2:
$-8\cdot(-2)<-1\cdot(-2)$
$16<2$ False

When an inequality is multiplied by a positive number, the statement is still true; however, when an inequality is multiplied by a negative number, the statement is false. Changing the direction of the inequality sign will yield a true statement.

11. $8>9-1$
$8>8$
The statement is false.

12. $-2\leq 5-7$
$-2\leq -2$
The statement is true.

13. $8\leq 9-1$
$8\leq 8$
The statement is true.

14. $-2>5-7$
$-2>-2$
The statement is false.

15. $\quad x+8>-1$
$x+8-8>-1-8$
$x>-9$

16. $\quad x-6\leq 7$
$x-6+6\leq 7+6$
$x\leq 13$

17. $\quad x+\dfrac{3}{4}>1$
$x+\dfrac{3}{4}-\dfrac{3}{4}>1-\dfrac{3}{4}$
$x>\dfrac{1}{4}$

18. $\quad x+\dfrac{3}{4}\leq\dfrac{1}{2}$
$x+\dfrac{3}{4}-\dfrac{3}{4}\leq\dfrac{2}{4}-\dfrac{3}{4}$
$x\leq -\dfrac{1}{4}$

19. $\quad x+0.04>0.6$
$x+0.04-0.04>0.6-0.04$
$x>0.56$

20. $\quad x-0.1<8$
$x-0.1+0.1<8+0.1$
$x<8.1$

21. Answers may vary. For example, Rachel has already spent $10 and was told that she must stay under her $100 limit. How much does she have left to spend?

22. $\quad x-4\geq -1$
$x-4+4\geq -1+4$
$x\geq 3$

23. $\quad x+3<2$
$x+3-3<2-3$
$x<-1$

24. The line includes numbers –1 and greater.
$x\geq -1$

25. The line includes the numbers greater than –1, up to, and including, 3.5.
$-1<x\leq 3.5$

26. The integers between 57 and 66 inclusive are 57, 58, 59, 60, 61, 62, 63, 64, 65, and 66.

For Exercises 27–31, let *t* represent the temperature in degrees Fahrenheit.

27. Answers may vary, depending on location. For example, $15 \le t \le 115$

28. A high temperature of 66°F can be represented by $t \le 66$.

29. A low temperature of 54°F can be represented by $t \ge 54$.

30. A temperature of 54°F can be represented by $t = 54$; an equality results.

31. An initial temperature with an increase of 5° for a final temperature between 70° and 80° can be represented by $70 \le t + 5 \le 80$ or $65 \le t \le 75$.

For Exercises 32–34, let *P* represent the number of spectators.

32. A stadium with fewer than 15,000 spectators can be represented by $1 \le P < 15{,}000$.

33. $P + 74 \le 450$
or $0 \le P \le 450 - 74$
$0 \le P \le 376$
The number of seats to be filled is between 0 and 376 inclusive.

34. $30 - 10 \le P \le 50 - 5$
$20 \le P \le 45$
The number of people left at the party is between 20 and 45 inclusive.

35. Let *M* represent the range in centimeters.
$42.3 - 0.5 \le M \le 42.3 + 0.5$
$41.8 \le M \le 42.8$
The measurement can be between 41.8 cm and 42.8 cm inclusive.

36. The inequality $70 \le C < 80$ means that to receive a C average, your average is at least 70 but less than 80.

37. Students earn a B if they average at least 78, but less than 89. This can be represented by the inequality $78 \le B < 89$.

PAGE 319, LOOK BACK

38. $|-4.5| = 4.5$

39. $|-9| = 9$

40. $|-3 + 4| = |1| = 1$

41. $|-2 + -6| = |-8| = 8$

42. $|(-2)(-6)| = |12| = 12$

43. $|-4| - |3| = 4 - 3 = 1$

44. $-\frac{2}{3} \cdot -\frac{3}{4} = \frac{2}{4} = \frac{1}{2}$

45. $2\frac{5}{8} + \left(-\frac{3}{4}\right) = \frac{21}{8} - \frac{6}{8}$
$= \frac{15}{8}$, or $1\frac{7}{8}$

46. $2\frac{3}{7} \div \left(-\frac{7}{9}\right) = \frac{17}{7} \cdot \left(-\frac{9}{7}\right)$
$= -\frac{153}{49}$, or $-3\frac{6}{49}$

47. $4\frac{1}{8} - 3\frac{2}{5} = \frac{33}{8} - \frac{17}{5}$
$= \frac{165}{40} - \frac{136}{40}$
$= \frac{29}{40}$

48. $9\frac{3}{4} \cdot \frac{8}{3} = \frac{39}{4} \cdot \frac{8}{3}$
$= 26$

49. $\frac{2}{3} \div \frac{2}{3} = \frac{2}{3} \cdot \frac{3}{2} = 1$

50. Let *d* represent the amount of discount in dollars.
$$d = (0.2)(120) = 24$$
The amount of discount is $24.

51. In order to roll less than 3 on a number cube, the only possibilities are to roll 1 or 2. The total number of different ways to roll less than 3 on both cubes are as follows: 1, 1; 1, 2; 2, 1; 2, 2. Total possible combinations of numbers are 6×6, or 36. Therefore, the theoretical probability that Dana rolls less than 3 on both cubes is $\frac{4}{36}$, or $\frac{1}{9}$.

52. Use the "Pythagorean" Right-Triangle Theorem to find the length of the hypotenuse of a right triangle.
$$a^2 + b^2 = c^2$$
$$120^2 + 90^2 = c^2$$
$$14{,}400 + 8100 = c^2$$
$$22{,}500 = c^2$$
$$150 = c$$
The length of the hypotenuse is 150 meters.

53. $x - 11 = -28$
$x - 11 + 11 = -28 + 11$
$x = -17$

54. $x + \frac{1}{2} = \frac{3}{4}$
$x + \frac{1}{2} - \frac{1}{2} = \frac{3}{4} - \frac{1}{2}$
$x = \frac{3}{4} - \frac{2}{4}$
$x = \frac{1}{4}$

55. $x - 5 = 16$
$x - 5 + 5 = 16 + 5$
$x = 21$

56. $\frac{2}{5} - x = \frac{1}{10}$
$\frac{2}{5} - x + x = \frac{1}{10} + x$
$\frac{2}{5} = \frac{1}{10} + x$
$\frac{2}{5} - \frac{1}{10} = \frac{1}{10} - \frac{1}{10} + x$
$\frac{4}{10} - \frac{1}{10} = x$
$\frac{3}{10} = x$

57. $2x < 8$
$$\frac{2x}{2} < \frac{8}{2}$$
$$x < 4$$

58. $4x + 5 \le 16$
$$4x + 5 - 5 \le 16 - 5$$
$$4x \le 11$$
$$x \le \frac{11}{4}, \text{ or } 2\frac{3}{4}$$

59. $8x - 3 > 33$
$$8x - 3 > 33 + 3$$
$$8x > 36$$
$$x > \frac{36}{8}$$
$$x > \frac{9}{2}, \text{ or } 4\frac{1}{2}$$

60. Use a table to organize your work.
Number of dimes: 2 2 1 1 1   1 0 0   0   0   0   0
Number of nickels: 1 0 3 2 1   0 5 4   3   2   1   0
Number of pennies: 0 5 0 5 10 15 0 5 10 15 20 25
There are 12 ways to make change for a quarter.

61. Draw a diagram like the ones shown to determine the number of regions created.
16 regions

---

1. $(6a - 1) + (5a - 4) = 6a - 1 + 5a - 4$
$$= (6a + 5a) + (-1 - 4)$$
$$= 11a - 5$$

2. $(7 - t) + (3t + 4) = 7 - t + 3t + 4$
$$= (-t + 3t) + (7 + 4)$$
$$= 2t + 11$$

3. $\left(\frac{x}{3} - 2\right) + \left(\frac{x}{2} + 4\right) = \frac{x}{3} - 2 + \frac{x}{2} + 4$
$$= \left(\frac{x}{3} + \frac{x}{2}\right) + (-2 + 4)$$
$$= \left(\frac{2x}{6} + \frac{3x}{6}\right) + 2$$
$$= \frac{5}{6}x + 2$$

4. $(1.4m - 6.2n) + (2.4m - 5.5n) = 1.4m - 6.2n + 2.4m - 5.5n$
$$= (1.4m + 2.4m) + (-6.2n - 5.5n)$$
$$= 3.8m - 11.7n$$

5. $(3x + 2y + z) + (6x - 4y - 3z) = 3x + 2y + z + 6x - 4y - 3z$
$$= (3x + 6x) + (2y - 4y) + (z - 3z)$$
$$= 9x - 2y - 2z$$

6. $3x - 5x = -2x$

7. $7y - (7 - 5y) = 7y - 7 + 5y$
$$= 7y + 5y - 7$$
$$= 12y - 7$$

8. $(8m - 4) - (6m - 3) = 8m - 4 - 6m + 3$
$$= (8m - 6m) + (-4 + 3)$$
$$= 2m - 1$$

9. $(6d + 3) - (4d - 7) + (3d - 5) = 6d + 3 - 4d + 7 + 3d - 5$
$$= (6d - 4d + 3d) + (3 + 7 - 5)$$
$$= 5d + 5$$

10. $(4a - 3b - c) - (6a + 5b - 4c) = 4a - 3b - c - 6a - 5b + 4c$
$$= (4a - 6a) + (-3b - 5b) + (-c + 4c)$$
$$= -2a - 8b + 3c$$

11. $x + 3 = 2 \qquad\qquad x + 3 - 3 = 2 - 3 \qquad\qquad x = -1$

12. $x - 1 = -2$ $\qquad$ $x - 1 + 1 = -2 + 1$ $\qquad$ $x = -1$

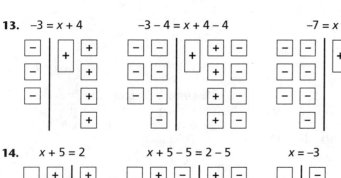

13. $-3 = x + 4$ $\qquad$ $-3 - 4 = x + 4 - 4$ $\qquad$ $-7 = x$

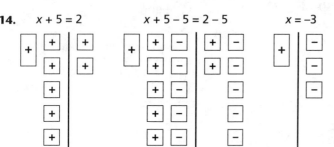

14. $x + 5 = 2$ $\qquad$ $x + 5 - 5 = 2 - 5$ $\qquad$ $x = -3$

15. $w + 16 = 25$
$w + 16 - 16 = 25 - 16$
$w = 9$

16. $r + 26 = 16$
$r + 26 - 26 = 16 - 26$
$r = -10$

17. $t + 7 = -5$
$t + 7 - 7 = -5 - 7$
$t = -12$

18. $a + 1.5 = 3.6$
$a + 1.5 - 1.5 = 3.6 - 1.5$
$a = 2.1$

19. $m + \frac{1}{2} = \frac{5}{6}$
$m + \frac{1}{2} - \frac{1}{2} = \frac{5}{6} - \frac{1}{2}$
$m = \frac{5}{6} - \frac{3}{6}$
$m = \frac{2}{6}$
$m = \frac{1}{3}$

20. $y - 13 = 12$
$y - 13 + 13 = 12 + 13$
$y = 25$

21. $24 = x - 19$
$24 + 19 = x - 19 + 19$
$43 = x$

22. $-6 = g - 17$
$-6 + 17 = g - 17 + 17$
$11 = g$

23. $h - \frac{1}{6} = \frac{2}{3}$
$h - \frac{1}{6} + \frac{1}{6} = \frac{4}{6} + \frac{1}{6}$
$h = \frac{5}{6}$

24. $7k - (6k + 5) = 7$
$7k - 6k - 5 = 7$
$k - 5 = 7$
$k - 5 + 5 = 7 + 5$
$k = 12$

25. $4 - (2 - 3z) = 6z - (4z + 3)$
$4 - 2 + 3z = 6z - 4z - 3$
$2 + 3z = 2z - 3$
$2 + 3z - 2z = 2z - 2z - 3$
$2 - 2 + z = -3 - 2$
$z = -5$

26. $(5x - 1) + (2x + 3) = (5x + 2x) + (-1 + 3)$
$\qquad = 7x + 2$

27. $(x^2 + 1) - (2x^2 - 4) = x^2 + 1 - 2x^2 + 4$
$\qquad = (x^2 - 2x^2) + (1 + 4)$
$\qquad = -x^2 + 5$

28. $(-4x^2 - 8) - (7x + 2) = -4x^2 - 8 - 7x - 2$
$\qquad = -4x^2 - 7x - 10$

29. $(3c - 8) + (-6c - 12) = (3c - 6c) + (-8 - 12)$
$\qquad = -3c - 20$

For Exercises 30–33 use guess-and-check to solve each inequality.

30. $x - 5 < -3$

Guessed value of x	Subtraction process	Simplified value	Less than -3?
5	5 − 5	0	no
4	4 − 5	−1	no
3	3 − 5	−2	no
2	2 − 5	−3	no
1	1 − 5	−4	yes

The solution is all numbers less than 2, or $x < 2$.

31. $x + 4 \geq 7$

Guessed value of x	Addition process	Simplified value	Greater than or equal to 7?
0	0 + 4	4	no
1	1 + 4	5	no
2	2 + 4	6	no
3	3 + 4	7	yes
4	4 + 4	8	yes

The solution is all numbers greater than or equal to 3, or $x \geq 3$.

32. $x - 7 > -9$

Guessed value of x	Subtraction process	Simplified value	Greater than −9?
−10	−10 − 7	−17	no
−5	−5 − 7	−12	no
−3	−3 − 7	−10	no
−2	−2 − 7	−9	no
−1	−1 − 7	−8	yes

The solution is all numbers greater than −2, or $x > -2$.

33. $x + \frac{1}{2} \le 3\frac{1}{2}$

Guessed value of x	Addition process	Simplified value	Less than or equal to $3\frac{1}{2}$?
5	$5 + \frac{1}{2}$	$5\frac{1}{2}$	no
4	$4 + \frac{1}{2}$	$4\frac{1}{2}$	no
3	$3 + \frac{1}{2}$	$3\frac{1}{2}$	yes
2	$2 + \frac{1}{2}$	$2\frac{1}{2}$	yes
1	$1 + \frac{1}{2}$	$1\frac{1}{2}$	yes

The solution is all numbers less than or equal to 3, or $x \le 3$.

34.
$$x + 5 > 10$$
$$x + 5 - 5 > 10 - 5$$
$$x > 5$$

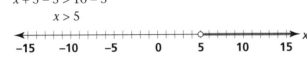

35.
$$n - 15 \le -3$$
$$n - 15 + 15 \le -3 + 15$$
$$n \le 12$$

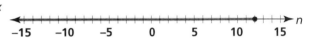

36.
$$y + 0.09 < 3.09$$
$$y + 0.09 - 0.09 < 3.09 - 0.09$$
$$y < 3$$

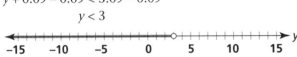

37.
$$d - \frac{2}{3} \ge \frac{1}{3}$$
$$d - \frac{2}{3} + \frac{2}{3} \ge \frac{1}{3} + \frac{2}{3}$$
$$d \ge 1$$

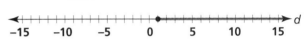

38. Let b represent the number of brushes, and let j represent the number of jars of paint.
Then the expression for the cost is $1.75b = 2.45j$.

39. Let p represent the money that can be spent by Rita in dollars.
$$p \le 15 - 3$$
$$p \le 12$$
The most that Rita can spend on other cards is $12.

PAGE 325 CHAPTER 5 ASSESSMENT

1. $(8n - 2) + (6n + 4) = 8n - 2 + 6n + 4$
$\qquad = (8n + 6n) + (-2 + 4)$
$\qquad = 14n + 2$

2. $5t - (9t - 6) = 5t - 9t + 6$
$\qquad = -4t + 6$

3. $(8 - 9z) - (7z + 15) = 8 - 9z - 7z - 15$
$\qquad = (-9z - 7z) + (8 - 15)$
$\qquad = -16z - 7$

4. $(7 - x) - (8 + 3x) - (6x - 1) = 7 - x - 8 - 3x - 6x + 1$
$\qquad = (-x - 3x - 6x) + (7 - 8 + 1)$
$\qquad = -10x$

5. $(17x + 20y - 15z) - (3x + 5y - z) = 17x + 20y - 15z - 3x - 5y + z$
$\qquad = (17x - 3x) + (20y - 5y) + (-15z + z)$
$\qquad = 14x + 15y - 14z$

For Exercises 6–7, let b represent one box of books, and the constant represent the number of single books.

6. $(5b + 5) + (2b + 2) = (5b + 2b) + (5 + 2)$
$\qquad = 7b + 7$
There are $7b + 7$ books in the storage room, where b represents the number of books in a box.

7. $(7b + 7) - (3b + 1) = 7b + 7 - 3b - 1$
$\qquad = (7b - 3b) + (7 - 1)$
$\qquad = 4b + 6$
There are $4b + 6$ books in the storage room, where b represents the number of books in a box.

8. $x - 5 = 8$ $x - 5 + 5 = 8 + 5$ $x = 13$

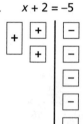

9. $x + 2 = -5$ $x + 2 - 2 = -5 - 2$ $x = -7$

10. $x + 4 = 2$ $x + 4 - 4 = 2 - 4$ $x = -2$

11. $c + 18 = 10$
$c + 18 - 18 = 10 - 18$
$c = -8$

12. $t - 36 = 19$
$t - 36 + 36 = 19 + 36$
$t = 55$

13. $8 + y = 14$
$8 - 8 + y = -14 - 8$
$y = -22$

14. $34 = h - 4$
$34 + 4 = h - 4 + 4$
$38 = h$

15. $w + \dfrac{2}{5} = \dfrac{7}{10}$
$w + \dfrac{2}{5} - \dfrac{2}{5} = \dfrac{7}{10} - \dfrac{2}{5}$
$w = \dfrac{7}{10} - \dfrac{4}{10}$
$w = \dfrac{3}{10}$

16. $4x - (2x + 2) = 3 + x$
$4x - 2x - 2 = 3 + x$
$2x - 2 = 3 + x$
$2x - x - 2 + 2 = 3 + 2 + x - x$
$x = 5$

17. Let c represent the measure of the complementary angle in degrees.
$c + 48 = 90$
$c + 48 - 48 = 90 - 48$
$c = 42$
The measure of the complementary angle is 42°.

18. $I = C + T$
$I - T = C + T - T$
$I - T = C$

19. $C + T = I$
$C = I - T$
$C = 25.19 - 1.20$
$C = 23.99$
The cost of the item without sales tax is \$23.99.

20. $x + 6 \geq 4$
$x + 6 - 6 \geq 4 - 6$
$x \geq -2$

21. $y - 2.3 < 1.4$
$y - 2.3 + 2.3 < 1.4 + 2.3$
$y < 3.7$

22. $t + \dfrac{1}{2} \geq 2$
$t + \dfrac{1}{2} - \dfrac{1}{2} \geq \dfrac{4}{2} - \dfrac{1}{2}$
$t \geq \dfrac{3}{2}$

23. $x - 8 > -4$
$x - 8 + 8 > -4 + 8$
$x > 4$

24. $x \geq 5$

25. Let P represent the number of people who can still sign up.
$P + 25 \leq 40$ or $0 \leq P \leq 15$
The number of people who can sign up is less than or equal to 15.

CHAPTER 6

MULTIPLICATION AND DIVISION IN ALGEBRA

8. $13r = 13(-4)$
$= -52$

9. $13r = 13(1.5)$
$= 19.5$

10. $13r = 13(7)$
$= 91$

11. $13r = 13\left(\frac{1}{2}\right)$
$= \frac{13}{2}$, or $6\frac{1}{2}$, or 6.5

12. $2t + 1 = 2(10) + 1$
$= 20 + 1$
$= 21$

13. $2t + 1 = 2(8.5) + 1$
$= 17 + 1$
$= 18$

14. $2t + 1 = 2(-6.2) + 1$
$= -12.4 + 1$
$= -11.4$

15. $2t + 1 = 2\left(\frac{3}{4}\right) + 1$
$= \frac{6}{4} + 1$
$= \frac{3}{2} + \frac{2}{2}$
$= \frac{5}{2}$, or $2\frac{1}{2}$, or 2.5

16. $2 \cdot 6x = (2.6)x$
$= 12x$

17. $-6x \cdot 2 = (-6 \cdot 2)x$
$= -12x$

18. $6x \cdot 2x = (6 \cdot 2)(x \cdot x)$
$= 12x^2$

19. $-66x \div 2 = \left(\frac{-66}{2}\right)x$
$= -33x$

20. $12x \cdot 3x = (12 \cdot 3)(x \cdot x)$
$= 36x^2$

21. $-2(6x + 3) = (-2 \cdot 6)x + (-2 \cdot 3)$
$= -12x + (-6)$
$= -12x - 6$

22. $-1.2x \cdot 3x = (-1.2 \cdot 3)(x \cdot x)$
$= -3.6x^2$

23. $-12x \div 3 = \left(\frac{-12}{3}\right)x$
$= -4x$

24. $7x - (3 - x) = 7x - 3 + x$
$= 7x + x - 3$
$= 8x - 3$

25. $-3(7x - 3) = (-3 \cdot 7x) + (-3 \cdot (-3))$
$= (-3 \cdot 7)x + 9$
$= -21x + 9$

26. $-2(4x - 1) = (-2 \cdot 4x) + (-2 \cdot (-1))$
$= (-2 \cdot 4)x + 2$
$= -8x + 2$

27. $3x \cdot 5 + 2x \cdot 2 = (3 \cdot 5)x + (2 \cdot 2)x$
$= 15x + 4x$
$= 19x$

28. $-2 \cdot 8x = (-2 \cdot 8)x$
$= -16x$

29. $8x \cdot 2x = (8 \cdot 2)(x \cdot x)$
$= 16x^2$

30. $-8x \div 2 = \left(\frac{-8}{2}\right)x$
$= -4x$

31. $-21x \cdot 3x = (-21 \cdot 3)(x \cdot x)$
$= -63x^2$

32. $2.1x \cdot 3x = (2.1 \cdot 3)(x \cdot x)$
$= 6.3x^2$

33. $-21x \div 7 = \left(\frac{-21}{7}\right)x$
$= -3x$

34. $8x - (2 - 5x) = 8x - 2 + 5x$
$= 8x + 5x - 2$
$= 13x - 2$

35. $8(x + 1) - (2 - 5x) = 8x + 8 - 2 + 5x$
$= 8x + 5x + 8 - 2$
$= 13x + 6$

36. $(3x + 2y - 9) - 2(x - y) = 3x + 2y - 9 - 2x + 2y$
$= 3x + 2x + 2y + 2y - 9$
$= x + 4y - 9$

37. $4(x - 5y) - (2x - 2y) = 4x - 20y - 2x + 2y$
$= 4x - 2x - 20y + 2y$
$= 2x - 18y$

38. $\frac{5w + 15}{-5} = \left(\frac{5}{-5}\right)w + \left(\frac{15}{-5}\right)$
$= -w + (-3)$
$= -w - 3$

39. $8(x - y) + 5(3x - 3y) = 8x - 8y + 15x - 15y$
$= 8x + 15x - 8y - 15y$
$= 23x - 23y$

40. $(3x + 5y - 9) - 7(x - y) = 3x + 5y - 9 - 7x + 7y$
$= 3x - 7x + 5y + 7y - 9$
$= -4x + 12y - 9$

41. $\frac{8 + 16w}{8} = \frac{8}{8} + \left(\frac{16}{8}\right)w$
$= 1 + 2w$

42. $\frac{-90x + 2.7}{-9} = \left(\frac{-90}{-9}\right)x + \left(\frac{2.7}{-9}\right)$
$= 10x - 0.3$

43. $-(x-y)-4(x-y+9) = -x+y-4x+4y-36$
$$= -x-4x+y+4y-36$$
$$= -5x+5y-36$$

44. $9(2x+y)-3(3x+3y) = 18x+9y-9x-9y$
$$= 18x-9x+9y-9y$$
$$= 9x+0$$
$$= 9x$$

45. $\frac{11-33y}{11} = \frac{11}{11} + \left(\frac{-33}{11}\right)y$
$$= 1+(-3y)$$
$$= 1-3y$$

46. $\frac{-10x+35}{5} = \left(\frac{-10}{5}\right)x + \frac{35}{5}$
$$= \frac{-10}{5}x + 7$$
$$= -2x+7$$

47. $-6(4x-y)-4(2x-3y) = -24x+6y-8x+12y$
$$= -24x-8x+6y+12y$$
$$= -32x+18y$$

48. $A = -5 \cdot B + B$
$$= (-5 \cdot 3) + 3$$
$$= -15 + 3$$
$$= -12$$

For Exercises 49–53, let *h* represent the number of hours worked for the day, and let *e* represent Nicole's earnings.

49. $e = 5.25h$
$$= 5.25(4)$$
$$= 21.00$$
Nicole earned $21.00 for 4 hours of work.

50. $e = 5.25h$
$$= 5.25(6.5)$$
$$= 34.13$$
Nicole earned $34.13 for 6.5 hours of work.

51. $e = 5.25(4) + 5.25(6.5)$
$e = 21.00 + 34.13$
$e = 55.13$
Nicole earned $55.13 on Friday and Saturday.

52. $e = 5.25h$

53. hours worked $= 4 + 6.5 + h$
$$= 10.5 + h$$
The expression $10.5 + h$ shows the number of hours Nicole worked.

54. $A = lw$
$A = 6 \cdot 4$
$A = 24$
The area is 24 square centimeters.

55. $V = lwh$
$V = 8 \cdot 3 \cdot 4$
$V = 24 \cdot 4$
$V = 96$
The volume is 96 cubic inches.

For Exercises 56–61, let *h* represent the time taken for the plumbing job, and let *C* represent the total cost.

56. $C = 35h + 20$
$$= 35(1) + 20$$
$$= 35 + 20$$
$$= 55$$
Charlotte charges $55.00 for a 1-hour job.

57. $C = 35h + 20$
$$= 35(3) + 20$$
$$= 105 + 20$$
$$= 125$$
Charlotte charges $125.00 for a 3-hour job.

58. $C = 35h + 20$

59. $C = 70h + 20$
$$= 70(1) + 20$$
$$= 70 + 20$$
$$= 90$$
Charlotte charges $90.00 for a 1-hour job on Sunday.

60. $C = 70h + 20$
$$= 70(3) + 20$$
$$= 210 + 20$$
$$= 230$$
Charlotte charges $230.00 for a 3-hour job on Sunday.

61. $C = 70h + 20$

PAGE 335, LOOK BACK

62. $(3x+2y)+(3x-2y)-(3x-2y) = 3x+2y+3x-2y-3x+2y$
$$= 3x+3x-3x+2y+2y-2y$$
$$= 6x-3x+4y-2y$$
$$= 3x+2y$$

63. $(x^2+2y+4)-(2x-3y-2) = x^2+2y+4-2x+3y+2$
$$= x^2-2x+2y+3y+4+2$$
$$= x^2-2x+5y+6$$

64. $x-4 \le 3$
$x \le 7$

65. $x+5 \ge -2$
$x \ge -7$

66. $x < -3 + 4$
$x < 1$

67.
$$x + \frac{1}{3} \leq \frac{1}{2}$$
$$x + \frac{1}{3} - \frac{1}{3} \leq \frac{1}{2} - \frac{1}{3}$$
$$x \leq \frac{3}{6} - \frac{2}{6}$$
$$x \leq \frac{1}{6}$$

68.
$$x - 16 \geq \frac{2}{5}$$
$$x - 16 + 16 \geq \frac{2}{5} + 16$$
$$x \geq 16\frac{2}{5}$$

69.
$$\frac{4}{5} + x > 7$$
$$\frac{4}{5} - \frac{4}{5} + x > 7 - \frac{4}{5}$$
$$x > \frac{35}{5} - \frac{4}{5}$$
$$x > \frac{31}{5}$$
$$x > 6\frac{1}{5}$$

 PAGE 335, LOOK BEYOND

70.
$$\frac{2x^2 + 4x}{4x} = \frac{2x^2}{4x} + \frac{4x}{4x}$$
$$= \left(\frac{2}{4}\right)\left(\frac{x^2}{x}\right) + \left(\frac{4}{4}\right)\left(\frac{x}{x}\right)$$
$$= \frac{1}{2}x + (1)(1)$$
$$= \frac{1}{2}x + 1 = \frac{x}{2} + 1$$

71.
$$\frac{5y^2 - 15y}{-5} = \frac{5y^2}{-5y} + \frac{-15y}{-5y}$$
$$= \left(\frac{5}{-5}\right)\left(\frac{y^2}{y}\right) + \left(\frac{-15}{-5}\right)\left(\frac{y}{y}\right)$$
$$= (-1)y + (3)(1)$$
$$= -y + 3$$

72.

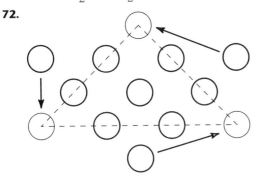

73. In the first round there are $\frac{64}{2}$, or 32 games. In the second round there are $\frac{32}{2}$, or 16 games. In the third round there are $\frac{16}{2}$, or 8 games. In the fourth round there are $\frac{8}{2}$, or 4 games. In the semi-finals there $\frac{4}{2}$, or 2 games, and 1 final game. Therefore, there are 32 + 16 + 8 + 4 + 2 + 1, or 63 games.

 6.2 **PAGES 343–344, PRACTICE & APPLY**

11. Multiplication Property of Equality
$$\frac{y}{3} = -13$$
$$\frac{y}{3}(3) = -13(3)$$
$$y = -39$$

12. Multiplication Property of Equality
$$\frac{x}{27} = -26$$
$$\frac{x}{27}(27) = -26(27)$$
$$x = -702$$

13. Addition Property of Equality
$$x - \frac{1}{3} = 2$$
$$x - \frac{1}{3} + \frac{1}{3} = 2 + \frac{1}{3}$$
$$x = 2\frac{1}{3}$$

14. Division Property of Equality
$$7x = 56$$
$$\frac{7x}{7} = \frac{56}{7}$$
$$x = 8$$

15. Multiplication Property of Equality
$$\frac{b}{-9} = 6$$
$$\frac{b}{-9}(-9) = 6(-9)$$
$$b = -54$$

16. Division Property of Equality
$$-12y = 84$$
$$\frac{-12y}{-12} = \frac{84}{-12}$$
$$y = -7$$

17. Addition Property of Equality
$$x - \frac{2}{3} = 2$$
$$x - \frac{2}{3} + \frac{2}{3} = 2 + \frac{2}{3}$$
$$x = 2\frac{2}{3}$$

18. Division Property of Equality
$$777x = -888$$
$$\frac{777x}{777} = \frac{-888}{777}$$
$$x = \frac{-888}{777}$$
$$x = \frac{-8}{7}$$

19. Division Property of Equality
$$5.6v = 7$$
$$\frac{5.6v}{5.6} = \frac{7}{5.6}$$
$$v = 1.25$$

20. Division Property of Equality
$$7 = -56w$$
$$\frac{7}{-56} = \frac{-56w}{-56}$$
$$-\frac{1}{8} = w$$

21. Multiplication Property of Equality
$$\frac{x}{-7} = -1.4$$
$$\frac{x}{-7}(-7) = -1.4(-7)$$
$$x = 9.8$$

22. Division Property of Equality
$$3x = 2$$
$$\frac{3x}{3} = \frac{2}{3}$$
$$x = \frac{2}{3}$$

23. $888x = 777$

$$\frac{888x}{888} = \frac{777}{888}$$

$$x = \frac{7}{8}, \text{ or } 0.875$$

24. $x + \frac{3}{4} = 12$

$$x + \frac{3}{4} - \frac{3}{4} = 12 - \frac{3}{4}$$

$$x = 11\frac{1}{4}$$

25. $x - 888 = 777$

$$x - 888 + 888 = 777 + 888$$

$$x = 1665$$

26. $-3f = 15$

$$\frac{-3f}{-3} = \frac{15}{-3}$$

$$f = -5$$

27. $\frac{x}{7} = -8$

$$\frac{x}{7}(7) = -8(7)$$

$$x = -56$$

28. $\frac{x}{0.5} = 6$

$$\frac{x}{0.5}(0.5) = 6(0.5)$$

$$x = 3$$

29. $w + 0 = -22$

$$w = -22$$

30. $-4x = -3228$

$$\frac{-4x}{-4} = \frac{-3228}{-4}$$

$$x = 807$$

31. $4b = -15$

$$\frac{4b}{4} = \frac{-15}{4}$$

$$b = -\frac{15}{4}, \text{ or } -3\frac{3}{4}, \text{ or } -3.75$$

32. $\frac{p}{111} = -10$

$$111\left(\frac{p}{111}\right) = 111(-10)$$

$$p = -1110$$

33. $\frac{s}{-1} = -40$

$$-1\left(\frac{s}{-1}\right) = -1(-40)$$

$$s = 40$$

34. $c + 7 = 63$

$$c = 56$$

35. $r - \frac{1}{5} = 2$

$$r - \frac{1}{5} + \frac{1}{5} = \frac{10}{5} + \frac{1}{5}$$

$$r = \frac{11}{5}, \text{ or } 2\frac{1}{5}, \text{ or } 2.2$$

36. $2a = 13$

$$\frac{2a}{2} = \frac{13}{2}$$

$$a = \frac{13}{2}, \text{ or } 6\frac{1}{2}, \text{ or } 6.5$$

37. $\frac{x}{10} = -1.9$

$$10\left(\frac{x}{10}\right) = 10(-1.9)$$

$$x = -19$$

38. $d - 7 = 35$

$$d = 42$$

39. $\frac{w}{-1.2} = 10$

$$-1.2\left(\frac{w}{-1.2}\right) = -1.2(10)$$

$$w = -12$$

40. $7e = -14$

$$\frac{7e}{7} = \frac{-14}{7}$$

$$e = -2$$

41. $\frac{m}{-9} = 0$

$$-9\left(\frac{m}{-9}\right) = -9(0)$$

$$m = 0$$

42. $\frac{b}{15} = 1$

$$15\left(\frac{b}{15}\right) = 15(1)$$

$$b = 15$$

43. $0.55x = 0.55$

$$\frac{0.55x}{0.55} = \frac{0.55}{0.55}$$

$$x = 1$$

44. $\frac{p}{-9} = 0.9$

$$-9\left(\frac{p}{-9}\right) = -9(0.9)$$

$$p = -8.1$$

45. $-3x = -4215$

$$\frac{-3x}{-3} = \frac{-4215}{-3}$$

$$x = 1405$$

46. $p + 2300 = 890$

$$p + 2300 - 2300 = 890 - 2300$$

$$p = -1410$$

47. Let t represent the number of rolls of tape that Max can buy.

$1.15t = 6.00$

$$\frac{1.15t}{1.15} = \frac{6.00}{1.15}$$

$$t \approx 5.2$$

Max can buy 5 rolls of tape.

48. Let r represent the cost of one roll of tape.

$4r = 4.32$

$$\frac{4r}{4} = \frac{4.32}{4}$$

$$4 = 1.08$$

One roll of tape costs $1.08. Yes, it costs more to buy a single roll.

49. Let t represent the number of tape measures that can be purchased.

$4.95t = 19.00$

$$\frac{4.95t}{4.95} = \frac{19.00}{4.95}$$

$$t \approx 3.84$$

Max's employer can buy 3 tape measures.

50. Let e represent the cost of one extension cord.

$6e = 7.26$

$$\frac{6e}{6} = \frac{7.26}{6}$$

$$e = 1.21$$

One extension cord costs $1.21.

51. Let b represent the price of one battery.

$4b = 2.52$

$$\frac{4b}{4} = \frac{2.52}{4}$$

$$b = 0.63$$

The price of one battery is 63¢.

52. Let s represent the average speed that Natalie's family must travel.

$(10 - 2)s = 400$

$$8s = 400$$

$$\frac{8s}{8} = \frac{400}{8}$$

$$s = 50$$

They must travel 50 miles per hour (mph).

53. Let d represent the distance Derrick traveled in the first 3 hr.

$d = 50 \cdot 3$

$d = 150$

Derrick drove 150 mi during the first 3 hr.

To find the total distance after driving 75 mi more, add 75 to 150.

$150 + 75 = 225$

Derrick will drive a total of 225 mi.

54. Let s represent the speed that Maria should drive.

$8s = 320$

$\dfrac{8s}{8} = \dfrac{320}{8}$

$s = 40$

Maria should drive 40 mph.

55. $r = \dfrac{d}{t}$

$t(r) = t\left(\dfrac{d}{t}\right)$

$rt = d$

56. $A = bh$

$\dfrac{A}{h} = \dfrac{bh}{h}$

$\dfrac{A}{h} = b$

57. $V = lwh$

$\dfrac{V}{lh} = \dfrac{lwh}{lh}$

$\dfrac{V}{lh} = w$

58. An equilateral triangle has 3 equal sides, so $n = 3$.

$m = \dfrac{180(n-2)}{n}$

$= \dfrac{180(3-2)}{3}$

$= \dfrac{180(1)}{3}$

$= \dfrac{180}{3}$

$= 60$

The measure of the interior angles of an equilateral triangle is 60°.

59. A square has 4 equal sides, so $n = 4$.

$m = \dfrac{180(n-2)}{n}$

$= \dfrac{180(4-2)}{4}$

$= \dfrac{180(2)}{4}$

$= \dfrac{360}{4}$

$= 90$

The measure of the interior angles of a square is 90°.

60. A pentagon has 5 equal sides, so $n = 5$.

$m = \dfrac{180(n-2)}{n}$

$= \dfrac{180(5-2)}{5}$

$= \dfrac{180(3)}{5}$

$= \dfrac{540}{5}$

$= 108$

The measure of the interior angles of a regular pentagon is 108°.

61. An octagon has 8 equal sides, so $n = 8$.

$m = \dfrac{180(n-2)}{n}$

$= \dfrac{180(8-2)}{8}$

$= \dfrac{180(6)}{8}$

$= \dfrac{1080}{8}$

$= 135$

The measure of the interior angles of a regular octagon is 135°.

62. The greater the number of angles in the regular polygons, the larger the measure of the angle.

63. $A = \dfrac{1}{2}mn$

$2A = 2\left(\dfrac{1}{2}\right)mn$

$2A = mn$

$\dfrac{2A}{m} = \dfrac{mn}{m}$

$\dfrac{2A}{m} = n$

64. $n = \dfrac{2A}{m}$

$= \dfrac{2(21)}{7}$

$= \dfrac{42}{7}$

$= 6$

The length of the other diagonal is 6 inches.

PAGE 344, LOOK BACK

65. $3 \cdot 2 = 6$

$6 \cdot 2 = 12$

$12 \cdot 2 = 24$

$24 \cdot 2 = 48$

The sequence of 5 numbers is 3, 6, 12, 24, and 48.

66. $\dfrac{a + b \cdot c}{3} = \dfrac{3 + 2 \cdot 0}{3}$

$= \dfrac{3 + 0}{3}$

$= \dfrac{3}{3}$, or 1

67. $\dfrac{a \cdot b}{b + c} = \dfrac{3 \cdot 2}{2 + 0}$

$= \dfrac{6}{2}$, or 3

68. $\dfrac{a + b}{b + c} = \dfrac{3 + 2}{2 + 0}$

$= \dfrac{5}{2}$, or $2\dfrac{1}{2}$, or 2.5

69. $(30 \cdot 7 - 4) \cdot 10 \div 2 \div 2 = 515$

70. $|0| = 0$

CHAPTER 6   **125**

71. $\left| -5 \right| = 5$

72. $\left| -\frac{1}{6} \right| = \frac{1}{6}$

73. $\left| 9 \right| = 9$

PAGE 344, LOOK BEYOND

74.
$$3y = 10 + 5y$$
$$3y - 5y = 10 + 5y - 5y$$
$$-2y = 10$$
$$y = -5$$

75.
$$4x + \frac{1}{2} = 5x$$
$$4x - 4x + \frac{1}{2} = 5x - 4x$$
$$\frac{1}{2} = x$$

76.
$$x + 4 = 3x - 2$$
$$x - x + 4 = 3x - x - 2$$
$$4 = 2x - 2$$
$$4 + 2 = 2x - 2 + 2$$
$$6 = 2x$$
$$3 = x$$

77.
$$6x - 2 = 14 - 2x$$
$$6x + 2x - 2 = 14 - 2x + 2x$$
$$8x - 2 = 14$$
$$8x - 2 + 2 = 14 + 2$$
$$8x = 16$$
$$x = 2$$

6.3 PAGES 349–350, PRACTICE & APPLY

5.

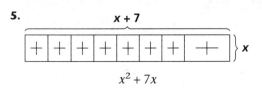

$x + 7$

$x^2 + 7x$

6.

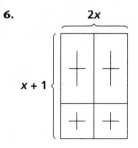

$2x$

$x + 1$

$2x$ and $x + 1$

7. $2x, 3x + 1;$
$2x(3x + 1) = 6x^2 + 2x$

8. $2x, 2x + 1;$
$2x(2x + 1) = 4x^2 + 2x$

9. $2x, x + 5; 2x(x + 5) = 2x^2 + 10x$

10. $3, x + 3; 3(x + 3) = 3x + 9$

11. $2, 3x + 1; 2(3x + 1) = 6x + 2$

12. $4, x + 3; 4(x + 3) = 4x + 12$

13. $4(x + 2) = 4x + 8$

14. $6(2x + 7) = 12x + 42$

15. $5(y + 10) = 5y + 50$

16. $3(m + 8) = 3m + 24$

17. $x(x + 2) = x^2 + 2x$

18. $2y(y - 4) = 2y^2 - 8y$

19. $3r(r^2 - 3) = 3r^3 - 9r$

20. $p^2(p + 7) = p^3 + 7p^2$

21. $8(3x - 4) = 24x - 32$

22. $4y(y - 4) = 4y^2 - 16y$

23. $5x(4x + 9) = 20x^2 + 45x$

24. $3w(w^2 - w) = 3w^3 - 3w^2$

25. $2y^2(y^2 + y) = 2y^4 + 2y^3$

26. $2t^2(2t^2 + 8t) = 4t^4 + 16t^3$

27. $3y^2(3y - 6) = 9y^3 - 18y^2$

28. $z(11z^2 + 22z) = 11z^3 + 22z^2$

29. $3x^2 + 6 = 3(x^2 + 2)$

30. $5x^2 - 20 = 5(x^2 - 4)$

31. $y^2 - y^3 = y^2(1 - y)$

32. $4p + 12p^3 = 4p(1 + 3p^2)$

33. $7y^4 + 49y = 7y(y^3 + 7)$

34. $m^4 - 6m^2 = m^2(m^2 - 6)$

35. $-4r^2 - 6r = -2r(2r + 3)$

36. $9n^2 - 27n^4 = 9n^2(1 - 3n^2)$

37. Let A represent the area of the flower bed in square yards $10x$

38. Let A represent the area of the lawn in square yards.
$25 \cdot 10$

39. Let A represent the area of the backyard in square yards.
$10(x + 25)$

40. The area of the backyard is equal to the area of the flower bed plus the area of the lawn

41. Let x represent the number of glasses, and let y represent the number of plates.
$0.25(1.50x + 2.50y)$

42. Let P represent the perimeter of the rectangle in linear units.
$$P = 2(2x + 3) + 2(3x)$$
$$= 4x + 6 + 6x$$
$$= 10x + 6$$

The perimeter of the rectangle is $10x + 6$ linear units.

43. $\frac{12}{35}$ and $\frac{18}{40}$

$\frac{12}{35} \cdot \frac{8}{8} = \frac{96}{280}$ $\frac{18}{40} \cdot \frac{7}{7} = \frac{126}{280}$

The LCD of $\frac{12}{35}$ and $\frac{18}{40}$ is 280.

Using the LCD, we can compare the two fractions.

$\frac{12}{35} < \frac{18}{40}$

44. $\frac{1}{4}$ and $\frac{3}{15}$

$\frac{1}{4} \cdot \frac{15}{15} = \frac{15}{60}$ $\frac{3}{15} \cdot \frac{4}{4} = \frac{12}{60}$

The LCD of $\frac{1}{4}$ and $\frac{3}{15}$ is 60.

Using the LCD, we can compare the two fractions.

$\frac{1}{4} > \frac{3}{15}$

45. $8 \div \frac{5}{6} = 8 \cdot \frac{6}{5}$

$= \frac{48}{5}$

$= 9\frac{3}{5}$

Since you cannot have $\frac{3}{5}$ of a plaque, only 9 plaques can be carved from the piece of wood.

46. $2^2 + 4^2 = 5^2$

$4 + 16 = 25$

$20 = 25$

Since this is not a true statement, the triangle having sides of 2, 4, and 5 is not a right triangle.

47. $10^2 + 24^2 = 26^2$

$100 + 576 = 676$

$676 = 676$

Since this is a true statement, the triangle having sides of 10, 24, and 26 is a right triangle.

48.

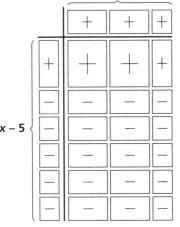

$(2x + 1)(x - 5) = 2x^2 - 9x - 5$

49.

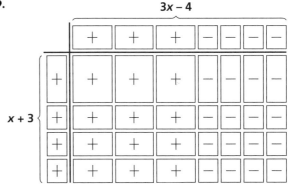

$(x + 3)(3x - 4) = 3x^2 + 5x - 12$

6.4 PAGES 355–356, PRACTICE & APPLY

7. The reciprocal of –2 or $\frac{-2}{1}$ is $-\frac{1}{2}$.

8. The reciprocal of $\frac{-1}{9}$ is $-\frac{9}{1}$ or –9.

9. The reciprocal of $4\frac{1}{5}$ or $\frac{21}{5}$ is $\frac{5}{21}$.

10. The reciprocal of $\frac{10}{3}$ is $\frac{3}{10}$.

11. The reciprocal of 1 is 1.

12. $\frac{3}{5}x = 3$

$\frac{5}{3}\left(\frac{3}{5}x\right) = \frac{5}{3}(3)$

$x = \frac{15}{3}$

$x = 5$

13. $\frac{1}{-7}y = -6$

$-7\left(\frac{1}{-7}y\right) = -7(-6)$

$y = 42$

14. $\frac{-5}{8}q = 10$

$\frac{8}{-5}\left(\frac{-5}{8}q\right) = \frac{8}{-5}(10)$

$q = \frac{80}{-5}$

$q = -16$

15. $-\frac{3}{4}x = -9$

$-\frac{4}{3}\left(-\frac{3}{4}x\right) = -\frac{4}{3}(-9)$

$x = 12$

16. $\frac{-y}{7} = 11$

$7\left(\frac{-y}{7}\right) = -7(11)$

$y = -77$

17. $\frac{p}{4} = -1.2$

$4\left(\frac{p}{4}\right) = 4(-1.2)$

$p = -4.8$

18. $\frac{p}{-11} = -5$

$-11\left(\frac{p}{-11}\right) = -11(-5)$

$p = 55$

19. $-\frac{t}{4} = -5$

$-4\left(-\frac{t}{4}\right) = -4(-5)$

$t = 20$

20. $-\dfrac{w}{8} = 9$

$$-8\left(-\dfrac{w}{8}\right) = -8(9)$$
$$w = -72$$

21. $\dfrac{-m}{-12} = -10$

$$\dfrac{m}{12} = -10$$
$$12\left(\dfrac{m}{12}\right) = 12(-10)$$
$$m = -120$$

22. $\dfrac{x}{5} = \dfrac{3}{4}$

$$5\left(\dfrac{x}{5}\right) = 5\left(\dfrac{3}{4}\right)$$
$$x = \dfrac{15}{4}, \text{ or } 3\tfrac{3}{4}, \text{ or } 3.75$$

23. $\dfrac{-x}{3} = \dfrac{2}{5}$

$$3\left(\dfrac{-x}{3}\right) = 3\left(\dfrac{2}{5}\right)$$
$$-x = \dfrac{6}{5}$$
$$x = -\dfrac{6}{5}, \text{ or } -1\tfrac{1}{5}, \text{ or } -1.2$$

24. $\dfrac{x}{4} = \dfrac{-3}{6}$

$$4\left(\dfrac{x}{4}\right) = 4\left(\dfrac{-3}{6}\right)$$
$$x = \dfrac{-12}{6}$$
$$x = -2$$

25. $\dfrac{p}{-3} = \dfrac{-4}{7}$

$$3\left(\dfrac{p}{-3}\right) = -3\left(\dfrac{-4}{7}\right)$$
$$p = \dfrac{12}{7}, \text{ or } 1\tfrac{5}{7}, \text{ or } \approx 1.714$$

26. $\dfrac{x}{16} = \dfrac{-3}{8}$

$$16\left(\dfrac{x}{16}\right) = 16\left(\dfrac{-3}{8}\right)$$
$$x = \dfrac{-48}{8}$$
$$x = -6$$

27. $\dfrac{x}{-25} = \dfrac{3}{-5}$

$$-25\left(\dfrac{x}{-25}\right) = -25\left(\dfrac{3}{-5}\right)$$
$$x = \dfrac{-75}{-5}$$
$$x = 15$$

28. $\dfrac{-x}{6} = \dfrac{5}{3}$

$$6\left(\dfrac{-x}{6}\right) = 6\left(\dfrac{5}{3}\right)$$
$$-x = \dfrac{30}{3}$$
$$x = -\dfrac{30}{3}$$
$$x = -10$$

29. $\dfrac{w}{-14} = \dfrac{6}{7}$

$$-14\left(\dfrac{w}{-14}\right) = -14\left(\dfrac{6}{7}\right)$$
$$w = \dfrac{-84}{7}$$
$$w = -12$$

30. $\dfrac{-x}{6} = \dfrac{3}{7}$

$$6\left(\dfrac{-x}{6}\right) = 6\left(\dfrac{3}{7}\right)$$
$$-x = \dfrac{18}{7}$$
$$x = -\dfrac{18}{7}, \text{ or } -2\tfrac{4}{7}, \text{ or } \approx -2.571$$

31. $\dfrac{-y}{7.5} = \dfrac{-2}{4}$

$$7.5\left(\dfrac{-y}{7.5}\right) = 7.5\left(\dfrac{-2}{4}\right)$$
$$-y = -\dfrac{15}{4}$$
$$y = \dfrac{15}{4}, \text{ or } 3\tfrac{3}{4}, \text{ or } 3.75$$

32. Let S represent the amount of Miguel's savings, and let P represent the amount that Miguel paid for the lawn mower.

$$\tfrac{2}{3}S = P$$
$$\tfrac{2}{3}S = 210$$
$$\left(\tfrac{3}{2}\right)\left(\tfrac{2}{3}S\right) = 210\left(\tfrac{3}{2}\right)$$
$$S = 315$$

Miguel had $315 in his savings before buying the lawn mower.

33. Let S represent the total number of free throws that Alicia is supposed to practice.

$$\tfrac{3}{4}S = 45$$
$$\left(\tfrac{4}{3}\right)\left(\tfrac{3}{4}S\right) = 45\left(\tfrac{4}{3}\right)$$
$$S = 60$$

Alicia is supposed to practice 60 free throws.

34. Let r represent the number of ribbons before the sale.

$$\tfrac{2}{3}r = 450$$
$$\left(\tfrac{3}{2}\right)\left(\tfrac{2}{3}r\right) = 450\left(\tfrac{3}{2}\right)$$
$$r = 675$$

The cheerleaders had 675 ribbons before the sale.

35. Let s represent the time it takes Mary to run 75 yards.

$$\dfrac{s}{75} = \dfrac{9}{50}$$
$$75\left(\dfrac{s}{75}\right) = 75\left(\dfrac{9}{50}\right)$$
$$s = \dfrac{675}{50}$$
$$s = 13.5$$

It will take Mary 13.5 seconds.

36. Let p represent the price of 16 cans of dog food in dollars and cents.

$$\dfrac{p}{16} = \dfrac{1.74}{6}$$
$$16\left(\dfrac{p}{16}\right) = 16\left(\dfrac{1.74}{6}\right)$$
$$p = 4.64$$

Since the food costs $4.64 and Miguel has $5, he has enough to buy 16 cans of dog food.

37. Let p represent the number of pesos exchanged for 63 crowns.

$$\dfrac{7}{9} = \dfrac{p}{63}$$
$$63\left(\dfrac{7}{9}\right) = 63\left(\dfrac{p}{63}\right)$$
$$\dfrac{441}{9} = p$$
$$49 = p$$

The number of pesos was 49.

38. Let x represent the total of Diophantus's life in years.

Then $\frac{1}{6}x$ represents his time as a child, $\frac{1}{12}x$ represents his time as a youth, $\frac{1}{7}x$

represents his time before marriage, and $\frac{1}{2}x$ represents the portion of his life that his son lived.

$$x = \frac{1}{6}x + \frac{1}{12}x + \frac{1}{7}x + 5 + \frac{1}{2}x + 4$$
$$84(x) = 84\left(\frac{1}{6}x + \frac{1}{12}x + \frac{1}{7}x + 5 + \frac{1}{2}x + 4\right)$$
$$84x = 14x + 7x + 12x + 420 + 42x + 336$$
$$84x = 75x + 756$$
$$9x = 756$$
$$x = 84$$

Diophantus lived 84 years.

PAGE 356, LOOK BACK

39. $6p - 3q + r = 6(3) - 3(4) + 10$
$= 18 - 12 + 10$
$= 6 + 10$
$= 16$

40. $\frac{4}{18} - \frac{5}{9} = \frac{4}{18} - \frac{10}{18}$
$= \frac{-6}{18}$
$= -\frac{1}{3}$

41. $\frac{5}{17} \div \frac{10}{17} = \frac{5}{17} \cdot \frac{17}{10}$
$= \frac{85}{170}$
$= \frac{1}{2}$

42. $\frac{3}{8} + \frac{1}{4} - \frac{5}{16} = \frac{6}{16} + \frac{4}{16} - \frac{5}{16}$
$= \frac{10}{16} - \frac{5}{16}$
$= \frac{5}{16}$

43. $(3x - 2) + (4x + 7) = 3x - 2 + 4x + 7$
$= 3x + 4x - 2 + 7$
$= 7x + 5$

44. $2(4q + 3) - (q - 2) = 8q + 6 - q + 2$
$= 8q - q + 6 + 2$
$= 7q + 8$

45. $(2a + 3b - 1) - 2(a - 2b - 1) = 2a + 3b - 1 - 2a + 4b + 2$
$= 2a - 2a + 3b + 4b - 1 + 2$
$= 7b + 1$

46. $x + 4 > -12$
$x + 4 - 4 > -12 - 4$
$x > -16$

47. $y - 0.05 \leq 10.5$
$y - 0.05 + 0.05 \leq 10.5 + 0.05$
$y \leq 10.55$

48. $w + 1.4 \geq 10.2$
$w + 1.4 - 1.4 \geq 10.2 - 1.4$
$w \geq 8.8$

PAGE 356, LOOK BEYOND

49. Choose one of the equations and solve for x.
Substitute that value into the other equation and solve for y.
Solve for x in $6x - 4 = 8$.

$$6x - 4 = 8$$
$$6x - 4 + 4 = 8 + 4$$
$$6x = 12$$
$$\frac{6x}{6} = \frac{12}{6}$$
$$x = 2$$

Substitute $x = 2$ in $3x + 2y = 14$
to solve for y.

$$3(2) + 2y = 14$$
$$6 + 2y = 14$$
$$6 - 6 + 2y = 14 - 6$$
$$2y = 8$$
$$y = 4$$
$$x = 2 \text{ and } y = 4$$

6.5 PAGES 361–364, PRACTICE & APPLY

6. $\frac{27}{18} = \frac{42}{n}$
$27 \cdot n = 18 \cdot 42$
$\frac{27n}{27} = \frac{756}{27}$
$n = 28$

7. $\frac{38}{19} = \frac{n}{20}$
$19n = 38 \cdot 20$
$\frac{19n}{19} = \frac{760}{19}$
$n = 40$

8. $\frac{42}{28} = \frac{36}{n}$
$42n = 28 \cdot 36$
$\frac{42n}{42} = \frac{1008}{42}$
$n = 24$

9. $\frac{n}{48} = \frac{72}{96}$
$96n = 48 \cdot 72$
$\frac{96n}{96} = \frac{3456}{96}$
$n = 36$

10. $\frac{21.5}{x} = \frac{64.5}{18}$
$64.5x = 21.5 \cdot 18$
$\frac{64.5x}{64.5} = \frac{387}{64.5}$
$x = 6$

11. $\frac{x}{37.2} = \frac{16}{24.8}$
$24.8x = 16 \cdot 37.2$
$\frac{24.8x}{24.8} = \frac{595.2}{24.8}$
$x = 24$

12. $\frac{30.8}{112} = \frac{y}{10}$
$112y = 30.8 \cdot 10$
$\frac{112y}{112} = \frac{308}{112}$
$y = 2.75$

13. $\frac{t}{25} = \frac{473}{15}$
$15t = 25 \cdot 473$
$\frac{15t}{15} = \frac{11,825}{15}$
$t = 788\frac{1}{3}$

14. $\dfrac{15}{9} \overset{?}{=} \dfrac{35}{21}$

$15 \cdot 21 \overset{?}{=} 35 \cdot 9$

$315 = 315$ True

This is a true proportion.

15. $\dfrac{12}{9} \overset{?}{=} \dfrac{18}{12}$

$12 \cdot 12 \overset{?}{=} 9 \cdot 18$

$144 \neq 162$ False

This is not a true proportion.

16. $\dfrac{56}{24} \overset{?}{=} \dfrac{49}{21}$

$56 \cdot 21 \overset{?}{=} 24 \cdot 49$

$1176 = 1176$ True

This is a true proportion.

17. $\dfrac{27}{21} \overset{?}{=} \dfrac{35}{28}$

$27 \cdot 28 \overset{?}{=} 21 \cdot 35$

$756 \neq 735$ False

This is not a true proportion.

18. $\dfrac{18}{8} \overset{?}{=} \dfrac{108}{48}$

$18 \cdot 48 \overset{?}{=} 8 \cdot 108$

$864 = 864$ True

This is a true proportion.

19. $\dfrac{3}{5} \overset{?}{=} \dfrac{81}{135}$

$135 \cdot 3 \overset{?}{=} 81 \cdot 5$

$405 = 405$ True

This is a true proportion.

20. $\dfrac{3}{13} \overset{?}{=} \dfrac{10}{65}$

$65 \cdot 3 \overset{?}{=} 10 \cdot 13$

$195 \neq 130$ False

This is not a true proportion.

21. $\dfrac{12}{20} \overset{?}{=} \dfrac{27}{45}$

$12 \cdot 45 \overset{?}{=} 20 \cdot 27$

$540 = 540$ True

This is a true proportion.

22. For similar triangles ABC and MNP, use the two corresponding sides that have measures given to calculate the ratio between the triangles.

$$\frac{BC}{NP} = \frac{1.12}{2.24} = \frac{1}{2}$$

Then use the ratio to compute the missing side lengths.

$\dfrac{AB}{MN} = \dfrac{1.26}{MN} = \dfrac{1}{2}$

$2(1.26) = 1(MN)$

$2.52 = MN$

$\dfrac{AC}{MP} = \dfrac{AC}{3.14} = \dfrac{1}{2}$

$2(AC) = 1(3.14)$

$\dfrac{2(AC)}{2} = \dfrac{3.14}{2}$

$AC = 1.57$

The measure of $\overline{MN}$ is 2.52 inches, and the measure of $\overline{AC}$ is 1.30 inches.

23. The ratio of cleaner to water for 200 square feet is 3 ounces of cleaner to 2 gallons of water. To clean 600 square feet she would need to multiply the amount of cleaner by 3 to get 9 ounces of cleaner.

24. $\dfrac{2}{3} \overset{?}{=} \dfrac{6}{9}$ Also $\dfrac{3}{2} = \dfrac{9}{6}$, $\dfrac{3}{9} = \dfrac{2}{6}$, and $\dfrac{9}{3} = \dfrac{6}{2}$

$2 \cdot 9 \overset{?}{=} 3 \cdot 6$

$18 = 18$ True

This is a true proportion.

25. False; for example, it is possible that the second team won 4 games out of 6 games played because $\dfrac{2}{3} = \dfrac{4}{6}$.

26. Let x represent the number of boys on the council.

$\dfrac{280}{360} = \dfrac{x}{72}$

$360x = 280 \cdot 72$

$\dfrac{360x}{360} = \dfrac{20{,}160}{360}$

$x = 56$

There must be 56 boys on the student council.

27. Let x represent the number of voters in favor of the bond issue.

$x = \dfrac{2}{3}(28{,}950)$

$x = 19{,}300$

19,300 eligible voters are in favor of the bond issue.

28. Let x represent the pounds of fertilizer needed to cover 2400 square feet.

$\dfrac{4}{1500} = \dfrac{x}{2400}$

$1500x = 4 \cdot 2400$

$\dfrac{1500x}{1500} = \dfrac{9600}{1500}$

$x = 6.4$

6.4 pounds of fertilizer are needed to cover 2400 square feet.

29. $\dfrac{3}{2} = \dfrac{36}{24}$, $\dfrac{2}{24} = \dfrac{3}{36}$, and $\dfrac{24}{2} = \dfrac{36}{3}$

30. $\dfrac{36}{14} = \dfrac{54}{21}$, $\dfrac{54}{36} = \dfrac{21}{14}$, and $\dfrac{14}{36} = \dfrac{21}{54}$

31. $\dfrac{48}{64} = \dfrac{27}{36}$, $\dfrac{64}{48} = \dfrac{36}{27}$, and $\dfrac{27}{48} = \dfrac{36}{64}$

32. $\dfrac{15}{10} = \dfrac{9}{6}$, $\dfrac{10}{15} = \dfrac{6}{9}$, and $\dfrac{9}{15} = \dfrac{6}{10}$

33. $\dfrac{12}{27} = \dfrac{20}{45}$, $\dfrac{27}{12} = \dfrac{45}{20}$, and $\dfrac{20}{12} = \dfrac{45}{27}$

34. $\dfrac{24}{54} = \dfrac{8}{18}$, $\dfrac{54}{24} = \dfrac{18}{8}$, and $\dfrac{8}{24} = \dfrac{18}{54}$

35. $\dfrac{2}{10} = \dfrac{13}{65}$, $\dfrac{10}{2} = \dfrac{65}{13}$, and $\dfrac{13}{2} = \dfrac{65}{10}$

36. $\dfrac{12}{18} = \dfrac{16}{24}$, $\dfrac{18}{12} = \dfrac{24}{16}$, and $\dfrac{16}{12} = \dfrac{24}{18}$

37.

Sale price	Regular price
6	8
9	12
12	16
15	20
18	24

38. $\dfrac{\text{Sale price}}{\text{Regular price}} = \dfrac{6}{8} = \dfrac{9}{12} = \dfrac{12}{16} = \dfrac{18}{24} = \dfrac{3}{4}$

The ratios are all equal to $\dfrac{3}{4}$.

39. Let x represent the regular price of the item.

$$\frac{3}{4} = \frac{56}{x}$$

$$3x = 56 \cdot 4$$

$$\frac{3x}{3} = \frac{224}{3}$$

$$x = 74\frac{2}{3}$$

The regular price of the item would be $74.67.

40. Let x represent the sale price of the item.

$$\frac{3}{4} = \frac{x}{36}$$

$$4x = 3 \cdot 36$$

$$\frac{4x}{4} = \frac{108}{4}$$

$$x = 27$$

The sale price of the item is $27.

41. $\dfrac{\text{Sale price}}{\text{Regular price}} = \dfrac{48}{60} = \dfrac{4}{5}$

The price ratio is not the same as in the original graph.

42. Let x represent the number of times Frank's heart beats in a minute (60 seconds).

$$\frac{20}{60} = \frac{24}{x}$$

$$20x = 60 \cdot 24$$

$$\frac{20x}{20} = \frac{1440}{20}$$

$$x = 72$$

Frank's heart beats 72 times in one minute.

43. Let x represent the number of females in the Senate.

$$\frac{23}{2} = \frac{92}{x}$$

$$23x = 92 \cdot 2$$

$$\frac{23x}{23} = \frac{184}{23}$$

$$x = 8$$

There were 8 female senators in the 104th Congress.

44. Let x represent the number of gallons of gasoline Matthew needs.

$$\frac{425}{18.2} = \frac{640}{x}$$

$$425x = 640 \cdot 18.2$$

$$\frac{425x}{425} = \frac{11648}{425}$$

$$x = 27.4$$

Matthew needs 27.4 gallons of gas.

45. Let x represent the length of the kennel.

$$\frac{48}{120} = \frac{16}{x}$$

$$48x = 120 \cdot 16$$

$$\frac{48x}{48} = \frac{1920}{48}$$

$$x = 40$$

The length of the kennel will be 40 ft.

46. Let x represent the height of the statue.

$$\frac{51}{48} = \frac{x}{16}$$

$$48x = 51 \cdot 16$$

$$\frac{48x}{48} = \frac{816}{48}$$

$$x = 17$$

The statue is 17 feet tall.

47. Let x represent the height of the building.

$$\frac{17}{16} = \frac{x}{52}$$

$$16x = 17 \cdot 52$$

$$\frac{16x}{16} = \frac{884}{16}$$

$$x = 55\frac{1}{4} = 55 \text{ ft 3 in.}$$

The building is 55 feet and 3 inches tall.

48. Let x represent the height of the road sign.

$$\frac{17}{16} = \frac{x}{10}$$

$$16x = 17 \cdot 10$$

$$\frac{16x}{16} = \frac{170}{16}$$

$$x = 10.625 \text{ or } 10\frac{5}{8}$$

The road sign is $10\frac{5}{8}$ feet tall.

49. Let x represent the number of pounds of ground beef.

$$\frac{12}{3} = \frac{50}{x}$$

$$12x = 3 \cdot 50$$

$$\frac{12x}{12} = \frac{150}{12}$$

$$x = 12.5$$

You would need 12.5 pounds of ground beef to make 50 servings.

50. Let x represent the number of pounds of ground beef needed.

$$\frac{12}{3} = \frac{65}{x}$$

$$12x = 3 \cdot 65$$

$$\frac{12x}{12} = \frac{195}{12}$$

$$x = 16.25$$

You would need 16.25 pounds of ground beef to make 65 servings.

51. Let x represent the number of servings.

$$\frac{12}{8} = \frac{x}{5}$$

$$8x = 12 \cdot 5$$

$$\frac{8x}{8} = \frac{60}{8}$$

$$x = 7.5$$

You could make approximately 7 servings with 5 tomatoes.

52. Let x represent the number of servings.

$$\frac{12}{3} = \frac{x}{4}$$

$$3x = 12 \cdot 4$$

$$\frac{3x}{3} = \frac{48}{3}$$

$$x = 16$$

You could make 16 complete servings with 4 pounds of ground beef.

53. $\dfrac{1}{12} - \dfrac{2}{30} = \dfrac{5}{60} - \dfrac{4}{60}$
$\qquad = \dfrac{1}{60}$

54. $0.4(100) = 40\%$

55. $1.25(100) = 125\%$

56. $0.003(100) = 0.3\%$

57. $\dfrac{3}{4}(100) = \dfrac{300}{4}$
$\qquad = 75\%$

58. $\dfrac{2}{3}(100) = \dfrac{200}{3}$
$\qquad = 66\dfrac{2}{3}\%$

59. $\dfrac{3}{8}(100) = \dfrac{300}{8}$
$\qquad = 37\dfrac{1}{2}\%$

60. $3 \cdot 5x = (3 \cdot 5)x$
$\qquad = 15x$

61. $-2y \cdot 3y = (-2 \cdot 3)(y \cdot y)$
$\qquad = -6y^2$

62. $7(x - 3) - (5 - 4x) = 7x - 21 - 5 + 4x$
$\qquad = 7x + 4x - 21 - 5$
$\qquad = 11x - 26$

63. $\dfrac{w}{-12} = 13$
$(-12)\left(\dfrac{w}{-12}\right) = (13)(-12)$
$\qquad w = -156$

64. $-18 = \dfrac{x}{12}$
$(12)(-18) = \left(\dfrac{x}{12}\right)(12)$
$\qquad -216 = x$

65. $\dfrac{12}{100} = \dfrac{x}{18}$
$18\left(\dfrac{12}{100}\right) = \left(\dfrac{x}{18}\right)18$
$\qquad \dfrac{216}{100} = x$
$\qquad \dfrac{54}{25} = x$
$\text{or } x = 2\dfrac{4}{25}, \text{ or } x = 2.16$

66. $(2x - 3) + x + 105 = 180$
$\qquad 3x - 3 + 105 = 180$
$\qquad 3x + 102 = 180$
$\qquad 3x = 78$
$\qquad x = 26$
x is $26°$.

67. $3x - 4 > 2x + 5$
$3x - 2x - 4 > 2x - 2x + 5$
$\qquad x - 4 > 5$
$\qquad x - 4 + 4 > 5 + 4$
$\qquad x > 9$

68. $8x - 16 \leq 5x + 92$
$8x - 5x - 16 \leq 5x - 5x + 92$
$\qquad 3x - 16 \leq 92$
$3x - 16 + 16 \leq 92 + 16$
$\qquad 3x \leq 108$
$\qquad \dfrac{3x}{3} \leq \dfrac{108}{3}$
$\qquad x \leq 36$

69. $\dfrac{2}{3}x + 9 \leq 87$
$\dfrac{2}{3}x + 9 - 9 \leq 87 - 9$
$\qquad \dfrac{2}{3}x \leq 78$
$\left(\dfrac{3}{2}\right)\left(\dfrac{2}{3}x\right) \leq \left(\dfrac{3}{2}\right)(78)$
$\qquad x \leq 117$

6.6 **PAGES 370–372, PRACTICE & APPLY**

11. $55\% = \dfrac{55}{100}$
$\qquad = 0.55$

12. $1.2\% = \dfrac{1.2}{100}$
$\qquad = 0.012$

13. $8\% = \dfrac{8}{100}$
$\qquad = 0.08$

14. $145\% = \dfrac{145}{100}$
$\qquad = 1.45$

15. $0.5\% = \dfrac{0.5}{100}$
$\qquad = 0.005$

16. $0.47 = 0.47 \cdot 100$
$\qquad = 47\%$

17. $0.019 = 0.019 \cdot 100$
$\qquad = 1.9\%$

18. $8.11 = 8.11 \cdot 100$
$\qquad = 811\%$

19. $0.001 = 0.001 \cdot 100$
$\qquad = 0.1\%$

20. $9.00 = 9.00 \cdot 100$
$\qquad = 900\%$

For Exercises 21–47, let x represent the answer.

21. 35% of 80

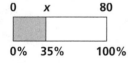

22. 5 is what percent of 25?

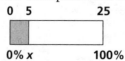

23. What number is 10% of 8?

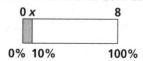

24. 150% of 40

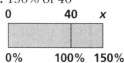

25. What percent of 90 is 40?

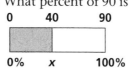

26. 18 is 20% of what number?

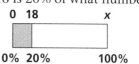

For Exercises 27–32, estimate each answer as more or less than 50 or 50% by changing percents to decimals or fractions.

27. 5% of 80

50% of a number is $\frac{50}{100}$, or $\frac{1}{2}$ of a number.

50% of 80 would be $\frac{80}{2}$ = 40.

Since 40 < 50, the answer is *less* than 50.

28. 18 is 20% of what number?

20% of a number is 0.02, or $\frac{20}{100}$, or $\frac{1}{5}$ of a number.

Since you know that 18 is part of a larger number that is 5 times more than 18 and $18 \times 5 = 90$, the answer is *more* than 50.

29. 150% of 40

100% of 40 is 40.

50% of 40 is $\frac{40}{2}$ = 20.

Since 100% of 40 plus 50% of 40 is 40 + 20 = 60, the answer is *more* than 50.

30. 2.5% of 100

50% of 100 would be $\frac{100}{2}$ = 50.

Since 2.5% < 50%, the answer is *less* than 50.

31. What percent of 90 is 40?

Since 50% of 90 would be $\frac{90}{2}$ = 45, and 45 > 40, the answer is *less* than 50%.

32. What percent of 60 is 120?

Since 100% of 60 is 60, and 200% of 60 is $2.00 \times 60 = 120$, the answer is *more* than 50%.

For Exercises 33–44, the equation method is shown. Another method is to solve by using a percent bar and forming a proportion.

33. 40% of 50

$(0.40)(50) = x$
$(0.40)(50) = 20$
40% of 50 is 20.

34. 125% of what number is 45?

$1.25x = 45$
$x = 36$
125% of 36 is 45.

35. 8 is 20% of what number?

$8 = 0.20x$
$40 = x$
8 is 20% of 40.

36. 200% of 50

$(2.00)(50) = x$
$100 = x$
200% of 50 is 100.

37. 30 is 60% of what number?

$30 = 0.60x$
$\frac{30}{0.60} = x$
$50 = x$
30 is 60% of 50.

38. What percent of 80 is 10?

x% of 80 is 10?
$(x)(80) = 10$
$x = 0.125$
10 is 12.5% of 80.

39. What number is 35% of 80?

$(0.35)(80) = x$
$28 = x$
28 is 35% of 80.

40. What number is 3.5% of 120?

$x = (0.035)(120)$
$x = 4.2$
4.2 is 3.5% of 120.

41. 3 is what percent of 3000?

$3 = (x)(3000)$
$3 = 3000x$
$\frac{3}{3000} = x$
$0.001 = x$
3 is 0.1% of 3000.

42. 75% of 900

$(0.75)(900) = x$
$675 = x$
675 is 75% of 900.

43. 72 is 9% of what number?

$72 = 0.09x$
$800 = x$
72 is 9% of 800.

44. What percent of 60 is 24?

$x \cdot 60 = 24$
$x = \frac{24}{60}$
$x = 0.40$
24 is 40% of 60.

45. Total income: $35,600
Amount over $22,100: $35,600 - 22,100 = \$13,500$
Federal income tax: $3315 + 13,500(0.28) = \$7095$

46. Total income: $24,850
Amount over $22,100: $24,850 - 22,100 = \$2750$
Federal income tax: $3315 + 2750(0.28) = \$4085$

47. Total income: $42,950
Amount over $22,100: $42,950 - 22,100 = \$20,850$
Federal income tax: $3315 + 20,850(0.28) = \$9,153$

48. Total income: $17,890
Federal income tax: $17,890(0.15) = \$2683.50$

49.　　　　Total income: $55,930
Amount over $53,500:　55,930 – 53,500 = $2430
　Federal income tax:　12,107 + 2430(0.31) =
　　　　　　　　　　　$12,860.30

50.　　　　Total income: $51,865
Amount over $22,100:　51,865 – 22,100 = $29,765
　Federal income tax:　3315 + 29,765(0.28)
　　　　　　　　　　　= $11,649.20

51.　　　　Total income: $112,050
Amount over $53,500:　112,050 – 53,500 = $58,550
　Federal income tax:　12,107 + 58,550(0.31) =
　　　　　　　　　　　$30,257.50

52.　　　　Total income: $53,500
Amount over $22,100:　53,500 – 22,100 = $31,400
　Federal income tax:　3315 + 31,400(0.28) =
　　　　　　　　　　　$12,107

	Taxable income	Amount of tax on income	Amount withheld	Amount owed　or　Amount to be refunded	
53.	$65,750	12,107 + 12,250(.31) = $15,904.50	$1856	$14,048.50	
54.	$55,930	12,107 + 2430(.31) = $12,860.30	$25,036		$12,175.70
55.	$43,100	3315 + 21,000(.28) = $9195	$5850	$3345	
56.	$108,426	12,107 +54,926(.31) = $29,134.06	$42,865		$13,730.94

57. Let x represent the percentage.
$\frac{1}{2}$ of 0.01% is what number?
0.5(0.1) = 0.05%

58. The statement is
$\frac{1}{2}$ of 0.1% is 0.05%.

59. Let x represent the number of students.
52% of 50 is what number?
(0.52)(50) = x
26 = x
These were 26 students who opposed the new policy.

60. Let p represent the sale price of the racket. If the discount is 30% off the original price of the racket, then the sale price will be 70% of the original price.
70% of 66 is what number?
(0.70)(66) = p
46.20 = p
The sale price of the tennis racket is $46.20.

Use the following method for Exercises 61–64:
To determine the percent of each type of vote, find the sum of each type of vote.

Let p represent the total number of popular votes, e represent the total number of electoral votes, and x represent the percentage of each type of vote.
p = 43,682,624 + 38,117,331 + 19,217,213 = 101,017,168
e = 370 + 168 + 0 = 538

61. Clinton:
43,682,624 is what percent of 101,017,168?

43,682,624 = (x)(101,017,168)

$\frac{43,682,624}{101,017,168} = \frac{(x)(101,017,168)}{101,017,168}$
43.24 ≈ x

Clinton received about 43.24% of the popular vote.

62. Bush:
38,117,331 is what percent of 101,017,168?

38,117,331 = (x)(101,017,168)

$\frac{38,117,331}{101,017,168} = \frac{(x)(101,017,168)}{101,017,168}$
37.73 ≈ x

Bush received about 37.73% of the popular vote.

63. Perot:
19,217,213 is what percent of 101,017,168?

19,217,213 = (x)(101,017,168)

$\frac{19,217,213}{101,017,168} = \frac{(x)(101,017,168)}{101,017,168}$
19.02 ≈ x

Perot received about 19.02% of the popular vote.

64. Number of votes Clinton received: 43,682,624
　Number of votes Bush received: 38,117,331
Number of votes received by both: 81,799,955
81,799,955 is what percent of 101,017,168?

81,799,955 = (x)(101,017,168)

$\frac{81,799,955}{101,017,168} = \frac{(x)(101,017,168)}{101,017,168}$
80.98 = x

Bush and Clinton received about 80.98% of the popular vote.

65. Let x represent the number of people who were registered.

42% of what number is 11,960?

$$(0.42)(x) = 11{,}960$$
$$\frac{(0.42)(x)}{0.42} = \frac{11{,}960}{0.42}$$
$$x \approx 28{,}476.19$$

There were about 28,476 registered voters.

66. Let l represent the length of the rectangle, w represent the width, and P represent the perimeter.

$$P = 2l + 2w$$
$$P = 2(l + 0.10l) + 2(w + 0.10w)$$
$$P = (2l + 0.20l) + (2w + 0.20w)$$
$$P = 2.20l + 2.20w$$

Find the percent increase in the perimeter.
$2.20l + 2.20w$ is what percent of $2l + 2w$?

$$2.20l + 2.20w = (x)(2l + 2w)$$
$$\frac{2.20l + 2.20w}{2l + 2w} = \frac{(x)(2l + 2w)}{2l + 2w}$$
$$\frac{2.20l + 2.20w}{2l + 2w} = x$$
$$\frac{2.20(l + w)}{2(l + w)} = x$$
$$1.10 = x$$

$2.20l + 2.20w$ is 1.10% of $2l + 2w$. Therefore, the perimeter has increased by 10%.

PAGE 372, LOOK BACK

68–71.

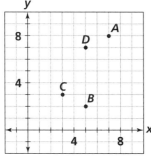

72. If x is an even integer, then the next two even integers are $x + 2$ and $x + 4$.

73. $-2 \cdot 3x = (-2 \cdot 3)x$
$ = -6x$

74. $-8x \div 4 = \frac{-8x}{4}$
$ = -2x$

75. $\frac{10x + 25}{-5} = \frac{10x}{-5} + \frac{25}{-5}$
$\phantom{\frac{10x + 25}{-5}} = \left(\frac{10}{-5}\right)x + (-5)$
$\phantom{\frac{10x + 25}{-5}} = -2x - 5$

76. $\frac{22 - 2y}{2} = \frac{22}{2} - \frac{2y}{2}$
$\phantom{\frac{22 - 2y}{2}} = 11 - \left(\frac{2}{2}\right)y$
$\phantom{\frac{22 - 2y}{2}} = 11 - y$

PAGE 372, LOOK BEYOND

77. $\quad 4x + 6 = 2x - 2$
$4x - 2x + 6 = 2x - 2x - 2$
$\quad 2x + 6 = -2$
$\quad\quad 2x = -8$
$\quad\quad\ x = -4$

78. $\quad 4x + \frac{1}{2} = 5x - \frac{3}{4}$
$\quad 4x + \frac{1}{2} + \frac{3}{4} = 5x - \frac{3}{4} + \frac{3}{4}$
$\quad 4x + \frac{2}{4} + \frac{3}{4} = 5x$
$\quad 4x - 4x + \frac{5}{4} = 5x - 4x$
$\quad\quad\quad \frac{5}{4} = x$
$\quad x = \frac{5}{4}$, or $1\frac{1}{4}$, or 1.25

PAGES 374–376 CHAPTER 6 REVIEW

1. $3 \cdot 9x = (3 \cdot 9)x$
$ = 27x$

2. $-33x \div 3 = -11x$

3. $-2(7y - 2) = (-2 \cdot 7y) - (-2) \cdot 2$
$ = -14y - (-4)$
$ = -14y + 4$

4. $-2.4x \cdot 2x = (-2.4 \cdot 2) \cdot (x \cdot x)$
$ = -4.8 \cdot x^2$
$ = -4.8x^2$

5. $\dfrac{-30y + 3.6}{-3} = \dfrac{-30y}{-3} + \dfrac{3.6}{-3}$
$= 10y + (-1.2)$
$= 10y - 1.2$

6. $9r^2 - 8(4 - 3r^2) = 9r^2 - (8 \cdot 4) - (8 \cdot (-3r^2))$
$= 9r^2 - 32 - (-24r^2)$
$= 9r^2 - 32 + 24r^2$
$= 9r^2 + 24r^2 - 32$
$= 33r^2 - 32$

7. $17x = -85$
$\dfrac{17x}{17} = \dfrac{-85}{17}$
$x = -5$

8. $-4g = -56$
$\dfrac{-4g}{-4} = \dfrac{-56}{-4}$
$g = 14$

9. $-2.2h = 33$
$\dfrac{-2.2h}{-2.2} = \dfrac{33}{-2.2}$
$h = -15$

10. $24f = 150$
$\dfrac{24f}{24} = \dfrac{150}{24}$
$f = 6\dfrac{1}{4}$

11. $\dfrac{w}{-8} = 0.5$
$-8\left(\dfrac{w}{-8}\right) = (0.5)(-8)$
$w = -4$

12. $\dfrac{y}{-2.4} = -10$
$-2.4\left(\dfrac{y}{-2.4}\right) = (-10)(-2.4)$
$y = 24$

13. $5(x - 5) = 5x - 5 \cdot 5$
$= 5x - 25$

14. $y(y + 4) = y \cdot y + y \cdot 4$
$= y^2 + 4y$

15. $4t(t^2 + 7) = 4t \cdot t^2 + 4t \cdot 7$
$= 4 \cdot (t \cdot t^2) + (7 \cdot 4)t$
$= 4 \cdot t^3 + 28t$
$= 4t^3 + 28t$

16. $2r^2(r^2 - 3r) = 2r^2 \cdot r^2 - 2r^2 \cdot 3r$
$= 2(r^2 \cdot r^2) - (2 \cdot 3)(r^2 \cdot r)$
$= 2(r^4) - 6(r^3)$
$= 2r^4 - 6r^3$

17. $b(12b^2 + 11b) = b \cdot 12b^2 + b \cdot 11b$
$= 12 \cdot (b \cdot b^2) + 11 \cdot (b \cdot b)$
$= 12 \cdot b^3 + 11 \cdot b^2$
$= 12b^3 + 11b^2$

18. $4y(y + 5) = 4y \cdot y + 4y \cdot 5$
$= 4y^2 + (4 \cdot 5)y$
$= 4y^2 + 20y$

19. $5x^2(2x^2 - x) = 5x^2 \cdot 2x^2 - 5x^2 \cdot x$
$= (5 \cdot 2)(x^2 \cdot x^2) - 5(x^2 \cdot x)$
$= 10x^4 - 5x^3$

20. $6d^2(d^2 - 1) = 6d^2 \cdot d^2 - 6d^2 \cdot 1$
$= 6(d^2 \cdot d^2) - 6d^2$
$= 6d^4 - 6d^2$

21. $6x^2 + 8 = 2(3x^2 + 4)$

22. $5c^3 - 25c = 5c(c^2 - 5)$

23. $n^4 + 2n^3 = n^3(n + 2)$

24. $-9w^2 - 21w^4 = -3w^2(3 + 7w^2)$
$= -3w^2(7w^2 + 3)$

25. $8y^2 - 3y = y(8y - 3)$

26. $-8p - 14p^2 = -2p(4 + 7p)$
$= -2p(7p + 4)$

27. $z^4 + 5z^2 = z^2(z^2 + 5)$

28. $16y^5 - 4y^3 = 4y^3(4y^2 - 1)$

29. $\dfrac{4}{7}x = 4$
$\dfrac{7}{4}\left(\dfrac{4}{7}x\right) = (4)\dfrac{7}{4}$
$x = 7$

30. $\dfrac{1}{-9}y = 2.5$
$\dfrac{-9}{1}\left(\dfrac{1}{-9}y\right) = (2.5)\dfrac{-9}{1}$
$y = -22.5$

31. $\dfrac{w}{-16} = \dfrac{3}{-4}$
$\dfrac{-16}{1}\left(\dfrac{w}{-16}\right) = \left(\dfrac{3}{-4}\right)\dfrac{-16}{1}$
$w = 12$

32. $-\dfrac{3}{5}m = \dfrac{8}{15}$
$-\dfrac{5}{3}\left(-\dfrac{3}{5}m\right) = \left(\dfrac{8}{15}\right)\dfrac{-5}{3}$
$m = -\dfrac{8}{9}$

33. $\dfrac{n}{6} = \dfrac{12}{9}$
$9n = 6 \cdot 12$
$\dfrac{9n}{9} = \dfrac{72}{9}$
$n = 8$

34. $\dfrac{13}{n} = \dfrac{39}{27}$
$39n = 13 \cdot 27$
$\dfrac{39n}{39} = \dfrac{351}{39}$
$n = 9$

35. $\dfrac{11.4}{8} = \dfrac{45.6}{x}$
$11.4x = 8 \cdot 45.6$
$\dfrac{11.4x}{11.4} = \dfrac{364.8}{11.4}$
$x = 32$

36. $\dfrac{16}{41} = \dfrac{x}{820}$
$41x = 16 \cdot 820$
$\dfrac{41x}{41} = \dfrac{13,120}{41}$
$x = 320$

37. $\dfrac{17}{11} \overset{?}{=} \dfrac{68}{44}$
$11 \cdot 68 \overset{?}{=} 17 \cdot 44$
$748 = 748$ True
The statement is a true proportion.

38. $\dfrac{7}{19} \overset{?}{=} \dfrac{20}{59}$
$7 \cdot 59 \overset{?}{=} 19 \cdot 20$
$413 \neq 380$ False
The statement is not a true proportion.

39. $\dfrac{2}{5} \overset{?}{=} \dfrac{82}{405}$
$2 \cdot 405 \overset{?}{=} 5 \cdot 82$
$810 \neq 410$ False
The statement is not a true proportion.

40. $\dfrac{23}{43} \overset{?}{=} \dfrac{45}{87}$
$23 \cdot 87 \overset{?}{=} 43 \cdot 45$
$2001 \neq 1935$ False
The statement is not a true proportion.

41. $55\% \cdot 60 = x$
$0.55 \cdot 60 = x$
$33 = x$
33 is 55% of 60.

42. $28 = 70\% \cdot x$
$28 = 0.70x$
$\dfrac{28}{0.70} = \dfrac{0.70x}{0.70}$
$40 = x$
28 is 70% of 40.

43. $200\% \cdot 40 = x$
$2.00 \cdot 40 = x$
$80 = x$
80 is 200% of 40.

44. $35\% \cdot 140 = x$
$0.35 \cdot 140 = x$
$49 = x$
49 is 35% of 140.

45. $x \cdot 90 = 40.5$

$\dfrac{x \cdot 90}{90} = \dfrac{40.5}{90}$

$x = 0.45$

40.5 is 45% of 90.

46. $4 = x \cdot 50$

$\dfrac{4}{50} = \dfrac{x \cdot 50}{50}$

$0.08 = x$

4 is 8% of 50.

47. Let h represent the height of the triangle. Use the formula $A = \frac{1}{2}bh$, where A is 21 square centimeters and b is 6 centimeters.

$A = \frac{1}{2}bh$

$21 = \frac{1}{2}(6)h$

$21 = 3h$

$\dfrac{21}{3} = \dfrac{3h}{3}$

$7 = h$

The height of the triangle is 7 centimeters.

48. Let x represent the number of pounds of French fries.

$x = 22\% \cdot 50$

$x = 0.22 \cdot 50$

$x = 11$

11 pounds of potatoes are made into French fries.

PAGE 377 CHAPTER 6 ASSESSMENT

1.

a. $(8x - 32) \div 4 = \dfrac{8x}{4} - \dfrac{32}{4}$
$= 2x - 8$

b. $(8x - 32)(0.25) = 8x \cdot 0.25 - 32 \cdot 0.25$
$= 2x - 8$

c. $\dfrac{32 - 8x}{4} = \dfrac{32}{4} - \dfrac{8x}{4}$
$= 8 - 2x$

d. $\dfrac{-32 + 8x}{4} = \dfrac{-32}{4} + \dfrac{8x}{4}$
$= -8 + 2x$
$= 2x - 8$

Expressions 1a, 1b, and 1d are equivalent. Expression 1c is different.

2. $-5x \cdot 7 = (-5 \cdot 7)x$
$= -35x$

3. $-3(4 - 11y) = -3 \cdot 4 + (-3) \cdot (-11y)$
$= -12 + ((-3) \cdot (-11))y$
$= -12 + 33y$
$= 33y - 12$

4. $\dfrac{-28q}{-14} = 2q$

5. $\dfrac{-10t + 35}{-5} = \dfrac{-10t}{-5} + \dfrac{35}{-5}$
$= 2t - 7$

6. $\dfrac{r}{5} = -22$
$5\left(\dfrac{r}{5}\right) = (-22)5$
$r = -110$

7. $-10f = 0.55$
$\dfrac{-10f}{-10} = \dfrac{0.55}{-10}$
$f = -0.055$

8. $\dfrac{z}{-3.5} = -7$
$-3.5\left(\dfrac{z}{-3.5}\right) = (-7)(-3.5)$
$z = 24.5$

9. $8(x - 7) = 8 \cdot x - 8 \cdot 7$
$= 8x - 56$

10. $3a^2(a - 1) = 3a^2 \cdot a - 3a^2 \cdot 1$
$= 3a^3 - 3a^2$

11. $q(2q^2 + q) = q \cdot 2q^2 + q \cdot q$
$= 2(q \cdot q^2) + q \cdot q$
$= 2q^3 + q^2$

12. $5y^2 + 10y = 5y(y + 2)$

13. $m^4 - 5m^3 = m^3(m - 5)$

14. $36x^5 + 18x^2 = 18x^2(2x^3 + 1)$

15. Not all rational numbers are integers. For example $\frac{1}{2}$ is a rational number but is not an integer.

16. 0 is the only rational number that does not have a reciprocal. The reason for this is that 0 in the denominator of a fraction is undefined.

17. $\dfrac{2}{3}y = -8$
$\dfrac{3}{2}\left(\dfrac{2}{3}y\right) = (-8)\dfrac{3}{2}$
$y = -12$

18. $\dfrac{-5}{11}p = -15$
$\dfrac{11}{-5}\left(\dfrac{-5}{11}p\right) = (-15)\dfrac{11}{-5}$
$p = 33$

19. $-\dfrac{c}{14} = -\dfrac{1}{7}$
$-14\left(\dfrac{-c}{14}\right) = \left(\dfrac{-1}{7}\right)(-14)$
$c = \dfrac{14}{7}$
$c = 2$

20. $\frac{x}{3} = \frac{-2}{5}$

$5x = 3 \cdot (-2)$

$\frac{5x}{5} = \frac{-6}{5}$

$x = -\frac{6}{5}$

21. $-\frac{a}{6} = \frac{4}{-9}$

$(-a)(-9) = 4 \cdot 6$

$9a = 24$

$\frac{9a}{9} = \frac{24}{9}$

$a = \frac{24}{9}$, or $\frac{8}{3}$, or $2\frac{2}{3}$, or 2.6

22. $\frac{r}{2.8} = -\frac{5}{7}$

$2.8\left(\frac{r}{2.8}\right) = \left(-\frac{5}{7}\right)2.8$

$r = -2$

23. $\frac{1}{3} \overset{?}{=} \frac{19}{57}$

$1 \cdot 57 \overset{?}{=} 3 \cdot 19$

$57 = 57$ True

This statement is a
true proportion.

24. $\frac{2}{9} \overset{?}{=} \frac{7}{26}$

$2 \cdot 26 \overset{?}{=} 9 \cdot 7$

$52 \neq 63$ False

This statement is
not a true proportion.

25. $\frac{113}{29} \overset{?}{=} \frac{1017}{261}$

$113 \cdot 261 \overset{?}{=} 29 \cdot 1017$

$29{,}493 = 29{,}493$ True

This statement is
a true proportion.

26. Let x represent the amount
Paula will earn in 10 weeks.

$\frac{350}{4} = \frac{x}{10}$

$4x = 350 \cdot 10$

$\frac{4x}{4} = \frac{3500}{4}$

$x = 875$

Paula will earn \$875 in 10 weeks.

27. Use the equation method.

$x = 35\% \cdot 90$

$x = 0.35 \cdot 90$

$x = 31.5$

31.5 is 35% of 90.

28. Use the equation method.

$x \cdot 15 = 3$

$x \cdot \frac{15}{15} = \frac{3}{15}$

$x = 0.2$

3 is 20% of 15.

29. Use the proportion method.

$\frac{28}{100\%} = \frac{x}{150\%}$

$\frac{28}{1.00} = \frac{x}{1.50}$

$1.00x = 28 \cdot 1.50$

$x = 42$

42 is 150% of 28.

30. Let x represent the number of free
throws that Jamie made.

$x = 80\% \cdot 15$

$x = 0.80 \cdot 15$

$x = 12$

Jamie made 12 free throws in his game last
night.

---

1. B

$2x + 1$	B > A	$4x - 3$
$2(6) + 1 = 13$	$21 > 13$	$4(6) - 3 = 21$

$\therefore$ B is the correct response.

2. B

$4\frac{1}{3} = 4\frac{8}{24}$ B > A $4\frac{3}{8} = 4\frac{9}{24}$

$4\frac{3}{8} > 4\frac{1}{3}$

$\therefore$ B is the correct response.

3. D

$(3y + 2) + (2y - 5) = (3y + 2y) + (2 - 5)$

$= 5y + (-3)$

$= 5y - 3$

$(2y + 6) - (y + 7) = 2y + 6 - y - 7$

$= (2y - y) + (6 - 7)$

$= y + (-1)$

$= y - 1$

D is the correct response because the relationship cannot be determined from
the given information.

4. $-\frac{3}{4}x = 3$

$\left(\frac{-4}{3}\right)\left(\frac{-3}{4}x\right) = (3)\left(\frac{-4}{3}\right)$ B > A

$x = -4$ $3 > -4$

$\therefore$ B is the correct response.

$-\frac{4}{3}x = -4$

$\left(\frac{-3}{4}\right)\left(\frac{-4}{3x}\right) = (-4)\left(\frac{-3}{4}\right)$

$x = 3$

5. d

$9 \div 3 \cdot 2^3 - 5 = 9 \div 3 \cdot 8 - 5$

$= 3 \cdot 8 - 5$

$= 24 - 5$

$= 19$

6. c

$$5\tfrac{5}{6} \cdot \tfrac{3}{5} = \tfrac{35}{6} \cdot \tfrac{3}{5}$$
$$= \tfrac{105}{30}$$
$$= 3\tfrac{15}{30}$$
$$= 3\tfrac{1}{2}$$

7. d

$$2(6.4) + 2(16.05) = 12.8 + 32.1$$
$$= 44.9$$

8. c

a. $3x - 2(x - 3) = 3x - (2 \cdot x) - (2 \cdot -3)$
$\qquad\qquad\quad = 3x - 2x - (-6)$
$\qquad\qquad\quad = x + 6$

b. $3x + 2(3 - x) = 3x + (2 \cdot 3) = (2 \cdot -x)$
$\qquad\qquad\quad = 3x + 6 + (-2x)$
$\qquad\qquad\quad = 3x - 2x + 6$
$\qquad\qquad\quad = x + 6$

c. $3x - 2(x + 3) = 3x - (2 \cdot x) - (2 \cdot 3)$
$\qquad\qquad\quad = 3x - 2x - 6$
$\qquad\qquad\quad = x - 6$

d. $3x - 2(-3 + x) = 3x - (2 \cdot -3) - (2 \cdot x)$
$\qquad\qquad\quad\ = 3x - (-6) - 2x$
$\qquad\qquad\quad\ = 3x - 2x - (-6)$
$\qquad\qquad\quad\ = 3x - 2x + 6$
$\qquad\qquad\quad\ = x + 6$

9. b

$$\frac{q}{139.2} = -58$$
$$139.2\left(\frac{q}{139.2}\right) = (-58)139.2$$
$$q = -8073.6$$

10. b

$$0.5 = \frac{50}{100}$$
$$= 50\%$$

11. $-25 + (-4) = -29$

12. $-36 + 6 + |-6| = -36 + 6 + 6$
$\qquad\qquad\qquad\ = -30 + 6$
$\qquad\qquad\qquad\ = -24$

13. $452 + (-452) = 0$

14. $\tfrac{7}{8}$ and $\tfrac{13}{16}$
LCD is 16.
$\tfrac{7}{8} = \tfrac{14}{16} \quad \tfrac{13}{16} = \tfrac{13}{16}$
So
$\tfrac{7}{8} > \tfrac{13}{16}$

15. Let x represent the angle.
$$90 - 23 = x$$
$$67 = x$$
Let y represent the supplement of the angle.
$$67 + y = 180$$
$$-67 + 67 + y = -67 + 180$$
$$y = 113$$
The supplement of the angle is $113°$.

16.

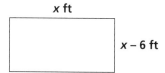

x ft
x – 6 ft

Let x represent the length of the rectangle; then $x - 6$ represents the width of the rectangle.
$$x + x + (x - 6) + (x - 6) = 52$$
$$x + x + x + x - 6 - 6 = 52$$
$$4x - 12 = 52$$
$$4x - 12 + 12 = 52 + 12$$
$$4x = 64$$
$$\frac{4x}{4} = \frac{64}{4}$$
$$x = 16$$
The length of the rectangle is 16 feet, and the width of the rectangle is $x - 6 = 16 - 6 = 10$ feet.

17. $6 - (3 + 2x) = -3x + (2x - 4)$
$\qquad 6 - 3 - 2x = -3x + 2x - 4$
$\qquad\quad 3 - 2x = -x - 4$
$\quad 3 - 2x + 2x = -x - 4 + 2x$
$\qquad\qquad\ 3 = x - 4$
$\qquad\quad 3 + 4 = x - 4 + 4$
$\qquad\qquad\ 7 = x$

18. $\qquad y + 4.5 \geq 6$
$\quad y + 4.5 - 4.5 \geq 6 - 4.5$
$\qquad\qquad y \geq 1.5$

19. $18x^3 - 12x^2 = 6x^2(3x - 2)$

20. $\quad \frac{15}{n} = \frac{20}{32}$
$\qquad 20n = 15 \cdot 32$
$\qquad \frac{20n}{20} = \frac{480}{20}$
$\qquad\qquad n = 24$

21. This is the same as adding $1 + 2 + 3 + \cdots + 12$:

$$\frac{12 \cdot 13}{2} = \frac{156}{2}$$
$$= 78$$

78 games will be played.

22. $\frac{1}{6} + \frac{1}{2} = \frac{1}{6} + \frac{3}{6}$
$$= \frac{4}{6}$$
$$= \frac{2}{3}$$

23.

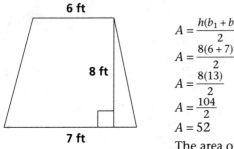

$$A = \frac{h(b_1 + b_2)}{2}$$
$$A = \frac{8(6 + 7)}{2}$$
$$A = \frac{8(13)}{2}$$
$$A = \frac{104}{2}$$
$$A = 52$$

The area of the trapezoid is 52 square feet.

24.

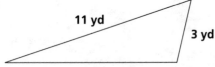 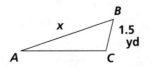

Let x represent the length of the longest side of triangle ABC.

$$\frac{3}{11} = \frac{1.5}{x}$$
$$3x = 11 \cdot 1.5$$
$$\frac{3x}{3} = \frac{16.5}{3}$$
$$x = 5.5$$

The longest side is $5\frac{1}{2}$ yards in length.

25. $\frac{c}{16} = \frac{3}{8}$
$$8c = 16 \cdot 3$$
$$\frac{8c}{8} = \frac{48}{8}$$
$$c = 6$$

CHAPTER 7

SOLVING EQUATIONS AND INEQUALITIES

6. $2m + 5 = 17$
$2m + 5 - 5 = 17 - 5$
$2m = 12$
$\frac{2m}{2} = \frac{12}{2}$
$m = 6$

7. $9p + 11 = -7$
$9p + 11 - 11 = -7 - 11$
$9p = -18$
$\frac{9p}{9} = \frac{-18}{9}$
$p = -2$

8. $5x + 9 = 39$
$5x + 9 - 9 = 39 - 9$
$5x = 30$
$\frac{5x}{5} = \frac{30}{5}$
$x = 6$

9. $3 + 2x = 21$
$3 + 2x - 3 = 21 - 3$
$2x = 18$
$\frac{2x}{2} = \frac{18}{2}$
$x = 9$

10. $6 - 8d = -42$
$6 - 8d - 6 = -42 - 6$
$-8d = -48$
$\frac{-8d}{-8} = \frac{-48}{-8}$
$d = 6$

11. $9 - 14z = 51$
$9 - 14z - 9 = 51 - 9$
$-14z = 42$
$\frac{-14z}{-14} = \frac{42}{-14}$
$z = -3$

12. $12 = 9x - 6$
$12 + 6 = 9x - 6 + 6$
$18 = 9x$
$\frac{18}{9} = \frac{9x}{9}$
$2 = x$

13. $16 = 5w - 9$
$16 + 9 = 5w - 9 + 9$
$25 = 5w$
$\frac{25}{5} = \frac{5w}{5}$
$5 = w$

14. $-4 - 11w = 18$
$-4 - 11w + 4 = 18 + 4$
$-11w = 22$
$\frac{-11w}{-11} = \frac{22}{-11}$
$w = -2$

15. $-7 - 13y = 32$
$-7 - 13y + 7 = 32 + 7$
$-13y = 39$
$\frac{-13y}{-13} = \frac{39}{-13}$
$y = -3$

16. $36 = -3y + 12$
$36 - 12 = -3y + 12 - 12$
$24 = -3y$
$\frac{24}{-3} = \frac{-3y}{-3}$
$-8 = y$

17. $58 = -8z + 18$
$58 - 18 = -8z + 18 - 18$
$40 = -8z$
$\frac{40}{-8} = \frac{-8z}{-8}$
$-5 = z$

18. $2(x - 3) = 14$
$2x - 6 = 14$
$2x - 6 + 6 = 14 + 6$
$2x = 20$
$\frac{2x}{2} = \frac{20}{2}$
$x = 10$

19. $4(x - 20) = 16$
$4x - 80 = 16$
$4x - 80 + 80 = 16 + 80$
$4x = 96$
$\frac{4x}{4} = \frac{96}{4}$
$x = 24$

20. $5(2x + 3) = 25$
$10x + 15 = 25$
$10x + 15 - 15 = 25 - 15$
$10x = 10$
$\frac{10x}{10} = \frac{10}{10}$
$x = 1$

21. $3(4x - 3) = 15$
$12x - 9 = 15$
$12x - 9 + 9 = 15 + 9$
$12x = 24$
$\frac{12x}{12} = \frac{24}{12}$
$x = 2$

22. $8 = 2(3x + 4)$
$8 = 6x + 8$
$8 - 8 = 6x + 8 - 8$
$0 = 6x$
$\frac{0}{6} = \frac{6x}{6}$
$0 = x$

23. $20 = 5(3x - 2)$
$20 = 15x - 10$
$20 + 10 = 15x - 10 + 10$
$30 = 15x$
$\frac{30}{15} = \frac{15x}{15}$
$2 = x$

24.
$$3x + 5 + 7x = 25$$
$$3x + 7x + 5 = 25$$
$$10x + 5 = 25$$
$$10x + 5 - 5 = 25 - 5$$
$$10x = 20$$
$$\frac{10x}{10} = \frac{20}{10}$$
$$x = 2$$

25.
$$9x + 6 + 4x = 45$$
$$9x + 4x + 6 = 45$$
$$13x + 6 = 45$$
$$13x + 6 - 6 = 45 - 6$$
$$13x = 39$$
$$\frac{13x}{13} = \frac{39}{13}$$
$$x = 3$$

26.
$$8x - 3 - 5x = 21$$
$$8x - 5x - 3 = 21$$
$$3x - 3 = 21$$
$$3x - 3 + 3 = 21 + 3$$
$$3x = 24$$
$$\frac{3x}{3} = \frac{24}{3}$$
$$x = 8$$

27.
$$17y - 9 - 9y = -41$$
$$17y - 9y - 9 = -41$$
$$8y - 9 = -41$$
$$8y - 9 + 9 = -41 + 9$$
$$8y = -32$$
$$\frac{8y}{8} = \frac{-32}{8}$$
$$y = -4$$

28.
$$56 = -5w + 15 + 3w - 7$$
$$56 = -5w + 3w + 15 - 7$$
$$56 = -2w + 8$$
$$56 - 8 = -2w + 8 - 8$$
$$48 = -2w$$
$$\frac{48}{-2} = \frac{-2w}{-2}$$
$$-24 = w$$

29.
$$-72 = -8y + 12 + 4y - 16$$
$$-72 = -8y + 4y + 12 - 16$$
$$-72 = -4y - 4$$
$$-72 + 4 = -4y - 4 + 4$$
$$-68 = -4y$$
$$\frac{-68}{-4} = \frac{-4y}{-4}$$
$$17 = y$$

30.
$$5x + \frac{1}{8} = \frac{1}{3}$$
$$5x + \frac{1}{8} - \frac{1}{8} = \frac{1}{3} - \frac{1}{8}$$
$$5x = \frac{8}{24} - \frac{3}{24}$$
$$5x = \frac{5}{24}$$
$$\frac{1}{5}(5x) = \left(\frac{5}{24}\right)\frac{1}{5}$$
$$x = \frac{5}{120}$$
$$x = \frac{1}{24}$$

31.
$$3x + \frac{2}{7} = \frac{1}{3}$$
$$3x + \frac{2}{7} - \frac{2}{7} = \frac{1}{3} - \frac{2}{7}$$
$$3x = \frac{7}{21} - \frac{6}{21}$$
$$3x = \frac{1}{21}$$
$$\frac{1}{3}(3x) = \frac{1}{3}\left(\frac{1}{21}\right)$$
$$x = \frac{1}{63}$$

32.
$$3 + \frac{1}{4} + 2x = \frac{5}{8}$$
$$\frac{12}{4} + \frac{1}{4} + 2x = \frac{5}{8}$$
$$\frac{13}{4} + 2x = \frac{5}{8}$$
$$\frac{13}{4} + 2x - \frac{13}{4} = \frac{5}{8} - \frac{13}{4}$$
$$2x = \frac{5}{8} - \frac{26}{8}$$
$$2x = \frac{-21}{8}$$
$$\frac{1}{2}(2x) = \left(\frac{-21}{8}\right)\frac{1}{2}$$
$$x = \frac{-21}{16}$$
$$x = -1\frac{5}{16}$$

33.
$$4\left(x - \frac{1}{3}\right) = \frac{1}{5}$$
$$4x - \frac{4}{3} = \frac{1}{5}$$
$$4x - \frac{4}{3} + \frac{4}{3} = \frac{1}{5} + \frac{4}{3}$$
$$4x = \frac{3}{15} + \frac{20}{15}$$
$$4x = \frac{23}{15}$$
$$\frac{1}{4}(4x) = \left(\frac{23}{15}\right)\frac{1}{4}$$
$$x = \frac{23}{60}$$

34.
$$\frac{1}{6} + 2x = \frac{7}{24}$$
$$\frac{1}{6} + 2x - \frac{1}{6} = \frac{7}{24} - \frac{1}{6}$$
$$2x = \frac{7}{24} - \frac{4}{24}$$
$$2x = \frac{3}{24}$$
$$\frac{1}{2}(2x) = \left(\frac{3}{24}\right)\frac{1}{2}$$
$$x = \frac{3}{48}$$
$$x = \frac{1}{16}$$

35.
$$8t = \frac{2}{3} - 3t + 7$$
$$8t + 3t = \frac{2}{3} - 3t + 7 + 3t$$
$$11t = \frac{2}{3} + 7$$
$$11t = \frac{2}{3} + \frac{21}{3}$$
$$11t = \frac{23}{3}$$
$$\frac{1}{11}(11t) = \left(\frac{23}{3}\right)\frac{1}{11}$$
$$t = \frac{23}{33}$$

36.
$$5x + 10 = \frac{5}{11}$$
$$5x + 10 - 10 = \frac{5}{11} - 10$$
$$5x = \frac{5}{11} - \frac{110}{11}$$
$$5x = \frac{-105}{11}$$
$$\frac{1}{5}(5x) = \left(\frac{-105}{11}\right)\frac{1}{5}$$
$$x = \frac{-105}{55}$$
$$x = -1\frac{50}{55}$$
$$x = -1\frac{10}{11}$$

37.
$$\frac{3}{4}x + 1 + \frac{1}{6} + x = \frac{7}{24}$$
$$\frac{3}{4}x + x + 1 + \frac{1}{6} = \frac{7}{24}$$
$$\frac{3}{4}x + \frac{4}{4}x + \frac{6}{6} + \frac{1}{6} = \frac{7}{24}$$
$$\frac{7}{4}x + \frac{7}{6} = \frac{7}{24}$$
$$\frac{7}{4}x + \frac{7}{6} - \frac{7}{6} = \frac{7}{24} - \frac{7}{6}$$
$$\frac{7}{4}x = \frac{7}{24} - \frac{28}{24}$$
$$\frac{7}{4}x = \frac{-21}{24}$$
$$\frac{4}{7}\left(\frac{7}{4}x\right) = \left(\frac{-21}{24}\right)\frac{4}{7}$$
$$x = \frac{-84}{168}$$
$$x = -\frac{1}{2}$$

38.
$$239(x + 20) = -956$$
$$239x + 4780 = -956$$
$$239x + 4780 - 4780 = -956 - 4780$$
$$239x = -5736$$
$$\frac{239x}{239} = \frac{-5736}{239}$$
$$x = -24$$

39. Let x represent the first of three consecutive whole numbers. Then $x + 1$ and $x + 2$ represent the other two numbers.

$$x + (x + 1) + (x + 2) = 48$$
$$x + x + x + 1 + 2 = 48$$
$$3x + 3 = 48$$
$$3x + 3 - 3 = 48 - 3$$
$$3x = 45$$
$$\frac{3x}{3} = \frac{45}{3}$$
$$x = 15$$

Substitute 15 for x to find the three numbers.
$$x = 15$$
$$x + 1 = 15 + 1 = 16$$
$$x + 2 = 15 + 2 = 17$$

The three numbers are 15, 16, and 17.

40. Let x represent the first of four consecutive whole numbers. Then $x + 1$, $x + 2$, and $x + 3$ represent the other three numbers.

$$x + (x + 1) + (x + 2) + (x + 3) = 58$$
$$x + x + x + x + 1 + 2 + 3 = 58$$
$$4x + 6 = 58$$
$$4x + 6 - 6 = 58 - 6$$
$$4x = 52$$
$$\frac{4x}{4} = \frac{52}{4}$$
$$x = 13$$

Substitute 13 for x to find the four numbers.
$$x = 13$$
$$x + 1 = 13 + 1 = 14$$
$$x + 2 = 13 + 2 = 15$$
$$x + 3 = 13 + 3 = 16$$

The four numbers are 13, 14, 15, and 16.

41. Let x represent the fourth score.
$$\frac{95 + 91 + 88 + x}{4} = 90$$
$$\frac{274 + x}{4} = 90$$
$$4\left(\frac{274 + x}{4}\right) = (90)\,4$$
$$274 + x = 360$$
$$274 + x - 274 = 360 - 274$$
$$x = 86$$
The fourth score must be 86.

42.
$$p = (x + 60) + (x + 60) + x + x$$
$$180 = x + x + x + x + 60 + 60$$
$$180 = 4x + 120$$
$$180 - 120 = 4x + 120 - 120$$
$$60 = 4x$$
$$\frac{60}{4} = \frac{4x}{4}$$
$$15 = x$$

Substitute 15 for x to get the length and width of the rectangle.

Length: $x + 60 = 15 + 60 = 75$

Width: $x = 15$

The length of the rectangle is 75 feet and the width is 15 feet.

43. Let x represent the number of compact discs.
$$C = 2.95 + 15.95x$$
$$98.65 = 2.95 + 15.95x$$
$$98.65 - 2.95 = 2.95 + 15.95x - 2.95$$
$$95.70 = 15.95x$$
$$\frac{95.70}{15.95} = \frac{15.95x}{15.95}$$
$$6 = x$$
Kara and her friend bought 6 compact discs.

44. Let x represent the percent sales tax.
$$x = \frac{(5.40 - 5.00)}{5.00} \cdot 100$$
$$x = \left(\frac{0.40}{5.00}\right) \cdot 100$$
$$x = 0.08 \cdot 100$$
$$x = 8$$
Felicia paid 8% sales tax on her sandwich.

45. Let x represent the subtotal for Dan's sandwich.
$$4.59 = x + 0.08x$$
$$4.59 = 1.08x$$
$$\frac{4.59}{1.08} = \frac{1.08x}{1.08}$$
$$4.25 = x$$
The subtotal for Dan's sandwich was $4.25.

46. Let x represent the amount of hekats in one basket.
$$1\tfrac{1}{2}x + 4 = 10$$
$$1\tfrac{1}{2}x + 4 - 4 = 10 - 4$$
$$1\tfrac{1}{2}x = 6$$
$$\frac{3}{2}x = 6$$
$$\frac{2}{3}\left(\frac{3}{2}x\right) = (6)\frac{2}{3}$$
$$x = \frac{12}{3}$$
$$x = 4$$
A basket holds 4 hekats.

47. Let A represent the area of the square, and let s represent the length of its side.
$$A = s^2$$
$$36 = s^2$$
$$\sqrt{36} = \sqrt{s^2}$$
$$6 = s$$
The side of the square is 6 feet.

48. $-(6c - 23d) = -6c + 23d$

49. $-(-s + t) = s - t$

50. $-(-a - c) = a + c$

51.
$$5 - x = -12$$
$$5 - x - 5 = -12 - 5$$
$$-x = -17$$
$$-1(-x) = -1(-17)$$
$$x = 17$$

52.
$$2.1 + x = -8.3$$
$$2.1 + x - 2.1 = -8.3 - 2.1$$
$$x = -10.4$$

53.
$$-\frac{2}{3} = x = -\frac{1}{6}$$
$$-\frac{2}{3} + x + \frac{2}{3} = -\frac{1}{6} + \frac{2}{3}$$
$$x = -\frac{1}{6} + \frac{4}{6}$$
$$x = \frac{3}{6}$$
$$x = \frac{1}{2}$$

54.
$$3x - 4 = 2x + 7$$
$$3x - 4 - 2x = 2x + 7 - 2x$$
$$x - 4 = 7$$
$$x - 4 + 4 = 7 + 4$$
$$x = 11$$

55.
$$5x + 8 = 2x - 10$$
$$5x + 8 - 2x = 2x - 10 - 2x$$
$$3x + 8 = -10$$
$$3x + 8 - 8 = -10 - 8$$
$$3x = -18$$
$$\frac{3x}{3} = \frac{-18}{3}$$
$$x = -6$$

56.
$$-8x + 12 = 2x - 48$$
$$-8x + 12 + 8x = 2x - 48 + 8x$$
$$12 = 10x - 48$$
$$12 + 48 = 10x - 48 + 48$$
$$60 = 10x$$
$$\frac{60}{10} = \frac{10x}{10}$$
$$6 = x$$

7.2 PAGES 393–394, PRACTICE & APPLY

6.
$$8y = 6y + 24$$
$$8y - 6y = 6y + 24 - 6y$$
$$2y = 24$$
$$\frac{2y}{2} = \frac{24}{2}$$
$$y = 12$$

7.
$$12w - 15 = 7w$$
$$12w - 15 - 7w = 7w - 7w$$
$$5w - 15 = 0$$
$$5w - 15 + 15 = 0 + 15$$
$$5w = 15$$
$$\frac{5w}{5} = \frac{15}{5}$$
$$w = 3$$

8.
$$4g + 1 = 12 - 8g$$
$$4g + 1 + 8g = 12 - 8g + 8g$$
$$12g + 1 = 12$$
$$12g + 1 - 1 = 12 - 1$$
$$12g = 11$$
$$\frac{12g}{12} = \frac{11}{12}$$
$$g = \frac{11}{12}$$

9.
$$3r - 8 = 5r - 20$$
$$3r - 8 - 3r = 5r - 20 - 3r$$
$$-8 = 2r - 20$$
$$-8 + 20 = 2r - 20 + 20$$
$$12 = 2r$$
$$\frac{12}{2} = \frac{2r}{2}$$
$$6 = r$$

10.
$$1 - 3x = 2x + 8$$
$$1 - 3x + 3x = 2x + 8 + 3x$$
$$1 = 5x + 8$$
$$1 - 8 = 5x + 8 - 8$$
$$-7 = 5x$$
$$\frac{-7}{5} = \frac{5x}{5}$$
$$-\frac{7}{5} = x$$
$$-1\frac{2}{5} = x$$

11.
$$15 - 2y = 12 - 8y$$
$$15 - 2y + 8y = 12 - 8y + 8y$$
$$15 + 6y = 12$$
$$15 + 6y - 15 = 12 - 15$$
$$6y = -3$$
$$\frac{6y}{6} = \frac{-3}{6}$$
$$y = \frac{-3}{6}$$
$$y = -\frac{1}{2}$$

12.
$$5 - 3y = 5y + 65$$
$$5 - 3y + 3y = 5y + 65 + 3y$$
$$5 = 8y + 65$$
$$5 - 65 = 8y + 65 - 65$$
$$-60 = 8y$$
$$\frac{-60}{8} = \frac{8y}{8}$$
$$\frac{-60}{8} = y$$
$$-7\frac{4}{8} = y$$
$$-7\frac{1}{2} = y$$

13.
$$18 + 2w = 7w - 13$$
$$18 + 2w - 2w = 7w - 13 - 2w$$
$$18 = 5w - 13$$
$$18 + 13 = 5w - 13 + 13$$
$$31 = 5w$$
$$\frac{31}{5} = \frac{5w}{5}$$
$$\frac{31}{5} = w$$
$$6\frac{1}{5} = w$$

14.
$$4(2w + 5) = 12w - 9$$
$$8w + 20 = 12w - 9$$
$$8w + 20 - 8w = 12w - 9 - 8w$$
$$20 = 4w - 9$$
$$20 + 9 = 4w - 9 + 9$$
$$29 = 4w$$
$$\frac{29}{4} = \frac{4w}{4}$$
$$\frac{29}{4} = w$$
$$7\frac{1}{4} = w$$

15.
$$5x - 7 = 2x + 2$$
$$5x - 2x - 7 = 2x + 2 - 2x$$
$$3x - 7 = 2$$
$$3x - 7 + 7 = 2 + 7$$
$$3x = 9$$
$$\frac{3x}{3} = \frac{9}{3}$$
$$x = 3$$

16.
$$7m - 2(m - 3) = 3m - 14$$
$$7m - 2m + 6 = 3m - 14$$
$$5m + 6 = 3m - 14$$
$$5m + 6 - 3m = 3m - 14 - 3m$$
$$2m + 6 = -14$$
$$2m + 6 - 6 = -14 - 6$$
$$2m = -20$$
$$\frac{2m}{2} = \frac{-20}{2}$$
$$m = -10$$

17.
$$2(y - 3) + 4y + 8 = 3(y + 6)$$
$$2y - 6 + 4y + 8 = 3y + 18$$
$$6y + 2 = 3y + 18$$
$$6y + 2 - 3y = 3y + 18 - 3y$$
$$3y + 2 = 18$$
$$3y + 2 - 2 = 18 - 2$$
$$3y = 16$$
$$\frac{3y}{3} = \frac{16}{3}$$
$$y = \frac{16}{3}$$
$$y = 5\frac{1}{3}$$

18.
$$8f - 3(f + 6) = 2f - 16$$
$$8f - 3f - 18 = 2f - 16$$
$$5f - 18 = 2f - 16$$
$$5f - 18 - 2f = 2f - 16 - 2f$$
$$3f - 18 = -16$$
$$3f - 18 + 18 = -16 + 18$$
$$3f = 2$$
$$\frac{3f}{3} = \frac{2}{3}$$
$$f = \frac{2}{3}$$

19.
$$4t - 5 + 8t = 7(t + 6)$$
$$12t - 5 = 7t + 42$$
$$12t - 5 - 7t = 7t + 42 - 7t$$
$$5t - 5 = 42$$
$$5t - 5 + 5 = 42 + 5$$
$$5t = 47$$
$$\frac{5t}{5} = \frac{47}{5}$$
$$t = \frac{47}{5}$$
$$t = 9\frac{2}{5}$$

20. Let x represent a free scoop of ice cream. Then $2x$ represents the number of scoops purchased.
$$2x + x = 33$$
$$3x = 33$$
$$\frac{3x}{3} = \frac{33}{3}$$
$$x = 11$$
11 scoops of ice cream were free.

21. Let x represent the number of cones ordered. Then $3x + 8$ represents the number of cups ordered.
$$3x + 8 = 263$$
$$3x + 8 - 8 = 263 - 8$$
$$3x = 255$$
$$\frac{3x}{3} = \frac{255}{3}$$
$$x = 85$$
85 cones were ordered.

22. Let x represent the amount earned on each of the first 3 days. Then $3x$ represents the amount earned during the first 3 days.
$$3x + 32 = 200$$
$$3x + 32 - 32 = 200 - 32$$
$$3x = 168$$
$$\frac{3x}{3} = \frac{168}{3}$$
$$x = 56$$
Franklin earned $56 on each of the first 3 days.

23. Let x represent the number of sundaes made. Then $5x - 4$ represents the number of sodas made.
$$5x - 4 = 96$$
$$5x - 4 + 4 = 96 + 4$$
$$5x = 100$$
$$\frac{5x}{5} = \frac{100}{5}$$
$$x = 20$$
Andalon made 20 sundaes.

24.
$$2(p-3) = 3(p-4)$$
$$2p - 6 = 3p - 12$$
$$2p - 6 - 2p = 3p - 12 - 2p$$
$$-6 = p - 12$$
$$-6 + 12 = p - 12 + 12$$
$$6 = p$$

25.
$$8.3y = 4.2y + 143.5$$
$$8.3y - 4.2y = 4.2y + 143.5 - 4.2y$$
$$4.1y = 143.5$$
$$\frac{4.1y}{4.1} = \frac{143.5}{4.1}$$
$$y = 35$$

26.
$$187a + 265 = -456a - 378$$
$$187a + 265 + 456a = -456a - 378 + 456a$$
$$643a + 265 = -378$$
$$643a + 265 - 265 = -378 - 265$$
$$643a = -643$$
$$\frac{643a}{643} = \frac{-643}{643}$$
$$a = -1$$

27
$$0.95q - 4.56 = 0.35(2.7q + 1.5)$$
$$0.95q - 4.56 = 0.945q + 0.525$$
$$0.95q - 4.56 - 0.945q = 0.945q + 0.525 - 0.945q$$
$$0.005q - 4.56 = 0.525$$
$$0.005q - 4.56 + 4.56 = 0.525 + 4.56$$
$$0.005q = 5.085$$
$$\frac{0.005q}{0.005} = \frac{5.085}{0.005}$$
$$q = 1017$$

28.
$$2.1(y-5) = 3(y-5)$$
$$2.1y - 10.5 = 3y - 15$$
$$2.1y - 10.5 - 2.1y = 3y - 15 - 2.1y$$
$$-10.5 = 0.9y - 15$$
$$-10.5 + 15 = 0.9y - 15 + 15$$
$$4.5 = 0.9y$$
$$\frac{4.5}{0.9} = \frac{0.9y}{0.9}$$
$$5 = y$$

29.
$$1.5(k+4) = 4(k+0.5)$$
$$1.5k + 6 = 4k + 2$$
$$1.5k + 6 - 1.5k = 4k + 2 - 1.5k$$
$$6 = 2.5k + 2$$
$$6 - 2 = 2.5k + 2 - 2$$
$$4 = 2.5k$$
$$\frac{4}{2.5} = \frac{2.5k}{2.5}$$
$$1.6 = k$$

30.
$$17.2a + 1291.5 = 14.2a$$
$$17.2a - 14.2a + 1291.5 = 14.2a - 14.2a$$
$$3a + 1291.5 = 0$$
$$3a + 1291.5 - 1291.5 = -1291.5$$
$$3a = -1291.5$$
$$\frac{3a}{3} = \frac{-1291.5}{3}$$
$$a = -430.5$$

31.
$$2.85b + 102.96 = 4.5b$$
$$2.85b + 102.96 - 2.85b = 4.5b - 2.85b$$
$$102.96 = 1.65b$$
$$\frac{102.96}{1.65} = \frac{1.65b}{1.65}$$
$$62.4 = b$$

32.
$$1.4m - 3.7 = 0.9m + 6.3$$
$$1.4m - 3.7 - 1.4m = 0.9m + 6.3 - 1.4m$$
$$-3.7 = -0.5m + 6.3$$
$$-3.7 - 6.3 = -0.5m + 6.3 - 6.3$$
$$-10 = -0.5m$$
$$\frac{-10}{-0.5} = \frac{-0.5m}{-0.5}$$
$$20 = m$$

33.
$$0.8n - 4.7 = 0.75n - 4.1$$
$$0.8n - 4.7 - 0.75n = 0.75n - 4.1 - 0.75n$$
$$0.05n - 4.7 = -4.1$$
$$0.05n - 4.7 + 4.7 = -4.1 + 4.7$$
$$0.05n = 0.6$$
$$\frac{0.05n}{0.05} = \frac{0.6}{0.05}$$
$$n = 12$$

34.
$$x + \frac{5}{8} + \frac{3x}{4} = \frac{2}{3} + 5x$$
$$\frac{4x}{4} + \frac{5}{8} + \frac{3x}{4} = \frac{2}{3} + 5x$$
$$\frac{7x}{4} + \frac{5}{8} = \frac{2}{3} + 5x$$
$$\frac{7x}{4} + \frac{5}{8} - \frac{7x}{4} = \frac{2}{3} + 5x - \frac{7x}{4}$$
$$\frac{5}{8} = \frac{2}{3} + \frac{20x}{4} - \frac{7x}{4}$$
$$\frac{5}{8} = \frac{2}{3} + \frac{13x}{4}$$
$$\frac{5}{8} - \frac{2}{3} = \frac{2}{3} + \frac{13x}{4} - \frac{2}{3}$$
$$\frac{15}{24} - \frac{16}{24} = \frac{13x}{4}$$
$$\frac{-1}{24} = \frac{13x}{4}$$
$$\left(\frac{4}{13}\right)\frac{-1}{24} = \left(\frac{13x}{4}\right)\frac{4}{13}$$
$$\frac{-4}{312} = x$$
$$\frac{-1}{78} = x$$

35.
$$3\left(x + \frac{1}{3}\right) = 6\left(x + \frac{1}{4}\right)$$
$$3x + 1 = 6x + \frac{6}{4}$$
$$3x + 1 - 3x = 6x + \frac{3}{2} - 3x$$
$$1 = 3x + \frac{3}{2}$$
$$1 - \frac{3}{2} = 3x + \frac{3}{2} - \frac{3}{2}$$
$$\frac{2}{2} - \frac{3}{2} = 3x$$
$$-\frac{1}{2} = 3x$$
$$\frac{1}{3}\left(\frac{-1}{2}\right) = (3x)\frac{1}{3}$$
$$\frac{-1}{6} = x$$

36. Set the perimeters equal to each other.
$$2x + 2x + x + x = (x + 12) + (x + 12) + (x - 3) + (x - 3)$$
$$6x = x + x + x + x + 12 + 12 - 3 - 3$$
$$6x = 4x + 18$$
$$6x - 4x = 4x + 18 - 4x$$
$$2x = 18$$
$$\frac{2x}{2} = \frac{18}{2}$$
$$x = 9$$

The value of x is 9.
Substitute 9 for x to calculate the perimeter.
$$6x = 6(9) = 54$$
The common perimeter is 54 units.

37. First compute last year's wages:
$6 \cdot 20 = \$120$. Next compute Clayton's current hourly wage: $6 + 20\% \cdot 6 = 6 + 0.20(6) = 6 + 1.2 = \$7.20$.

Let x represent the number of hours worked.
$$7.20x = 120$$
$$\frac{7.20x}{7.20} = \frac{120}{7.20}$$
$$x \approx 16.67$$
Since Clayton gets paid by the hour, he must work about 17 hours a week to earn the same weekly wage.

38. Let x represent the number of football programs sold last week. This means that $x - 54$ represents the number of football programs sold this week.
$$x - 54 = 192$$
$$x - 54 + 54 = 192 + 54$$
$$x = 246$$
246 football programs were sold last week.

39. Let x represent the number of trees planted in March. Then $2x + 3$ represents the number of trees planted in April.
$$2x + 3 = 71$$
$$2x + 3 - 3 = 71 - 3$$
$$2x = 68$$
$$\frac{2x}{2} = \frac{68}{2}$$
$$x = 34$$
There were 34 trees planted in March.

40. Let x represent the number of votes Jill received. Then $2x$ represents the number of votes Morgan received, and $2x + 7$ represents the number of votes Patricia received.
$$x + 2x + (2x + 7) = 327$$
$$x + 2x + 2x + 7 = 327$$
$$5x + 7 = 327$$
$$5x + 7 - 7 = 327 - 7$$
$$5x = 320$$
$$\frac{5x}{5} = \frac{320}{5}$$
$$x = 64$$
Jill received 64 votes, Morgan received $2x = 2(64) = 128$ votes, and Patricia received $2x + 7 = 2(64) + 7 = 128 + 7 = 135$ votes.

41. Let x represent the number of foreign coins. Then $3x - 26$ represents the number of U.S. coins.
$$x + (3x - 26) = 998$$
$$x + 3x - 26 = 998$$
$$4x - 26 = 998$$
$$4x - 26 + 26 = 998$$
$$4x - 26 + 26 = 998 + 26$$
$$4x = 1024$$
$$\frac{4x}{4} = \frac{1024}{4}$$
$$x = 256$$
Alfredo has 256 foreign coins and $3x - 26 = 3(256) - 26 = 742$ U.S. coins.

PAGE 394, LOOK BACK

42. $8\% = 0.08$

43. Angle 5 and angle 7 are alternate interior angles. Angle 6 and angle 8 are alternate interior angles.

44. $60 \cdot 1.8\% = 60 \cdot 0.018$
$$= 1.08$$
There are 1.08 milliliters of acid in the solution.

45. Let x represent the number of points needed in the sixth game.
$$\frac{24 + 18 + 27 + 32 + 21 + x}{6} = 25$$
$$\frac{122 + x}{6} = 25$$
$$6\left(\frac{122 + x}{6}\right) = 6(25)$$
$$122 + x = 150$$
$$122 + x - 122 = 150 - 122$$
$$x = 28$$
Ben needs to score 28 points in the sixth game.

46.
$$x - 4 \geq 2x + 5$$
$$x - 4 - x \geq 2x + 5 - x$$
$$-4 \geq x + 5$$
$$-4 - 5 \geq x + 5 - 5$$
$$-9 \geq x$$

7.3 PAGES 398–400, PRACTICE & APPLY

5. Let h represent the number of hours Orthea works.
$$600 = 110 + 8h$$
$$600 - 110 = 110 + 8h - 110$$
$$490 = 8h$$
$$\frac{490}{8} = \frac{8h}{8}$$
$$61\frac{1}{4} = h$$

Since Orthea gets paid by the hour, Orthea must work 61 hours and 15 minutes to earn $600.

7. Let s represent Holly's weekly sales.
$$200 = 120 + 2.5\%(s)$$
$$200 = 120 + 0.025s$$
$$200 - 120 = 120 + 0.025s - 120$$
$$80 = 0.025s$$
$$\frac{80}{0.025} = \frac{0.025s}{0.025}$$
$$3200 = s$$

Holly must have weekly sales of $3200 to earn $200 per week.

9. Let s represent Kendall's weekly sales.
$$400 = 150 + 5.2\%(s)$$
$$400 = 150 + 0.052s$$
$$400 - 150 = 150 + 0.052s - 150$$
$$250 = 0.052s$$
$$\frac{250}{0.052} = \frac{0.052s}{0.052}$$
$$4807.69 = s$$

Kendall must sell $4807.69 per week.

11. Let x represent the number of tickets.
$$7.50x - 2400 = 6000$$
$$7.50x - 2400 + 2400 = 6000 + 2400$$
$$7.50x = 8400$$
$$\frac{7.50x}{7.50} = \frac{8400}{7.50}$$
$$x = 1120$$

1120 tickets must be sold.

6. Let h represent the number of hours the plumber worked.
$$92 = 32 + 18h$$
$$92 - 32 = 32 + 18h - 32$$
$$60 = 18h$$
$$\frac{60}{18} = \frac{18h}{18}$$
$$3\frac{1}{3} = h$$

The plumber must work $3\frac{1}{3}$ hours, or 3 hours and 20 minutes, to earn $92.

8. Let s represent the weekly sales at the restaurant.
$$700 = 400 + 1.2\%(s)$$
$$700 = 400 + 0.012s$$
$$700 - 400 = 400 + 0.012s - 400$$
$$300 = 0.012s$$
$$\frac{300}{0.012} = \frac{0.012s}{0.012}$$
$$25,000 = s$$

The weekly sales must be $25,000 for Denny to make $700 per week.

10. Let x represent the number of football programs.
$$2x - 1240 = 600$$
$$2x - 1240 + 1240 = 600 + 1240$$
$$2x = 1840$$
$$\frac{2x}{2} = \frac{1840}{2}$$
$$x = 920$$

The booster club must sell 920 football programs to earn a $600 profit.

12.

	First solution	Second solution	New solution
Percent acid	2% = 0.02	100% = 1.00	2.5% = 0.025
Amount of solution	40 oz	x	$40 + x$
Amount of acid	40(0.02)	x(1.00)	40(0.02) + 1.00x = 0.025(40 + x)

$$40(0.02) + 1.00x = 0.025(40 + x)$$
$$0.8 + x = 1 + 0.025x$$
$$0.8 + x - 0.025x = 1 + 0.025x - 0.025x$$
$$0.8 + 0.975x = 1$$
$$0.8 + 0.975x - 0.8 = 1 - 0.8$$
$$0.975x = 0.2$$
$$\frac{0.975x}{0.975} = \frac{0.2}{0.975}$$
$$x \approx 0.205$$

The chemist should add approximately 0.2 ounces of acid.

13.

	First solution	Second solution	New solution
Percent acid	3% = 0.03	0%	2.2% = 0.022
Amount of solution	60 mL	x	$60 + x$
Amount of acid	60(0.03)	$0(x) = 0$	$60(0.03) + 0 = (60 + x)0.022$

$$60(0.03) = (60 + x)0.022$$
$$1.8 = 1.32 + 0.022x$$
$$1.8 - 1.32 = 1.32 + 0.022x - 1.32$$
$$0.48 = 0.022x$$
$$\frac{0.48}{0.022} = \frac{0.022x}{0.022}$$
$$21.81 = x$$

Abigail should add approximately 21.8 milliliters of pure water to the solution.

14.

	First solution	Second solution	New solution
Percent salt	48% = 0.48	30% = 0.30	38% = 0.38
Amount of solution	48 oz	x	$48 + x$
Amount of salt	48(0.48)	0.30x	$48(0.48) + 0.30x = 0.38(48 + x)$

$$48(0.48) + 0.30x = 0.38(48 + x)$$
$$23.04 + 0.30x = 18.24 + 0.38x$$
$$23.04 + 0.30x - 0.30x = 18.24 + 0.38x - 0.30x$$
$$23.04 = 18.24 + 0.08x$$
$$23.04 - 18.24 = 18.24 + 0.08x - 18.24$$
$$4.8 = 0.08x$$
$$\frac{4.8}{0.08} = \frac{0.08x}{0.08}$$
$$60 = x$$

Laura should add 60 ounces of the second solution.

15.

	First solution	Second solution	New solution
Percent antifreeze	25% = 0.25	32% = 0.32	30% = 0.30
Amount of solution	2 L	x	$2 + x$
Amount of antifreeze	0.25(2)	0.32x	$0.25(2) + 0.32x = 0.30(2 + x)$

$$0.25(2) + 0.32x = 0.30(2 + x)$$
$$0.5 + 0.32x = 0.6 + 0.30x$$
$$0.5 + 0.32x - 0.30x = 0.6 + 0.30x - 0.30x$$
$$0.5 + 0.02x = 0.6$$
$$0.5 + 0.02x - 0.5 = 0.6 - 0.5$$
$$0.02x = 0.1$$
$$\frac{0.02x}{0.02} = \frac{0.1}{0.02}$$
$$x = 5$$

Gary should add 5 liters of the 32% solution.

16. Let x represent the number of games played last season. Then $x + 4$ represents the number of games played this season.

$$55\% \cdot x = 50\% \cdot (x + 4)$$
$$0.55x = 0.50(x + 4)$$
$$0.55x = 0.50x + 2$$
$$0.55x - 0.50x = 0.50x + 2 - 0.50x$$
$$0.05x = 2$$
$$\frac{0.05x}{0.05} = \frac{2}{0.05}$$
$$x = 40$$

The basketball team won 40 games last season and 44 games this season.

17. Let x represent the number of girls who tried out. Then $x + 4$ represents the number of boys who tried out.

$$75\% \cdot x = 60\% \cdot (x + 4)$$
$$0.75x = 0.60(x + 4)$$
$$0.75x = 0.60x + 2.4$$
$$0.75x - 0.60x = 0.60x + 2.4 - 0.60x$$
$$0.15x = 2.4$$
$$\frac{0.15x}{0.15} = \frac{2.4}{0.15}$$
$$x = 16$$

The number of girls who tried out was 16, and the number of boys was $16 + 4 = 20$.

18. Let x represent the number of batteries in stock at the beginning of July. Then $x + 40$ represents the number of oil filters in stock.

$$40\% \cdot x = 30\% \cdot (x + 40)$$
$$0.40x = 0.30(x + 40)$$
$$0.40x = 0.30x + 12$$
$$0.40x - 0.30x = 0.30x + 12 - 0.30x$$
$$0.10x = 12$$
$$\frac{0.10x}{0.10} = \frac{12}{0.10}$$
$$x = 120$$

There were 120 batteries in stock and $x + 40 = 120 + 40 = 160$ oil filters in stock.

19. Let C represent the cost of making the cages, and let n represent the number of cages.

$$C = 155 + 4.25n$$

20. Let R represent the revenue made from selling the cages, and let n represent the number of cages.

$$R = 12.50n$$

21. Let P represent the profit, and let n represent the number of cages. Profit is computed by subtracting the cost, C, from the revenue, R.

$$P = R - C$$
$$P = 12.50n - (155 + 4.25n)$$
$$P = 12.50n - 4.25n - 155$$
$$P = 8.25n - 155$$

22. In order for Jesse to break even, the cost must equal the revenue.

$$C = R$$
$$155 + 4.25n = 12.50n$$
$$155 + 4.25n - 4.25n = 12.50n - 4.25n$$
$$155 = 8.25n$$
$$\frac{155}{8.25} = \frac{8.25n}{8.25}$$
$$18.78 = n$$

In order for Jesse to at least break even, he must sell 19 cages since he cannot sell 0.78 of a cage.

23. Substitute 450 for P in $P = 8.25n - 155$.

$$P = 8.25n - 155$$
$$450 = 8.25n - 155$$
$$605 = 8.25n$$
$$\frac{605}{8.25} = \frac{8.25n}{8.25}$$
$$73.3 \approx n$$

Jesse must sell 74 cages to earn \$450 in profit.

24. Graph the line $P = 200$ and the line $P = 8.25n - 155$ on the same set of coordinate axes. The n–coordinate of the point of intersection is the number of cages Jesse must sell.

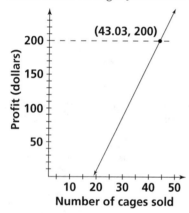

Since he cannot sell 43.03 cages, Jesse must sell 44 cages to earn a profit of \$200.

25. Let d represent the number of days, and let n represent the number of cages. Graph the line $n = 44$ and the line $n = 8d$ on the same set of coordinate axes. The d-coordinate of the point of intersection is the number of days necessary.

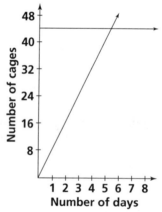

Jesse will have to make cages for about 5.5 days to earn a profit of \$200.

26. Let n represent the number of packages, and let C represent the cost.

$$C = 24 + 2.50n$$

27. Let n represent the number of packages, and let R represent the revenue.

$$R = 4n$$

28. The amount of profit is equal to the revenue minus the cost.

Let P represent the amount of profit.

$$P = R - C$$
$$= 4n - (24 + 2.50n)$$
$$= 1.5n - 24$$

29. To break even, the total revenue must equal the total cost.

$$R = C$$
$$4n = 24 + 2.50n$$
$$4n - 2.50n = 24 + 2.50n - 2.50n$$
$$1.5n = 24$$
$$\frac{1.5n}{1.5n} = \frac{24}{1.5}$$
$$n = 16$$

The French Club must sell 16 packages to break even.

30. Substitute 300 for P in the formula $P = 1.5n - 24$.

$$P = 1.5n - 24$$
$$300 = 1.5n - 24$$
$$300 + 24 = 1.5n - 24 + 24$$
$$324 = 1.5n$$
$$\frac{324}{1.5} = \frac{1.5n}{1.5}$$
$$216 = n$$

The French Club must sell 216 packages of wrapping paper.

31. Since the angles are vertical angles formed by intersecting lines, they are equal.

$$4w + 9 = 6w - 7$$
$$4w + 9 - 4w = 6w - 7 - 4w$$
$$9 = 2w - 7$$
$$9 + 7 = 2w - 7 + 7$$
$$16 = 2w$$
$$\frac{16}{2} = \frac{2w}{2}$$
$$8 = w$$

Left angle: $4w + 9 = 4(8) + 9 = 41°$
Right angle: $6w - 7 = 6(8) - 7 = 41°$

PAGE 400, LOOK BACK

32. $-8 < -3.2$ or $-3.2 > -8$

33. $12 > -17$ or $-17 < 12$

34. $-\frac{1}{2} > -\frac{2}{3}$ or $-\frac{2}{3} < -\frac{1}{2}$

35. Both numbers must be positive, or both numbers must be negative.

36. The sum of two supplementary angles is 180°.

37. Opposite angles of a parallelogram are equal. The sum of two adjacent angles is 180°. The sum of all the angles in a parallelogram is 360°.

38. $P = 2(x + 3) + 2(24)$

39. $A = 24(x + 3)$

40.
$$3x + 6 + 4x = 8$$
$$7x + 6 = 8$$
$$7x + 6 - 6 = 8 - 6$$
$$7x = 2$$
$$\frac{7x}{7} = \frac{2}{7}$$
$$x = \frac{2}{7}$$

41.
$$2(x - 8) = 3x + 24$$
$$2x - 16 = 3x + 24$$
$$2x - 16 - 2x = 3x + 24 - 2x$$
$$-16 = x + 24$$
$$-16 - 24 = x + 24 - 24$$
$$-40 = x$$

PAGE 400, LOOK BEYOND

42. $|x| < 10$

To determine the set of numbers that satisfies this inequality, consider two cases.

Case 1
The quantity within the absolute-value sign is positive.
$$|x| < 10$$
$$x < 10$$

Case 2
The quantity within the absolute-value sign is negative.
$$|x| < 10$$
$$-x < 10$$
$$x > -10$$

The inequality is true when $x < 10$ and when $x > -10$. We write the set of numbers for $x < 10$ and $x > -10$ as $-10 < x < 10$.

43. $|x - 2| < 10$

Case 1
The quantity within the absolute-value sign is positive.
$$|x - 2| < 10$$
$$x - 2 < 10$$
$$x - 2 + 2 < 10 + 2$$
$$x < 12$$

Case 2
The quantity within the absolute-value sign is negative.
$$|x - 2| < 10$$
$$-(x - 2) < 10$$
$$-x + 2 < 10$$
$$-x + 2 - 2 < 10 - 2$$
$$-x < 8$$
$$-1(-x) > -1(8)$$
$$x > -8$$

The inequality is true when $x < 12$ and when $x > -8$. We write this set of numbers as $-8 < x < 12$.

44. $|x| \geq 3$

Consider two cases.

Case 1

The quantity x is positive.

$$|x| \geq 3$$
$$x \geq 3$$

Case 2

The quantity x is negative.

$$|x| \geq 3$$
$$-x \geq 3$$
$$-1(-x) \geq 3(-1)$$
$$x \leq -3$$

The inequality is true when $x \leq -3$ or when $x \geq 3$.

For Exercises 5–8, complementary angles are angles whose sum is 90°, so let m∠1 + m∠2 = 90.

5.
$$\text{m}\angle 1 + \text{m}\angle 2 = 90$$
$$(x + 9) + (2x + 3) = 90$$
$$3x + 12 = 90$$
$$3x + 12 - 12 = 90 - 12$$
$$3x = 78$$
$$\frac{3x}{3} = \frac{78}{3}$$
$$x = 26$$
$$\text{m}\angle 1 = x + 9 = 26 + 9 = 35°$$
$$\text{m}\angle 2 = 3x + 3 = 2(26) + 3 = 55°$$

6.
$$\text{m}\angle 1 + \text{m}\angle 2 = 90$$
$$(5x + 2) + (3x) = 90$$
$$8x + 2 = 90$$
$$8x + 2 - 2 = 90 - 2$$
$$8x = 88$$
$$\frac{8x}{8} = \frac{88}{8}$$
$$x = 11$$
$$\text{m}\angle 1 = 5x + 2 = 5(11) + 2 = 55 + 2 = 57°$$
$$\text{m}\angle 2 = 3x = 3(11) = 33°$$

7.
$$\text{m}\angle 1 + \text{m}\angle 2 = 90$$
$$(4x + 17) + (5x - 8) = 90$$
$$9x + 9 = 90$$
$$9x + 9 - 9 = 90 - 9$$
$$9x = 81$$
$$\frac{9x}{9} = \frac{81}{9}$$
$$x = 9$$
$$\text{m}\angle 1 = 4x + 17 = 4(9) + 17 = 36 + 17 = 53°$$
$$\text{m}\angle 2 = 5x - 8 = 5(9) - 8 = 45 - 8 = 37°$$

8.
$$\text{m}\angle 1 + \text{m}\angle 2 = 90$$
$$\left(\frac{x}{2} + 18\right) + 4x = 90$$
$$\frac{1}{2}x + 4x + 18 = 90$$
$$\frac{9}{2}x + 18 = 90$$
$$\frac{9}{2}x + 18 - 18 = 90 - 18$$
$$\frac{9}{2}x = 72$$
$$\frac{2}{9}\left(\frac{9}{2}x\right) = (72)\frac{2}{9}$$
$$x = \frac{144}{9}$$
$$x = 16$$
$$\text{m}\angle 1 = \frac{x}{2} + 18 = \frac{16}{2} + 18 = 8 + 18 = 26°$$
$$\text{m}\angle 2 = 4x = 4(16) = 64°$$

For Exercises 9–11, the sum of the measures of the angles of a triangle is 180°, so m∠A + m∠B + m∠C = 180°.

9.
$$\text{m}\angle A + \text{m}\angle B + \text{m}\angle C = 180$$
$$7x + (4x + 9) + (15 + x) = 180$$
$$12x + 24 = 180$$
$$12x + 24 - 24 = 180 - 24$$
$$12x = 156$$
$$\frac{12x}{12} = \frac{156}{12}$$
$$x = 13$$
$$\text{m}\angle A = 7x = 7(13) = 91°$$
$$\text{m}\angle B = 4x + 9 = 4(13) + 9 = 61°$$
$$\text{m}\angle C = 15 + x = 15 + 13 = 28°$$

10.
$$\text{m}\angle A + \text{m}\angle B + \text{m}\angle C = 180$$
$$(6x - 7) + 4x + (2x + 11) = 180$$
$$12x + 4 = 180$$
$$12x + 4 - 4 = 180 - 4$$
$$12x = 176$$
$$\frac{12x}{12} = \frac{176}{12}$$
$$x = \frac{44}{3}$$
$$\text{m}\angle A = 6x - 7 = 6\left(\frac{44}{3}\right) - 7 = 88 - 7 = 81°$$
$$\text{m}\angle B = 4x = 4\left(\frac{44}{3}\right) = \frac{176}{3} = 58\frac{2}{3}°$$
$$\text{m}\angle C = 2x + 11 = 2\left(\frac{44}{3}\right) + 11 = \frac{88}{3} + 11 = 40\frac{1}{3}°$$

11. $m\angle A + m\angle B + m\angle C = 180$

$$\frac{x}{3} + \left(\frac{1}{3} + x\right) + 6x = 180$$

$$\frac{1}{3}x + x + 6x + \frac{1}{3} = 180$$

$$7\frac{1}{3}x + \frac{1}{3} = 180$$

$$\frac{22}{3}x + \frac{1}{3} - \frac{1}{3} = 180 - \frac{1}{3}$$

$$\frac{22}{3}x = 179\frac{2}{3}$$

$$\frac{3}{22}\left(\frac{22}{3}x\right) = \left(\frac{539}{3}\right)\frac{3}{22}$$

$$x = \frac{1617}{66}$$

$$x = 24\frac{1}{2}, \text{ or } \frac{49}{2}$$

$m\angle A = \frac{x}{3} = \frac{1}{3}\left(\frac{49}{2}\right) = \frac{49}{6} = 8\frac{1}{6}°$

$m\angle B = \frac{1}{3} + x = \frac{1}{3} + \frac{49}{2} = \frac{2}{6} + \frac{147}{6} = \frac{149}{6} = 24\frac{5}{6}°$

$m\angle C = 6x = 6\left(\frac{49}{2}\right) = \frac{294}{2} = 147°$

12. Since line r is parallel to line s, $m\angle 1 = m\angle 3$.

$$m\angle 1 = m\angle 3$$

$$2x + 2 = 4x - 5$$

$$2x + 2 - 2x = 4x - 5 - 2x$$

$$2 = 2x - 5$$

$$2 + 5 = 2x - 5 + 5$$

$$7 = 2x$$

$$\frac{7}{2} = \frac{2x}{2}$$

$$\frac{7}{2} = x$$

$m\angle 1 = 2x + 2 = 2\left(\frac{7}{2}\right) + 2 = \frac{14}{2} + 2 = 7 + 2 = 9°$

$m\angle 3 = 4x - 5 = 4\left(\frac{7}{2}\right) - 5 = \frac{28}{2} - 5 = 14 - 5 = 9°$

13. Since $m\angle 6$ and $m\angle 7$ are supplementary, $m\angle 6 + m\angle 7 = 180$.

$$m\angle 6 + m\angle 7 = 180$$

$$(4x + 7) + (8x + 9) = 180$$

$$12x + 16 = 180$$

$$12x = 164$$

$$\frac{12x}{12} = \frac{164}{12}$$

$$x = \frac{164}{12}, \text{ or } \frac{41}{3}$$

$m\angle 6 = 4x + 7 = 4\left(\frac{41}{3}\right) + 7 = \frac{164}{3} + 7 = \frac{164}{3} + \frac{21}{3} = \frac{185}{3} = 61\frac{2}{3}°$

$m\angle 7 = 8x + 9 = 8\left(\frac{41}{3}\right) + 9 = \frac{328}{3} + 9 = \frac{328}{3} + \frac{27}{3} = \frac{355}{3} = 188\frac{1}{3}°$

14. Since $m\angle 5$ and $m\angle 6$ are supplementary, $m\angle 5 + m\angle 6 = 180°$.

$$m\angle 5 + m\angle 6 = 180$$

$$(4x + 1) + (2x + 2) = 180$$

$$6x + 3 = 180$$

$$6x = 177$$

$$\frac{6x}{6} = \frac{177}{6}$$

$$x = \frac{177}{6} = \frac{59}{2}, \text{ or } 29\frac{1}{2}$$

$m\angle 5 = 4x + 1 = 4\left(\frac{59}{2}\right) + 1 = 118 + 1 = 119°$

$m\angle 6 = 2x + 2 = 2\left(\frac{59}{2}\right) + 2 = 59 + 2 = 61°$

15. Since line r is parallel to line s, $m\angle 4 = m\angle 8$.

$$m\angle 4 = m\angle 8$$

$$2x + 8 = 6x$$

$$8 = 4x$$

$$2 = x$$

$m\angle 4 = 2x + 8 = 2(2) + 8 = 12°$

$m\angle 8 = 6x = 6(2) = 12°$

16. Let A represent the area of the triangle, b represent the base, and h represent the height.

$$A = \frac{1}{2}bh$$

$$48 = \frac{1}{2}(24)h$$

$$48 = 12h$$

$$\frac{48}{12} = \frac{12h}{12}$$

$$4 = h$$

The height of the triangle is 4 meters.

17. Let A represent the area of the trapezoid, and let b_1 and b_2 represent the bases.

$$A = \frac{1}{2}h(b_1 + b_2)$$

$$121 = \frac{1}{2}h(15.5 + 14.75)$$

$$121 = h\left(\frac{1}{2}\right)(30.25)$$

$$121 = h(15.125)$$

$$\frac{121}{15.125} = \frac{15.125h}{15.125}$$

$$8 = h$$

The height of the trapezoid is 8 feet.

18. Let x represent the smaller angle. This means that $4x$ will represent the larger angle. Since the angles are complementary, their sum is 90°.

$$4x + x = 90$$

$$5x = 90$$

$$\frac{5x}{5} = \frac{90}{5}$$

$$x = 18$$

The measure of the smaller angle is 18°. The measure of the larger angle is $4x = 4(18) = 72°$.

19. Let x represent the smaller angle. This means that $2x - 60$ will represent the larger angle. Since the angles are supplementary, their sum is 180°.

$$x + (2x - 60) = 180$$
$$3x - 60 = 180$$
$$3x - 60 + 60 = 180 + 60$$
$$3x = 240$$
$$\frac{3x}{3} = \frac{240}{3}$$
$$x = 80$$

The measure of the smaller angle is 80°. The measure of the larger angle is $2x - 60 = 160 - 60 = 100°$.

20.

$$l = 1\tfrac{1}{2}w$$

w

Let w represent the width of the rectangular screen. Then $1\tfrac{1}{2}w$ represents the length of the screen.

$$P = 2l + 2w$$
$$400 = 2\left(\tfrac{3}{2}w\right) + 2(w)$$
$$400 = \tfrac{6}{2}w + 2w$$
$$400 = 3w + 2w$$
$$400 = 5w$$
$$\frac{400}{5} = \frac{5w}{5}$$
$$80 = w$$

The width of the screen is 80 feet. The length of the screen is $\tfrac{3}{2}w = \tfrac{3}{2}(80) = \tfrac{240}{2} = 120$ feet.

21.

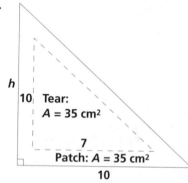

h
10 Tear:
$A = 35$ cm^2
7
Patch: $A = 35$ cm^2
10

Area of the tear $= \tfrac{1}{2}bh$

$= \tfrac{1}{2}(7)(10)$

$= \tfrac{1}{2}(70)$

$= 35$

Area of the patch $= \tfrac{1}{2}bh$

$(350)(2) = \tfrac{1}{2}(10)h$

$70 = 5h$

$\dfrac{70}{5} = \dfrac{5h}{5}$

$14 = h$

The height of the patch is 14 centimeters. The width of the patch is 10 centimeters.

22.
$$A = \tfrac{1}{2}h(b_1 + b_2)$$
$$2A = 2\left[\tfrac{1}{2}h(b_1 + b_2)\right]$$
$$2A = 2\left(\tfrac{1}{2}\right)h(b_1 + b_2)$$
$$2A = h(b_1 + b_2)$$
$$\frac{2A}{h} = \frac{h(b_1 + b_2)}{h}$$
$$\frac{2A}{h} = b_1 + b_2$$
$$\frac{2A}{h} - b_2 = b_1 + b_2 - b_2$$
$$\frac{2A}{h} - b_2 = b_1$$

23.
$$s = (n - 2)180$$
$$\frac{s}{180} = \frac{(n - 2)\,180}{180}$$
$$\frac{s}{180} = n - 2$$
$$\frac{s}{180} + 2 = n - 2 + 2$$
$$\frac{s}{180} + 2 = n$$

24.
$$3x + g + 2h = t - y$$
$$3x + g + 2h - 3x = t - y - 3x$$
$$g + 2h = t - y - 3x$$
$$g + 2h - g = t - y - 3x - g$$
$$2h = t - y - 3x - g$$
$$\frac{2h}{2} = \frac{t - y - 3x - g}{2}$$
$$h = \frac{t - y - 3x - g}{2}$$

25.
$$x + 4y = r$$
$$x + 4y - x = r - x$$
$$4y = r - x$$
$$\frac{4y}{4} = \frac{r - x}{4}$$
$$y = \frac{r - x}{4}$$

26.
$$\frac{x}{y} = \frac{4}{5}$$
$$y\left(\frac{x}{y}\right) = \left(\frac{4}{5}\right)y$$
$$x = \frac{4y}{5}$$

27.
$$\tfrac{9}{5}C + 32 = F$$
$$\tfrac{9}{5}C + 32 - 32 = F - 32$$
$$\tfrac{9}{5}C = F - 32$$
$$\tfrac{5}{9}\left(\tfrac{9}{5}C\right) = \tfrac{5}{9}(F - 32)$$
$$C = \tfrac{5}{9}(F - 32)$$

28.
$$\text{heat transfer} = A \cdot U(i - o)$$
$$= 200 \cdot 0.58(65 - 80)$$
$$= 200 \cdot 0.58(-15)$$
$$= 116(-15)$$
$$= -1740$$
The heat transfer would be −1740 BTUs per hour.

29.
$$\text{heat transfer} = A \cdot U(i - o)$$
$$= 400 \cdot 0.43(72 - 85)$$
$$= 400 \cdot 0.43(-13)$$
$$= 172(-13)$$
$$= -2236$$
The heat transfer would be −2236 BTUs per hour.

30. The greater the heat transfer factor, the greater the heat transfer. The heat transfer factor for a concrete wall 6 inches thick is greater than the heat transfer factor for a brick wall 8 inches thick. Therefore the heat transfer through a concrete wall that is 6 inches thick is greater.

31. There will be a heat loss in the interior. For example, assume that you have a 100-square-foot wall of concrete that is 6 inches thick.
$$\text{heat transfer} = A \cdot U(i - o)$$
$$= 100 \cdot 0.58(71 - 30)$$
$$= 100 \cdot 0.58(41)$$
$$= 58(41)$$
$$= 2378$$
Since the heat transfer is positive, there is a heat loss in the interior.

PAGE 407, LOOK BACK

32. $\left|-3\right| + \left|7\right| = 3 + 7 = 10$

33. $\left|-5 - 8\right| = \left|-13\right| = 13$

34. $\left|10 - 24\right| = \left|-14\right| = 14$

35.
$$0.25x = 7$$
$$\frac{0.25x}{0.25} = \frac{7}{0.25}$$
$$x = 28$$

36.
$$5x = 3x - 10$$
$$5x - 3x = 3x - 10 - 3x$$
$$2x = -10$$
$$\frac{2x}{2} = \frac{-10}{2}$$
$$x = -5$$

37.
$$9x - 10 = 5x - 16$$
$$9x - 10 - 5x = 5x - 16 - 5x$$
$$4x - 10 = -16$$
$$4x - 10 + 10 = -16 + 10$$
$$4x = -6$$
$$\frac{4x}{4} = \frac{-6}{4}$$
$$x = \frac{-6}{4}$$
$$x = -\frac{3}{2}$$

38. Let x represent the number of figurines, C represent the cost of making the figurines, R the revenue received for selling the figurines, and P the profit made for selling the figurines. The cost, C, can be computed in the following manner:
$$c = 7 + 0.65x$$
The revenue made from selling the figurines can be computed in this way:
$$R = 3.25x$$
The profit received from the sale is equal to the revenue minus the cost:
$$P = R - C$$
$$P = 3.25x - (7 + 0.65x)$$
$$P = 3.25x - 0.65x - 7$$
$$P = 2.6x - 7$$

Now substitute 250 for P:
$$P = 2.6x - 7$$
$$250 = 2.6x - 7$$
$$250 = 2.6x - 7$$
$$250 + 7 = 2.6x - 7 + 7$$
$$257 = 2.6x$$
$$\frac{257}{2.6} = \frac{2.6x}{2.6}$$
$$98.85 \approx x$$
Since Juanita cannot sell 98.85 figurines, she will have to sell 99 figurines to earn a profit of $250.

PAGE 407, LOOK BEYOND

39.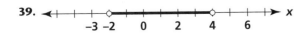

9. $L > W$

10. $r \geq 4$

11. $3.1 \leq V \leq 3.2$

12. $x \neq 0$

13. $m > 0$

14. $y \geq 0$

15. True; $4.2 \geq 4.2$ means $4.2 > 4.2$ *or* $4.2 = 4.2$, which is true.

16. True; $9.22 \leq 9.22$ means $9.22 < 9.22$ *or* $9.22 = 9.22$, which is true.

17. false; $3\frac{1}{10} > 3\frac{1}{100}$

18. true; $8\frac{55}{100} > 8\frac{505}{1000}$

19. False; $\frac{1}{7}$ and $\frac{1}{6}$ can be expressed as the equivalent fractions $\frac{6}{42}$ and $\frac{7}{42}$ but $\frac{6}{42} \leq \frac{7}{42}$.

20. True; $\frac{3}{4} \leq \frac{4}{5}$ can be expressed in decimal form as $0.75 \leq 0.8$ *or* $0.75 < 0.8$, which is true.

21. true; $-8 < -4$

22. True; $0 \geq -3$ means $0 = -3$ *or* $0 > -3$, which is true.

23. $x + 8 \geq 11$
$x \geq 3$

24. $x - 11 < -20$
$x < -9$

25. $G - 6 \leq 9$
$G \leq 15$

26. $8 - H > 9$
$-H > 1$
$H < -1$

27. $6 - x > -1$
$-x > -7$
$x < 7$

28. $5 - y \geq 2$
$-y \geq -3$
$y \leq 3$

29. $\frac{x}{8} < 1$
$8\left(\frac{x}{8}\right) < 8(1)$
$x < 8$

30. $\frac{u}{-3} \geq 21$
$-3\left(\frac{u}{-3}\right) \leq -3(21)$
$u \leq -63$

31. $5b > 3$
$b > \frac{3}{5}$

32. $9c \geq -21$
$c \geq -\frac{21}{9}$
$c \geq -\frac{7}{3}$, or $-2\frac{1}{3}$

33. $2d + 1 < 5$
$2d < 4$
$d < 2$

34. $5x - 2 > 2x + 9$
$3x - 2 > 9$
$3x > 11$
$x > \frac{11}{3}$, or $3\frac{2}{3}$

35. $\frac{x}{3} + 4 < 10$
$3\left(\frac{x}{3} + 4\right) < 3(10)$
$x + 12 < 30$
$x < 18$

36. $\frac{-x}{5} - 1 < 3$
$5\left(\frac{-x}{5} - 1\right) < 5(3)$
$-x - 5 < 15$
$-x < 20$
$x > -20$

37. $8x - 3 \leq 9$
$8x \leq 12$
$x \leq \frac{12}{8}$
$x \leq \frac{3}{2}$, or $1\frac{1}{2}$

38. $15 + \frac{y}{4} > 10$
$\frac{y}{4} > -5$
$4\left(\frac{y}{4}\right) > 4(-5)$
$y > -20$

39. Let C represent the cost of the shoes for a year.
Lowest cost: $C = 15 \cdot 17 = 255$
Highest cost:
$C = 15 \cdot 20 = 300$
$255 \leq C \leq 300$
The cost ranges between $255 and $300 inclusive.

40. $p = 2$
$2p = 4$
3 is the next prime number after 2, and $3 < 4$, so $3 < 2p$.

41. $p = 3$
$2p = 6$
5 is the next prime number after 3, and $5 < 6$, so $5 < 2p$.

42. $p = 5$
$2p = 10$
7 is the next prime number after 5, and $7 < 10$, so $7 < 2p$.

43. $p = 89$
$2p = 178$
97 is the next prime number after 89, and $97 < 178$, so $97 < 2p$.

For Exercise 44–45, let *l* represent the length of the rectangle, and let *w* represent the width.

44. $l \geq 5 + w$

45. $w = 20$
$l \geq 5 + w$
$l \geq 5 + 20$
$l \geq 25$
The length of the rectangle is at least 25 cm.

46. Let v represent the number of videos that Robin can buy.

a. $14.99v + 3.95 \leq 50.00$

b. Robin can buy a minimum of 0 videos but purchasing 0 videos is unrealistic; therefore the lower boundary is $v \geq 1$.

47. Robin can buy 1, 2, or 3 videos. The minimum number of videotapes is not included because Robin would not want to pay a $3.95 handling charge for an order of 0 tapes.

48. Let v represent the number of videos that can be bought.
$$14.99v + 3.95 \leq 80.00$$
$$14.99v + 3.95 - 3.95 \leq 80.00 - 3.95$$
$$14.88v \leq 76.05$$
$$v \leq 5.07$$
Robin and her friends can buy 1, 2, 3, 4, or 5 tapes.

PAGE 413, LOOK BACK

49. $89 - (-14) = 89 + 14$
$= 103$

50. $400 - (-111) = 400 + 111$
$= 511$

51. $-16 - (-3) = -16 + 3$
$= -13$

52. $-674 - 9(-900) = -674 - (-8100)$
$= -674 + 8100$
$= 7426$

53. There are 4 negative signs in the expression, so the result should be positive.
$(-3)(-3)(-1)(-1) = 9(1) = 9$

54. There are 3 negative signs in the expression, so the result should be negative.
$(-1)(1)(-1)(-1) = -1(1) = -1$

55. There is 1 negative sign in the expression, so the result should be negative.
$-\frac{22}{2} = -11$

56. There are 2 negative signs in the expression, so the result should be positive.
$\frac{-16}{-4} = 4$

57. $(3x - 2y + 1) - 3(x + 2y - 1) = 3x - 2y + 1 - 3x - 6y + 3$
$= 3x - 3x - 2y - 6y + 1 + 3$
$= -8y + 4$

58. $3(a + b) - 2(a - b) = 3a + 3b - 2a + 2b$
$= 3a - 2a + 3b + 2b$
$= a + 5b$

PAGE 413, LOOK BEYOND

59. If $y = \frac{1}{x - 2}$, then $x \neq 2$. The denominator cannot equal 0 because then the function would be undefined.

60. If $y = \sqrt{x + 3}$, then $x \geq -3$. The radicand will be greater than or equal to 0.

7.6 PAGES 419–420, PRACTICE & APPLY

6. $|x - 5| = 3$
Case 1:
$x - 5 = 3$
$x - 5 + 5 = 3 + 5$
$x = 8$
Case 2:
$-(x - 5) = 3$
$-x + 5 = 3$
$-x = 3 - 5$
$-x = -2$
$x = 2$

7. $|x - 1| = 6$
Case 1:
$x - 1 = 6$
$x = 6 + 1$
$x = 7$
Case 2:
$-(x - 1) = 6$
$-x + 1 = 6$
$-x = 6 - 1$
$x = -5$

8. $|x - 2| = 4$
Case 1:
$x - 2 = 4$
$x = 4 + 2$
$x = 6$
Case 2:
$-(x - 2) = 4$
$-x + 2 = 4$
$-x = 4 - 2$
$-x = 2$
$x = -2$

9. $|x - 8| = 5$
Case 1:
$x - 8 = 5$
$x = 5 + 8$
$x = 13$
Case 2:
$-(x - 8) = 5$
$-x + 8 = 5$
$-x = 5 - 8$
$-x = -3$
$x = 3$

10. $|5x - 1| = 4$
Case 1:
$5x - 1 = 4$
$5x = 5$
$\frac{5x}{5} = \frac{5}{5}$
$x = 1$
Case 2:
$-(5x - 1) = 4$
$-5x + 1 = 4$
$-5x = 4 - 1$
$-5x = 3$
$x = -\frac{3}{5}$, or -0.6

11. $|2x + 4| = 7$
Case 1:
$2x + 4 = 7$
$2x = 7 - 4$
$2x = 3$
$x = \frac{3}{2}$, or $1\frac{1}{2}$, or 1.5
Case 2:
$-(2x + 4) = 7$
$-2x - 4 = 7$
$-2x = 7 + 4$
$-2x = 11$
$x = -\frac{11}{2}$, or $-5\frac{1}{2}$, or -5.5

12. $|4x + 5| = 1$
Case 1:
$4x + 5 = 1$
$4x = 1 - 5$
$4x = -4$
$x = -1$
Case 2:
$-(4x + 5) = 1$
$-4x - 5 = 1$
$-4x = 1 + 5$
$-4x = 6$
$\frac{-4x}{-4} = \frac{6}{-4}$
$x = -\frac{3}{2}$, or $-1\frac{1}{2}$

13. $|-1 + x| = 3$
Case 1:
$-1 + x = 3$
$x = 3 + 1$
$x = 4$
Case 2:
$-(-1 + x) = 3$
$1 - x = 3$
$-x = 3 + 1$
$-x = 2$
$x = -2$

14. $|x - 3| < 7$

Case 1:

$x - 3 < 7$

$\quad x < 10$

Case 2:

$-(x - 3) < 7$

$\quad -x + 3 < 7$

$\quad\quad -x < 4$

$\quad\quad\quad x > -4$

$-4 < x < 10$

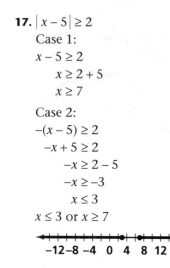

15. $|x + 4| > 8$

Case 1:

$x + 4 > 8$

$\quad x > 8 - 4$

$\quad x > 4$

Case 2:

$-(x + 4) > 8$

$\quad -x - 4 > 8$

$\quad\quad -x > 8 + 4$

$\quad\quad -x > 12$

$\quad\quad\quad x < -12$

$x > 4$ or $x < -12$

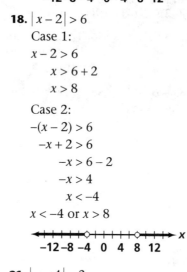

16. $|x - 8| \le 4$

Case 1:

$x - 8 \le 4$

$\quad x \le 4 + 8$

$\quad x \le 12$

Case 2:

$-(x - 8) \le 4$

$\quad -x + 8 \le 4$

$\quad\quad -x \le 4 - 8$

$\quad\quad -x \le -4$

$\quad\quad\quad x \ge 4$

$4 \le x \le 12$

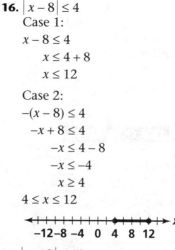

17. $|x - 5| \ge 2$

Case 1:

$x - 5 \ge 2$

$\quad x \ge 2 + 5$

$\quad x \ge 7$

Case 2:

$-(x - 5) \ge 2$

$\quad -x + 5 \ge 2$

$\quad\quad -x \ge 2 - 5$

$\quad\quad -x \ge -3$

$\quad\quad\quad x \le 3$

$x \le 3$ or $x \ge 7$

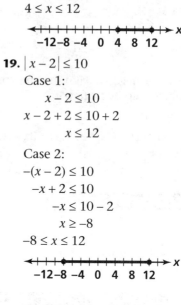

18. $|x - 2| > 6$

Case 1:

$x - 2 > 6$

$\quad x > 6 + 2$

$\quad x > 8$

Case 2:

$-(x - 2) > 6$

$\quad -x + 2 > 6$

$\quad\quad -x > 6 - 2$

$\quad\quad -x > 4$

$\quad\quad\quad x < -4$

$x < -4$ or $x > 8$

19. $|x - 2| \le 10$

Case 1:

$\quad x - 2 \le 10$

$x - 2 + 2 \le 10 + 2$

$\quad\quad x \le 12$

Case 2:

$-(x - 2) \le 10$

$\quad -x + 2 \le 10$

$\quad\quad -x \le 10 - 2$

$\quad\quad\quad x \ge -8$

$-8 \le x \le 12$

20. $|x + 1| < 5$

Case 1:

$\quad x + 1 < 5$

$x + 1 - 1 < 5 - 1$

$\quad\quad x < 4$

Case 2:

$-(x + 1) < 5$

$\quad -x - 1 < 5$

$\quad\quad -x < 5 + 1$

$\quad\quad\quad x > -6$

$-6 < x < 4$

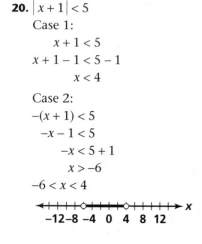

21. $|x - 4| > 2$

Case 1:

$\quad x - 4 > 2$

$x - 4 + 4 > 2 + 4$

$\quad\quad x > 6$

Case 2:

$-(x - 4) > 2$

$\quad -x + 4 > 2$

$\quad\quad -x > 2 - 4$

$\quad\quad -x > -2$

$\quad\quad\quad x < 2$

$x < 2$ or $x > 6$

22. Let w represent the ideal weight in pounds. For the acceptable weight range, $113 \le w \le 123$. For the unacceptable weight ranges, $w \le 113$ or $w \ge 123$

23. Let w represent the weight at the boundary in pounds. Then $|w - 118| = 5$ represents the acceptable weight values in pounds.

Case 1: $\quad w - 118 = 5$

$\quad\quad w - 118 + 118 = 5 + 118$

$\quad\quad\quad\quad w = 123$

Case 2: $\quad -(w - 118) = 5$

$\quad\quad -w + 118 = 5$

$\quad\quad -w + 118 - 118 = 5 - 118$

$\quad\quad\quad\quad -w = -113$

$\quad\quad\quad\quad w = 113$

The boundary values are 123 lb and 113 lb.

24. Let w represent the weight at the boundary in pounds. Then $|w - 118| \le 5$ represents the acceptable weight range.

Case 1: $w - 118 \le 5$

$\quad\quad w \le 5 + 118$

$\quad\quad w \le 123$

Case 2: $-(w - 118) \le 5$

$\quad\quad -w + 118 \le 5$

$\quad\quad -w \le -113$

$\quad\quad w \ge 113$

$113 \le w \le 123$

25.

26. $|x - 2| = 7$
Check 1:
$x - 2 = 7$
$x = 9$
Check 2:
$-(x - 2) = 7$
$-x + 2 = 7$
$-x = 5$
$x = -5$

27. $|x - 3| < 4$; the distance between x and 3 is less than 4 units.

28. $|x - 3| < 4$
Case 1:
$x - 3 < 4$
$x < 7$
Case 2:
$-(x - 3) < 4$
$-x + 3 < 4$
$-x < 1$
$x > -1$
$-1 < x < 7$

29. The solution for $|x - 3| < 4$ is all numbers between but not including –1 and 7.

30. Answers may vary. Five numbers that satisfy $|x - 3| < 4$ are 0, 1, 2, 3, and 4.

31. $|x - 3| > 4$; the distance between x and 3 is greater than 4 units.

32. To find the boundary, solve the absolute-value inequality $|x - 3| > 4$.

Case 1:
$x - 3 > 4$
$x > 7$

Case 2:
$-(x - 3) > 4$
$-x + 3 > 4$
$-x > 1$
$x < -1$

$x < -1$ or $x > 7$

33. The solution is all numbers that are greater than 7 or less than –1.

34. Answers may vary. Five numbers that satisfy the inequality are –2, –3, –4, 8, and 9.

35. The upper boundary is $(50 + 3)\%$, or 53%. The lower boundary is $(50 - 3)\%$, or 47%.

36. Let A represent the percent of voters favoring candidate A.
$47 \leq A \leq 53$
$|A - 50| \leq 3$

37. Yes, candidate A could lose because he could get a percent of votes in the range $47\% \leq A \leq 50\%$. If candidate A receives less than 50% of the vote, while another candidate receives more than 50% of the vote, candidate A could lose.

38. The graph $y = 2x - 6$ is a straight line with a slope of 2 and a y-intercept of –6.
The graph $y = |2x - 6|$ is a V that opens upwards and whose lowest point (vertex) is at (3, 0). The portion of the line $y = 2x - 6$ that lies above the x-axis is the right half of the V.

39. The graph $y = -x + 5$ is a straight line with a slope of –1 and a y-intercept of 5. The graph $y = |-x + 5|$ is a V that opens upward and whose lowest point (vertex) is at (5, 0). The portion of the line $y = -x + 5$ that lies above the x-axis is the left side of the V.

40. $pqr - q = 4(1)(2) - 1$
$= 8 - 1$
$= 7$

41. $\dfrac{pq}{r} = \dfrac{4(1)}{2}$
$= \dfrac{4}{2}$
$= 2$

42. $\dfrac{pqr}{q} + pqr = \dfrac{4(1)(2)}{1} + 4(1)(2)$
$= \dfrac{8}{1} + 8$
$= 8 + 8$
$= 16$

43. $-5(8c + 3) = -40c - 15$

44. $9(7b + 2) = 63b + 18$

45. $-4(-5k + 8) = 20k - 32$

46. $4x + 5 < 25$
$4x + 5 - 5 < 25 - 5$
$4x < 20$
$\dfrac{4x}{4} < \dfrac{20}{4}$
$x < 5$

47. $6y - 10 > 5$
$6y - 10 + 10 > 5 + 10$
$6y > 15$
$\dfrac{6y}{6} > \dfrac{15}{6}$
$y > \dfrac{15}{6}$
$y > \dfrac{5}{2}$, or $2\dfrac{1}{2}$, or 2.5

48. $9m - 8 < 4 + 8m$
$9m - 8 - 8m < 4 + 8m - 8m$
$m - 8 < 4$
$m - 8 + 8 < 4 + 8$
$m < 12$

49. What percent of 480 is 60?
$(x)(480) = 60$
$\dfrac{(x)(480)}{480} = \dfrac{60}{480}$
$x = \dfrac{60}{480} = \dfrac{1}{8} = 0.125$
$x = 0.125 \times 100 = 12.5\%$

50. $3x - 4 = 5$
$3x - 4 + 4 = 5 + 4$
$3x = 9$
$\dfrac{3x}{3} = \dfrac{9}{3}$
$x = 3$

51. $8x - 7 = 25$
$8x - 7 + 7 = 25 + 7$
$8x = 32$
$\dfrac{8x}{8} = \dfrac{32}{8}$
$x = 4$

52. $4(2 - x) = 20$
$8 - 4x = 20$
$8 - 4x - 8 = 20 - 8$
$-4x = 12$
$\dfrac{-4x}{-4} = \dfrac{12}{-4}$
$x = -3$

53. $x^2 - x + 5 - (x^2 + 4) = x^2 - x + 5 - x^2 - 4$
$= x^2 - x^2 - x + 5 - 4$
$= -x + 1$

54. $x^2 + 10 - (x^2 + 2x + 3) = x^2 + 10 - x^2 - 2x - 3$
$= x^2 - x^2 - 2x + 10 - 3$
$= -2x + 7$

PAGES 422–424 # CHAPTER 7 REVIEW

1. $3x + 7 = 31$
$3x + 7 - 7 = 31 - 7$
$3x = 24$
$\dfrac{3x}{3} = \dfrac{24}{3}$
$x = 8$

2. $7n - 6 = 29$
$7n - 6 + 6 = 29 + 6$
$7n = 35$
$\dfrac{7n}{7} = \dfrac{35}{7}$
$n = 5$

3. $34 = -6 + 8m$
$34 + 6 = -6 + 8m + 6$
$40 = 8m$
$\dfrac{40}{8} = \dfrac{8m}{8}$
$5 = m$

4. $7(2y + 18) = 28$
$14y + 126 = 28$
$14y + 126 - 126 = 28 - 126$
$14y = -98$
$\dfrac{14y}{14} = \dfrac{-98}{14}$
$y = -7$

5. $8\left(z - \dfrac{1}{3}\right) = 4$
$8z - \dfrac{8}{3} = 4$
$8z - \dfrac{8}{3} + \dfrac{8}{3} = 4 + \dfrac{8}{3}$
$8z = \dfrac{20}{3}$
$\dfrac{1}{8}(8z) = \left(\dfrac{20}{3}\right)\dfrac{1}{8}$
$z = \dfrac{20}{24}$
$z = \dfrac{5}{6}$

6. $\dfrac{1}{3} + 2t = 1$
$\dfrac{1}{3} + 2t - \dfrac{1}{3} = 1 - \dfrac{1}{3}$
$2t = \dfrac{2}{3}$
$\dfrac{1}{2}(2t) = \left(\dfrac{2}{3}\right)\dfrac{1}{2}$
$t = \dfrac{2}{6}$
$t = \dfrac{1}{3}$

7. $10x = 7x - 12$
$10x - 7x = 7x - 12 - 7x$
$3x = -12$
$\dfrac{3x}{3} = \dfrac{-12}{3}$
$x = -4$

8. $11t + 9 = 61 - 2t$
$11t + 9 + 2t = 61 - 2t + 2t$
$13t + 9 = 61$
$13t + 9 - 9 = 61 - 9$
$13t = 52$
$\dfrac{13t}{13} = \dfrac{52}{13}$
$t = 4$

9.
$$4s - 4 = 6s - 21$$
$$4s - 4 - 4s = 6s - 21 - 4s$$
$$-4 = 2s - 21$$
$$-4 + 21 = 2s - 21 + 21$$
$$17 = 2s$$
$$\frac{17}{2} = \frac{2s}{2}$$
$$\frac{17}{2} = s$$
$$s = \frac{17}{2}, \text{ or } 8\frac{1}{2}$$

10.
$$8(d - 1) = 15d + 6$$
$$8d - 8 = 15d + 6$$
$$8d - 8 - 8d = 15d + 6 - 8d$$
$$-8 = 7d + 6$$
$$-8 - 6 = 7d + 6 - 6$$
$$-14 = 7d$$
$$\frac{-14}{7} = \frac{7d}{7}$$
$$-2 = d$$

11.
$$5(y - 1) = 4(10 - y)$$
$$5y - 5 = 40 - 4y$$
$$5y - 5 + 4y = 40 - 4y + 4y$$
$$9y - 5 = 40$$
$$9y - 5 + 5 = 40 + 5$$
$$9y = 45$$
$$\frac{9y}{9} = \frac{45}{9}$$
$$y = 5$$

12.
$$0.6z + 1.4 = -6.7 - 0.3z$$
$$0.6z + 1.4 + 0.3z = -6.7 - 0.3z + 0.3z$$
$$0.9z + 1.4 = -6.7$$
$$0.9z + 1.4 - 1.4 = -6.7 - 1.4$$
$$0.9z = -8.1$$
$$\frac{0.9z}{0.9} = \frac{-8.1}{0.9}$$
$$z = -9$$

13. Let S represent the total sales for the month.
$$3400 = 1000 + 4\% \cdot S$$
$$3400 = 1000 + 0.04S$$
$$3400 - 1000 = 1000 + 0.04S - 1000$$
$$2400 = 0.04S$$
$$\frac{2400}{0.04} = \frac{0.04S}{0.04}$$
$$60,000 = S$$

Janice had total sales of $60,000 for the month.

14.

	First solution	Second solution	New solution
Percent acid	3% = 0.03	5% = 0.05	x
Amount of solution	30 mL	10 mL	30 + 10 = 40 mL
Amount of acid	0.03(30)	0.05(10)	0.03(30) + 0.05(10) = x(40)

$$0.03(30) + 0.05(10) = x(40)$$
$$0.9 + 0.5 = 40x$$
$$1.4 = 40x$$
$$\frac{1.4}{40} = \frac{40x}{40}$$
$$0.035 = x$$
$$0.035 = 3.5\%$$

3.5% of the new solution is acid. There are $40(3.5\%) = 40(0.035) = 1.4$ milliliters of acid in the new solution.

15. Since line r is parallel to line s, $\angle 1$ and $\angle 3$ are corresponding angles and $m\angle 1 = m\angle 3$.
$$m\angle 1 = m\angle 3$$
$$3x - 1 = x + 2$$
$$3x - 1 - x = x + 2 - x$$
$$2x - 1 = 2$$
$$2x - 1 + 1 = 2 + 1$$
$$2x = 3$$
$$\frac{2x}{2} = \frac{3}{2}$$
$$x = \frac{3}{2}$$
$$m\angle 1 = 3x - 1 = 3\left(\frac{3}{2}\right) - 1 = \frac{9}{2} - 1 = \frac{7}{2}^\circ, \text{ or } 3\frac{1}{2}^\circ$$
$$m\angle 2 = x + 2 = \frac{3}{2} + 2 = \frac{7}{2}^\circ, \text{ or } 3\frac{1}{2}^\circ$$

16. Since they form a straight angle, $m\angle 5 + m\angle 6 = 180^\circ$.
$$m\angle 5 + m\angle 6 = 180$$
$$(6x - 1) + (3x + 1) = 180$$
$$6x + 3x - 1 + 1 = 180$$
$$9x = 180$$
$$\frac{9x}{9} = \frac{180}{9}$$
$$x = 20$$
$$m\angle 5 = 6x - 1 = 6(20) - 1 = 120 - 1 = 119^\circ$$
$$m\angle 6 = 3x + 1 = 3(20) + 1 = 60 + 1 = 61^\circ$$

17. Since they are vertical angles formed by two intersecting lines, $m\angle 1 = m\angle 7$.
$$m\angle 1 = m\angle 7$$

$$8x - 2 = 4x$$
$$8x - 2 - 4x = 4x - 4x$$
$$4x - 2 = 0$$
$$4x - 2 + 2 = 0 + 2$$
$$4x = 2$$
$$\frac{4x}{4} = \frac{2}{4}$$
$$x = \frac{2}{4}, \text{ or } \frac{1}{2}$$
$$m\angle 1 = 8x - 2 = 8\left(\frac{1}{2}\right) - 2 = 4 - 2 = 2^\circ$$
$$m\angle 2 = 4x = 4\left(\frac{1}{2}\right) = 2^\circ$$

18. Since line r is parallel to line s and $\angle 2$ and $\angle 3$ consecutive angles, $\angle 2$ and $\angle 3$ are supplementary to each other. Therefore, $m\angle 2 + m\angle 3 = 180$.
$$m\angle 2 + m\angle 3 = 180$$
$$(x + 5) + (6x - 7) = 180$$
$$x + 6x + 5 - 7 = 180$$
$$7x - 2 = 180$$
$$7x - 2 + 2 = 180 + 2$$
$$7x = 182$$
$$\frac{7x}{7} = \frac{182}{7}$$
$$x = 26$$
$$m\angle 2 = x + 5 = 26 + 5 = 31^\circ$$
$$m\angle 3 = 6x - 7 = 6(26) - 7 = 156 - 7 = 149^\circ$$

19. Let x represent the smaller angle. Then $3x + 20$ represents the larger angle.

$$x + (3x + 20) = 180$$
$$4x + 20 = 180$$
$$4x + 20 - 20 = 180 - 20$$
$$4x = 160$$
$$\frac{4x}{4} = \frac{160}{4}$$
$$x = 40$$

The smaller angle is 40°. The larger angle is $3x + 20 = 3(40) + 20 = 120 + 20 = 140°$.

20.

16 yd

$$A = \frac{1}{2}bh$$
$$56 = \left(\frac{1}{2}\right)(16)(h)$$
$$56 = 8h$$
$$\frac{56}{8} = \frac{8h}{8}$$
$$7 = h$$

The height of the triangle is 7 yards.

21.
$$x + 4 < 6$$
$$x + 4 - 4 < 6 - 4$$
$$x < 2$$

22.
$$8 - y \geq 7$$
$$8 - y - 8 \geq 7 - 8$$
$$-y \geq -1$$
$$-1(-y) \leq (-1)-1$$
$$y \leq 1$$

23. $5r > -60$
$$\frac{5r}{5} > \frac{-60}{5}$$
$$r > -12$$

24.
$$\frac{-p}{8} \leq -3$$
$$8\left(\frac{-p}{8}\right) \leq (-3)8$$
$$-p \leq -24$$
$$(-1)(-p) \geq (-24)(-1)$$
$$p \geq 24$$

25.
$$x + 3 \geq 9 - x$$
$$x + 3 + x \geq 9 - x + x$$
$$2x + 3 \geq 9$$
$$2x + 3 - 3 \geq 9 - 3$$
$$2x \geq 6$$
$$\frac{2x}{2} \geq \frac{6}{2}$$
$$x \geq 3$$

26.
$$t + \frac{1}{2} < \frac{t}{4} + 2$$
$$t + \frac{1}{2} - \frac{1}{4}t < \frac{t}{4} + 2 - \frac{1}{4}t$$
$$\frac{3}{4}t + \frac{1}{2} < 2$$
$$\frac{3}{4}t + \frac{1}{2} - \frac{1}{2} < 2 - \frac{1}{2}$$
$$\frac{3}{4}t < \frac{3}{2}$$
$$\frac{4}{3}\left(\frac{3}{4}t\right) < \left(\frac{3}{2}\right)\frac{4}{3}$$
$$t < \frac{12}{6}, \text{ or } 2$$

27. $|x - 4| = 8$

Case 1

The quantity $x - 4$ is positive.
$$|x - 4| = 8$$
$$x - 4 = 8$$
$$x - 4 + 4 = 8 + 4$$
$$x = 12$$

Case 2

The quantity $x - 4$ is negative.
$$|x - 4| = 8$$
$$-(x - 4) = 8$$
$$-x + 4 = 8$$
$$-x + 4 - 4 = 8 - 4$$
$$-x = 4$$
$$-1(-x) = (4) - 1$$
$$x = -4$$

$x = 12$ or $x = -4$

28. $|3x + 2| = 8$

Case 1

The quantity $3x + 2$ is positive.
$$|3x + 2| = 8$$
$$3x + 2 = 8$$
$$3x = 6$$
$$x = 2$$

$x = 2$ or $x = -\frac{10}{3}$

Case 2

The quantity $3x + 2$ is negative.
$$|3x + 2| = 8$$
$$-(3x + 2) = 8$$
$$-3x - 2 = 8$$
$$-3x = 10$$
$$x = -\frac{10}{3}, \text{ or } -3\frac{1}{3}$$

29. $|x - 3| \leq 8$

Case 1

The quantity $x - 3$ is positive.
$$|1x - 3| \leq 8$$
$$x - 3 \leq 8$$
$$x - 3 + 3 \leq 8 + 3$$
$$x \leq 11$$

Case 2

The quantity $x - 3$ is negative.
$$|x - 3| \leq 8$$
$$-(x - 3) \leq 8$$
$$-x + 3 \leq 8$$
$$-x + 3 - 3 \leq 8 - 3$$
$$-x \leq 5$$
$$-1(-x) \leq (5)-1$$
$$x \geq -5$$

The inequality is true when $x \geq -5$ and when $x \leq 11$. We write this as $-5 \leq x \leq 11$.

30. $|x - 6| < 8$

Case 1

The quantity $x - 6$ is positive.
$$|x - 6| < 8$$
$$x - 6 < 8$$
$$x - 6 + 6 < 8 + 6$$
$$x < 14$$

Case 2

The quantity $x - 6$ is negative.
$$|x - 6| < 8$$
$$-(x - 6) < 8$$
$$-x + 6 < 8$$
$$-x + 6 - 6 < 8 - 6$$
$$-x < 2$$
$$-1(-x) > (2)-1$$
$$x > -2$$

The inequality is true when $x > -2$ and when $x < 14$. We write this as $-2 < x < 14$.

31.

	First solution	Second solution	New solution
Percent glucose	16% = 0.16	80% = 0.80	30% = 0.30
Amount of solution	20 oz	x	20 + x
Amount of glucose	0.16(20)	0.80x	0.30(20 + x)

$$0.16\,(20) + 0.80x = 0.30(20 + x)$$
$$3.2 + 0.80x = 6 + 0.30x$$
$$3.2 + 0.80x - 0.30x = 6 + 0.30x - 0.30x$$
$$3.2 + 0.50x = 6$$
$$3.2 + 0.50x - 3.2 = 6 - 3.2$$
$$0.50x = 2.8$$
$$\frac{0.50x}{0.50} = \frac{2.8}{0.50}$$
$$x = 5.6$$

5.6 ounces of the 80% solution should be added.

32. Let x represent the possible actual value of Mr. Greene's percent in the election.

$$|x - 51| \le 3.5$$

Case 1

$x - 51$ is positive
$$|x - 51| \le 3.5$$
$$x - 51 \le 3.5$$
$$x \le 54.5$$

Case 2

$x - 51$ is negative.
$$|x - 51| \le 3.5$$
$$-(x - 51) \le 3.5$$
$$-x + 51 \le 3.5$$
$$-x \le -47.5$$
$$x \ge 47.5$$

$$47.5 \le x \le 54.5$$

Yes, it is possible for Mr. Greene to lose the election because the actual percentage of votes he might receive can be less than 50%.

PAGE 425 CHAPTER 7 ASSESSMENT

1.
$$2x - 9 = 23$$
$$2x - 9 + 9 = 23 + 9$$
$$2x = 32$$
$$\frac{2x}{2} = \frac{32}{2}$$
$$x = 16$$

2.
$$53 = -7 + 2s$$
$$53 + 7 = -7 + 2s + 7$$
$$60 = 2s$$
$$\frac{60}{2} = \frac{2s}{2}$$
$$30 = s$$

3.
$$4(15 - 5r) = 90$$
$$60 - 20r = 90$$
$$60 - 20r - 60 = 90 - 60$$
$$-20r = 30$$
$$\frac{-20r}{-20} = \frac{30}{-20}$$
$$r = \frac{30}{-20}, \text{ or } -1\frac{10}{20}, \text{ or } -1\frac{1}{2}$$

4.
$$-16x + 3 = 37 + x$$
$$-16x + 3 + 16x = 37 + x + 16x$$
$$3 = 37 + 17x$$
$$3 - 37 = 37 + 17x - 37$$
$$-34 = 17x$$
$$\frac{-34}{17} = \frac{17x}{17}$$
$$-2 = x$$

5.
$$2\left(t + \frac{1}{4}\right) = 4t - 1$$
$$2t + \frac{1}{2} = 4t - 1$$
$$2t + \frac{1}{2} - 2t = 4t - 1 - 2t$$
$$\frac{1}{2} = 2t - 1$$
$$\frac{1}{2} + 1 = 2t - 1 + 1$$
$$\frac{3}{2} = 2t$$
$$\frac{1}{2}\left(\frac{3}{2}\right) = (2t)\frac{1}{2}$$
$$\frac{3}{4} = t$$

6.
$$1.1y - 8 = 0.5 + 0.25y$$
$$1.1y - 8 - 0.25y = 0.5 + 0.25y - 0.25y$$
$$0.85y - 8 = 0.5$$
$$0.85y - 8 + 8 = 0.5 + 8$$
$$0.85y = 8.5$$
$$\frac{0.85y}{0.85} = \frac{8.5}{0.85}$$
$$y = 10$$

7.
$$4v - 5(v - 2) = 6v - 46$$
$$4v - 5v + 10 = 6v - 46$$
$$-v + 10 = 6v - 46$$
$$-v + 10 + v = 6v - 46 + v$$
$$10 = 7v - 46$$
$$10 + 46 = 7v - 46 + 46$$
$$56 = 7v$$
$$\frac{56}{7} = \frac{7v}{7}$$
$$8 = v$$

8.
$$-2z + 4(z - 7) = 9z + 7(-2 + z)$$
$$-2z + 4z - 28 = 9z - 14 + 7z$$
$$2z - 28 = 16z - 14$$
$$2z - 28 - 2z = 16z - 14 - 2z$$
$$-28 = 14z - 14$$
$$-28 + 14 = 14z - 14 + 14$$
$$-14 = 14z$$
$$\frac{-14}{14} = \frac{14z}{14}$$
$$-1 = z$$

9. Let x represent the grade on the third test.
$$\frac{100 + 75 + x}{3} = 85$$
$$3\left(\frac{100 + 75 + x}{3}\right) = (85)3$$
$$100 + 75 + x = 255$$
$$175 + x = 255$$
$$175 + x - 175 = 255 - 175$$
$$x = 80$$
Alberto must receive a grade of 80.

10.
$$3x + (5x - 1) + (15 - x) = (4x + 4) + (2x - 2) + (8x - 10)$$
$$3x + 5x - x - 1 + 15 = 4x + 2x + 8x + 4 - 2 - 10$$
$$7x + 14 = 14x - 8$$
$$7x + 14 - 7x = 14x - 8 - 7x$$
$$14 = 7x - 8$$
$$14 + 8 = 7x - 8 + 8$$
$$22 = 7x$$
$$\frac{22}{7} = x$$
The value of x is $\frac{22}{7}$, or $3\frac{1}{7}$.

11. Using the value of x from Exercise 10, $x = \frac{22}{7}$. Substitute this value for x in either perimeter.

Let P_1 represent the perimeter of the triangle on the left, and let P_2 represent the perimeter of the triangle on the right. Since we know that the perimeters are equal, $P_1 = P_2$.
$$P_1 = 3x + (5x - 1) + (15 - x)$$
$$P_1 = 3x + 5x - x + 15 - 1$$
$$P_1 = 7x + 14$$
$$P_1 = 7\left(\frac{22}{7}\right) + 14$$
$$P_1 = \frac{154}{7} + 14$$
$$P_1 = 22 + 14$$
$$P_1 = 36$$
The perimeter of both triangles is 36 units.

12. Let x represent the number of games the team played last year. Then $x - 6$ represents the number of games played this year.
$$60\% \cdot (x - 6) = 50\% \cdot x$$
$$0.60(x - 6) = 0.50x$$
$$0.60x - 3.6 = 0.50x$$
$$0.60x - 3.6 - 0.50x = 0.50x - 0.50x$$
$$0.10x - 3.6 = 0$$
$$0.10x - 3.6 + 3.6 = 0 + 3.6$$
$$0.10x = 3.6$$
$$\frac{0.10x}{0.10} = \frac{3.6}{0.10}$$
$$x = 36$$
The baseball team played 36 games last year and $x - 6 = 36 - 6 = 30$ games this year.

13.
$$m\angle A + m\angle B + m\angle C = 180$$
$$5x + (3x + 11) + (29 - x) = 180$$
$$5x + 3x - x + 11 + 29 = 180$$
$$7x + 40 = 180$$
$$7x + 40 - 40 = 180 - 40$$
$$7x = 140$$
$$\frac{7x}{7} = \frac{140}{7}$$
$$x = 20$$
$m\angle A = 5x = 5(20) = 100°$
$m\angle B = 3x + 11 = 3(20) + 11 = 60 + 11 = 71°$
$m\angle C = 29 - x = 29 - 20 = 9°$

14.
$$m\angle A + m\angle B + m\angle C = 180$$
$$(2x - 10) + (5x - 100) + (x + 10) = 180$$
$$2x + 5x + x - 10 - 100 + 10 = 180$$
$$8x - 100 = 180$$
$$8x - 100 + 100 = 180 + 100$$
$$8x = 280$$
$$\frac{8x}{8} = \frac{280}{8}$$
$$x = 35$$
$m\angle A = 2x - 10 = 2(35) - 10 = 70 - 10 = 60°$
$m\angle B = 5x - 100 = 5(35) - 100 = 175 - 100 = 75°$
$m\angle C = x + 10 = 35 + 10 = 45°$

15.
$$m\angle A + m\angle B + m\angle C = 180$$
$$\left(\frac{x}{8} + 25\right) + \left(\frac{x}{2} + 80\right) + (90 - x) = 180$$
$$\frac{x}{8} + \frac{x}{2} - x + 25 + 80 + 90 = 180$$
$$-\frac{3}{8}x + 195 = 180$$
$$-\frac{3}{8}x + 195 - 195 = 180 - 195$$
$$-\frac{3}{8}x = -15$$
$$-\frac{8}{3}\left(-\frac{3}{8}x\right) = (-15)-\frac{8}{3}$$
$$x = \frac{120}{3}, \text{ or } 40$$

$m\angle A = \frac{x}{8} + 25 = \frac{40}{8} + 25 = 5 + 25 = 30°$

$m\angle B = \frac{x}{2} + 80 = \frac{40}{2} + 80 = 20 + 80 = 100°$

$m\angle C = 90 - x = 90 - 40 = 50°$

16. $s = mph$

$\dfrac{s}{ph} = \dfrac{mph}{ph}$

$\dfrac{s}{ph} = m$

17.

$A = \dfrac{x}{2}h(b_1 + b_2)$

$2A = 2\left[\dfrac{x}{2}h(b_1 + b_2)\right]$

$2A = xh(b_1 + b_2)$

$\dfrac{2A}{x} = \dfrac{xh(b_1 + b_2)}{x}$

$\dfrac{2A}{x} = h(b_1 + b_2)$

$\left(\dfrac{1}{b_1 + b_2}\right)\left(\dfrac{2A}{x}\right) = \left[h\,(b_1 + b_2)\right]\left(\dfrac{1}{b_1 + b_2}\right)$

$\dfrac{2A}{x\,(b_1 + b_2)} = h$

18. $x - 8 < 15$

$x - 8 + 8 < 15 + 8$

$x < 23$

19. $7 + y \geq 23$

$7 + y - 7 \geq 23 - 7$

$y \geq 16$

20. $4t \leq -16$

$\dfrac{4t}{4} \leq \dfrac{-16}{4}$

$t \leq -4$

21. $-5z > 45$

$\dfrac{-5z}{-5} < \dfrac{45}{-5}$

$z < -9$

22. $|x - 8| = 14$

Case 1

The quantity $x - 8$ is positive.

$|x - 8| = 14$

$x - 8 = 14$

$x - 8 + 8 = 14 + 8$

$x = 22$

Case 2

The quantity $x - 8$ is negative.

$|x - 8| = 14$

$-(x - 8) = 14$

$-x + 8 = 14$

$-x + 8 - 8 = 14 - 8$

$-x = 6$

$-1(-x) = (6)-1$

$x = -6$

$x = 22$ or $x = -6$

23. $|4x + 3| = 7$

Case 1

The quantity $4x + 3$ is positive.

$|4x + 3| = 7$

$4x + 3 = 7$

$4x + 3 - 3 = 7 - 3$

$4x = 4$

$\dfrac{4x}{4} = \dfrac{4}{4}$

$x = 1$

Case 2

The quantity $4x + 3$ is negative.

$|4x + 3| = 7$

$-(4x + 3) = 7$

$-4x - 3 = 7$

$-4x - 3 + 3 = 7 + 3$

$-4x = 10$

$\dfrac{-4x}{-4} = \dfrac{10}{-4}$

$x = \dfrac{-10}{4}$, or $-2\dfrac{2}{4}$, or $-2\dfrac{1}{2}$

$x = 1$ or $x = -2\dfrac{1}{2}$

24. $|x - 6| \leq 17$

Case 1

The quantity $x - 6$ is positive.

$|x - 6| \leq 17$

$x - 6 \leq 17$

$x - 6 + 6 \leq 17 + 6$

$x \leq 23$

Case 2

The quantity $x - 6$ is negative.

$|x - 6| \leq 17$

$-(x - 6) \leq 17$

$-x + 6 \leq 17$

$-x + 6 + 6 \leq 17 - 6$

$-x \leq 11$

$-1(-x) \geq (11)-1$

$x \geq -11$

The inequality is true when $x \leq 23$ and when $x \geq -11$. We write this as $-11 \leq x \leq 23$.

25. $x + 2 > 4$

Case 1

The quantity $x + 2$ is positive.

$|x + 2| > 4$

$x + 2 > 4$

$x + 2 - 2 > 4 - 2$

$x > 2$

Case 2

The quantity $x + 2$ is negative.

$|x + 2| > 4$

$-(x + 2) > 4$

$-x - 2 > 4$

$-x - 2 + 2 > 4 + 2$

$-x > 6$

$-1(-x) > (6)-1$

$x < -6$

The inequality is true when $x > 2$ or when $x < -6$.

26. $A = \dfrac{1}{2}bh$

$336 = \left(\dfrac{1}{2}\right)(24)h$

$336 = 12h$

$\dfrac{336}{12} = \dfrac{12h}{12}$

$28 = h$

The height of the triangle is 28 centimeters.

CHAPTER 8

LINEAR FUNCTIONS

7. The points lie on a straight line.

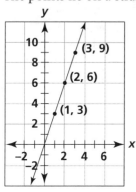

8. The points do not lie on a straight line.

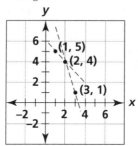

9. The points do not lie on a straight line.

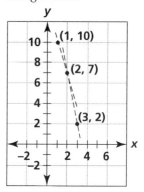

10. The points lie on a straight line.

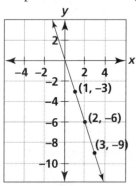

11. The points lie on a straight line.

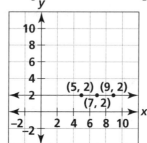

12. The points lie on a straight line.

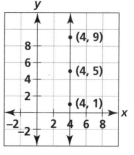

13. A(0, 7)

14. B(7, 7)

15. C(5, 4)

16. D(6, 0)

For Exercises 17–18, substitute values for *x* and *y*. Plot the points or use a calculator to graph each function. Points may vary.

17–18.

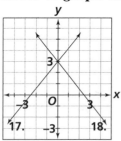

When there is a plus sign in front of *x*, the line goes up from left to right. When there is a minus sign in front of *x*, the line goes down from the left to right.

For Exercises 19–22 substitute values for *x* and *y*. Plot the points or use a calculator to graph each function. Points may vary.

19–22.

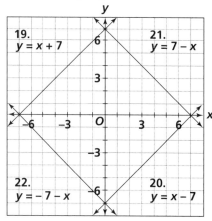

19.
$y = x + 7$

21.
$y = 7 - x$

22.
$y = -7 - x$

20.
$y = x - 7$

They are all linear functions. The lines $y = x + 7$ and $y = x - 7$ are parallel to each other. The lines $y = 7 - x$ and $y = -7 - x$ are parallel to each other. The lines $y = x + 7$ and $y = x - 7$ appear to be perpendicular to the lines $y = 7 - x$ and $y = -7 - x$.

For Exercises 23–26, substitute values for *x* and solve for *y*.

23.

x	$x + 3$	y
1	$1 + 3$	4
2	$2 + 3$	5
3	$3 + 3$	6
4	$4 + 3$	7
5	$5 + 3$	8

24.

x	$x + 4$	y
1	$1 + 4$	5
2	$2 + 4$	6
3	$3 + 4$	7
4	$4 + 4$	8
5	$5 + 4$	9

25.

x	$2x$	y
1	$2 \cdot 1$	2
2	$2 \cdot 2$	4
3	$2 \cdot 3$	6
4	$2 \cdot 4$	8
5	$2 \cdot 5$	10

26.

x	$2x + 5$	y
1	$2 \cdot 1 + 5$	7
2	$2 \cdot 2 + 5$	9
3	$2 \cdot 3 + 5$	11
4	$2 \cdot 4 + 5$	13
5	$2 \cdot 5 + 5$	15

27. $d = 3h$

28.

h	$3h$	d
0	$3 \cdot 0$	0
1	$3 \cdot 1$	3
2	$3 \cdot 2$	6
3	$3 \cdot 3$	9

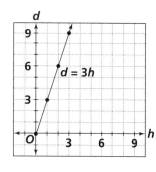

29. Since we do not measure negative time, a reasonable domain would be $h \geq 0$. Likewise, since we do not measure negative distances, a reasonable range would be $d \geq 0$.

30. The dependent variable is *d*, and the independent variable is *h*. The distance traveled depends on the length of time that Don walks.

31. Cost = $8x + 3$
   $= 8(2) + 3$
   $= 16 + 3$
   $= 19$
An order for 2 T-shirts costs $19.

32. Cost = $8x + 3$
   $= 8(5) + 3$
   $= 40 + 3$
   $= 43$
An order for 5 T-shirts costs $43.

33.

x	$8x + 3$	y
1	$8(1)+ 3$	11
2	$8(2)+ 3$	19
5	$8(5)+ 3$	43

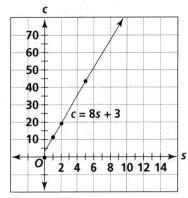

The points do lie on a straight line.

34. We cannot order negative amounts of shirts, so a reasonable domain is $x \geq 0$. Therefore, the resulting range for cost is $y \geq 0$.

PAGE 433, LOOK BACK

35.

Sequence	1		1		4		10		19		[31]		[46]		[64]
First differences		0		3		6		9		[12]		[15]		[18]	
Second differences			3		3		3		3		3		3		

The next three terms are 31, 46, and 64.

36. $2 \cdot 14 \div 2 + 5 = 28 \div 2 + 5$
$\qquad\qquad\qquad = 14 + 5$
$\qquad\qquad\qquad = 19$

37. $6 + 12 \div 6 - 4 = 6 + 2 - 4$
$\qquad\qquad\qquad = 8 - 4$
$\qquad\qquad\qquad = 4$

38. $4[(12 - 3) \cdot 2] \div 11 = 4[9 \cdot 2] \div 11$
$\qquad\qquad\qquad\qquad = 4(18) \div 11$
$\qquad\qquad\qquad\qquad = 72 \div 11$
$\qquad\qquad\qquad\qquad = \frac{72}{11}, \text{ or } 6\frac{6}{11}$

39. $[3(4) - 6] - [(15 - 7) \div 4] = (12 - 6) - (8 \div 4)$
$\qquad\qquad\qquad\qquad\qquad = 6 - 2$
$\qquad\qquad\qquad\qquad\qquad = 4$

40.

Sequence	1		2		6		15		31
First differences		1		4		9		16	
Second differences			3		5		7		
Third differences				2		2			

Three differences are needed to reach the constant difference of 2.

41.

Sequence	1		1		2		3		5		8
First differences		0		1		1		2		3	
Second differences			1		0		1		1		

The next two terms of the sequence are 13 and 21. The first differences are the same as the Fibonacci sequence. The pattern is adding the previous two terms.

42. Try $x = 4$.
$\qquad 3x + 406 = 421$
$\qquad 3(4) + 406 \overset{?}{=} 421$
$\qquad\qquad\quad 418 = 421 \quad$ False
Try $x = 5$.
$\qquad 3x + 406 = 421$
$\qquad 3(5) + 406 \overset{?}{=} 421$
$\qquad\qquad\quad 421 = 421 \quad$ True
The solution is $x = 5$.

43. Substitute values for x. Values may vary.

x	$7x + 4$	y
4	$7(4) + 4$	32
5	$7(5) + 4$	39
6	$7(6) + 4$	46

The solution is a number between 5 and 6.
Try $5\frac{1}{7}$.
$7\left(5\frac{1}{7}\right) + 4 = 40$
$7\left(\frac{36}{7}\right) + 4 = 40$
$\qquad\quad 36 + 4 = 40$
$\qquad\qquad\quad 40 = 40 \quad$ True
The solution is $x = 5\frac{1}{7}$.

44.

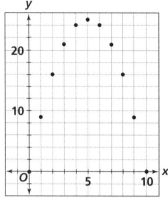

The vertex is (5, 25).

8.2 **PAGES 438–441, PRACTICE & APPLY**

7. positive (slope is up and to the right)

8. neither (the line slopes neither up nor down)

9. negative (slope is down and to the right)

10. Answers may vary. Draw a line to represent a steep ski slope. Calculate the slope. Draw a line to calculate a slightly sloping beginner's slope. Calculate the slope. Study the following graphs for examples.

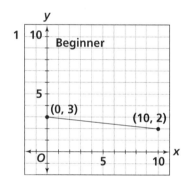

$$\text{slope} = \frac{2-3}{10-0} = -\frac{1}{10}$$

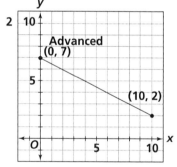

$$\text{slope} = \frac{2-7}{10-0} = -\frac{5}{10} \text{ or } -\frac{1}{2}$$

11. $\text{slope} = \frac{\text{rise}}{\text{run}} = \frac{6}{2} = 3$

12. $\text{slope} = \frac{\text{rise}}{\text{run}} = \frac{1}{7}$

13. $\text{slope} = \frac{\text{rise}}{\text{run}} = -\frac{1}{7}$

14. $\text{slope} = \frac{\text{rise}}{\text{run}} = \frac{0}{5} = 0$

15. $\text{slope} = \frac{\text{rise}}{\text{run}} = \frac{5-3}{-3-1} = \frac{2}{-4} = -\frac{1}{2}$

16. $\text{slope} = \frac{\text{rise}}{\text{run}} = \frac{-7+2}{3-1} = -\frac{5}{2}$

17. Answers may vary. A sample answer is shown.

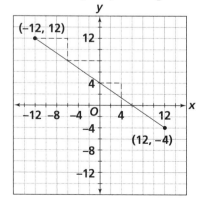

$$\text{slope} = \frac{-4-12}{12-(-12)}$$
$$= \frac{-16}{24}$$
$$= -\frac{2}{3}$$

The shape is a line with a slope of $-\frac{2}{3}$.

18.

Difference in x	$2-1=1$	$3-2=1$	$4-3=1$	$8-4=4$
Difference in y	$6-3=3$	$9-6=3$	$12-9=3$	$24-12=12$

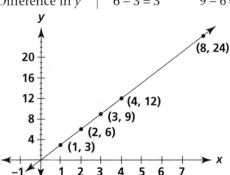

$$\text{Slope} = \frac{\text{rise}}{\text{run}} = \frac{6}{12} = 3$$

$$\text{slope} = \frac{\text{difference in } y}{\text{difference in } x} = \frac{6}{2} = \frac{9}{3} = \frac{12}{4} = \frac{24}{8} = 3$$

The slope can be found by using any corresponding set of points on the line.

19. Answers may vary. The slope of the roof for the house in the picture is about 0.5. The angle is about 26°.

20. distance traveled = 140 miles

$$\text{rate} = \frac{\text{distance}}{\text{time}} = \frac{140}{10} = 14 \text{ miles per hour}$$

21. distance traveled = 240 miles

$$\text{rate} = \frac{\text{distance}}{\text{time}} = \frac{240}{4} = 60 \text{ miles per hour}$$

22. distance traveled = 160 miles

rate from 0–2 hours: $\dfrac{\text{distance}}{\text{time}} = \dfrac{80}{2} = 40$ miles per hour

rate from 3–5 hours: $\dfrac{\text{distance}}{\text{time}} = \dfrac{80}{2} = 40$ miles per hour

23. From the graph, the distance from Jarel's house to his grandmother's house is 15 miles.

24. Yes; Jarel stopped and rested 70 minutes after leaving his grandmother's house. He rested for 30 minutes before continuing his journey.

25. Jarel traveled at 3 different rates.

Rate 1 $= \dfrac{\text{distance}}{\text{time}} = \dfrac{15-5}{70-0} = \dfrac{10}{70} = \dfrac{1}{7}$, or 1 mile every 7 minutes

Rate 2 $= \dfrac{\text{distance}}{\text{time}} = \dfrac{5-5}{100-70} = \dfrac{0}{30} = 0$ miles per minute

Rate 3 $= \dfrac{\text{distance}}{\text{time}} = \dfrac{5-0}{160-100} = \dfrac{5}{60} = \dfrac{1}{12}$, or 1 mile over 12 minutes

26. From the graph, Jarel took 160 minutes, or 2 hours and 40 minutes, to get home.

27. amount climbed per mile $= \dfrac{\text{rise}}{\text{run}} = \dfrac{5280-744}{600-0}$

$$= \dfrac{4536}{600} = 7\dfrac{14}{25} = 7.56$$

You climb 7.56 feet per mile.

28. Average slope of the land $= \dfrac{\text{rise}}{\text{run}} = \dfrac{12{,}992-5280}{70} = \dfrac{7712}{70} = \dfrac{3856}{35}$, or $110\dfrac{6}{35} \approx 110.17$

The average slope of the land is approximately 110.17 feet per mile.

29. slope $= \dfrac{\text{rise}}{\text{run}} = \dfrac{27}{25} = 1.08$

30. slope $= \dfrac{\text{rise}}{\text{run}} = \dfrac{29.7}{27.5} = 1.08$

The slope of the average step is the same as the slope of the pyramid.

31. slope $= \dfrac{\text{rise}}{\text{run}} = \dfrac{1}{2}$

32. slope $= \dfrac{\text{rise}}{\text{run}} = \dfrac{2}{-1} = -2$

33. slope $\dfrac{\text{rise}}{\text{run}} = \dfrac{-2}{2} = -1$

34. slope $= \dfrac{\text{rise}}{\text{run}} = \dfrac{3}{1} = 3$

35. slope $= \dfrac{\text{rise}}{\text{run}} = \dfrac{1}{3}$

36. slope $= \dfrac{\text{rise}}{\text{run}} = -\dfrac{3}{4}$

37. slope $= 0$

38. The slope is undefined.

39. slope $= \dfrac{\text{rise}}{\text{run}} = \dfrac{3}{2}$

40. slope $= \dfrac{\text{rise}}{\text{run}}$

$$= \dfrac{4-6}{1-9}$$

$$= \dfrac{-2}{-8} = \dfrac{1}{4}$$

41. slope $= \dfrac{\text{rise}}{\text{run}}$

$$= \dfrac{5-3}{1-1} = \dfrac{2}{0}$$

The slope is undefined.

42. slope $= \dfrac{\text{rise}}{\text{run}}$

$$= \dfrac{6-1}{2-(-3)}$$

$$= \dfrac{5}{5} = 1$$

43. slope $= \dfrac{\text{rise}}{\text{run}}$

$$= \dfrac{0-2}{3-0}$$

$$= -\dfrac{2}{3}$$

44. slope $= \dfrac{\text{rise}}{\text{run}}$

$$= \dfrac{6-5}{7-(-3)}$$

$$= \dfrac{1}{10}$$

45. slope $= \dfrac{\text{rise}}{\text{run}}$

$$= \dfrac{9-(-4)}{5-2}$$

$$= \dfrac{13}{3}$$

46. slope $= \dfrac{\text{rise}}{\text{run}}$

$$= \dfrac{7.2-8.9}{9.1-3.2}$$

$$= -\dfrac{1.7}{5.9}$$

$$\dfrac{-1.7}{5.9} \times \dfrac{10}{10} = -\dfrac{17}{59}$$

47. slope $= \dfrac{\text{rise}}{\text{run}}$

$= \dfrac{7 - 10}{8 - 8}$

$= -\dfrac{3}{0}$

The slope is undefined.

48. slope $= \dfrac{\text{rise}}{\text{run}}$

$= \dfrac{4 - 4}{7 - 10}$

$= \dfrac{0}{-3} = 0$

49. From the graph, there were 100 gallons of water in the tank when the pump was turned on.

50. From the graph, the pump was on for 10 minutes.

51. rate $= \dfrac{\text{number of gallons}}{\text{time}} = \dfrac{450 - 100}{10} = \dfrac{350}{10} = 35$

The water was pumped at a rate of 35 gallons per minute.

52. Answers may vary.
The points should fit the line very closely. The slope of the line should be between 3.1 and 3.2. This ratio of circumference to diameter is near $3.14 \approx \pi$.

PAGE 441, LOOK BACK

53. $|-7| = 7$

54. $|50| = 50$

55. $-|-9| = -9$

56. $-|99| = -99$

57. Let x represent the amount each person would have to contribute.

$8x = 98$

$\dfrac{8x}{8} = \dfrac{98}{8}$

$x = 12.25$

Each person would have to contribute \$12.25.

58.
$3x + 16 = 19$
$3x + 16 - 16 = 19 - 16$
$3x = 3$
$\dfrac{3x}{3} = \dfrac{3}{3}$
$x = 1$

59.
$28 = -4 + 4x$
$28 + 4 = -4 + 4 + 4x$
$32 = 4x$
$\dfrac{32}{4} = \dfrac{4x}{4}$
$8 = x$

60.
$2x - 7 = 4x - 9$
$2x - 7 - 2x = 4x - 9 - 2x$
$-7 = 2x - 9$
$-7 + 9 = 2x - 9 + 9$
$2 = 2x$
$\dfrac{2}{2} = \dfrac{2x}{2}$
$1 = x$

61.
$7(x - 1) = 2(3 - 3x)$
$7x - 7 = 6 - 6x$
$7x + 6x - 7 = 6 - 6x + 6x$
$13x - 7 = 6$
$13x - 7 + 7 = 6 + 7$
$13x = 13$
$\dfrac{13x}{13} = \dfrac{13}{13}$
$x = 1$

62.
$\dfrac{2}{5} + x = \dfrac{1}{3} - 4x$
$\dfrac{2}{5} + x + 4x = \dfrac{1}{3} - 4x + 4x$
$\dfrac{2}{5} + 5x = \dfrac{1}{3}$
$\dfrac{2}{5} + 5x - \dfrac{2}{5} = \dfrac{1}{3} - \dfrac{2}{5}$
$5x = \dfrac{5}{15} - \dfrac{6}{15}$
$5x = -\dfrac{1}{15}$
$\dfrac{1}{5}(5x) = \left(-\dfrac{1}{15}\right)\dfrac{1}{5}$
$x = -\dfrac{1}{75}$

63.
$2x - (x + 3) = 3x - 4$
$2x - x - 3 = 3x - 4$
$x - 3 = 3x - 4$
$x - 3 - x = 3x - 4 - x$
$-3 = 2x - 4$
$-3 + 4 = 2x - 4 + 4$
$1 = 2x$
$\dfrac{1}{2} = \dfrac{2x}{2}$
$\dfrac{1}{2} = x$

64.
$2m + n = 10$
$2m + n - 2m = 10 - 2m$
$n = 10 - 2m$

65.
$3q - p = 4$
$3q - p - 3q = 4 - 3q$
$-p = 4 - 3q$
$-1(-p) = (4 - 3q)-1$
$p = -4 + 3q$
$p = 3q - 4$

66. Graph $y = 4x - 2$. Substitute values for x and solve for y. Points may vary.

x	0	1	2	3
y	−2	2	6	10

$m = \dfrac{10 - 6}{3 - 2} = 4$

Graph $y = 4x + 3$. Substitute values for x and solve for y. Points may vary.

x	0	1	2	3
y	3	7	11	15

$m = \dfrac{15 - 11}{3 - 2} = 4$

Graph $y = 4x$. Substitute values for x and solve for y. Points may vary.

x	0	1	2	3
y	0	4	8	12

$m = \dfrac{12 - 8}{3 - 2} = 4$

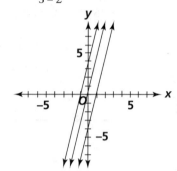

The lines are parallel; they have the same slope, but they cross the y-axis at different points.

67. Answers may vary. The curve goes up and to the right. It rises faster as it moves right.

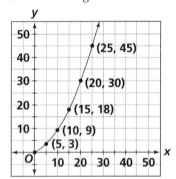

8.

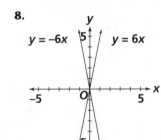

Both lines have y-intercepts at $(0, 0)$. They have the same steepness, but one has a positive slope and the other has a negative slope.

9.

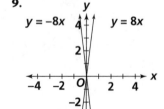

Both lines have y-intercepts at $(0, 0)$. They have the same steepness, but one has a positive slope and the other has a negative slope.

10.

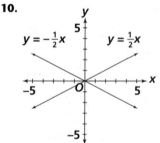

Both lines have y-intercepts at $(0, 0)$. They have the same steepness, but one has a positive slope and the other has a negative slope.

11.

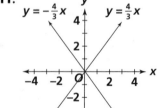

Both lines have y-intercepts at $(0, 0)$. They have the same steepness, but one has a positive slope and the other has a negative slope.

12.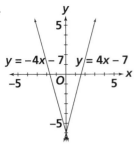

Both lines have y-intercepts at $(0, -7)$. They have the same steepness, but one has a positive slope and the other has a negative slope.

13.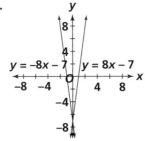

Both lines have y-intercepts at $(0, -7)$. They have the same steepness, but one has a positive slope and the other has a negative slope.

14. The line $y = -mx$ has a slope that is opposite the slope of the line $y = mx$, but the y-intercept is the same.

15. $M = w + 30$

16. $m = \dfrac{5 - 0}{2 - 0} = \dfrac{5}{2}$

The equation is $y = \dfrac{5}{2}x$.

17. $m = \dfrac{8 - 0}{5 - 0}$

$m = \dfrac{8}{5}$

The equation is $y = \dfrac{8}{5}x$.

18. $m = \dfrac{9 - 0}{1 - 0}$

$m = \dfrac{9}{1}$

The equation is $y = 9x$.

19. $m = \dfrac{2 - 0}{4 - 0}$

$m = \dfrac{2}{4}$ or $\dfrac{1}{2}$

The equation is $y = \dfrac{1}{2}x$.

20. $m = \dfrac{3 - 0}{7 - 0}$

$m = \dfrac{3}{7}$

The equation is $y = \dfrac{3}{7}x$.

21.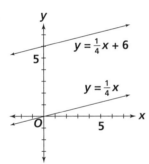

The lines are parallel, and both have a slope of $\dfrac{1}{4}$. They cross the y-axis at different points: $(0, 0)$ and $(0, 6)$.

22.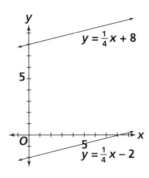

The lines are parallel, and both have a slope of $\dfrac{1}{4}$. They cross the y-axis at different points: $(0, 8)$ and $0, -2)$.

23. The value of b is where the line crosses the y-axis. The lines are parallel; they have the same slope but different y-intercepts.

24. $l = 0.8d + 32$

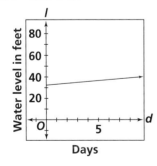

25. $l = 34 - 0.5d$

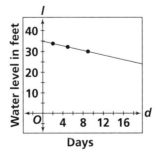

The rate of change is -0.5 feet/day.
The water level will be 26 feet after 16 days.

26. slope -5, crosses the y-axis at 0

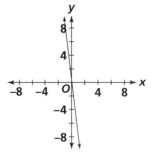

27. slope –6, crosses the y-axis at 3

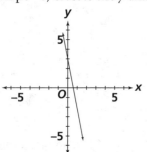

28. horizontal line at $y = 7$

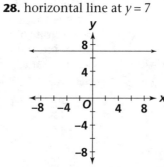

29. horizontal line at $y = -6$

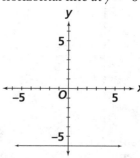

30. slope –5, crosses y-axis at –1

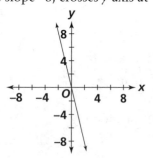

31. horizontal line at $y = -2$

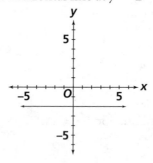

32. slope –1, crosses y-axis at –3

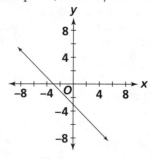

33. slope 2, crosses y-axis at 3

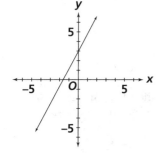

34. slope 3, crosses y-axis at 7

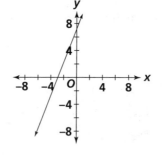

35. slope –1, crosses y-axis at 7

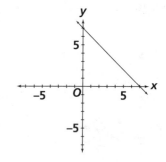

36. slope $\frac{1}{2}$, crosses y-axis at –3

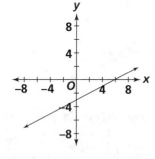

37. slope 1, crosses y-axis at 4

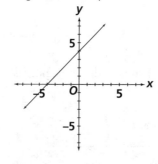

38. (1) slope $= \dfrac{250 \text{ cubits}}{180 \text{ cubits}} \approx 1.4$

(2) slope $= \dfrac{429 \text{ feet}}{309 \text{ feet}} \approx 1.4$

(3) The slope is approximately the same using either measuring unit.

PAGE 449, LOOK BACK

---

39. Earnings = $8 × number of hours worked

$$E = 8n$$
$$= 8 \times 33$$
$$= 264$$

Calvin's earnings for 33 hours would be $264.

40. For each box sold Dan earns 15% of $20.

$$15\% \times 20 = 3$$
$$\frac{100}{3} = 33\frac{1}{3}$$

To earn at least $100, Dan needs to sell 34 boxes.

41. $3x + 4y = 24$

$$4y = -3x + 24$$
$$\frac{4y}{4} = \frac{-3x + 24}{4}$$
$$y = -\frac{3}{4}x + 6$$

42. $w = \frac{1}{2}n + 3$

$$51 = \frac{1}{2}n + 3$$
$$48 = \frac{1}{2}n$$
$$96 = n$$

There are 96 oranges in the carton.

43. neither   **44.** negative   **45.** positive   **46.** seked $= \frac{180}{250}$

slope $= \frac{\text{rise}}{\text{run}} = \frac{250}{180}$
The seked is the reciprocal of the slope.

PAGE 449, LOOK BEYOND

47. No; the lines have the same slope, $\frac{1}{2}$, but different y-intercepts. They are parallel.

8.4 **PAGES 456-458, PRACTICE & APPLY**

For Exercises 8–10, use the differences shown.

x	0	2	4	6	8	10
y	4	10	16	22	28	34

Find the first differences of the y-values.

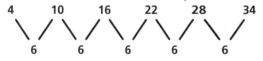

Find the first differences of the x-values.

The first differences of the y-values are constant, 6. The first differences of the x-values are constant, 2.

8. $m = \dfrac{y\text{-value differences}}{x\text{-value differences}} = \dfrac{6}{2} = 3$

9. 4; when the x-coordinate of a point is 0, the point is on the y-axis. The line crosses the y-axis at (0, 4).

10. Since the slope is 3 and the line crosses the y-axis at 4, $y = mx + b$ can be written as $y = 3x + 4$.

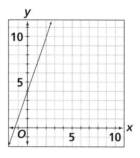

11. (0, 5)   **12.** (0, −1)   **13.** (0, 7)   **14.** (0, −9)   **15.** line k **16.** line n

17. $\dfrac{\text{difference in } y}{\text{difference in } x} = \dfrac{6 - 0}{0 - 5} = \dfrac{6}{-5} = -\dfrac{6}{5}$

18. $\dfrac{\text{difference in } y}{\text{difference in } x} = \dfrac{4 - (-2)}{3 - (-1)} = \dfrac{6}{4} = \dfrac{3}{2}$

19. $\dfrac{\text{difference in } y}{\text{difference in } x} = \dfrac{7 - 3}{1 - 5} = \dfrac{4}{-4} = -1$

20. $\dfrac{\text{difference in } y}{\text{difference in } x} = \dfrac{2 - (-2)}{7} - (-4) = \dfrac{4}{11}$

21. $\dfrac{\text{difference in } y}{\text{difference in } x} = \dfrac{0 - (-4)}{-5 - 8} = \dfrac{4}{-13} = -\dfrac{4}{13}$

22. $\dfrac{\text{difference in } y}{\text{difference in } x} = \dfrac{-7 - (-3)}{7 - (-4)} = \dfrac{-4}{11} = -\dfrac{4}{11}$

23. $\dfrac{\text{difference in } y}{\text{difference in } x} = \dfrac{-3 - (-6)}{-4 - (-2)} = \dfrac{3}{-2} = -\dfrac{3}{2}$

24. $\dfrac{\text{difference in } y}{\text{difference in } x} = \dfrac{6 - (-2)}{6 - (-2)} = \dfrac{8}{8} = 1$

25. $\dfrac{\text{difference in } y}{\text{difference in } x} = \dfrac{1 - (-7)}{-1 - 5} = \dfrac{8}{-6} = -\dfrac{4}{3}$

26. $y = mx + b$
$y = -x$

27. $y = mx + b$
$y = -4x - 4$

28. $y = mx + b$
$y = 11x + 15$

29. $y = mx + b$
$y = -5x + 7$

30. $y = mx + b$
$y = x + 5$

31. $y = mx + b$
$y = -3x - 1$

32. $y = mx + b$
$y = 3x + 3$

33. $y = mx + b$
$y = \dfrac{2}{3}x + 2$

For Exercises 34–39, find the slope for each line. Write $y = mx + b$, substitute values for the slope, and choose x- and y-values from one of the given points.

34. $m = \dfrac{0-3}{-1-0} = \dfrac{-3}{-1} = 3$

In $y = 3x + b$, substitute $x = -1$ and $y = 0$.

$y = 3x + b$

$0 = 3(-1) + b$

$3 = b$

The equation is $y = 3x + 3$.

35. $ml = \dfrac{9-(-2)}{7-3} = \dfrac{11}{4}$

In $y = \dfrac{11}{4}x + b$, substitute $x = 3$ and $y = -2$.

$y = \dfrac{11}{4}x + b$

$-2 = \dfrac{11}{4}(3) + b$

$-2 - \dfrac{33}{4} = b$

$-\dfrac{41}{4} = b$

Substitute $\dfrac{11}{4}$ for x and $-\dfrac{41}{4}$ for b in $y = mx + b$.

The equation is $y = \dfrac{11}{4}x - \dfrac{41}{4}$.

36. $m = \dfrac{5-(-2)}{4-(-1)} = \dfrac{7}{5}$

In $y = \dfrac{7}{5}x + b$, substitute $x = -1$ and $y = -2$.

$y = \dfrac{7}{5}x + b$

$-2 = \dfrac{7}{5}(-1) + b$

$-2 + \dfrac{7}{5} = b$

$-\dfrac{3}{5} = b$

The equation is $y = \dfrac{7}{5}x - \dfrac{3}{5}$.

37. $m = \dfrac{3-(-6)}{3-(-2)} = \dfrac{9}{5}$

In $y = \dfrac{9}{5}x + b$, substitute $x = 3$ and $y = 3$.

$y = \dfrac{9}{5}x + b$

$3 = \dfrac{9}{5}(3)$

$3 - \dfrac{27}{5} = b$

$-\dfrac{12}{5} = b$

The equation is $y = \dfrac{9}{5}x - \dfrac{12}{5}$.

38. $m = \dfrac{-3-(-2)}{-8-6} = \dfrac{-1}{-14} = \dfrac{1}{14}$

In $y = \dfrac{1}{14}x + b$, substitute $x = 6$ and $y = -2$.

$y = \dfrac{1}{14}x + b$

$-2 = \dfrac{1}{14}(6) + b$

$-2 - \dfrac{3}{7} = b$

$-\dfrac{17}{7} = b$

The equation is $y = \dfrac{1}{14}x - \dfrac{17}{7}$.

39. $m = \dfrac{-4-(-5)}{-1-(-3)} = \dfrac{1}{2}$

In $y = \dfrac{1}{2}x + b$, substitute $x = -1$ and $y = -4$.

$y = \dfrac{1}{2}x + b$

$-4 = \dfrac{1}{2}(-1) + b$

$-4 + \dfrac{1}{2} = b$

$-\dfrac{7}{2} = b$

The equation is $y = \dfrac{1}{2}x - \dfrac{7}{2}$.

40. $c = 0.50p + 2$; this is a linear equation written in slope-intercept form.

41. Find the slope from the given points.

$m = \dfrac{4-1}{0-(-1)} = \dfrac{3}{1} = 3$

Since the line crosses the y-axis at $(0, 4)$, the y-intercept, b, is 4.

$y = mx + b$

$y = 3x + 4$

42. Find the slope from the given points.

$m = \dfrac{-3-(-7)}{0-4} = \dfrac{4}{-4} = -1$

Since the line crosses the y-axis at $(0, -3)$, the y-intercept, b, is -3.

$y = mx + b$

$y = -x - 3$

43. Let x represent the number of animals Josh sells, and let y represent the profit. Then, $y = 6.50x - 43.80$.

44. Make a table to find how many figures Josh must sell for his income to be more than his cost.

6.50
13.00
19.50
26.00
32.50
39.00
45.50
45.50 > 43.80

Josh will need to sell 7 figures in order for his income to be more than the cost of materials.

45.

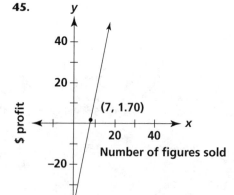

46. $\dfrac{d}{t} = k$, where d represents distance, and t represents time

$\dfrac{d}{t} = 65$

$\dfrac{d}{3} = 65$

$d = 3(65)$

$d = 195$

After 3 hr the car had traveled 195 mi.

47. Answers may vary. Use a spring scale and a rubber band to measure the force required to stretch a rubber band; record the amount of force and the length of the rubber band in two tables.

The first list, L1, is measured in newtons (N).
The second list, L2, is measured in millimeters (mm).

The force in newtons is the independent variable, while the amount of stretch is the dependent variable. For example:

Weight in newtons	Length in millimeters
0	10
1	12
2	15.5
3	21
4	27

Line of best fit: $y = 4.3x + 8.5$

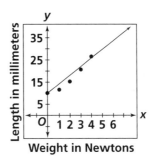

Weight in Newtons

48. $\dfrac{V}{h} = k$

$\dfrac{27}{3} = k$

$9 = k$

When $h = 12$, $\dfrac{V}{12} = 9$.

$V = 12(9) = 108$

When the height is 12 centimeters, the volume is 108 cubic centimeters.

PAGE 458, LOOK BACK

49.

Year	Population
0	12,345
1	13,023
2	13,701
3	14,379
4	15,057
5	15,735
6	16,413
7	17,091
8	17,769
9	18,447
10	19,125
11	19,803
12	20,481

It takes between 11 and 12 years to reach 20,000 people.

50. $p = 678y + 12{,}345$

51.

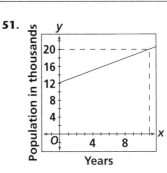

Years

The population will reach 20,000 in approximately 11 years.

52. $(3a - 2) + (2a - 2) = 5a - 4$

53. $(4x + 3y) - (3x - 2y) = 4x + 3y - 3x + 2y$
$= x + 5y$

54. $x + 7 \le -2$
$x \le -9$

55. $x - 4 \ge 6$
$x \ge 10$

56. $x - 5 < 21$
$x < 26$

PAGE 458, LOOK BEYOND

57. If the line is horizontal, the rise is 0.

58. If the line is vertical, the run is 0. The slope is undefined.

8.5 | PAGES 464–465, PRACTICE & APPLY

For Exercises 7–14, write equations in the form Ax + By = C.

7. $4x = -3y + 24$
$4x + 3y = 24$

8. $7y = -5x - 35$
$5x + 7y = -35$

9. $6x + 4y + 12 = 0$
$6x + 4y = -12$

10. $2x = 4y$
$2x - 4y = 0$

11. $6x - 8 = 2y + 6$
$6x - 2y = 14$

12. $x = \frac{2}{3}y + 6$
$x - \frac{2}{3}y = 6$
$3x - 2y = 18$

13. $2 + 7x + 14y = 3x - 10$
$7x - 3x + 14y = -10 - 2$
$4x + 14y = -12$

14. $5 = y - x$
$x - y = -5$

For Exercises 15–18, substitute 0 for x and then solve for y to find the x-intercept. Substitute 0 for y and then solve for x to find the y-intercept.

15. $x + y = 10$

For the y-intercept, substitute $x = 0$.
$0 + y = 10$
$y = 10$
The y-intercept is (0, 10).

For the x-intercept, substitute $y = 0$.
$x + 0 = 10$
$x = 10$
The x-intercept is (10, 0).

16. $3x - 2y = 12$

For the y-intercept, substitute $x = 0$.
$3(0) - 2y = 12$
$y = -6$
The y-intercept is (0, –6).

For the x-intercept, substitute $y = 0$.
$3x - 2(0) = 12$
$3x = 12$
$x = 4$
The x-intercept is (4, 0).

17. $5x + 4y = 20$

For the y-intercept, substitute $x = 0$.
$5(0) + 4y = 20$
$4y = 20$
$y = 5$
The y-intercept is (0, 5).

For the x-intercept, substitute $y = 0$.
$5x + 4(0) = 20$
$5x = 20$
$x = 4$
The x-intercept is (4, 0).

18. $x = 2y$

For the x-intercept, substitute $x = 0$.
$0 = 2y$
$0 = y$
The x- and y-intercepts are the same.

19.

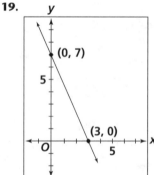

20. $2x + 6y = 18$

Substitute $x = 0$.
$2(0) + 6y = 18$
$y = 3$
The y-intercept is (0, 3).
Substitute $y = 0$.
$2x = 18$
$x = 9$

The x-intercept is (9, 0).

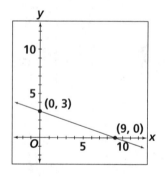

21. $6x + 2y - 6x = 40$
$2y = -6x + 40$
$y = -\frac{6}{2}x + \frac{40}{2}$
$y = -3x + 20$

The slope is –3.

22. $4a + 2s = 588$
intercepts: (0, 294), (147, 0)
$2a + s = 294$
intercepts: (0, 294), (147, 0)
These equations describe the same line.

23. Substitute 50 for y.
$$4x + 2y = 588$$
$$4x + 2(50) = 588$$
$$4x + 100 = 588$$
$$4x + 100 - 100 = 588 - 100$$
$$4x = 488$$
$$\frac{4x}{4} = \frac{488}{4}$$
$$x = 122$$
122 adult tickets must be sold.

24. Substitute values in the point-slope formula.
$$y - y_1 = m(x - x_1)$$
$$y - 2 = -8(x - 5)$$
$$y = -8x + 42$$

25. Use the points $(7, 0)$ and $(0, 2)$ to find the slope.
$m = \frac{0 - 2}{7 - 0} = -\frac{2}{7}$
Substitute the values for m and b in $y = mx + b$.
$y = -\frac{2}{7}x + 2$

26. $y - y_1 = m(x - x_1)$
$\quad y - 2 = 8(x - 5)$
$\quad\quad y = 8x - 38$

27. A slope of 0 indicates a horizontal line.
$\quad y = 0x + 2$
$\quad y = 2$

28. $m = \frac{0 - \pi}{1 - 0} = -\pi$
$\quad y = -\pi x + \pi$

29. $m = \frac{3 - (-3)}{2 - 8} = \frac{6}{-6} = -1$
$\quad y - 3 = -1(x - 2)$
$\quad\quad y = -x + 5$

30. $m = \frac{9 - 9}{5 - 10} = 0$
$\quad y = 0x + 9$
$\quad y = 9$

31. slope-intercept form;
$y = mx + b$

32. $2x + 3y = 12$
$\quad 3y = -2x + 12$
$\quad\; y = -\frac{2}{3}x + 4$

33. $y - 2 = 3(x - 7)$
$\quad\; y = 3x - 21 + 2$
$\quad\; y = 3x - 19$

34. $2x + 2y + 5 = 0$
$\quad\quad 2y = -2x - 5$
$\quad\quad\; y = -x - \frac{5}{2}$

35. $3x + 4y = 6 + 5y$
$\quad\quad -y = -3x + 6$
$\quad\quad\;\; y = 3x - 6$

36. $\frac{x}{2} + \frac{y}{3} = 18$
$\quad 6\left(\frac{x}{2} + \frac{y}{3}\right) = 6(18)$
$\quad\quad 3x + 2y = 108$
$\quad\quad\quad 2y = -3x + 108$
$\quad\quad\quad\; y = -\frac{3}{2}x + 54$

37. $\frac{5x - y}{7} = 14$
$\quad 5x - y = 7(14)$
$\quad\quad -y = -5x + 98$
$\quad\quad\;\; y = 5x - 98$

38. $0.05n + 0.10d = 5$ (in dollars)

39. $5(40) = \$200$

40. $3(20) + 5(37)$

41. $3s + 5a$

42. $3s + 5a = 700$
This equation is in standard form.

43. $s = 90$
$\quad 3(90) + 5a = 700$
$\quad\quad\quad\; 5a = 700 - 270$
$\quad\quad\quad\; 5a = 430$
$\quad\quad\quad\;\; a = \frac{430}{5}$
$\quad\quad\quad\;\; a = 86$
86 adult tickets were sold.

44. $a = 80$
$\quad 3s + 5(80) = 700$
$\quad\quad\quad 3s = 700 - 400$
$\quad\quad\quad 3s = 300$
$\quad\quad\quad\; s = 100$
100 student tickets were sold.

45. October 1, 1908; 10-01-08

46. 1-31-58; 580131

47. July 20, 1969; 690720

48. Because two digits spaces must be assigned to allow for all possible months.
$01, \ldots, 12$

PAGE 465, LOOK BACK

---

49. $x^2 + y + z^2 = 1^2 + 1 + 2^2$
$\quad\quad\quad\quad\quad = 1 + 1 + 4$
$\quad\quad\quad\quad\quad = 6$

50. $x - y + z = 1 - 1 + 2 = 2$

51. $x + y - z = 1 + 1 - 2 = 0$

52. $-(x + y + z) = -(1 + 1 + 2)$
$\quad\quad\quad\quad\quad\; = -4$

53. $\frac{12x - 18}{-6} = \frac{12x}{-6} - \frac{18}{-6}$
$\quad\quad\quad\quad\; = -2x + 3$

54. $-5y = 30$
$\quad \frac{-5y}{-5} = \frac{30}{-5}$
$\quad\quad\; y = -6$

55. $3x = 420$
$\quad \frac{3x}{3} = \frac{420}{3}$
$\quad\;\; x = 140$

56. $\frac{y}{9} = 36$
$\quad 9\left(\frac{y}{9}\right) = 9(36)$
$\quad\quad\; y = 324$

57. $\frac{x}{2} = 108$
$\quad 2\left(\frac{x}{2}\right) = 2(108)$
$\quad\quad\; x = 216$

58. $m = \frac{6 - 0}{3 - 0} = \frac{6}{3} = 2$
$\quad y = 2x$

59. $m = \frac{8 - 0}{2 - 0} = \frac{8}{2} = 4$
$\quad y = 4x$

60. $m = \frac{3-0}{6-0} = \frac{3}{6} = \frac{1}{2}$

$y = \frac{1}{2}x$

61. $m = \frac{-7-0}{-5-0} = \frac{-7}{-5} = \frac{7}{5}$

$y = \frac{7}{5}x$

PAGE 465, LOOK BEYOND

have
one point in common.

63. Two parallel lines have no points in common.

64. Fill the 3 L bottle. Pour the contents into the 5 L bottle. Fill the 3 L bottle again. Pour water from it into the 5 L bottle, which needs 2 L more to be full. Then 1 L will remain in the 3 L bottle.

8.6 PAGES 470–471, PRACTICE & APPLY

8. $y = 5$, $m = 0$

horizontal line

9. $x = 7$, m is undefined

vertical line

10. $y = 9x$, $m = 9$

11 $x = 5y$, $y = \frac{1}{5}x$, $m = \frac{1}{5}$

12. $y = \frac{1}{3}x$, $m = \frac{1}{3}$

8–9.

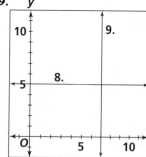

10–12.

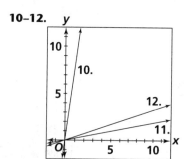

13. from the word *horizon*

14. E; $x + y = 9$ has a slope of –1 and a y-intercept of 9.

15. F; $xy = 9$ or $y = \frac{9}{x}$ is a reciprocal function.

16. B; $x = 9$ has an undefined slope; it is a vertical line through $(9, 0)$.

17. A; $y = 9$ has a slope of 0; it is a horizontal line through $(0, 9)$.

18. C; $y = 9x$ has a slope of 9 and a y-intercept of 0.

19. D; $x = 9y$ or $y = \frac{1}{9}x$ has a slope of $\frac{1}{9}$ and a y-intercept of 0.

	Given	Slope-intercept	Standard
20.	$x = 1$	undefined slope	$1x + 0y = 1$
21.	$y = 4$	$y = 4$	$0x + 1y = 4$
22.	$x + y = 5$	$y = -x + 5$	$1x + 1y = 5$
23.	$y = 4x$	$y = 4x$	$4x - y = 0$
24.	$x = 4y$	$y = \frac{1}{4}x$	$1x - 4y = 0$

For Exercises 25–28, determine the slope, or graph the lines to find out if the lines are vertical or horizontal.

25. $y = 8$, $m = 0$; horizontal

26. $x = -2$, $m =$ undefined; vertical

27. $y = -4$, $m = 0$; horizontal

28. $x = 9$, $m =$ undefined; vertical

29. The answer will depend on the calculator used. Press GRAPH and then DRAW, and select VERTICAL.

30. $y = 6x$, $m = 6$

$x = 6y$

$y = \frac{1}{6}x$, $m = \frac{1}{6}$

Both lines pass through $(0, 0)$.

31. $\frac{1}{0.25} = \frac{1}{\frac{1}{4}} = 1 \div \frac{1}{4} = 1 \cdot \frac{4}{1} = 4$

32. $\frac{1}{-4\frac{1}{2}} = \frac{1}{-\frac{9}{2}} = 1 \div -\frac{9}{2} = 1 \cdot -\frac{2}{9} = -\frac{2}{9}$

33. $\frac{40}{3} = 13\frac{1}{3}$

Saul must attend at least 14 times for the movie pass to benefit his father.

34. $8 \times 2 = 16$

Paying $2 per visit is cheaper.

35. $29 \times 2 = 58$

The $25 season pass is cheaper.

36. Make a table.

3.00	21.00
6.00	24.00
9.00	27.00
12.00	30.00
15.00	33.00
18.00	36.00

After 12 or more visits, the season pass is cheaper.

37. Points; you cannot visit the pool a fractional number of times. Another example could be population growth. To indicate a constant population growth during the year for a community, you would show the growth with a graph of lines, not points. You cannot indicate a partial person.

PAGE 471, LOOK BACK

38. $30 \cdot 2 \div 1 + 10 = 60 \div 1 + 10$
$= 70$

39. $[2(105 - 5)] \div 2 = 2(100) \div 2$
$= 200 \div 2$
$= 100$

40. $\frac{(3+9)^2 - 4}{22 \cdot 15 - 10} = \frac{(12^2 - 4)}{4 \cdot 15 - 10}$
$= \frac{144 - 4}{60 - 10}$
$= \frac{140}{50}$
$= \frac{14}{5}$, or $2\frac{4}{5}$, or 2.8

41. $(6a + 3) + (2a + 6) = 8a + 9$

42. $(x + y + z) + (3x + y + 4z) = 4x + 2y + 5z$

43. $-7 + 3p - 9 - 7p = -16 - 4p$

44. $5 \div 1\frac{1}{3} = 5 \div \frac{4}{3}$
$= 5 \times \frac{3}{4}$
$= \frac{15}{4} = 3\frac{3}{4}$

Mary can make 3 skirts.

45. 7% of $15.50 is what number?

$(0.07)(15.50) = x$
$1.09 = x$

The tax is $1.09.

46. Tip $= (15.50) + 1.09) \times 0.15$
$= 16.59 \times 0.15$
$= \$2.49$

47. $m = \frac{5 - (-2)}{3 - (-4)} = \frac{7}{7} = 1$

In $y = 1x + b$, substitute $x = 3$ and $y = 5$.
$5 = 3 + b$
$2 = b$
The equation is $y = x + 2$.

PAGE 471, LOOK BEYOND

48. right angle

49. No; two different vertical lines are parallel.

50. No; two different horizontal lines are parallel.

8.7 **PAGE 477, PRACTICE & APPLY**

8–9. Answers may vary.

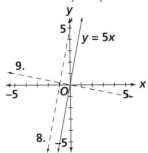

8. Answers may vary. Any line of the form $y = 5x + b$ is parallel, such as $y = 5x - 6$. The slope must be 5 to be parallel, but the y-intercept may vary.

9. Answers may vary. Any line of the form $y = -\frac{1}{5} + b$ is perpendicular, such as $y = -\frac{1}{5}x$. The slope must be $-\frac{1}{5}$ to be perpendicular, but the y-intercept may vary.

10. The line $y = 3x + 2$ has a slope of 3, and the line $y = -3x + 2$ has a slope of -3; both lines have a y-intercept of 2. The lines are not perpendicular.

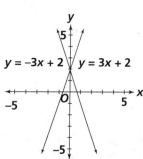

11. 0; the line is horizontal and has a slope of 0.

12. Undefined; the line is vertical and has an undefined slope.

13. Undefined; the line is vertical and has an undefined slope.

14. 0; the line is horizontal and has a slope of 0.

15. Find the slope of the line.
$$5x - 2y = 10$$
$$-2y = -5x + 10$$
$$y = \frac{5}{2}x - 5$$
$m = \frac{5}{2}$, so the parallel slope is $\frac{5}{2}$.
To find the new equation, use the point-slope formula.
$$y - (-5) = \frac{5}{2}(x - 3)$$
$$y + 5 = \frac{5}{2}(x - 3)$$
$$2y + 10 = 5x - 15$$
$$2y = 5x - 25$$
$$5x - 2y = 25$$

16. $5x - 2y = 10$; from Exercise 15, $m = \frac{5}{2}$, so the perpendicular slope is $-\frac{2}{5}$.
$$y - (-5) = -\frac{2}{5}(x - 3)$$
$$y + 5 = -\frac{2}{5}(x - 3)$$
$$5y + 25 = -2x + 6$$
$$2x + 5y = -19$$

17. $y = 3x - 4$; $m = 3$, so the parallel slope is 3.
For the new equation:
$$y - 7 = 3(x - (-2))$$
$$y - 7 = 3(x + 2)$$
$$y - 7 = 3x + 6$$
$$-3x + y = 13$$
$$3x - y = -13$$

18. $y = 3x - 4$; $m = 3$; the perpendicular slope is $-\frac{1}{3}$.
$$y - 7 = \frac{1}{3}(x - (-2))$$
$$y - 7 = -\frac{1}{3}(x + 2)$$
$$3y - 21 = -x - 2$$
$$x + 3y = 19$$

19. $y = 7$; $m = 0$; the parallel slope is 0.
$$y - 4 = 0(x - 2)$$
$$y = 4$$

20. $y = 7$; $m = 0$; the perpendicular slope is undefined.
The new equation is $x = 2$.

21. $y = 3x + 14$; $m = 3$; the parallel slope is 3.

22. $2x + y = 6$
$$y = -2x + 6$$
$m = -2$; the parallel slope is -2.

23. $8 = -4x + 2y$
$$-2y + 8 = -4x$$
$$-2y = -4x - 8$$
$$y = 2x + 4$$
$m = 2$; the parallel slope is 2.

24. $-2x + \frac{1}{2}y = 16$
$$\frac{1}{2}y = 2x + 16$$
$$y = 4x + 32$$
$m = 4$; the parallel slope is 4.

25. $y = -\frac{1}{3}x + 10$
$m = -\frac{1}{3}$;
the perpendicular slope is 3.

26. $-\frac{1}{2}x - y = 20$
$$2y = \frac{1}{2}x + 20$$
$$y = -\frac{1}{2}x - 20$$
$m = -\frac{1}{2}$; the perpendicular slope is 2.

27. $13 = -x + y$
$$y = x + 13$$
$m = 1$; the perpendicular slope is -1.

28. $3x + 12y = 12$
$$12y = -3x + 12$$
$$y = -\frac{1}{4}x + 1$$
$m = -\frac{1}{4}$; the perpendicular slope is 4.

29. Answers may vary. For example: $x = 2$, $x = 4$, $y = 2$, $y = 4$

30. Answers may vary. For example: $y = x$, $y = x - 2$, $y = -x$, $y = -x + 2$

PAGE 477, LOOK BACK

31. $2(7 + 35) \div 7 - 10 = 2$
$$2(42) \div 7 - 10 = 2$$
$$84 \div 7 - 10 = 2$$
$$12 - 10 = 2$$
$$2 = 2$$

32. $-4 + (-3) + 1 = -6$

33. $-2 + 3 + (-7) + 3 = 1 + (-7) + 3$
$$= -6 + 3$$
$$= -3$$

34. $-12 + 4 - (-4) = -8 + 4 = -4$

35. $2x^2 + 3y + 4y + 3x^2 = 5x^2 + 7y$

36. $3x + 2 + 4y + 2 + 3y = 3x + 7y + 4$

37. $2x + 3xy + 5x^2 + 7xy = 5x^2 + 2x + 10xy$

38. Parallel lines have no points in common, so *no* ordered pairs satisfy both simultaneosuly.

39. Perpendicular lines have one intersection point, so *one* ordered pair satisfies both simultaneously.

6. $y < 2x - 1$

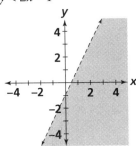

7. $y \leq -\frac{3}{4}x - 3$

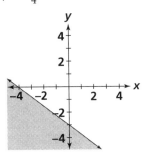

8. $y \geq \frac{1}{3}x - 3$

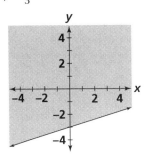

9. $y > -\frac{2}{5}x + 3$

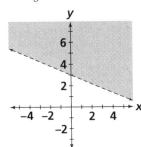

10.
$$2x + y < 8$$
$$2x - 2x + y < 8 - 2x$$
$$y < -2x + 8$$

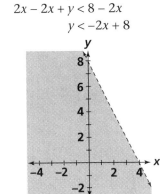

11.
$$5x - 3y \leq 6$$
$$5x - 5x - 3y \leq 6 - 5x$$
$$-3y \leq -5x + 6$$
$$\frac{-3y}{-3} \geq \frac{-5x}{-3} + \frac{6}{-3}$$
$$y \geq \frac{5}{3}x - 2$$

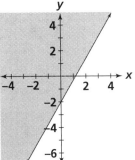

12.
$$x + y \geq 5$$
$$x + y - x \geq 5 - x$$
$$y \geq -x + 5$$

13.
$$2x + y < -2$$
$$2x - 2x + y < -2 - 2x$$
$$y < -2x - 2$$

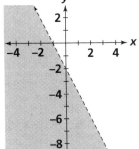

14.
$$x + 4y \leq 4$$
$$x - x + 4y \leq 4 - x$$
$$4y \leq -x + 4$$
$$\frac{1}{4}(4y) \leq \frac{1}{4}(-x + 4)$$
$$y \leq -\frac{1}{4}x + 1$$

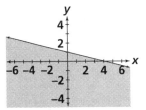

15.
$$3x + 2y \leq 2$$
$$3x - 3x + 2y \leq 2 - 3x$$
$$2y \leq -3x + 2$$
$$\frac{1}{2}(2y) \leq \frac{1}{2}(-3x + 2)$$
$$y \leq -\frac{3}{2}x + 1$$

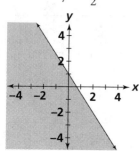

16.
$$3x + y \geq -3$$
$$3x - 3x + y \geq -3 - 3x$$
$$y > -3x - 3$$

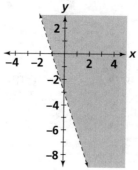

17.
$$4x + 5y < -20$$
$$4x - 4x + 5y < -20 - 4x$$
$$5y < -4x - 20$$
$$\frac{1}{5}(5y) < \frac{1}{5}(-4x - 20)$$
$$y < -\frac{4}{5}x - 4$$

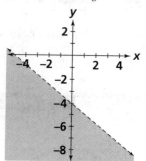

18. $2y > 10$
$$\frac{2y}{2} > \frac{10}{2}$$
$$y > 5$$

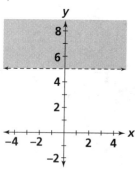

19. $y \leq -3$

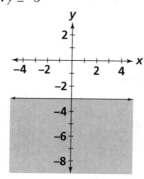

20. $x \geq 3$

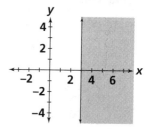

21. $2x < -6$
$$\frac{2x}{2} < \frac{-6}{2}$$
$$x < -3$$

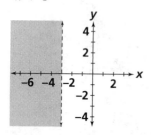

22.
$$-3x + y - 5 > 0$$
$$-3x + 3x + y - 5 > 0 + 3x$$
$$y - 5 > 3x$$
$$y - 5 + 5 > 3x + 5$$
$$y > 3x + 5$$

23.
$$2x + y + 3 < 0$$
$$2x - 2x + y + 3 < 0 - 2x$$
$$y + 3 < -2x$$
$$y + 3 - 3 < -2x - 3$$
$$y < -2x - 3$$

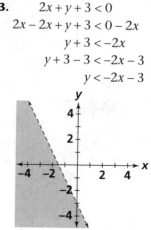

24. $4x + y \leq 6$
$4x - 4x + y \leq 6 - 4x$
$y \leq -4x + 6$

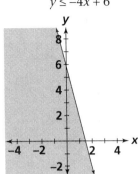

25. $-5x + y \geq 2$
$-5x + 5x + y \geq 2 + 5x$
$y \geq 5x + 2$

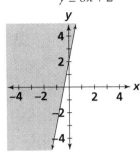

26. $x - y \leq -3$
$x - x - y \leq -3 - x$
$2y \leq -x - 3$
$-1(-y) \geq -1(-x - 3)$
$y \geq x + 3$

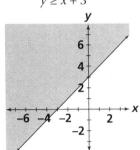

27. $\frac{1}{3}y < x - 5$
$3\left(\frac{1}{3}y\right) < 3(x - 5)$
$y < 3x - 15$

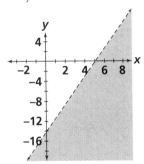

28. $-\frac{1}{5}y \leq -x + 2$
$-5\left(-\frac{1}{5}y\right) \geq -5(-x + 2)$
$y \geq 5x - 10$

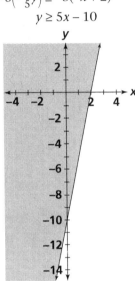

29. $2x - 3y > 6$
$2x - 2x - 3y > 6 - 2x$
$-3y > -2x + 6$
$\frac{1}{3}(-3y) > \frac{1}{3}(-2x + 6)$
$-y > -\frac{2}{3}x + 2$
$-1(-y) < -1\left(-\frac{2}{3}x + 2\right)$
$y < \frac{2}{3}x - 2$

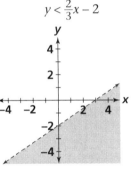

30. $y > \frac{1}{3}x + 8$

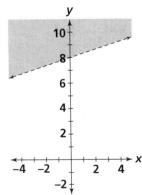

31. $y \geq \frac{5}{2}x - 2$

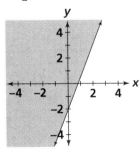

32. $-9x - y \leq 3$
$-9x + 9x - y \leq 3 + 9x$
$-y \leq 9x + 3$
$-1(-y) \geq -1(9x + 3)$
$y \geq -9x - 3$

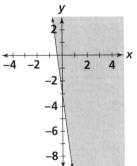

33. $y < 3x - 1$

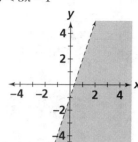

34. $y < -2x + 2$

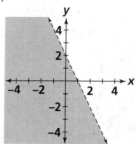

35. $y > -x + 3$

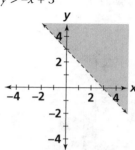

36. $y > 3$

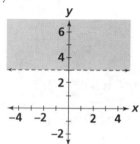

37. $x > 3$

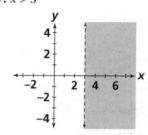

38. $y \geq \frac{1}{2}x - 3$

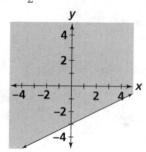

39.
$$-3x + 2y - 2 > 0$$
$$-3x + 2y - 2 + 2 > 0 + 2$$
$$-3x + 2y > 2$$
$$-3x + 3x + 2y > 2 + 3x$$
$$2y > 3x + 2$$
$$\frac{1}{2}(2y) > \frac{1}{2}(3x + 2)$$
$$y > \frac{3}{2}x + 1$$

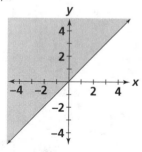

40.
$$-\frac{1}{3}x + y \leq 1$$
$$-\frac{1}{3}x + \frac{1}{3}x + y \leq 1 + \frac{1}{3}x$$
$$y \leq \frac{1}{3}x + 1$$

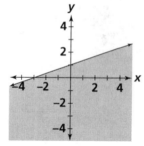

41.
$$x \leq -y - 3$$
$$x + 3 \leq -y - 3 + 3$$
$$x + 3 \leq -y$$
$$-1(x + 3) \geq (-y) - 1$$
$$-x - 3 \geq y$$
$$y \leq -x - 3$$

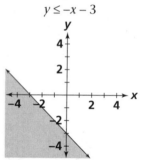

42. $y \geq x$

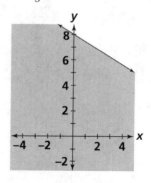

43. $y \leq -\frac{3}{5}x + 8$

44. $y \ge \frac{1}{2}x - 4$

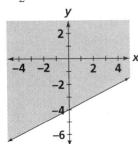

45. $y > \frac{2}{3}x + 5$

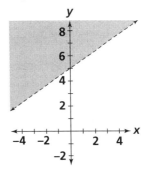

46. $y < -x$ **47.** $y < 5$ **48.** $y \ge -2x + 2$ **49.** $y < 3x + 6$ **50.** $y \ge \frac{2}{3}x - 3$ **51.** $x \le 2$

52. Let y represent the number of gold coins; then $14y$ represents the weight of gold coins in grams. Let x represent the number of silver coins; then $7x$ represents the weight of silver coins in grams.

$$14y + 7x \ge 25,000$$
$$14y + 7x - 7x \ge 25,000 - 7x$$
$$14y \ge -7x + 25,000$$
$$\frac{1}{14}(14y) \ge \frac{1}{14}(-7x + 25,000)$$
$$y \ge -\frac{1}{2}x + \frac{25,000}{14}$$
$$y \ge -\frac{1}{2}x + 1785.7$$

Since you cannot have fractional pieces of gold or silver, the reasonable domain and range are all whole numbers such that $x \ge 0$, $y \ge 0$, and

$$y \ge -\frac{1}{2}x + 1785.7$$

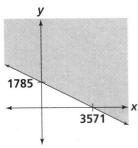

53. Let d represent the number of days the car is to be rented. Let m represent the number of miles the car is to be driven.

$$25d + 0.30m < 140$$
$$25d < -0.30m + 140$$
$$d < -0.012m + 5.6$$

The reasonable domain for this function is all rational numbers such that $m \le 466.66$. The reasonable range is all rational numbers such that $d \le 5.6$.

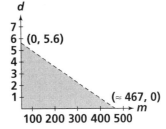

54. Let x represent a correct answer; then $5x$ represents the number of points Alice receives for correct answers. Let y represent a wrong answer; then $-2y$ represents the number of points Alice receives for wrong answers.

$$5x + (-2y) \ge 80$$
$$-2y \ge -5x + 80$$
$$y \le \frac{5}{2}x - 40$$

To determine if Alice will score at least 80 if she gets 18 correct answers and 4 incorrect answers, locate the point (18, 4) on the graph. The point (18, 4) is within the shaded region, so Alice will score at least 80 on her test.

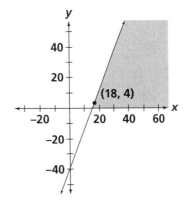

55. Let s represent the number of student tickets; then $4s$ represents the revenue from student tickets. Let a represent the number of adult tickets; then $5a$ represents the revenue from adult tickets.

$$4s + 5a \geq 2000$$
$$4s - 4s + 5a \geq 2000 - 4s$$
$$5s \geq -4s + 2000$$
$$\frac{1}{5}(5a) \geq \frac{1}{5}(-4s + 2000)$$
$$a \geq -\frac{4}{5}s + 400$$

No; they will not meet their goal if they sell 200 student tickets and 90 adult tickets because the point (200, 90) is not in the shaded region.

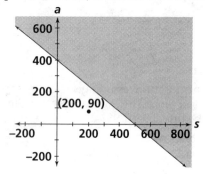

56. Let p represent the number of pizzas; then $8p$ represents the cost of the pizzas. Let d represent the number of soft drinks; then $2d$ represents the cost of soft drinks.

$$8p + 2d \leq 60$$
$$8p - 8p + 2d \leq 60 - 8p$$
$$2d \leq -8p + 60$$
$$\frac{1}{2}(2d) \leq \frac{1}{2}(-8p + 60)$$
$$d \leq -4p + 30$$

Yes; Will can purchase 5 pizzas and 4 sodas for less than \$60 because the point (5, 4) is in the shaded region.

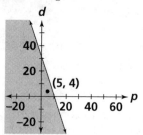

57. Let x represent the number of blouses; then $5x$ represents the amount of money made on blouses. Let y represent the number of shirts; then $4y$ represents the amount of money made on shirts.

$$5x + 4y \geq 60$$
$$5x - 5x + 4y \geq 60 - 5x$$
$$4y \geq -5x + 60$$
$$\frac{1}{4}(4y) \geq \frac{1}{4}(-5x + 60)$$
$$y \geq -\frac{5}{4}x + 15$$

Yes; Jenna can earn at least \$60 selling 8 blouses and 7 shirts because the point (8, 7) is within the shaded region.

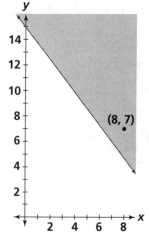

58. Let x represent the number of 2-point baskets; then $2x$ represents the number of points made shooting 2-point baskets. Let y represent the number of 3-point baskets; then $3y$ represents the number of points made shooting 3-point baskets.

$$2x + 3y \geq 24$$
$$2x - 2x + 3y \geq 24 - 2x$$
$$3y \geq -2x + 24$$
$$\frac{1}{3}(3y) \geq \frac{1}{3}(-2x + 24)$$
$$y \geq -\frac{2}{3}x + 8$$

No; Mike could not have scored five 2-point baskets and four 3-point baskets in one game because the point (5, 4) is outside the shaded region.

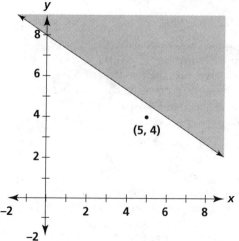

59.

In a parallelogram, opposite angles have the same measure, and consecutive angles are supplementary.

$m\angle X = m\angle Z$ $m\angle X + m\angle Y = 180$
$m\angle W = m\angle Y$ $m\angle W + m\angle Z = 180$

Let a represent the measure of $\angle Y$. Then $2a - 15$ represents the measure of $\angle X$.

$$m\angle X + m\angle Y = 180$$
$$(2a - 15) + a = 180$$
$$2a + a - 15 = 180$$
$$3a - 15 = 180$$
$$3a - 15 + 15 = 180 + 15$$
$$3a = 195$$
$$\frac{3a}{3} = \frac{195}{3}$$
$$a = 65$$
$$2a - 15 = 2(65) - 15$$
$$= 130 - 15$$
$$= 115$$

$m\angle X = 2a - 15 = 115°$
$m\angle Y = a = 65°$
$m\angle Z = 115°$
$m\angle W = 65°$

60.
$$\frac{7}{18} = \frac{21}{x}$$
$$7x = 18 \cdot 21$$
$$7x = 378$$
$$\frac{7x}{7} = \frac{378}{7}$$
$$x = 54$$

61.
$$\frac{15}{32} = \frac{x}{20}$$
$$32x = 15 \cdot 20$$
$$32x = 300$$
$$\frac{32x}{32} = \frac{300}{32}$$
$$x = \frac{75}{8}, \text{ or } 9\frac{3}{8}$$

62.
$$\frac{3}{x} = \frac{14}{9}$$
$$14x = 27$$
$$\frac{14x}{14} = \frac{27}{14}$$
$$x = \frac{27}{14}, \text{ or } 1\frac{13}{14}$$

63.

	First solution	**Second solution**	**New solution**
Percent acid	2% = 0.02	3% = 0.03	2.4% = 0.024
Amount of solution	x	$48 - x$	48 mL
Amount of acid	$0.02x$	$0.03(48 - x)$	$0.02x + 0.03(48 - x) = 0.024(48)$

$$0.02x + 0.03(48 - x) = 0.024(48)$$
$$0.02x + 1.44 - 0.03x = 1.152$$
$$0.02x - 0.03x + 1.44 = 1.152$$
$$-0.01x + 1.44 = 1.152$$
$$-0.01x + 1.44 - 1.44 = 1.152 - 1.44$$
$$-0.01x = -0.288$$
$$\frac{-0.01x}{-0.01} = \frac{-0.288}{-0.01}$$
$$x = 28.8$$

Carter should use 28.8 milliliters of the 2% solution and 48 − 28.8, or 19.2, milliliters of the 3% solution.

64.
$$\begin{cases} x < 2 \\ y < 2x - 4 \end{cases}$$

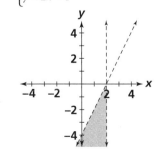

65.
$$\begin{cases} y > -2 \\ 2x - y < 5 \Rightarrow -y < -2x + 5 \end{cases}$$
$$\Rightarrow y > 2x - 5$$

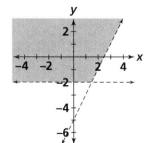

1.

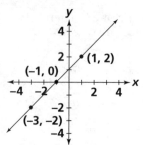

Yes, the points lie on a straight line.

2.

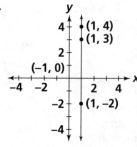

Yes, the points lie on a straight line.

3.

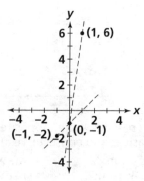

No, the points do not lie on a straight line.

4. $m = \dfrac{\text{difference in } y\text{-values}}{\text{difference in } x\text{-values}} = \dfrac{3-2}{2-(-3)} = \dfrac{1}{5}$
The slope is $\dfrac{1}{5}$.

5. $m = \dfrac{\text{difference in } y\text{-values}}{\text{difference in } x\text{-values}} = \dfrac{4-4}{1-(-5)} = \dfrac{0}{6} = 0$
The slope is 0.

6. $m = \dfrac{\text{difference in } y\text{-values}}{\text{difference in } x\text{-values}} = \dfrac{3-(-1)}{-3-(-3)} = \dfrac{3+1}{-3+3} = \dfrac{4}{0}$
The slope is undefined.

7. $m = \dfrac{2-0}{-3-0} = \dfrac{2}{-3} = -\dfrac{2}{3}$
The equation is
$y = -\dfrac{2}{3}x.$

8. $m = \dfrac{3-0}{2-0} = \dfrac{3}{2}$

The equation is $y = \dfrac{3}{2}x.$

9. $m = \dfrac{-5-0}{-2-0} = \dfrac{-5}{-2} = \dfrac{5}{2}$
The equation is $y = \dfrac{5}{2}x.$

10. $m = \dfrac{4-0}{-5-0} = -\dfrac{4}{5}$
The equation is $y = -\dfrac{4}{5}x.$

11. slope: 2, y-intercept: 1
$y = 2x + 1$

12. $m = \dfrac{-1-(-1)}{-3-2} = \dfrac{-1+1}{-5} = \dfrac{0}{5} = 0$
$y = mx + b$
$-1 = 0(2) + b$
$-1 = 0 + b$
$-1 = 0 + b$
$-1 = b$
The equation is $y = 0x + (-1)$ or $y = -1.$

13.
$$y + 9 = 4x - 8$$
$$y + 9 - 4x = 4x - 8 - 4x$$
$$-4x + y + 9 - 9 = -8 - 9$$
$$-4x + y = -17$$
$$-1(-4x + y) = -1(-17)$$
$$4x - y = 17$$

14.
$$y - 4 = -x + 1$$
$$y - 4 + x = -x + 1 + x$$
$$y - 4 + x = 1$$
$$y - 4 + x + 4 = 1 + 4$$
$$y + x = 5$$
$$x + y = 5$$

15.
$$y - 13 = 2x + 4$$
$$y - 13 - 2x = 2x + 4 - 2x$$
$$y - 13 - 2x = 4$$
$$y - 13 - 2x + 13 = 4 + 13$$
$$y - 2x = 17$$
$$-2x + y = 17$$
$$-1(-2x + y) = -1(17)$$
$$2x - y = -17$$

16.
$$3x + y + 6 = 9$$
$$3x + y + 6 - 6 = 9 - 6$$
$$3x + y = 3$$

17. Use the point $(0, -1)$ for (x_1, y_1).
$$y - y_1 = m(x - x_1)$$
$$y - (-1) = 2(x - 0)$$
$$y + 1 = 2(x - 0)$$

18. $m = \dfrac{2-4}{1-0} = \dfrac{-2}{1} = -2$
Use the point $(0, 4)$ for (x_1, y_1).
$$y - y_1 = m(x - x_1)$$
$$y - 4 = -2(x - 0)$$

or

Use the point $(1, 2)$ for (x_1, y_1).
$$y - y_1 = m(x - x_1)$$
$$y - 2 = -2(x - 1)$$

19. horizontal line
slope = 0

20. vertical line
slope undefined

21. horizontal line
slope = 0

22. vertical line
slope undefined

23. Parallel lines have the same slope. The slope of a line parallel to $y = \frac{2}{3}x + 4$ is $m = \frac{2}{3}$. Perpendicular lines have slopes that are opposite reciprocals. The slope of a line perpendicular to $y = \frac{2}{3}x + 4$ is $m = -\frac{3}{2}$.

24. Slope of parallel line: $m = -7$.
Slope of perpendicular line: $m = \frac{1}{7}$.

25. Use the point-slope form.
$$m = -2$$
Use the point (1, 5) for (x_1, y_1).
$$y - y_1 = m(x - x_1)$$
$$y - 5 = -2(x - 1)$$
$$y - 5 = -2x + 2$$
$$y = -2x + 7$$

26. The slope of a perpendicular line is $m = \frac{1}{2}$.
Use the point (1, 5) for (x_1, y_1).
$$y - y_1 = m(x - x_1)$$
$$y - 5 = \frac{1}{2}(x - 1)$$
$$y - 5 = \frac{1}{2}x - \frac{1}{2}$$
$$y = \frac{1}{2}x + \frac{9}{2}$$

27. $y > x + 1$

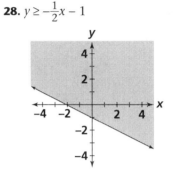

28. $y \geq -\frac{1}{2}x - 1$

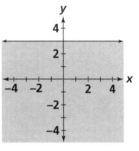

29. $x + y < 4$
$$y < -x + 4$$

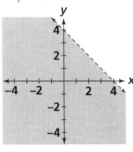

30. $y \leq 3$

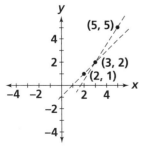

Let d represent the distance driven, and let h represent the number of hours. Then $d = 50h + 110$.

31. 1.6 hours
$$d = 50(1.6) + 110$$
$$= 80 + 110$$
$$= 190$$
Marie had driven 190 miles after 1.6 hours.

32. 2.9 hours
$$d = 50(2.0) + 110$$
$$= 145 + 110$$
$$= 255$$
Marie had driven 255 miles after 29 hours.

33. 3.3 hours
$$d = 50(3.3) + 110$$
$$d = 50(3.3) + 110$$
$$= 165 + 110$$
$$= 275$$
Marie had driven 275 miles after 3.3 hours.

PAGE 491 CHAPTER 8 ASSESSMENT

1.

No, they are not on a straight line.

2.
$$y + 3 = -5x + 6$$
$$y + 3 + 5x = -5x + 6 + 5x$$
$$y + 3 + 5x = 6$$
$$y + 3 + 5x - 3 = 6 - 3$$
$$y + 5x = 3$$
$$5x + y = 3$$

3.
$$4x + 2y + 8 = 10$$
$$4x + 2y + 8 - 8 = 10 - 8$$
$$4x + 2y = 2$$

4.
$$2x + y = 10 - 3x$$
$$2x + y - 2x = 10 - 3x - 2x$$
$$y = 10 - 5x$$
$$y = -5x + 10$$

5.
$$3x - y = 2y - 5$$
$$3x - y - 2y = 2y - 5 - 2y$$
$$3x - 3y = -5$$
$$3x - 3y - 3x = -5 - 3x$$
$$-3y = -3x - 5$$
$$\frac{1}{3}(-3y) = \frac{1}{3}(-3x - 5)$$
$$-y = -x - \frac{5}{3}$$
$$-1(-y) = -1\left(-x - \frac{5}{3}\right)$$
$$y = x + \frac{5}{3}$$

6.
$$3x + 6y = 12$$
$$3x + 6y - 3x = 12 - 3x$$
$$6y = -3x + 12$$
$$\frac{1}{6}(6y) = \frac{1}{6}(-3x + 12)$$
$$y = -\frac{1}{2}x + 2$$
$$m = -\frac{1}{2}$$
$$b = 2$$

7.
$$2x + 3y = -3$$
$$2x + 3y - 2x = -3 - 2x$$
$$3y = -2x - 3$$
$$\frac{1}{3}(3y) = \frac{1}{3}(-2x - 3)$$
$$y = -\frac{2}{3}x - 1$$
$$m = -\frac{2}{3}$$
$$b = -1$$

8. $y = 3x + 1$

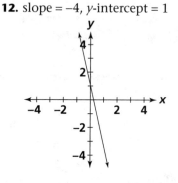

9. slope $= \dfrac{\text{difference in } y\text{-values}}{\text{difference in } x\text{-values}}$

$$= \frac{-2 - 3}{8 - 5} = -\frac{5}{3}$$

10. Use $m = -3$ and the point $(2, 4)$ for (x_1, y_1).
$$y - y_1 = m(x - x_1)$$
$$y - 4 = -3(x - 2)$$
$$y - 4 = -3x + 6$$
$$y - 4 + 4 = -3x + 6 + 4$$
$$y = -3x + 10$$

11.
$$2x + y = 13$$
$$2x + y - 2x = 13 - 2x$$
$$y = -2x + 13$$
The slope of a perpendicular line is $\frac{1}{2}$. Use the point $(0, 13)$ for (x_1, y_1).
$$y - y_1 = m(x - x_1)$$
$$y - 13 = \frac{1}{2}(x - 0)$$
$$y - 13 = \frac{1}{2}x$$
$$y - 13 + 13 = \frac{1}{2}x + 13$$
$$y = \frac{1}{2}x + 13$$
The equation of the perpendicular line is $y = \frac{1}{2}x + 13$.

12. slope $= -4$, y-intercept $= 1$

13. $y = -\frac{2}{3}x + 5$

14. $m = -3$
Use the point $(2, -3)$ for (x_1, y_1).
$$y - y_1 = m(x - x_1)$$
$$y - (-3) = -3(x - 2)$$

15. $m = \dfrac{5 - (-1)}{1 - (-5)} = \dfrac{5 + 1}{1 + 5} = \dfrac{6}{6} = 1$
Use the point $(1, 5)$ for (x_1, y_1).
$$y - y_1 = m(x - x_1)$$
$$y - 5 = 1(x - 1)$$
$$y - 5 = x - 1$$
$$y - 5 + 5 = x - 1 + 5$$
$$y = x + 4$$

16. $y = \frac{2}{3}x + 2$

17. Slope $= \dfrac{\text{difference in } y\text{-values}}{\text{difference in } x\text{-values}} = \dfrac{8 - 8}{-2 - 1} = \dfrac{0}{-3} = 0$

18. $y > 2x - 1$

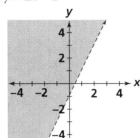

19. $y \leq 3x + 2$

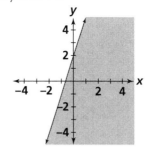

20. $\quad x - y \geq 4$
$\quad x - y - x \geq 4 - x$
$\quad\quad -y \geq 2x + 4$
$\quad -1(-y) \leq -1(-x + 4)$
$\quad\quad\quad y \leq x - 4$

21. $y < \frac{1}{2}x$

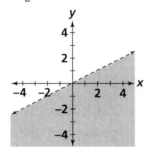

22. Use a table.

Days	Daily rate
1	15(1) = 15
2	15(2) = 30
3	15(3) = 45
4	15(4) = 60
5	15(5) = 75
6	15(6) = 90
7	15(7) = 105

Steve must use the mower for 7 days before it would benefit him to pay the flat rate.

PAGES 492–493 CHAPTERS 1-8 CUMULATIVE ASSESSMENT

1. C: $-18 + 4 = -10 + (-4) = -14$

2. B: $\frac{37}{10} = 3.7$
$3.7 > 0.37$

3. A: $\quad x + 3 \geq 4 \quad\quad\quad\quad x - 7 < -6$
$\quad x + 3 - 3 \geq 4 - 3 \quad\quad x - 7 + 7 < -6 + 7$
$\quad\quad\quad\quad x \geq 1 \quad\quad\quad\quad\quad\quad x < 1$
$\quad$ smallest integer = 1 $\quad$ largest integer = 0

4. C: The slopes are equal.

Column A	Column B
slope $= \frac{3-2}{0-1} = \frac{1}{-1} = -1$	$4x + 4y = 12$
	$4x + 4y - 4x = 12 - 4x$
	$4y = -4x + 12$
	$\frac{1}{4}(4y) = \frac{1}{4}(-4x + 12)$
	$y = -x + 3$
	slope $= -1$

5.

Sequence	5		8		11		14		17		[20]		[23]		[26]
First differences		3		3		3		3		3		3		3	

a: The next three terms are 20, 23, and 26.

6. d: $y = -7.5$
$\quad 16y = -120$
$\quad \frac{16y}{16} = \frac{-120}{16}$
$\quad\quad y = -7.5$

7. c: $\quad\quad x \geq -2$
$\quad\quad -2x + 3 \leq 7$
$\quad\quad 2x + 3 - 3 \leq 7 - 3$
$\quad\quad\quad\quad -2x \leq 4$
$\quad\quad\quad\quad \frac{-2x}{-2} > \frac{4}{-2}$
$\quad\quad\quad\quad\quad x \geq -2$

8. d: $\quad 2x - y = 11$
$\quad\quad y + 4 = 2x - 7$
$\quad y + 4 - 2x = 2x - 7 - 2x$
$\quad\quad y + 4 - 2x = -7$
$\quad y + 4 - 2x - 4 = -7 - 4$
$\quad\quad\quad y - 2x = -11$
$\quad\quad\quad -2x + y = -11$
$\quad -1(-2x + y) = -1(-11)$
$\quad\quad\quad 2x - y = 11$

9. b: $x = 3$

10. c: $y = 2x + 4$

Slope $= m = 2$

Let the point $(-1, 2)$ be (x_1, y_1).
$$y - y_1 = m(x - x_1)$$
$$y - 2 = 2(x - (-1))$$
$$y - 2 = 2(x + 1)$$
$$y - 2 = 2x + 2$$
$$y - 2 + 2 = 2x + 2 + 2$$
$$y = 2x + 4$$

11. c: trapezoid

12.

$\frac{1}{12}$	$\frac{1}{12}$	$\frac{1}{12}$	$\frac{1}{12}$	$\frac{1}{12}$	$\frac{1}{12}$	$\frac{1}{12}$	$\frac{1}{12}$	$\frac{1}{12}$	$\frac{1}{12}$	$\frac{1}{12}$	$\frac{1}{12}$

$\frac{1}{6}$	$\frac{1}{6}$	$\frac{1}{6}$	$\frac{1}{6}$	$\frac{1}{6}$	$\frac{1}{6}$

$$\frac{9}{12} \leq \frac{5}{6}$$

13. $(7x^2 + 2) - (3x - 2x^2) = 7x^2 + 2 - 3x + 2x^2$
$$= 7x^2 + 2x^2 - 3x + 2$$
$$= 9x^2 - 3x + 2$$

14. $(9w - 5) - (3w - 4) = 9w - 5 - 3w + 4$
$$= 9w - 3w - 5 + 4$$
$$= 6w - 1$$

15. $-54s \div 6s = \frac{-54s}{6s} = -9$

16. $4x^2 - 4(3x^2 + 7) = 4x^2 - 12x^2 - 28$
$$= -8x^2 - 28$$

17.
$$\frac{x}{12} = \frac{-3}{20}$$
$$20x = -3 \cdot 12$$
$$20x = -36$$
$$\frac{20x}{20} = \frac{-36}{20}$$
$$x = -\frac{36}{20} = -\frac{9}{5}, \text{ or } -1\frac{4}{5}$$

18.
$$0.4x + 5.4 = -(3.2 - x)$$
$$0.4x + 5.4 = -3.2 + x$$
$$0.4x + 5.4 - 0.4x = -3.2 + x - 0.4x$$
$$5.4 = -3.2 + 0.6x$$
$$5.4 + 3.2 = -3.2 + 0.6x + 3.2$$
$$8.6 = 0.6x$$
$$\frac{8.6}{0.6x} = \frac{0.6x}{0.6}$$
$$14.3 = x$$

19.
$$2x + 3y = 4$$
$$2x + 3y - 2x = 4 - 2x$$
$$3y = -2x + 4$$
$$\frac{1}{3}(3y) = \frac{1}{3}(-2x + 4)$$
$$y = -\frac{2}{3}x + \frac{4}{3}$$

The y-intercept is $(0, 1)$.

Slope $= -\frac{2}{3}$

Use the point $(3, -1)$ for (x_1, y_1).
$$y - y_1 = m(x - x_1)$$
$$y - (-1) = -\frac{2}{3}(x - 3)$$
$$y + 1 = -\frac{2}{3}x + 2$$
$$y + 1 - 1 = -\frac{2}{3}x + 2 - 1$$
$$y = -\frac{2}{3}x + 1$$

20. $y \leq \frac{1}{2}x + 3$

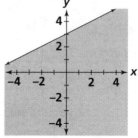

21. $4^2 \div 8 + 5(8 - 2) \cdot 2 = 4^2 \div 8 + 5(6) \cdot 2$
$$= 16 \div 8 + 5(6) \cdot 2$$
$$= 2 + 5(6) \cdot 2$$
$$= 2 + 30 \cdot 2$$
$$= 2 + 60$$
$$= 62$$

22.
$$\frac{5}{8} - x = \frac{1}{2}$$
$$\frac{5}{8} - x - \frac{5}{8} = \frac{1}{2} - \frac{5}{8}$$
$$-x = \frac{4}{8} - \frac{5}{8}$$
$$-x = -\frac{1}{8}$$
$$-1(-x) = -1\left(-\frac{1}{8}\right)$$
$$x = \frac{1}{8}$$

23. Let x represent the score needed on the fourth test.
$$\frac{88 + 90 + 80 + x}{4} = 85$$
$$\frac{258 + x}{4} = 85$$
$$4\left(\frac{258 + x}{4}\right) = (85)4$$
$$258 + x = 340$$
$$258 + x - 258 = 340 - 258$$
$$x = 82$$

Maurice must score an 82 on the next test.

24. $A = \frac{1}{2}bh$
$$27 = \frac{1}{2}(10)h$$
$$27 = 5h$$
$$\frac{27}{5} = \frac{5h}{5}$$
$$5.4 = h$$

The height of the triangle is 5.4 meters.

25. $m = \frac{2 - 0}{4 - 0} = \frac{2}{4} = \frac{1}{2}$

CHAPTER 9

SYSTEMS OF EQUATIONS AND INEQUALITIES

4. solution = (4, 1)

5. solution = (0, 6)

6. solution = (–2, –3)

7. solution = (–2, 3)

8. solution = $\left(5, \frac{1}{2}\right)$

9. solution ≈ (–2.3, –0.4)

10. $\begin{cases} 2x + y = 1 \\ 3x + y = 2 \end{cases}$

$2x + y = 1$	$3x + y = 2$
$2x + y - 2x = 1 - 2x$	$3x + y - 3x = 2 - 3x$
$y = -2x + 1$	$y = -3x + 2$

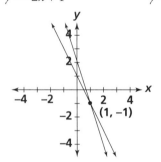

solution = (1, –1)

11. $\begin{cases} x + y = 2 \\ 2x + y = 6 \end{cases}$

$x + y = 2$	$2x + y = 6$
$x + y - x = 2 - x$	$2x + y - 2x = 6 - 2x$
$y = -x + 2$	$y = -2x + 6$

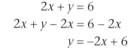
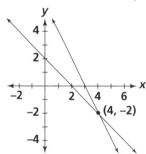

solution = (4, –2)

12. $\begin{cases} 3x - y = 4 \\ 2x + y = 6 \end{cases}$

$3x - y = 4$	$2x + y = 6$
$3x - y - 3x = 4 - 3x$	$2x + y - 2x = 6 - 2x$
$-y = -3x + 4$	$y = -2x + 6$
$-1(-y) = -1(-3x + 4)$	
$y = 3x - 4$	

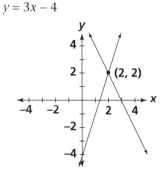

solution = (2, 2)

13. $\begin{cases} 2x + y = 7 \\ x - y = 2 \end{cases}$

$2x + y = 7$	$x - y = 2$
$2x + y - 2x = 7 - 2x$	$x - y - x = 2 - x$
$y = -2x + 7$	$-y = -x + 2$
	$-1(-y) = -1(-x + 2)$
	$y = x - 2$

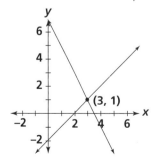

solution = (3, 1)

14. $\begin{cases} 3x - y = 6 \\ y = 4x - 4 \end{cases}$

$3x - y = 6$
$3x - y - 3x = 6 - 3x$
$-y = -3x + 6$
$-1(-y) = -1(-3x + 6)$
$y = 3x - 6$

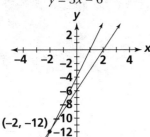

solution = (−2, −12)

15. $\begin{cases} 3x - 2y = 10 \\ y = x - 4 \end{cases}$

$3x - 2y = 10$
$3x - 2y - 3x = 10 - 3x$
$-2y = -3x + 10$
$-\frac{1}{2}(-2y) = -\frac{1}{2}(-3x + 10)$
$y = \frac{3}{2}x - 5$

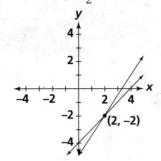

solution = (2, −2)

16. $\begin{cases} 3x - y = 6 \\ y = 4 \end{cases}$

$3x - y = 6$
$3x - y - 3x = 6 - 3x$
$-y = -3x + 6$
$-1(-y) = -1(-3x + 6)$
$y = 3x - 6$

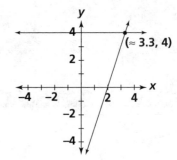

solution ≈ (3.3, 4)

17. $\begin{cases} 3x - y = 8 \\ x = -2 \end{cases}$

$3x - y = 8$
$3x - y - 3x = 8 - 3x$
$-y = -3x + 8$
$1(-y) = -1(-3x + 8)$
$y = 3x - 8$

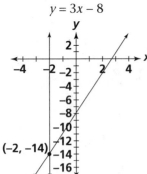

solution = (−2, −14)

18. $\begin{cases} x = -4 \\ y = 5 \end{cases}$

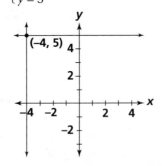

solution = (−4, 5)

19. $\begin{cases} y = -\frac{1}{2}x + 1 \\ y = 2x + 4 \end{cases}$

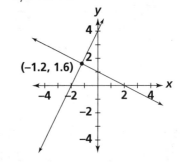

solution ≈ (−1.2, 1.6)

20. $\begin{cases} y = \frac{3}{4}x + 2 \\ y = x + 1 \end{cases}$

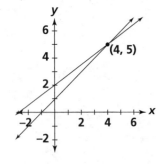

solution = (4, 5)

21. $\begin{cases} y = -\frac{1}{3}x + 2 \\ y = x + 2 \end{cases}$

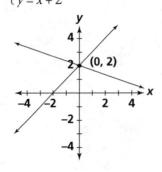

solution = (0, 2)

22. Let y represent the number of bull calves, and let x represent the number of heifer calves.

$\begin{cases} y = 2x \\ y + x = 50 \end{cases} \Rightarrow y = -x + 50$

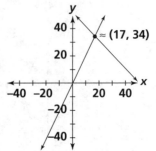

Answers may vary. One approximate solution is 17 heifer calves and 34 bull calves.

23. Let x represent the number of pounds of raisins.
Let y represent the number of pounds of peanuts.

$$\begin{cases} 2x + 3y = 6 \\ x + y = 2\frac{1}{2} \end{cases}$$

$2x + 3y = 6$
$2x + 3y - 2x = 6 - 2x$
$3y = -2x + 6$
$\frac{1}{3}(3y) = \frac{1}{3}(-2x + 6)$
$y = -\frac{2}{3}x + 2$

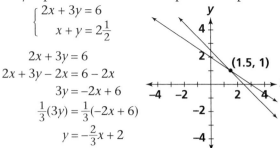

Answers may vary. There are approximately $1\frac{1}{2}$ pounds of raisins and 1 pound of peanuts in the mixture.

24. Let x represent the number of grams of saturated fat and let y represent the number of grams of unsaturated fat.

$$\begin{cases} x + y = 15 \\ y = 5x \end{cases}$$

$x + y = 15$
$x + y - x = 15$
$y = -x + 15$

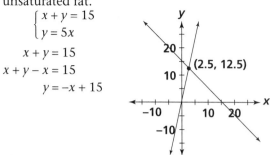

Answers may vary. There are approximately $2\frac{1}{2}$ grams of saturated fat and approximately $12\frac{1}{2}$ grams of unsaturated fat in the crackers.

25. Let a represent the number of adult tickets sold.
Let s represent the number of student tickets sold.

$$\begin{cases} 5a + 2s = 5766 \\ a + s + 254 = 2000 \end{cases}$$

$5a + 2s = 5766$
$5a + 2s - 5a = 5766 - 5a$
$2s = -5a + 5766$
$\frac{1}{2}(2s) = \frac{1}{2}(-5a + 5766)$
$s = -\frac{5}{2}a + 2883$

$a + s + 254 = 2000$
$a + s + 254 - 254 = 2000 - 254$
$a + s = 1746$
$a + s - a = 1746 - a$
$s = -a + 1746$

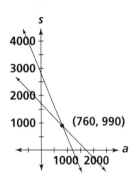

Approximately 760 adult tickets and approximately 990 student tickets were sold for the game. The exact solution is 758 adult tickets and 988 student tickets.

PAGE 503, LOOK BACK

---

26. $(2.8\%)(420) = (0.028)(420)$
$= 11.76$
There are 11.76 milliliters of acid in the mixture.

27.
$3x + 5 > -4$
$3x + 5 - 5 > -4 - 5$
$3x > -9$
$\frac{3x}{3} > \frac{-9}{3}$
$x > -3$

28.
$3 - z \le 18$
$3 - z - 3 \le 18 - 3$
$-z \le 15$
$-1(-z) \ge (15) - 1$
$z \ge -15$

29.
$18 < 15 + 4a$
$18 - 15 < 15 + 4a - 15$
$3 < 4a$
$\frac{3}{4} < \frac{4a}{4}$
$\frac{3}{4} < a$

30. The slope of a vertical line is undefined. The slope of a horizontal line is 0.

31. Substitute $(-2, 5)$ for x and y in the inequality.
$x + 5y < 12$
$-2 + 5(5) \overset{?}{<} 12$
$-2 + 25 \overset{?}{<} 12$
$23 < 12$ False
No; $(-2, 5)$ does not satisfy the inequality.

32. Substitute $(0, 0)$ for x and y in the inequality.
$3x - 4y < 10$
$3(0) - 4(0) < 10$
$0 - 0 < 10$
$0 < 10$ True
Yes; $(0, 0)$ satisfies the inequality.

33. Substitute 3 for m in the equation $3m + 4v = 23$
and solve for v.

$$3m + 4v = 23$$
$$3(3) + 4v = 23$$
$$9 + 4v = 23$$
$$9 + 4v - 9 = 23 - 9$$
$$4v = 14$$
$$\frac{4v}{4} = \frac{14}{4}$$
$$v = \frac{14}{4}, \text{ or } \frac{7}{2}, \text{ or } 3\frac{1}{2}, \text{ or } 3.5$$

9.2 PAGES 508–509, PRACTICE & APPLY

For Exercises 4–39, substitutions may vary.

Solve one equation for a variable with a coefficient of 1, substitute, and solve for
the other variable. Substitute the value you find in the other equation to solve.

4. $\begin{cases} y = 4x \\ x + y = 20 \end{cases}$

Substitute $4x$ for y.
$$x + y = 20$$
$$x + 4x = 20$$
$$5x = 20$$
$$\frac{1}{5}(5x) = \frac{1}{5}(20)$$
$$x = 4$$
Substitute 4 for x.
$$y = 4x$$
$$y = 4(4)$$
$$y = 16$$
$$x = 4 \text{ and } y = 16$$

5. $\begin{cases} x = 5y \\ x + 3y = 24 \end{cases}$

Substitute $5y$ for x.
$$x + 3y = 24$$
$$5y + 3y = 24$$
$$8y = 24$$
$$\frac{1}{8}(8y) = \left(\frac{1}{8}\right)24$$
$$y = 3$$
Substitute 3 for y.
$$x = 5y$$
$$x = 5(3)$$
$$x = 15$$
$$x = 15 \text{ and } y = 3$$

6. $\begin{cases} x = y - 3 \\ x + 3y = 13 \end{cases}$

Substitute $y - 3$ for x.
$$x + 3y = 13$$
$$(y - 3) + 3y = 13$$
$$4y - 3 = 13$$
$$4y = 16$$
$$\frac{1}{4}(4y) = \frac{1}{4}(16)$$
$$y = 4$$
Substitute 4 for y.
$$x = y - 3$$
$$x = 4 - 3$$
$$x = 1$$
$$x = 1 \text{ and } y = 4$$

7. $\begin{cases} m = n + 7 \\ m + 5n = 37 \end{cases}$

Substitute $n + 7$ for m.
$$m + 5n = 37$$
$$(n + 7) + 5n = 37$$
$$6n + 7 = 37$$
$$6n = 30$$
$$\frac{1}{6}(6n) = \frac{1}{6}(30)$$
$$n = 5$$
Substitute 5 for n.
$$m = n + 7$$
$$m = 5 + 7$$
$$m = 12$$
$$m = 12 \text{ and } n = 5$$

8. $\begin{cases} y = 9 - x \\ x - y = 5 \end{cases}$

Substitute $9 - x$ for y.
$$x - y = 5$$
$$x - (9 - x) = 5$$
$$x + x - 9 = 5$$
$$2x - 9 = 5$$
$$2x - 9 + 9 = 5 + 9$$
$$2x = 14$$
$$\frac{1}{2}(2x) = \frac{1}{2}(14)$$
$$x = 7$$
Substitute 7 for x.
$$y = 9 - x$$
$$y = 9 - 7$$
$$y = 2$$
$$x = 7 \text{ and } y = 2$$

9. $\begin{cases} t = 11 - z \\ z - t = 15 \end{cases}$

Substitute $11 - z$ for t.
$$z - t = 15$$
$$z - (11 - z) = 15$$
$$z + z - 11 = 15$$
$$2z - 11 = 15$$
$$2z - 11 + 11 = 15 + 11$$
$$2z = 26$$
$$\frac{1}{2}(2z) = \frac{1}{2}(26)$$
$$z = 13$$
Substitute 13 for z.
$$t = 11 - z$$
$$t = 11 - 13$$
$$t = -2$$
$$t = -2 \text{ and } z = 13$$

10. $\begin{cases} w = 5 - 2y \\ y - 3w = 23 \end{cases}$

Substitute $5 - 2y$ for w.
$$y - 3w = 23$$
$$y - 3(5 - 2y) = 23$$
$$y - 15 + 6y = 23$$
$$7y - 15 = 23$$
$$7y - 15 + 15 = 23 + 15$$
$$7y = 38$$
$$\frac{7y}{7} = \frac{38}{7}$$
$$y = \frac{38}{7}, \text{ or } 5\frac{3}{7}$$

Substitute $\frac{38}{7}$ for y.
$$w = 5 - 2y$$
$$w = 5 - 2\left(\frac{38}{7}\right)$$
$$w = 5 - \frac{76}{7}$$
$$w = \frac{35}{7} - \frac{76}{7}$$
$$w = -\frac{41}{7}, \text{ or } -5\frac{6}{7}$$
$$w = -\frac{41}{7} \text{ and } y = \frac{38}{7}$$

11. $\begin{cases} c = 9 + 3d \\ 3d - 4c = 36 \end{cases}$

Substitute $9 + 3d$ for c.
$$3d - 4c = 36$$
$$3d - 4(9 + 3d) = 36$$
$$3d - 36 - 12d = 36$$
$$-9d - 36 = 36$$
$$-9d - 36 + 36 = 36 + 36$$
$$-9d = 72$$
$$-\frac{1}{9}(-9d) = -\frac{1}{9}(72)$$
$$d = -8$$

Substitute -8 for d.
$$c = 9 + 3d$$
$$c = 9 + 3(-8)$$
$$c = 9 - 24$$
$$c = -15$$
$$c = -15 \text{ and } d = -8$$

12. $\begin{cases} 2x + y = 11 \\ x + y = 14 \end{cases}$

$$x + y = 14$$
$$x + y - x = 14 - x$$
$$y = 14 - x$$

Substitute $14 - x$ for y.
$$2x + y = 11$$
$$2x + (14 - x) = 11$$
$$2x + 14 - x = 11$$
$$x + 14 = 11$$
$$x + 14 - 14 = 11 - 14$$
$$x = -3$$

Substitute -3 for x.
$$x + y = 14$$
$$(-3) + y = 14$$
$$-3 + y + 3 = 14 + 3$$
$$y = 17$$
$$x = -3 \text{ and } y = 17$$

13. $\begin{cases} 3w + 5z = 19 \\ w - z = 3 \end{cases}$

$$w - z = 3$$
$$w - z + z = 3 + z$$
$$w = 3 + z$$

Substitute $3 + z$ for w.
$$3w + 5z = 19$$
$$3(3 + z) + 5z = 19$$
$$9 + 3z + 5z = 19$$
$$9 + 8z = 19$$
$$9 + 8z - 9 = 19 - 9$$
$$8z = 10$$
$$\frac{1}{8}(8z) = \frac{1}{8}(10)$$
$$z = \frac{10}{8}, \text{ or } \frac{5}{4}, \text{ or } 1\frac{1}{4}$$

Substitute $\frac{5}{4}$ for z.
$$w = 3 + z$$
$$w = 3 + \frac{5}{4}$$
$$w = \frac{17}{4}, \text{ or } 4\frac{1}{4}$$
$$w = 4\frac{1}{4} \text{ and } z = 1\frac{1}{4}$$

14. $\begin{cases} m - 2n = 20 \\ 2m + n = 5 \end{cases}$

$$m - 2n = 20$$
$$m - 2n + 2n = 20 + 2n$$
$$m = 20 + 2n$$

Substitute $20 + 2n$ for m.
$$2m + n = 5$$
$$2(20 + 2n) + n = 5$$
$$40 + 4n + n = 5$$
$$40 + 5n = 5$$
$$40 + 5n - 40 = 5 - 40$$
$$5n = -35$$
$$\frac{1}{5}(5n) = \frac{1}{5}(-35)$$
$$n = -7$$

Substitute -7 for n.
$$m = 20 + 2n$$
$$m = 20 + 2(-7)$$
$$m = 6$$
$$m = 6 \text{ and } n = -7$$

15. $\begin{cases} x + 2y = 11 \\ 3x + y = 3 \end{cases}$

$$x + 2y = 11$$
$$x + 2y - 2y = 11 - 2y$$
$$x = 11 - 2y$$

Substitute $11 - 2y$ for x.
$$3x + y = 3$$
$$3(11 - 2y) + y = 3$$
$$33 - 6y + y = 3$$
$$33 - 5y = 3$$
$$33 - 5y - 33 = 3 - 33$$
$$-5y = -30$$
$$-\frac{1}{5}(-5y) = -\frac{1}{5}(-30)$$
$$y = 6$$

Substitute 6 for y.
$$x = 11 - 2y$$
$$x = 11 - 2(6)$$
$$x = 1 - 12$$
$$x = -1$$
$$x = -1 \text{ and } y = 6$$

16. $\begin{cases} x + y = 13 \\ x - 2y = -2 \end{cases}$

$x + y = 13$

$x + y - y = 13 - y$

$x = 13 - y$

Substitute $13 - y$ for x.

$x - 2y = -2$

$(13 - y) - 2y = -2$

$13 - 3y = -2$

$13 - 3y - 13 = -2 - 13$

$-3y = -15$

$-\frac{1}{3}(-3y) = -\frac{1}{3}(-15)$

$y = 5$

Substitute 5 for y.

$x = 13 - y$

$x = 13 - 5$

$x = 8$

$x = 8$ and $y = 5$

19. $\begin{cases} 2z - 3w = 15 \\ z - 2w = 16 \end{cases}$

$z - 2w = 16$

$z - 2w + 2w = 16 + 2w$

$z = 16 + 2w$

Substitute $16 + 2w$ for z.

$2z - 3w = 15$

$2(16 + 2w) - 3w = 15$

$32 + 4w - 3w = 15$

$32 + w = 15$

$32 + w - 32 = 15 - 32$

$w = -17$

Substitute -17 for w.

$z = 16 + 2w$

$z = 16 + 2(-17)$

$z = 16 - 34$

$z = -18$

$z = -18$ and $w = -17$

17. $\begin{cases} m - n = 16 \\ m + 3n = 12 \end{cases}$

$m - n = 16$

$m - n + n = 16 + n$

$m = 16 + n$

Substitute $16 + n$ for m.

$m + 3n = 12$

$(16 + n) + 3n = 12$

$16 + 4n = 12$

$16 + 4n - 16 = 12 - 16$

$4n = -4$

$\frac{1}{4}(4n) = \frac{1}{4}(-4)$

$n = -1$

Substitute -1 for n.

$m = 16 + n$

$m = 16 + (-1)$

$m = 15$

$m = 15$ and $n = -1$

20. $\begin{cases} y = x - 4 \\ 2x - 5y = 2 \end{cases}$

Substitute $x - 4$ for y.

$2x - 5y = 2$

$2x - 5(x - 4) = 2$

$2x - 5x + 20 = 2$

$-3x + 20 = 2$

$-3x + 20 - 20 = 2 - 20$

$-3x = -18$

$-\frac{1}{3}(-3x) = -\frac{1}{3}(-18)$

$x = 6$

Substitute 6 for x.

$y = x - 4$

$y = 6 - 4$

$y = 2$

$x = 6$ and $y = 2$

18. $\begin{cases} z - 2h = 18 \\ z + 3h = -2 \end{cases}$

$z - 2h = 18$

$z - 2h + 2h = 18 + 2h$

$z = 18 + 2h$

Substitute $18 + 2h$ for z.

$z + 3h = -2$

$(18 + 2h) + 3h = -2$

$18 + 5h = -2$

$18 + 5h - 18 = -2 - 18$

$5h = -20$

$\frac{1}{5}(5h) = \frac{1}{5}(-20)$

$h = -4$

Substitute -4 for h.

$z = 18 + 2h$

$z = 18 + 2(-4)$

$z = 18 - 8$

$z = 10$

$z = 10$ and $h = -4$

21. $\begin{cases} y = -x + 2 \\ 2x - y = 1 \end{cases}$

Substitute $-x + 2$ for y.

$2x - y = 1$

$2x - (-x + 2) = 1$

$2x + x - 2 = 1$

$3x - 2 = 1$

$3x - 2 + 2 = 1 + 2$

$3x = 3$

$\frac{1}{3}(3x) = \frac{1}{3}(3)$

$x = 1$

Substitute 1 for x.

$y = -x + 2$

$y = -1 + 2$

$y = 1$

$x = 1$ and $y = 1$

22. $\begin{cases} x = 2y - 1 \\ y = -2x + 3 \end{cases}$

Substitute $2y - 1$ for x.
$$y = -2x + 3$$
$$y = -2(2y - 1) + 3$$
$$y = -4y + 2 + 3$$
$$y = -4y + 5$$
$$y + 4y = -4y + 5 + 4y$$
$$5y = 5$$
$$\tfrac{1}{5}(5y) = \tfrac{1}{5}(5)$$
$$y = 1$$
Substitute 1 for y.
$$x = 2y - 1$$
$$x = 2(1) - 1$$
$$x = 2 - 1$$
$$x = 1$$
$x = 1$ and $y = 1$

23. $\begin{cases} 4x - 8 = y \\ 5x - 10 = -3y \end{cases}$

Substitute $4x - 8$ for y.
$$5x - 10 = -3y$$
$$5x - 10 = -3(4x - 8)$$
$$5x - 10 = -12x + 24$$
$$5x - 10 + 12x = -12x + 24 + 12x$$
$$17x - 10 = 24$$
$$17x - 10 + 10 = 24 + 10$$
$$17x = 34$$
$$\frac{17x}{17} = \frac{34}{17}$$
$$x = 2$$
Substitute 2 for x.
$$4x - 8 = y$$
$$4(2) - 8 = y$$
$$8 - 8 = y$$
$$0 = y$$
$x = 2$ and $y = 0$

24. $\begin{cases} x - y = 4 \\ 2x - 3y = -2 \end{cases}$
$$x - y = 4$$
$$x - y + y = 4 + y$$
$$x = 4 + y$$
Substitute $4 + y$ for x.
$$2x - 3y = -2$$
$$2(4 + y) - 3y = -2$$
$$8 + 2y - 3y = -2$$
$$8 - y = -2$$
$$8 - y - 8 = -2 - 8$$
$$-y = -10$$
$$-1(-y) = -1(-10)$$
$$y = 10$$
Substitute 10 for y.
$$x - y = 4$$
$$x - 10 = 4$$
$$x - 10 + 10 = 4 + 10$$
$$x = 14$$
$x = 14$ and $y = 10$

25. $\begin{cases} 5x + y = -15 \\ x - y = 3 \end{cases}$
$$x - y = 3$$
$$x - y + y = 3 + y$$
$$x = 3 + y$$
Substitute $3 + y$ for x.
$$5x + y = -15$$
$$5(3 + y) + y = -15$$
$$15 + 5y + y = -15$$
$$15 + 6y = -15$$
$$15 + 6y - 15 = -15 - 15$$
$$6y = -30$$
$$\tfrac{1}{6}(6y) = \tfrac{1}{6}(-30)$$
$$y = -5$$
Substitute -5 for y.
$$x - y = 3$$
$$x - (-5) = 3$$
$$x + 5 = 3$$
$$x + 5 - 5 = 3 - 5$$
$$x = -2$$
$x = -2$ and $y = -5$

26. $\begin{cases} x = y - 4 \\ 2y - 5x = 2 \end{cases}$

Substitute $y - 4$ for x.
$$2y - 5x = 2$$
$$2y - 5(y - 4) = 2$$
$$2y - 5y + 20 = 2$$
$$-3y + 20 = 2$$
$$-3y + 20 - 20 = 2 - 20$$
$$-3y = -18$$
$$-\tfrac{1}{3}(-3y) = -\tfrac{1}{3}(-18)$$
$$y = 6$$
Substitute 6 for y.
$$x = y - 4$$
$$x = 6 - 4$$
$$x = 2$$
$x = 2$ and $y = 6$

27. $\begin{cases} x = -y + 2 \\ 2y - x = 1 \end{cases}$

Substitute $-y + 2$ for x.
$$2y - x = 1$$
$$2y - (-y + 2) = 1$$
$$2y + y - 2 = 1$$
$$3y - 2 = 1$$
$$3y - 2 + 2 = 1 + 2$$
$$3y = 3$$
$$\tfrac{1}{3}(3y) = \tfrac{1}{3}(3)$$
$$y = 1$$
Substitute 1 for y.
$$x = -y + 2$$
$$x = -1 + 2$$
$$x = 1$$
$x = 1$ and $y = 1$

28. $\begin{cases} 4x - 8 = -y \\ 5x - 3 = -3y \end{cases}$

$4x - 8 = -y$

$-1(4x - 8) = (-y) -1$

$-4x + 8 = y$

Substitute $-4x + 8$ for y.

$5x - 3 = -3y$

$5x - 3 = -3(-4x + 8)$

$5x - 3 = 12x - 24$

$5x - 5x - 3 = 12x - 24 - 5x$

$-3 = 7x - 24$

$-3 + 24 = 7x - 24 + 24$

$21 = 7x$

$\frac{1}{7}(21) = \frac{1}{7}(7x)$

$3 = x$

Substitute 3 for x.

$4x - 8 = -y$

$4(3) - 8 = -y$

$12 - 8 = -y$

$4 = -y$

$-1(4) = (-y)(-1)$

$-4 = y$

$x = 3$ and $y = -4$

29. $\begin{cases} 3x - 16 = -2y \\ 7x - 19 = -y \end{cases}$

$7x - 19 = -y$

$-1(7x - 19) = (-y) -1$

$-7x + 19 = y$

Substitute $-7x + 19$ for y.

$3x - 16 = -2y$

$3x - 16 = -2(-7x + 19)$

$3x - 16 = 14x - 38$

$3x - 16 - 3x = 14x - 38 - 3x$

$-16 = 11x - 38$

$-16 + 38 = 11x - 38 + 38$

$22 = 11x$

$\frac{1}{11}(22) = \frac{1}{11}(11x)$

$2 = x$

Substitute 2 for x.

$7x - 19 = -y$

$7(2) - 19 = -y$

$14 - 19 = -y$

$-5 = -y$

$-1(-5) = -1(-y)$

$5 = y$

$x = 2$ and $y = 5$

30. $\begin{cases} x - 2y = -2 \\ 2x - 3y = 2 \end{cases}$

$x - 2y = -2$

$x - 2y + 2y = -2 + 2y$

$x = -2 + 2y$

Substitute $-2 + 2y$ for x.

$2x - 3y = 2$

$2(-2 + 2y) - 3y = 2$

$-4 + 4y - 3y = 2$

$-4 + y = 2$

$-4 + y + 4 = 2 + 4$

$y = 6$

Substitute 6 for y.

$x - 2y = -2$

$x - 2(6) = -2$

$x - 12 = -2$

$x - 12 + 12 = -2 + 12$

$x = 10$

$x = 10$ and $y = 6$

31. $\begin{cases} 2x + y = 5 \\ 8x - y = 45 \end{cases}$

$8x - y = 45$

$8x - y + y = 45 + y$

$8x = 45 + y$

$8x - 45 = 45 + y - 45$

$8x - 45 = y$

Substitute $8x - 45$ for y.

$2x + y = 5$

$2x + (8x - 45) = 5$

$10x - 45 = 5$

$10x = 50$

$x = 5$

Substitute 5 for x.

$8x - y = 45$

$8(5) - y = 45$

$40 - y = 45$

$-y = 5$

$y = -5$

$x = 5$ and $y = -5$

32. $\begin{cases} x + 2y = 5 \\ -3x - 2y = -3 \end{cases}$

$x + 2y = 5$

$x + 2y - 2y = 5 - 2y$

$x = 5 - 2y$

Substitute $5 - 2y$ for x.

$-3x - 2y = -3$

$-3(5 - 2y) - 2y = -3$

$-15 + 6y - 2y = -3$

$-15 + 4y = -3$

$-15 + 4y + 15 = -3 + 15$

$4y = 12$

$y = 3$

Substitute 3 for y.

$x + 2y = 5$

$x + 2(3) = 5$

$x + 6 = 5$

$x + 6 - 6 = 5 - 6$

$x = -1$

$x = -1$ and $y = 3$

33. $\begin{cases} y = 2.4x - 1.6 \\ y = -3.6x + 1.4 \end{cases}$

Substitute $2.4x - 1.6$ for y.

$y = -3.6x + 1.4$

$2.4x - 1.6 = -3.6x + 1.4$

$2.4x - 1.6 + 3.6x = -3.6x + 1.4 + 3.6x$

$6x - 1.6 = 1.4$

$6x - 1.6 + 1.6 = 1.4 + 1.6$

$6x = 3$

$\frac{1}{6}(6x) = \frac{1}{6}(3)$

$x = 0.5$

Substitute 0.5 for x.

$y = 2.4x - 1.6$

$y = 2.4(0.5) - 1.6$

$y = 1.2 - 1.6$

$y = -0.4$

$x = 0.5$ and $y = -0.4$

34. $\begin{cases} -5.7x + 1.8y = 9 \\ y = 1.5x + 3 \end{cases}$

Substitute $1.5x + 3$ for y.
$$-5.7x + 1.8y = 9$$
$$-5.7x + 1.8(1.5x + 3) = 9$$
$$-5.7x + 2.7x + 5.4 = 9$$
$$-3x + 5.4 = 9$$
$$-3x + 5.4 - 5.4 = 9 - 5.4$$
$$-3x = 3.6$$
$$-\tfrac{1}{3}(-3x) = -\tfrac{1}{3}(3.6)$$
$$x = -1.2$$

Substitute -1.2 for x.
$$y = 1.5x + 3$$
$$y = 1.5(-1.2) + 3$$
$$y = -1.8 + 3$$
$$y = 1.2$$
$x = -1.2$ and $y = 1.2$

37. $\begin{cases} y - 3 = \tfrac{1}{4}x - 3 \\ y + 2 = -x + 3 \end{cases}$

$$y - 3 = \tfrac{1}{4}x - 3$$
$$y - 3 + 3 = \tfrac{1}{4}x - 3 + 3$$
$$y = \tfrac{1}{4}x$$

Substitute $\tfrac{1}{4}x$ for y.
$$y + 2 = -x + 3$$
$$\tfrac{1}{4}x + 2 = -x + 3$$
$$\tfrac{1}{4}x + 2 + x = -x + 3 + x$$
$$\tfrac{5}{4}x + 2 = 3$$
$$\tfrac{5}{4}x + 2 - 2 = 3 - 2$$
$$\tfrac{5}{4}x = 1$$
$$\tfrac{4}{5}\left(\tfrac{5}{4}x\right) = \tfrac{4}{5}(1)$$
$$x = \tfrac{4}{5}$$

Substitute $\tfrac{4}{5}$ for x.
$$y - 3 = \tfrac{1}{4}x - 3$$
$$y - 3 = \tfrac{1}{4}\left(\tfrac{4}{5}\right) - 3$$
$$y - 3 = \tfrac{4}{20} - 3$$
$$y - 3 + 3 = \tfrac{4}{20} - 3 + 3$$
$$y = \tfrac{4}{20} = \tfrac{1}{5}$$
$x = \tfrac{4}{5}$ and $y = \tfrac{1}{5}$

35. $\begin{cases} y = \tfrac{5}{2}x - 2 \\ 11x - 4y = 8 \end{cases}$

Substitute $\tfrac{5}{2}x - 2$ for y.
$$11x - 4y = 8$$
$$11x - 4\left(\tfrac{5}{2}x - 2\right) = 8$$
$$11x - 10x + 8 = 8$$
$$x + 8 = 8$$
$$x + 8 - 8 = 8 - 8$$
$$x = 0$$

Substitute 0 for x.
$$y = \tfrac{5}{2}x - 2$$
$$y = \tfrac{5}{2}(0) - 2$$
$$y = 0 - 2$$
$$y = -2$$
$x = 0$ and $y = -2$

38. $\begin{cases} x + y = 320 \\ 0.1x + 0.18y = 0.15 \end{cases}$

$$x + y = 320$$
$$x + y - y = 320 - y$$
$$x = 320 - y$$

Substitute $320 - y$ for x.
$$0.1x + 0.18y = 0.15$$
$$0.1(320 - y) + 0.18y = 0.15$$
$$32 - 0.1y + 0.18y = 0.15$$
$$32 + 0.08y = 0.15$$
$$32 + 0.08y - 32 = 0.15 - 32$$
$$0.08y = -31.85$$
$$y = -398.125$$

Substitute -398.125 for y.
$$x = 320 - y$$
$$x = 320 - (-398.125)$$
$$x = 320 + 398.125$$
$$x = 718.125$$
$x = 718.125$ and $y = -398.125$

36. $\begin{cases} x = -\tfrac{3}{2}y + 2 \\ 2x + 4y = 4 \end{cases}$

Substitute $-\tfrac{3}{2}y + 2$ for x.
$$2x + 4y = 4$$
$$2\left(-\tfrac{3}{2}y + 2\right) + 4y = 4$$
$$-3y + 4 + 4y = 4$$
$$y + 4 = 4$$
$$y + 4 - 4 = 4 - 4$$
$$y = 0$$

Substitute 0 for y.
$$x = -\tfrac{3}{2}y + 2$$
$$x = -\tfrac{3}{2}(0) + 2$$
$$x = 0 + 2$$
$$x = 2$$
$x = 2$ and $y = 0$

39. $\begin{cases} x = \tfrac{1}{2}y - 3 \\ y = -4x + 3 \end{cases}$

Substitute $-4x + 3$ for y.
$$x = \tfrac{1}{2}y - 3$$
$$x = \tfrac{1}{2}(-4x + 3) - 3$$
$$x = -2x + \tfrac{3}{2} - 3$$
$$2x + x = -2x + 2x - \tfrac{3}{2}$$
$$3x = -\tfrac{3}{2}$$
$$x = -\tfrac{3}{6}, \text{ or } -\tfrac{1}{2}$$

Substitute $-\tfrac{1}{2}$ for x.
$$y = -4x + 3$$
$$y = -4\left(-\tfrac{1}{2}\right) + 3$$
$$y = 2 + 3$$
$$y = 5$$
$x = -\tfrac{1}{2}$ and $y = 5$

40. Let x represent the larger angle.
Let y represent the smaller angle.
$$\begin{cases} x + y = 180 \\ x = 3y \end{cases}$$
Substitute $3y$ for x.
$$x + y = 180$$
$$3y + y = 180$$
$$4y = 180$$
$$y = \frac{180}{4} = 45$$
Substitute 45 for y.
$$x = 3y$$
$$x = 3(45)$$
$$x = 135$$
The measure of the smaller angle is 45°.
The measure of the larger angle is 135°.

41. Let x represent the larger angle.
Let y represent the smaller angle.
$$\begin{cases} x + y = 90 \\ x = y + 10 \end{cases}$$
Substitute $y + 10$ for x.
$$x + y = 90$$
$$(y + 10) + y = 90$$
$$2y + 10 = 90$$
$$2y = 80$$
$$y = 40$$
Substitute 40 for y.
$$x = y + 10$$
$$x = 40 + 10$$
$$x = 50$$
The measure of the larger angle is 50°.
The measure of the smaller angle is 40°.

42. Let x represent the amount invested at 5%.
Let y represent the amount invested at 7%.
$$\begin{cases} 0.05x + 0.07y = 290 \\ x + y = 4500 \end{cases}$$
$$x + y = 4500$$
$$x = 4500 - y$$
Substitute $4500 - y$ for x.
$$0.05x + 0.07y = 290$$
$$0.05(4500 - y) + 0.07y = 290$$
$$225 - 0.05y + 0.07y = 290$$
$$225 + 0.02y = 290$$
$$225 + 0.02y - 225 = 290 - 225$$
$$0.02y = 65$$
$$y = 3250$$
Substitute 3250 for y.
$$x + y = 4500$$
$$x + 3250 = 4500$$
$$x = 1250$$
Margaret should invest $1250 at 5% and $3250 at 7%.

43. Let x represent the amount of the 30% solution.
Let y represent the amount of pure acid.
$$\begin{cases} x + y = 42 \\ 0.30x + 1.00y = 0.50(42) \Rightarrow 0.30x + y = 21 \end{cases}$$
$$x + y = 42$$
$$x = 42 - y$$
Substitute $42 - y$ for x.
$$0.30x + y = 21$$
$$0.30(42 - y) + y = 21$$
$$12.6 - 0.30y + y = 21$$
$$12.6 + 0.70y = 21$$
$$0.70y = 8.4$$
$$y = 12$$
Substitute 12 for y.
$$x + y = 42$$
$$x + 12 = 42$$
$$x = 30$$
The chemist should use 30 milliliters of the 30% solution and 12 milliliters of pure acid.

44. Let m represent the number of thermal mugs. Let b represent the number of baseball caps.
$$\begin{cases} 2m + 8b = 1422 \\ b = 2m \end{cases}$$
Substitute $2m$ for b.
$$2m + 8(2m) = 1422$$
$$2m + 16m = 1422$$
$$18m = 1422$$
$$m = 79$$
Substitute 79 for m.
$$b = 2m$$
$$b = 2(79)$$
$$b = 158$$
They sold 79 thermal mugs and 158 baseball caps.

45. Let x represent the larger number.
Let y represent the smaller number.
$$\begin{cases} x + y = 17 \\ y = x - 33 \end{cases}$$
Substitute $x - 33$ for y.
$$x + y = 17$$
$$x + (x - 33) = 17$$
$$2x - 33 = 17$$
$$2x = 50$$
$$x = 25$$
Substitute 25 for x.
$$y = x - 33$$
$$y = 25 - 33$$
$$y = -8$$
The smaller number is –8.
The larger number is 25.

46. Let x represent the larger number.
Let y represent the smaller number.
$$\begin{cases} x + y = 8 \\ 4x = 4y + 2 \end{cases}$$
$$x + y = 8$$
$$x = 8 - y$$
Substitute $8 - y$ for x.
$$4x = 4y + 2$$
$$4(8 - y) = 4y + 2$$
$$32 - 4y = 4y + 2$$
$$32 = 8y + 2$$
$$30 = 8y$$
$$\frac{30}{8} = y, \text{ or } y = \frac{15}{4}, \text{ or } 3\frac{3}{4}$$
Substitute $\frac{15}{4}$ for y.
$$x + \frac{15}{4} = 8$$
$$x = 4\frac{1}{4}$$
The smaller number is $3\frac{3}{4}$.

The larger number is $4\frac{1}{4}$.

47. Let m represent the larger number.
Let n represent the smaller number.

$$\begin{cases} m + n = 28 \\ m - n = 3 \end{cases}$$

$$m + n = 28$$
$$m = 28 - n$$

Substitute $28 - n$ for m.

$$m - n = 3$$
$$(28 - n) - n = 3$$
$$28 - 2n = 3$$
$$-2n = -25$$
$$n = \frac{25}{2}, \text{ or } 12\frac{1}{2}$$

Substitute $\frac{25}{2}$ for n.

$$m + n = 28$$
$$m + \frac{25}{2} = 28$$
$$m + \frac{25}{2} - \frac{25}{2} = 28 - \frac{25}{2}$$
$$m = 28 - \frac{25}{2}$$
$$m = \frac{31}{2}, \text{ or } 15\frac{1}{2}$$

The larger number is $15\frac{1}{2}$.

The smaller number is $12\frac{1}{2}$.

48. Let a represent the number of adult tickets sold.
Let s represent the number of student tickets sold.

$$a + s + 254 = 2000$$
or
$$\begin{cases} a + s = 1746 \\ 5a + 2s = 5766 \end{cases}$$

$$a + s = 1746$$
$$a = 1746 - s$$

Substitute $1746 - s$ for a.

$$5a + 2s = 5766$$
$$5(1746 - s) + 2s = 5766$$
$$8730 - 5s + 2s = 5766$$
$$8730 - 3s = 5766$$
$$-3s = -2964$$
$$s = 988$$

Substitute 988 for s.

$$a + s = 1746$$
$$a + 988 = 1746$$
$$a = 758$$

There were 758 adult tickets and 988 student tickets sold.

PAGE 509, LOOK BACK

49. $m = -3$
Use $(-2, 5)$ for (x_1, y_1)
in $y - y_1 = m(x - x_1)$.

$$y - 5 = -3(x - (-2))$$
$$y - 5 = -3(x + 2)$$
$$y - 5 = -3x - 6$$
$$y - 5 + 5 = -3x - 6 + 5$$
$$y = -3x - 1$$

50. $m = \frac{8 - 7}{3 - (-2)} = \frac{8 - 7}{3 + 2} = \frac{1}{5}$
Use $(3, 8)$ for (x_1, y_1).

$$y - 8 = \frac{1}{5}(x - 3)$$
$$y - 8 = \frac{1}{5}x - \frac{3}{5}$$
$$y - 8 + 8 = \frac{1}{5}x - \frac{3}{5} + 8$$
$$y = \frac{1}{5}x + \frac{37}{5}$$

51. Since the x-coordinates are the same, this is the vertical line $x = -3$.

52. Since the y-coordinates are the same, this is the horizontal line $y = 2$.

53.
$$2x - 3y = 5$$
$$2x - 3y - 2x = -2x + 5$$
$$-3y = -2x + 5$$
$$-\frac{1}{3}(-3y) = -\frac{1}{3}(-2x + 5)$$
$$y = \frac{2}{3}x - \frac{5}{3}$$
$$\text{slope} = \frac{2}{3}$$

A line perpendicular to
$y = \frac{2}{3}x - \frac{5}{3}$ has a slope of $-\frac{3}{2}$.
Answers may vary. One perpendicular line would be
$y = -\frac{3}{2}x$.

PAGE 509, LOOK BEYOND

54. $2xy \cdot 2x = 4x^2y$
$4x^2 \cdot y = 4x^2y$
The least common multiple of $2xy$ and $4x^2$ is $4x^2y$.

55. $3xz \cdot 5xy = 15x^2yz$
$5x^2y \cdot 3z = 15x^2yz$
The least common multiple of $3xz$ and $5x^2y$ is $15x^2yz$.

5. $\begin{cases} 3x + y = 7 \\ 2x + y = 3 \end{cases}$

$\begin{cases} 3x + y = 7 \rightarrow -1(3x) + -1(y) = -1(7) \rightarrow -3x - y = -7 \\ 2x + y = 3 \rightarrow \qquad\qquad 2x + y = 3 \qquad \rightarrow \underline{\quad 2x + y = 3} \\ \qquad\qquad\qquad\qquad\qquad\qquad\qquad\qquad\qquad -x = -4 \end{cases}$
$\qquad\qquad\qquad\qquad\qquad\qquad\qquad\qquad\qquad\qquad\qquad\quad x = 4$

Substitute 4 for x.
$$3x + y = 7$$
$$3(4) + y = 7$$
$$12 + y = 7$$
$$12 + y - 12 = 7 - 12$$
$$y = -5$$
$$(x, y) = (4, -5)$$

6. $\begin{cases} 3x + y = 6 \\ \underline{\ x - y = -2} \\ \ 4x = 4 \end{cases}$

$$\frac{4x}{4} = \frac{4}{4}$$
$$x = 1$$

Substitute 1 for x.
$$x - y = -2$$
$$1 - y = -2$$
$$1 - y - 1 = -2 - 1$$
$$-y = -3$$
$$y = 3$$
$$(x, y) = (1, 3)$$

7. $\begin{cases} 4x - 2y = 10 \\ \underline{3x + 2y = 4} \\ \ 7x = 14 \end{cases}$

$$\frac{7x}{7} = \frac{14}{7}$$
$$x = 2$$

Substitute 2 for x.
$$4x - 2y = 10$$
$$4(2) - 2y = 10$$
$$8 - 2y = 10$$
$$8 - 2y - 8 = 10 - 8$$
$$-2y = 2$$
$$\frac{-2y}{-2} = \frac{2}{-2}$$
$$y = -1$$
$$(x, y) = (2, -1)$$

8. $\begin{cases} 3x - y = 4 \\ 2x - y = 2 \end{cases}$

$\begin{cases} 3x - y = 4 \rightarrow -1(3x) - (-1)(y) = -1(4) \rightarrow -3x + y = -4 \\ 2x - y = 2 \rightarrow \qquad\qquad 2x - y = 2 \qquad \rightarrow \underline{\quad 2x - y = 2} \\ \qquad\qquad\qquad\qquad\qquad\qquad\qquad\qquad\qquad -x = -2 \end{cases}$
$\qquad\qquad\qquad\qquad\qquad\qquad\qquad\qquad\qquad\qquad\qquad\quad x = 2$

Substitute 2 for x.
$$2x - y = 2$$
$$2(2) - y = 2$$
$$4 - y = 2$$
$$4 - y - 4 = 2 - 4$$
$$-y = -2$$
$$-1(-y) = -1(-2)$$
$$y = 2$$
$$(x, y) = (2, 2)$$

9. $\begin{cases} 3x + y = 10 \\ 2x + y = 8 \end{cases}$

$\begin{cases} 3x + y = 10 \rightarrow \qquad\qquad 3x + y = 10 \qquad \rightarrow \ 3x + y = 10 \\ 2x + y = 8 \ \rightarrow -1(2x) + -1(y) = -1(8) \rightarrow \underline{-2x - y = -8} \\ \qquad\qquad\qquad\qquad\qquad\qquad\qquad\qquad\qquad\qquad x = 2 \end{cases}$

Substitute 2 for x.
$$3x + y = 10$$
$$3(2) + y = 10$$
$$6 + y = 10$$
$$6 + y - 6 = 10 - 6$$
$$y = 4$$
$$(x, y) = (2, 4)$$

10. $\begin{cases} 5x + 7y = 11 \\ 5x + 3y = 3 \end{cases}$

$\begin{cases} 5x + 7y = 11 \rightarrow \qquad\qquad 5x + 7y = 11 \qquad \rightarrow \ 5x + 7y = 11 \\ 5x + 3y = 3 \ \rightarrow -1(5x) + -1(3y) = -1(3) \rightarrow \underline{-5x - 3y = -3} \\ \qquad\qquad\qquad\qquad\qquad\qquad\qquad\qquad\qquad\qquad 4y = 8 \\ \qquad\qquad\qquad\qquad\qquad\qquad\qquad\qquad\qquad\qquad\ y = 2 \end{cases}$

Substitute 2 for y.
$$5x + 7y = 11$$
$$5x + 7(2) = 11$$
$$5x + 14 = 11$$
$$5x + 14 - 14 = 11 - 14$$
$$5x = -3$$
$$\frac{5x}{5} = \frac{-3}{5}$$
$$x = -\frac{3}{5}$$
$$(x, y) = \left(-\frac{3}{5}, 2\right)$$

11. $\begin{cases} x - y = 4 \\ x + y = 2 \end{cases}$

$2x = 6$

$\dfrac{2x}{2} = \dfrac{6}{2}$

$x = 3$

Substitute 3 for x.

$x - y = 4$

$3 - y = 4$

$-y = 1$

$y = -1$

$(x, y) = (3, -1)$

12. $\begin{cases} 2x + y = 5 \\ x + y = -2 \end{cases} \quad \to \quad \begin{array}{l} 2x + y = 5 \\ -1(x + y) = (-2) \end{array} \quad \to \quad \begin{array}{l} 2x + y = 5 \\ \underline{-x - y = 2} \\ x = 7 \end{array}$

Substitute 7 for x.

$2x + y = 5$

$2(7) + y = 5$

$14 + y = 5$

$14 + y - 14 = 5 - 14$

$y = -9$

$(x, y) = (7, -9)$

13. $\begin{cases} 4x + y = 2 \\ x - y = 3 \end{cases}$

$5x = 5$

$\dfrac{5x}{5} = \dfrac{5}{5}$

$x = 1$

Substitute 1 for x.

$x - y = 3$

$1 - y = 3$

$1 - y - 1 = 3 - 1$

$-y = 2$

$y = -2$

$(x, y) = (1, -2)$

14. $\begin{cases} 3x - 2y = -13 \\ 3x + y = 2 \end{cases} \quad \to \quad \begin{array}{l} 3x - 2y = -13 \\ 2(3x + y) = 2(2) \end{array} \quad \to \quad \begin{array}{l} 3x - 2y = -13 \\ \underline{6x + 2y = 4} \\ 9x = -9 \\ x = -1 \end{array}$

Substitute -1 for x.

$3x + y = 2$

$3(-1) + y = 2$

$-3 + y = 2$

$y = 5$

$(x, y) = (-1, 5)$

15. $\begin{cases} x + 2y = 3 \\ 3x - 2y = 5 \end{cases}$

$4x = 8$

$\dfrac{4x}{4} = \dfrac{8}{4}$

$x = 2$

Substitute 2 for x.

$x + 2y = 3$

$2 + 2y = 3$

$2y = 1$

$y = \dfrac{1}{2}$

$(x, y) = \left(2, \dfrac{1}{2}\right)$

16. $\begin{cases} x - y = 3 \\ 2x - y = 2 \end{cases} \quad \to \quad \begin{array}{l} -1(x - y) = -1(3) \\ 2x - y = 2 \end{array} \quad \to \quad \begin{array}{l} -x + y = -3 \\ \underline{2x - y = 2} \\ x = -1 \end{array}$

Substitute -1 for x.

$x - y = 3$

$-1 - y = 3$

$-y = 4$

$y = -4$

$(x, y) = (-1, -4)$

17. $\begin{cases} x + 4y = 10 \\ x + 3y = 13 \end{cases} \quad \to \quad \begin{array}{l} -1(x + 4y) = -1(10) \\ x + 3y = 13 \end{array} \quad \to \quad \begin{array}{l} -x - 4y = -10 \\ \underline{x + 3y = 13} \\ -y = 3 \\ y = -3 \end{array}$

Substitute -3 for y.

$x + 4y = 10$

$x + 4(-3) = 10$

$x - 12 = 10$

$x = 22$

$(x, y) = (22, -3)$

18. $\begin{cases} 7a + 5c = 37 \\ 2a - 5c = 8 \end{cases}$

$9a = 45$

$\dfrac{9a}{9} = \dfrac{45}{9}$

$a = 5$

Substitute 5 for a.

$7a + 5c = 37$

$7(5) + 5c = 37$

$35 + 5c = 37$

$35 + 5c - 35 = 37 - 35$

$5c = 2$

$\dfrac{5c}{5} = \dfrac{2}{5}$

$c = \dfrac{2}{5}$

$(a, c) = \left(5, \dfrac{2}{5}\right)$

19. $\begin{cases} 4w - 2z = 15 \\ 3w + 2z = 13 \end{cases}$

$7w = 28$

$\dfrac{7w}{7} = \dfrac{28}{7}$

$w = 4$

Substitute 4 for w.

$3w + 2z = 13$

$3(4) + 2z = 13$

$12 + 2z = 13$

$12 + 2z - 12 = 13 - 12$

$2z = 1$

$\dfrac{2z}{2} = \dfrac{1}{2}$

$z = \dfrac{1}{2}$

$w = 4$ and $z = \dfrac{1}{2}$

20. $\begin{cases} 4w + 5c = 12 \\ 4w + 6c = 16 \end{cases}$ $\begin{array}{l} \rightarrow -1(4w+5c) = -1(12) \rightarrow -4w - 5c = -12 \\ \rightarrow 4w + 6c = 16 \rightarrow \underline{4w + 6c = 16} \\ c = 4 \end{array}$

Substitute 4 for c.
$$4w + 5c = 12$$
$$4w + 5(4) = 12$$
$$4w + 20 = 12$$
$$4w + 20 - 20 = 12 - 20$$
$$4w = -8$$
$$\frac{4w}{4} = \frac{-8}{4}$$
$$w = -2$$
$$c = 4 \text{ and } w = -2$$

21. $\begin{cases} 2m - 3n = 16 \\ 5m - 3n = 13 \end{cases}$ $\begin{array}{l} \rightarrow 2m - 3n = 16 \rightarrow 2m - 3n = 16 \\ \rightarrow -1(5m - 3n) = -1(13) \rightarrow \underline{-5m + 3n = -13} \\ -3m = 3 \\ \frac{-3m}{-3} = \frac{3}{-3} \\ m = -1 \end{array}$

Substitute -1 for m.
$$2m - 3n = 16$$
$$2(-1) - 3n = 16$$
$$-2 - 3n = 16$$
$$-2 - 3n + 2 = 16 + 2$$
$$-3n = 18$$
$$\frac{-3n}{-3} = \frac{18}{-3}$$
$$n = -6$$
$$m = -1 \text{ and } n = -6$$

22. $\begin{cases} 4p - 5q = 11 \\ 2p - 5q = 17 \end{cases}$ $\begin{array}{l} \rightarrow 4p - 5q = 11 \rightarrow 4p - 5q = 11 \\ \rightarrow -1(2p - 5q) = -1(17) \rightarrow \underline{-2p + 5q = -17} \\ 2p = -6 \\ \frac{2p}{2} = \frac{-6}{2} \\ p = -3 \end{array}$

Substitute -3 for p.
$$4p - 5q = 11$$
$$4(-3) - 5q = 11$$
$$-12 - 5q = 11$$
$$-12 - 5q + 12 = 11 + 12$$
$$-5q = 23$$
$$\frac{-5q}{-5} = \frac{23}{-5}$$
$$q = -\frac{23}{5}, \text{ or } -4\frac{3}{5}$$
$$p = -3 \text{ and } q = -4\frac{3}{5}$$

23. $\begin{cases} 3x - y = 12 \\ y = -3x + 5 \end{cases}$ $\begin{array}{l} \rightarrow 3x - y = 12 \\ \rightarrow \underline{3x + y = 5} \\ 6x = 17 \\ \frac{6x}{6} = \frac{17}{6} \\ x = \frac{17}{6}, \text{ or } 2\frac{5}{6} \end{array}$

Substitute $\frac{17}{6}$ for x.
$$y = -3x + 5$$
$$y = -3\left(\frac{17}{6}\right) + 5$$
$$y = \frac{-51}{6} + 5$$
$$y = \frac{-51}{6} + \frac{30}{6}$$
$$y = \frac{-21}{6}$$
$$y = -3\frac{3}{6}, \text{ or } -3\frac{1}{2}$$
$$(x, y) = \left(2\frac{5}{6}, -3\frac{1}{2}\right)$$

24. $\begin{cases} 4m + 3n = 15 \\ 4m = -2n + 10 \end{cases}$ $\begin{array}{l} \rightarrow 4m + 3n = 15 \rightarrow 4m + 3n = 15 \rightarrow 4m + 3n = 15 \\ \rightarrow 4m + 2n = 10 \rightarrow -1(4m + 2n) = -1(10) \rightarrow \underline{-4m - 2n = -10} \\ n = 5 \end{array}$

Substitute 5 for n.
$$4m = -2n + 10$$
$$4m = -2(5) + 10$$
$$4m = -10 + 10$$
$$4m = 0$$
$$m = 0$$
$$(m, n) = (0, 5)$$

25. $\begin{cases} \frac{4}{5}x + 2y = 6 \\ \frac{4}{5}x + 5y = 21 \end{cases} \to \begin{matrix} -1\left(\frac{4}{5}x + 2y\right) = -1(6) \\ \frac{4}{5}x + 5y = 21 \end{matrix} \to \begin{matrix} -\frac{4}{5}x - 2y = -6 \\ \frac{4}{5}x + 5y = 21 \\ \hline 3y = 15 \\ y = 5 \end{matrix}$

Substitute 5 for y.

$\frac{4}{5}x + 2y = 6$

$\frac{4}{5}x + 2(5) = 6$

$\frac{4}{5}x + 10 = 6$

$\frac{4}{5}x = -4$

$\frac{5}{4}\left(\frac{4}{5}x\right) = \frac{5}{4}(-4)$

$x = -5$

$(x, y) = (-5, 5)$

26. $\begin{cases} x + 3y = \frac{4}{5} \\ x - 3y = -\frac{1}{5} \\ \hline 2x = \frac{3}{5} \end{cases}$

$\frac{1}{2}(2x) = \frac{1}{2}\left(\frac{3}{5}\right)$

$x = \frac{3}{10}$

Substitute $\frac{3}{10}$ for x.

$x + 3y = \frac{4}{5}$

$\frac{3}{10} + 3y = \frac{4}{5}$

$3y = \frac{4}{5} - \frac{3}{10}$

$3y = \frac{8}{10} - \frac{3}{10}$

$3y = \frac{5}{10}$

$\frac{1}{3}(3y) = \frac{1}{3}\left(\frac{5}{10}\right)$

$y = \frac{5}{30}, \text{ or } \frac{1}{6}$

$(x, y) = \left(\frac{3}{10}, \frac{1}{6}\right)$

27. $\begin{cases} 5x - y = -\frac{3}{5} \\ 2x - y = \frac{3}{5} \end{cases} \to \begin{matrix} -1(5x - y) = -1\left(-\frac{3}{5}\right) \\ 2x - y = \frac{3}{5} \end{matrix} \to \begin{matrix} -5x + y = \frac{3}{5} \\ 2x - y = \frac{3}{5} \\ \hline -3x = \frac{6}{5} \end{matrix}$

$-\frac{1}{3}(-3x) = -\frac{1}{3}\left(\frac{6}{5}\right)$

$x = -\frac{6}{15}, \text{ or } -\frac{2}{5}$

Substitute $-\frac{2}{5}$ for x.

$5x - y = -\frac{3}{5}$

$5\left(-\frac{2}{5}\right) - y = -\frac{3}{5}$

$-\frac{10}{5} - y = -\frac{3}{5}$

$-y = -\frac{3}{5} + \frac{10}{5}$

$-y = \frac{7}{5}$

$y = -\frac{7}{5}$

$(x, y) = \left(-\frac{2}{5}, -\frac{7}{5}\right)$

28. $\begin{cases} 5y = 2x - 1 \\ y = -2x + 3 \\ \hline 6y = 2 \end{cases}$

$y = \frac{2}{6}, \text{ or } \frac{1}{3}$

Substitute $\frac{1}{3}$ for y.

$5y = 2x - 1$

$5\left(\frac{1}{3}\right) = 2x - 1$

$\frac{5}{3} = 2x - 1$

$\frac{5}{3} + 1 = 2x$

$\frac{8}{3} = 2x$

$\frac{1}{2}\left(\frac{8}{3}\right) = \frac{1}{2}(2x)$

$\frac{8}{6} = x, \text{ or } x = \frac{4}{3}$

$(x, y) = \left(\frac{4}{3}, \frac{1}{3}\right)$

29. $\begin{cases} 1.3x = 2.5y - 1 \\ y = -1.3x + 3 \end{cases} \to \begin{matrix} 1.3x - 2.5y = -1 \\ 1.3x + y = 3 \end{matrix} \to \begin{matrix} -1(1.3x - 2.5y) = -1(-1) \\ 1.3x + y = 3 \end{matrix} \to \begin{matrix} -1.3x + 2.5y = 1 \\ 1.3x + y = 3 \\ \hline 3.5y = 4 \\ \frac{3.5y}{3.5} = \frac{4}{3.5} \\ y = \frac{8}{7} \end{matrix}$

Substitute $\frac{8}{7}$ for y.

$y = -1.3x + 3$

$\frac{8}{7} = -1.3x + 3$

$\frac{8}{7} - 3 = -1.3x$

$-\frac{13}{7} = -1.3x$

$\left(-\frac{1}{1.3}\right)\left(-\frac{13}{7}\right) = (-1.3x)\left(-\frac{1}{1.3}\right)$

$\frac{10}{7} = x$

$(x, y) = \left(\frac{10}{7}, \frac{8}{7}\right)$

30. $\begin{cases} 0.2m - 0.3n = 1.4 \ \rightarrow \\ 0.2m - 1.5n = 6.2 \ \rightarrow \end{cases}$ $\begin{aligned} 0.2m - 0.3n &= 1.4 \\ -1(0.2m - 1.5n) &= -1(6.2) \end{aligned}$ $\rightarrow$ $\begin{aligned} 0.2m - 0.3n &= 1.4 \\ \underline{-0.2m + 1.5n} &= \underline{-6.2} \\ 1.2n &= -4.8 \\ \frac{1.2n}{1.2} &= \frac{-4.8}{1.2} \\ n &= -4 \end{aligned}$

Substitute -4 for n.
$$0.2m - 0.3n = 1.4$$
$$0.2m - 0.3(-4) = 1.4$$
$$0.2m + 1.2 = 1.4$$
$$0.2m + 1.2 - 1.2 = 1.4 - 1.2$$
$$0.2m = 0.2$$
$$\frac{0.2m}{0.2} = \frac{0.2}{0.2}$$
$$m = 1$$
$$(m, n) = (1, -4)$$

31. Let x represent the number of adult tickets.
Let y represent the number of children's tickets.
$\begin{cases} 2x + 1y = 656 \ \rightarrow \\ x + y = 400 \ \rightarrow \end{cases}$ $\begin{aligned} 2x + y &= 656 \\ 1(x + y) &= -1(400) \end{aligned}$ $\rightarrow$ $\begin{aligned} 2x + y &= 656 \\ \underline{-x - y} &= \underline{-400} \\ x &= 256 \end{aligned}$

Substitute 256 for x.
$$x + y = 400$$
$$256 + y = 400$$
$$256 + y - 256 = 400 - 256$$
$$y = 144$$

The drama club sold 256 adult tickets and 144 children's tickets.

32. Let b represent the number of buttons sold.
Let p represent the number of programs sold.
$\begin{cases} b + p = 150 \ \rightarrow \\ b + 2p = 285 \ \rightarrow \end{cases}$ $\begin{aligned} -1(b + p) &= -1(150) \\ b + 2p &= 285 \end{aligned}$ $\rightarrow$ $\begin{aligned} -b - p &= -150 \\ \underline{b + 2p} &= \underline{285} \\ p &= 135 \end{aligned}$

Substitute 135 for p.
$$b + p = 150$$
$$b + 135 = 150$$
$$b + 135 - 135 = 150 - 135$$
$$b = 15$$

The Booster club sold 15 buttons and 135 programs

33. Let x represent the amount invested in the secured fund.
Let y represent the amount invested in the unsecured fund.
$\begin{cases} 0.04x + 0.06y = 216 \ \rightarrow \\ 0.04x + 0.08y = 272 \ \rightarrow \end{cases}$ $\begin{aligned} -0.04x - 0.06y &= -216 \\ \underline{0.04x + 0.08y} &= \underline{272} \\ 0.02y &= 56 \\ y &= 2800 \end{aligned}$

Substitute 2800 for y.
$$0.04x + 0.08y = 272$$
$$0.04x + 0.08(2800) = 272$$
$$0.04x + 224 = 272$$
$$0.04x + 224 - 224 = 272 - 224$$
$$0.04x = 48$$
$$\frac{0.04x}{0.04} = \frac{48}{0.04}$$
$$x = 1200$$

Morris is planning to invest \$1200 in a secured account and \$2800 in an unsecured account.

PAGE 516, LOOK BACK

34. $\begin{aligned} d + h - k &= 3l \\ d + h - k + k &= 3l + k \\ d + h &= 3l + k \\ d + h - 3l &= 3l + k - 3l \\ d + h - 3l &= k \end{aligned}$

35. $\begin{aligned} kxh &= r \\ \frac{1}{xh}(kxh) &= \frac{1}{xh}(r) \\ k &= \frac{r}{xh} \end{aligned}$

36. $\begin{aligned} mk - 4t &= 8s \\ mk - 4t + 4t &= 8s + 4t \\ mk &= 8s + 4t \\ \frac{mk}{m} &= \frac{8s + 4t}{m} \\ k &= \frac{8s + 4t}{m} \end{aligned}$

37. $\begin{aligned} -k + m &= x \\ -k + m + k &= x + k \\ m &= x + k \\ m - x &= x + k - x \\ m - x &= k \end{aligned}$

38. $\begin{aligned} 2x - 5 &< 8x - 4 \\ 2x - 5 - 2x &< 8x - 2x - 4 \\ -5 &< 6x - 4 \\ -5 + 4 &< 6x - 4 + 4 \\ -1 &< 6x \\ \frac{-1}{6} &< \frac{6x}{6} \\ -\frac{1}{6} &< x \end{aligned}$
or
$$x > -\frac{1}{6}$$

39. $\begin{aligned} 3(x - 4) &\geq 4(x + 7) - 3 \\ 3x - 12 &\geq 4x + 28 - 3 \\ 3x - 12 &\geq 4x + 25 \\ 3x - 12 - 3x &\geq 4x - 3x + 25 \\ -12 &\geq x + 25 \\ -12 - 25 &\geq x + 25 - 25 \\ -37 &\geq x \end{aligned}$
or
$$x \leq -37$$

40. $\begin{cases} 2x - y = 6 \;\rightarrow\; -y = -2x + 6 \;\rightarrow\; y = 2x - 6 \\ y = 3x - 4 \;\rightarrow\; \quad y = 3x - 4 \quad \rightarrow\; y = 3x - 4 \end{cases}$

Substitute $3x - 4$ for y.

$$2x - y = 6$$
$$2x - (3x - 4) = 6$$
$$-x + 4 = 6$$
$$-x + 4 - 4 = 6 - 4$$
$$-x = 2$$
$$x = -2$$

Substitute -2 for x.

$$y = 3x - 4$$
$$y = 3(-2) - 4$$
$$y = -6 - 4$$
$$y = -10$$
$$(x, y) = (-2, -10)$$

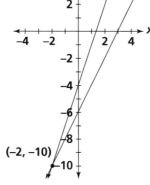

41. $\begin{cases} 2x + 3y = 7 \;\rightarrow\; 3y = 2x + 7 \;\rightarrow\; y = -\frac{2}{3}x + \frac{7}{3} \\ x + y = 2 \;\rightarrow\; \quad y = -x + 2 \;\rightarrow\; y = -x + 2 \end{cases}$

Substitute $-x + 2$ for y.

$$2x + 3y = 7$$
$$2x + 3(-x + 2) = 7$$
$$2x - 3x + 6 = 7$$
$$-x + 6 = 7$$
$$-x + 6 - 6 = 7 - 6$$
$$-x = 1$$
$$x = -1$$

Substitute -1 for x.

$$x + y = 2$$
$$-1 + y = 2$$
$$-1 + y + 1 = 2 + 1$$
$$y = 3$$

$$(x, y) = (-1, 3)$$

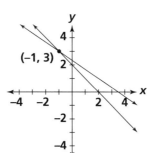

42. $\begin{cases} y = -5x + 9 \\ 3x - 4y = 10 \;\rightarrow\; -4y = -3x + 10 \;\rightarrow\; y = \frac{3}{4}x - \frac{10}{4} \end{cases}$

Substitute $-5x + 9$ for y.

$$3x - 4y = 10$$
$$3x - 4(-5x + 9) = 10$$
$$3x + 20x - 36 = 10$$
$$23x - 36 = 10$$
$$23x = 46$$
$$\frac{23x}{23} = \frac{46}{23}$$
$$x = 2$$

Substitute 2 for x.

$$y = -5x + 9$$
$$y = -5(2) + 9$$
$$y = -10 + 9$$
$$y = -1$$
$$(x, y) = (2, -1)$$

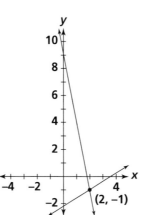

43.

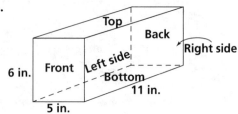

Area of bottom $= l \cdot w =$ Area of top
$$= 5 \cdot 11$$
$$= 55 \text{ square inches}$$
Area of front $= l \cdot w =$ Area of back
$$= 6 \cdot 5$$
$$= 30 \text{ square inches}$$
Area of left side $= l \cdot w =$ Area of right side
$$= 6 \cdot 11$$
$$= 66 \text{ square inches}$$

44. $y = 2x - 3$

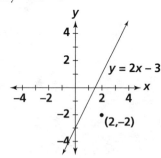

Answers may vary. $(2, -2)$ satisfies the inequality $y < 2x - 3$ because $-2 < 2(2) - 3$ or $-2 < 1$ is a true statement.

9.4 **PAGES 521–523, PRACTICE & APPLY**

7. $\begin{cases} x + 2y = 7 \rightarrow & x + 2y = 7 & \rightarrow & x + 2y = 7 \\ 2x - y = 4 \rightarrow & 2(2x - y) = 2(4) & \rightarrow & 4x - 2y = 8 \end{cases}$

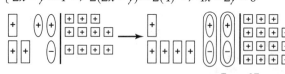

$$5x = 15$$
$$\frac{5x}{5} = \frac{15}{5}$$
$$x = 3$$

Substitute 3 for x.
$$x + 2y = 7$$
$$3 + 2y = 7$$
$$3 + 2y - 3 = 7 - 3$$
$$2y = 4$$
$$\frac{2y}{2} = \frac{4}{2}$$
$$y = 2$$
$$(x, y) = (3, 2)$$

8. $\begin{cases} 2x + y = 5 \rightarrow & -2(2x + y) = -2(5) & \rightarrow & -4x - 2y = -10 \\ 3x + 2y = 4 \rightarrow & 3x + 2y = 4 & \rightarrow & 3x + 2y = 4 \end{cases}$

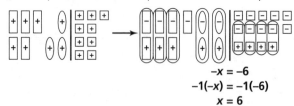

$$-x = -6$$
$$-1(-x) = -1(-6)$$
$$x = 6$$

Substitute 6 for x.
$$2x + y = 5$$
$$2(6) + y = 5$$
$$12 + y = 5$$
$$12 + y - 12 = 5 - 12$$
$$y = -7$$
$$(x, y) = (6, -7)$$

9. $\begin{cases} 5x - 4y = 6 \rightarrow & 5x - 4y = 6 & \rightarrow & 5x - 4y = 6 \\ 3x + y = 7 \rightarrow & 4(3x + y) = 4(7) & \rightarrow & 12x + 4y = 28 \end{cases}$

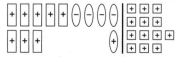

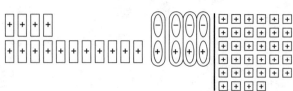

$$17x = 34$$
$$\frac{17x}{17} = \frac{34}{17}$$
$$x = 2$$

Substitute 2 for x.
$$5x - 4y = 6$$
$$5(2) - 4y = 6$$
$$10 - 4y = 6$$
$$10 - 4y - 10 = 6 - 10$$
$$-4y = -4$$
$$\frac{-4y}{-4} = \frac{-4}{-4}$$
$$y = 1$$
$$(x, y) = (2, 1)$$

10. $\begin{cases} 20x + 9y = 10 & \to & 20x + 9y = 10 & \to & 20x + 9y = 10 \\ 5x + 2y = 3 & \to & -4(5x + 2y) = -4(3) & \to & -20x - 8y = -12 \end{cases}$

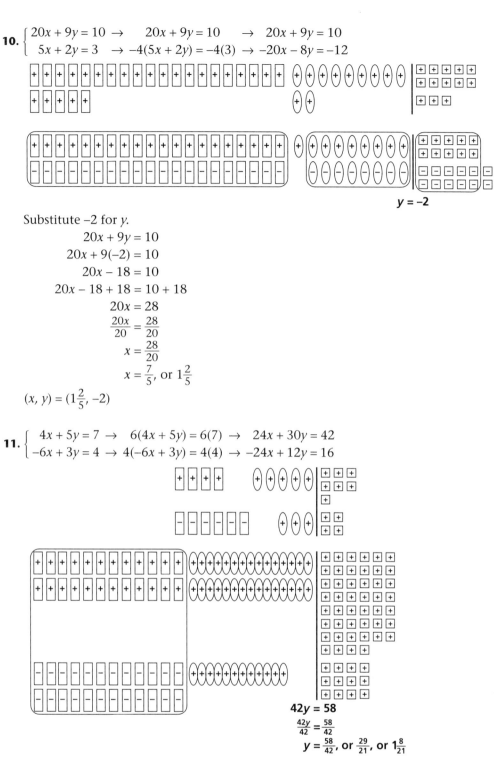

$$y = -2$$

Substitute -2 for y.

$$20x + 9y = 10$$
$$20x + 9(-2) = 10$$
$$20x - 18 = 10$$
$$20x - 18 + 18 = 10 + 18$$
$$20x = 28$$
$$\frac{20x}{20} = \frac{28}{20}$$
$$x = \frac{28}{20}$$
$$x = \frac{7}{5}, \text{ or } 1\frac{2}{5}$$

$(x, y) = \left(1\frac{2}{5}, -2\right)$

11. $\begin{cases} 4x + 5y = 7 & \to & 6(4x + 5y) = 6(7) & \to & 24x + 30y = 42 \\ -6x + 3y = 4 & \to & 4(-6x + 3y) = 4(4) & \to & -24x + 12y = 16 \end{cases}$

$$42y = 58$$
$$\frac{42y}{42} = \frac{58}{42}$$
$$y = \frac{58}{42}, \text{ or } \frac{29}{21}, \text{ or } 1\frac{8}{21}$$

Substitute $\frac{29}{21}$ for y.

$$4x + 5y = 7$$
$$4x + 5\left(\frac{29}{21}\right) = 7$$
$$4x + \frac{145}{21} = 7$$
$$4x + \frac{145}{21} - \frac{145}{21} = 7 - \frac{145}{21}$$
$$4x = \frac{2}{21}$$
$$\frac{1}{4}(4x) = \frac{1}{4}\left(\frac{2}{21}\right)$$
$$x = \frac{2}{84} = \frac{1}{42}$$

$(x, y) = \left(\frac{1}{42}, 1\frac{8}{21}\right)$

12. $\begin{cases} 2a - 4c = 5 \\ a - 3c = 7 \end{cases}$ $\begin{array}{l} \rightarrow \\ \rightarrow \end{array}$ $\begin{array}{l} 2a - 4c = 5 \\ -2(a - 3c) = -2(7) \end{array}$ $\begin{array}{l} \rightarrow \\ \rightarrow \end{array}$ $\begin{array}{l} 2a - 4c = 5 \\ -2a + 6c = -14 \end{array}$

Substitute $-\frac{9}{2}$ for c.

$$a - 3c = 7$$
$$a - 3\left(-\frac{9}{2}\right) = 7$$
$$a + \frac{27}{2} = 7$$
$$a + \frac{27}{2} - \frac{27}{2} = 7 - \frac{27}{2}$$
$$a = \frac{14}{2} - \frac{27}{2}$$
$$a = -\frac{13}{2}, \text{ or } -6\frac{1}{2}$$
$$(a, c) = \left(-6\frac{1}{2}, -4\frac{1}{2}\right)$$

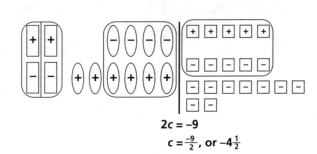

$$2c = -9$$
$$c = \frac{-9}{2}, \text{ or } -4\frac{1}{2}$$

13. $\begin{cases} 2x + 3y = 6 \\ 4x + y = 2 \end{cases}$ $\begin{array}{l} \rightarrow \\ \rightarrow \end{array}$ $\begin{array}{l} 2x + 3y = 6 \\ -3(4x + y) = -3(2) \end{array}$ $\begin{array}{l} \rightarrow \\ \rightarrow \end{array}$ $\begin{array}{l} 2x + 3y = 6 \\ \underline{-12x - 3y = -6} \end{array}$

$$-10x = 0$$
$$\frac{-10x}{-10} = \frac{0}{-10}$$
$$x = 0$$

Substitute 0 for x.

$$2x + 3y = 6$$
$$2(0) + 3y = 6$$
$$3y = 6$$
$$\frac{3y}{3} = \frac{6}{3}$$
$$y = 2$$
$$(x, y) = (0, 2)$$

14. $\begin{cases} 3x + y = 2 \\ x - 2y = 10 \end{cases}$ $\begin{array}{l} \rightarrow \\ \rightarrow \end{array}$ $\begin{array}{l} 2(3x + y) = 2(2) \\ x - 2y = 10 \end{array}$ $\begin{array}{l} \rightarrow \\ \rightarrow \end{array}$ $\begin{array}{l} 6x + 2y = 4 \\ \underline{x - 2y = 10} \end{array}$

$$7x = 14$$
$$\frac{7x}{7} = \frac{14}{7}$$
$$x = 2$$

Substitute 2 for x.

$$3x + y = 2$$
$$3(2) + y = 2$$
$$6 + y = 2$$
$$6 + y - 6 = 2 - 6$$
$$y = -4$$
$$(x, y) = (2, -4)$$

15. $\begin{cases} y = 2x + 3 \\ 6x - 12y = 6 \end{cases}$ $\begin{array}{l} \rightarrow \\ \rightarrow \end{array}$ $\begin{array}{l} -2x + y = 3 \\ 6x - 12y = 6 \end{array}$ $\begin{array}{l} \rightarrow \\ \rightarrow \end{array}$ $\begin{array}{l} 3(-2x + y) = 3(3) \\ 6x - 12y = 6 \end{array}$ $\begin{array}{l} \rightarrow \\ \rightarrow \end{array}$ $\begin{array}{l} 6x + 3y = 9 \\ \underline{6x - 12y = 6} \end{array}$

$$-9y = 15$$
$$\frac{-9y}{-9} = \frac{15}{-9}$$
$$y = -\frac{15}{9} = -\frac{5}{3}, \text{ or } -1\frac{2}{3}$$

Substitute $-\frac{5}{3}$ for y.

$$6x - 12y = 6$$
$$6x - 12\left(-\frac{5}{3}\right) = 6$$
$$6x + \frac{60}{3} = 6$$
$$6x + 20 = 6$$
$$6x + 20 - 20 = 6 - 20$$
$$6x = -14$$
$$\frac{6x}{6} = -\frac{14}{6}$$
$$x = -\frac{14}{6}, \text{ or } -\frac{7}{3}, \text{ or } -2\frac{1}{3}$$
$$(x, y) = \left(-2\frac{1}{3}, -1\frac{2}{3}\right)$$

16. $\begin{cases} 2a - 4c = 5 \\ 2a - 2c = 7 \end{cases}$ $\begin{aligned} \to & -1(2a - 4c) = -1(5) \to -2a + 4c = -5 \\ \to & \quad 2a - 2c = 7 \quad \to \underline{\quad 2a - 2c = 7 \quad} \end{aligned}$

$$2c = 2$$
$$\frac{2c}{2} = \frac{2}{2}$$
$$c = 1$$

Substitute 1 for c.
$$2a - 2c = 7$$
$$2a - 2(1) = 7$$
$$2a - 2 = 7$$
$$2a = 9$$
$$a = \frac{9}{2}, \text{ or } 4\frac{1}{2}$$
$$(a, c) = (4\tfrac{1}{2}, 1)$$

17. $\begin{cases} 5x - 4y = 1 \\ x + 2y = 8 \end{cases}$ $\begin{aligned} \to & \quad 5x - 4y = 1 \quad \to 5x + 4y = 1 \\ \to & \, 2(x + 2y) = 2(8) \to \underline{\, 2x + 4y = 16 \,} \end{aligned}$

$$7x = 17$$
$$\frac{7x}{7} = \frac{17}{7}$$
$$x = \frac{17}{7}, \text{ or } 2\frac{3}{7}$$

Substitute $\frac{17}{7}$ for x.
$$x + 2y = 8$$
$$\frac{17}{7} + 2y = 8$$
$$\frac{17}{7} + 2y - \frac{17}{7} = 8 - \frac{17}{7}$$
$$2y = \frac{39}{7}$$
$$\frac{1}{2}(2y) = \frac{1}{2}\left(\frac{39}{7}\right)$$
$$y = \frac{39}{14}, \text{ or } 2\frac{11}{14}$$
$$(x, y) = \left(2\tfrac{3}{7}, 2\tfrac{11}{14}\right)$$

18. $\begin{cases} 2x + y = 9 \\ 3x - 4y = 8 \end{cases}$ $\begin{aligned} \to & \, 4(2x + y) = 4(9) \to 8x + 4y = 36 \\ \to & \quad 3x - 4y = 8 \quad \to \underline{\, 3x - 4y = 8 \,} \end{aligned}$

$$11x = 44$$
$$x = 4$$

Substitute 4 for x.
$$2x + y = 9$$
$$2(4) + y = 9$$
$$8 + y = 9$$
$$y = 1$$
$$(x, y) = (4, 1)$$

19. $\begin{cases} 3x - 5y = 11 \\ 2x - 3y = 1 \end{cases}$ $\begin{aligned} \to & \, 2(3x - 5y) = 2(11) \to 6x - 10y = 22 \\ \to & \, -3(2x - 3y) = -3(1) \to \underline{\, -6x + 9y = -3 \,} \end{aligned}$

$$-y = 19$$
$$y = -19$$

Substitute -19 for y.
$$2x - 3y = 1$$
$$2x - 3(-19) = 1$$
$$2x + 57 = 1$$
$$2x = -56$$
$$x = -28$$
$$(x, y) = (-28, -19)$$

20. $\begin{cases} 9x + 2y = 2 \\ -21x + 6y = 4 \end{cases}$ $\begin{aligned} \to & \, -3(9x + 2y) = -3(2) \to -27x - 6y = -6 \\ \to & \quad -21x + 6y = 4 \quad \to \underline{\, -21x + 6y = 4 \,} \end{aligned}$

$$-48x = -2$$
$$\frac{-48x}{-48} = \frac{-2}{-48}$$
$$x = \frac{1}{24}$$

Substitute $\frac{1}{24}$ for x.
$$9x + 2y = 2$$
$$9\left(\frac{1}{24}\right) + 2y = 2$$
$$\frac{9}{24} + 2y = 2$$
$$2y = 2 - \frac{9}{24}$$
$$2y = \frac{48}{24} - \frac{9}{24}$$
$$2y = \frac{39}{24}$$
$$\frac{1}{2}(2y) = \frac{1}{2}\left(\frac{39}{24}\right)$$
$$y = \frac{39}{48}, \text{ or } \frac{13}{16}$$
$$(x, y) = \left(\frac{1}{24}, \frac{13}{16}\right)$$

21. $\begin{cases} 1.6x - 2.4y = 2 \\ 0.2x - 2.4y = 9 \end{cases}$ $\begin{aligned} \to & \quad 1.6x + 2.4y = 2 \quad \to 1.6x - 2.4y = 2 \\ \to & \, -1(0.2x - 2.4y) = -1(9) \to \underline{\, -0.2x + 2.4y = -9 \,} \end{aligned}$

$$1.4x = -7$$
$$\frac{1.4x}{1.4} = \frac{-7}{1.4}$$
$$x = -5$$

Substitute -5 for x.
$$0.2x - 2.4y = 9$$
$$0.2(-5) - 2.4y = 9$$
$$-1 - 2.4y = 9$$
$$-1 - 2.4y + 1 = 9 + 1$$
$$-2.4y = 10$$
$$\frac{-2.4y}{-2.4} = \frac{10}{-2.4}$$
$$y = -4.1\overline{6}, \text{ or } -4\frac{1}{6}$$
$$(x, y) = \left(-5, -4\tfrac{1}{6}\right)$$

22. Let x represent the amount of the 90% solution, and let y represent the amount of the 40% solution.

$$\begin{cases} x + y = 4 \\ 0.9x + 0.4y = 2.1 \end{cases} \begin{array}{l} \rightarrow \ -0.4(x+y) = -0.4(4) \rightarrow -0.4x - 0.4y = -1.6 \\ \rightarrow \ 0.9x + 0.4y = 2.1 \qquad\qquad \rightarrow \ \underline{0.9x + 0.4y = 2.1} \end{array}$$

Substitute 1 for x.
$$y + y = 4$$
$$1 + y = 4$$
$$1 + y - 1 = 4 - 1$$
$$y = 3$$

$$0.5x = 0.5$$
$$\frac{0.5x}{0.5} = \frac{0.5}{0.5}$$
$$x = 1$$

1 liter of the 90% solution and 3 liters of the 40% solution should be used.

23.

	First solution	Second solution	New solution
Percent antifreeze	25% = 0.25	100% = 1.00	40% = 0.40
Amount of solution	x	y	40 oz
Amount of antifreeze	0.25x	1.00$y = y$	0.25$x + y = 0.40(40)$

$$\begin{cases} x + y = 40 \\ 0.25x + y = 16 \end{cases} \begin{array}{l} \rightarrow \ -1(x+y) = -1(40) \rightarrow \ -x - y = -40 \\ \rightarrow \ 0.25x + y = 16 \qquad \rightarrow \underline{0.25x + y = 16} \end{array}$$

$$-0.75x = -24$$
$$\frac{-0.75x}{-0.75} = \frac{-24}{-0.75}$$
$$x = 32$$

Substitute 32 for x.
$$x + y = 40$$
$$32 + y = 40$$
$$32 + y - 32 = 40 - 32$$
$$y = 8$$

8 ounces of pure antifreeze should be added to 32 ounces of the 25% solution.

24. Let x represent the number of servings of cranberry juice. Let y represent the number of servings of apple juice.

$$\begin{cases} 1.20x + 1.00y = 8.50 \\ x + y = 8 \end{cases} \begin{array}{l} \rightarrow \ 1.2x + y = 8.5 \rightarrow -1(1.2x + y) = -1(8.5) \rightarrow -1.2x - y = -8.5 \\ \rightarrow \ x + y = 8 \qquad \rightarrow \qquad x + y = 8 \qquad \rightarrow \ \underline{x + y = 8} \end{array}$$

$$-0.2x = -0.5$$
$$x = 2.5, \text{ or } 2\tfrac{1}{2}$$

Substitute 2.5 for x.
$$x + y = 8$$
$$2.5 + y = 8$$
$$2.5 + y - 2.5 = 8 - 2.5$$
$$y = 5.5, \text{ or } 5\tfrac{1}{2}$$

The house blend contains $2\tfrac{1}{2}$ servings of cranberry juice and $5\tfrac{1}{2}$ servings of apple juice.

25. Let x represent the number of ounces of seeds. Let y represent the number of ounces of nuts.

$$\begin{cases} x + y = 42 \\ 0.20x + 0.30y = 11.00 \end{cases} \begin{array}{l} \rightarrow \ -0.20(x+y) = -0.20(42) \rightarrow -0.20x - 0.20y = -8.4 \\ \rightarrow \ 0.20x + 0.30y = 11.00 \qquad \rightarrow \underline{0.20x + 0.30y = 11.00} \end{array}$$

$$0.1y = 2.6$$
$$\frac{0.1y}{0.1} = \frac{2.6}{0.1}$$
$$y = 26$$

Substitute 26 for y.
$$x + y = 42$$
$$x + 26 = 42$$
$$x + 26 - 26 = 42 - 26$$
$$x = 16$$

The owner used 16 ounces of seeds and 26 ounces of nuts.

26.

	First solution	Second solution	New solution
Percent salt	10% = 0.10	18% = 0.18	15% = 0.15
Amount of solution	x	y	320 g
Amount of salt	$0.10x$	$0.18y$	$0.15(320) = 48$ g

$$\begin{cases} x + y = 320 \\ 0.1x + 0.18y = 48 \end{cases} \rightarrow \begin{matrix} -0.1(x) + -0.1(y) = -0.1(320) \\ 0.1x + 0.18y = 48 \end{matrix} \rightarrow \begin{matrix} -0.1x - 0.1y = -32 \\ \underline{0.1x + 0.18y = 48} \end{matrix}$$

Substitute 200 for y.

$$x + y = 320$$
$$x + 200 = 320$$
$$x + 200 - 200 = 320 - 200$$
$$x = 120$$

$$0.08y = 16$$
$$\frac{-0.08y}{0.08} = \frac{16}{0.08}$$
$$y = 200$$

120 grams of the 10% solution and 200 grams of the 18% solution are needed.

27. $\begin{cases} 6m - 3n = -12 \\ \underline{5m + 3n = 1} \end{cases}$

$$11m = -11$$
$$\frac{11m}{11} = \frac{-11}{11}$$
$$m = -1$$

Substitute –1 for m.
$$6m - 3n = -12$$
$$6(-1) - 3n = -12$$
$$-6 - 3n = -12$$
$$-6 - 3n + 6 = -12 + 6$$
$$-3n = -6$$
$$\frac{-3n}{-3} = \frac{-6}{-3}$$
$$n = 2$$

$(m, n) = (-1, 2)$

28. $\begin{cases} 3a + 4c = 5 \\ 5a + 2c = 13 \end{cases} \rightarrow \begin{matrix} 3a + 4c = 5 \\ -2(5a + 2c) = -2(13) \end{matrix} \rightarrow \begin{matrix} 3a + 4c = 5 \\ \underline{-10a - 4c = -26} \end{matrix}$

$$-7a = -21$$
$$\frac{-7a}{-7} = \frac{-21}{-7}$$
$$a = 3$$

Substitute 3 for a.
$$3a + 4c = 5$$
$$3(3) + 4c = 5$$
$$9 + 4c = 5$$
$$9 + 4c - 9 = 5 - 9$$
$$4c = -4$$
$$\frac{4c}{4} = \frac{-4}{4}$$
$$c = -1$$

$(a, c) = (3, -1)$

29. $\begin{cases} 4w + 5z = 7 \\ 2w + z = -1 \end{cases} \rightarrow \begin{matrix} 4w + 5z = 7 \\ -2(2w + z) = -2(-1) \end{matrix} \rightarrow \begin{matrix} 4w + 5z = 7 \\ \underline{-4w - 2z = 2} \end{matrix}$

$$3z = 9$$
$$\frac{3z}{3} = \frac{9}{3}$$
$$z = 3$$

Substitute 3 for z.
$$2w + z = -1$$
$$2w + 3 = -1$$
$$2w + 3 - 3 = -1 - 3$$
$$2w = -4$$
$$\frac{2w}{2} = \frac{-4}{2}$$
$$w = -2$$

$(w, z) = (-2, 3)$

30. $\begin{cases} 7x = 4y + 22 \\ 3x + 2y = 2 \end{cases} \rightarrow \begin{matrix} 7x - 4y = 22 \\ 3x + 2y = 2 \end{matrix} \rightarrow \begin{matrix} 7x - 4y = 22 \\ 2(3x + 2y) = 2(2) \end{matrix} \rightarrow \begin{matrix} 7x - 4y = 22 \\ \underline{6x + 4y = 4} \end{matrix}$

$$13x = 26$$
$$\frac{13x}{13} = \frac{26}{13}$$
$$x = 2$$

Substitute 2 for x.
$$3x + 2y = 2$$
$$3(2) + 2y = 2$$
$$6 + 2y = 2$$
$$6 + 2y - 6 = 2 - 6$$
$$2y = -4$$
$$\frac{2y}{2} = \frac{-4}{2}$$
$$y = -2$$

$(x, y) = (2, -2)$

31. $\begin{cases} 5w + 7z = 10 \\ w + z = 4 \end{cases}$ $\begin{matrix} \to \\ \to \end{matrix}$ $\begin{matrix} 5w + 7z = 10 \\ -5(w + z) = -5(4) \end{matrix}$ $\begin{matrix} \to \\ \to \end{matrix}$ $\begin{matrix} 5w + 7z = 10 \\ \underline{-5w - 5z = -20} \end{matrix}$

Substitute -5 for z.

$$2z = -10$$
$$\frac{2z}{2} = \frac{-10}{2}$$
$$z = -5$$

$$w + z = 4$$
$$w + (-5) = 4$$
$$w - 5 + 5 = 4 + 5$$
$$w = 9$$

$(w, z) = (9, -5)$

32. $\begin{cases} 2a - 3c = 9 \\ a - c = 7 \end{cases}$ $\begin{matrix} \to \\ \to \end{matrix}$ $\begin{matrix} 2a - 3c = 9 \\ -2(a - c) = -2(9) \end{matrix}$ $\begin{matrix} \to \\ \to \end{matrix}$ $\begin{matrix} 2a - 3c = 9 \\ \underline{-2a + 2c = -14} \end{matrix}$

Substitute 5 for c.

$$-c = -5$$
$$-1(-c) = -1(-5)$$
$$c = 5$$

$$a - c = 7$$
$$a - 5 = 7$$
$$a - 5 + 5 = 7 + 5$$
$$a = 12$$

$(a, c) = (12, 5)$

33. $\begin{cases} 3m = 8 + n \\ 10m - 4n = 7 \end{cases}$ $\begin{matrix} \to \\ \to \end{matrix}$ $\begin{matrix} 3m - n = 8 \\ 10m - 4n = 7 \end{matrix}$ $\begin{matrix} \to \\ \to \end{matrix}$ $\begin{matrix} -4(3m - n) = -4(8) \\ 10m - 4n = 7 \end{matrix}$ $\begin{matrix} \to \\ \to \end{matrix}$ $\begin{matrix} -12m + 4n = -32 \\ \underline{10m - 4n = 7} \end{matrix}$

$$-2m = -25$$
$$\frac{-2m}{-2} = \frac{-25}{-2}$$
$$m = \frac{25}{2}, \text{ or } 12\tfrac{1}{2}$$

Substitute $\frac{25}{2}$ for m.
$$10m - 4n = 7$$
$$10\left(\frac{25}{2}\right) - 4n = 7$$
$$125 - 4n = 7$$
$$125 - 4n - 125 = 7 - 125$$
$$-4n = -118$$
$$\frac{-4n}{-4} = \frac{-118}{-4}$$
$$n = 29\tfrac{1}{2}$$

$(m, n) = \left(12\tfrac{1}{2}, 29\tfrac{1}{2}\right)$

34. $\begin{cases} 5a - 3c = 13 \\ 3a + 2c = 4 \end{cases}$ $\begin{matrix} \to \\ \to \end{matrix}$ $\begin{matrix} 2(5a - 3c) = 2(13) \\ 3(3a + 2c) = 3(4) \end{matrix}$ $\begin{matrix} \to \\ \to \end{matrix}$ $\begin{matrix} 10a - 6c = 26 \\ \underline{9a + 6c = 12} \end{matrix}$

Substitute 2 for a.

$$19a = 38$$
$$\frac{19a}{19} = \frac{38}{19}$$
$$a = 2$$

$$5a - 3c = 13$$
$$5(2) - 3c = 13$$
$$10 - 3c = 13$$
$$10 - 3c - 10 = 13 - 10$$
$$-3c = 3$$
$$\frac{-3c}{-3} = \frac{3}{-3}$$
$$c = -1$$

$(a, c) = (2, -1)$

35. $\begin{cases} 3x + 4y = 6 \\ 5x + 3y = -1 \end{cases}$ $\begin{matrix} \to \\ \to \end{matrix}$ $\begin{matrix} 3(3x + 4y) = 3(6) \\ -4(5x + 3y) = -4(-1) \end{matrix}$ $\begin{matrix} \to \\ \to \end{matrix}$ $\begin{matrix} 9x + 12y = 18 \\ \underline{-20x - 12y = 4} \end{matrix}$

Substitute -2 for x.

$$-11x = 22$$
$$\frac{-11x}{-11} = \frac{22}{-11}$$
$$x = -2$$

$$3x + 4y = 6$$
$$3(-2) + 4y = 6$$
$$-6 + 4y = 6$$
$$-6 + 4y + 6 = 6 + 6$$
$$4y = 12$$
$$\frac{4y}{4} = \frac{12}{4}$$
$$y = 3$$

$(x, y) = (-2, 3)$

36. $\begin{cases} 2x - y = 6 & \to & -5(2x - y) = -5(6) & \to & -10x + 5y = -30 \\ 4x - 5y = 2 & \to & 4x - 5y = 2 & \to & \underline{4x - 5y = 2} \end{cases}$

$$-6x = -28$$
$$\frac{-6x}{-6} = \frac{-28}{-6}$$
$$x = \frac{28}{6}, \text{ or } \frac{14}{3}, \text{ or } 4\frac{2}{3}$$

Substitute $\frac{14}{3}$ for x.
$$4x - 5y = 2$$
$$4\left(\frac{14}{3}\right) - 5y = 2$$
$$\frac{56}{3} - 5y = 2$$
$$\frac{56}{3} - 5y - \frac{56}{3} = 2 - \frac{56}{3}$$
$$-5y = \frac{-50}{3}$$
$$-\frac{1}{5}(-5y) = -\frac{1}{5}\left(-\frac{50}{3}\right)$$
$$y = \frac{50}{15}, \text{ or } \frac{10}{3}, \text{ or } 3\frac{1}{3}$$

$(x, y) = \left(4\frac{2}{3}, 3\frac{1}{3}\right)$

37. $\begin{cases} 3x - 5y = 7 & \to & 3(3x - 5y) = 3(7) & \to & 9x - 15y = 21 \\ 4x - 3y = 2 & \to & -5(4x - 3y) = -5(2) & \to & -20x + 15y = -10 \end{cases}$

$$-11x = 11$$
$$\frac{-11x}{-11} = \frac{11}{-11}$$
$$x = -1$$

Substitute -1 for x.
$$3x - 5y = 7$$
$$3(-1) - 5y = 7$$
$$-3 - 5y = 7$$
$$-3 - 5y + 3 = 7 + 3$$
$$-5y = 10$$
$$\frac{-5y}{-5} = \frac{10}{-5}$$
$$y = -2$$

$(x, y) = (-1, -2)$

38. $\begin{cases} 2y = 3x + 1 & \to & 2(2y) = 2(3x + 1) & \to & 4y = 6x + 2 \\ -4y = 2x + 1 & \to & -4y = 2x + 1 & \to & \underline{-4y = 2x + 1} \end{cases}$

$$0 = 8x + 3$$
$$-3 = 8x$$
$$\frac{-3}{8} = \frac{8x}{8}$$
$$-\frac{3}{8} = x$$

Substitute $\frac{-3}{8}$ for x.
$$2y = 3x + 1$$
$$2y = 3\left(\frac{-3}{8}\right) + 1$$
$$2y = \frac{-9}{8} + 1$$
$$2y = -\frac{1}{8}$$
$$\frac{1}{2}(2y) = \frac{1}{2}\left(-\frac{1}{8}\right)$$
$$y = -\frac{1}{16}$$

$(x, y) = \left(-\frac{3}{8}, -\frac{1}{16}\right)$

39. $\begin{cases} y = 2x - 8 & \to & -2x + y = -8 & \to & -2x + y = -8 & \to & -2x + y = -8 \\ x - 5y = 9 & \to & x - 5y = 9 & \to & 2(x - 5y) = 2(9) & \to & \underline{2x - 10y = 18} \end{cases}$

$$-9y = 10$$
$$\frac{-9y}{-9} = \frac{10}{-9}$$
$$y = -\frac{10}{9}, \text{ or } -1\frac{1}{9}$$

Substitute $-\frac{10}{9}$ for y.
$$x - 5y = 9$$
$$x - 5\left(-\frac{10}{9}\right) = 9$$
$$x + \frac{50}{9} = 9$$
$$x + \frac{50}{9} - \frac{50}{9} = 9 - \frac{50}{9}$$
$$x = \frac{31}{9}, \text{ or } 3\frac{4}{9}$$

$(x, y) = \left(3\frac{4}{9}, -1\frac{1}{9}\right)$

40. $\begin{cases} 3g - 2h = 4 \\ 5h = -3g + 2 \end{cases}$ $\begin{matrix} \to & 3g - 2h = 4 & \to & -1(3g - 2h) = -1(4) & \to & -3g + 2h = -4 \\ \to & 3g + 5h = 2 & \to & 3g + 5h = 2 & \to & \underline{3g + 5h = 2} \end{matrix}$

$$7h = -2$$
$$\frac{7h}{7} = \frac{-2}{7}$$
$$h = -\frac{2}{7}$$

Substitute $-\frac{2}{7}$ for h.
$$3g - 2h = 4$$
$$3g - 2\left(-\frac{2}{7}\right) = 4$$
$$3g + \frac{4}{7} = 4$$
$$3g + \frac{4}{7} - \frac{4}{7} = 4 - \frac{4}{7}$$
$$3g = \frac{24}{7}$$
$$\frac{1}{3}(3g) = \frac{1}{3}\left(\frac{24}{7}\right)$$
$$g = \frac{24}{21}, \text{ or } \frac{8}{7}, \text{ or } 1\frac{1}{7}$$
$$(g, h) = \left(1\frac{1}{7}, -\frac{2}{7}\right)$$

41. $\begin{cases} 0.5x - 2y = 9 \\ -\frac{1}{4}x - \frac{1}{2}y = 2 \end{cases}$ $\begin{matrix} \to & 0.5x - 2y = 9 & \to & 0.5x - 2y = 9 \\ \to & -4\left(-\frac{1}{4}x - \frac{1}{2}y\right) = -4(2) & \to & \underline{x + 2y = -8} \end{matrix}$

$$\frac{3}{2}x = 1$$
$$\frac{2}{3}\left(\frac{3}{2}x\right) = \frac{2}{3}(1)$$
$$x = \frac{2}{3}$$

Substitute $\frac{2}{3}$ for x.
$$-\frac{1}{4}x - \frac{1}{2}y = 2$$
$$-\frac{1}{4}\left(\frac{2}{3}\right) - \frac{1}{2}y = 2$$
$$-\frac{2}{12} - \frac{1}{2}y = 2$$
$$-\frac{1}{6} - \frac{1}{2}y + \frac{1}{6} = 2 + \frac{1}{6}$$
$$-\frac{1}{2}y = \frac{13}{6}$$
$$-2\left(-\frac{1}{2}y\right) = -2\left(\frac{13}{6}\right)$$
$$y = \frac{-26}{6}, \text{ or } -\frac{13}{3}, \text{ or } -4\frac{1}{3}$$

$$(x, y) = \left(\frac{2}{3}, -4\frac{1}{3}\right)$$

42. $\begin{cases} 5.2w + 0.5c = -19.3 \\ 3.1w + 2.5c = -4.9 \end{cases}$ $\begin{matrix} \to & -5(5.2w + 0.5c) = -5(-19.3) & \to & -26w - 2.5c = 96.5 \\ \to & 3.1w + 2.5c = -4.9 & \to & \underline{3.1w + 2.5c = -4.9} \end{matrix}$

$$-22.9w = 91.6$$
$$\frac{-22.9w}{-22.9} = \frac{91.6}{-22.9}$$
$$w = -4$$

Substitute -4 for w.
$$3.1w + 2.5c = -4.9$$
$$3.1(-4) + 2.5c = -4.9$$
$$-12.4 + 2.5c = -4.9$$
$$2.5c = 7.5$$
$$\frac{2.5c}{2.5} = \frac{7.5}{2.5}$$
$$c = 3$$
$$(c, w) = (3, -4)$$

43. Let x represent John's age. Let y represent his grandfather's age.

$\begin{cases} x = y - 56 \\ x + y = 78 \end{cases}$ $\begin{matrix} \to & x - y = -56 \\ \to & \underline{x + y = 78} \end{matrix}$

$$2x = 22$$
$$\frac{2x}{2} = \frac{22}{2}$$
$$x = 11$$

Substitute 16 for x.
$$x + y = 78$$
$$11 + y = 78$$
$$y = 67$$

John is 11 years old. His grandfather is 67 years old.

44.

	First solution	Second solution	New solution
Percent chlorine	10% = 0.10	15% = 0.15	12% = 0.12
Amount of solution	x	20 g	y
Amount of chlorine	$0.10x$	$0.15(20) = 3$	$0.12y$

$$\begin{cases} x + 20 = y & \rightarrow -0.1(x+20) = -0.1(y) \rightarrow -0.1x - 2 = -0.1y \\ 0.1x + 3 = 0.12y \rightarrow & \quad 0.1x + 3 = 0.12y \quad \rightarrow \underline{\quad 0.1x + 3 = 0.12y} \end{cases}$$

$$1 = 0.02y$$
$$\frac{1}{0.02} = \frac{0.02y}{0.02}$$
$$50 = y$$

Substitute 50 for y.
$$x + 20 = y$$
$$x + 20 = 50$$
$$x + 20 - 20 = 50 - 20$$
$$x = 30$$

There are 30 grams of the 10% solution and 50 grams of the 12% solution.

45. Answers may vary. Suppose that you mix 20 milliliters of a 40% acid solution with 10 milliliters of a 30% acid solution. Let x represent the percent of acid in the mixture.

	First solution	Second solution	New solution
Percent acid	40% = 0.4	30% = 0.3	x
Amount of solution	20 mL	10 mL	30 mL
Amount of acid	$0.4(20) = 8$	$0.3(10) = 3$	$30x$

$$8 + 3 = 30x$$
$$11 = 30x$$
$$\frac{11}{30} = \frac{30x}{30}$$
$$0.3\overline{66} = x$$

The resulting mixture would have $36.\overline{66}$% acid in the mixture.

46. Let x represent the amount invested at 5%. Let y represent the amount invested at 8%.

$$\begin{cases} x + y = 3000 & \rightarrow -0.05(x+y) = -0.05(3000) \rightarrow -0.05x - 0.05y = -150 \\ 0.05x + 0.08y = 202.38 \rightarrow 0.05x + 0.08y = 202.38 & \rightarrow \underline{\quad 0.05x + 0.08y = 202.38} \end{cases}$$

$$0.03y = 52.38$$
$$\frac{0.03y}{0.03} = \frac{52.38}{0.03}$$
$$y = 1746$$

Substitute 1746 for y.
$$x + y = 3000$$
$$x + 1746 = 3000$$
$$x + 1746 - 1746 = 3000 - 1746$$
$$x = 1254$$

Becky invested $1254 in the account earning 5% and $1746 in the account earning 8%.

47. Let x represent the number of innings Brandi played. Let y represent the number of innings Denise played.

$$\begin{cases} 2x+2=y \\ x+4=y \end{cases} \rightarrow \begin{array}{l} 2x+2=y \\ -2(x+4)=-2(y) \end{array} \rightarrow \begin{array}{l} 2x+2=y \\ \underline{-2x-8=-2y} \\ -6=-y \\ 6=y \end{array}$$

Substitute 6 for y.

$$\begin{aligned} x+4 &= y \\ x+4 &= 6 \\ x+4-4 &= 6-4 \\ x &= 2 \end{aligned}$$

Brandi played 2 innings and Denise played 6 innings.

48. $\begin{cases} 2l+2w=43 \\ w=l-9 \end{cases} \rightarrow \begin{array}{l} 2l+2w=43 \\ -l+w=-9 \end{array} \rightarrow \begin{array}{l} 2l+2w=43 \\ 2(-l+w)=2(-9) \end{array} \rightarrow \begin{array}{l} 2l+2w=43 \\ \underline{-2l+2w=-18} \\ 4w=25 \\ \dfrac{4w}{4}=\dfrac{25}{4} \\ w=\dfrac{25}{4},\text{ or }6\tfrac{1}{4} \end{array}$

Substitute $\dfrac{25}{4}$ for w.

$$\begin{aligned} w &= l-9 \\ \frac{25}{4} &= l-9 \\ \frac{25}{4}+9 &= l-9+9 \\ \frac{61}{4} &= l \\ \text{or } l &= 15\tfrac{1}{4} \end{aligned}$$

The length of the rectangle is $15\tfrac{1}{4}$ centimeters. The width of the rectangle is $6\tfrac{1}{4}$ centimeters.

49. Let a represent the number of adult tickets sold. Let s represent the number of student tickets sold.

$$\begin{cases} 5a+2s=5766 \\ a+s+254=2000 \end{cases} \rightarrow \begin{array}{l} 5a+2s=5766 \\ a+s=1746 \end{array} \rightarrow \begin{array}{l} 5a+2s=5766 \\ -2(a+s)=-2(1746) \end{array} \rightarrow \begin{array}{l} 5a+2s=5766 \\ \underline{2a-2s=-3492} \\ 3a=2274 \\ \dfrac{3a}{3}=\dfrac{2274}{3} \\ a=758 \end{array}$$

Substitute 758 for a.

$$\begin{aligned} 5a+2s &= 5766 \\ 5(758)+2s &= 5766 \\ 3790+2s &= 5766 \\ 3790+2s-3790 &= 5766-3790 \\ 2s &= 1976 \\ \frac{2s}{2} &= \frac{1976}{2} \\ s &= 988 \end{aligned}$$

There were 758 adult tickets and 988 student tickets sold.

PAGE 523, LOOK BACK

50.
$$\begin{aligned} 5t+7t &= 9 \\ 12t &= 9 \\ \frac{12t}{12} &= \frac{9}{12} \\ t &= \frac{9}{12},\text{ or }\frac{3}{4} \end{aligned}$$

51.
$$\begin{aligned} 8t-9 &= 2t+1 \\ 8t-9-2t &= 2t+1-2t \\ 6t-9 &= 1 \\ 6t-9+9 &= 1+9 \\ 6t &= 10 \\ \frac{6t}{6} &= \frac{10}{6} \\ t &= \frac{10}{6},\text{ or }\frac{5}{3},\text{ or }1\tfrac{2}{3} \end{aligned}$$

52.
$$\begin{aligned} \tfrac{1}{5}t+1 &= 7(t+1) \\ \tfrac{1}{5}t+1 &= 7t+7 \\ \tfrac{1}{5}t+1-\tfrac{1}{5}t &= 7t+7-\tfrac{1}{5}t \\ 1 &= \frac{34}{5}t+7 \\ 1-7 &= \frac{34}{5}t+7-7 \\ -6 &= \frac{34}{5}t \\ \frac{5}{34}(-6) &= \frac{5}{34}\left(\frac{34}{5}t\right) \\ -\frac{30}{34} &= t \\ \text{or } t &= -\frac{15}{17} \end{aligned}$$

53.
$$\begin{aligned} 3t+5k &= r \\ 3t+5k-5k &= r-5k \\ 3t &= r-5k \\ \tfrac{1}{3}(3t) &= \tfrac{1}{3}(r-5k) \\ t &= \frac{r-5k}{3} \end{aligned}$$

54. $|x + 7| = 8$

Case 1

The quantity $x + 7$ is positive.

$$|x + 7| = 8$$
$$x + 7 = 8$$
$$x + 7 - 7 = 8 - 7$$
$$x = 1$$

Case 2

The quantity $x + 7$ is negative.

$$|x + 7| = 8$$
$$-(x + 7) = 8$$
$$-x - 7 = 8$$
$$-x - 7 + 7 = 8 + 7$$
$$-x = 15$$
$$x = -15$$

$$x = 1 \text{ or } x = -15$$

55. $|x - 8| \leq 4$

Case 1

The quantity $x - 8$ is positive.

$$|x - 8| \leq 4$$
$$x - 8 \leq 4$$
$$x - 8 + 8 \leq 4 + 8$$
$$x \leq 12$$

Case 2

The quantity $x - 8$ is negative.

$$|x - 8| \leq 4$$
$$-(x - 8) \leq 4$$
$$-x + 8 \leq 4$$
$$-x + 8 - 8 \leq 4 - 8$$
$$-x \leq -4$$
$$-1(-x) \geq -1(-4)$$
$$x \geq 4$$

The inequality is true when $4 \leq x \leq 12$.

56. $|x - 2| > 10$

Case 1

The quantity $x - 2$ is positive.

$$|x - 2| > 10$$
$$x - 2 > 10$$
$$x > 12$$

Case 2

The quantity $x - 2$ is negative.

$$|x - 2| > 10$$
$$-(x - 2) > 10$$
$$-x + 2 > 10$$
$$-x > 8$$
$$x < -8$$

The inequality is true when $x < -8$ or when $x > 12$.

PAGE 523, LOOK BEYOND

57. $y = x^2$ $\qquad\qquad\qquad\qquad$ $y = 2^x$

Tables may vary.

x	-3	-2	-1	0	1	2	3
y	9	4	1	0	1	4	9

x	-3	-2	-1	0	1	2	3
y	$\frac{1}{8}$	$\frac{1}{4}$	$\frac{1}{2}$	1	2	4	8

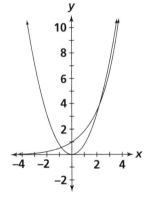

58. The graphs of $y = x^2$ and $y = 2^x$ both increase as they move in the positive x-direction. The graph of $y = x^2$ also increases as it moves in the negative x-direction, but the graph of $y = 2^x$ decreases toward the x-axis as it moves in the negative x-direction.

9.5 **PAGES 529–530, PRACTICE & APPLY**

6. b, $(4, 7)$

$$\begin{cases} 2x - 3y > 10 \rightarrow 2(4) - 3(-7) > 10 \rightarrow 8 + 21 > 10 \rightarrow 29 > 10 \quad \text{True} \\ x + 4y < 6 \rightarrow 4 + 4(-7) < 6 \rightarrow 4 - 28 < 6 \rightarrow -24 < 6 \quad \text{True} \end{cases}$$

7. b, $(6, -5)$

$$\begin{cases} x + 2y \leq 12 \rightarrow 6 + 2(-5) \leq 12 \rightarrow 6 - 10 \leq 12 \rightarrow -4 \leq 12 \quad \text{True} \\ x - y > 5 \rightarrow 6 - (-5) > 5 \rightarrow 6 + 5 > 5 \rightarrow 11 > 5 \quad \text{True} \end{cases}$$

8. a, (18, –20) and **b,** (15, –10)

$$\begin{cases} 18x - 12y > 80 \ \to\ 18(18) - 12(-20) > 80 \ \to\ 324 + 240 > 80 \ \to\ 564 > 80 \quad \text{True} \\ 12x - 11y > 12 \ \to\ 12(18) - 11(-20) > 12 \ \to\ 216 + 220 > 12 \ \to\ 436 > 12 \quad \text{True} \end{cases}$$

$$\begin{cases} 18x - 12y > 80 \ \to\ 18(15) - 12(-10) > 80 \ \to\ 270 + 120 > 80 \ \to\ 390 > 80 \quad \text{True} \\ 12x - 11y > 12 \ \to\ 12(15) - 11(-10) > 12 \ \to\ 180 + 110 > 12 \ \to\ 290 > 12 \quad \text{True} \end{cases}$$

9. none

When substituted for x and y, none of the points satisfy both of the inequalities.

10. $\begin{cases} y \le x + 4 \\ y \ge x - 6 \end{cases}$

11. $\begin{cases} y < -\frac{1}{2}x + 3 \\ y > 2x + 3 \end{cases}$

12. $\begin{cases} y \le 4 \\ y > -x - 3 \end{cases}$

13. $\begin{cases} y \le -\frac{3}{5}x + 3 \\ y > \frac{2}{3}x - 4 \end{cases}$

14. Let x represent the number of pounds of small-sized gravel. Let y represent the number of pounds of large-sized gravel.

$$\begin{cases} 1.25x + 1.75y \ge 7.50 \\ x + y \le 10 \end{cases}$$

$1.25x + 1.75y \ge 7.50$

$1.75y \ge -1.25x + 7.50$

$y \ge \frac{-1.25}{1.75}x + 4.28$

$x + y \le 10$

$y \le -x + 10$

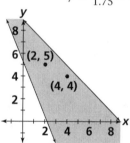

Answers may vary. The points (2, 5) and (4, 4) lie in the shaded region, so possible answers include the following:

1. 2 pounds of small-sized gravel mixed with 5 pounds of large-sized gravel
2. 4 pounds of small-sized gravel mixed with 4 pounds of large-sized gravel

Since you cannot have negative pieces of gravel, the reasonable domain and range are all rational numbers greater than or equal to 0 such that:

$0 \le x \le 10$ domain

$0 \le y \le 10$ range

15. Let x represent the number of wreaths made. Let y represent the number of baskets made.

$$\begin{cases} 2x + y \le 40 \\ 3x + 2y \le 72 \end{cases}$$

$2x + y \le 40$

$2x + y - 2x \le 40 - 2x$

$y \le -2x + 40$

$3x + 2y \le 72$

$3x + 2y - 3x \le 72 - 3x$

$2y \le -3x + 72$

$\frac{1}{2}(2y) \le \frac{1}{2}(-3x + 72)$

$y \le -\frac{3}{2}x + 36$

Answers may vary. One possible answer is for Janice to make 10 wreaths and 5 baskets. The reasonable domain and range of this system of inequalities are the set of positive integers and 0 such that:

$0 \le x \le 20$ domain

$0 \le y \le 36$ range

16.

	First solution	Second solution	New solution
Percent salt	22% = 0.22	30% = 0.30	———
Amount of solution	x	y	48 oz
Amount of salt	$0.22x$	$0.30y$	12 oz

$$\begin{cases} x + y \geq 48 \\ 0.22x + 0.30y \geq 12 \end{cases}$$

$x + y \geq 48$
$x + y - x \geq 48 - x$
$y \geq -x + 48$

$0.22x + 0.30y \geq 12$
$0.22x + 0.30y - 0.22x \geq 12 - 0.22x$
$0.30y \geq -0.22x + 12$
$\frac{1}{0.30}(0.30y) \geq \frac{1}{0.30}(-0.22x + 12)$
$y \geq -0.73x + 40$

Answers may vary. One possible answer is to mix 80 ounces of the 22% solution with 100 ounces of the 30% solution. The reasonable domain and range of this system of inequalities are the set of positive real numbers and 0 such that:

$x \geq 0$ domain
$y \geq 0$ range

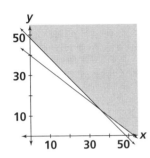

17. $\begin{cases} y > 2 \\ y > 3x - 2 \end{cases}$

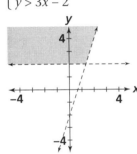

18. $\begin{cases} y < 1 \\ y \geq \frac{2}{3}x + 1 \end{cases}$

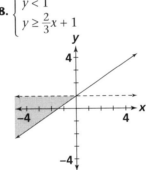

19. $\begin{cases} x < 2 \\ y \leq -\frac{1}{2}x + 3 \end{cases}$

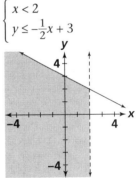

20. $\begin{cases} x + 2y \leq 6 \\ 2x + 4y \geq 4 \end{cases}$

$x + 2y \leq 6$
$x + 2y - x \leq 6 - x$
$2y \leq -x + 6$
$\frac{1}{2}(2y) \leq \frac{1}{2}(-x + 6)$
$y \leq -\frac{1}{2}x + 3$

$2x + 4y \geq 4$
$2x + 4y - 2x \geq 4 - 2x$
$4y \geq -2x + 4$
$\frac{1}{4}(4y) \geq \frac{1}{4}(-2x + 4)$
$y \geq -\frac{1}{2}x + 1$

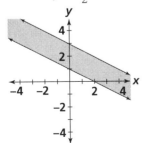

21. $\begin{cases} y + 2x > 3 \\ 3x - 4y < 8 \end{cases}$

$y + 2x > 3$
$y + 2x - 2x > 3 - 2x$
$y > -2x + 3$

$3x - 4y < 8$
$3x - 4y - 3x < 8 - 3x$
$-4y < -3x + 8$
$-\frac{1}{4}(-4y) > -\frac{1}{4}(-3x + 8)$
$y > \frac{3}{4}x - 2$

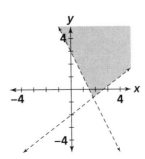

22. $\begin{cases} 2x + y < 3 \\ 3x - 2y \geq 4 \end{cases}$

$\quad\quad 2x + y < 3 \quad\quad\quad\quad\quad 3x - 2y \geq 4$

$\quad 2x + y - 2x < 3 - 2x \quad\quad 3x - 2y - 3x \geq 4 - 3x$

$\quad\quad\quad\quad y < -2x + 3 \quad\quad\quad\quad -2y \geq -3x + 4$

$\quad\quad\quad\quad\quad\quad\quad\quad\quad\quad\quad -\frac{1}{2}(-2y) \geq -\frac{1}{2}(-3x + 4)$

$\quad\quad\quad\quad\quad\quad\quad\quad\quad\quad\quad\quad y \leq \frac{3}{2}x - 4$

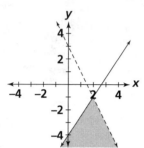

23. $\begin{cases} 4x + 3y \leq 6 \\ x - 2y \geq 4 \end{cases}$

$\quad\quad 4x + 3y \leq 6 \quad\quad\quad\quad\quad x - 2y \geq 4$

$\quad 4x + 3y - 4x \leq 6 - 4x \quad\quad x - 2y - x \geq 4 - x$

$\quad\quad\quad\quad 3y \leq -4x + 6 \quad\quad\quad\quad -2y \geq -x + 4$

$\quad\quad \frac{1}{3}(3y) \leq \frac{1}{3}(-4x + 6) \quad\quad -\frac{1}{2}(-2y) \leq -\frac{1}{2}(-x + 4)$

$\quad\quad\quad\quad y \leq -\frac{4}{3}x + 2 \quad\quad\quad\quad\quad y \leq \frac{1}{2}x - 2$

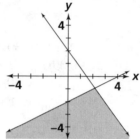

24. $\begin{cases} y \leq 3x + 4 \\ 2x + y \geq 1 \end{cases}$

$\quad\quad\quad\quad 2x + y \geq 1$

$\quad\quad 2x + y - 2x \geq 1 - 2x$

$\quad\quad\quad\quad\quad y \geq -2x + 1$

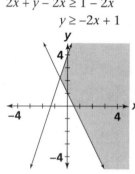

25. $\begin{cases} y - 7 \leq 2x \\ 3y + 6 \leq 6x \end{cases}$

$\quad\quad y - 7 \leq 2x \quad\quad\quad\quad 3y + 6 \leq 6x$

$\quad y - 7 + 7 \leq 2x + 7 \quad\quad 3y + 6 - 6 \leq 6x - 6$

$\quad\quad\quad y \leq 2x + 7 \quad\quad\quad\quad 3y \leq 6x - 6$

$\quad\quad\quad\quad\quad\quad\quad\quad\quad \frac{1}{3}(3y) \leq \frac{1}{3}(6x - 6)$

$\quad\quad\quad\quad\quad\quad\quad\quad\quad\quad y \leq 2x - 2$

26. $\begin{cases} y + 2 > 3x \\ 3x - y < 7 \end{cases}$

$\quad\quad y + 2 > 3x \quad\quad\quad\quad 3x - y < 7$

$\quad y + 2 - 2 > 3x - 2 \quad\quad 3x - y - 3x < 7 - 3x$

$\quad\quad\quad y > 3x - 2 \quad\quad\quad\quad -y < -3x + 7$

$\quad\quad\quad\quad\quad\quad\quad\quad\quad -1(-y) < -1(-3x + 7)$

$\quad\quad\quad\quad\quad\quad\quad\quad\quad\quad y > 3x - 7$

27. $\begin{cases} 3x + y < 3 \\ 6x + 2y \geq 12 \end{cases}$

$\quad\quad 3x + y < 3 \quad\quad\quad\quad 6x + 2y \geq 12$

$\quad 3x + y - 3x < 3 - 3x \quad\quad 6x + 2y - 6x \geq 12 - 6x$

$\quad\quad\quad y < -3x + 3 \quad\quad\quad\quad 2y \geq -6x + 12$

$\quad\quad\quad\quad\quad\quad\quad\quad\quad \frac{1}{2}(2y) \geq \frac{1}{2}(-6x + 12)$

$\quad\quad\quad\quad\quad\quad\quad\quad\quad\quad y \geq -3x + 6$

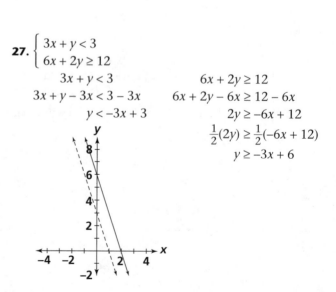

28. $\begin{cases} x + y < 4 \\ x - y < -4 \end{cases}$

$\begin{aligned} x + y &< 4 \\ x + y - x &< 4 - x \\ y &< -x + 4 \end{aligned}$

$\begin{aligned} x - y &< -4 \\ x - y - x &< -4 - x \\ -y &< -x - 4 \\ -1(y) &> -1(-x - 4) \\ y &> x + 4 \end{aligned}$

29. $\begin{cases} y \geq -2 \\ x < -3 \end{cases}$

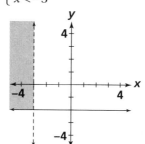

30. $\begin{cases} 6x + 5y \leq 10 \\ x + 4y > 5 \\ y < 2 \end{cases}$

$\begin{aligned} 6x + 5y &\leq 10 \\ 6x + 5y - 6x &\leq 10 - 6x \\ 5y &\leq -6x + 10 \\ \tfrac{1}{5}(5y) &\leq \tfrac{1}{5}(-6x + 10) \\ y &\leq -\tfrac{6}{5}x + 2 \end{aligned}$

$\begin{aligned} x + 4y &> 5 \\ x + 4y - x &> 5 - x \\ 4y &> -x + 5 \\ \tfrac{1}{4}(4y) &> \tfrac{1}{4}(-x + 5) \\ y &> -\tfrac{1}{4}x + \tfrac{5}{4} \end{aligned}$

31. $\begin{cases} y \leq 5 \\ x + y \geq -2 \\ x + y < 8 \end{cases}$

$\begin{aligned} x + y &\geq -2 \\ x + y - x &\geq -2 - x \\ y &\geq -x - 2 \end{aligned}$

$\begin{aligned} x + y &< 8 \\ x + y - x &< 8 - x \\ y &< -x + 8 \end{aligned}$

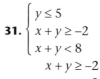

32. $\begin{cases} 2x > 6 \\ x - 5y < 15 \\ 2x + 3y > 6 \end{cases}$

$\begin{aligned} 2x &> 6 \\ \tfrac{2x}{2} &> \tfrac{6}{2} \\ x &> 3 \end{aligned}$

$\begin{aligned} x - 5y &< 15 \\ x - 5y - x &< 15 - x \\ -5y &< -x + 15 \\ -\tfrac{1}{5}(-5y) &> -\tfrac{1}{5}(-x + 15) \\ y &> \tfrac{1}{5}x - 3 \end{aligned}$

$\begin{aligned} 2x + 3y &> 6 \\ 2x + 3y - 2x &> 6 - 2x \\ 3y &> -2x + 6 \\ \tfrac{1}{3}(3y) &> \tfrac{1}{3}(-2x + 6) \\ y &> -\tfrac{2}{3}x + 2 \end{aligned}$

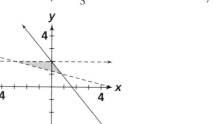

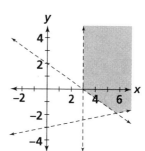

PAGE 530, LOOK BACK

33. $\begin{aligned} 4 \cdot 2 + 3 - 6 &= 8 + 3 - 6 \\ &= 11 - 6 \\ &= 5 \end{aligned}$

34. $\begin{aligned} 9 - 6 \div 2 + 7 &= 9 - 3 + 7 \\ &= 6 + 7 \\ &= 13 \end{aligned}$

35. $\begin{aligned} 10 \div 5 \cdot 3 + 6 &= 2 \cdot 3 + 6 \\ &= 6 + 6 \\ &= 12 \end{aligned}$

36. $\begin{cases} y = 3x - 4 \\ 2x - y = 12 \end{cases}$

Substitute $3x - 4$ for y.

$$2x - y = 12$$
$$2x - (3x - 4) = 12$$
$$-x + 4 = 12$$
$$-x + 4 - 4 = 12 - 4$$
$$-x = 8$$
$$-1(-x) = -1(8)$$
$$x = -8$$

Substitute -8 for x.

$$y = 3x - 4$$
$$y = 3(-8) - 4$$
$$y = -24 - 4$$
$$y = -28$$
$$(x, y) = (-8, -28)$$

37. $\begin{cases} x - y = 14 \\ 2x + 3y = 12 \end{cases}$

$$x - y = 14$$
$$x - y + y = 14 + y$$
$$x = 14 + y$$

Substitute $14 + y$ for x.

$$2x + 3y = 12$$
$$2(14 + y) + 3y = 12$$
$$28 + 2y + 3y = 12$$
$$28 + 5y = 12$$
$$28 + 5y - 28 = 12 - 28$$
$$5y = -16$$
$$\frac{1}{5}(5y) = \frac{1}{5}(-16)$$
$$y = -\frac{16}{5}, \text{ or } -3\frac{1}{5}$$

Substitute $-\frac{16}{5}$ for y.

$$x = 14 + y$$
$$x = 14 + \left(-\frac{16}{5}\right)$$
$$x = \frac{54}{5}, \text{ or } 10\frac{4}{5}$$
$$(x, y) = \left(10\frac{4}{5}, -3\frac{1}{5}\right)$$

38. $\begin{cases} 4a - 3c = 12 \\ 2a + c = 10 \end{cases} \rightarrow \begin{aligned} & 4a - 3c = 12 \\ & 3(2a + c) = 3(10) \end{aligned} \rightarrow \begin{aligned} 4a - 3c &= 12 \\ \underline{6a + 3c} &= \underline{30} \end{aligned}$

$$10a = 42$$
$$\frac{10a}{10} = \frac{42}{10}$$
$$a = \frac{42}{10}, \text{ or } \frac{21}{5}, \text{ or } 4\frac{1}{5}$$

Substitute $\frac{21}{5}$ for a.

$$2a + c = 10$$
$$2\left(\frac{21}{5}\right) + c = 10$$
$$\frac{42}{5} + c = 10$$
$$\frac{42}{5} + c - \frac{42}{5} = 10 - \frac{42}{5}$$
$$c = \frac{8}{5}, \text{ or } 1\frac{3}{5}$$
$$(a, c) = \left(4\frac{1}{5}, 1\frac{3}{5}\right)$$

39. $\begin{cases} 0.5m + 0.3n = 1.4 \\ 0.7m + 0.3n = 2.8 \end{cases} \rightarrow \begin{aligned} & -1(0.5m + 0.3n) = -1(1.4) \\ & 0.7m + 0.3n = 2.8 \end{aligned} \rightarrow \begin{aligned} -0.5m - 0.3n &= -1.4 \\ \underline{0.7m + 0.3n} &= \underline{2.8} \end{aligned}$

$$0.2m = 1.4$$
$$\frac{0.2m}{0.2} = \frac{1.4}{0.2}$$
$$m = 7$$

Substitute 7 for m.

$$0.7m + 0.3n = 2.8$$
$$0.7(7) + 0.3n = 2.8$$
$$4.9 + 0.3n = 2.8$$
$$4.9 + 0.3n - 4.9 = 2.8 - 4.9$$
$$0.3n = -2.1$$
$$\frac{0.3n}{0.3} = \frac{-2.1}{0.3}$$
$$n = -7$$
$$(m, n) = (7, -7)$$

PAGE 530, LOOK BEYOND

40. $\begin{cases} 2x + y \geq 1 \\ x - 2y > 1 \\ x < 6 \end{cases}$

$$2x + y \geq 1$$
$$2x + y - 2x \geq 1 - 2x$$
$$y \geq -2x + 1$$

$$x - 2y > 1$$
$$x - 2y - x > 1 - x$$
$$-2y > -x + 1$$
$$-\frac{1}{2}(-2y) < -\frac{1}{2}(-x + 1)$$
$$y < \frac{1}{2}x - \frac{1}{2}$$

The solution region is a triangular shape with the following vertices:

$$\left(6, \frac{5}{2}\right)$$
$$\left(\frac{3}{5}, -\frac{1}{5}\right)$$
$$(6, -11)$$

1. $\begin{cases} 2x - y = 3 \\ x + 2y = 4 \end{cases}$

$2x - y = 3$

$2x - y - 2x = 3 - 2x$ $x + 2y = 4$

$-y = -2x + 3$ $x + 2y - x = 4 - x$

$-1(-y) = -1(-2x + 3)$ $2y = -x + 4$

$y = 2x - 3$ $\frac{1}{2}(2y) = \frac{1}{2}(-x + 4)$

$y = -\frac{1}{2}x + 2$

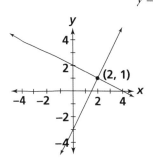

solution = (2, 1)

2. $\begin{cases} 4x + y = 5 \\ 3x - y = 9 \end{cases}$

$4x + y = 5$ $3x - y = 9$

$4x + y - 4x = 5 - 4x$ $3x - y - 3x = 9 - 3x$

$y = -4x + 5$ $-y = -3x + 9$

$-1(-y) = -1(-3x + 9)$

$y = 3x - 9$

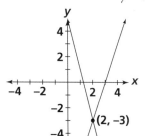

solution = (2, −3)

3. $\begin{cases} y = -2x \\ x - y = -6 \end{cases}$

$x - y = -6$

$x - y - x = -6 - x$

$-y = -x - 6$

$-1(-y) = -1(-x - 6)$

$y = x + 6$

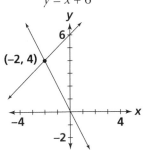

solution = (−2, 4)

4. $\begin{cases} x + y = 4 \\ 2x - 2y = 10 \end{cases}$

$x + y = 4$ $2x - 2y = 10$

$x + y - x = 4 - x$ $2x - 2y - 2x = 10 - 2x$

$y = -x + 4$ $-2y = -2x + 10$

$-\frac{1}{2}(-2y) = -\frac{1}{2}(-2x + 10)$

$y = x - 5$

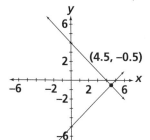

solution = (4.5, −0.5)

5. $\begin{cases} y = 3x \\ x + y = 12 \end{cases}$

Substitute $3x$ for y.

$x + y = 12$

$x + 3x = 12$

$4x = 12$

$\frac{4x}{4} = \frac{12}{4}$

$x = 3$

Substitute 3 for x.

$y = 3x$

$y = 3(3)$

$y = 9$

$(x, y) = (3, 9)$

6. $\begin{cases} y = 2x - 6 \\ x - y = 4 \end{cases}$

Substitute $2x - 6$ for y.

$x - y = 4$

$x - (2x - 6) = 4$

$-x + 6 = 4$

$-x + 6 - 6 = 4 - 6$

$-x = -2$

$-1(-x) = -1(-2)$

$x = 2$

Substitute 2 for x.

$y = 2x - 6$

$y = 2(2) - 6$

$y = 4 - 6$

$y = -2$

$(x, y) = (2, -2)$

7. $\begin{cases} 3x + 2y = 14 \\ 4 - 2x = y \end{cases}$

Substitute $4 - 2x$ for y.

$3x + 2y = 14$

$3x + 2(4 - 2x) = 14$

$3x + 8 - 4x = 14$

$-x + 8 = 14$

$-x + 8 - 8 = 14 - 8$

$-x = 6$

$-1(-x) = -1(6)$

$x = -6$

Substitute −6 for x.

$4 - 2x = y$

$4 - 2(-6) = y$

$4 + 12 = y$

$16 = y$

$(x, y) = (-6, 16)$

8. $\begin{cases} x - y = 16 \\ x + y = 74 \end{cases}$

$x - y = 16$

$x - y + y = 16 + y$

$x = 16 + y$

Substitute $16 + y$ for x.

$x + y = 74$

$(16 + y) + y = 74$

$16 + 2y = 74$

$16 + 2y - 16 = 74 - 16$

$2y = 58$

$\dfrac{2y}{2} = \dfrac{58}{2}$

$y = 29$

Substitute 29 for y.

$x - y = 16$

$x - 29 = 16$

$x - 29 + 29 = 16 + 29$

$x = 45$

$(x, y) = (45, 29)$

9. $\begin{cases} x + y = 6 \\ x - y = 12 \end{cases}$

$\quad 2x = 18$

$\quad \dfrac{2x}{2} = \dfrac{18}{2}$

$\quad x = 9$

Substitute 9 for x.

$x - y = 12$

$9 - y = 12$

$9 - y - 9 = 12 - 9$

$-y = 3$

$-1(-y) = -1(3)$

$y = -3$

$(x, y) = (9, -3)$

10. $\begin{cases} 5x - 2y = 30 \\ x + 2y = 6 \end{cases}$

$\quad 6x = 36$

$\quad \dfrac{6x}{6} = \dfrac{36}{6}$

$\quad x = 6$

Substitute 6 for x.

$x + 2y = 6$

$6 + 2y = 6$

$6 + 2y - 6 = 6 - 6$

$2y = 0$

$\dfrac{1}{2}(2y) = \dfrac{1}{2}(0)$

$y = 0$

$(x, y) = (6, 0)$

11. $4x - 3y = 14$

$\quad 5x + 3y = 31$

$\quad 9x = 45$

$\quad \dfrac{9x}{9} = \dfrac{45}{9}$

$\quad x = 5$

Substitute 5 for x.

$5x + 3y = 31$

$5(5) + 3y = 31$

$25 + 3y = 31$

$25 + 3y - 25 = 31 - 25$

$3y = 6$

$\dfrac{3y}{3} = \dfrac{6}{3}$

$y = 2$

$(x, y) = (5, 2)$

12. $\begin{cases} 4x - 5y = 44 \\ 4x + 9y = -12 \end{cases}$ $\begin{array}{l} \rightarrow -1(4x - 5y) = -1(44) \rightarrow -4x + 5y = -44 \\ \rightarrow \quad\quad 4x + 9y = -12 \quad\quad \rightarrow \quad 4x + 9y = -12 \end{array}$

$14y = -56$

$\dfrac{14y}{14} = \dfrac{-56}{14}$

$y = -4$

Substitute -4 for y.

$4x - 5y = 44$

$4x - 5(-4) = 44$

$4x + 20 = 44$

$4x + 20 - 20 = 44 - 20$

$4x = 24$

$\dfrac{4x}{4} = \dfrac{24}{4}$

$x = 6$

$(x, y) = (6, -4)$

13. $\begin{cases} 4x - 3y = 1 \\ 2x + y = 3 \end{cases}$ $\begin{array}{l} \rightarrow \quad\quad 4x - 3y = 1 \quad\quad \rightarrow \quad 4x - 3y = 1 \\ \rightarrow -2(2x + y) = -2(3) \rightarrow -4x - 2y = -6 \end{array}$

$-5y = -5$

$\dfrac{-5y}{-5} = \dfrac{-5}{-5}$

$y = 1$

Substitute 1 for y.

$2x + y = 3$

$2x + 1 = 3$

$2x + 1 - 1 = 3 - 1$

$2x = 2$

$\dfrac{2x}{2} = \dfrac{2}{2}$

$x = 1$

$(x, y) = (1, 1)$

14. $\begin{cases} 5x - y = 14 \\ 3x + 3y = 3 \end{cases}$ $\begin{array}{l} \rightarrow 3(5x - y) = 3(14) \rightarrow 15x - 3y = 42 \\ \rightarrow \quad\quad 3x - 3y = 3 \quad\quad \rightarrow \quad 3x + 3y = 3 \end{array}$

$18x = 45$

$\dfrac{18x}{8} = \dfrac{45}{18}$

$x = \dfrac{45}{18},\ \text{or } \dfrac{5}{2},\ \text{or } 2\dfrac{1}{2}$

Substitute $\dfrac{5}{2}$ for x.

$5x - y = 14$

$5\left(\dfrac{5}{2}\right) - y = 14$

$\dfrac{25}{2} - y = 14$

$\dfrac{25}{2} - y - \dfrac{25}{2} = 14 - \dfrac{25}{2}$

$-y = \dfrac{3}{2}$

$-1(-y) = -1\left(\dfrac{3}{2}\right)$

$y = -\dfrac{3}{2},\ \text{or } -1\dfrac{1}{2}$

$(x, y) = \left(2\dfrac{1}{2}, -1\dfrac{1}{2}\right)$

15. $\begin{cases} 3x + 2y = 13 \\ 2x + 5y = 16 \end{cases}$ $\begin{array}{l} \to \quad 2(3x + 2y) = -2(13) \\ \to \quad 3(2x + 5y) = 3(16) \end{array}$ $\begin{array}{l} \to \quad -6x - 4y = -26 \\ \to \quad \underline{6x + 15y = 48} \\ \qquad\qquad 11y = 22 \\ \qquad\qquad \dfrac{11y}{11} = \dfrac{22}{11} \\ \qquad\qquad\quad y = 2 \end{array}$

Substitute 2 for y.
$$3x + 2y = 13$$
$$3x + 2(2) = 13$$
$$3x + 4 = 13$$
$$3x + 4 - 4 = 13 - 4$$
$$3x = 9$$
$$\frac{3x}{3} = \frac{9}{3}$$
$$x = 3$$
$$(x, y) = (3, 2)$$

16. $\begin{cases} -3x - 3y = 6 \\ x - 2y = 7 \end{cases}$ $\begin{array}{l} \to \quad -3x - 3y = 6 \\ \to \quad 3(x - 2y) = 3(7) \end{array}$ $\begin{array}{l} \to \quad -3x - 3y = 6 \\ \to \quad \underline{3x - 6y = 21} \\ \qquad\qquad -9y = 27 \\ \qquad\qquad \dfrac{-9y}{-9} = \dfrac{27}{-9} \\ \qquad\qquad\quad y = -3 \end{array}$

Substitute -3 for y.
$$x - 2y = 7$$
$$x - 2(-3) = 7$$
$$x + 6 = 7$$
$$x + 6 - 6 = 7 - 6$$
$$x = 1$$
$$(x, y) = (1, -3)$$

17. $\begin{cases} x < 4 \\ y \geq 3 \end{cases}$

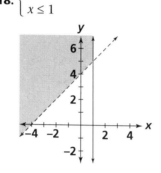

18. $\begin{cases} y > x + 4 \\ x \leq 1 \end{cases}$

19. $\begin{cases} y \leq 2x - 4 \\ y > \dfrac{1}{2}x - 5 \end{cases}$

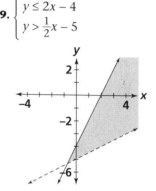

20. $\begin{cases} 3x - 4y \leq 12 \\ x - y > 1 \end{cases}$

$$3x - 4y \leq 12$$
$$3x - 4y - 3x \leq 12 - 3x$$
$$-4y \leq -3x + 12$$
$$-\frac{1}{4}(-4y) \geq -\frac{1}{4}(-3x + 12)$$
$$y \geq \frac{3}{4}x - 3$$

$$x - y > 1$$
$$x - y - x > 1 - x$$
$$-y > -x + 1$$
$$-1(-y) < -1(-x + 1)$$
$$y < x - 1$$

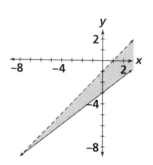

21. Let x represent the number of adults. Let y represent the number of students.

$\begin{cases} 5.50x + 3.50y = 2850 \\ x + y = 700 \end{cases}$ $\begin{array}{l} \to \quad 5.50x + 3.50y = 2850 \\ \to \quad -3.50(x + y) = -3.50(700) \end{array}$ $\begin{array}{l} \to \quad 5.50x + 3.50y = 2850 \\ \to \quad \underline{-3.50x - 3.50y = -2450} \\ \qquad\qquad 2x = 400 \\ \qquad\qquad \dfrac{2x}{2} = \dfrac{400}{2} \\ \qquad\qquad\quad x = 200 \end{array}$

Substitute 200 for x.
$$x + y = 700$$
$$200 + y = 700$$
$$200 + y - 200 = 700 - 200$$
$$y = 500$$
There were 200 adults and 500 students at the game.

1. $\begin{cases} 3x - 2y = 6 \\ x + y = 2 \end{cases}$

$3x - 2y = 6$ $x + y = 2$

$3x - 2y - 3x = 6 - 3x$ $x + y - x = 2 - x$

$-2y = -3x + 6$ $y = -x + 2$

$-\frac{1}{2}(-2y) = -\frac{1}{2}(-3x + 6)$

$y = \frac{3}{2}x - 3$

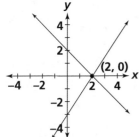

solution = (2, 0)

2. $\begin{cases} x + 2y = 5 \\ 5x + 3y = -3 \end{cases}$

$x + 2y = 5$ $5x + 3y = -3$

$x + 2y - x = 5 - x$ $5x + 3y - 5x = -3 - 5x$

$2y = -x + 5$ $3y = -5x - 3$

$\frac{1}{2}(2y) = \frac{1}{2}(-x + 5)$ $\frac{1}{3}(3y) = \frac{1}{3}(-5x - 3)$

$y = -\frac{1}{2}x = \frac{5}{2}$ $y = -\frac{5}{3}x - 1$

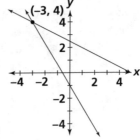

solution = (−3, 4)

3. $\begin{cases} 3x - 2y = 4 \\ 2x + y = 5 \end{cases}$

$3x - 2y = 4$ $2x + y = 5$

$-2y = -3x + 4$ $y = -2x + 5$

$y = \frac{3}{2}x - 2$

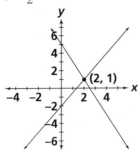

solution = (2, 1)

4. $\begin{cases} y = 2x \\ x + y = 12 \end{cases}$

Substitute 2x for y.

$x + y = 12$

$x + 2x = 12$

$3x = 12$

$\frac{3x}{3} = \frac{12}{3}$

$x = 4$

Substitute 4 for x.

$y = 2x$

$y = 2(4)$

$y = 8$

$(x, y) = (4, 8)$

5. $\begin{cases} x + y = 15 \\ y = x + 3 \end{cases}$

Substitute x + 3 for y.

$x + y = 15$

$x + (x + 3) = 15$

$2x + 3 = 15$

$2x + 3 - 3 = 15 - 3$

$2x = 12$

$\frac{2x}{2} = \frac{12}{12}$

$x = 6$

Substitute 6 for x.

$y = x + 3$

$y = 6 + 3$

$y = 9$

$(x, y) = (6, 9)$

6. $\begin{cases} 2x + 2y = 4 \\ x - y = 6 \end{cases}$

$x - y = 6$

$x - y + y = 6 + 4$

$x = 6 + y$

Substitute 6 + y for x.

$2x + 2y = 4$

$2(6 + y) + 2y = 4$

$12 + 2y + 2y = 4$

$12 + 4y = 4$

$12 + 4y - 12 = 4 - 12$

$4y = -8$

$y = -2$

Substitute −2 for y.

$x - y = 6$

$x - (-2) = 6$

$x + 2 = 6$

$x + 2 - 2 = 6 - 2$

$x = 4$

$(x, y) = (4, -2)$

7. $\begin{cases} 2x + 9y = 24 \\ -2x + 5y = 4 \end{cases}$

$14y = 28$

$\frac{14y}{14} = \frac{28}{14}$

$y = 2$

Substitute 2 for y.

$2x + 9y = 24$

$2x + 9(2) = 24$

$2x + 18 = 24$

$2x - 18 - 18 = 24 - 18$

$2x = 6$

$x = 3$

$(x, y) = (3, 2)$

8. $\begin{cases} 3x + 2y = 13 \\ 5x - 2y = 11 \end{cases}$

$8x = 24$

$\frac{8x}{8} = \frac{24}{8}$

$x = 3$

Substitute 3 for x.

$3x + 2y = 13$

$3(3) + 2y = 13$

$9 + 2y = 13$

$9 + 2y - 9 = 13 - 9$

$2y = 4$

$y = 2$

$(x, y) = (3, 2)$

9. $\begin{cases} x + y = 32 \\ x - y = 4 \end{cases}$

$2x = 36$

$\dfrac{2x}{2} = \dfrac{36}{2}$

$x = 18$

Substitute 18 for x.

$x + y = 32$

$18 + y = 32$

$18 + y - 18 = 32 - 18$

$y = 14$

$(x, y) = (18, 14)$

10. $\begin{cases} 5x - 2y = 3 \rightarrow 2(5x - 2y) = 2(3) \rightarrow 10x - 4y = 6 \\ 2x + 7y = 9 \rightarrow -5(2x + 7y) = -5(9) \rightarrow \underline{-10x - 35y = -45} \end{cases}$

$-39y = -39$

$\dfrac{-39y}{-39} = \dfrac{-39}{-39}$

$y = 1$

Substitute 1 for y.

$5x - 2y = 3$

$5x - 2(1) = 3$

$5x - 2 = 3$

$5x - 2 + 2 = 3 + 2$

$5x = 5$

$\dfrac{5x}{5} = \dfrac{5}{5}$

$x = 1$

$(x, y) = (1, 1)$

11. $\begin{cases} 5x + 2y = 9 \rightarrow 3(5x + 2y) = 3(9) \rightarrow 15x + 6y = 27 \\ 3x + 7y = 17 \rightarrow -5(3x + 7y) = -5(17) \rightarrow \underline{-15x - 35y = -85} \end{cases}$

$-29y = -58$

$\dfrac{-29y}{-29} = \dfrac{-58}{-29}$

$y = 2$

Substitute 2 for y.

$3x + 7y = 17$

$3x + 7(2) = 17$

$3x + 14 = 17$

$3x = 3$

$x = 1$

$(x, y) = (1, 2)$

12. $\begin{cases} 10x - 5y = 50 \rightarrow 2(10x - 5y) = 2(50) \rightarrow 20x - 10y = 100 \\ 6x + 2y = 28 \rightarrow 5(6x + 2y) = 5(28) \rightarrow \underline{30x + 10y = 140} \end{cases}$

$50x = 240$

$\dfrac{50x}{50} = \dfrac{240}{50}$

$x = \dfrac{24}{5}$, or $4\dfrac{4}{5}$

Substitute $\dfrac{24}{5}$ for x.

$6x + 2y = 28$

$6\left(\dfrac{24}{5}\right) + 2y = 28$

$\dfrac{144}{5} + 2y = 28$

$\dfrac{144}{5} + 2y - \dfrac{144}{5} = 28 - \dfrac{144}{5}$

$2y = -\dfrac{4}{5}$

$\dfrac{1}{2}(2y) = \dfrac{1}{2}\left(-\dfrac{4}{5}\right)$

$y = -\dfrac{4}{10}$, or $-\dfrac{2}{5}$

$(x, y) = \left(4\dfrac{4}{5}, -\dfrac{2}{5}\right)$

13. Let a represent the number of pounds of almonds. Let p represent the number of pounds of pecans.

$\begin{cases} a = 4p \rightarrow a - 4p = 0 \rightarrow 3(a - 4p) = 3(0) \rightarrow 3a - 12p = 0 \\ 4.50a + 3.00p = 21.00 \rightarrow 4.5a + 3p = 21 \rightarrow 4(4.5a + 3p) = 4(21) \rightarrow \underline{18a + 12p = 84} \end{cases}$

$21a = 84$

$\dfrac{21a}{21} = \dfrac{84}{21}$

$a = 4$

Substitute 4 for a.

$a = 4p$

$4 = 4p$

$\dfrac{4}{4} = \dfrac{4p}{4}$

$1 = p$

There are 4 pounds of almonds and 1 pound of pecans in a package of mixed nuts.

14. Let n represent the number of nickels. Let d represent the number of dimes.

$$\begin{cases} n + d = 2d + 1 \\ 0.05n + 0.10d = 0.95 \end{cases} \to \begin{array}{l} n - d = 1 \\ 0.05n + 0.10d = 0.95 \end{array} \to \begin{array}{l} 0.10(n-d) = 0.10(1) \\ 0.05n + 0.10d = 0.95 \end{array} \to \begin{array}{l} 0.10n - 0.10d = 0.10 \\ \underline{0.05n + 0.10d = 0.95} \end{array}$$

$$0.15n = 1.05$$
$$\frac{0.15n}{0.15} = \frac{1.05}{0.15}$$
$$n = 7$$

Substitute 7 for n.

$$n - d = 1$$
$$7 - d = 1$$
$$7 - d - 7 = 1 - 7$$
$$-d = -6$$
$$-1(-d) = -1(-6)$$
$$d = 6$$

Alex has 6 dimes and 7 nickels.

15. $\begin{cases} x < 2 \\ y \geq -1 \end{cases}$

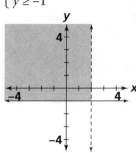

16. $\begin{cases} 3x - 5y < 10 \\ 2x + 3y \leq 3 \end{cases}$

$$\begin{array}{l} 3x - 5y < 10 \\ 3x - 5y - 3x < 10 - 3x \\ -5y < -3x + 10 \\ -\frac{1}{5}(-5y) > -\frac{1}{5}(-3x + 10) \\ y > \frac{3}{5}x - 2 \end{array} \qquad \begin{array}{l} 2x + 3y \leq 3 \\ 2x + 3y - 2x \leq 3 - 2x \\ 3y \leq -2x + 3 \\ \frac{1}{3}(3y) \leq \frac{1}{3}(-2x + 3) \\ y \leq -\frac{2}{3}x + 1 \end{array}$$

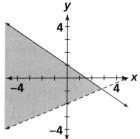

17. $\begin{cases} 3x - 2y < 2 \\ 2y - 3x < 4 \end{cases}$

$$\begin{array}{l} 3x - 2y < 2 \\ 3x - 2y - 3x < 2 - 3x \\ -2y < -3x + 2 \\ -\frac{1}{2}(-2y) > -\frac{1}{2}(-3x + 2) \\ y > \frac{3}{2}x - 1 \end{array} \qquad \begin{array}{l} 2y - 3x < 4 \\ 2y - 3x + 3x < 4 + 3x \\ 2y < 3x + 4 \\ \frac{1}{2}(2y) < \frac{1}{2}(3x + 4) \\ y < \frac{3}{2}x + 2 \end{array}$$

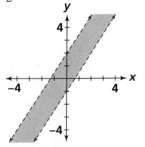

18. Let b represent the number of boxes of brownies. Let c represent the number of boxes of cookies.

$$\begin{cases} 8b + 6c \geq 120 \\ b + c \leq 50 \end{cases}$$

$$\begin{array}{l} 8b + 6c \geq 120 \\ 6c \geq -8b + 120 \\ c \geq -\frac{4}{3}b + 20 \end{array} \qquad \begin{array}{l} b + c \leq 50 \\ c \leq -b + 50 \end{array}$$

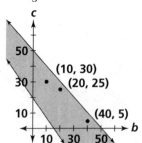

19. Since you cannot have negative boxes of anything, the reasonable domain and range are all positive numbers such that:

$$0 \leq b \leq 50 \quad \text{domain}$$
$$0 \leq c \leq 50 \quad \text{range}$$

20. Answers may vary. Three possible solutions are (10, 30), (20, 25), and (40, 5).

CHAPTER 10

A PREVIEW OF FUNCTIONS

9. 5, 10, 20, 40, 80

10. Multiply each term by 3. 24,300; 72,900; 218,700

11. Add 200 to each term. 1100, 1300, 1500

12. Divide each term by 10. 0.001, 0.0001, 0.00001

13. Subtract 5 from each term. 15, 10, 5

14. The sequence in Exercise 10 shows exponential growth.

15. The sequences in Exercises 11 and 13 are linear.

16. Each term is $\frac{1}{4}$ of the previous one; the sequence is exponential.

17.

x	3^x	y
1	3^1	3
2	3^2	9
3	3^3	27
4	3^4	81
5	3^5	243

18. 0.5, 0.25, 0.125, 0.0625, 0.03125; each successive product is one-half of the previous term. The terms get closer and closer to zero, but never equal zero.

19. When does $1000(1.05)^x = 2000$?

Try $x = 10$.
$1000(1.05)^{10} = 1628.89$
10 is too small.

Try $x = 15$.
$1000(1.05)^{15} = 2078.92$
15 is too large.

Try $x = 14$.
$1000(1.05)^{14} = 1979.93$
14 is too small.

It takes between 14 and 15 years for Jacy's money to double; 15 years.

20. Second bounce: $10 \times \frac{1}{2} = 5$

After the second bounce, the ball bounces to a height of 5 ft.

21. Third bounce: $5 \times \frac{1}{2} = 2\frac{1}{2}$

After the third bounce, the ball bounces to a height of $2\frac{1}{2}$ ft.

22. Fourth bounce: $2\frac{1}{2} \times \frac{1}{2} = \frac{5}{2} \times \frac{1}{2} = \frac{5}{4}$

After the fourth bounce, the ball bounces to a height of $1\frac{1}{4}$ ft.

23. Fifth bounce: $\frac{5}{4} \times \frac{1}{2} = \frac{5}{8}$

After the sixth bounce, the ball bounces to a height of $\frac{5}{8}$ ft, or 0.625 ft.

24. 1, 3, 9, 27, 81, 243, . . .

25. The sequence is linear because each term is 10 less than the previous term. The difference is a fixed amount.

26. A fixed rate means that each term is a constant multiple of the previous one.

27. A constant amount is added to or subtracted from the previous term.

28. Compound interest is the interest computed on the current balance after each time period; the compounded amount is growing exponentially.

29. 8, 16, 32, 64, 128, 256
After doubling 5 times you get 256.

30.

Month	Balance	Payment
1	1000.00	50.00
2	950.00	47.50
3	902.50	45.13
4	857.37	42.87
5	814.50	40.73
6	773.77	38.69
7	735.08	

After 6 months the balance is $735.08.

31. Add 4 to each term.
23, 27

32. Divide by 2 to obtain the
next term.
$\frac{1}{8}, \frac{1}{16}$

33. Subtract 3 from each term.
18, 15

34. Add 2 to the constant to
find each successive term,
$66 + 19 = 85$ and $85 + 21 = 106$.
The next two terms are 85
and 106.

35. Alternately subtract 21 and
6 to find successive terms.
24, 18

36–39.

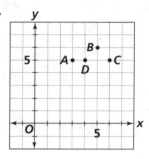

40. 100, –200, 400, –800, 1600, –3200, . . .
The sequence does not get close to any particular
number.

41. 100, –50, 25, –12.5, 6.25, . . .
The numbers get closer and closer to 0.

10.2 **PAGES 548–549, PRACTICE & APPLY**

10. The second difference is a
constant of 2.
c. Quadratic

11. Each term is 2 times the
previous one.
b. Exponential

12. The first difference is a
constant of –1.
a. Linear

13. The first difference is a
constant of 2.
a. Linear

14. The second difference is
a constant of 2.
c. Quadratic

15. Each term is half of the previous
one.
b. Exponential

16. If the length of each side is
tripled, the area is 3^2, or 9
times as much.

17. If the length of each side is
multiplied by 10, the area is
multiplied by 10^2, or 100.

18. If the length of each side is
$\frac{1}{3}$ as large, the area is $\left(\frac{1}{3}\right)^2$, or
$\frac{1}{9}$ of the original area.

19. Area of a 10-in. pizza $= \pi(5)^2$
$= 78.5$ in.^{2}

Area of a 15-in. pizza $= \pi(7.5)^2$
$= 176.63$ in.^{2}

20. Price per square inch:
10-in. pizza $= \frac{4.50}{78.5} = 5.7$ cents
15-in. pizza $= \frac{9.00}{176.7} = 5.1$ cents
The 15-in. pizza is the better buy.

21. c. Quadratic   **22. b.** Exponential   **23. a.** Linear   **24. d.** None of these

25. A side of the larger square is 4 in., and a side of
the smaller square is 2 in., so the side of the larger
square is twice the side of the smaller square.

26. Plot the points on a coordinate grid. Draw a
parabola to connect the points. Find the point
on the parabola that is symmetrical to the point
(5, 3). The point will have the same y-value as
(5, 3). Another point is (11, 3).

27. The parabola opens
upward.

28. $h = 16t^2$
$h = 16(1)^2$
$h = 16$
The waterfall is
16 feet high.

29. $h = 16t^2$
$h = 16(2)^2$
$h = 16(4)$
$h = 64$
The waterfall is
64 feet high.

30. $h = 16t^2$
$h = 16(5)^2$
$h = 16(25)$
$h = 400$
The waterfall is
400 feet high.

31.

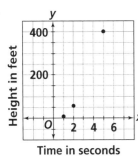

Time in seconds

Answers will vary, however most of the world's tallest waterfalls are under 2000 feet in height, so a reasonable domain would be $0 \le x \le 12$ seconds and a reasonable range would be $0 \le y \le 2300$ feet.

32. Extend the graph in Exercise 31. From a height of 600 feet, it would take just over 6 seconds.

PAGE 549, LOOK BACK

33. Multiply each term by 3.
$891 \times 3 = 2673$

34. Multiply each term by $\frac{1}{5}$.
$25 \times \frac{1}{5} = 5$

35. Multiply each term by $\frac{2}{2}$.
$\frac{32}{40} \times \frac{2}{2} = \frac{64}{80}$

36. $3xy = 3(2)(1) = 6$

37. $4z = 4(4) = 16$

38. $21yz = 21(1)(4) = 84$

39. $xyz = (2)(1)(4) = 8$

40. cost $= 5 \times (1.29) = 6.45$
The cost of 5 packages of notebook paper is $6.45.

41. Points may vary.

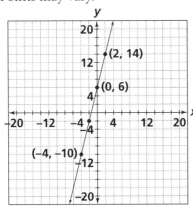

42. Points may vary.

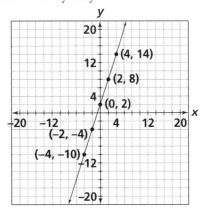

PAGE 549, LOOK BEYOND

43. The variable t is the independent variable in $h = 16t^2$.

44. Points may vary.

x	$(x-2)^2 + 7$	y
4	$(4-2)^2 + 7$	11
3	$(3-2)^2 + 7$	8
2	$(2-2)^2 + 7$	7
1	$(1-2)^2 + 7$	8
0	$(0-2)^2 + 7$	11
-1	$(-1-2)^2 + 7$	18

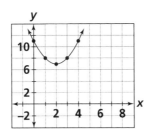

The vertex is (2, 7).

45. Points may vary.

x	$(x^2 + 2x) + 1$	y
3	$3^2 + 2(3) + 1$	16
2	$2^2 + 2(2) + 1$	9
1	$1^2 + 2(1) + 1$	4
0	$0^2 + 2(0) + 1$	1
-1	$(-1)^2 + 2(-1) + 1$	0
-2	$(-2)^2 + 2(-2) + 1$	1
-3	$(-3)^2 + 2(-3) + 1$	4

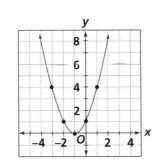

The vertex is (-1, 0).

9.

x	6	5	3	1	$\frac{1}{3}$	$\frac{1}{5}$	$\frac{1}{6}$
y	$\frac{1}{6}$	$\frac{1}{5}$	$\frac{1}{3}$	1	3	5	6

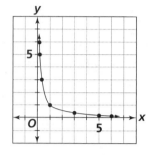

10.

time, t	4	?
speed, s	45	60

distance = speed × time $\qquad d = st$

$\qquad\qquad = 4 \times 45 \qquad\qquad 180 = 60t$

$\qquad\qquad = 180 \qquad\qquad\qquad t = 3$

At 60 mph the trip will take 3 hours.

11. $\frac{1}{7}$ **12.** $\frac{1}{5}$ **13.** $\frac{1}{25}$ **14.** 4 **15.** 10 **16.** 7

17. Division by 0 is not defined.

18. 1 is its own reciprocal because $\frac{1}{1} = 1$.

19. Find the relationship of the new length of string to the original 60-cm string.

$$30 \text{ cm} = \frac{1}{2} \cdot 60 \text{ cm}$$

The 30-cm string is half as long. By the reciprocal relationship, a string half as long doubles the frequency of 300 vps.

$$2 \times 300 = 600 \text{ vps}$$

A 30-cm string has a frequency of 600 vibrations per second.

20. Find the relationship of the 20-cm string to the 30-cm string.

$$20 \text{ cm} = \frac{1}{3} \cdot 60 \text{ cm}$$

A string $\frac{1}{3}$ as long triples the frequency of 300 vps.

$$3 \times 300 = 900 \text{ vps}$$

A 20-cm string has a frequency of 900 vibrations per second.

21. Find the relationship of the 90-cm string to the 60-cm string.

$$90 \text{ cm} = \frac{3}{2} \cdot 60 \text{ cm}$$

A string $\frac{3}{2}$ as long multiplies the frequency by $\frac{2}{3}$.

$$\frac{2}{3} \times 300 = \frac{600}{3} = 200 \text{ vps}$$

A 90-cm string has a frequency of 200 vibrations per second.

22. Find the relationship of the 96-cm string to the 32-cm string.

$$96 \text{ cm} = 3 \cdot 32 \text{ cm}$$

A string 3 times as long multiplies the frequency of 660 vps by $\frac{1}{3}$.

$$\frac{1}{3} \times 660 = 220 \text{ vps}$$

A 96-cm string has a frequency of 220 vibrations per second.

23. Find the relationship of the 16-cm string to the 32-cm string.

$$16 \text{ cm} = \frac{1}{2} \cdot 32 \text{ cm}$$

A string half as long doubles the frequency.

$$2 \times 660 = 1320 \text{ vps}$$

A 16-cm string has a frequency of 1320 vibrations per second.

24. Find the relationship of the 24-cm string to the 32-cm string.

$$24 \text{ cm} = \frac{3}{4} \cdot 32 \text{ cm}$$

A string $\frac{3}{4}$ as long multiplies the frequency by $\frac{4}{3}$.

$$\frac{4}{3} \times 660 = \frac{2640}{3} = 880 \text{ vps}$$

A 24-cm string has a frequency of 880 vibrations per second.

25. Points may vary.

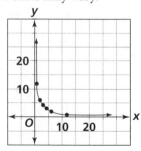

26. Points may vary.

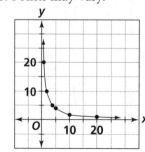

27. Points may vary.

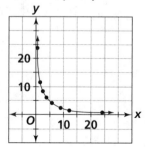

28. $\frac{100}{10} = 10$

Each person contributes $10.

29. $\frac{100}{20} = 5$

Each person contributes $5.

30. $\frac{100}{100} = 1$

Each person contributes $1.

31. $\frac{100}{1000} = 0.10$

Each person contributes $0.10.

32. $\frac{60}{3} = 20$

If each car holds 3 passengers, 20 cars are needed.

33. $\frac{60}{4} = 15$

If each car holds 4 passengers, 15 cars are needed.

34. $\frac{60}{5} = 12$

If each car holds 5 passengers, 12 cars are needed.

35. distance = speed × time

$240 = s \times 6$

$40 = s$

To complete the trip in 6 hours, you need to average 40 mph.

36. $240 = s \times 5$

$48 = s$

To complete the trip in 5 hours, you need to average 48 mph.

37. $240 = s \times 4$

$60 = s$

To complete the trip in 4 hours, you need to average 60 mph.

38. $240 = s \times 3$

$80 = s$

To complete the trip in 3 hours, you need to average 80 mph.

39. $240 = s \times 1$

$240 = s$

To complete the trip in 1 hour, you need to average 240 mph.

40. $240 = s \times \frac{1}{2}$

$480 = s$

To complete the trip in $\frac{1}{2}$ hour, you need to average 480 mph.

41. distance = $50 \times 4 = 200$

$40t = 200$

$t = 5$

At 40 mph, the trip will take 5 hours.

42. frequency = constant × $\frac{1}{\text{length}}$

$400 = k \times \frac{1}{48}$

$21{,}120 = k$

The constant is 21,120 centimeters per second.

PAGE 555, LOOK BACK

43.
$$\text{m}\angle 1 + \text{m}\angle 2 = 90$$
$$(2x + 9) + \left(\frac{3}{4} + x\right) = 90$$
$$2x + x + 9 + \frac{3}{4} = 90$$
$$3x + \frac{39}{4} = 90$$
$$3x + \frac{39}{4} - \frac{39}{4} = 90 - \frac{39}{4}$$
$$3x = \frac{321}{4}$$
$$\frac{1}{3}(3x) = \frac{1}{3}\left(\frac{321}{4}\right)$$
$$x = \frac{321}{12}, \text{ or } 26\frac{3}{4}, \text{ or } 26.75$$

44.
$$\text{m}\angle 1 + \text{m}\angle 2 = 90$$
$$(1.7x - 0.98) + (1.4 + 7.9) = 90$$
$$1.7x + 1.4x - 0.98 + 7.9 = 90$$
$$3.1x + 6.92 = 90$$
$$3.1x + 6.92 - 6.92 = 90 - 6.92$$
$$3.1x = 83.08$$
$$\frac{3.1x}{3.1} = \frac{83.08}{3.1}$$
$$x \approx 26.8$$

45. Let x represent the number of hardcover books sold. Let y represent the number of paperback books sold.

$$\begin{cases} 7x + 3y = 48 \\ y = 3x \end{cases}$$

Substitute $3x$ for y.

$$7x + 3y = 48$$
$$7x + 3(3x) = 48$$
$$7x + 9x = 48$$
$$16x = 48$$
$$\frac{16x}{16} = \frac{48}{16}$$
$$x = 3$$

Substitute 3 for x.

$$y = 3(3)$$
$$y = 9$$

Each member should sell 3 hardcover books and 9 paperbacks.

46.

	First solution	Second solution	New solution
Percent acid	1.5% = 0.015	3% = 0.03	1.8% = 0.018
Amount of solution	x	y	150 g
Amount of acid	0.015x	0.03y	0.018(150) = 2.7

$$\begin{cases} x + y = 150 \\ 0.015x + 0.03y = 2.7 \end{cases} \rightarrow \begin{matrix} -0.03(x+y) = -0.03(150) \\ 0.015x + 0.03y = 2.7 \end{matrix} \rightarrow \begin{matrix} -0.03x - 0.03y = -4.5 \\ 0.015x + 0.03y = 2.7 \end{matrix}$$

$$-0.015x = -1.8$$
$$\frac{-0.015x}{-0.015} = \frac{-1.8}{-0.015}$$
$$x = 120$$

Substitute 120 for x.

$$x + y = 150$$
$$120 + y = 150$$
$$120 + y - 120 = 150 - 120$$
$$y = 30$$

120 grams of the 1.5% solution and 30 grams of the 3% solution are needed.

47. $\begin{cases} 3x + y < -3 \\ x - y \geq 2 \end{cases}$

$$\begin{matrix} 3x + y < -3 & x - y \geq 2 \\ 3x + y - 3x < -3 - 3x & x - y - x \geq 2 - x \\ y < -3x - 3 & -y \geq -x + 2 \\ & -1(-y) \leq -1(-x + 2) \\ & y \leq x - 2 \end{matrix}$$

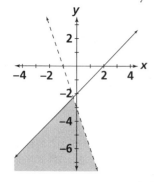

48. $\begin{cases} y > -x - 2 \\ y > x + 2 \end{cases}$

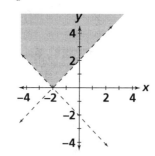

49. $\begin{cases} y \leq -2x + 1 \\ y \leq 2x - 3 \end{cases}$

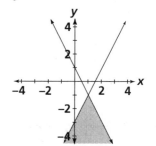

PAGE 555, LOOK BEYOND

50. $y = \dfrac{3}{x}$

Substitute values for x and solve for y.

x	$\frac{3}{x}$	y	x	$\frac{3}{x}$	y	x	$\frac{3}{x}$	y	x	$\frac{3}{x}$	y
1	$\frac{3}{1}$	3	$\frac{1}{2}$	$\frac{3}{2}$	6	-1	$\frac{3}{-1}$	-3	$-\frac{1}{2}$	$\frac{3}{-\frac{1}{2}}$	-6
2	$\frac{3}{2}$	$\frac{3}{2}$	$\frac{1}{4}$	$\frac{3}{4}$	12	-2	$\frac{3}{-2}$	$-\frac{3}{2}$	$-\frac{1}{4}$	$\frac{3}{-\frac{1}{4}}$	-12
4	$\frac{3}{4}$	$\frac{3}{4}$	$\frac{1}{5}$	$\frac{3}{5}$	15	-4	$\frac{3}{-4}$	$-\frac{3}{4}$			
5	$\frac{3}{5}$	$\frac{3}{5}$				-5	$\frac{3}{-5}$	$-\frac{3}{5}$	$-\frac{1}{5}$	$\frac{3}{-\frac{1}{5}}$	-15

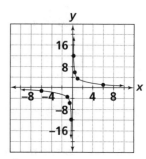

11. 52 seconds is less than 1 minute, so the student's estimate was under the correct amount.

12. 60 − 52 = 8

The student's error was 8 seconds under, or −8 seconds.

13. The absolute value is $|-8| = 8$.

14. $|17| = 17$

15. $|-33| = 33$

16. $|8.67| = 8.67$

17. $|-7.11| = 7.11$

18. $|4.8| = 4.8$

19. $|-3.2| = 3.2$

20. INT(5.8) = 5

21. $\text{INT}\left(\frac{11}{2}\right) = 5$

22. ABS(5.8) = 5.8

23. $\text{ABS}\left(\frac{11}{2}\right) = 5.5$

24. INT(17) = 17

25. $\text{INT}\left(\frac{33}{4}\right) = \text{INT}\left(8\frac{1}{4}\right) = 8$

26. INT(−8.67) = −9

27. INT(−7.11) = −8

28. 8

29. 8

30. −8

31. −8

32.

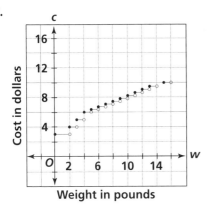

This is a step function because the graph resembles a flight of stairs. This is not the greatest-integer function because the cost does not round down to a whole dollar (integer) in many cases.

For Exercises 33–36, you cannot make part of a place mat.

33. 6 place mats

34. 3 place mats

35. 5 place mats

36. no place mat because $\frac{9}{10}$ yard < 1 yard

37–38.

	A	B	C	D
1	Student	Time	Error	Abs. error
2	Buster	57	−3	3
3	Tony	74	14	14
4	Charlotte	59	−1	1
5	Amy	60	0	0
6	Gerti	71	11	11
7	Nathan	56	−4	4
8	Jamie	58	−2	2
9	Marni	70	10	10
10	Lee	58	−2	2
11	Wei	62	2	2
12	Ned	68	8	8
13	Debbie	74	14	14
14	Wynton	70	10	10
15	Bob	73	13	13
16	Jill	65	5	5

39. Answers may vary.

40. Since the person riding always stops riding as he encounters the person walking and does not pass the person walking, we can assume that they arrive at the same time. Therefore, they have walked the same distance and ridden the same distance, that is, halfway.

Riding at 5 mph:

$$t = \frac{d}{r} = \frac{10}{5} = 2$$

Riding 10 miles takes 2 hours.

Walking at 3 mph:

$$t = \frac{d}{r} = \frac{10}{3} = 3\frac{1}{3}$$

Walking 10 miles takes $3\frac{1}{3}$ hours.

The trip takes $2 + 3\frac{1}{3}$, hours, or 5 hours and 20 minutes.

41. $x^2 + 3x - 2x^2 + 4x = -x^2 + 7x$ **42.** $2x^2 - (-4x + 3) = 2x^2 + 4x - 3$ **43.** $(2x + 5) + (3x + 4) = 2x + 3x + 5 + 4$
$$= 5x + 9$$

44. $(4x + 3) - (2x - 5) = 4x + 3 - 2x + 5$ **45.** $-4x(3x - 2) = -12x^2 + 8x$
$$= 4x - 2x + 3 + 5$$
$$= 2x + 8$$

46. $2y^2(-5y + 1) = -10y^3 + 2y^2$ **47.** $6(-x^2 + 4x) = -6x^2 + 24x$ **48.** $3x(x^2 - x) = 3x^3 - 3x^2$

49. $3m + 24 = 3(m + 8)$ **50.** $6x^4 + 36x = 6x(x^3 + 6)$ **51.** $4u - 20u^3 = 4u(1 - 5u^2)$

52. $9x^2 - 36x^3 = 9x^2(1 - 4x)$ **53.** The vertex is (2, 3).

For Exercises 54–55, substitute values for *x* and solve for *y*. Points may vary. Examples are shown.

54. $y = |x| + 3$

x	$|x| + 3$	y
-3	$|-3| + 3$	6
-2	$|-2| + 3$	5
-1	$|-1| + 3$	4
0	$|0| + 3$	3
1	$|1| + 3$	4
2	$|2| + 3$	5
3	$|3| + 3$	6

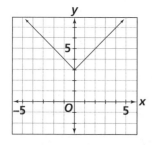

55. $y = |x + 3|$

x	$|x + 3|$	y
-6	$|-6 + 3|$	3
-5	$|-5 + 3|$	2
-4	$|-4 + 3|$	1
-3	$|-3 + 3|$	0
-2	$|-2 + 3|$	1
-1	$|-1 + 3|$	2
0	$|0 + 3|$	3

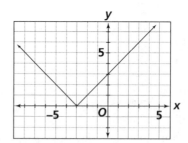

10.5 **PAGES 568–569, PRACTICE & APPLY**

11. a. Linear **12. c.** Quadratic **13. b.** Exponential

14. d. Reciprocal **15. f.** Step **16. e.** Absolute value

17.

y-values	2		6		18		54		162
First differences		4		12		36		108	
Second differences			8		24		72		

Each term is 3 times the previous one. This is an exponential function; it is neither linear nor quadratic.

18.

y-values	44		55		66		77		88
First differences		11		11		11		11	

The first differences are constant; this is a linear relationship.

19.

y-values	8		15		24		35		48
First differences		7		9		11		13	
Second differences			2		2		2		

The second differences are constant; this is a quadratic relationship.

20.

y-values	1		1		2		3		5
First differences		0		1		1		2	
Second differences			1		0		1		

The second differences are not constant; this is neither linear nor quadratic.

21.

y-values	1		3		6		10		15
First differences		2		3		4		5	
Second differences			1		1		1		

The second differences are constant; this is a quadratic relationship.

22.

y-values	45		54		63		72		81
First differences		9		9		9		9	

The first differences are constant; this is a linear relationship.

23.

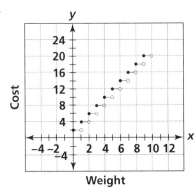

The points fit nicely near a line with one exception. The players near the line all score about the same number of points per minute. However, Trina does not score at the same rate as her teammates.

24. When the x-values are positive, $y = x$. When the x-values are negative, $y = -x$. The absolute value function can be described as two linear functions with $y \geq 0$ that meet at a vertex.

25.

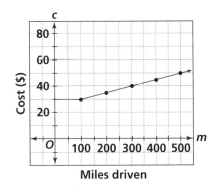

26. It is a step function.

27.

Miles driven	0	100	200	300	400	500
Cost($)	30	30	35	40	45	50

28. The function in Exercise 27 is a piecewise function.

29. $\dfrac{72}{4} = 18$ years

30. $\dfrac{72}{6} = 12$ years

31. $\dfrac{72}{9} = 8$ years

32. $t = \dfrac{72}{x}$, where t is the number of years and x the number of hundredths of the percent of interest

33. It is a reciprocal function.

PAGE 569, LOOK BACK

34.

32 ft = 384 in.

20 ft, 8 in. = 248 in.

$$\frac{\text{length}}{\text{width}} = \frac{384}{248} = \frac{384 \div 8}{248 \div 8} = \frac{48}{31}$$

The ratio of the length to the width is 48 to 31.

35. Let D represent the distance from Earth to Mars. Let r represent the rate of travel for a radio signal, and let t represent the time (in seconds) it takes for the signal to travel from Earth to Mars.

$$D = rt$$
$$35,000,000 = 186,000t$$
$$\frac{35,000,000}{186,000} = \frac{186,000t}{186,000}$$
$$188.17 \approx t$$

It will take approximately 188 seconds (or about 3 minutes, 8 seconds) for the radio signal to reach Mars.

36. End of year 1: $1000(1.20) = \$1200.00$
End of year 2: $1200(1.20) = \$1440.00$
End of year 3: $1440(1.20) = \$1728.00$
End of year 4: $1728(1.20) = \$2073.60$
End of year 5: $2073.60(1.20) = \$2488.32$

It takes 4 years to double an amount compounded annually at 20%.

PAGE 569, LOOK BEYOND

37.

x	a. $y = \lvert x \rvert$	b. $y = \lvert x + 2 \rvert$	c. $y = \lvert x - 1 \rvert$	d. $y = \lvert x \rvert - 3$	e. $y = \lvert x \rvert + 1$
−5	5	3	6	2	6
−4	4	2	5	1	5
−3	3	1	4	0	4
−2	2	0	3	−1	3
−1	1	1	2	−2	2
0	0	2	1	−3	1
1	1	3	0	−2	2
2	2	4	1	−1	3
3	3	5	2	0	4
4	4	6	3	1	5
5	5	7	4	2	6

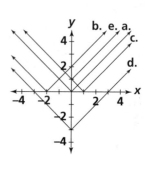

b. The graph of $y = \lvert x + 2 \rvert$ is the same as the graph of $y = \lvert x \rvert$ shifted to the left 2 units.

c. The graph of $y = \lvert x - 1 \rvert$ is the same as the graph of $y = \lvert x \rvert$ shifted to the right 1 unit.

d. The graph of $y = \lvert x \rvert - 3$ is the same as the graph of $y = \lvert x \rvert$ shifted down 3 units.

e. The graph of $y = \lvert x \rvert + 1$ is the same as the graph of $y = \lvert x \rvert$ shifted up 1 unit.

6. $y = |x| - 3$

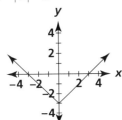

7. $y = |x| + 1$

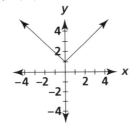

8. $y = |x| - 4$

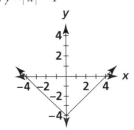

9. $y = |x - 1|$

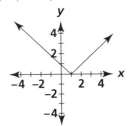

10. $y = (x + 1)^2$

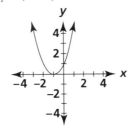

11. $y = |x + 3|$

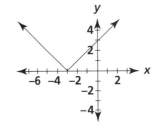

12. $y = |x - 1| + 2$

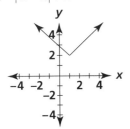

13. $y = (x - 1)^2 + 1$

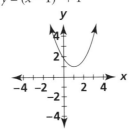

14. $y = |x + 3| - 1$

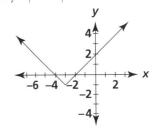

15. $y = -(x + 1)^2$

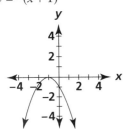

16. $y = -|x + 3|$

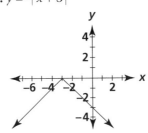

17. $y = |x + 1| - 2$

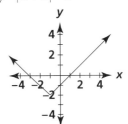

18. $y = -|x - 1|$

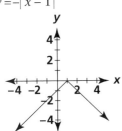

19. $y = (x - 4)^2 - 3$

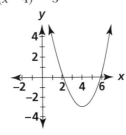

20. $y = |x + 2| + 1$

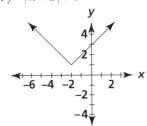

21. $y = -|x| - 3$

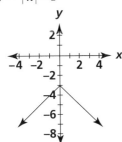

22. $y = -|x| + 1$

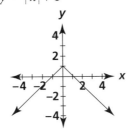

23. $y = -|x| - 4$

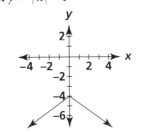

24. $y = |x| + 3$ **25.** $y = |x| - 4$ **26.** $y = |x - 6|$ **27.** $y = |x + 2|$ **28.** $y = |x - 1|$

29. $y = |x| + 4.5$ **30.** $y = |x - 3| + 2$ **31.** $y = |x + 2| - 1$ **32.** $y = |x + 5| + 6$ **33.** $y = |x - 17| - 100$

34. $y = (x - 3)^2$ **35.** $y = (x + 2)^2$ **36.** $y = x^2 - 1$ **37.** $y = x^2 + 5$ **38.** $y = x^2 - 40$

39. $y = x^2 + 21$ **40.** $y = (x - 17)^2$ **41.** $y = (x + 19)^2$ **42.** $y = x^2 + 25$ **43.** $y = (x - 3)^2 + 2$

44. $y = (x - 1)^2 + 12$ **45.** $y = (x + 2)^2 - 10$ **46.** $y = (x + 9)^2 + 6$ **47.** $y = (x - 7)^2 - 1$ **48.** $y = (x + 7)^2 - 40$

49. Translation; the boat is sliding across the survace of the water. A transformation in which you slide a figure to a new position is called a translation.

50. Rotation; the arm of the pendulum rotates about the fixed point where the arm is attached.

51. Rotation; a transformation in which a figure rotates about a point, called the center, is a rotation.

52. Translation; the plane is sliding across the sky. A transformation in which you slide a figure to a new position is called a translation.

53. Rotation; the Earth is rotating about the sun (the center of rotation).

54. reflection

55. $y = |x + 2|$ **56.** $y = |x + 1| - 2$ **57.** $y = |x - 1|$ **58.** $y = -x^2$ **59.** $y = x^2 - 3$ **60.** $y = (x - 1)^2 - 3$

PAGE 575, LOOK BACK

61. $\frac{7}{21}$ does not belong to the set. The other fractions are equal to $\frac{1}{2}$.

62. slope = 2
Answers may vary. Two possible equations are $y = 2x$ and $y = 2x + 3$.

63. The slope of a line perpendicular to $y = 2x - 1$ is $-\frac{1}{2}$.
Answers may vary. Two possible equations are $y = -\frac{1}{2}x$ and $y = -\frac{1}{2}x + 1$.

PAGE 575, LOOK BEYOND

64. $(-2, 2) \times 2 = (-4, 4)$
$(-2, -4) \times 2 = (-4, -8)$
$(6, -4) \times 2 = (12, -8)$

$(-2, 2) \times \frac{1}{2} = (-1, 1)$
$(-2, -4) \times \frac{1}{2} = (-1, -2)$
$(6, -4) \times \frac{1}{2} = (3, -2)$

The scale factors are 2 and $\frac{1}{2}$.

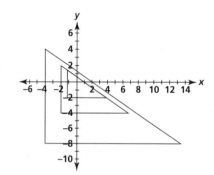

65. As $|a|$ gets larger, the parabola gets more narrow. As $|a|$ approaches a value of 0, the parabola gets wider or more open.

PAGES 578–580 CHAPTER 10 REVIEW

1.

Sequence	45		43		41		39		37		[35]		[33]		[31]
First differences		2		2		2		2		2		2		2	

The first differences are constant, so the sequence is linear.

2. 0.09, 0.009, 0.0009
The sequence is exponential. Each term is $\frac{1}{10}$ of the previous term.

3. 729, 2187, 6561
The sequence is exponential. Each term is 3 times the previous term.

4. Since you are multiplying by a quantity greater than 1, the function shows growth.

5. The vertex is (4, 9).

6.

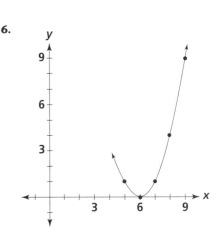

The vertex is (6, 0).

7.

y-values	2		5		10		17		26
First differences		3		5		7		9	
Second differences			2		2		2		

The second differences are constant; this is a quadratic function.

8.

y-values	6		12		24		48		96
First differences		6		12		24		48	
Second differences			6		12		24		

Each y-value is 2 times the previous term. The second differences are not constant; this is not a quadratic function.

9.

y-values	3		12		27		48		75
First differences		9		15		21		27	
Second differences			6		6		6		

The second differences are constant; this is a quadratic function.

10. The reciprocal of 6 is $\frac{1}{6}$.

11. The reciprocal of $\frac{6}{7}$ is $1 \div \frac{6}{7} = 1 \cdot \frac{7}{6} = \frac{7}{6}$.

12. The reciprocal of 3.5 is $1 \div 3.5 = 1 \div \frac{7}{2} = 1 \cdot \frac{2}{7} = \frac{2}{7}$.

13. The reciprocal of $\frac{1}{15}$ is $1 \div \frac{1}{15} = 1 \cdot \frac{15}{1} = 15$.

14. $|-3| = 3$

15. $|6.7| = 6.7$

16. $|-1.7| = 1.7$

17. ABS(-45) = 45

18. INT(45) = 45

19. INT(3.68) = 3

20. INT(7.5) = 7

21. INT(36) = 36

22. exponential function

23. absolute-value function

24. quadratic function

25. $y = |x| - 2$

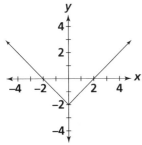

26. $y = |x - 2|$

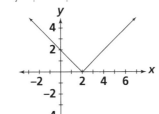

27. $y = -|x + 4|$

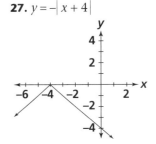

28. $y = x^2 - 2$

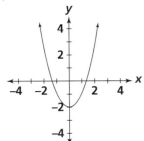

29. $y = (x - 2)^2$

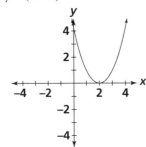

30. $y = -(x + 4)^2$

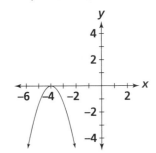

31. Since you are adding 100% to 7.9%, multiply 1000 by 1.079 repeatedly to find how many years it will take to double $1000 at 7.9%. Use a calculator or spreadsheet.

1079.00	1578.08
1164.24	1702.75
1256.22	1837.26
1355.46	1982.41
1462.54	2139.02

At 7.9% it takes 10 years for Roy's money to double.

1. 320, 640, 1280
Each term is 2 times the previous term; the sequence is exponential.

2. 80, 76, 72
Each term is 4 less than the previous term; the sequence is linear.

3. The sequence shows exponential decay. Each term is $\frac{1}{100}$ of the previous term. The terms of the sequence are decreasing.

4.

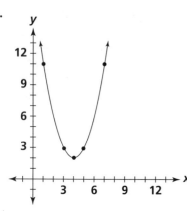

The vertex is (4, 2).

5. $\frac{500}{10} = 50$
Each team member needs to raise $50.

6. $\frac{1}{6}$

7. 12

8. $\frac{1}{5.5} = \frac{1}{5\frac{1}{2}} = \frac{1}{\frac{11}{2}} = \frac{2}{11}$

9. $|-10| = 10$

10. ABS(7.9) = 7.9

11. INT(9.75) = 9

12. The first differences for the y-values are a constant of -5; the relationship is linear.

13.
y-values	4		7		12		19		28
First differences		3		5		7		9	
Second differences			2		2		2		

The second differences are constant; the relationship is quadratic.

14. a. Linear

15. f. Step

16. c. Quadratic

17. d. Reciprocal

18. e. Absolute value

19. b. Exponential

20. $y = |x + 1|$

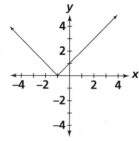

21. $y = (x - 3)^2$

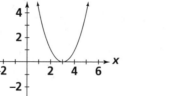

22. $y = -|x| + 2$

23. $y = x^2 + 4$

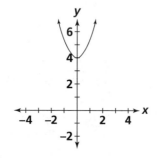

1. A

$(-18)(-4) = 72 \quad 18(-2) = -36$

$72 > -36$

2. C

$-6 = x + 1 \qquad x + 4 = -3$

$-6 - 1 = x + 1 - 1 \quad x + 4 - 4 = -3 - 4$

$-7 = x \qquad\qquad x = -7$

$-7 = -7$

3. C

$0.20(15) = 3 \text{ mL} \quad 0.15(20) = 3 \text{ mL}$

$3 \text{ mL} = 3 \text{ mL}$

4. A

$|-4.8| = 4.8 \quad |3.2| = 3.2$

$4.8 > 3.2$

5. c.

$\dfrac{5^2 + 11}{9 \cdot 3 + 9} = \dfrac{25 + 11}{27 + 9}$

$= \dfrac{36}{36}$

$= 1$

6. b.

$\dfrac{7}{3} = \dfrac{n}{12}$

$12 \cdot \dfrac{7}{3} = \dfrac{n}{12} \cdot 12$

$28 = n$

both sides multiplied by 12

7. b. scalene and right

8. d.

$|x - 6| = 10$

Case 2

The value of $x - 6$ is negative.

$|x - 6| = 10$

$-(x - 6) = 10$

$-x + 6 = 10$

$-x + 6 - 6 = 10 - 6$

$-x = 4$

$-1(-x) = -1(4)$

$x = -4$

9. d.

Two sequences show growth:

a. 2, 4, 6, 8, 10 . . .

d. 2, 4, 8, 16, 32, . . .

The sequence in **a** has a constant 1st difference of 2 and is linear. In **d** the sequence is developed by multiplying the previous term by 2.

10. b. 400, 350, 300, 250, 200, . . .

There is a constant first difference of 50.

11. $\dfrac{7}{8} \cdot 100 = 0.875(100)$

$= 87.5\%$

12. $(2x - 4) - (x - 9) - (5x + 2) = 2x - 4 - x + 9 - 5x - 2$

$= 2x - x - 5x - 4 + 9 - 2$

$= -4x + 3$

13. $\dfrac{15n^2 - 25n}{-5n} = \dfrac{15n^2}{-5n} - \dfrac{25n}{-5n}$

$= -3n + 5$

14.

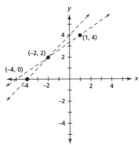

No; the points $(-2, 2)$, $(1, 4)$ and $(-4, 0)$ are not on a straight line.

15. $m = -2$

Use $(-1, 0)$ for (x_1, y_1).

$y - y_1 = m(x - x_1)$

$y - 0 = -2[x - (-1)]$

$y = -2(x + 1)$

$y = -2x - 2$

16. $\begin{cases} 4x - y = 7 \\ -6x + 2y = -14 \end{cases} \to \begin{array}{l} 2(4x - y) = 2(7) \\ -6x + 2y = -14 \end{array} \to \begin{array}{l} 8x - 2y = 14 \\ \underline{-6x + 2y = -14} \\ 2x = 0 \\ \dfrac{2x}{2} = \dfrac{0}{2} \\ x = 0 \end{array}$

Substitute 0 for x.

$4x - y = 7$

$4(0) - y = 7$

$0 - y = 7$

$-y = 7$

$-1(-y) = -1(7)$

$y = -7$

$(x, y) = (0, -7)$

17. $\begin{cases} x - 2y = 5 \\ 3x - 2y = 47 \end{cases}$

$x - 2y = 5$

$x - 2y + 2y = 5 + 2y$

$x = 5 + 2y$

Substitute $5 + 2y$ for x.

$3x - 2y - 47$

$3(5 + 2y) - 2y = 47$

$15 + 6y - 2y = 47$

$15 + 4y = 47$

$\underline{15 + 4y - 15 = 47 - 15}$

$4y = 32$

$y = 8$

Substitute 8 for y.

$x = 5 + 2y$

$x = 5 + 2(8)$

$x = 5 + 16$

$x = 21$

$(x, y) = (21, 8)$

18. $\begin{cases} 9x - 10y = 96 \\ 3x + 8y = -36 \end{cases}$ $\rightarrow$ $\begin{array}{l} 9x - 10y = 96 \\ -3(3x + 8y) = -3(-36) \end{array}$ $\rightarrow$ $\begin{array}{l} 9x - 10y = 96 \\ -9x - 24y = 108 \\ \hline -34y = 204 \end{array}$

$$\frac{-34y}{-34} = \frac{204}{-34}$$
$$y = -6$$

Substitute -6 for y.

$$3x + 8y = -36$$
$$3x + 8(-6) = -36$$
$$3x - 48 = -36$$
$$3x - 48 + 48 = -36 + 48$$
$$3x = 12$$
$$\frac{3x}{3} = \frac{12}{3}$$
$$x = 4$$
$$(x, y) = (4, -6)$$

19. absolute value

20. linear

21. Use the "Pythagorean" Right-Triangle Theorem.
Since the hypotenuse is always the longest side, use 78 for c.
$$a^2 + b^2 = c^2$$
$$a^2 + 72^2 = 78^2$$
$$a^2 + 5184 = 6084$$
$$a^2 + 5184 - 5184 = 6084 - 5184$$
$$a^2 = 900$$
$$\sqrt{a^2} = \sqrt{900}$$
$$a = 30$$

The length of the other leg is 30.

22. 70% of $45 = 0.70 \times 45$
$$= 31.5$$

23.
$$8(y - 2) = -6(20 - 4y)$$
$$8y - 16 = -120 + 24y$$
$$8y - 16 - 8y = -120 + 24y - 8y$$
$$-16 = -120 + 16y$$
$$-16 + 120 = -120 + 16y + 120$$
$$104 = 16y$$
$$\frac{104}{16} = \frac{16y}{16}$$
$$\frac{104}{16} = y$$
$$\text{or } y = \frac{13}{2}, \text{ or } 6\frac{1}{2}$$

24. slope $= \dfrac{\text{change in } y\text{-values}}{\text{change in } x\text{-values}} = \dfrac{-3 - (-5)}{1 - (-7)} = \dfrac{-3 + 5}{1 + 7} = \dfrac{2}{8} = \dfrac{1}{4}$

Parallel lines have equal slopes, so a line parallel to the first line has a slope of $\frac{1}{4}$.

25. $\dfrac{136}{16} = \dfrac{17}{2} = 8\frac{1}{2}$
Each person would have to contribute \$8.50 toward the gift.

CHAPTER 11

APPLYING STATISTICS

9. Madrid, July

10. Moscow, January

11. Moscow, approximately 55°

12. Moscow, approximately 25°

13. Rio de Janeiro, Moscow, and London approximately 75°

14. $957{,}000 \cdot 10\% = 957{,}000 \cdot 0.10$
$= 95{,}700$

There were 95,700 house fires caused by smoking.

15. $957{,}000 \cdot 26\% = 957{,}000 \cdot 0.26$
$= 248{,}820$

There were 248,820 house fires caused by faulty electrical wiring.

16. Faulty electrical wiring is the most likely cause for a house fire.

17. Answers may vary. A sample answer is to stop smoking in the house, be careful when cooking and when using open flames (stoves and fireplaces), check the wiring periodically, and watch children carefully.

18. orthopedic injury

19. other

20. There were 1000 patients diagnosed with an orthopedic injury and 150 patients diagnosed with a spinal cord injury.

21. $200 - 150 = 50$

There was an increase of 50 patients diagnosed with a head injury from 1996 to 1997.

22. Different; to compute the percent increase, subtract the 1996 total from the 1997 total. Then divide the resulting difference by the 1996 total.

Type of injury	1996	1997	Percent increase
Other	50	100	100%
Spinal cord injury	100	150	50%
Head injury	150	200	33%
Stroke	350	450	29%
Orthopedic injury	800	1000	25%

23. $253{,}000{,}000 \cdot 24\% = 253{,}000{,}000 \cdot 0.24$
$= 60{,}720{,}000$

60,720,000 people lived in the West.

24. Percent of Midwesterners in 1995:

$\frac{58{,}3000{,}000}{265{,}000{,}000} = 0.22 = 22\%$

Percent change from 1990 to 1995:

$22\% - 20\% = 2\%$

There was a 2% increase in the population from 1990 to 1995.

25. day 2, approximately $57

26. day 7, approximately $35

27. day 7, approximately $87

28. New Century Software

29. New Century Software

30. The two graphs can be misleading because they concern the same number of days, but the dollar increments are different.

31. $x + 3x - 1 = \left(\frac{2}{7}\right) + 3\left(\frac{2}{7}\right) - 1$

$\qquad = \frac{2}{7} + \frac{6}{7} - 1$

$\qquad = \frac{8}{7} - 1$

$\qquad = \frac{8-7}{7}$

$\qquad = \frac{1}{7}$

32. $\qquad \frac{x+70}{4} = 23$

$\qquad 4\left(\frac{x+70}{4}\right) = 4(23)$

$\qquad x + 70 = 92$

$\qquad x + 70 - 70 = 92 - 70$

$\qquad x = 22$

33. $\qquad 2x - 3 < 4x + 7$

$\qquad 2x - 3 - 2x < 4x + 7 - 2x$

$\qquad -3 < 2x + 7$

$\qquad -3 - 7 < 2x + 7 - 7$

$\qquad -10 < 2x$

$\qquad \frac{-10}{2} < \frac{2x}{2}$

$\qquad -5 < x, \text{ or } x > -5$

34. $|3x - 4| = 16$

Case 1

The quantity $3x - 4$ is positive.

$|3x - 4| = 16$

$3x - 4 = 16$

$3x - 4 + 4 = 16 + 4$

$3x = 20$

$\frac{3x}{3} = \frac{20}{3}$

$x = \frac{20}{3}, \text{ or } 6\frac{2}{3}$

Case 2

The quantity $3x - 4$ is negative.

$|3x - 4| = 16$

$-(3x - 4) = 16$

$-3x + 4 = 16$

$-3x + 4 - 4 = 16 - 4$

$-3x = 12$

$-\frac{1}{3}(-3x) = -\frac{1}{3}(12)$

$x = -4$

$x = 6\frac{2}{3} \text{ or } x = -4$

35. $|2x - 5| \geq 15$

Case 1

The quantity $2x - 5$ is positive.

$|2x - 5| \geq 15$

$2x - 5 \geq 15$

$2x - 5 + 5 \geq 15 + 5$

$2x \geq 20$

$\frac{2x}{2} \geq \frac{20}{2}$

$x \geq 10$

Case 2

The quantity $2x - 5$ is negative.

$|2x - 5| \geq 15$

$-(2x - 5) \geq 15$

$-2x + 5 \geq 15$

$-2x + 5 - 5 \geq 15 - 5$

$-2x \geq 10$

$-\frac{1}{2}(-2x) \leq -\frac{1}{2}(10)$

$x \leq -5$

The inequality is true when $x \leq -5$ or when $x \geq 10$.

36.

	First solution	Second solution	New solution
Percent glucose	50% = 0.50	0% = 0	24% = 0.24
Amount of solution	60 oz	x	60 + x
Amount of glucose	0.50(60) = 30	0x = 0	0.24(60 + x)

$30 = 0.24(60 + x)$

$30 = 14.4 + 0.24x$

$30 - 14.4 = 14.4 + 0.24x - 14.4$

$15.6 = 0.24x$

$\frac{15.6}{0.24} = \frac{0.24x}{0.24}$

$65 = x$

The chemist should add 65 ounces of pure water.

For Exercises 37–39, methods of solving may vary.

37. $\begin{cases} 7g + 2h = -4 \\ 5h = -g + 12 \quad \rightarrow \quad g = -5h + 12 \end{cases}$

Substitute $-5h + 12$ for g:

$7g + 2h = -4$

$7(-5h + 12) + 2h = -4$

$-35h + 84 + 2h = -4$

$-33h + 84 = -4$

$-33h + 84 - 84 = -4 - 84$

$-33h = -88$

$\frac{-33h}{-33} = \frac{-88}{-33}$

$h = \frac{8}{3}, \text{ or } 2\frac{2}{3}$

Substitute $\frac{8}{3}$ for h in $5h = -g + 12$:

$5h = -g + 12$

$5\left(\frac{8}{3}\right) = -g + 12$

$\frac{40}{3} = -g + 12$

$\frac{40}{3} - 12 = -g + 12 - 12$

$\frac{40}{3} - \frac{36}{3} = -g$

$\frac{4}{3} = -g$

$-1\left(\frac{4}{3}\right) = -1(-g)$

$-\frac{4}{3} = g, \text{ or } g = -1\frac{1}{3}$

$(g, h) = \left(-1\frac{1}{3}, 2\frac{2}{3}\right)$

38. $\begin{cases} 2g - h = 3 & \rightarrow \quad 2g - 3 = h \\ 3h = 12 - g \end{cases}$

Substitute $2g - 3$ for h:

$$3h = 12 - g$$
$$3(2g - 3) = 12 - g$$
$$6g - 9 = 12 - g$$
$$6g - 9 + g = 12 - g + g$$
$$7g - 9 = 12$$
$$7g - 9 + 9 = 12 + 9$$
$$7g = 21$$
$$\frac{7g}{7} = \frac{21}{7}$$
$$g = 3$$

Substitute 3 for g in $2g - h = 3$:

$$2g - h = 3$$
$$2(3) - h = 3$$
$$6 - h = 3$$
$$6 - h + h = 3 + h$$
$$6 = 3 + h$$
$$6 - 3 = 3 + h - 3$$
$$3 = h$$

$(g, h) = (3, 3)$

39. $\begin{cases} 3x - y = 2 & \rightarrow \quad 4(3x - y) = 4(2) \quad \rightarrow \quad 12x - 4y = 8 \\ x + 4y = 5 & \rightarrow \quad\quad x + 4y = 5 \quad\quad \rightarrow \quad\quad \underline{x + 4y = 5} \end{cases}$

$$13x = 13$$
$$\frac{13x}{13} = \frac{13}{13}$$
$$x = 1$$

Substitute 1 for x in $x + 4y = 5$:

$$x + 4y = 5$$
$$1 + 4y = 5$$
$$1 - 1 + 4y = 5 - 1$$
$$4y = 4$$
$$\frac{4y}{4} = \frac{4}{4}$$
$$y = 1$$

$(x, y) = (1, 1)$

PAGE 592, LOOK BEYOND

40. Answers may vary. Kevin could choose the middle number, 80. He could also choose the average: $\frac{82 + 80 + 79 + 70 + 90}{5} = \frac{401}{5} = 80.2$.

41. Answers may vary. One possible answer is $\frac{1}{15} + \frac{2}{15} + \frac{1}{5} + \frac{4}{15} + \frac{1}{3} = 1$.

11.2 PAGES 598–600, PRACTICE & APPLY

For Exercises 6–9, to determine the mean, find the sum of the data and then divide by the number of data points. To determine the median, order the data from least to greatest and find the middle term. To determine the mode, find the most frequently occurring data point. To determine the range, subtract the least data point from the greatest data point.

6. mean $= \frac{12 + 12 + 11 + 9 + 10 + 20 + 18 + 11 + 9}{9} = \frac{112}{9} = 12\frac{4}{9}$, or $12.\overline{4}$

median: 9, 9, 10, 11, ⑪, 12, 12, 18, 20
　　The median is 11.

mode: There are three modes; 9, 11 and 12 each occur twice.

range $= 20 - 9 = 11$
　　The range is 11.

7. mean $= \frac{22 + 27 + 11 + 29 + 18 + 27 + 18 + 31 + 29}{9} = \frac{212}{9} = 23\frac{5}{9}$, or $23.\overline{5}$

median 11, 18, 18, 22, ㉗, 27, 29, 29 31
　　The median is 27.

mode: There are three modes; 18, 27, and 29 each occur twice.

range $= 31 - 11 = 20$
　　The range is 20.

8. mean $= \frac{2 + 2 + 1 + 9 + 1 + 2 + 8 + 1 + 9 + 2 + 1 + 7 + 5 + 6}{14} = \frac{56}{14} = 4$

median: 1, 1, 1, 1, 2, 2, ②, ②, 5, 6, 7, 8, 9, 9,
　　The mean is the average of the middle two numbers. $\frac{2 + 2}{2} = \frac{4}{2} = 2$

mode: The numbers 1 and 2 are the modes. They both occur four times.

range $= 9 - 1 = 8$
　　The range is 8.

9. mean $= \frac{127 + 312 + 191 + 99 + 160 + 210 + 178 + 116 + 119 + 172}{10} = \frac{1684}{10} = 168.4$

median: 99, 116, 119, 127, ⟨160, 172⟩, 178, 191, 210, 312
　　The median is the average of the middle two numbers. $\frac{160 + 172}{2} = \frac{332}{2} = 166$

mode: There is no mode in the sequence. No number appears more than once.

range $= 312 - 99 = 213$
　　The range is 213.

10. The biologist most likely used the mode. The number 2 appears 65 times in the data sequence.

11. List the data points and count the number of times each score occurs.

Points scored	0	2	3	4	5	6	7	8	9	10	11	12	15	16	18	26	27
Frequency	III	I	II	II	HHT	II	II	I	I	I	I	II	I	I	IIII	II	I

12. To determine the median, order the data from least to greatest and find the middle number.

0, 0, 0, 2, 3, 3, 4, 4, 5, 5, 5, 5, 5, 6, 6, (7, 7), 8, 9, 10, 11, 12, 12, 15, 16, 18, 18, 18, 18, 26, 26, 27

The median is the average of the middle two numbers. $\frac{7+7}{2} = \frac{14}{2} = 7$

13. mean $= \frac{\text{sum of data}}{32} = \frac{311}{32} \approx 9.7$
The mean is approximately 9.7.

14. The number 5 is the mode; it occurs five times.

15. Answers may vary. The mean would leave the best impression of the player's abilities. The mean is approximately 9.7, which is higher than the median, 7, or the mode, 5.

16. mean $= \frac{\text{total number of viewing hours}}{\text{number of age groups}} = \frac{273}{10} = 27.3$
The mean number of viewing hours was 27.3 hours.

17. To determine the median, order the data from least to greatest and find the middle number.

20, 21, 21, 22, (24, 25), 28, 30, 38, 44

The median is the average of the middle two numbers. $\frac{24+25}{2} = \frac{49}{2} = 24.5$

18. The mode number of viewing hours is 21. The number 21 occurs twice.

19. To determine the range, subtract the least from the greatest number of viewing hours.
range $= 44 - 20 = 24$
The range of the data is 24.

20. The only change would be the mean number of viewing hours.
The new mean would be $\frac{275}{10}$, or 27.5.
The mode would still be 21 because the number 21 shows up more than once. The median would still be 24.5 because 24 and 25 would still be the middle two numbers.

21.

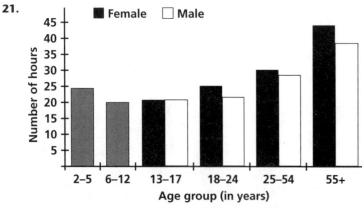

22. To determine the number of survey respondents, count the number of tick marks in the table. There were 27 students that responded to the survey.

23. The mode was 3 hours. There were 10 students that watched television 3 hours each day.

24. False; 15 out of the 27 respondents watched television less than 4 hours per day.
$\frac{15}{27} \approx 55.6\%$

25. To determine the mean, add the data and divide by the number of respondents.
mean $= \frac{106}{27} \approx 3.9$
The mean number of hours was approximately 3.9.

26. No; only 6 out of 27 students watched more than 5 hours of television.
$\frac{6}{27} < \frac{1}{4}$

27. Michael Jordan

28. Bob Pettit

29. To calculate the average points per game, you must know the total number of points scored and the number of games in which a player competed.

30. To determine the number of games played, divide the total points scored by the average points per game.
$$\frac{31,419}{30.1} \approx 1044$$
Wilt Chamberlain played in 1044 games during his career.

31. To determine the total number of points, multiply the average points per game by the number of games.
$$32.2 \times 684 \approx 22,025$$
Michael Jordon scored a total of 22,025 points.

32. To determine the median, add the scores and divide by the number of participants.
$$\text{mean} = \frac{511.57}{9} \approx 56.84$$
The mean number of points scored was 56.84.

33. To determine the median, order the scores from least to greatest and find the middle number.

50.26, 52.50, 54.25, 58.22, ⟮58.50⟯, 58.52, 59.64, 59.80, 59.88

The median number of points scored was 58.50.

34. There is no mode for this set of data. Each score occurs only once.

35. To determine the range, subtract the lowest score from the highest.
range = 59.88 − 50.26 = 9.62
The range for this set of data is 9.62.

36. To determine the effect on the mean, median, and mode, relist the data and include the 10th score.

50.26, 52.50, 54.25, 58.22, ⟮58.50, 58.52⟯, 59.64, 59.80, 59.88, 60.00

$$\text{mean} = \frac{571.57}{10} \approx 57.157 \approx 57.16$$

$$\text{median} = \frac{58.50 + 58.52}{2} = \frac{117.02}{2} = 58.51$$

mode = no mode

range = 60.00 − 50.26 = 9.74

The mean, median, and range have increased. The mode remains unchanged.

37. To determine how many students took the exam, count the number of tick marks in the table; 33 students took the exam.

38. To determine the median, order the scores from lowest to highest and find the middle score.

50, 50, 55, 55, 60, 60, 60, 65, 65, 65, 65, 70, 70, 70, 75, 75, ⟮75⟯, 75, 80, 80, 80, 80, 80, 85, 85, 85, 85, 90, 90, 90, 95, 95, 100

The median score was 75.

39. The mode is 80. 80 occurs 5 times in the set of data.

40. To compute the mean, add the scores and divide by the number of scores.
$$\text{mean} = \frac{2460}{33} \approx 74.54$$
The mean score was approximately 74.5.

41. $\frac{2460 + 75}{34} \approx 74.6$; median would not change; new modes of 75 and 80; mean would change to approximately 74.6.

42.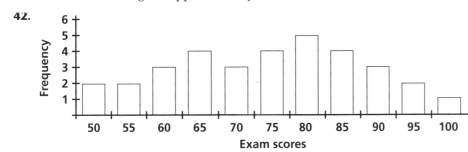

43. $|-2 - 7| = |-9| = 9$

44. $2x - 5 - 5x + 4 = 2x - 5x - 5 + 4$
$= -3x - 1$

45. $-2(5x - 3) = -10x + 6$

46. Let x represent the amount of phosphate in the fertilizer.
$$\frac{15}{10} = \frac{x}{24}$$
$$10x = 15 \cdot 24$$
$$10x = 360$$
$$x = 36$$

There are 36 ounces of phosphate in the fertilizer.

47. $percent = \dfrac{\text{number of students spending 2 hours a day}}{\text{total number of students surveyed}} \cdot 100$
$$= \frac{275}{450} \cdot 100$$
$$= \frac{27{,}500}{450}$$
$$\approx 61.1$$

Approximately 61% of the students surveyed spend 2 hours a day doing homework.

48. Perimeter $= 2l + 2w$
$$56 = 2(2x + 7) + 2(x - 3)$$
$$56 = 4x + 14 + 2x - 6$$
$$56 = 6x + 8$$
$$56 - 8 = 6x + 8 - 8$$
$$48 = 6x$$
$$\frac{48}{6} = \frac{6x}{6}$$
$$8 = x$$

Substitute 8 for x.
$$2x + 7 = 2(8) + 7 = 16 + 7 = 23$$
$$x - 3 = 8 - 3 = 5$$

The length of the rectangle is 23 centimeters.
The width of the rectangle is 5 centimeters.

49. To determine the percent of students scoring in each range, count the number of students in that range, divide by the total number of students, and then multiply by 100.

Percentage of students scoring 60 or below $= \dfrac{7}{33} \cdot 100 = \dfrac{700}{33} \approx 21\%$

Percentage of students scoring from 61 to 70 $= \dfrac{7}{33} \cdot 100 = \dfrac{700}{33} \approx 21\%$

Percentage of students scoring from 71 to 80 $= \dfrac{9}{33} \cdot 100 = \dfrac{900}{33} \approx 27\%$

Percentage of students scoring from 81 to 90 $= \dfrac{7}{33} \cdot 100 = \dfrac{700}{33} \approx 21\%$

Percentage of students scoring from 91 to 100 $= \dfrac{3}{33} \cdot 100 = \dfrac{300}{33} \approx 9\%$

50.

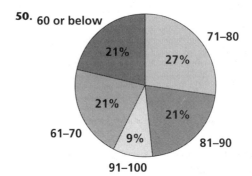

5. To make a stem-and-leaf plot, let the whole numbers be the stems and let the tenths be the leaves.

key $\boxed{14 \mid 1 = 14.1}$

Duration of Humpback Whale Songs

Stems	Leaves
14	1, 5, 9
15	0, 2, 3, 5, 6
16	1, 2, 3, 6
17	2, 2, 4, 8
18	1, 2, 9
19	3, 3, 7, 9
20	0

6. To determine the range, subtract the smallest number from the greatest number.

$$20.0 - 14.1 = 5.9$$

The range of the data is 5.9 minutes.

7. To determine the median of the data, find the middle term. The median is the average of the middle two terms.

$$\text{median} = \frac{16.6 + 17.2}{2} = \frac{33.8}{2} = 16.9$$

The median is 16.9 minutes.

8. To determine the mean, add the data and divide by the number of data points.

$$\text{mean} = \frac{\text{sum of the data}}{\text{number of data points}} = \frac{408.3}{24} = 17.0125$$

The mean of the data is 17.0125 minutes.

9. The mode is the data point which appears most often. There are two modes, 17.2, and 19.3. Each of these numbers appears twice.

10. Answers may vary. To determine the average duration of the whale songs, use the mean of the data. The mean is 17.0125 hours.

11.

original mean	$= \frac{1842}{29} \approx 63.52$	new mean	$= \frac{1902}{30} = 63.4$
original range	$= 104 - 35 = 69$	new range	$= 104 - 35 = 69$
original median	$= 60$	new median	$= 60$
original mode	$= 59$	new mode	$= 59$ and 60

12. To compute the percent of players scoring more than 80 runs, count the number of players scoring more than 80, divide by the total number of players, and then multiply by 100.

$$\text{percent} = \frac{5}{29} \cdot 100 = \frac{500}{29} \approx 17.2\%$$

The percent of players scoring more than 80 runs was 17.2%.

13. Count the number of players scoring fewer than 60 runs, divide by the total number of players, and then multiply by 100.

$$\text{percent} = \frac{13}{29} \cdot 100 = \frac{1300}{29} \approx 44.8\%$$

The percent of players scoring fewer than 60 runs was 44.8%.

14.

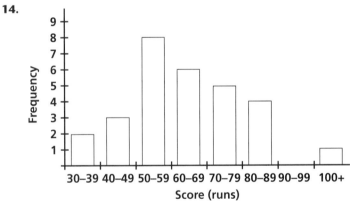

15. First draw a number line. Mark the least value and the greatest value. Find and mark the median. Find the median of the lower half of the data; this is called the lower quartile. Find the median of the upper half; this is called the upper quartile.

$$\text{lower quartile} = \frac{52 + 55}{2} = \frac{107}{2} = 53.5 \qquad \text{upper quartile} = \frac{77 + 79}{2} = \frac{156}{2} = 78$$

Mark the upper and lower quartile with vertical marks above the number line.

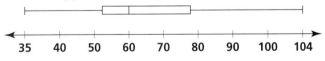

16. class A

17. All classes had a high score of 100.

18. class A

19. class A

20. The median for class A was approximately 95.

21. No; since we don't know the individual scores, the mean cannot be determined.

22. between the median and the upper quartile

23. between the median and the lower quartile

24. The median score of class C is below 80 since the line indicating the median score is below 80.

25. No; since we have information only on the highest, lowest, median, and upper and lower quartiles, we cannot determine how many students were tested.

26. Let the tens digits be the stems and the ones digits be the leaves.

key $\boxed{2\,|\,0} = 20$

Points Scored

Stems	Leaves
2	0
3	1, 2, 3, 4, 7, 8, 8, 8
4	0, 1, 1, 2, 2, 2, 9, 9
5	0, 3, 6

27. To determine the range, subtract the lowest score from the highest.

$$\text{range} = 56 - 20 = 36$$

The range is 36.

28. To determine the median, find the middle score. The median is the average of the two middle scores.

$$\text{median} = \frac{40 + 41}{2} = \frac{81}{2} = 40.5$$

The median score was 40.5.

29. The mode is the number which occurs most often. There are two modes, 38 and 42.

30. $\text{mean} = \dfrac{\text{total points scored}}{\text{number of data points}}$

$$= \frac{806}{20}$$

$$= 40.3$$

The mean number of points scored is 40.3.

31. The mean would increase.

$\text{mean} = \dfrac{\text{total number of points}}{\text{number of data points}}$

$$= \frac{811}{20}$$

$$= 40.55$$

The new mean would be 40.55. The median and mode would not be affected.

32.

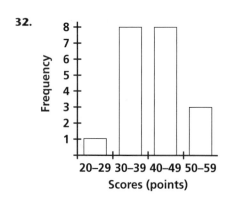

33. First draw a number line. Mark the least value and the greatest value. Find and mark the median with a vertical line. Find the median of the lower half of the data and the median of the upper half of the data and mark them with a vertical line. These are the lower and upper quartiles.

lower quartile = 35.5   upper quartile = 45.5

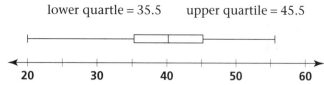

34. Let the tens digits be the stems and the ones digits be the leaves. key $\boxed{10\,|\,6} = 106$

Dollars Spent on Dental Care

Stems	Leaves
10	6, 6, 8
11	4, 8, 9
12	0, 4, 5
13	0, 1, 7
14	1, 1, 2, 6
15	2, 3, 3, 9
16	8, 8, 9
17	0, 2, 2, 6, 8, 8
18	1, 4, 4, 5
19	4, 6
20	2, 8
21	0
22	
23	
24	5
25	5

35. To find the median, find the middle two terms and compute their average.

$$\text{median} = \frac{159 + 168}{2} = \frac{327}{2} = 163.5$$

The median is $163.50.

36. To determine the lower quartile, find the median of the lower half of the data. To determine the upper quartile, find the median of the upper half of the data.

The lower quartile is the average of the middle two terms in the lower half of the data.

$$\text{lower quartile} = \frac{130 + 131}{2} = \frac{261}{2} = 130.5$$

The upper quartile is the average of the middle two terms in the upper half of the data.

$$\text{upper quartile} = \frac{181 + 184}{2} = \frac{365}{2} = 182.5$$

The lower quartile is 130.5 and the upper quartile is 182.5.

37. First draw a number line. Find and mark the median, lower quartile, and upper quartile with a vertical line. Draw a box using these lines. Find and mark the least and the greatest values. Connect these points to your box.

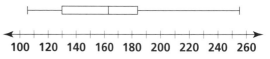

38. Let the hundreds digits be the stems and the remaining digits be the leaves. key $2 \mid 49 = 249$

Weight of Bottle-nosed Dolphins (in pounds)

Stems	Leaves
2	49, 75
3	43, 45, 83, 99
4	78, 84, 91, 97, 97, 99
5	12, 49, 67, 74, 76, 86, 88, 89

39. To determine the range, subtract the lowest number from the highest.

$$\text{range} = 589 - 249 = 340$$

The range of the data is 340.

40. To determine the median, find the middle term. The median is 497.

41. To determine the mean, add the data and divide by the number of data points.

$$\text{mean} = \frac{9481}{20} = 474.05$$

The mean of the data is 474.05.

42. Yes; the mode is 497.

43. Answers may vary. Possible answers include the mean value, 474, or the median value, 497. The average dolphin weight is approximately 474 pounds.

PAGE 608, LOOK BACK

44. $8 \cdot 1\frac{1}{4} = 8 \cdot \frac{5}{4}$
$= \frac{40}{4}$
$= 10$

45. $\frac{2}{3} \cdot 2\frac{3}{5} = \frac{2}{3} \cdot \frac{13}{5}$
$= \frac{26}{15}$
$= 1\frac{11}{15}$

46. $6\frac{1}{5} \cdot 3\frac{3}{10} = \frac{31}{5} \cdot \frac{33}{10}$
$= \frac{1023}{50}$
$= 20\frac{23}{50}$

47. $80\% = \frac{80}{100} = \frac{4}{5}$

48. $38\% = \frac{38}{100} = \frac{19}{50}$

49. $3.5\% = \frac{3.5}{100} = \frac{7}{200}$

50. Let x represent the amount of profit from the sale. Then the school's income is $150 + 0.20x$.

51. The book dealer's income is represented by $0.8x - 150$, that is, the profit after giving the school their share.

$$0.8x - 150 = 700$$
$$0.8x - 150 + 150 = 700 + 150$$
$$0.8x = 850$$
$$\frac{0.8x}{0.8} = \frac{850}{0.8}$$
$$x = 1062.5$$

The book dealer needs to have $1062.50 in sales.

52. $\frac{86.4}{4.5} = 19.2$

The wildebeast runs at a speed of 19.2 meters per second.

53.
$$4y - 3 = 6y - 2$$
$$4y - 3 - 4y = 6y - 2 - 4y$$
$$-3 = 2y - 2$$
$$-3 + 2 = 2y - 2 + 2$$
$$-1 = 2y$$
$$\frac{1}{2}(-1) = (2y)\frac{1}{2}$$
$$-\frac{1}{2} = y$$

PAGE 608, LOOK BEYOND

54.
$$C = \pi d$$
$$C = \pi(18)$$

The circumference of the smaller circle is 18π centimeters, or about 56.5 centimeters.

$$C = \pi d$$
$$C = \pi(24)$$

The circumference of the larger circle is 24π centimeters, or about 75.4 centimeters.

11.4 PAGES 614–616, PRACTICE & APPLY

5. The rent is between $550 and $700.

6. The rent is less than $400.

7. 2 categories account for less than $\frac{1}{4}$ of the apartments. The rent in these categories is either less than $400 or greater than $1000.

8. The $700–$1000 category and the $400–$550 category each contain approximately 25% of the apartments.

9. $35\% \cdot 75{,}000 = 0.35 \cdot 75{,}000 = 26{,}250$

Approximately 26,250 apartments would have rents between $550 and $700.

10. $\text{percent} = \frac{15{,}000}{80{,}000} \cdot 100 = 18.75\%$

Approximately 18.8% of the apartments in Kerrville have rents between $700 and $1000. In Mortonville, approximately 25% of the apartments are in this category, so Kerrville has approximately 6% fewer than Mortonville.

11. $14{,}500 + 8400 + 6800 + 4200 + 3500 = 37{,}400$

There are 37,400 customers using these services.

12. To compute the percent, divide the number of customers in each category by the total number of customers.

	United Long Distance	ABC Service	Advanced Services	Multi Media Services	Fast Phones Long Distance
Number of customers	14,500	8400	6800	4200	3500
Percent	$\frac{14{,}500}{37{,}400} \approx 39\%$	$\frac{8400}{37{,}400} \approx 23\%$	$\frac{6800}{37{,}400} \approx 18\%$	$\frac{4200}{37{,}400} \approx 11\%$	$\frac{3500}{37{,}400} \approx 9\%$

13.

	Number of customers	Percent	Number of degrees
United Long Distance	14,500	$\frac{14{,}500}{37{,}400} \approx 0.39 \approx 39\%$	$0.39 \cdot 360 = 140.4°$
ABC Service	8400	$\frac{8400}{37{,}400} \approx 0.23 \approx 23\%$	$0.23 \cdot 360 = 82.8°$
Advanced Services	6800	$\frac{6800}{37{,}400} \approx 0.18 \approx 18\%$	$0.18 \cdot 360 = 64.8°$
Multi Media Services	4200	$\frac{4200}{37{,}400} \approx 0.11 \approx 11\%$	$0.11 \cdot 360 = 39.6°$
Fast Phones Long Distance	3500	$\frac{3500}{37{,}400} \approx 0.09 \approx 9\%$	$0.09 \cdot 360 = 32.4°$
Total	37,400	100%	360°

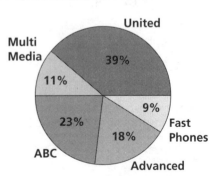

14. The new number of ABC Service customers is 8400 − 400 = 8000. The number of Advanced Services customers is 6800 + 400 = 7200.

	Number of customers	Percent	Number of degrees
ABC Service	8000	$\frac{8000}{37,400} \approx 0.21 \approx 21\%$	$0.21 \cdot 360 = 75.6°$
Advanced Services	7200	$\frac{7200}{37,400} \approx 0.19 \approx 19\%$	$0.19 \cdot 360 = 68.4°$

The angle for ABC Service would change to 76° and the angle for Advanced Services would change to 68°. The others would stay the same.

15. Add 200 to each category. The new total number of customers is 37,400 + 1000 = 38,400.

	Number of customers	Percent	Number of degrees
United Long Distance	14,700	$\frac{14,700}{38,400} \approx 0.38 \approx 38\%$	$0.38 \cdot 360 = 136.8°$
ABC Service	8600	$\frac{8600}{38,400} \approx 0.22 \approx 22\%$	$0.22 \cdot 360 = 79.2°$
Advanced Services	7000	$\frac{7000}{38,400} \approx 0.18 \approx 18\%$	$0.18 \cdot 360 = 64.8°$
Multi Media Services	4400	$\frac{4400}{38,400} \approx 0.12 \approx 12\%$	$0.12 \cdot 360 = 43.2°$
Fast Phones Long Distance	3700	$\frac{3700}{38,400} \approx 0.10 \approx 10\%$	$0.10 \cdot 360 = 36°$
Total	38,400	100%	360°

The new percents are very close to the old percents, so the circle graph would not change significantly.

16. 12% of 850,000 = 0.12 · 850,000 = 102,000
The sales in the hardware department were $102,000.

17. 40% of 850,000 = 0.40 · 850,000 = 340,000
The sales in the household and electronics department were $340,000.

18. auto: 8% of 850,000 = 0.08 · 850,000 = 68,000
clothing: 28% of 850,000 = 0.28 · 850,000 = 238,000
The sales in the auto and clothing departments were $68,000 + $238,000 = $306,000.

19. clothing, other, and hardware

20. percent of 1996 sales in the household and electronics department $= \frac{415,000}{980,000} \approx 0.42 \approx 42\%$
Since 42% is greater than 40%, there was a 2% increase in sales for this department.

21. 28% of 950,000 = 0.28 · 950,000 = 266,000
The 1997 clothing sales were $266,000.

22. Answers may vary. A possible answer is that a circle graph would be the best way to compare percents of different categories to the whole.

23. Answers may vary. Sample answer: A circle graph would not be the best way to represent data if you are trying to show how something changes over a period of time. A better way to represent the data would be to use a line graph or a bar graph.

24.

	Number of cars	Percent	Degrees
Hart	17	$\frac{17}{146} \approx 0.116 \approx 11.6\%$	$0.116 \cdot 360 \approx 42°$
Morton	26	$\frac{26}{146} \approx 0.178 \approx 17.8\%$	$0.178 \cdot 360 \approx 64°$
Kelley	15	$\frac{15}{146} \approx 0.103 \approx 10.3\%$	$0.103 \cdot 360 \approx 37°$
Washington	30	$\frac{30}{146} \approx 0.206 \approx 20.6\%$	$0.21 \cdot 360 \approx 74°$
Jarvis	22	$\frac{22}{146} \approx 0.151 \approx 15.1\%$	$0.151 \cdot 360 \approx 54°$
Gonzales	19	$\frac{19}{146} \approx 0.13 \approx 13\%$	$0.13 \cdot 360 \approx 47°$
Swenson	17	$\frac{17}{146} \approx 0.116 \approx 11.6\%$	$0.116 \cdot 360 \approx 42°$
Total	146	100%	360°

25.

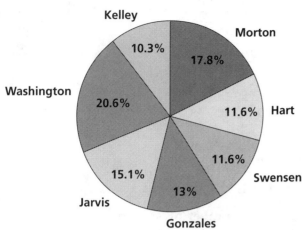

Kelley 10.3%
Morton 17.8%
Hart 11.6%
Washington 20.6%
Swensen 11.6%
Jarvis 15.1%
Gonzales 13%

26. approximately 15%   **27.** Washington

28. Add the total number of cars and divide by the number of people.

$$\text{average} = \frac{146}{7} \approx 20.86 \approx 21$$

The average number of cars sold was approximately 21.

29. To determine the median, order the data from least to greatest and find the middle number. The median number of cars is 19. Gonzales sold the median number of cars.

30. The most frequently occurring number is 17. The mode is 17.

31. Answers may vary. One possible answer is that a bar graph could be used to show the amount of sales for a given time period.

32. Answers may vary. A sample answer is that a bar graph would not be the best way to show how different categories are related to the whole. A circle graph would be a better way to display the data.

33. To determine the total number of employees, add the number of employees in each category.

$$8 + 15 + 20 + 10 + 2 = 55$$

The company has 55 employees.

34. The $20,000 to $29,999 category has the greatest percent of the employees. Since this category has the greatest number of employees, it has the greatest percent of the total.

35.

	Amount	Percent	Degrees
Less than $12,000	12	$\frac{12}{72} = 0.1\overline{6} = 16.\overline{6}\%$	$\frac{1}{6} \cdot 360 = 60°$
$12,000 to $19,999	18	$\frac{18}{72} = 0.25 = 25\%$	$0.25 \cdot 360 = 90°$
$20,000 to $29,999	32	$\frac{32}{72} = 0.4\overline{4} = 44.\overline{4}\%$	$\frac{4}{9} \cdot 360 = 160°$
$30,000 to $50,000	9	$\frac{9}{72} = 0.125 = 12.5\%$	$0.13 \cdot 360 = 45°$
Over $50,000	1	$\frac{1}{72} = 0.013\overline{8} = 1.3\overline{8}\%$	$\frac{1}{72} \cdot 360 = 5°$
Total	72	100%	360°

36.

$12,000 to $19,999 25%
Less than $12,000 16.6%
1.38% Over $50,000
12.5% $30,000 to $50,000
44.4% $20,000 to $29,999

37. The median salary lies in the $20,000 to $29,999 category.

38. Although we do know the total number of employees and the general range of their salaries, we do not know anything about the individual salaries. Therefore, we cannot compute the mean or find the most frequently occurring salary.

39. No; the median salary would still lie in the $20,000 to $29,999 category.

40. Answers may vary. A sample answer is that if the total number of employees in the $30,000 to $50,000 category and the over $50,000 category increased to over 32, the median would change.

41. Answers may vary.

PAGE 617, LOOK BACK

42. $abc^2 = (-2)(3)(-6)^2$
$= (-2)(3)(36)$
$= (-6)(36)$
$= -216$

43. $2ab^2c = 2(-2)(3)^2(-6)$
$= 2(-2)(9)(-6)$
$= (-4)(9)(-6)$
$= (-36)(-6)$
$= 216$

44. $a^2b^3 = (-2)^2(3)^3$
$= (4)(27)$
$= 108$

45. $(6)^2 + (8)^2 \overset{?}{=} (10)^2$
$36 + 64 = 100$
Since $a^2 + b^2 = c^2$, this is a right triangle.

46. $(14)^2 + (20)^2 \overset{?}{=} (26)^2$
$196 + 400 \neq 676$
Since $a^2 + b^2 \neq c^2$, this is not a right triangle.

47. $(8)^2 + (19)^2 \overset{?}{=} (25)^2$
$64 + 361 \neq 625$
Since $a^2 + b^2 \neq c^2$, this is not a right triangle.

48. Under 5 is the smallest population group. 65 and over is the second smallest population group.

49. Since the 5 to 19 population group is approximately 20%, you can estimate that the number of Americans from 5 to 19 years old is 20% of 250,000,000 ($0.20 \times 250,000,000$). The approximate number of Americans from 5 to 19 years old is 50,000,000.

50. 22% of $248,709,873 = 0.22 \cdot 248,709,873$
$= 54,716,172$
The number of Americans from 5 to 19 years old is 54,716,172.

PAGE 617, LOOK BEYOND

51. $2(40) = 80$
Mary is 80 miles from the city after 2 hours.

52. Let d represent the distance Mary drives, and let h represent the number of hours.
$$d = 40h$$

53.

Time (in hours)	Distance (in miles)
1	40
2	80
3	120
4	160
5	200

54.

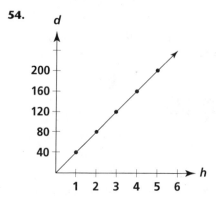

The graph is a ray.

8. little or none

9. strong positive correlation

10.

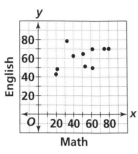

There is little or no correlation between math scores and English scores.

11.

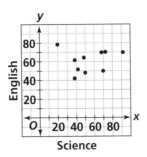

There is little or no correlation between science scores and English scores.

12. no obvious tendency in elevations

13. Yes; as the latitude north increases, the temperature decreases.

14. There is no correlation between latitude and elevation.

15. There is a strong negative correlation between latitude and temperature.

16.

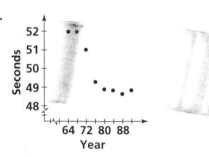

17. There is a strong negative correlation between the year and the time.

18a.

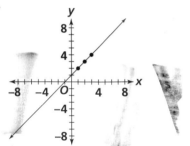

18b.

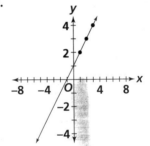

19. Graph **b** is steeper.

20. The vertical axis has a scale that is stretched. On graph **b** the vertical axis has 2 squares for each unit.

21. By stretching the vertical scale, you make the line look steeper.

22. Not really. If there is a positive correlation the linear pattern will still go up to the right: it will just be a steeper line if the scale is stretched.

PAGE 623, LOOK BACK

23. $\begin{cases} 3x + 3y < -3 \\ 4x - 4y \ge 2 \end{cases}$

$$3x + 3y < -3 \qquad\qquad 4x - 4y \ge 2$$
$$3x + 3y - 3x < -3 - 3x \qquad 4x - 4y - 4x \ge 2 - 4x$$
$$3y < -3x - 3 \qquad\qquad -4y \ge -4x + 2$$
$$\tfrac{1}{3}(3y) < \tfrac{1}{3}(-3x - 3) \qquad -\tfrac{1}{4}(-4y) \le -\tfrac{1}{4}(-4x + 2)$$
$$y < -x - 1 \qquad\qquad y \le x - \tfrac{1}{2}$$

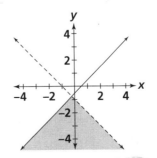

24. $\begin{cases} 2y > -x - 4 \\ 3y > x + 2 \end{cases}$

$2y > -x - 4$ $3y > x + 2$

$\frac{1}{2}(2y) > \frac{1}{2}(-x - 4)$ $\frac{1}{3}(3y) > \frac{1}{3}(x + 2)$

$y > -\frac{1}{2}x - 2$ $y > \frac{1}{3}x + \frac{2}{3}$

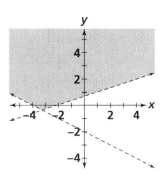

25. $\begin{cases} y \leq -x + 3 \\ y \leq 4x - 5 \end{cases}$ **26.** $\begin{cases} y > \frac{1}{2}x \\ y < 3x \end{cases}$ **27.** $\begin{cases} y \geq \frac{1}{3}x - 1 \\ y \geq 3x - 2 \end{cases}$ **28.** $\begin{cases} x \leq 1 \\ y \leq 1 \end{cases}$

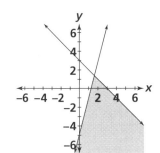   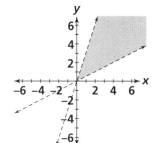   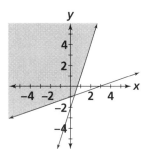   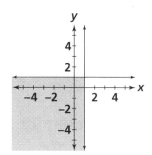

PAGE 623, LOOK BEYOND

29.

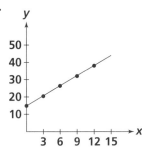

30. When x is 15, y is 44.

11.6 PAGES 626–627, PRACTICE & APPLY

6. increase   **7.** positive

8. close to 1   **9.** rises; no   **10.** falls; yes

11. rises; yes   **12.** falls; no   **13.** 1   **14.** 0

15. Line 1; it is as close to as many data points as possible.

16. A   **17. C**   **18. B**

19.

20. Answers may vary; approximately $1.65.

21.

Sequence	1		4		7		10		13		[16]		[19]
First differences		3		3		3		3		3		3	

The next two terms are 16 and 19.

22.

Sequence	2		5		10		17		26		[37]		[50]
First differences		3		5		7		9		11		13	
Second differences			2		2		2		2		2		

The next two terms are 37 and 50.

23. By following the pattern 1, 2, 3, 4, 0, 1, the next terms are 3 and –1.

1		2		3		4		0		1		2		3		–1
	1		1		1		–4		1		1		1		–4	

24. $A = s^2$

$A = 8^2 = 64$

The area is 64 square centimeters.

25. slope $= \dfrac{\text{difference in } y\text{-values}}{\text{difference in } x\text{-values}}$

$m = \dfrac{3-2}{-4-1} = \dfrac{1}{-5} = -\dfrac{1}{5}$

The slope is $-\dfrac{1}{5}$.

26. $m = \dfrac{0-(-2)}{-4-(0)} = \dfrac{2}{-4} = -\dfrac{1}{2}$

The slope is $-\dfrac{1}{2}$.

27. $m = \dfrac{-1-4}{3-3} = \dfrac{-5}{0}$

The slope is undefined.

28. $2x + 4 = 12$

$2x = 12 - 4$

$2x = 8$

$x = \dfrac{8}{2}$

$x = 4$

Check: $2x + 4 = 12$

$2(4) + 4 = 12$ True

The value $x = 4$ makes the equality true.

29. $32 - 2n = 10$

$-2n = 10 - 32$

$-2n = -22$

$n = \dfrac{-22}{-2}$

$n = 11$

Check: $32 - 2n = 10$

$32 - 2(11) = 10$ True

The value $n = 11$ makes the equality true.

1. 20% of 1000 = 0.20 · 1000 = 200
You would expect 200 tires to last between 40,000 and 50,000 miles.

2. Add up the percent for anything over 30,000 miles.

51% + 20% = 71%

71% of 550 = 0.71 · 550 = 390.5

You would expect 390 tires to last at least 30,000 miles.

3. mean: $\dfrac{6+8+8+11+7}{5} = \dfrac{40}{5} = 8$

median: Arrange the numbers in order: 6, 7, 8, 8, 11. The middle number is 8.

mode: The number that appears most often is 8.

range: The range is 11 – 6 = 5.

4. mean: $\dfrac{5+7+10+13+21+3}{6} = \dfrac{59}{6} \approx 9.8$

median: Arrange the numbers in order: 3, 5, 7, 10, 13, 21. The median is the
average of the middle two numbers. $\dfrac{7+10}{2} = \dfrac{17}{2} = 8.5$

mode: There is no mode for this set of data. Each number appears only once.

range: The range is 21 – 3 = 18.

5. mean: $\dfrac{55 + 85 + 96 + 102 + 135 + 85 + 55 + 96 + 55 + 206}{10} = \dfrac{970}{10} = 97$

median: Arrange the numbers in order: 55, 55, 55, 85, 85, 96, 96, 102, 135, 206.

The median is the average of the middle two numbers. $\dfrac{85 + 96}{2} = \dfrac{181}{2} = 90.5$

mode: The number 55 appears most often.

range: The range is $206 - 55 = 151$.

6. From the box-and-whisker plot, the lower quartile is 23.

7. From the box-and-whisker plot, the upper quartile is 46.

8. The median is the average of the middle two scores. $\dfrac{31 + 34}{2} = \dfrac{65}{2} = 32.5$

9. The range is $56 - 18 = 38$.

10. Let the tens digits be the stems and the ones digits be the leaves. key $\boxed{5\,|\,0 = 50}$

Test Scores

Stems	Leaves
5	0, 8
6	0, 5, 8
7	4, 5, 6, 8, 9
8	0, 1, 4, 5, 5, 8
9	2, 2, 3, 8, 9

11.

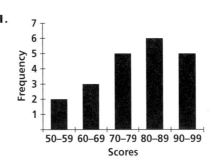

12. First draw a number line. Find and mark the lowest and highest scores. Find and mark the median (or middle) grade with a vertical line above the axis. Find and mark the lower quartile (the median of the lower half) with a vertical line above the axis. Find and mark the upper quartile (the median of the upper half) with a vertical line above the axis. Draw your box-and-whisker plot.

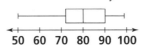

13.

	Amount	Percent	Degrees
Gasoline	800	$\dfrac{800}{2200} \approx 0.36 \approx 36\%$	$0.36 \cdot 360 = 129.6°$
Maintenance	200	$\dfrac{200}{2200} \approx 0.09 \approx 9\%$	$0.09 \cdot 360 = 32.4°$
Repairs	200	$\dfrac{200}{2200} \approx 0.09 \approx 9\%$	$0.09 \cdot 360 = 32.4°$
Insurance	900	$\dfrac{900}{2200} \approx 0.41 \approx 41\%$	$0.41 \cdot 360 = 147.6°$
Misc.	100	$\dfrac{100}{2200} \approx 0.05 \approx 5\%$	$0.05 \cdot 360 = 18°$
Total	2200	100%	360°

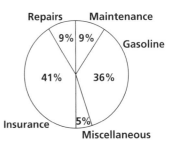

14. strong positive

15. strong negative

16. little or none

17. line rises; not a good fit

18. line falls; is a good fit

19. line rises; is a good fit

20. 1

21. −1

22. 0

23. mean: $\dfrac{11{,}800 + 14{,}500 + 12{,}500 + 17{,}000 + 18{,}600}{5} = \dfrac{74{,}400}{5} = \$14{,}880$

median: Arrange the salaries in order: 11,800, 12,500, 14,500, 17,000, 18,600.

The median salary is $14,500.

mode: There is no mode. Each value appears once in the data set.

range: The range is $18{,}600 - 11{,}800 = \$6{,}800$.

24.

	Amount	Percent	Degrees
Food	6500	$\frac{6500}{30,100} \approx 0.22 \approx 22\%$	$0.22 \cdot 360 = 79.2°$
Housing	10,300	$\frac{10,300}{30,100} \approx 0.34 \approx 34\%$	$0.34 \cdot 360 = 122.4°$
Clothing	2500	$\frac{2500}{30,100} \approx 0.08 \approx 8\%$	$0.08 \cdot 360 = 28.8°$
Transportation	7000	$\frac{7000}{30,100} \approx 0.23 \approx 23\%$	$0.23 \cdot 360 = 82.8°$
Health & personal care	1800	$\frac{1800}{30,100} \approx 0.06 \approx 6\%$	$0.06 \cdot 360 = 21.6°$
Misc.	2000	$\frac{2000}{30,100} \approx 0.07 \approx 7\%$	$0.07 \cdot 360 = 25.2°$
Total	30,100	100%	360°

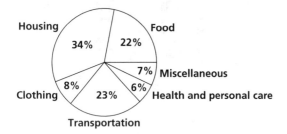

PAGE 633 CHAPTER 11 ASSESSMENT

1. approximately $290

2. approximately $140

3. $260 - 100 = 160$
The WMB stock increased by approximately $160.

4. $160 - 100 = 60$
The CBC stock increased by approximately $60.

5. $150 - 100 = 50$
The WMB increased by approximately $50.

6. mean: $\frac{10 + 15 + 30 + 55 + 78}{5} = \frac{188}{5} = 37.6$

median: Arrange the numbers in order: 10, 15, 30, 55, 78. The middle number is 30.

mode: There is no mode. Each number appears once.

range: The range is $78 - 10 = 68$.

7. mean: $\frac{12 + 5 + 9 + 12 + 2 + 15}{6} = \frac{55}{6} \approx 9.2$

median: Arrange the numbers in order: 2, 5, 9, 12, 12, 15. The median is the average of the middle two numbers. $\frac{9 + 12}{2} = \frac{21}{2} = 10.5$

mode: The number 12 appears most often.

range: The range is $15 - 2 = 13$.

8. mean: $\frac{83 + 23 + 29 + 31 + 41 + 43 + 53 + 83 + 23 + 83 + 6 + 9}{12} = \frac{507}{12} = 42.25$

median: Arrange the numbers in order: 6, 9, 23, 23, 29, 31, 41, 43, 53, 83, 83, 83. The median is the average of the middle two numbers. $\frac{31 + 41}{2} = \frac{72}{2} = 36$

mode: The number 83 appears most often.

range: The range is $83 - 6 = 77$.

9. Let the tens digits be the stems, and let the ones digits be the leaves. key $5\,|\,2 = 52$

Stems	Leaves
5	2, 2, 8, 9
6	0, 2, 5, 6, 9
7	3, 4, 7, 7
8	1, 1, 2, 4, 4
9	0

10.

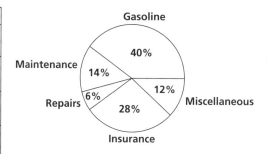

11. First draw a line. Find and mark the lowest and highest weights. Find and mark the median with a vertical line above the axis. Find and mark the lower quartile (the median of the lower half) with a vertical line above the axis. Find and mark the upper quartile (the median of the upper half) with a vertical line above the axis. Draw your box-and-whisker plot.

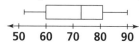

12.

	Amount	Percent	Degrees
Gasoline	1000	$\frac{1000}{2500} = 0.40 = 40\%$	$0.40 \cdot 360 = 144°$
Maintenance	350	$\frac{350}{2500} = 0.14 = 14\%$	$0.14 \cdot 360 = 50.4°$
Repairs	150	$\frac{150}{2500} = 0.06 = 6\%$	$0.06 \cdot 360 = 21.6°$
Insurance	700	$\frac{700}{2500} = 0.28 = 28\%$	$0.28 \cdot 360 = 100.8°$
Misc.	300	$\frac{300}{2500} = 0.12 = 12\%$	$0.12 \cdot 360 = 43.2°$
Total	2500	100%	360°

13. From the circle graph, insurance is about 30% of the total cost.

14. Repairs are 6% of the total cost.

15. From the chart above, gasoline makes up 144° of the circle graph.

16.

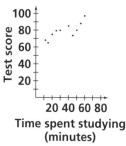

17. strong positive

18. 1

19.

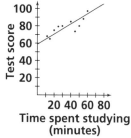

From the graph, a student who spends 35 minutes studying will score approximately 78 points on the test.

CHAPTER 12

APPLICATIONS IN GEOMETRY

For Exercise 6–11, to find the circumference, C, use either $C = 2\pi r$ or $C = \pi d$, where r is radius and d is diameter; to find the area, A, use $A = \pi r^2$.

6. $C = 2\pi r$ $A = \pi r^2$

$= 2\pi \cdot 2$ $= \pi \cdot 2^2$

$= 4\pi$ $= 4\pi$

≈ 12.6 ≈ 12.6

The circumference of the circle is approximately 12.6 inches, and the area of the circle is approximately 12.6 square inches.

7. $C = 2\pi r$ $A = \pi r^2$

$= 2\pi(4.5)$ $= \pi(4.5)^2$

$= 9\pi$ $= 20.25\pi$

≈ 28.3 ≈ 63.6

The circumference is approximately 28.3 centimeters, and the area is approximately 63.6 square centimeters.

8. $C = \pi d$ $r = \frac{1}{2}d$ $A = \pi r^2$

$= \pi \cdot 6$ $= \frac{1}{2}(6)$ $= \pi \cdot 3^2$

≈ 18.8 $= 3$ $= 9\pi$

                     ≈ 28.3

The circumference is approximately 18.8 inches, and the area is approximately 28.3 square inches.

9. $C = \pi d$ $r = \frac{1}{2}d$ $A = \pi r^2$

$= \pi(4.6)$ $= \frac{1}{2}(4.6)$ $= \pi(2.3)^2$

≈ 14.5 $= 2.3$ $= 5.29\pi$

                    ≈ 16.6

The circumference is approximately 14.5 meters, and the area is approximately 16.6 square meters.

10. $C = \pi d$ $r = \frac{1}{2}d$ $A = \pi r^2$

$= \pi \cdot 7$ $= \frac{1}{2}(7)$ $= \pi(3.5)^2$

≈ 22.0 $= 3.5$ $= 12.25\pi$

                    ≈ 38.5

The circumference is approximately 22.0 meters, and the area is approximately 38.5 square meters.

11. $C = 2\pi r$ $A = \pi r^2$

$= 2\pi\left(3\frac{1}{4}\right)$ $= \pi\left(3\frac{1}{4}\right)^2$

$= 2\pi(3.25)$ $= \pi(3.25)^2$

$= 6.5\pi$ $= \pi(10.5625)$

≈ 20.4 ≈ 33.2

The circumference is approximately 20.4 inches, and the area is approximately 33.2 square inches.

12. Answers may vary. Sample answer: a bicycle tire with a diameter of 27 inches has a circumference of 27π, or approximately 84.82 inches. Convert 1 mile to inches: 1 mile = 5280 feet = 63,360 inches. The tire must travel 63,360 inches, so, the total number of rotations is $\frac{63,360}{27\pi}$, or approximately 747. The tire will rotate approximately 747 times per mile.

13. Area of a medium pizza $= \pi r^2$

$= \pi(6)^2$

$= 36\pi$

≈ 113

Area of a large pizza $= \pi r^2$

$= \pi(7.5)^2$

$= 56.25\pi$

≈ 177

Area of a jumbo pizza $= l \times w$

First, convert feet to inches, and then substitute $l \times w = 24 \cdot 12 = 288$

The area of the medium pizza is approximately 113 square inches. The area of the large pizza is approximately 177 square inches. The area of a jumbo pizza is 288 square inches.

14. Area of 3 medium pizzas $\approx 3(113)$

≈ 339

Area of 2 large pizzas $\approx 2(177)$

≈ 354

The area of 2 large pizzas is greater by approximately 15 square inches.

15. Area of 2 medium pizzas $\approx 2(113)$

≈ 226

Area of 1 jumbo pizza = 288 sq in.

The area of 1 jumbo pizza is greater by approximately 62 square inches.

16. Calculate the price per square inch to find which option is the better bargain.

1 jumbo: $\frac{8.99}{288} \approx 0.031$ 3-for-2 mediums: $\frac{2(5.99)}{339.3} \approx 0.035$

The jumbo costs approximatley 3.1¢ per square inch while the 3-for-2 mediums cost approximately 3.5¢ per square inch. The jumbo 1-topping is the better bargain.

	Radius r	Diameter $2r$	Area πr^2	Circumference $2\pi r$
17.	4.5 centimeters	9 centimeters	$\approx$ 63.6 square centimeters	$\approx$ 28.3 centimeters
18.	2 yards	4 yards	$\approx$ 12.6 square yards	$\approx$ 12.6 yards
19.	2.5 inches	5 inches	$\approx$ 19.6 square inches	$\approx$ 15.7 inches
20.	3 yards	6 yards	$\approx$ 28.3 square yards	$\approx$ 18.8 yards
21.	7 inches	14 inches	$\approx$ 153.9 square inches	$\approx$ 44.0 inches
22.	16 feet	32 feet	$\approx$ 804.2 square feet	$\approx$ 100.5 feet
23.	1.5 inches	3 inches	$\approx$ 7.1 square inches	$\approx$ 9.4 inches
24.	15 centimeters	30 centimeters	$\approx$ 706.9 square centimeters	$\approx$ 94.2 centimeters
25.	$\approx$ 2.4 meters	$\approx$ 4.8 meters	$\approx$ 17.9 square meters	15 meters
26.	$\approx$ 2.3 meters	$\approx$ 4.5 meters	16 square meters	$\approx$ 14.2 meters

27. Add the distance of the two lengths of the rectangle to the circumference of the circular region formed by the 2 half-circles. Let D represent the distance around the track, and let d represent the diameter of the circular region.

$$D = 2(200) + \pi d$$
$$= 400 + 70\pi$$
$$\approx 400 + 219.91$$
$$\approx 619.9 \text{ yd}$$

The distance around the track is approximately 620 yards.

28. Add the area of the rectangular region to the area of the circle formed by the 2 half-circles. Let l represent the length of the rectangle, and let w represent the width (note that the width of the rectangle is the same as the diameter of the half-circles). Let A represent the area that needs to be covered with grass.

$$A = l \cdot w + \pi\left(\frac{w}{2}\right)^2$$
$$= 200 \cdot 70 + \pi\left(\frac{70}{2}\right)^2$$
$$= 14,000 + \pi(35)^2$$
$$= 14,000 + 1225\pi$$
$$\approx 14,000 + 3848$$
$$\approx 17,848 \text{ sq yd}$$

There are approximately 17,848 square yards which need to be covered.

29. The circumference of the circular base is greater. The height of the can is $3d$, while the circumference is πd. Since π, or approximately 3.14, is greater than 3, the circumference of the can is greater than the height.

For Exercises 30–31, subtract the area of the unshaded region from the area of the larger figure.

30. Area of square $= 6 \cdot 6$
$$= 36 \text{ sq in.}$$
Area of circle $= \pi r^2$
$$= \pi(3)^2$$
$$= 9\pi$$
$$\approx 28.3 \text{ sq in.}$$
Area of shaded region $=$ Area of square $-$ Area of circle
$$\approx 36 - 28.3$$
$$\approx 7.7 \text{ sq in.}$$
The area of the shaded region is approximately 7.7 square inches.

31. Area of outer circle $= \pi r^2$
$$= \pi(4)^2$$
$$= 16\pi$$
Area of inner circle $= 2(\pi r^2)$
$$= 2\pi(2)^2$$
$$= 2 \cdot 4\pi$$
$$= 8\pi$$
Area of shaded region $= 16\pi - 8\pi$
$$= 8\pi$$
$$\approx 25.1$$
The area of the shaded region is 8π, or approximately 25.1 square inches.

32. Perimeter of semicircle $= \frac{1}{2}$ circumference + diameter

$P = \frac{1}{2}C + d \qquad A = \frac{1}{2}\pi r^2$

$P = \frac{1}{2}\pi d + d \qquad\quad = \frac{1}{2}(\pi)(4)^2$

$\qquad = \frac{1}{2}(\pi)(8) + 8 \qquad = \frac{1}{2}(16)(\pi)$

$\qquad = 4\pi + 8 \qquad\qquad = 8\pi$

$\qquad \approx 20.6 \qquad\qquad \approx 25.1$

The perimeter of the semi-circle is approximately 20.6 yards. The area of the semi-circle is approximately 25.1 square yards.

PAGE 642, LOOK BACK

33. $V = e^3$
$\quad = 2^3$
$\quad = 8$

The volume is 8 cubic centimeters.

34. $V = e^3$
$\quad = (4.5)^3$
$\quad \approx 91.1$

The volume is approximately 91.1 cubic centimeters.

35. $V = e^3$
$\quad = 1^3$
$\quad = 1$ cubic yard

The volume is 1 cubic yard.

36. Since opposite sides of a parallelogram are equal, $AB = DC$.

$AB = DC$
$2y - 4 = y + 34$
$2y - 4 - y = y + 34 - y$
$y - 4 = 34$
$y - 4 + 4 = 34 + 4$
$y = 38$

37. Let l represent the length of the gym, then $l - 13$ represents the width of the gym.

$p = 2l + 2w$
$194 = 2l + 2(l - 13)$
$194 = 2l + 2l - 26$
$194 = 4l - 26$
$220 = 4l$
$55 = l$

The gym is 55 feet long.

38. Let m represent the amount of time (in seconds) Maria takes to run the race. Let j represent the amount of time (in seconds) Janel takes to run the race.

$\begin{cases} j = m - 5 \\ m + j = 59 \end{cases}$

Substitute $m - 5$ for j.   Substitute 32 for m.

$m + j = 59$ $j = m - 5$
$m + (m - 5) = 59$ $j = 32 - 5$
$2m - 5 = 59$ $j = 27$
$2m = 64$
$m = 32$

Maria ran the race in 32 seconds, and Janel ran the race in 27 seconds.

PAGE 642, LOOK BEYOND

39. First find the area of the entire target, and then find the area of the shaded region. The area of the target represents the sample space, and the area of the shaded region represents the desired event. To determine the theoretical probability of hitting the shaded region, divide the desired event by the sample space.

Area of target $= \pi r^2$
$\qquad\qquad\quad = \pi(8)^2$
$\qquad\qquad\quad = 64\pi$

The sample space is 64π.

To compute the area of the shaded region, subtract the area of the inner circle from the area of the circle with a radius of 4.

Area of inner circle $= \pi r^2$ Area of shaded region = Area of middle circle − Area of inner circle
$\qquad\qquad\qquad = \pi(2)^2$ $= 16\pi - 4\pi$
$\qquad\qquad\qquad = 4\pi$ $= 12\pi$

Area of middle circle $= \pi r^2$
$\qquad\qquad\qquad\quad = \pi(4)^2$
$\qquad\qquad\qquad\quad = 16\pi$

Now divide the desired event, 12π, by the sample space 64π.

$\frac{12\pi}{64\pi} = \frac{3}{16}$

The theoretical probability of hitting the shaded region is $\frac{3}{16}$, or 18.75%.

To determine the surface area of a cube for Exercises 5–12, use the formula $S = 6e^2$, where S represents the surface area and e represents the length of an edge of the cube. To determine the volume of a cube, use the formula $V = e^3$, where V represents the volume and e represents an edge of the cube.

5. $S = 6e^2$
$= 6(10)^2$
$= 6(100)$
$= 600$ square meters

$V = e^3$
$= (10)^3$
$= 1000$ cubic meters

6. $S = 6e^2$
$= 6(7)^2$
$= 6(49)$
$= 294$ square inches

$V = e^3$
$= (7)^3$
$= 343$ cubic inches

7. $S = 6e^2$
$= 6(15)^2$
$= 6(225)$
$= 1350$ square centimeters

$V = e^3$
$= (15)^3$
$= 3375$ cubic centimeters

8. $S = 6e^2$
$= 6(16)^2$
$= 6(256)$
$= 1536$ square feet

$V = e^3$
$= (16)^3$
$= 4096$ cubic feet

9. $S = 6e^2$
$= 6(2.5)^2$
$= 6(6.25)$
$= 37.5$ square meters

$V = e^3$
$= (2.5)^3$
≈ 15.6 cubic meters

10. $S = 6e^2$
$= 6(5.25)^2$
$= 6(27.5625)$
≈ 165.4 square meters

$V = e^3$
$= (5.25)^3$
≈ 144.7 cubic meters

11. $S = 6e^2$
$= 6(11)^2$
$= 6 \cdot 121$
$= 726$ square inches

$V = e^3$
$= 11^3$
$= 1331$ cubic inches

12. $S = 6e^2$
$= 6(6.25)^2$
≈ 234.4 square centimeters

$V = e^3$
$= (6.25)^3$
≈ 244.1 cubic centimeters

13. $S = 2(l \cdot w + h \cdot w + l \cdot h)$
$= 2(5 \cdot 3 + 2 \cdot 3 + 5 \cdot 2)$
$= 2(15 + 6 + 10)$
$= 2(31)$
$= 62$ square meters

$V = l \cdot w \cdot h$
$= 5 \cdot 3 \cdot 2$
$= 30$ cubic meters

14. $S = 2(l \cdot w + h \cdot w + l \cdot h)$
$= 2(4 \cdot 3 + 2 \cdot 3 + 4 \cdot 2)$
$= 2(12 + 6 + 8)$
$= 2(26)$
$= 52$ square yards

$V = l \cdot w \cdot h$
$= 4 \cdot 3 \cdot 2$
$= 24$ cubic yards

15. $S = 2(l \cdot w + h \cdot w + l \cdot h)$
$= 2(7 \cdot 4 + 9 \cdot 4 + 7 \cdot 9)$
$= 2(28 + 36 + 63)$
$= 2(127)$
$= 254$ square inches

$V = l \cdot w \cdot h$
$= 7 \cdot 4 \cdot 9$
$= 252$ cubic inches

16. $S = 2(l \cdot w + h \cdot w + l \cdot h)$
$= 2(1.5 \cdot 8 + 3 \cdot 8 + 1.5 \cdot 3)$
$= 2(12 + 24 + 4.5)$
$= 2(40.5)$
$= 81$ square centimeters

$V = l \cdot w \cdot h$
$= 1.5 \cdot 8 \cdot 3$
$= 36$ cubic centimeters

17. $S = 2(l \cdot w + h \cdot w + l \cdot h)$
$= 2(1 \cdot 1 + 2.3 \cdot 1 + 1 \cdot 2.3)$
$= 2(1 + 2.3 + 2.3)$
$= 2(5.6)$
$= 11.2$ square meters

$V = l \cdot w \cdot h$
$= 1 \cdot 1 \cdot 2.3$
$= 2.3$ cubic meters

18. $S = 2(l \cdot w + h \cdot w + l \cdot h)$
$= 2(3 \cdot 2 + 1 \cdot 2 + 3 \cdot 1)$
$= 2(6 + 2 + 3)$
$= 2(11)$
$= 22$ square inches

$V = l \cdot w \cdot h$
$= 3 \cdot 2 \cdot 1$
$= 6$ cubic inches

	Length	Width	Height	Surface area	Volume
19.	4 cm	4 cm	4 cm	96 cm^2	64 cm^3
20.	4 in.	3 in.	2 in.	52 in.^{2}	24 in.^{3}
21.	3.5 ft	7.2 ft	1.6 ft	84.64 ft^2	40.32 ft^3
22.	34 cm	57 cm	88 cm	19,892 cm^2	170,544 cm^3
23.	$\frac{1}{2}$ in.	$3\frac{1}{4}$ in.	2 in.	$20\frac{3}{4}$ in.^{2}	$3\frac{3}{4}$ in.^{3}
24.	102 ft	117 ft	300 ft	155,268 ft^2	3,580,200 ft^3
25.	248 ft	118 ft	12 ft	67,312 ft^2	351,168 ft^3
26.	20 cm	15 cm	1 cm	670 cm^2	300 cm^3

	Length	Width	Height	Surface area	Volume
27.	5 m	5 m	6 m	170 m^2	150 m^3
28.	6 m	6 m	$7\frac{1}{9}$ m	$242\frac{2}{3}$ m^2	256 m^3
29.	4 in.	8 in.	$21\frac{7}{8}$ in.	589 in.^{2}	700 in.^{3}
30.	5 cm	8 cm	10 cm	340 cm^2	400 cm^3

	Dimensions of removed squares	Height	Length	Width	Volume
31.	1 cm · 1 cm	1 cm	14 cm	8 cm	112 cm^3
32.	2 cm · 2 cm	2 cm	12 cm	6 cm	144 cm^3
33.	3 cm · 3 cm	3 cm	10 cm	4 cm	120 cm^3
34.	4 cm · 4 cm	4 cm	8 cm	2 cm	64 cm^3

35. The box with a height of 2 centimeters has the greatest volume.

Dimensions of removed squares	Height	Length	Width	Volume
1.5 cm · 1.5 cm	1.5 cm	13 cm	7 cm	136.5 cm^3
2.5 cm · 2.5 cm	2.5 cm	11 cm	5 cm	137.5 cm^3
3.5 cm · 3.5 cm	3.5 cm	9 cm	3 cm	94.5 cm^3
4.5 cm · 4.5 cm	4.5 cm	7 cm	1 cm	31.5 cm^3

36. Since the width of the piece of sheet metal is only 10 centimeters, a box with a height of 5 centimeters would have a width of 0, which is impossible.

37.
$$S = 6e^2$$
$$= 6(5)^2$$
$$= 6(25)$$
$$= 150 \text{ square meters}$$

$$V = e^3$$
$$= (5)^3$$
$$= 125 \text{ cubic meters}$$

38.
$$S = 2(l \cdot w + l \cdot h + w \cdot h)$$
$$= 2(13 \cdot 10 + 13 \cdot 5 + 10 \cdot 5)$$
$$= 2(130 + 65 + 50)$$
$$= 2(245)$$
$$= 490 \text{ square inches}$$

$$V = l \cdot w \cdot h$$
$$= 13 \cdot 10 \cdot 5$$
$$= 650 \text{ cubic inches}$$

39.
$$S = 2(l \cdot w + l \cdot h + w \cdot h)$$
$$= 2(8 \cdot 2 + 8 \cdot 3 + 2 \cdot 3)$$
$$= 2(16 + 24 + 6)$$
$$= 2(46)$$
$$= 92 \text{ square centimeters}$$

$$V = l \cdot w \cdot h$$
$$= 8 \cdot 2 \cdot 3$$
$$= 48 \text{ cubic centimeters}$$

40.
$$1 \text{ yd} = 3 \text{ ft}$$
$$(1 \text{ yd})^3 = (3 \text{ ft})^3$$
$$1 \text{ cu yd} = 27 \text{ cu ft}$$
There are 27 cubic feet in 1 cubic yard.

41. Since there are 3 feet in 1 yard, a cubic yard would have $3 \times 3 \times 3$, or 27 cubic feet. Multiply the number of cubic yards, 4, by 27 to convert to cubic feet.

4 cubic yards = 108 cubic feet

42. 1 cubic yard has $3 \times 3 \times 3$, or 27 cubic feet, so divide 108 by 27 to convert to cubic yards.
$$\frac{108}{27} = 4 \text{ cubic yards}$$

43. To determine the number of cubic yards of concrete needed, first convert the dimensions of the patio into yards, and then find the volume.

$$20 \text{ feet} = 6\frac{2}{3} \text{ yards}$$
$$\frac{1}{2} \text{ foot} = \frac{1}{6} \text{ yard}$$
$$V = l \cdot w \cdot h$$
$$= \left(6\frac{2}{3}\right) \cdot \left(6\frac{2}{3}\right) \cdot \left(\frac{1}{6}\right)$$
$$= \frac{20}{3} \cdot \frac{20}{3} \cdot \frac{1}{6}$$
$$= \frac{400}{54}$$
$$= \frac{200}{27} \approx 7.4$$

Approximately 7.4 cubic yards of concrete are needed.

44.
$$2.5x - 2 = 1$$
$$2.5x - 2 + 2 = 1 + 2$$
$$2.5x = 3$$
$$\frac{2.5x}{2.5} = \frac{3}{2.5}$$
$$x = 1.2$$

45.
$$5x = 2x + 16$$
$$5x - 2x = 2x - 2x + 16$$
$$3x = 16$$
$$\frac{3x}{3} = \frac{16}{3}$$
$$x = \frac{16}{3}, \text{ or } 5\frac{1}{3}$$

46.
$$x - 1 \le 2x + 5$$
$$x - 2x - 1 \le 2x - 2x + 5$$
$$-x - 1 \le 5$$
$$-x - 1 + 1 \le 5 + 1$$
$$-x \le 6$$
$$-1(-x) \ge -1(6)$$
$$x \ge -6$$

47. $m = \dfrac{4 - 0}{0 - 4} = \dfrac{4}{-4} = -1$
Use (4, 0) for (x_1, y_1).
$$y - y_1 = m(x - x_1)$$
$$y - 0 = -1(x - 4)$$
$$y = -x + 4$$

48. $m = \dfrac{3 - (-2)}{2 - (-1)} = \dfrac{5}{3}$
Use (2, 3) for (x_1, y_1).
$$y - y_1 = m(x - x_1)$$
$$y - 3 = \frac{5}{3}(x - 2)$$
$$y - 3 = \frac{5}{3}x - \frac{10}{3}$$
$$y - 3 + 3 = \frac{5}{3}x - \frac{10}{3} + 3$$
$$y = \frac{5}{3}x - \frac{1}{3}$$

49. $m = \dfrac{3 - 3}{5 - 4} = \dfrac{0}{1} = 0$
Use (4, 3) for (x_1, y_1).
$$y - y_1 = m(x - x_1)$$
$$y - 3 = 0(x - 4)$$
$$y - 3 = 0$$
$$y - 3 + 3 = 0 + 3$$
$$y = 3$$

50.
$C = 2\pi r$
$= 2\pi(2)$
$= 4\pi$
≈ 12.6 centimeters

$A = \pi r^2$
$= \pi(2)^2$
$= 4\pi$
≈ 12.6 square centimeters

51.
$C = \pi d$
$= \pi(4.5)$
$= 4.5\pi$
≈ 14.1 centimeters

$A = \pi r^2$
$= \pi(2.25)^2$
$= 5.0625\pi$
≈ 15.9 square centimeters

52.
$C = \pi d$
$= \pi(1)$
≈ 3.1 yards

$A = \pi r^2$
$= \pi\left(\frac{1}{2}\right)^2$
$= \pi\left(\frac{1}{4}\right)$
≈ 0.8 square yards

53. If x represents the length of the square removed, then x also represents the height of the box. The length is represented by 16 minus the 2 squares removed, or $2x$, and the width by 10 minus the 2 squares, or $2x$. The dimensions of the box are: x, $16 - 2x$, and $10 - 2x$. To compute the volume, multiply length times width times height.
$$V = l \cdot w \cdot h = (16 - 2x)(10 - 2x)x$$

54. Let x represent the side length of the square or height. Let $Y_1 = (16 - 2x)(10 - 2x)x$, represent the volume.

X	Y₁	
1	112	
1.5	136.5	
2	144	
2.5	137.5	
3	120	
3.5	94.5	
4	64	
X=2		

From the table you can see that a side length of 2 centimeters yields the greatest volume.

55. Let x represent the side length of the square piece of material to be removed. Let $Y_1 = (30 - 2x)(20 - 2x)x$ represent the volume.

X	Y₁	
3.6	1050.6	
3.7	1053.6	
3.8	1055.5	
3.9	1056.3	
4	1056	
4.1	1054.7	
4.2	1052.4	
X=3.9		

From the table, you can see that when $x = 3.9$, the volume is greatest. Therefore, to produce the greatest volume, a square with side lengths of 3.9 centimeters should be removed.

12.3 **PAGES 655–657, PRACTICE & APPLY**

5.
$V = Bh$
$= (4)(6)$
$= 24$ cubic meters

6.
$L = hp$
$= (8)(16)$
$= 128$ square centimeters

7.
$L = hp$
$= (4)(32)$
$= 128$ square centimeters

8.
$V = Bh$
$= (16.25)(18.5)$
$= 300.625$
≈ 300.6 cubic meters

9. Find the lateral surface area.

$L = hp$
$= (7)(17)$
$= 119$ square
   centimeters

Find the total surface area.

$S = L + 2B$
$= 119 + 2(8)$
$= 119 + 16$
$= 135$ square
   centimeters

10. $V = Bh$
$= (7)(8)$
$= 56$ cubic feet

11. $V = Bh$
$= (4.5)(20)$
$= 90$ cubic feet

12. 1 cubic yard is 27 cubic feet, so, divide 90 cubic feet by 27 cubic feet to convert to cubic yards.
$\frac{90}{27} = \frac{10}{3}$, or $3\frac{1}{3}$ cubic yards

13. Each pillar has a volume of $3\frac{1}{3}$ cubic yards, so the volume of 4 pillars is as follows:

$V = 4\left(3\frac{1}{3}\right)$
$= 4\left(\frac{10}{3}\right)$
$= \frac{40}{3}$, or $13\frac{1}{3}$ cubic yards

Cost = (number of cubic yards) $\times$ (cost per yard)
$= \left(13\frac{1}{3}\right)(65)$
≈ 866.67

It will cost approximately \$867 to pour four pillars.

14. Find the area of a base.

$B = \frac{1}{2}bh$
$= \frac{1}{2}(9)(12)$
$= 54$ square inches

Find the lateral surface area.

$L = hp$
$= (16)(9 + 12 + 15)$
$= (16)(36)$
$= 576$ square inches

Find the total surface area.

$S = L + 2B$
$= 576 + 2(54)$
$= 576 + 108$
$= 684$ square inches

Find the volume of the prism.

$V = Bh$
$= (54)(16)$
$= 864$ cubic inches

15. Find the area of a base.

$B = \frac{1}{2}bh$
$= \frac{1}{2}(3)(2.6)$
$= 3.9$ square centimeters

Find the lateral surface area.

$L = hp$
$= 8(3 + 3 + 3)$
$= 8(9)$
$= 72$ square centimeters

Find the total surface area.

$S = L + 2B$
$= 72 + 2(3.9)$
$= 72 + 7.8$
$= 79.8$ square centimeters

Find the volume of the prism.

$V = Bh$
$= (3.9)(8)$
$= 31.2$ cubic centimeters

16. $S = 2(lw + lh + wh)$
$= 2(4 \cdot 3 + 4 \cdot 1.5 + 3 \cdot 1.5)$
$= 2(12 + 6 + 4.5)$
$= 2(22.5)$
$= 45$ square meters

$V = lwh$
$= 4 \cdot 3 \cdot 1.5$
$= 18$ cubic meters

17. Find the area of the base.

$B = \frac{(b_1 + b_2)h}{2}$
$= \frac{(6 + 4)5}{2}$
$= \frac{(10)(5)}{2}$
$= \frac{50}{2}$
$= 25$ square feet

Find the lateral surface area.

$L = hp$
$= 5(6 + 4 + 4 + 4)$
$= 5(18)$
$= 90$ square feet

Find the total surface area.

$S = L + 2B$
$= 90 + 2(25)$
$= 90 + 50$
$= 140$ square feet

Find the volume of the prism.

$V = Bh$
$= (25)(5)$
$= 125$ cubic feet

18. Find the area of the base.

$B = 6\left(\frac{1}{2}bh\right)$
$= 6\left[\left(\frac{1}{2}\right)(5)(4.3)\right]$
$= 6(10.75)$
$= 64.5$ square feet

Find the lateral surface area.

$L = hp$
$= (2)(5 + 5 + 5 + 5 + 5 + 5)$
$= (2)(30)$
$= 60$ square feet

Find the total surface area.

$S = L + 2B$
$= 60 + 2(64.5)$
$= 60 + 129$
$= 189$ square feet

Find the volume of the prism.

$V = Bh$
$= (64.5)(2)$
$= 129$ cubic feet

19. Find the area of the base.

$$B = 6\left(\tfrac{1}{2}bh\right)$$
$$= 6\left[\left(\tfrac{1}{2}\right)(8)(7)\right]$$
$$= 6(28)$$
$$= 168 \text{ square meters}$$

Find the lateral surface area.

$$L = hp$$
$$= (3)(8 + 8 + 8 + 8 + 8 + 8)$$
$$= (3)(48)$$
$$= 144 \text{ square meters}$$

Find the total surface area.

$$S = L + 2B$$
$$= 144 + 2(168)$$
$$= 144 + 336$$
$$= 480 \text{ square meters}$$

Find the volume of the prism.

$$V = Bh$$
$$= (168)(3)$$
$$= 504 \text{ cubic meters}$$

20.
$$B = 6\left(\tfrac{1}{2}bh\right)$$
$$= 6\left[\left(\tfrac{1}{2}\right)(10)(8.6)\right]$$
$$= 6(43)$$
$$= 258 \text{ square feet}$$

The area of the base is 258 square feet.

21. Find the lateral surface area.

$$L = hp$$
$$= (10)(10 + 10 + 10 + 10 + 10 + 10)$$
$$= (10)(60)$$
$$= 600 \text{ square feet}$$

Since the top is left open, the total amount of material will be equal to the area of one base plus the lateral surface area. Let x represent the amount of material needed

$$x = B + L$$
$$= 258 + 600$$
$$= 858 \text{ square feet}$$

They will need 858 square feet of material.

22.
$$V = Bh$$
$$= (258)(10)$$
$$= 2580 \text{ cubic feet}$$

The volume of the aquarium is 2580 cubic feet.

23. Multiply the number of cubic feet of water by 7.5.

$$(2580)(7.5) = 19,350$$

The aquarium would hold approximately 19,350 gallons of water.

	Shape of base	Vertices, v	Faces, f	Edges, e	$v + f$
24.	Triangle	6	5	9	11
25.	Rectangle	8	6	12	14
26.	Pentagon	10	7	15	17
27.	Hexagon	12	8	18	20
28.	Heptagon	14	9	21	23
29.	Octogon	16	10	24	26
30.	n-gon	$2n$	$n + 2$	$3n$	$3n + 2$

31. Let $Y_1 = 2x$

$$Y_2 = x + 2$$
$$Y_3 = 3x$$
$$Y_4 = Y_1 + Y_2$$

Set up a table for $x = 3, 4, 5, \ldots$ where Y_1 computes the number of vertices, Y_2 computes the number of faces, Y_3 computes the number of edges, and Y_4 computes $v + f$ for the prism.

32. Using the pattern developed in Exercise 31, substitute 100 for n.

number of vertices $= 2n = 2(100) = 200$
number of faces $= n + 2 = 100 + 2 = 102$
number of edges $= 3n = 3(100) = 300$

33. In the 100-gon, $V = 200$ and $f = 102$. This means that $v + f = 200 + 102 = 302$. Therefore, $v + f$ is 2 more than the number of edges in the 100-gon. One possible conjecture is that the larger v becomes, the closer $v + f$ gets to e.

34. $y = 1 - 2x$

x	-3	-2	-1	0	1	2	3
y	7	5	3	1	-1	-3	-5

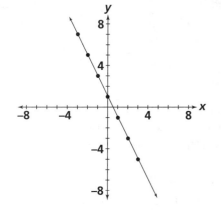

35. $y = -4$

x	-3	-2	-1	0	1	2	3
y	-4	-4	-4	-4	-4	-4	-4

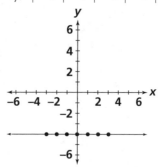

36. $y = \dfrac{x}{2} + 1$

x	-3	-2	-1	0	1	2	3
y	$-\frac{1}{2}$	0	$\frac{1}{2}$	1	$\frac{3}{2}$	2	$\frac{5}{2}$

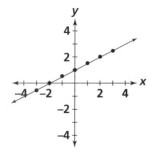

37. $C = 2\pi r$
$= 2\pi \cdot 5$
$= 10\pi$
≈ 31.4 centimeters

$A = \pi r^2$
$= \pi(5)^2$
$= 25\pi$
≈ 78.5 square centimeters

38. $C = \pi d$
$= 5\pi$
≈ 15.7 centimeters

$A = \pi r^2$
$= \pi(2.5)^2$
$= 6.25\pi$
≈ 19.6 square centimeters

39. $C = \pi d$
$= 0.5\pi$
≈ 1.6 yards

$A = \pi^2$
$= \pi(0.25)^2$
$= 0.0625\pi$
≈ 0.2 square yards

40.

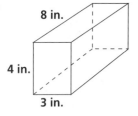

8 in.

4 in.

3 in.

Volume of a right rectangular prism $= Bh$
$= lwh$
$= (8)(3)(4)$
$= 96$ cubic inches

Volume of a right triangular prism $= Bh$
$= \left(\frac{1}{2}lw\right)h$
$= \left[\frac{1}{2}(8)(3)\right]4$
$= 48$ cubic inches

5. $S = 2\pi r^2 + 2\pi rh$ $V = Bh$
     $= 2\pi(2)^2 + 2\pi(2)(10)$ $= \pi r^2 h$
     $= 2\pi(4) + 2\pi(20)$ $= \pi(2)^2(10)$
     $= 8\pi + 40\pi$ $= \pi(4)(10)$
     $= 48\pi$ $= 40\pi$
     ≈ 150.8 square inches ≈ 125.7 cubic inches

6. $S = 2\pi r^2 + 2\pi rh$ $V = Bh$
     $= 2\pi(6)^2 + 2\pi(6)(4)$ $= \pi r^2 h$
     $= 2\pi(36) + 2\pi(24)$ $= \pi(6)^2(4)$
     $= 72\pi + 48\pi$ $= \pi(36)(4)$
     $= 120\pi$ $= 144\pi$
     ≈ 377.0 square yards ≈ 452.4 cubic yards

7. $S = 2\pi r^2 + 2\pi rh$ $V = Bh$
     $= 2\pi(3)^2 + 2\pi(3)(3)$ $= \pi r^2 h$
     $= 2\pi(9) + 2\pi(9)$ $= \pi(3)^2(3)$
     $= 18\pi + 18\pi$ $= \pi(9)(3)$
     $= 36\pi$ $= 27\pi$
     ≈ 113.1 square ≈ 84.8 cubic
         centimeters   centimeters

8. $S = 2\pi r^2 + 2\pi rh$ $V = Bh$
     $= 2\pi(3.5)^2 + 2\pi(3.5)(8)$ $= \pi r^2 h$
     $= 2\pi(12.25) + 2\pi(28)$ $= \pi(3.5)^2(8)$
     $= 24.5\pi + 56\pi$ $= \pi(12.25)(8)$
     $= 80.5\pi$ $= 98\pi$
     ≈ 252.9 square meters ≈ 307.9 cubic meters

9. $S = 2\pi r^2 + 2\pi rh$ $V = Bh$
     $= 2\pi(1.5)^2 + 2\pi(1.5)(8.5)$ $= \pi r^2 h$
     $= 2\pi(2.25) + 2\pi(12.75)$ $= \pi(1.5)^2(8.5)$
     $= 4.5\pi + 25.5\pi$ $= \pi(2.25)(8.5)$
     $= 30\pi$ $= 19.125\pi$
     ≈ 94.2 square feet ≈ 60.1 cubic feet

10. $S = 2\pi r^2 + 2\pi rh$ $V = Bh$
     $= 2\pi(4)^2 + 2\pi(4)(8.2)$ $= \pi r^2 h$
     $= 2\pi(16) + 2\pi(32.8)$ $= \pi(4)^2(8.2)$
     $= 32\pi + 65.6\pi$ $= \pi(16)(8.2)$
     $= 97.6\pi$ $= 131.2\pi$
     ≈ 306.6 square feet ≈ 412.2 cubic feet

11. Let x represent the number of gallons in the cylinder. Convert cubic inches to cubic feet.

$$1 \text{ foot} = 12 \text{ inches}$$
$$(1 \text{ foot})^3 = (12 \text{ inches})^3$$
$$1 \text{ cubic foot} = 1728 \text{ cubic inches}$$

Now use this conversion to convert 125.63 cubic inches to cubic feet.

$$\frac{125.63}{1728} \approx 0.073 \text{ cubic feet}$$

Convert 0.073 cubic feet to gallons.

$$\frac{x \text{ gallons}}{0.073 \text{ cubic feet}} = \frac{7.5 \text{ gallons}}{1 \text{ cubic foot}}$$
$$\frac{x}{0.073} = \frac{7.5}{1}$$
$$x = (0.073)(7.5)$$
$$x \approx 0.5$$

125.63 cubic inches is about 0.5 gallons.

12. Let x represent the number of gallons in the cylinder. Convert cubic yards to cubic feet.

$$1 \text{ yard} = 3 \text{ feet}$$
$$(1 \text{ yard})^3 = (3 \text{ feet})^3$$
$$1 \text{ cubic yard} = 27 \text{ cubic feet}$$

Now convert 452.4 cubic yards to cubic feet.

$$(452.4)(27) = 12{,}214.8 \text{ cubic feet}$$

Convert 12,214.8 cubic feet to gallons.

$$\frac{x \text{ gallons}}{12{,}214.8 \text{ cubic feet}} = \frac{7.5 \text{ gallons}}{1 \text{ cubic foot}}$$
$$\frac{x}{12{,}214.8} = \frac{7.5}{1}$$
$$x = (7.5)(12{,}214.8)$$
$$x \approx 91{,}611$$

452.4 cubic yards is about 91,611 gallons.

13. Let x represent the number of gallons in the cylinder. Convert 60.1 cubic feet to gallons.

$$\frac{x \text{ gallons}}{60.1 \text{ cubic feet}} = \frac{7.5 \text{ gallons}}{1 \text{ cubic foot}}$$
$$\frac{x}{60.1} = \frac{7.5}{1}$$
$$x = (7.5)(60.1)$$
$$x = 450.8$$

60.1 cubic feet is about 450.8 gallons.

14. $S = 2\pi r^2 + 2\pi rh$ $V = Bh$
     $= 2\pi(10)^2 + 2\pi(10)(15)$ $= \pi r^2 h$
     $= 2\pi(100) + 2\pi(150)$ $= \pi(10)^2(15)$
     $= 200\pi + 300\pi$ $= \pi(100)(15)$
     $= 500\pi$ $= 1500\pi$
     ≈ 1570.8 square feet ≈ 4712.4 cubic feet

15. $S = 2\pi r^2 + 2\pi rh$
     $= 2\pi(6)^2 + 2\pi(6)(5)$
     $= 2\pi(36) + 2\pi(30)$
     $= 72\pi + 60\pi$
     $= 132\pi$
     ≈ 414.7 square meters
 $V = Bh$
     $= \pi r^2 h$
     $= \pi(6)^2(5)$
     $= \pi(36)(5)$
     $= 180\pi$
     ≈ 565.5 cubic meters

16. $S = 2\pi r^2 + 2\pi rh$
     $= 2\pi(4)^2 + 2\pi(4)(12)$
     $= 2\pi(16) + 2\pi(48)$
     $= 32\pi + 96\pi$
     $= 128\pi$
     ≈ 402.1 square inches
 $V = Bh$
     $= \pi r^2 h$
     $= \pi(4)^2(12)$
     $= \pi(16)(12)$
     $= 192\pi$
     ≈ 603.2 cubic inches

17. $S = 2\pi r^2 + 2\pi rh$
     $= 2\pi(5.5)^2 + 2\pi(5.5)(14)$
     $= 2\pi(30.25) + 2\pi(77)$
     $= 60.5\pi + 154\pi$
     $= 214.5\pi$
     ≈ 673.9 square centimeters
 $V = Bh$
     $= \pi r^2 h$
     $= \pi(5.5)^2(14)$
     $= \pi(30.25)(14)$
     $= 423.5\pi$
     ≈ 1330.5 cubic centimeters

18. $S = 2\pi r^2 + 2\pi rh$
$= 2\pi(2.5)^2 + 2\pi(2.5)(6.5)$
$= 2\pi(6.25) + 2\pi(16.25)$
$= 12.5\pi + 32.5\pi$
$= 45\pi$
≈ 141.4 square yards

$V = Bh$
$= \pi r^2 h$
$= \pi(2.5)^2(6.5)$
$= \pi(6.25)(6.5)$
$= 40.625\pi$
≈ 127.6 cubic yards

19. $S = 2\pi r^2 + 2\pi rh$
$= 2\pi(4.1)^2 + 2\pi(4.1)(6.2)$
$= 2\pi(16.81) + 2\pi(25.42)$
$= 33.62\pi + 50.84\pi$
$= 84.46\pi$
≈ 265.3 square meters

$V = Bh$
$= \pi r^2 h$
$= \pi(4.1)^2(6.2)$
$= \pi(16.81)(6.2)$
$= 104.222\pi$
≈ 327.4 cubic meters

20. $S = 2\pi r^2 + 2\pi rh$
$= 2\pi(11)^2 + 2\pi(11)(45)$
$= 2\pi(121) + 2\pi(495)$
$= 242\pi + 990\pi$
$= 1232\pi$
≈ 3870.4 square feet

$V = Bh$
$= \pi r^2 h$
$= \pi(11)^2(45)$
$= \pi(121)(45)$
$= 5445\pi$
$\approx 17,106$ cubic feet

21. $S = 2\pi r^2 + 2\pi rh$
$= 2\pi(6.25)^2 + 2\pi(6.25)(5.7)$
$= 2\pi(39.0625) + 2\pi(35.625)$
$= 78.125\pi + 71.25\pi$
$= 149.375\pi$
≈ 469.3 square centimeters

$V = Bh$
$= \pi r^2 h$
$= \pi(6.25)^2(5.7)$
$= \pi(39.0625)(5.7)$
$= 222.65625\pi$
≈ 699.5 cubic centimeters

22. $S = 2\pi r^2 + 2\pi rh$
$= 2\pi(9)^2 + 2\pi(9)(22)$
$= 2\pi(81) + 2\pi(198)$
$= 162\pi + 396\pi$
$= 558\pi$
≈ 1753 square inches

$V = Bh$
$= \pi r^2 h$
$= \pi(9)^2(22)$
$= \pi(81)(22)$
$= 1782\pi$
≈ 5598.3 cubic inches

23. $S = 2\pi r^2 + 2\pi rh$
$= 2\pi(1.555)^2 + 2\pi(1.555)(1.42)$
$= 2\pi(2.418025) + 2\pi(2.2081)$
$= 4.83605\pi + 4.4162\pi$
$= 9.25225\pi$
≈ 29.1 square centimeters

$V = Bh$
$= \pi r^2 h$
$= \pi(1.555)^2(1.42)$
$= \pi(2.418025)(1.42)$
$= 3.4335955\pi$
≈ 10.8 cubic centimeters

24. $S = 2\pi r^2 + 2\pi rh$
$= 2\pi(16)^2 + 2\pi(16)(26)$
$= 2\pi(256) + 2\pi(416)$
$= 512\pi + 832\pi$
$= 1344\pi$
≈ 4222.3 square meters

$V = Bh$
$= \pi r^2 h$
$= \pi(16)^2(26)$
$= \pi(256)(26)$
$= 6656\pi$
$\approx 20,910.4$ cubic meters

25. $S = 2\pi r^2 + 2\pi rh$
$= 2\pi(100)^2 + 2\pi(100)(153)$
$= 2\pi(10,000) + 2\pi(15,300)$
$= 20,000\pi + 30,600\pi$
$= 50,600\pi$
$\approx 158,964.6$ square feet

$V = Bh$
$= \pi r^2 h$
$= \pi(100)^2(153)$
$= \pi(10,000)(153)$
$= 1,530,000\pi$
$\approx 4,806,636.8$ cubic feet

26. $S = 2\pi r^2 + 2\pi rh$
$= 2\pi(4.6)^2 + 2\pi(4.6)(7.5)$
$= 2\pi(21.16) + 2\pi(34.5)$
$= 42.32\pi + 69\pi$
$= 111.32\pi$
≈ 349.7 square meters

$V = Bh$
$= \pi r^2 h$
$= \pi(4.6)^2(7.5)$
$= \pi(21.16)(7.5)$
$= 158.7\pi$
≈ 498.6 cubic meters

27. $S = 2\pi r^2 + 2\pi rh$
$= 2\pi(55)^2 + 2\pi(55)(54)$
$= 2\pi(3025) + 2\pi(2970)$
$= 6050\pi + 5940\pi$
$= 11,990\pi$
$\approx 37,667.7$ square
centimeters

$V = Bh$
$= \pi r^2 h$
$= \pi(55)^2(54)$
$= \pi(3025)(54)$
$= 163,350\pi$
$\approx 513,179.2$ cubic
centimeters

28. $S = 2\pi r^2 + 2\pi rh$
$= 2\pi(7)^2 + 2\pi(7)(8)$
$\approx 2\pi(49) + 2\pi(56)$
$= 98\pi + 112\pi$
$= 210\pi$
≈ 659.7 square yards

$V = Bh$
$= \pi r^2 h$
$= \pi(7)^2(8)$
$= \pi(49)(8)$
$= 392\pi$
≈ 1231.5 cubic yards

29. $S = 2\pi r^2 + 2\pi rh$
$= 2\pi(2.55)^2 + 2\pi(2.55)(8.9)$
$= 2\pi(6.5025) + 2\pi(22.695)$
$= 13.005\pi + 45.39\pi$
$= 58.395\pi$
≈ 183.5 square meters

$V = Bh$
$= \pi r^2 h$
$= \pi(2.55^2(8.9)$
$= \pi(6.5025)(8.9)$
$= 57.87225\pi$
≈ 181.8 cubic meters

30. $S = 2\pi r^2 + 2\pi rh$
$\quad = 2\pi(4)^2 + 2\pi(4)(6)$
$\quad = 2\pi(16) + 2\pi(24)$
$\quad = 32\pi + 48\pi$
$\quad = 80\pi$
$\quad \approx 251.3$ square yards

$V = Bh$
$\quad = \pi r^2 h$
$\quad = \pi(4)^2(6)$
$\quad = \pi(16)(6)$
$\quad = 96\pi$
$\quad \approx 301.6$ cubic yards

31. $S = 2\pi r^2 + 2\pi rh$
$\quad = 2\pi(0.75)^2 + 2\pi(0.75)(12)$
$\quad = 2\pi(0.5625) + 2\pi(9)$
$\quad = 1.125\pi + 18\pi$
$\quad = 19.125\pi$
$\quad \approx 60.1$ square centimeters

$V = Bh$
$\quad = \pi r^2 h$
$\quad = \pi(0.75)^2(12)$
$\quad = \pi(0.5625)(12)$
$\quad = 6.75\pi$
$\quad \approx 21.2$ cubic centimeters

For Exercises 32–38 answers may vary. Sample answers are given.

	Object	Radius r	Height h	Lateral surface area $2\pi rh$	Surface area $2\pi r^2 + 2\pi rh$	Volume $\pi r^2 h$
32.	Soft drink can	1.3 in.	5 in.	≈ 40.8 in.^{2}	≈ 51.5 in.^{2}	≈ 26.5 in.^{3}
33.	Coffee can	3 in.	10 in.	≈ 188.50 in.^{2}	≈ 245 in.^{2}	≈ 282.7 in.^{3}
34.	Vegetable can	1.5 in.	4 in.	≈ 37.70 in.^{2}	≈ 51.8 in.^{2}	≈ 28.3 in.^{3}
35.	Roll of paper towels	5 in.	12 in.	≈ 377 in.^{2}	≈ 534.1 in.^{2}	≈ 942.5 in.^{3}
36.	Drinking cup	2 in.	6 in.	≈ 75.4 in.^{2}	≈ 100.5 in.^{2}	≈ 75.4 in.^{3}
37.	Soda straw	0.2 in.	7 in.	≈ 8.3 in.^{2}	≈ 9.0 in.^{2}	≈ 0.8 in.^{3}
38.	Drain pipe	3 in.	120 in.	≈ 2262 in.^{2}	≈ 2318.5 in.^{2}	≈ 3392.9 in.^{3}

39. $V = Bh$
$\quad = \pi r^2 h$
$\quad = \pi(4)^2(10)$
$\quad = \pi(16)(10)$
$\quad = 160\pi$
$\quad \approx 502.7$

The volume of the drink can is approximately 502.7 cubic centimeters.

40. $(502.65)(125\%) = (502.65)(1.25)$
$\quad\quad\quad\quad\quad\quad\quad \approx 628.3$

The volume of the new can is approximately 628.3 cubic centimeters.

41. Answers may vary. Sample answers are given.

New diameter	New height, h	Volume $\pi r^2 h$
8.6 cm	10.8 cm	≈ 627.4 cu cm
8.7 cm	10.5 cm	≈ 624.2 cu cm
8.8 cm	10.3 cm	≈ 626.5 cu cm

42. Answers may vary.
For the can having a diameter of 8.6 centimeters and a height of 10.8 centimeters:

$S = 2\pi r^2 + 2\pi rh$
$\quad = 2\pi(4.3)^2 + 2\pi(4.3)(10.8)$
$\quad = 2\pi(18.49) + 2\pi(46.44)$
$\quad = 36.98\pi + 92.88\pi$
$\quad = 129.86\pi$
$\quad \approx 408$ square centimeters

For the can having a diameter of 8.7 centimeters and a height of 10.5 centimeters:

$S = 2\pi r^2 + 2\pi rh$
$\quad = 2\pi(4.35)^2 + 2\pi(4.35)(10.5)$
$\quad = 2\pi(18.9225) + 2\pi(45.675)$
$\quad = 37.845\pi + 91.35\pi$
$\quad = 129.195\pi$
$\quad \approx 405.9$ square centimeters

For the can having a diameter of 8.8 centimeters and height of 10.3 centimeters:

$S = 2\pi r15^2 + 2\pi rh$
$\quad = 2\pi(4.4)^2 + 2\pi(4.4)(10.3)$
$\quad = 2\pi(19.36) + 2\pi(45.32)$
$\quad = 38.72\pi + 90.64\pi$
$\quad = 129.36\pi$
$\quad \approx 406.4$ square centimeters

This can has the least amount of surface area; thus, it requires the least amount of material.

43. $V = \pi r^2 h$
$\quad = \pi(1.5)^2(20)$
$\quad = \pi(2.25)(20)$
$\quad = 45\pi$
$\quad \approx 141.4$

Each pillar has a volume of about 141.4 cubic feet.

44. There are 27 cubic feet in 1 cubic yard. Divide the volume of the column by 27 to determine the amount of concrete needed.
$\quad \frac{141.37}{27} \approx 5.2$
About 5.2 cubic yards of concrete are needed for each pillar.

45. The cost for 4 pillars would be $5.2 \cdot 4 \cdot 65 = 1352$. It would cost approximately \$1352 to pour four pillars.

46. Let c represent the hypotenuse, a represent the leg that is 0.3 meters long, and b represent the leg that is 0.4 meters long.

$$a^2 + b^2 = c^2$$
$$(0.3)^2 + (0.4)^2 = c^2$$
$$(0.09) + (0.16) = c^2$$
$$0.25 = c^2$$
$$\sqrt{0.25} = \sqrt{c^2}$$
$$0.5 = c$$

The hypotenuse is 0.5 meters long.

48–49.

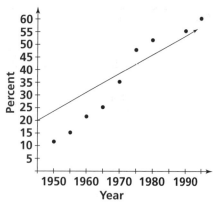

Answers may vary. Possible predictions for the years 2000 and 2010 are about 62% and about 67% respectively.

47. Answers may vary. The slope of the line $y = 2x + 1$ is $m = 2$. A line parallel to $y = 2x + 1$ will have the same slope but a different y-intercept; for example: $y = 2x$, $y = 2x + 2$, and $y = 2x - 1$. A line perpendicular to $y = 2x + 1$ will have a slope that is the negative reciprocal of $m = 2$. Some examples of lines perpendicular to $2x + 1$ are:
$y = -\frac{1}{2}x$, $y = -\frac{1}{2}x + 1$, and $y = -\frac{1}{2}x - 1$.

50. No; a line is not the best model for the data. There are many factors that can cause the data to change drastically. Some examples are a population increase or decrease for the community, gaining or losing an economic base for the community (industry moving in or out), and so on.

51. Answers may vary. Represent a right cylinder with a stack of pennies (Figure 1). The pennies each represent a cross section of the cylinder. Shift the stack of pennies to form an oblique cylinder (Figure 2). The cross sections of the oblique cylinder are still represented by pennies and thus have the same area as the cross sections of the original cylinder. According to Cavalieri's Principle, the volume of an oblique cylinder is the same as the volume of a right cylinder.

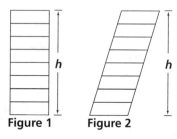

Figure 1   Figure 2

5. $V = \frac{Bh}{3}$
$= \frac{\pi r^2 h}{3}$
$= \frac{\pi (5)^2 (17)}{3}$
$= \frac{\pi (25)(17)}{3}$
$= \frac{425\pi}{3}$
$= 141\frac{2}{3}\pi$
≈ 445.1 cubic inches

6. $V = \frac{Bh}{3}$
$= \frac{\pi r^2 h}{3}$
$= \frac{\pi (5)^2 (6.5)}{3}$
$= \frac{\pi (25)(6.5)}{3}$
$= \frac{162.5\pi}{3}$
≈ 170.2 cubic centimeters

7. $V = \frac{Bh}{3}$
$= \frac{\pi r^2 h}{3}$
$= \frac{\pi (2.5)^2 (6)}{3}$
$= \frac{\pi (6.25)(6)}{3}$
$= \frac{37.5\pi}{3}$
$= 12.5\pi$
≈ 39.3 cubic meters

8. $V = \frac{Bh}{3}$
$= \frac{\pi r^2 h}{3}$
$= \frac{\pi (3.6)^2 (1.9)}{3}$
$= \frac{\pi (12.96)(1.9)}{3}$
$= \frac{24.624\pi}{3}$
$= 8.208\pi$
≈ 25.8 cubic meters

9. $V = \dfrac{Bh}{3}$

$= \dfrac{\pi r^2 h}{3}$

$= \dfrac{\pi\left(2\frac{1}{2}\right)^2\left(3\frac{3}{4}\right)}{3}$

$= \dfrac{\pi\left(\frac{5}{2}\right)^2\left(\frac{15}{4}\right)}{3}$

$= \dfrac{\pi\left(\frac{25}{4}\right)\left(\frac{15}{4}\right)}{3}$

$= \dfrac{\pi\left(\frac{375}{16}\right)}{3}$

$= \dfrac{1}{3}\left(\dfrac{375}{16}\right)\pi$

$= \dfrac{375}{48}\pi$

$= 7\dfrac{13}{16}\pi$

≈ 24.5 cubic inches

10. $V = \dfrac{Bh}{3}$

$= \dfrac{\pi r^2 h}{3}$

$= \dfrac{\pi\left(4\frac{1}{5}\right)^2\left(1\frac{2}{5}\right)}{3}$

$= \dfrac{\pi\left(\frac{21}{5}\right)^2\left(\frac{7}{5}\right)}{3}$

$= \dfrac{\pi\left(\frac{441}{25}\right)\left(\frac{7}{5}\right)}{3}$

$= \dfrac{\pi\left(\frac{3087}{125}\right)}{3}$

$= \dfrac{1}{3}\left(\dfrac{3087}{125}\right)\pi$

$= \dfrac{3087}{375}\pi$

$= 8\dfrac{87}{375}\pi$

≈ 25.9 cubic feet

11. $V = \dfrac{Bh}{3}$

$= \dfrac{\pi r^2 h}{3}$

$= \dfrac{\pi(4.45)^2(7.5)}{3}$

$= \dfrac{\pi(19.8025)(7.5)}{3}$

$= \dfrac{148.51875\pi}{3}$

$= 49.50625\pi$

≈ 155.5 cubic feet

12. $V = \dfrac{Bh}{3}$

$= \dfrac{\pi r^2 h}{3}$

$= \dfrac{\pi(8)^2(34)}{3}$

$= \dfrac{\pi(64)(34)}{3}$

$= \dfrac{2176\pi}{3}$

$= 725\dfrac{1}{3}\pi$

≈ 2278.7 cubic centimeters

13. $V = \dfrac{Bh}{3}$

$= \dfrac{\pi r^2 h}{3}$

$= \dfrac{\pi(6)^2(7)}{3}$

$= \dfrac{\pi(36)(7)}{3}$

$= \dfrac{252\pi}{3}$

$= 84\pi$

≈ 263.9 cubic inches

14. $V = \dfrac{Bh}{3}$

$= \dfrac{\pi r^2 h}{3}$

$= \dfrac{\pi(12)^2(15)}{3}$

$= \dfrac{\pi(144)(15)}{3}$

$= \dfrac{2160\pi}{3}$

$= 720\pi$

≈ 2261.9 cubic feet

15. $V = \dfrac{Bh}{3}$

$= \dfrac{(13)(30)}{3}$

$= \dfrac{390}{3}$

$= 130$ cubic inches

16. $V = \dfrac{Bh}{3}$

$= \dfrac{(12)(9)}{3}$

$= \dfrac{108}{3}$

$= 36$ cubic meters

17. $V = \dfrac{Bh}{3}$

$= \dfrac{(16)(15)}{3}$

$= \dfrac{240}{3}$

$= 80$ cubic yards

18. $V = \dfrac{Bh}{3}$

$= \dfrac{(8)(4)}{3}$

$= \dfrac{32}{3}$

$= 10\dfrac{2}{3}$

≈ 10.7 cubic centimeters

19. $V = \dfrac{Bh}{3}$

$= \dfrac{(7)(9)}{3}$

$= \dfrac{63}{3}$

$= 21$ cubic feet

20. $V = \dfrac{Bh}{3}$

$= \dfrac{(14)(10)}{3}$

$= \dfrac{140}{3}$

$= 46\dfrac{2}{3}$

≈ 46.7 cubic meters

21. $V = \dfrac{Bh}{3}$

$= \dfrac{(25)(6)}{3}$

$= \dfrac{150}{3}$

$= 50$ cubic millimeters

22. $V = \dfrac{Bh}{3}$

$= \dfrac{(36)(6)}{3}$

$= \dfrac{216}{3}$

$= 72$ cubic feet

23. $V = \dfrac{Bh}{3}$

$= \dfrac{(20)(7)}{3}$

$= \dfrac{140}{3}$

$= 46\dfrac{2}{3}$

≈ 46.7 cubic inches

24. $V = \dfrac{Bh}{3}$

$= \dfrac{(26)(37)}{3}$

$= \dfrac{962}{3}$

≈ 320.7 cubic centimeters

25. $V = \dfrac{Bh}{3}$

$= \dfrac{l \cdot w \cdot h}{3}$

$= \dfrac{(40)(40)(35)}{3}$

$= \dfrac{56000}{3}$

$= 18{,}666\dfrac{2}{3}$

$\approx 18{,}666.7$

The volume of the building is approximately 18,666.7 cubic feet.

26. Find the volume of the cone. Let V represent the volume,

$V = \dfrac{Bh}{3}$

$= \dfrac{\pi r^2 h}{3}$

$= \dfrac{\pi(4)^2(16)}{3}$

$= \dfrac{\pi(16)(16)}{3}$

$= \dfrac{256\pi}{3}$

$= 85\dfrac{1}{3}\pi$

≈ 268.1

It takes approximately 268.1 cubic centimeters of ice cream to fill the cone.

27. Substitute 56.5 for V and substitute 16 for h.

$V = \dfrac{Bh}{3}$

$56.5 = \dfrac{\pi r^2 h}{3}$

$56.5 = \dfrac{\pi r^2(16)}{3}$

$\left(\dfrac{3}{16\pi}\right)(56.5) = \left(\dfrac{\pi r^2(16)}{3}\right)\left(\dfrac{3}{16\pi}\right)$

$\dfrac{169.5}{16\pi} = r^2$

$\sqrt{\dfrac{169.5}{16\pi}} = \sqrt{r^2}$

$1.8 \approx r$

A radius of approximately 1.8 centimeters will give a volume of 56.5 cubic centimeters.

28. Answers may vary. Sample answers are given. For a volume of 75π cubic centimeters:

$$V = \frac{\pi r^2 h}{3}$$
$$75\pi = \pi \cdot \frac{r^2 h}{3}$$
$$75 = \frac{r^2 h}{3}$$
$$225 = r^2 h$$

Cone 1: Let $r = 3$; then $225 = 9h$ and $h = 25$.
Cone 2: Let $r = 5$; then $225 = 25h$ and $h = 9$.

29. Answers may vary. Sample answers are given. For a volume of 45 cubic meters:

$$V = \frac{Bh}{3}$$
$$45 = \frac{Bh}{3}$$
$$135 = Bh$$

Pyramid 1: Let $B = 9$; then $135 = 9h$ and $h = 15$.
$\quad\quad\quad B = s^2$, so $9 = s^2$ and $3 = s$.

Pyramid 2: Let $B = 25$; then $135 = 25h$ and $h = 5.4$.
$\quad\quad\quad B = s^2$, so $25 = s^2$ and $5 = s$.

Pyramid 3: Let $B = 15$; then $135 = 15h$ and $h = 9$.
$\quad\quad\quad B = s^2$, so $15 = s^2$ and $s \approx 3.9$.

PAGE 669, LOOK BACK

30. $(227 + 98) + 273 = (98 + 227) + 273$ Commutative Property
$\quad\quad\quad\quad\quad\quad\quad = 98 + (227 + 273)$ Associative Property
$\quad\quad\quad\quad\quad\quad\quad = 98 + 500$
$\quad\quad\quad\quad\quad\quad\quad = 598$

31. $(25 \cdot 323) \cdot 8 = (323 \cdot 25) \cdot 8$ Commutative Property
$\quad\quad\quad\quad\quad\quad = 323 \cdot (25 \cdot 8)$ Associative Property
$\quad\quad\quad\quad\quad\quad = 323 \cdot 200$
$\quad\quad\quad\quad\quad\quad = 64{,}600$

32. $(5 \cdot 976) \cdot 20 = (976 \cdot 5) \cdot 20$ Commutative Property
$\quad\quad\quad\quad\quad\quad = 976 \cdot (5 \cdot 20)$ Associative Property
$\quad\quad\quad\quad\quad\quad = 976 \cdot 100$
$\quad\quad\quad\quad\quad\quad = 97{,}600$

33. 26.2% of 3682

$$\frac{x}{0.262} = \frac{3682}{1.0}$$
$$(0.262)\left(\frac{x}{0.262}\right) = \left(\frac{3682}{1.0}\right)(0.262)$$
$$x \approx 965$$

34. $6\frac{2}{3}$% of $119.99

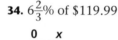
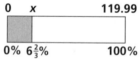

$$\frac{x}{0.667} = \frac{119.99}{1.0}$$
$$(0.0667)\left(\frac{x}{0.0667}\right) = \left(\frac{119.99}{1.0}\right)(0.0667)$$
$$x \approx 8$$

35. 39.5% of 200

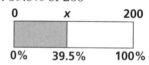

$$\frac{x}{0.395} = \frac{200}{1.0}$$
$$(0.395)\left(\frac{x}{0.395}\right) = \left(\frac{200}{1.0}\right)(0.395)$$
$$x \approx 79$$

36. 6.5% of 642

$$\frac{x}{0.065} = \frac{642}{1.0}$$
$$(0.065)\left(\frac{x}{0.065}\right) = \left(\frac{642}{1.0}\right)(0.065)$$
$$x \approx 42$$

37. 137% of $20.00

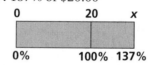

$$\frac{x}{1.37} = \frac{20}{1.0}$$
$$(1.37)\left(\frac{x}{1.37}\right) = \left(\frac{20}{1.0}\right)(1.37)$$
$$x \approx 27$$

38. 0.05% of 500

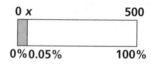

$$\frac{x}{0.0005} = \frac{500}{1.0}$$
$$(0.0005)\left(\frac{x}{0.0005}\right) = \frac{500}{1.0}(0.0005)$$
$$x \approx 0.25$$

39. $(2x - 1) + 3x \leq -2$
$\quad 2x + 3x - 1 \leq -2$
$\quad\quad\quad 5x - 1 \leq -2$
$\quad\quad\quad\quad 5x \leq -1$
$\quad\quad\quad\quad\quad x \leq -\frac{1}{5}$

40. $4x - 6 = -x + 1$
$\quad\quad 5x - 6 = 1$
$\quad\quad\quad 5x = 7$
$\quad\quad\quad\quad x = \frac{7}{5}$, or $1\frac{2}{5}$, or 1.4

41. $3 - (x - 4) = x$
$\quad 3 - x + 4 = x$
$\quad\quad 7 - x = x$
$\quad\quad\quad 7 = 2x$
$\quad\quad\quad \frac{7}{2} = x$, or $x = 3\frac{1}{2}$, or 3.5

42. Substitute x for r and y for h in the formula
$V = \frac{Bh}{3} = \frac{\pi r^2 h}{3}$ and solve for y. Let $V = 75$ cubic
centimeters.

$$V = \frac{Bh}{3}$$
$$V = \frac{\pi r^2 h}{3}$$
$$V = \frac{\pi x^2 y}{3}$$
$$75 = \frac{\pi x^2 y}{3}$$
$$75 \cdot 3 = \frac{\pi x^2 y}{3} \cdot 3$$
$$\frac{75 \cdot 3}{\pi x^2} = \frac{\pi x^2 y}{\pi x^2}$$
$$\frac{75 \cdot 3}{\pi x^2} = y$$

Therefore, $y = \frac{75 \cdot 3}{\pi x^2}$ can be used to describe the
volume of this cone.

43. Answers may vary.
Let x represent the radius of the cone and Y_1 represent the height of the cone.
Set $Y_1 = (75 \cdot 3) \div (\pi x \char`\^ 2)$. Create a table of Y_1
with ΔTb1 $= 0.5$. From this table it is likely that
the manufacturer would choose a cone with a
radius of 3 centimeters and a height of about 8
centimeters. If the manufacturer chose a smaller
radius, the cone would be too long and skinny. If
the manufacturer chose a larger radius, the cone
would be too short and difficult to hold.

X	Y_1	
1	1.7321	
2	6.9282	
3	15.588	
4	27.713	
5	43.301	
6	62.345	
7	84.87	

X=1

12.6 PAGES 673–675, PRACTICE & APPLY

6. Slant height, s, is found by using the "Pythagorean"
Right-Triangle Theorem, with the height and half of
the length of a side of the base as the legs.

$s^2 = 5^2 + 2^2$ $\qquad$ $B = l \cdot w B = l \cdot w$
$\quad = 25 + 4$ $\qquad\quad = 4 \cdot 4$
$\quad = 29$ $\qquad\qquad = 16$
$s = \sqrt{29} \approx 5.4$ centimeters

$L = \frac{1}{2}ps$ $\qquad\qquad\quad s = L + B$
$\quad \approx \frac{1}{2}(16)(5.4)$ $\qquad \approx 43.2 + 16$
$\quad \approx 43.2$ square $\qquad \approx 59.2$ square
$\qquad$ centimeters $\qquad\qquad$ centimeters

7. $s^2 = 12^2 + 8^2$ $\qquad\qquad c = 2\pi r$
$\quad = 208$ $\qquad\qquad\qquad = 2\pi(12)$
$s = \sqrt{208}$ $\qquad\qquad\qquad = 24\pi$
$s \approx 14.4$ $\qquad\qquad\qquad \approx 75.4$

$L = \frac{1}{2}Cs$ $\qquad\qquad\qquad B = \pi r^2$
$\quad \approx \frac{1}{2}(75.4)(14.4)$ $\qquad = \pi(12)^2$
$\quad \approx 542.9$ $\qquad\qquad\quad = 144\pi \approx 452.4$

$s = L + B$
$\quad \approx 542.9 + 452.4$
$\quad \approx 995.3$ square centimeters

8. $L = \frac{1}{2}Cs$
$\quad = \frac{1}{2}(\pi d)(s)$
$\quad = \frac{1}{2}\pi(12)(8)$
$\quad = 48\pi$
$\quad \approx 150.8$ square meters

$S = L + B$
$\quad = 48\pi + \pi r^2$
$\quad = 48\pi + \pi(6)^2$
$\quad = 48\pi + 36\pi$
$\quad = 84\pi$
$\quad \approx 263.9$ square meters

9. $L = \frac{1}{2}Cs$
$\quad = \frac{1}{2}(2\pi r)(s)$
$\quad = \frac{1}{2}(2)(\pi)(4)(9)$
$\quad = 36\pi$
$\quad \approx 113.1$ square inches

$S = L + B$
$S = 36\pi + \pi r^2$
$\quad = 36\pi + \pi(4)^2$
$\quad = 36\pi + 16\pi$
$\quad = 52\pi$
$\quad \approx 163.4$ square inches

10. $L = \frac{1}{2}Cs$
$\quad = \frac{1}{2}(2\pi r)(s)$
$\quad = \frac{1}{2}(2)(\pi)(20)(3.2)$
$\quad = 64\pi$
$\quad \approx 201.1$ square
$\qquad$ centimeters

$S = L + B$
$\quad = 64\pi + \pi r^2$
$\quad = 64\pi + \pi(20)^2$
$\quad = 64\pi + 400\pi$
$\quad = 464\pi$
$\quad \approx 1457.7$ square
$\qquad$ centimeters

11. $L = \frac{1}{2}Cs$
$\quad = \frac{1}{2}(\pi d)(s)$
$\quad = \frac{1}{2}\pi(10)(11)$
$\quad = 55\pi$
$\quad \approx 172.8$ square
$\qquad$ meters

$S = L + B$
$\quad = 55\pi + \pi r^2$
$\quad = 55\pi + \pi(5)^2$
$\quad = 55\pi + 25\pi$
$\quad = 80\pi$
$\quad \approx 251.3$ square
$\qquad$ meters

12. $L = \frac{1}{2}Cs$

$\quad = \frac{1}{2}(\pi d)(s)$

$\quad = \frac{1}{2}\pi(8)(8)$

$\quad = 32\pi$

$\quad \approx 100.5$ square feet

$S = L + B$

$\quad = 32\pi + \pi r^2$

$\quad = 32\pi + \pi(4)^2$

$\quad = 32\pi + 16\pi$

$\quad = 48\pi$

$\quad \approx 150.8$ square feet

13. $L = \frac{1}{2}Cs$

$\quad = \frac{1}{2}(2\pi r)(s)$

$\quad = \frac{1}{2}(2)(\pi)(2.5)(4)$

$\quad = 10\pi$

$\quad \approx 31.4$ square yards

$S = L + B$

$\quad = 10\pi + \pi r^2$

$\quad = 10\pi + \pi(25)2$

$\quad = 10\pi + 6.25\pi$

$\quad = 16.25\pi$

$\quad \approx 51.1$ square yards

14. $L = \frac{1}{2}ps$

$\quad = \frac{1}{2}(4 \cdot 8)(6)$

$\quad = \frac{1}{2}(32)(6)$

$\quad = 96$ square centimeters

$S = L + B$

$\quad = 96 + s^2$

$\quad = 96 + (8)^2$

$\quad = 96 + 64$

$\quad = 160$ square centimeters

15. $L = \frac{1}{2}ps$

$\quad = \frac{1}{2}(4 \cdot 16)(10)$

$\quad = \frac{1}{2}(64)(10)$

$\quad = 320$ square yards

$S = L + B$

$\quad = 320 + s^2$

$\quad = 320 + (16)^2$

$\quad = 320 + 256$

$\quad = 576$ square yards

16. $L = \frac{1}{2}ps$

$\quad = \frac{1}{2}(4 \cdot 4)(5)$

$\quad = \frac{1}{2}(16)(5)$

$\quad = 40$ square inches

$S = L + B$

$\quad = 40 + s^2$

$\quad = 40 + (4)^2$

$\quad = 40 + 16$

$\quad = 56$ square inches

17. $L = \frac{1}{2}ps$

$\quad = \frac{1}{2}(4 \cdot 7)(9)$

$\quad = \frac{1}{2}(28)(9)$

$\quad = 126$ square meters

$S = L + B$

$\quad = 126 + s^2$

$\quad = 126 + 7^2$

$\quad = 126 + 49$

$\quad = 175$ square meters

18. $S = L + B$

$\quad = \frac{1}{2}Cs + \pi r^2$

$\quad = \frac{1}{2}(2\pi r)(s) + \pi r^2$

$\quad = \frac{1}{2}(2)(\pi)(6)(7) + \pi(6)^2$

$\quad = 42\pi + 36\pi$

$\quad = 78\pi$

$\quad \approx 245$ square inches

19. $S = L + B$

$\quad = \frac{1}{2}Cs + \pi r^2$

$\quad = \frac{1}{2}(2\pi r)(s) + \pi r^2$

$\quad = \frac{1}{2}(2)(\pi)(2.5)(6) + \pi(2.5)^2$

$\quad = 15\pi + 6.25\pi$

$\quad = 21.25\pi$

$\quad \approx 66.8$ square meters

20. $S = L + B$

$\quad = \frac{1}{2}Cs + \pi r^2$

$\quad = \frac{1}{2}(\pi d)(s) + \pi r^2$

$\quad = \frac{1}{2}(\pi)(8)(5) + \pi(4)^2$

$\quad = 20\pi + 16\pi$

$\quad = 36\pi$

$\quad \approx 113.1$ square feet

21. $S = L + B$

$\quad = \frac{1}{2}Cs + \pi r^2$

$\quad = \frac{1}{2}(\pi d)(s) + \pi r^2$

$\quad = \frac{1}{2}(\pi)(9)(9) + \pi(4.5)^2$

$\quad = 40.5\pi + 20.25\pi$

$\quad = 60.75\pi$

$\quad \approx 190.9$ square centimeters

22. $S = L + B$

$\quad = \frac{1}{2}Cs + \pi r^2$

$\quad = \frac{1}{2}(\pi r)(s) + \pi r^2$

$\quad = \frac{1}{2}(2)(\pi)(17) + \pi(5)^2$

$\quad = 85\pi + 25\pi$

$\quad = 110\pi$

$\quad \approx 345.6$ square inches

23. $S = L + B$

$\quad = \frac{1}{2}Cs + \pi r^2$

$\quad = \frac{1}{2}(2\pi r)(s) + \pi r^2$

$\quad = \frac{1}{2}(2)(\pi)(5)(6.5) + \pi(5)^2$

$\quad = 32.5\pi + 25\pi$

$\quad = 57.5\pi$

$\quad \approx 180.6$ square centimeters

24. $S = L + B$

$\quad = \frac{1}{2}Cs + \pi r^2$

$\quad = \frac{1}{2}(\pi d)(s) + \pi r^2$

$\quad = \frac{1}{2}(\pi)(4)(15) + \pi(2)^2$

$\quad = 30\pi + 4\pi$

$\quad = 34\pi$

$\quad \approx 106.8$ square yards

25. $S = L + B$

$\quad = \frac{1}{2}Cs + \pi r^2$

$\quad = \frac{1}{2}(\pi d)(s) + \pi r^2$

$\quad = \frac{1}{2}(\pi)(7.2)(1.9) + \pi(3.6)^2$

$\quad = 68.4\pi + 12.96\pi$

$\quad = 19.8\pi$

$\quad \approx 62.2$ square meters

26. $S = L + B$

$\quad = \frac{1}{2}Cs + \pi r^2$

$\quad = \frac{1}{2}(2\pi r)(s) + \pi r^2$

$\quad = \frac{1}{2}(2)(\pi)\left(2\frac{1}{2}\right)\left(3\frac{3}{4}\right) + \pi\left(2\frac{1}{2}\right)^2$

$\quad = 9\frac{3}{8}\pi + 6\frac{1}{4}\pi$

$\quad = 15\frac{5}{8}\pi$

$\quad \approx 49.1$ square inches

27. $S = L + B$

$\quad = \frac{1}{2}Cs + \pi r^2$

$\quad = \frac{1}{2}(2\pi r)(s) + \pi r^2$

$\quad = \frac{1}{2}(2)(\pi)\left(4\frac{1}{5}\right)\left(1\frac{2}{5}\right) + \pi\left(4\frac{1}{5}\right)^2$

$\quad = 588\pi + 17.64\pi$

$\quad = 23.52\pi$

$\quad \approx 73.9$ square feet

28. $S = L + B$

$\quad = \frac{1}{2}Cs + \pi r^2$

$\quad = \frac{1}{2}(\pi d)(s) + \pi r^2$

$\quad = \frac{1}{2}(\pi)(8.9)(7.5) + \pi(4.45)^2$

$\quad = 33.375\pi + 19.8025\pi$

$\quad = 53.1775\pi$

$\quad \approx 167.1$ square feet

29. $S = L + B$

$\quad = \frac{1}{2}Cs + \pi r^2$

$\quad = \frac{1}{2}(\pi d)(s) + \pi r^2$

$\quad = \frac{1}{2}(\pi)(16)(34) + \pi(8)^2$

$\quad = 272\pi + 64\pi$

$\quad = 336\pi$

$\quad \approx 1055.6$ square centimeters

30. To find the surface area of a paper cone, find only the lateral surface area. There is no base.

$\quad S = L$

$\quad = \frac{1}{2}Cs$

$\quad = \frac{1}{2}(\pi d)(s)$

$\quad = \frac{1}{2}(\pi)(3)(4)$

$\quad = 6\pi$

$\quad \approx 18.8$

The surface area of the cone is approximately 18.8 square inches.

31. Use the Pythagorean Theorem. Let b represent the height of the cone, a represent the radius, and c represent the slant height.

$\quad a^2 + b^2 = c^2$

$\quad b^2 = c^2 - a^2$

$\quad b^2 = (4)^2 - (1.5)^2$

$\quad b^2 = 16 - 2.25$

$\quad b^2 = 13.75$

$\quad \sqrt{b^2} = \sqrt{13.75}$

$\quad b \approx 3.7$

The height of the cone is approximately 3.7 inches.

32. Use the Pythagorean Theorem. Let b represent the height of the cone, a represent the radius, and c represent the slant height.

$\quad a^2 + b^2 = c^2$

$\quad (1.5)^2 + (4)^2 = c^2$

$\quad 2.25 + 16 = c^2$

$\quad 18.25 = c^2$

$\quad \sqrt{18.95} = \sqrt{c^2}$

$\quad 4.3 \approx c$

The slant height of the cone is approximately 4.3 inches.

33. To find the surface area of a paper cone, find only the lateral surface area. There is no base.

$\quad S = L$

$\quad = \frac{1}{2}Cs$

$\quad = \frac{1}{2}(\pi d)(s)$

$\quad = \frac{1}{2}(\pi)(2)(4)$

$\quad = 4\pi$

$\quad \approx 12.57$

The surface area of the paper cone is approximately 12.6 square inches.

34. To find the area of the roof, find only the lateral surface area. There is no base.

$\quad S = L$

$\quad = \frac{1}{2}ps$

$\quad = \frac{1}{2}(12 + 12 + 12 + 12)(16)$

$\quad = \frac{1}{2}(48)(16)$

$\quad = 384$

The area of the roof is 384 square feet.

35. Multiply the number of square feet of area by 4.

$\quad 384 \cdot 4 = 1536$

It will cost $1536 to cover the roof.

36. Let a represent $\frac{1}{2}$ of the length of a side of the triangular face, b represent the height of the triangular face, and c represent the other side of the triangular face.

$\quad a^2 + b^2 = c^2$

$\quad b^2 = c^2 - a^2$

$\quad b^2 = (8)^2 - (4)^2$

$\quad b^2 = 64 - 16$

$\quad b^2 = 48$

$\quad \sqrt{b^2} = \sqrt{48}$

$\quad b = \sqrt{48}$

Therefore, the height of each triangular face is $\sqrt{48}$ centimeters.

37. $A = \frac{1}{2}bh$

$\quad = \frac{1}{2}(8)(\sqrt{48})$

$\quad = 4\sqrt{48}$

$\quad \approx 27.7$

The area of one triangular face is $4\sqrt{48}$, or approximately 27.7 square centimeters. To find the total surface area, multiply the area of one face by 4.

$\quad 4 \cdot 4\sqrt{48} = 16\sqrt{48} \approx 110.9$

The total surface area is approximately 110.9 square centimeters.

38.

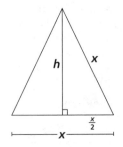

To find h, use the "Pythagorean" Right-Triangle Theorem.

$$h^2 + \left(\frac{x}{2}\right)^2 = x^2$$
$$h^2 + \frac{x^2}{4} = x^2$$
$$h^2 = x^2 - \frac{x^2}{4}$$
$$h = \frac{3x^2}{4}$$
$$\sqrt{h^2} = \sqrt{\frac{3x^3}{4}}$$
$$h = \frac{x\sqrt{3}}{2}$$

39. Let $Y_1 = X^2 * \sqrt{3}$.

X	Y_1
1	1.7321
2	6.9282
3	15.588
4	27.713
5	43.301
6	62.354
7	84.87
X=1	

To find the area of one triangular face:

$$A = \frac{1}{2}bh$$
$$= \frac{1}{2}(x)\left(\frac{x\sqrt{3}}{2}\right)$$
$$= \frac{x^2\sqrt{3}}{4}$$

$$s = 4A$$
$$= 4\left(\frac{x^2\sqrt{3}}{4}\right)$$
$$= x^2\sqrt{3}$$

PAGE 675, LOOK BACK

40. $C = 2\pi r$
$= 2\pi(5.78)$
$= 11.56\pi$
≈ 36.3 meters

$A = \pi r^2$
$= \pi(5.78)^2$
$= 33.4084\pi$
≈ 105 square meters

41. $C = 2\pi r$
$= 2\pi\left(\frac{4}{3}\right)$
$= \frac{8\pi}{3}$
≈ 8.4 inches

$A = \pi r^2$
$= \pi\left(\frac{4}{3}\right)^2$
$= \frac{16\pi}{9}$
≈ 5.6 square inches

42. $C = \pi d$
$= \pi\left(2\frac{3}{8}\right)$
≈ 7.5 inches

$A = \pi r^2$
$= \pi\left(1\frac{3}{16}\right)^2$
≈ 4.4 square inches

43. $C = \pi d$
$= 63\pi$
≈ 197.9 centimeters

$A = \pi r^2$
$= \pi(31.5)^2$
$= 992.25\pi$
≈ 3117.2 square centimeters

44. $C = 2\pi r$
$= 2(\pi)(2.01)$
$= 4.02\pi$
≈ 12.6 meters

$A = \pi r^2$
$= \pi(2.01)^2$
$= 4.0401\pi$
≈ 12.7 square meters

45. $C = \pi d$
$= 5.2\pi$
$= 16.3$ feet

$A = \pi r^2$
$= \pi(2.6)^2$
$= 6.76\pi$
≈ 21.2 square feet

46. $S = 2(l \cdot w + l \cdot h + w \cdot h)$
$= 2[(3.4 \cdot 2.5) + (3.4 \cdot 1.5) + (2.5 \cdot 1.5)]$
$= 2(8.5 + 5.1 + 3.75)$
$= 2(17.35)$
$= 34.7$ square meters

$V = Bh$
$= lwh$
$= (3.4)(2.5)(1.5)$
≈ 12.8 cubic centimeters

47. $S = 2(l \cdot w + l \cdot h + w \cdot h)$
$= 2[(2.4 \cdot 1.9) + (2.4 \cdot 3.6) + (1.9 \cdot 3.6)]$
$= 2(4.56 + 8.64 + 6.84)$
$= 2(20.04)$
$= 40.1$ square centimeters

$V = Bh$
$= lwh$
$= (2.4)(1.9)(3.6)$
≈ 16.4 cubic centimeters

48. $S = 2(l \cdot w + l \cdot h + w \cdot h)$
$\quad = 2[(1 \cdot 1) + (1 \cdot 5) + (1 \cdot 5)]$
$\quad = 2(1 + 5 + 5)$
$\quad = 2(11)$
$\quad = 22$ square centimeters

$V = Bh$
$\quad = lwh$
$\quad = 1 \cdot 1 \cdot 5$
$\quad \approx 5$ cubic centimeters

PAGE 675, LOOK BEYOND

49.

Base sides	Vertices, V	Faces, F	Edges, E
3	4	4	6
4	5	5	8
5	6	6	10
6	7	7	12
7	8	8	14
8	9	9	16
n	$n + 1$	$n + 1$	$2n$

Yes; the generalization for n satisfies Euler's formula $V + F - E = 2$.
$V + F - E = (n + 1) + (n + 1) - (2n)$
$V + F - E = n + n - 2n + 1 + 1$
$V + F - E = 2n - 2n + 2$
$V + F - E = 0 + 2$
$V + F - E = 2$

12.7 PAGES 679–681, PRACTICE & APPLY

5. $S = 4\pi r^2$
$\quad = 4(\pi)(3)^2$
$\quad = 4(\pi)(9)$
$\quad = 36\pi$
$\quad \approx 113.1$ square inches

$V = \dfrac{4\pi r^3}{3}$
$\quad = \dfrac{4(\pi)(3)^3}{3}$
$\quad = \dfrac{4(\pi)(27)}{3}$
$\quad = \dfrac{108\pi}{3}$
$\quad = 36\pi$
$\quad \approx 113.1$ cubic inches

6. $S = 4\pi r^2$
$\quad = 4(\pi)(2.75)^2$
$\quad = 4(\pi)(7.5625)$
$\quad = 30.25\pi$
$\quad \approx 95$ square centimeters

$V = \dfrac{4\pi r^3}{3}$
$\quad = \dfrac{4(\pi)(2.75)^3}{3}$
$\quad = \dfrac{4(\pi)(20.796875)}{3}$
$\quad = \dfrac{83.1875\pi}{3}$
$\quad \approx 87.1$ cubic centimeters

7. $S = 4\pi r^2$
$\quad = 4(\pi)(6)^2$
$\quad = 4(\pi)(36)$
$\quad = 144\pi$
$\quad \approx 452.4$ square yards

$V = \dfrac{4\pi r^3}{3}$
$\quad = \dfrac{4(\pi)(6)^3}{3}$
$\quad = \dfrac{4(\pi)(216)}{3}$
$\quad = \dfrac{864\pi}{3}$
$\quad = 288\pi$
$\quad \approx 904.8$ cubic yards

8. $S = 4\pi r^2$
$\quad = 4(\pi)(9)^2$
$\quad = 4(\pi)(81)$
$\quad = 324\pi$
$\quad \approx 1017.9$ square centimeters

$V = \dfrac{4\pi r^3}{3}$
$\quad = \dfrac{4(\pi)(9)^3}{3}$
$\quad = \dfrac{4(\pi)(729)}{3}$
$\quad = \dfrac{2916\pi}{3}$
$\quad = 972\pi$
$\quad \approx 3053.6$ cubic centimeters

9. $S = 4\pi r^2$
$\quad = 4(\pi)(13)^2$
$\quad = 4(\pi)(169)$
$\quad = 676\pi$
$\quad \approx 2123.7$ square yards

$V = \dfrac{4\pi r^3}{3}$
$\quad = \dfrac{4(\pi)(13)^3}{3}$
$\quad = \dfrac{4(\pi)(2197)}{3}$
$\quad = \dfrac{8788\pi}{3}$
$\quad \approx 9202.8$ cubic yards

10. $S = 4\pi r^2$
$\quad = 4(\pi)\left(\dfrac{5}{2\pi}\right)^2$
$\quad = 4(\pi)\left(\dfrac{25}{4\pi^2}\right)$
$\quad = \dfrac{25}{\pi}$
$\quad \approx 8$ square feet

$V = \dfrac{4\pi r^3}{3}$
$\quad = \dfrac{4(\pi)\left(\frac{5}{2\pi}\right)^3}{3}$
$\quad = \dfrac{4(\pi)\left(\frac{125}{8\pi^3}\right)}{3}$
$\quad = \dfrac{\frac{125}{2\pi^2}}{3}$
$\quad = 2.1$ cubic feet

11. Divide the formula for the surface area of a sphere by 2.
$$S = \frac{4\pi r^2}{2} = 2\pi r^2$$
Now substitute 3.5 for r.
$S = 2\pi r^2$
$\quad = 2\pi(3.5)^2$
$\quad = 2(\pi)(12.25)$
$\quad = 24.5\pi$
$\quad \approx 77$

The surface area of a bowl shaped like a hemisphere is approximately 77 square centimeters.

12. Divide the formula for the volume of a sphere by 2.

$$V = \left(\frac{4\pi r^3}{3}\right)\left(\frac{1}{2}\right) = \frac{4\pi r^3}{6}$$

Now substitute 3.5 for r.

$$V = \frac{4\pi r^3}{6}$$

$$= \frac{4\pi(3.5)^3}{6}$$

$$= \frac{4(\pi)(42.875)}{6}$$

$$= \frac{171.5\pi}{6}$$

$$\approx 89.8$$

The volume of a hemisphere with a radius of 3.5 centimeters is approximately 89.8 cubic centimeters.

13. $S = 4\pi r^2$
$= 4(\pi)(7)^2$
$= 4(\pi)(49)$
$= 196\pi$
≈ 615.8 square inches

$$V = \frac{4\pi r^3}{3}$$

$$= \frac{4(\pi)(7)^3}{3}$$

$$= \frac{4(\pi)(343)}{3}$$

$$= \frac{1372\pi}{3}$$

≈ 1436.8 cubic inches

14. $S = 4\pi r^2$
$= 4(\pi)(8)^2$
$= 4(\pi)(64)$
$= 256\pi$
≈ 804.2 square centimeters

$$V = \frac{4\pi r^3}{3}$$

$$= \frac{4(\pi)(8)^3}{3}$$

$$= \frac{4(\pi)(512)}{3}$$

$$= \frac{2048\pi}{3}$$

≈ 2144.7 cubic centimeters

15. $S = 4\pi r^2$
$= 4(\pi)(10)^2$
$= 4(\pi)(100)$
$= 400\pi$
≈ 1256.6 square meters

$$V = \frac{4\pi r^3}{3}$$

$$= \frac{4(\pi)(10)^3}{3}$$

$$= \frac{4(\pi)(1000)}{3}$$

$$= \frac{4000\pi}{3}$$

≈ 4188.8 cubic meters

16. $S = 4\pi r^2$
$= 4(\pi)(4.25)^2$
$= 4(\pi)(18.0625)$
$= 72.25\pi$
≈ 227 square yards

$$V = \frac{4\pi r^3}{3}$$

$$= \frac{4(\pi)(4.25)^3}{3}$$

$$= \frac{4(\pi)(76.765625)}{3}$$

$$= \frac{307.0625\pi}{3}$$

≈ 321.6 cubic yards

17. $S = 4\pi r^2$
$= 4(\pi)(9)^2$
$= 4(\pi)(81)$
$= 324\pi$
$= 1017.9$ square inches

$$V = \frac{4\pi r^3}{3}$$

$$= \frac{4(\pi)(9)^3}{3}$$

$$= \frac{4(\pi)(729)}{3}$$

$$= \frac{2916\pi}{3}$$

$= 972\pi$
≈ 3053.6 cubic inches

18. $S = 4\pi r^2$
$= 4(\pi)(11.4)^2$
$= 4(\pi)(129.96)$
$= 519.84\pi$
≈ 1633.1 square centimeters

$$V = \frac{4\pi r^3}{3}$$

$$= \frac{4(\pi)(11.4)^3}{3}$$

$$= \frac{4(\pi)(1481.544)}{3}$$

$$= \frac{5926.176\pi}{3}$$

≈ 6205.9 cubic centimeters

19. $S = 4\pi r^2$
$= 4(\pi)(3.5)^2$
$= 4(\pi)(12.25)$
$= 49\pi$
≈ 153.9 square feet

$$V = \frac{4\pi r^3}{3}$$

$$= \frac{4(\pi)(3.5)^3}{3}$$

$$= \frac{4(\pi)(42.875)}{3}$$

$$= \frac{171.5\pi}{3}$$

≈ 179.6 cubic feet

20. $S = 4\pi r^2$
$= 4(\pi)(2)^2$
$= 4(\pi)(4)$
$= 16\pi$
≈ 50.3 square meters

$$V = \frac{4\pi r^3}{3}$$

$$= \frac{4(\pi)(2)^3}{3}$$

$$= \frac{4(\pi)(8)}{3}$$

$$= \frac{32\pi}{3}$$

≈ 33.5 cubic meters

21. $S = 4\pi r^2$
$= 4(\pi)(3.2)^2$
$= 4(\pi)(10.24)$
$= 40.96\pi$
≈ 128.7 square meters

$$V = \frac{4\pi r^3}{3}$$

$$= \frac{4(\pi)(3.2)^3}{3}$$

$$= \frac{4(\pi)(32.768)}{3}$$

$$= \frac{131.072\pi}{3}$$

≈ 137.3 cubic meters

22. $S = 4\pi r^2$
$= 4(\pi)(2.5)^2$
$= 4(\pi)(6.25)$
$= 25\pi$
≈ 78.5 square centimeters

$$V = \frac{4\pi r^3}{3}$$

$$= \frac{4(\pi)(2.5)^3}{3}$$

$$= \frac{4(\pi)(15.625)}{3}$$

$$= \frac{62.5\pi}{3}$$

≈ 65.4 cubic centimeters

23. $S = 4\pi r^2$
$= 4(\pi)(12)^2$
$= 4(\pi)(144)$
$= 576\pi$
≈ 1809.6 square inches

$$V = \frac{4\pi r^3}{3}$$

$$= \frac{4(\pi)(12)^3}{3}$$

$$= \frac{4(\pi)(1728)}{3}$$

$$= \frac{6912\pi}{3}$$

$= 2304\pi$
≈ 7238.2 cubic inches

24. $S = 4\pi r^2$
$= 4(\pi)(1.95)^2$
$= 4(\pi)(3.8025)$
$= 15.21\pi$
≈ 47.8 square meters

$$V = \frac{4\pi r^3}{3}$$

$$= \frac{4(\pi)(1.95)^3}{3}$$

$$= \frac{4(\pi)(7.414875)}{3}$$

$$= \frac{29.6595\pi}{3}$$

≈ 31.1 cubic meters

25. $S = 4\pi r^2$
$= 4(\pi)(6)^2$
$= 4(\pi)(36)$
$= 144\pi$
≈ 452.4 square feet

$$V = \frac{4\pi r^3}{3}$$

$$= \frac{4(\pi)(6)^3}{3}$$

$$= \frac{4(\pi)(216)}{3}$$

$$= \frac{864\pi}{3}$$

$= 288\pi$
≈ 904.8 cubic feet

26. $S = 4\pi r^2$
$= 4(\pi)(3)^2$
$= 4(\pi)(9)$
$= 36\pi$
≈ 113.1 square feet

$$V = \frac{4\pi r^3}{3}$$

$$= \frac{4(\pi)(3)^3}{3}$$

$$= \frac{4(\pi)(27)}{3}$$

$$= \frac{108\pi}{3}$$

$= 36\pi$
≈ 113.1 cubic feet

27. $S = 4\pi r^2$
$= 4(\pi)(1.04)^2$
$= 4(\pi)(1.0816)$
$= 4.3264\pi$
≈ 13.6 square meters

$V = \dfrac{4\pi r^3}{3}$
$= \dfrac{4(\pi)(1.04)^3}{3}$
$= \dfrac{4(\pi)(1.124864)}{3}$
$= \dfrac{4.499456\pi}{3}$
≈ 4.7 cubic meters

28. $S = 4\pi r^2$
$= 4\pi(4.3)^2$
$= 4\pi(18.49)$
$= 73.96\pi$
≈ 232.4 square meters

$V = \dfrac{4\pi r^3}{3}$
$= \dfrac{4\pi(4.3)^3}{3}$
$= \dfrac{4\pi(79.507)}{3}$
$= \dfrac{318.028\pi}{3}$
≈ 333 cubic meters

29. $S = 4\pi r^2$
$= 4(\pi)(6)^2$
$= 4(\pi)(36)$
$= 144\pi$
≈ 452.4 square inches

$V = \dfrac{4\pi r^3}{3}$
$= \dfrac{4(\pi)(6)^3}{3}$
$= \dfrac{4(\pi)(216)}{3}$
$= \dfrac{864\pi}{3}$
$= 288\pi$
≈ 904.8 cubic inches

30. $S = 4\pi r^2$
$= 4(\pi)(6.5)^2$
$= 4(\pi)(42.25)$
$= 169\pi$
≈ 530.9 square centimeters

$V = \dfrac{4\pi r^3}{3}$
$= \dfrac{4(\pi)(6.5)^3}{3}$
$= \dfrac{4(\pi)(274.625)}{3}$
$= \dfrac{1098.5\pi}{3}$
≈ 1150.3 cubic centimeters

31. $S = 4\pi r^2$
$= 4(\pi)(9.35)^2$
$= 4(\pi)(87.4225)$
$= 349.69\pi$
≈ 1098.6 square centimeters

$V = \dfrac{4\pi r^3}{3}$
$= \dfrac{4(\pi)(9.35)^3}{3}$
$= \dfrac{4(\pi)(817.400375)}{3}$
$= \dfrac{3269.6015\pi}{3}$
≈ 3423.9 cubic centimeters

32. $S = 4\pi r^2$
$= 4(\pi)(19)^2$
$= 4(\pi)(361)$
$= 1444\pi$
≈ 4536.5 square inches

$V = \dfrac{4\pi r^3}{3}$
$= \dfrac{4(\pi)(19)^3}{3}$
$= \dfrac{4(\pi)(6859)}{3}$
$= \dfrac{27,436\pi}{3}$
$\approx 28,730.9$ cubic inches

33. $S = 4\pi r^2$
$= 4\pi(7.4)^2$
$= 4\pi(54.76)$
$= 219.04\pi$
≈ 688.1 square meters

$V = \dfrac{4\pi r^3}{3}$
$= \dfrac{4\pi(7.4)^3}{3}$
$= \dfrac{4\pi(405.224)}{3}$
$= \dfrac{1620.896\pi}{3}$
≈ 1697.4 cubic meters

34. $S = 4\pi r^2$
$= 4(\pi)(13.5)^2$
$= 4(\pi)(182.25)$
$= 729\pi$
≈ 2290.2 square feet

$V = \dfrac{4\pi r^3}{3}$
$= \dfrac{4(\pi)(13.5)^3}{3}$
$= \dfrac{4(\pi)(2460.375)}{3}$
$= \dfrac{9841.5\pi}{3}$
$\approx 10,306$ cubic feet

35. $S = 4\pi r^2$
$= 4(\pi)(3.85)^2$
$= 4(\pi)(14.8225)$
$= 59.29\pi$
≈ 186.3 square feet

$V = \dfrac{4\pi r^3}{3}$
$= \dfrac{4(\pi)(3.85)^3}{3}$
$= \dfrac{4(\pi)(57.066625)}{3}$
$= \dfrac{228.2665\pi}{3}$
≈ 239.0 cubic feet

36. $S = 4\pi r^2$
$= 4(\pi)(4.23)^2$
$= 4(\pi)(17.8929)$
$= 71.5716\pi$
≈ 224.8 square meters

$V = \dfrac{4\pi r^3}{3}$
$= \dfrac{4(\pi)(4.23)^3}{3}$
$= \dfrac{4(\pi)(75.686967)}{3}$
$= \dfrac{302.747868\pi}{3}$
≈ 317 cubic meters

37. $S = 4\pi r^2$
$= 4(\pi)(18)^2$
$= 4(\pi)(324)$
$= 1296\pi$
≈ 4071.5 square centimeters

$V = \dfrac{4\pi r^3}{3}$
$= \dfrac{4(\pi)(18)^3}{3}$
$= \dfrac{4(\pi)(5832)}{3}$
$= \dfrac{23,328\pi}{3}$
$= 7776\pi$
$\approx 24,429$ cubic centimeters

38. $S = 4\pi r^2$
$= 4(\pi)(17)^2$
$= 4(\pi)(289)$
$= 1156\pi$
≈ 3631.7 square meters

$V = \dfrac{4\pi r^3}{3}$
$= \dfrac{4(\pi)(17)^3}{3}$
$= \dfrac{4(\pi)(4913)}{3}$
$= \dfrac{19,652\pi}{3}$
$\approx 20,579.5$ cubic meters

39. $S = 4\pi r^2$
$= 4(\pi)\left(1\frac{3}{7}\right)^2$
$= 4(\pi)\left(\frac{10}{7}\right)^2$
$= 4(\pi)\left(\frac{100}{49}\right)$
$= \frac{400}{49}\pi$
≈ 25.6 square feet

$V = \dfrac{4\pi r^3}{3}$
$= \dfrac{4(\pi)\left(1\frac{3}{7}\right)^3}{3}$
$= \dfrac{4(\pi)\left(\frac{10}{7}\right)^3}{3}$
$= \dfrac{4\dfrac{(\pi)\left(\frac{1000}{343}\right)}{3}}{}$
≈ 12.2 cubic feet

40. $S = 4\pi r^2$
$= 4(\pi)\left(5\frac{1}{5}\right)^2$
$= 4(\pi)\left(\frac{26}{5}\right)^2$
$= 4(\pi)\left(\frac{676}{25}\right)$
$= \frac{2704}{25}\pi$
≈ 339.8 square feet

$V = \dfrac{4\pi r^3}{3}$
$= \dfrac{4(\pi)\left(5\frac{1}{5}\right)^3}{3}$
$= \dfrac{4(\pi)\left(\frac{26}{5}\right)^3}{3}$
$= \dfrac{4(\pi)\left(\frac{17,576}{125}\right)}{3}$
≈ 589 cubic feet

41. $S = 4\pi r^2$

$\quad = 4(\pi)\left(2\frac{1}{4}\right)^2$

$\quad = 4(\pi)\left(\frac{9}{4}\right)^2$

$\quad = 4(\pi)\left(\frac{81}{16}\right)$

$\quad = \frac{324}{16}\pi$

$\quad \approx 63.6$ square feet

$V = \frac{4\pi r^3}{3}$

$\quad = \frac{4(\pi)\left(2\frac{1}{4}\right)^3}{3}$

$\quad = \frac{4(\pi)\left(\frac{9}{4}\right)^3}{3}$

$\quad = \frac{4(\pi)\left(\frac{729}{64}\right)}{3}$

$\quad \approx 47.7$ cubic feet

42. $S = 4\pi r^2$

$\quad = 4(\pi)\left(3\frac{3}{4}\right)^2$

$\quad = 4(\pi)\left(\frac{15}{4}\right)^2$

$\quad = 4(\pi)\left(\frac{225}{16}\right)$

$\quad = \frac{900}{16}\pi$

$\quad \approx 176.7$ square feet

$V = \frac{4\pi r^3}{3}$

$\quad = \frac{4(\pi)\left(3\frac{3}{4}\right)^3}{3}$

$\quad = \frac{4(\pi)\left(\frac{15}{4}\right)^3}{3}$

$\quad \approx 220.9$ cubic feet

For Exercises 43–45, answers may vary. Sample answers are given.

	Object	Circumference	Radius	Surface area	Volume
43.	tennis ball	$3\pi \approx 9.4$ in.	1.5 in.	$9\pi \approx 28.3$ in.^{2}	$4.5\pi \approx 14.1$ in.^{3}
44.	basketball	$10\pi \approx 31.4$ in.	5 in.	$100\pi \approx 314.2$ in.^{2}	$166.67\pi \approx 523.6$ in.^{3}
45.	bowling	$9\pi \approx 28.3$ in.	4.5 in.	$81\pi \approx 254.5$ in.^{2}	$121.5\pi \approx 381.7$ in.^{3}

46. The surface area quadruples. Substitute $2r$ for r in the equation $S = 4\pi r^2$.

$\quad S = 4\pi r^2$

$\quad S = 4\pi(2r)^2$

$\quad S = 4\pi(4r^2)$

$\quad S = 4(4\pi r^2)$

47. The volume increases by a factor of 8. Substitute $2r$ for r in the equation $V = \frac{4\pi r^3}{3}$.

$\quad V = \frac{4\pi r^3}{3}$

$\quad V = \frac{4\pi(2r)^3}{3}$

$\quad V = \frac{4\pi(8r^3)}{3}$

$\quad V = 8\left(\frac{4\pi r^3}{3}\right)$

48. The surface area increases by a factor of 9. Substitute $3r$ for r in the equation $S = 4\pi r^2$.

$\quad S = 4\pi r^2$

$\quad S = 4\pi(3r)^2$

$\quad S = 4\pi(9r^2)$

$\quad S = 9(4\pi r^2)$

49. The volume increases by a factor of 27. Substitute $3r$ for r in the equation $V = \frac{4\pi r^3}{3}$.

$\quad V = \frac{4\pi r^3}{3}$

$\quad V = \frac{4\pi(3r)^3}{3}$

$\quad V = \frac{4\pi(27r^3)}{3}$

$\quad V = 27\left(\frac{4\pi r^3}{3}\right)$

50. When the radius is multiplied by n, the surface area increases by a factor of n^2 and the volume increases by a factor of n^3.

51. Substitute for C and solve for r.

$\quad C = 2\pi r$

$\quad 24{,}900 = 2\pi r$

$\quad 3963 \approx r$

52. Substitute for r and solve for S.

$\quad S = 4\pi r^2$

$\quad S = 4\pi(3963)^2$

$\quad S \approx 197{,}359{,}487.5$

53. Multiply 197,359,487.5 by 29% to find the land area.

$\quad (29\%)(197{,}359{,}487.5) = (0.29)(197{,}359{,}487.5)$
$\quad\quad\quad\quad\quad\quad\quad\quad\quad\quad \approx 57{,}234{,}251.4$

54. $D = \dfrac{\text{population}}{\text{land area}}$

$\quad D = \dfrac{6{,}000{,}000{,}000 \text{ people}}{57{,}233{,}040.63 \text{ sq mi}} \approx 104.8$

55. Answers may vary. One way is to use a spread sheet with the Year column starting at 1 and ending at 100. The population would start at 6,000,000,000 and increase 1.7% per year (that is, multiply the population by 1.017 to get the next year's population figure). The population density can then be determined by dividing a particular year's population figure by the total land area of the Earth (57,234,251.4 square miles).

	A	B	C
1	Year	Population	Pop. density
2	1	6,000,000,000.0	104.8
3	2	6,102,000,000.0	106.6
4	3	6,205,734,000.0	108.4
5	4	6,311,231,478.0	110.3
6	5	6,418,522,413.1	112.1
7	6	6,527,637,294.1	114.1
8	7	6,638,607,128.1	116.0
9	8	6,751,463,449.3	118.0
10	9	6,866,238,328.0	120.0
11	10	6,982,964,379.5	122.0

	A	B	C
92	91	27,355,018,538.2	477.9
93	92	27,820,052,853.4	486.1
94	93	28,292,994,768.9	494.3
95	94	28,773,975,680.0	502.7
96	95	29,263,133,266.5	511.3
97	96	29,760,606,532.0	520.0
98	97	30,266,536,843.1	528.8
99	98	30,781,067,969.4	537.8
100	99	31,304,346,124.9	547.0
101	100	31,836,520,009.0	556.2

56. $y = 0.5x + 3$

x	-3	-2	-1	0	1	2	3
y	1.5	2	2.5	3	3.5	4	4.5

57. $y = x - 1$

x	-3	-2	-1	0	1	2	3
y	4	-3	-2	-1	0	1	2

58. $y = 5 - 2x$

x	-3	-2	-1	0	1	2	3
y	11	9	7	5	3	1	-1

59. Since $\sqrt{147}$ is between $\sqrt{144}$ and $\sqrt{169}$, a reasonable estimate for $\sqrt{147}$ is between 12 and 13. Since 147 is closer to 144 than to 169, estimate $\sqrt{147}$ to be closer to 12. A reasonable estimate is about 12.1.

60. $\sqrt{19}$ is between $\sqrt{16}$ and $\sqrt{25}$. Since $\sqrt{19}$ is closer to $\sqrt{16}$ than to $\sqrt{25}$, a reasonable estimate is $\sqrt{19} \approx 4.4$.

61. $\sqrt{10}$ is between $\sqrt{9}$ and $\sqrt{16}$. Since $\sqrt{10}$ is closer to $\sqrt{9}$ than to $\sqrt{16}$, a reasonable estimate is $\sqrt{10} \approx 3.2$.

62.
$$x^2 = 15$$
$$\sqrt{x^2} = \sqrt{15}$$
$$x = \pm\sqrt{15}$$
$$x \approx \pm 3.9$$

63.
$$x - 6 = -x + 1$$
$$2x - 6 = 1$$
$$2x = 7$$
$$x = \frac{7}{2}, \text{ or } 3\frac{1}{2}$$

64.
$$3 - (x - 4) = x$$
$$3 - x + 4 = x$$
$$7 - x = x$$
$$7 = 2x$$
$$\frac{7}{2} = x \text{ or } x = 3\frac{1}{2}$$

65. $\begin{cases} x - y = 4 \\ 2x - y = -3 \end{cases} \begin{array}{l} \to \quad -1(x-4) = -1(4) \to \quad -x + y = -4 \\ \to \qquad 2x - y = -3 \quad\; \to \quad \underline{2x - y = -3} \\ \qquad\qquad\qquad\qquad\qquad\qquad\qquad\quad x = -7 \end{array}$

Substitute -7 for x.
$$x - y = 4$$
$$-7 - y = 4$$
$$-y = 11$$
$$y = -11$$
$$(x, y) = (-7, -11)$$

66. Solving for r in the equation
$V = \frac{4\pi r^3}{3}$ gives $r = \sqrt[3]{\frac{3V}{4\pi}}$.
$$V = \frac{4\pi r^3}{3}$$
$$3V = 4\pi r^3$$
$$\frac{3V}{4\pi} = r^3$$
$$\sqrt[3]{\frac{3V}{4\pi}} = \sqrt[3]{r^3 5}$$
$$\sqrt[3]{\frac{3V}{4\pi}} = r$$

67. Substitute 1000 for V.
$$r = \sqrt[3]{\frac{3V}{4\pi}}$$
$$= \sqrt[3]{\frac{3(1000)}{4\pi}}$$
$$= \sqrt[3]{\frac{750}{\pi}}$$
$$\approx 6.2$$
The radius of the sphere is approximately 6.2 centimeters.

68. Find the surface area of the sphere.
$$S = 4\pi r^2$$
$$= 4\pi(s)^2$$
$$= 100\pi$$
$$\approx 314.2 \text{ square centimeters}$$
Find the surface area of the cube.
$$S = 6e^2$$
$$= 6(10)^2$$
$$= 600 \text{ square centimeters}$$
Find the surface area of the cylinder.
$$S = L + B$$
$$= 2\pi rh + 2\pi r^2$$
$$= 2\pi(5)(10) + 2\pi(5)^2$$
$$= 100\pi + 50\pi$$
$$= 150\pi$$
$$\approx 471.2 \text{ square centimeters}$$
The surface area of the sphere is smallest.

69. Let x represent the volume of the sphere and $Y_1 = ((3 * x) \div (4 * \pi)) \,\hat{}\, (1 \div 3)$. Set Tb1 Start = 100 and ΔTb1 = 100.

X	Y₁	
1.000	6.2035	
1.100	6.4038	
1.200	6.5922	
1.300	6.7705	
1.400	6.9398	
1.500	7.1012	
1.600	7.2557	

X=1.200

From the table, a radius of about 6.7 centimeters will give a volume between 1200 and 1300 cubic centimeters.

1. $C = 2\pi r$ $\qquad\qquad$ $A = \pi r^2$
$\quad = 2\pi(4)$ $\qquad\qquad\quad = \pi(4)^2$
$\quad = 8\pi$ $\qquad\qquad\qquad = 16\pi$
$\quad \approx 25.1$ inches $\qquad\quad \approx 50.3$ square inches

2. $C = 2\pi r$ $\qquad\qquad$ $A = \pi r^2$
$\quad = 2\pi(4.25)$ $\qquad\quad = \pi(4.25)^2$
$\quad = 8.5\pi$ $\qquad\qquad\quad = 18.0625\pi$
$\quad \approx 26.7$ feet $\qquad\quad \approx 56.7$ square feet

3. $C = 2\pi r$ $\qquad\qquad\qquad\qquad$ $A = \pi r^2$
$\quad = 2\pi\left(5\frac{1}{2}\right)$ $\qquad\qquad\qquad = \pi\left(5\frac{1}{2}\right)^2$
$\quad = 2\pi\left(\frac{11}{2}\right)$ $\qquad\qquad\qquad = \pi\left(\frac{11}{2}\right)^2$
$\quad = \frac{22}{2}\pi$ $\qquad\qquad\qquad\qquad = \frac{121}{4}\pi$
$\quad = 11\pi$ $\qquad\qquad\qquad\qquad \approx 95.0$ square centimeters
$\quad \approx 34.6$ centimeters

4. $S = 2(l \cdot w + l \cdot h + w \cdot h)$ $\qquad\qquad$ $V = lwh$
$\quad = 2[(5.5 \cdot 10) + (5.5 \cdot 14) + (10 \cdot 14)]$ $\qquad = (5.5)(10)(14)$
$\quad = 2(55 + 77 + 140)$ $\qquad\qquad\qquad\qquad = 770$ cubic
$\quad = 2(272)$ $\qquad\qquad\qquad\qquad\qquad\qquad$ inches
$\quad = 544$ square inches

5. $S = 2(l \cdot w + l \cdot h + w \cdot h)$ $\qquad\qquad$ $V = lwh$
$\quad = 2[(3 \cdot 8.2) + (3 \cdot 15.6) + (8.2 \cdot 15.6)]$ $\qquad = (3)(8.2)(15.6)$
$\quad = 2(24.6 + 46.8 + 127.92)$ $\qquad\qquad\qquad \approx 383.8$ cubic meters
$\quad = 2(199.32)$
$\quad \approx 398.6$ square meters

6. $S = 2(l \cdot w + l \cdot h + w \cdot h)$ $\qquad\qquad$ $V = lwh$
$\quad = 2\left[\left(7\frac{1}{2} \cdot 4\frac{1}{2}\right) + \left(7\frac{1}{2} \cdot 6\frac{3}{4}\right) + \left(4\frac{1}{2} \cdot 6\frac{3}{4}\right)\right]$ $\qquad = \left(7\frac{1}{2}\right)\left(4\frac{1}{2}\right)\left(6\frac{3}{4}\right)$
$\quad = 2\left[\left(\frac{15}{2} \cdot \frac{9}{2}\right) + \left(\frac{15}{2} \cdot \frac{27}{4}\right) + \left(\frac{9}{2} \cdot \frac{27}{4}\right)\right]$ $\qquad = \left(\frac{15}{2}\right)\left(\frac{9}{2}\right)\left(\frac{27}{4}\right)$
$\quad = 2\left(\frac{135}{4} + \frac{405}{8} + \frac{243}{8}\right)$ $\qquad\qquad\qquad\qquad = \frac{3645}{16}$
$\quad = 2\left(\frac{270}{8} + \frac{405}{8} + \frac{243}{8}\right)$ $\qquad\qquad\qquad\qquad \approx 227.8$ cubic yards
$\quad = 2\left(\frac{918}{8}\right)$
$\quad = \frac{1836}{8}$
$\quad = 229.5$ square yards

7. $S = 6e^2$ $\qquad\qquad\qquad$ $V = e^3$
$\quad = 6(9.4)^2$ $\qquad\qquad\quad = (9.4)^3$
$\quad = 6(88.36)$ $\qquad\qquad \approx 830.6$ cubic
$\quad \approx 530.2$ square meters $\qquad$ meters

8. Find the area of the base. $\qquad$ Find the volume.
$\qquad B = \frac{1}{2}bh$ $\qquad\qquad\qquad\qquad V = Bh$
$\qquad\quad = \frac{1}{2}(2)(1.7)$ $\qquad\qquad\qquad\quad = (1.7)(3.5)$
$\qquad\quad = 1.7$ square meters $\qquad\qquad \approx 6.0$ cubic
$\qquad\qquad\qquad\qquad\qquad\qquad\qquad\qquad$ meters
Find the total surface area.
$\qquad S = L + 2B$
$\qquad\quad = hp + 2B$
$\qquad\quad = (3.5)(2 + 2 + 2) + 2(1.7)$
$\qquad\quad = (3.5)(6) + 3.4$
$\qquad\quad = 21 + 3.4$
$\qquad\quad = 24.4$ square meters

9. Find the area of the base. $\qquad$ Find the volume.
$\qquad B = bh$ $\qquad\qquad\qquad\qquad V = Bh$
$\qquad\quad = (5)(3)$ $\qquad\qquad\qquad\quad = (15)(6)$
$\qquad\quad = 15$ square feet $\qquad\qquad\quad = 90$ cubic feet
Find the total surface area.
$\qquad S = L + 2B$
$\qquad\quad = hp + 2B$
$\qquad\quad = 6[2(5) + 2(3.5)] + 2(15)$
$\qquad\quad = 6(10 + 7) + 30$
$\qquad\quad = 6(17) + 30$
$\qquad\quad = 102 + 30$
$\qquad\quad = 132$ square feet

10. Find the area of the base. $\qquad$ Find the volume.
$\qquad B = \frac{(b_1 + b_2)h}{2}$ $\qquad\qquad\qquad V = Bh$
$\qquad\quad = \frac{(4 + 2)(2.3)}{2}$ $\qquad\qquad\qquad = (6.9)(5)$
$\qquad\quad = \frac{(6)(2.3)}{2}$ $\qquad\qquad\qquad\qquad = 34.5$ cubic
$\qquad\qquad\qquad\qquad\qquad\qquad\qquad\qquad$ inches
$\qquad\quad = 6.9$ square inches
Find the total surface area.
$\qquad S = L + 2B$
$\qquad\quad = hp + 2B$
$\qquad\quad = 5[2 + 4 + 2(2.5)] + 2(6.9)$
$\qquad\quad = 5(2 + 4 + 5) + 2(6.9)$
$\qquad\quad = 5(11) + 2(6.9)$
$\qquad\quad = 55 + 13.8$
$\qquad\quad = 68.8$ square inches

11.
$$S = L + 2B$$
$$= 2\pi rh + 2\pi r^2$$
$$= 2\pi(2.5)(6) + 2\pi(2.5)^2$$
$$= 30\pi + 12.5\pi$$
$$= 42.5\pi$$
$$\approx 133.5 \text{ square inches}$$

$$V = Bh$$
$$= \pi r^2 h$$
$$= \pi(2.5)^2(6)$$
$$= 37.5\pi$$
$$\approx 117.8 \text{ cubic inches}$$

12.
$$S = L + 2B$$
$$= 2\pi rh + 2\pi r^2$$
$$= 2\pi(9)(45) + 2\pi(9)^2$$
$$= 810\pi + 162\pi$$
$$= 972\pi$$
$$\approx 3053.6 \text{ square}$$
$$\text{centimeters}$$

$$V = Bh$$
$$= \pi r^2 h$$
$$= \pi(9)^2(45)$$
$$= 3645\pi$$
$$\approx 11{,}451.1 \text{ cubic}$$
$$\text{centimeters}$$

13.
$$S = L + 2B$$
$$= 2\pi rh + 2\pi r^2$$
$$= 2\pi(9.5)(18.5) + 2\pi(9.5)^2$$
$$= 351.5\pi + 180.5\pi$$
$$= 532\pi$$
$$\approx 1671.3 \text{ square meters}$$

$$V = Bh$$
$$= \pi r^2 h$$
$$= \pi(9.5)^2(18.5)$$
$$= 1669.625\pi$$
$$\approx 5245.3 \text{ cubic}$$
$$\text{meters}$$

14.
$$S = L + 2B$$
$$= 2\pi rh + 2\pi r^2$$
$$= 2\pi(50)(150) + 2\pi(50)^2$$
$$= 15{,}000\pi + 5000\pi$$
$$= 20{,}000\pi$$
$$\approx 62{,}831.9 \text{ square}$$
$$\text{yards}$$

$$V = Bh$$
$$= \pi r^2 h$$
$$= \pi(50)^2(150)$$
$$= 375{,}000\pi$$
$$\approx 1{,}178{,}097.2 \text{ cubic}$$
$$\text{yards}$$

15.
$$V = \frac{Bh}{3}$$
$$= \frac{(1200)(25)}{3}$$
$$= 10{,}000 \text{ cubic meters}$$

16.
$$V = \frac{Bh}{3}$$
$$= \frac{\left(2\frac{1}{4}\right)\left(13\frac{1}{3}\right)}{3}$$
$$= 10 \text{ cubic}$$
$$\text{millimeters}$$

17.
$$V = \frac{Bh}{3}$$
$$= \frac{(15.6)(7)}{3}$$
$$= 36.4 \text{ cubic meters}$$

18.
$$V = \frac{Bh}{3}$$
$$= \frac{(30)(13)}{3}$$
$$= 130 \text{ cubic inches}$$

19.
$$L = \frac{1}{2}Cs$$
$$= \frac{1}{2}(2\pi r)s$$
$$= \pi rs$$
$$= \pi(10)(26)$$
$$= 260\pi$$
$$\approx 816.8 \text{ square yards}$$

$$S = L + B$$
$$= 260\pi + \pi r^2$$
$$= 260\pi + \pi(10)^2$$
$$= 260\pi + 100\pi$$
$$= 360\pi$$
$$\approx 1131 \text{ square yards}$$

20.
$$L = \frac{1}{2}Cs$$
$$= \frac{1}{2}(2\pi r)s$$
$$= \pi rs$$
$$= \pi(4.3)(6.4)$$
$$= 27.52\pi$$
$$\approx 86.5 \text{ square meters}$$

$$S = L + B$$
$$= 27.52\pi + \pi r^2$$
$$= 27.52\pi + \pi(4.3)^2$$
$$= 27.52\pi + 18.49\pi$$
$$= 46.01\pi$$
$$\approx 144.5 \text{ square meters}$$

21.
$$L = \frac{1}{2}ps$$
$$= \frac{1}{2}(4e)s$$
$$= 2es$$
$$= (2)(6.5)(10)$$
$$= 130 \text{ square}$$
$$\text{centimeters}$$

$$S = L + B$$
$$= 130 + e^2$$
$$= 130 + (6.5)^2$$
$$= 130 + 42.25$$
$$\approx 172.3 \text{ square}$$
$$\text{centimeters}$$

22.
$$L = \frac{1}{2}ps$$
$$= \frac{1}{2}(5e)s$$
$$= \frac{5}{2}es$$
$$= \left(\frac{5}{2}\right)(20)(30)$$
$$= 1500 \text{ square feet}$$

$$S = L + B$$
$$= 1500 + 450$$
$$= 1950 \text{ square feet}$$

23.
$$S = 4\pi r^2$$
$$= 4\pi(12)^2$$
$$= 576\pi$$
$$\approx 1809.6 \text{ square}$$
$$\text{yards}$$

$$V = \frac{4}{3}\pi r^3$$
$$= \frac{4}{3}\pi(12)^3$$
$$= 2304\pi$$
$$\approx 7238.2 \text{ cubic}$$
$$\text{yards}$$

24.
$$S = 4\pi r^2$$
$$= 4\pi(0.9)^2$$
$$= 3.24\pi$$
$$\approx 10.2 \text{ square inches}$$

$$V = \frac{4}{3}\pi r^3$$
$$= \frac{4}{3}\pi(0.9)^3$$
$$= 0.972\pi$$
$$\approx 3.1 \text{ cubic inches}$$

25.
$$S = 4\pi r^2$$
$$= 4\pi\left(5\frac{1}{4}\right)^2$$
$$= 4\pi\left(\frac{21}{4}\right)^2$$
$$= 110\frac{1}{4}\pi$$
$$\approx 346.4 \text{ square miles}$$

$$V = \frac{4}{3}\pi r^3$$
$$= \frac{4}{3}\pi\left(5\frac{1}{4}\right)^3$$
$$= \frac{4}{3}\pi\left(2\frac{1}{4}\right)^3$$
$$= 192\frac{15}{16}\pi$$
$$\approx 606.1 \text{ cubic miles}$$

26. Let x represent the cost of the second pizza.

area of the smaller pizza:
$$A = \pi r^2 = \pi(5)^2 = 25\pi$$

area of the larger pizza:
$$A = \pi r^2 = \pi(7.5)^2 = 56.25\pi$$

ratio of cost to area for the small pizza:
$$\frac{8}{25}\pi$$

To find the price of the second pizza, solve the proportion.
$$\frac{8}{25}\pi = \frac{x}{56.25\pi}$$
$$\frac{8}{25} = \frac{x}{56.25}$$
$$25x = 8(56.25)$$
$$25x = 450$$
$$x = 18$$

The second pizza should be $18.

27. Volume of first box = lwh

$$= (2)(9)(10.5)$$
$$= 189 \text{ cubic inches}$$

Volume of second box = lwh

$$= (3)(7.5)(8.5)$$
$$= 191.25 \text{ cubic inches}$$

The second box can hold more supplies.

28. $B = \pi r^2$
$$= \pi(0.5)^2$$
$$= 0.25\pi$$
$$\approx 0.8$$

The base area of the aquarium is 0.25π, or about 0.8 square feet.

29. Add the area of one base to the lateral surface area.

$$A = B + L$$
$$= B + 2\pi rh$$
$$= 0.25\pi + 2\pi(0.5)(3)$$
$$= 0.25\pi + 3\pi$$
$$= 3.25\pi$$
$$\approx 10.2$$

Approximately 10.2 square feet of material is needed.

30. $V = Bh$
$$= \pi r^2 h$$
$$= \pi(0.5)^2(3)$$
$$= 0.75\pi$$
$$\approx 2.4$$

The volume of the aquarium is approximately 2.4 cubic feet.

31. Multiply the number of cubic feet by 7.5 gallons.

$$(2.36)(7.5) = 17.7$$

The tank will hold approximately 17.7 gallons of water.

PAGE 689 CHAPTER 12 ASSESSMENT

1. $C = 2\pi r$
$$= 2\pi(7)$$
$$= 14\pi$$
$$\approx 44.0 \text{ feet}$$

2. $A = 2\pi r^2$
$$= \pi(7)^2$$
$$= 49\pi$$
$$\approx 153.9 \text{ square feet}$$

3. $S = 2(l \cdot w + l \cdot h + w \cdot h)$
$$= 2[(18 \cdot 10.5) + (18 \cdot 3) + (10.5 \cdot 3)]$$
$$= 2(189 + 54 + 31.5)$$
$$= 2(274.5)$$
$$= 549 \text{ square inches}$$

4. $V = lwh$
$$= (18)(10.5)(3)$$
$$= 567 \text{ cubic inches}$$

5. $S = L + 2B$

Find the area of the base.
$$B = \frac{(b_1 + b_2)h}{2}$$
$$= \frac{(9.4 + 2.8)3}{2}$$
$$= \frac{(12.2)3}{2}$$
$$= 18.3 \text{ square meters}$$

Find the surface area.
$$S = L + 2B$$
$$= ph + 2(18.3)$$
$$= (9.4 + 5 + 2.8 + 4)(12) + 36.6$$
$$= (21.2)(12) + 36.6$$
$$= 291 \text{ square meters}$$

6. $V = Bh$
$$= (18.3)(12)$$
$$= 219.6 \text{ cubic meters}$$

7. $S = L + 2B$
$$= 2\pi rh + 2\pi r^2$$
$$= 2\pi\left(9\tfrac{1}{4}\right)(14) + 2\pi\left(9\tfrac{1}{4}\right)^2$$
$$= 259\pi + 171\tfrac{1}{8}\pi$$
$$= 430\tfrac{1}{8}\pi$$
$$\approx 1351.3 \text{ square yards}$$

8. $V = Bh$
$$= \pi r^2 h$$
$$= \pi\left(9\tfrac{1}{4}\right)^2(14)$$
$$= \pi\left(\tfrac{37}{4}\right)^2(14)$$
$$= \left(\tfrac{1369}{16}\right)(14)\pi$$
$$= \tfrac{19166}{16}\pi$$
$$= 1197\tfrac{7}{8}\pi$$
$$\approx 3763.2 \text{ cubic yards}$$

9. $V = \dfrac{Bh}{3}$
$$= \frac{\pi r^2 h}{3}$$
$$= \frac{\pi(5)^2(12)}{3}$$
$$= \frac{300\pi}{3}$$
$$= 100\pi$$
$$\approx 314.2 \text{ cubic centimeters}$$

10. $S = L + B$
$$= \tfrac{1}{2}Cs + \pi r^2$$
$$= \tfrac{1}{2}(2\pi r)s + \pi r^2$$
$$= \pi rs + \pi r^2$$
$$= \pi(5)(13) + \pi(5)^2$$
$$= 65\pi + 25\pi$$
$$= 90\pi$$
$$\approx 282.7 \text{ square centimeters}$$

11. $V = \dfrac{Bh}{3}$

$= \dfrac{(41.6)(9.38)}{3}$

≈ 130.1 cubic millimeters

12. $S = L + B$

$= 6\left(\dfrac{1}{2} \cdot e \cdot s\right) + B$

$= 6)\dfrac{1}{2} \cdot 4 \cdot 10) + 41.6$

$= 6(20) + 41.6$

$= 120 + 41.6$

$= 161.6$ square millimeters

13. $S = 4\pi r^2$

$= 4\pi(6.3)^2$

$= 158.76\pi$

≈ 498.8 square feet

14. $V = \dfrac{4}{3}\pi r^3$

$= \dfrac{4}{3}\pi(6.3)^3$

$= 333.396\pi$

≈ 1047.4 cubic feet

15. $L = \dfrac{1}{2}Cs$

$= \dfrac{1}{2}(2\pi r)s$

$= \pi rs$

$= \pi(2.5)(6.5)$

$= 16.25\pi$

≈ 51.1

The approximate area of the chocolate layer will be 51.1 square inches.

CHAPTERS 1-12 CUMULATIVE ASSESSMENT

1. C

$-6 \cdot 9 = -54$

$6 \cdot (-9) = -54$

2. B

$\dfrac{90}{15} = 6$

$\dfrac{84}{12} = 7$

3. B

Slope of $y = -2$ is 0.

Slope of $y = x - 2$ is 1.

4. A

The correlation co-efficient of a line of best fit that rises is positive. The corre-lation coefficient of a line of best fit that falls is negative.

5. c; 30

$\dfrac{4}{15} \cdot \dfrac{2}{2} = \dfrac{8}{30}$

$\dfrac{3}{10} \cdot \dfrac{3}{3} = \dfrac{9}{30}$

6. a; an angle with a measure less than 90° is an acute angle.

7. a; $t < -3$

$6 - 4t > 18$

$-4t > 12$

$-t > 3$

$t < -3$

8. b; $-\dfrac{2}{3}$

$2x + 3y = -5$

$3y = -2x - 5$

$y = -\dfrac{2}{3}x - \dfrac{5}{3}$

$m = -\dfrac{2}{3}$

A parallel line will have the same slope.

9. d; $(1, -1)$ is the vertex of the parabola.

10. c; 49π

$A = \pi r^2$

$= \pi(7)^2$

$= 49\pi$

11. Let x represent the scale factor.

$12x = 18$

$x = \dfrac{18}{12}$, or $\dfrac{3}{2}$

To find the missing leg, multiply 30 by the scale factor.

$30 \cdot \dfrac{3}{2} = \dfrac{90}{2} = 45$

The length of the longer leg of the second triangle is 45.

12. $x < -3$ or $x \geq 3$

13. $\dfrac{x}{-10} = \dfrac{-3}{5}$

$5x = (-3)(-10)$

$5x = 30$

$x = 6$

14. $m = \dfrac{4}{5}$

Use the point $(-4, 2)$ for (x_1, y_1).

$y - y_1 = m(x - x_1)$

$y - 2 = \dfrac{4}{5}(x - (-4))$

$y - 2 = \dfrac{4}{5}(x + 4)$

15. $\begin{cases} y \le x + 2 & \to y \le x + 2 \\ x + y > -1 & \to y > -x - 1 \end{cases}$

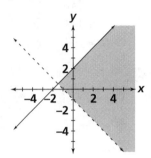

16. strong negative

17. -1; the correlation is strong negative.

18. $V = \dfrac{Bh}{3}$

$\quad = \dfrac{\pi r^2 h}{3}$

$\quad = \dfrac{\pi (5)^2 (15)}{3}$

$\quad = 125\pi$

$\quad \approx 392.7$

The volume of the cone is approximately 392.7 cubic feet.

19. $\begin{cases} 4x - 3y = 5 & \to 3(4x - 3y) = 3(5) \to 12x - 9y = 15 \\ 8x + 9y = 3 & \to \quad\quad 8x + 9y = 3 \quad\to \quad \underline{8x + 9y = 3} \end{cases}$
$$20x = 18$$

$20x = 18$

$x = \dfrac{18}{20} = \dfrac{9}{10}, \text{ or } 0.9$

20. slope $= \dfrac{\text{change in } y}{\text{change in } x} = \dfrac{4 - (-2)}{3 - (-1)} = \dfrac{6}{4} = \dfrac{3}{2}$

21. INT(5.6) $= 5$

22. $S = L + B$

$\quad = \dfrac{1}{2}ps + e^2$

$\quad = \dfrac{1}{2}(4e)s + e^2$

$\quad = 2es + e^2$

$\quad = 2(12)(24) + 12^2$

$\quad = 576 + 144$

$\quad = 720$

The surface area of the pyramid is 720 square inches.